Critical Civic Literacy: A Reader

"*Critical Civic Literacy: A Reader* is an inspiration for all who believe that the fundamental purpose of public schooling ought to be to develop the knowledge, skills, dispositions, and habits necessary for democracy to function and flourish. At a time when citizenship is too often reduced to consumption, and individual rights are heralded much more than community responsibility, the authors in this wide-ranging collection give us hope that another vision for schools and society is possible. Thoughtfully combining theory and practice, they provide numerous models and resources for education that enable genuine social and political engagement, help us to build community, and foster the development of the kinds of critical citizens we need to forge a more caring, compassionate, and socially just world."

> —*Kathy Hytten, Professor, Department of Educational Administration and Higher Education, Southern Illinois University, Carbondale; Past President, American Educational Studies Association*

"The urgency to incorporate critical civic literacy into the practice and thought of education in a democracy is evident in the essays that Joseph L. DeVitis has collected [here]. The contributors to this volume explore both the idea and ideal of critical civic literacy as it relates to 21st-century America. Their diverse voices are highly relevant to both the practitioner and the theorist. Throughout this book essential connections are made between critical civic literacy and the culture, the community, the curriculum, and the classroom."

> —*John A. Beineke, Distinguished Professor of Educational Leadership and Curriculum, Arkansas State University*

Critical
Civic
Literacy

This book is part of the Peter Lang Education list.
Every volume is peer reviewed and meets
the highest quality standards for content and production.

PETER LANG
New York • Washington, D.C./Baltimore • Bern
Frankfurt • Berlin • Brussels • Vienna • Oxford

Critical
Civic
Literacy
A READER

Joseph L. DeVitis, Editor

PETER LANG
New York • Washington, D.C./Baltimore • Bern
Frankfurt • Berlin • Brussels • Vienna • Oxford

Library of Congress Cataloging-in-Publication Data

Critical civic literacy: a reader / edited by Joseph L. DeVitis.
p. cm.
Includes bibliographical references.
1. Critical pedagogy—United States.
2. Civics—Study and teaching (Secondary)—United States.
3. Critical thinking—Study and teaching (Secondary)—United States.
4. Education, Secondary—Curricula—United States.
5. Democracy and education—United States. I. DeVitis, Joseph L.
LC196.5.U6C745   372.83'044—dc23   2011021143
978-1-4331-1172-3 (hardcover)
ISBN 978-1-4331-1171-6 (paperback)
ISBN 978-1-4539-0139-7 (e-book)

Bibliographic information published by **Die Deutsche Nationalbibliothek**.
Die Deutsche Nationalbibliothek lists this publication in the "Deutsche
Nationalbibliografie"; detailed bibliographic data is available
on the Internet at http://dnb.d-nb.de/.

The paper in this book meets the guidelines for permanence and durability
of the Committee on Production Guidelines for Book Longevity
of the Council of Library Resources.

© 2011 Peter Lang Publishing, Inc., New York
29 Broadway, 18th floor, New York, NY 10006
www.peterlang.com

Printed in the United States of America

*For their passion in
fostering the promise
and possibilities of
democratic education,
this book is dedicated
in memory of:*

Landon E. Beyer

Joe L. Kincheloe

David E. Purpel

Mary Anne Raywid

Adam Renner

Contents

Preface

A wise and enlightened constituency will refuse to invest a reckless and profligate man with office. . . . [If] we do not prepare children to become good citizens . . . then our republic must go down to destruction.

—Horace Mann

In the early part of the 21st century, one that seems to cast dark clouds over enlightened citizenship, Mann's words appear to have been lost or forgotten. Civic education, a cornerstone of 19th-century common schools, has been shunted to the back burner in public education today as often mindless high-stakes testing sets the larger agenda in our classrooms, board rooms, and media outlets. That striking devolution of interest in civics itself is one of the main reasons for this book's inception. The contributors to the volume do not speak in the same ways about citizenship education as did Mann, who was profoundly in favor of melioristic social harmony and consensus. But they all seek to lift civic literacy to its rightful place in nurturing and sustaining human rights in government and society. They realize that we now need critical civic literacy perhaps more than ever before.

American society is not structured to enhance the dignity of many, but unfortunately, is structured to foster a dehumanizing quest for status, power, and wealth. We live…in a fundamentally racist, materialistic society which, through a process of rewards and punishments, cultivates the quest for status, power, and wealth in such a way so as to use people and institutions effectively to protect vested interests.

—Clarence J. Karier

Karier, a leading historian of American education in the latter part of the 20th century, is a powerful critic of Mann's notion of social harmony and consensus. He perceives a plethora of contested areas of discourse and practice in American life, most notably our marked social stratification, excessive materialism, and so-called "meritocratic" system of governance. In one manner or another, each of our contributors tackles some important aspects of those dilemmas. Like Karier, they see obstacles and possibilities that many others do not see—or simply wish to ignore. They view injustice and want to correct it. They find inequities and seek to join forces with those who act to overcome them. Some may call many of our contributors "radical," forgetting that "radical" means getting to the roots of real problems. The latter is the definition that each of our contributors would acknowledge; and, because of that acceptance, they seek to construct stronger forms of critical civic literacy.

> You cannot have a secure self-location in a period where every movement is half-assed and not deep into the corruption of this society of which we are sensitive....I believe that our ambiguity has to do with the uneasiness of self-location and insecurity—which make(s) us strive to be politically happy when we know in our souls that [t]his is not the answer to anything we are really interested in on the political sphere.
>
> —C. WRIGHT MILLS

Mills was no ordinary sociologist. Of course, he used his "sociological imagination" to view events and trends. Yet he also employed self-observation and critical self-engagement in his academic endeavors. In almost existential fashion, he put his self-reflection into action, prodding the public and its power brokers to solve the problems of society. Indeed, he is among that rare breed we refer to as "public intellectuals." In large part, this volume was created in the hope that our contributors would choose to take a similar path in their writing and reflection. They have not disappointed. They also realize that there is something terribly wrong in our social structures; and they are striving to locate and eradicate those debilitating sociopolitical deficiencies. They, too, know that we are in drastic need of critical civic literacy.

> To refuse to participate in the shaping of our future is to give it up. Each of us must find our work and do it.
>
> —AUDRE LORDE

Lorde's message brings up one of my own misgivings about being a college professor in the oftentimes dim landscape of 21st-century America. I have, from time to time, been both amused and disheartened by those colleagues who, in the name of "liberation," obfuscate and mystify the larger public (that is, the relatively few who actually read their work). The convoluted nature of their language is accepted, and presumably perused, by perhaps several dozen of their scholarly comrades (some of whom privately admit to not understanding a word of such academic jargon). Too many educators, in both public schools and the academy, have also been too content to play the role of armchair philosopher—one who swings robust imaginary clubs at the Establishment while barely lifting him or herself out of the Lazy Boy. This book is meant for them only in the faint hope of an awakening. Above all, it is written for those interested citizens, educators, students, policymakers, and all others who seek to put civic literacy into social and political action. Yes, we need to reflect deeply about contested issues and come to deliberative conclusions—and then we need to get off our arses. Critical civic literacy is sorely needed if we are ever really going to practice democracy in our institutions, especially in school hallways and classrooms.

> We will constantly be drawn from our reflection into activism, making theory real….Indeed, this struggle toward a deeper understanding of classroom and structure of inequality is a moral struggle that compels all educators and those who work for the betterment of the lives of others to engage it fully. In order to avoid the socially reproductive tendencies of injustice, we must recognize the tremendous stakes and the pressing nature of the work. We can wait no longer.
>
> —ADAM RENNER

In December 2010, Adam Renner passed away at age 40. He had been a tenured faculty member at Bellarmine University in Louisville, Kentucky, for a number of years. In August 2010, he had left that position to become a teacher at the June Jordan School for Equity in San Francisco. Adam died before he could complete his original essay for this book. He embodied the ideal of the scholar/activist. Thus, in a certain and real sense, this volume is dedicated to Adam and people like him: Those who do not just sit on the sidelines and pontificate, those who practice what they preach in the realm of civic education. In this troubled, wildly fragmented world, we need far fewer silly sound bites, fewer goofy media images, fewer political candidates who are caricatures of unreason, and more substantial voices articulating and acting upon humane possibilities. In a word, we need more Adam Renners in our world if we are to survive and thrive today and tomorrow—especially in a public life still worth living.

CHAPTER ONE

The Tangled Web We Weave

Critical Literacy and Critical Thinking

CARA M. MULCAHY

Critical literacy and critical thinking are sometimes confused with one another even though they have different goals and educate for different purposes. Therefore, it is important that educators are aware of how the two differ in order to disrupt the conservative monopoly on the educative practices of secondary teachers. This chapter begins with a preliminary discussion of the terms "critical literacy" and "critical thinking," followed by an examination of the ways critical literacy and critical thinking compare to one another, particularly on issues such as fair-mindedness, problem solving, point of view, and questioning. The chapter concludes by considering the importance of acknowledging the differences between critical literacy and critical thinking and addresses the necessity for including critical literacy in the teaching of content area literacy.

Literacies and the Content Area

William S. Gray, a pioneer of content area reading, is recognized for coining the phrase "Every teacher is a teacher of reading" (Gray as quoted in Vacca, 2002, p. 186). As we enter the twenty-first century, it may be more accurate to say every teacher is a teacher of literacy. In recent years the term "content area reading" has been replaced with the term "content area literacy." Content area literacy no longer applies only to reading and writing but "refers to all the literacies in students' lives—whether in school or out of school—and the myriad forms that today's texts can take, whether textbook or trade book, e-mail, electronic messaging, or Internet sites" (Moss, 2005,

p. 48). Similarly, literacy is no longer viewed as merely a set of skills one must master, but as a set of practices, beliefs, and values as well as a way of being in the world. Therefore, as we engage in the teaching of content area literacy, we need to be cognizant of the kinds of literacies we are teaching toward. Critical literacy distinguishes itself from other kinds of literacy in the way it addresses issues of power, social injustice, and transformative action.

Critical Literacy Defined

Critical literacy is a mindset; it is a way of viewing and interacting with the world, not a set of teaching skills and strategies. From a pedagogical perspective, critical literacy is a philosophy that recognizes the connections between power, knowledge, language, and ideology, and recognizes the inequalities and injustices surrounding us in order to move toward transformative action and social justice. In order to do so, critical literacy examines texts in order to identify and challenge social constructs, underlying assumptions and ideologies, and power structures that intentionally or unintentionally perpetuate social inequalities and injustices. Furthermore, it examines the way in which texts use language to position readers, transmit information, and perpetuate the status quo. Critical literacy aims to delve deeply into the sociopolitical and sociocultural issues embedded in texts in order to identify the root causes of social inequities. By employing critical literacy, one questions the construction of knowledge and searches for hidden agendas in school curricula, governmental legislation, corporation policies, and the media.

Critical literacy separates itself from literacies such as functional, informational, cultural, and progressive literacy in that it works toward praxis. Praxis, as defined by Freire (1970), combines reflection and action in order to transform society. In this way, critical literacy is transformative. Such transformation attempts to eradicate social injustices and inequalities so as to create better social conditions for all. Grounded in critical theory, it recognizes that while literacy can be used to empower oneself, it can also be used as a means to control society. Thus, analyzing a text or being asked to think critically does not mean that one is engaging in critical literacy. Similarly, merely embedding a selection of critical questions and terminology into one's discourse does not necessarily mean one is teaching toward critical literacy.

Much has been written on the differences between critical literacy and critical thinking, and although many caution of the dangers in using the terms interchangeably, confusion continues.

Unraveling Critical Literacy and Critical Thinking

Here I shall rely upon Paul and Elder's (2005) framework for critical thinking and Lewison, Flint, and Van Sluys's (2002) definition of critical literacy to frame my discussion of the differences and similarities between the two concepts. As defined by Paul and Elder (2005), a critical thinker is skilled in the following three dimensions: analytic, evaluative, and creative thinking. In addition to forming analytical, evaluative, and creative thinkers, critical thinking is also a process whereby a person reflects upon his/her own thinking process so as to create clear, well-reasoned ideas for the benefit of him/herself and others.

Paul and Elder (2005) identify eight elements of critical thought that, when used in combination, allow us to be critical thinkers in accordance with the above understanding. These eight elements are:

1. Purpose, goal, or end in view: Whenever we reason we do so with an objective in mind, with an end goal we wish to reach.
2. Questions at issue (or problems to be solved): As we begin to reason, there is usually a question or a problem that needs to be solved.
3. Point of view or frame of reference: As we engage in reasoning, we do so from a specific standpoint or perspective. This point of view is constructed by our mind.
4. The information we use in reasoning: Whenever we reason we do so about some phenomenon.
5. The conceptual dimensions of our reasoning: Certain ideas and concepts created by the mind are used when we reason.
6. Assumptions: To begin reasoning, we must have a starting point. To establish a starting point, we must take some things for granted.
7. Our inferences, interpretations, and conclusions: As we reason, we create inferences in an attempt to understand the issue at hand.
8. Implications and consequences—where our reasoning takes us: The process of reasoning leads us somewhere new. Reasoning is not static. Implications and consequences are creations of our reasoning and they affect our thoughts and actions.

Once again the emphasis here is on one's ability to rationalize one's inner dialogue and thought process with the goal of being able to evaluate one's thinking, feelings, and actions in a disciplined manner.

Critical literacy, on the other hand, can be described as having four dimensions: (1) disrupting the commonplace, (2) interrogating multiple viewpoints, (3) focusing on sociopolitical issues, and (4) taking action and promoting social justice (Lewison, Flint, & Van Sluys, 2002). These four dimensions relate closely to Freire's notion of a liberating education, which allows one to problem-pose, engage in dialogue, and examine the world in a way that uncovers social oppressions and encourages people to understand ways in which their world can be transformed. Unlike the "banking" approach to education whereby students are seen as receptacles or bins to be filled and "in which the scope of action allowed to the students extends only as far as receiving, filling, and storing the deposits" (p. 72), critical literacy aims to actively engage the students in their learning and reading of texts by addressing these four dimensions of critical literacy.

Through problem posing, critique, and transformation, students are taught to question social constructs such as race, gender, ethnicity, and sexuality and the ways in which texts position them as readers, consumers, and sociopolitical beings. By suggesting that readers learn to interrogate texts from multiple viewpoints, consider sociopolitical issues, and disrupt commonplace notions of gender, race, and class, critical literacy scholars changed our relationship to the text and the world from unidirectional to dialectical.

Goals and Purposes

The goal of teaching critical thinking is to help students focus on developing their ability to reason, analyze, evaluate, and create in a way that is disciplined and that expresses their thoughts, feelings, and actions in a rational and clear manner. The goal of educating toward critical literacy, however, is to uncover the inequalities that exist within society, identify the root causes that may be perpetuating the inequalities, and to take social action so as to create a more just and equal society. Immediately one can begin to understand that critical literacy is concerned not only with the individual and one's ability to think rationally, but also with societal issues that reach beyond the individual—issues relating to social injustice, social inequalities, and unequal power relations. Shannon quoted in McDaniel (2004) points out,

> critical perspectives push the definition of literacy beyond traditional decoding or encoding of words in order to reproduce the meaning of text or society until it becomes a means for understanding one's own history and culture, to recognize connections between one's life and the social structure, to believe that change in one's life, and the lives of others and society are possible as well as desirable, and to act on this new knowledge in order to foster equal and just participation in all the decisions that affect and control our lives. (p. 171)

Similar to critical literacy, proponents of critical thinking, too, are concerned with how a person thinks, feels, and acts. However, critical thinking appears to be more concerned with just the individual, with developing "a powerful inner voice of reason" (Elder & Paul, 1998, p. 300) and in this respect is unlike critical literacy which also considers the impact of thinking in relation to societal matters. This can be evidenced more clearly when Paul and Elder (2005) state:

> Without the active knowledge that Critical Thinking empowers, we are unlikely to be personally transformed by our learning. Without the cultivation of our intellectual capacities such as fairmindedness, we are unlikely to notice our inconsistencies and contradictions. We are apt to uncritically conform in many domains of our personal lives. (p. 22)

Clearly then, while advocates of critical literacy would agree it is important that we not "uncritically conform" in our personal lives, critical theorists would argue that it is just as important that we not uncritically conform at a societal level as well.

In order to reach beyond the individual realm and move to the societal realm, critical literacy advocates contend that it is not enough to identify facts or argue against "demonstrably false beliefs" (Burbules & Berk, 1999). One must also examine the larger impact of those facts and false beliefs at the societal level. For example, on completing a policy analysis of *Reading First* (the federal initiative in reading that was signed into law in 2002) from a critical literacy perspective, it became evident that although the goal to have all children reading by grade three is ideal, it is unrealistic (Mulcahy, 2003). Not only does it assume all students develop at the same rate, it discounts the many variables that affect student learning: economic status, cultural background, biased testing practices, auditory processing delays, as well as other physiological and psychological factors. In addition to considering the multiple variables that influence student learning, one also needs to ask who is benefiting from this initiative. Who will be negatively impacted by it? What economic, business, and political interests are being brought to bear on the initiative? Therefore, when engaging in critical literacy one is examining not only the logic and reasoning that is supporting an idea or an argument, one is also challenging the underlying societal factors involved. Burbules and Berk (1999) point out that, unlike critical thinking, critical pedagogy, which has much in common with critical literacy, looks to how an issue relates to "deeper" explanations—deeper in the sense that they refer to the basic functioning of power on institutional and societal level. For Critical Pedagogy, it makes no sense to talk about issues on a nonrelational, item-by-item basis. Where Critical Thinking emphasizes the immediate reasons and assumptions of an argument, Critical Pedagogy wants to draw in for consideration factors that may appear at first of less immediate relevance. (p. 9)

Many aspects of the four dimensions put forth by Lewison, Flint, and Van Sluys incorporate cultural and social levels of transformation. Under the dimension "disrupting the commonplace," they explain how critical literacy examines language so as to understand "how it shapes identity, constructs cultural discourses, and supports or disrupts the status quo." Similarly under the dimension "focusing on sociopolitical issues," they explain that redefining literacy is a "form of cultural citizenship and politics that increases opportunities for subordinate groups to participate in society" (p. 383). Lewison et al. are making a connection between the individual, society, and a move to action. One can become critically conscious by developing an awareness of oneself, of one's place in a larger system of networks, and of one's own thinking while at the same time developing a sense of interrelatedness and interconnectivity among social, cultural, and political dimensions.

In addition, at the heart of critical consciousness is the importance of taking action and making change. In fact, for Freire, the two, reflection and action, must occur together. Burbules and Berk (1999) explain it well when they state:

> Critical Pedagogy would never find it sufficient to reform the habits of thought of thinkers, however effectively, without challenging and transforming the institutions, ideologies, and relations that engender distorted, oppressed thinking in the first place—not as an additional act beyond the pedagogical one, but as an inseparable part of it. For Critical Thinking, at most, the development of more discerning thinkers might make them more likely to undermine discreditable institutions, to challenge misleading authorities, and so on—but this would be a separate consequence of the attainment of Critical Thinking, not part of it. (p. 6)

This need for a move to action is not evident in Paul and Elder's framework for critical thinking. Although they talk about creativity and analytic thought as important dimensions, the need for social transformation does not appear to be a necessary component. And while social transformation may result from one's ability to critically examine a given issue, many critical theorists would argue it is more a byproduct of critical thinking than a purposeful outcome.

Fair-Mindedness and Neutrality

When discussing the importance of developing critical thought, Paul and Elder refer to the development of fair-mindedness as a way to cultivate intellectual capacities. Without fair-mindedness, readers and thinkers can not be objective and recognize their contradictions and inconsistencies. Supporters of critical literacy also believe it important to acknowledge the inconsistencies and contradictions within ourselves and within society. Such inconsistencies and contradictions may be referred to as tensions or binary opposites. However, a difference arises between critical literacy and critical thinking when we examine why fair-mindedness is important to teach. Paul and Elder underline the importance of fair-mindedness in one's thinking so that we can be transformed by our learning. Without fair-mindedness our inconsistencies and contradictions will prevent us from "critically examining" many domains of our lives. The implication here is that by becoming rational and applying the skills of critical thinking one is empowered. This, again, focuses on the individual, overlooking the social, cultural, and political aspects that surround us. Becoming empowered and changing one's own circumstances may be difficult or impossible without also transforming certain aspects of society. Kincheloe (2005) reminds us, "We cannot simply attempt to cultivate the intellect without changing the unjust social context in which such minds operate" (p. 21).

The belief that one can cultivate fair-mindedness also implies that one can analyze facts or problems in a neutral or unbiased way, thereby creating the belief that information or data can be examined objectively. Followers of critical literacy would strongly disagree. To believe knowledge is neutral overlooks "how sociopolitical systems, power relationships, and language are intertwined and inseparable" (Lewison, Flint, & Van Sluys, 2002, p. 383). Furthermore, due to personal biases, cultivating fair-mindedness may not be possible. In critical literacy, there is no pretense at being objective: All interpretations and analyses are value-laden and tied to the social, cultural, and historical context in which the text was examined. Being aware of our contradictions, inconsistencies, and biases allows us and others to understand how we are positioned and how others might be positioning us with their inferences, interpretations, and conclusions.

Critical theorists do not believe that there is one truth to be found or that reality exists outside of language, culture, and ideology. Instead they acknowledge that many truths may exist and it is only through dialogue and "interrogating multiple viewpoints" that we come to understand and acknowledge the many ways in which truth and knowledge can be grasped. The elements listed under the dimension "interrogating multiple viewpoints" address this aspect of critical literacy. Lewison et al. suggest we reflect on "multiple and contradictory perspectives," use multiple voices to interrogate texts, to pay attention to and seek out "the voices of those who have been silenced or marginalized," to write "counternarratives to dominant discourses," and to "make difference visible" (p. 383).

Acknowledging one's own contradictions and inconsistencies is important. Doing so allows one to become aware of who he or she is and how he or she operates and interacts with the world. Critical literacy, instead of attempting to achieve fair-mindedness, encourages one to make contradictions, inconsistencies, and biases known.

Inferences

In explaining the element of critical thought that addresses our inferences, interpretations, and conclusions, critical literacy and critical thinking may have much in common. According to Paul and Elder, it is not the information or the data that determines how we arrive at certain understandings. Instead drawing on "the powers of origination of our own minds," (pp. 24–25) it is our own concepts and understanding that lead us to infer, interpret, and draw conclusions.

Here both critical literacy and critical thinking can be related to transactional reading theory—that is, the way the text, the reader, and the context interact with one another to construct meaning. When applying transactional reading theory to the notion of drawing inferences, it is understood that one may come away with knowledge that differs from the author's original intent or from another person's analysis of the same text. Inferences are created by combining the reader's background knowledge with information from the text, which in turn creates new meaning. Therefore, there may be many possible inferences to be drawn from any one piece of text. With this understanding, it makes it difficult to say, categorically, that one's inference or reasoning is defective. However, advocates of critical thinking suggest that an inference can be incorrect because of some fault with a person's reasoning, which implies that there is one truth that can be found in the text.

From the standpoint of critical literacy, many possible inferences, interpretations, and conclusions may emerge from an analysis—with no one being more correct than another. Furthermore, one's opinions, inferences, and conclusions are open to debate. Information and data alone are not what cause us to arrive at certain conclusions or interpretations. This we do for ourselves as inferring, interpreting, and drawing conclusions are meaning-making constructions or creations.

Questioning and Problem Posing

Although asking questions is important to think critically and be critically literate, the purposes for questioning are somewhat different in each case. Critical thinking suggests we pose questions in order to reason through an issue. In the scholarship on critical thinking, Paul and Elder explain that the purpose of setting questions is to be clear about what we are asking in order to find a reasonable answer. They write, "If we are not clear about the question we are asking, or how the question relates to our basic purpose or goal, we will not be able to find a reasonable answer to it, or an answer that will serve our purpose" (p. 23). Questions that guide critical thinking might include: What examples were used to support the author's claim? Do you agree with the author's argument? Does the author include differing points of view?

Critical literacy, on the other hand, proposes we ask questions that interrogate the status quo and challenge commonly accepted social practices. Questioning is not solely for the purpose of ascertaining reasonable answers. Instead, critical literacy questions focus on uncovering inequalities and injustices, and on identifying why and how such inequalities are perpetuated. When "disrupting the commonplace" one problematizes "subjects of study" and interrogates texts by "asking questions" such as how is gender being constructed by this text? Or how does this text reify or disrupt stereotypes? Similarly, when "interrogating multiple view points," one poses questions about the voices included or excluded in the text: Who is missing from this text? Whose story is being told and whose is ignored? And, when focusing on sociopolitical issues, Lewison et al. suggest, one is constantly "challenging the unquestioned legitimacy of unequal power relations" (p. 382): How do I benefit from racism? Sexism? When engaging in critical pedagogy, students need to be problem posing instead of trying to find logical answers, as critical thinking asks us to.

In addition, both critical thinking and critical literacy demand that readers problematize assumptions inherent in texts. If our assumptions go unquestioned, we disallow the possibility of realizing alternative ways of being in the world. Holding to our assumptions without question leads to a passive acceptance of the status quo:

> All reasoning must begin somewhere, and must take some things for granted. Any defect in the starting points of our reasoning, any problem in what we are taking for granted, is a possible source of problems. Only we can create the assumptions on the basis of which we will reason. We (i.e. create) our minds' starting point. (p. 24)

Our assumptions, if unquestioned, can lead to problems in our reasoning. Critical literacy educators, too, would argue that false or misleading assumptions are problematic as they can lead to an unquestioning acceptance of the status quo.

While Paul and Elder acknowledge our assumptions may be a "possible source of problems," Lewison et al. encourage us to challenge commonly held assumptions, particularly those about race, class, gender, and sexuality. Accepting that our assumptions may be problematic allows us to reconceptualize the "every-day through new lenses." In so doing, we challenge unquestioned power relationships and interrogate popular culture and media to uncover how we are being positioned and constructed by television, video games, comics, and the like (p. 383).

Multiple Viewpoints

The importance of being aware of one's point of view is common to both critical literacy and critical thinking. Both recognize that points of view are human constructions. However, critical thinking warns readers against "defects in our point of view and frame of reference" as a possible "source of problem in our reasoning" (Paul & Elder, p. 24). It acknowledges that one's own point of view may be too narrow, imprecise, and contradictory. Again, as with other elements of thought discussed by Paul and Elder, the word "defect" suggests that something may be wrong with an individual's point of view. It further suggests that there is a correct point of view or frame of reference from which we should begin reasoning, while critical pedagogues maintain that there is no one correct position from which to construct meaning.

Critical literacy advocates ask readers to move beyond individual points of view to incorporate the importance of understanding multiple viewpoints. In so doing, critical literacy attempts to put readers in the shoes of others viewing a situation from other perspectives. This is important, as it allows readers to see that many possibilities may exist. It further reinforces the notion that there may not be one truth, but many possible ways of understanding the truth. Critical literacy invites students to read from many different perspectives and to always keep in mind whose voices are being heard and whose are missing, because who is missing from texts is as important as who is included.

In sum, the purpose of interrogating multiple viewpoints in critical literacy is not to find fault with a certain person's or group's point of view but to understand more fully the many perspectives from which people view the world. Who is to say an individual's point of view is defective? It is defective according to whom? Critical literacy understands that language, thoughts, beliefs, and actions are influenced by society and that our attitudes and understandings are often constructed by the context in which we operate. Therefore, one person's point of view is going to differ from another's depending on the context in which they operate.

The Importance of Critical Literacy for Content Area Literacy

In the field of content area literacy, a paradigm shift is underway from a "cognition and learning paradigm" that emerged in the 1970s and remained popular through the 1980s to a "social constructivist paradigm" of the 1990s. With this shift came "an emphasis on understanding the sociocultural underpinnings of teaching and learning in content classrooms" (Vacca, 2002, p. 193). Because critical literacy focuses on social transformation as well as individual transformation, integrating critical literacy into the teaching of the content areas allows us to further this paradigm shift toward a transformative and liberating education.

Another advantage of integrating critical literacy with content area literacy is that, apart from encouraging students to connect classroom learning with their everyday lives, it also allows for students to make connections across the disciplines, something that is often overlooked by a fragmented approach to the curriculum. While critical thinking often focuses on issues "item-by-item," critical literacy strives to make students aware of the interrelatedness and interconnectiveness of the world:

> Hence, Critical Thinking tends to address issues in an item-by-item fashion, not within a grand scheme with other issues. The issues themselves may have relations to one another, and they may have connections to broader themes, but those relations and connections are not the focus of investigation. What is crucial to the issue at hand is the interplay of an immediate cluster of evidence, reason, and arguments. For Critical Thinking, what is important is to describe the issue, give the various reasons for and against, and draw out any assumptions (and only those) that have immediate and direct bearing on the argument. This tends to produce a more analytical and less holistic mode of critique. (Burbules & Berk, 1999, p. 55)

In contrast to critical thinking, critical literacy encourages students to examine how the issues under examination may connect to one another and to broader themes. Making such connections is important because it discourages students from viewing things in isolation from one another and instead encourages them to understand the far-reaching impact any issue may have on the larger society.

In keeping with this sentiment, while critical thinking is crucially important in supplying students with the skills to analyze arguments and ideas presented to them in their texts, critical literacy challenges students to identify issues such as gender bias, cultural bias, omissions of narratives by marginalized groups from texts, and rewrite the text to represent a more complete picture. Thus, critical literacy pedagogy is transformative and accepts nothing less than social and political equality for all American citizens by educating students to upset the status quo.

In conclusion, although both critical literacy and critical thinking are important for students, it is necessary that educators be aware of how they differ and understand that the two ideas are not synonymous. Failing to disentangle critical literacy and critical thinking from one another could lead to a neutralization of critical literacy. McLaren (1998) cautions us of this. He argues, taxonomies promoting critical thinking have allowed neoconservatives and liberals to "neutralize the term critical by repeated and imprecise usage, removing its political and cultural dimensions and laundering its analytic potency to mean 'thinking skills'" (p. 161). To avoid such a fate, critical pedagogues must persist in making the distinction between critical literacy and critical thinking.

Bibliography

Burbules, N.C., & Berk, R. (1999). Critical thinking and critical pedagogy: Relations, differences and limits in critical theories in education. In T.S. Popkewitz & L. Fendler (Eds.), *Critical Theories in Education* (pp. 45–65). New York: Routledge.

Elder, L., & Paul. R. (1998). The role of Socratic questioning in thinking, teaching, and learning. *Clearing House*, 71(5), 297–302.

Freire, P. (1970). *Pedagogy of the oppressed.* New York: Herder & Herder.

Kincheloe, J.L. (2005). *Critical pedagogy.* New York: Peter Lang.

Lewison, M., Flint, A.S., & Van Sluys, K. (2002). Taking on critical literacy: The journey of newcomers and novices. *Language Arts*, 79(5), 382–392.

McDaniel, C. (2004). Critical literacy: A questioning stance and the possibility for change. *The Reading Teacher*, 57(5), 472–481.

McLaren, P. (1998). *Life in schools: An introduction to critical pedagogy in the field of education.* White Plains, NY: Longman.

Moss, B. (2005). Making a case and a place for effective content area literacy instruction in the elementary grades. *The Reading Teacher*, 59(1), 46–55.

Mulcahy, C.M. (2003). Emergent federal government policy on literacy in the USA. *Irish Educational Studies*, 22 (Autumn), 91–100.

Paul, R., & Elder, L. (2005). *The thinkers guide to the nature and functions of critical & creative thinking.* Dillon Beach, CA: Foundation for Critical Thinking

Shannon, P. (1995). *Text, lies, & and videotape: Stories about life, literacy, & learning.* Portsmouth, NH: Heinemann.

Shor, I. (1992). *Empowering education: Critical teaching for social change.* Chicago: University of Chicago Press.

Vacca, R.T. (2002). Making a difference in adolescents' school lives: Visible and invisible aspects of content area reading. In A.E. Farstrup & S.J. Samuels (Eds.), *What research has to say about reading instruction* (pp. 184–204). Newark, DE: International Reading Association.

Vasquez, V.M. (2004). *Negotiating critical literacies with young children.* Mahwah, NJ: Lawrence Erlbaum Associates.

This chapter originally appeared in Laraine Wallowitz (ed.), *Critical Literacy as Resistance: Teaching for Social Justice Across the Secondary Curriculum* (New York: Peter Lang, 2008).

CHAPTER TWO

Critical Civic Literacy in Schools

Adolescents Seeking to Understand and Improve The(ir) World

KENNETH TEITELBAUM

I still have materials I used when I taught high school United States history classes many years ago, including a supplemental "textbook" I developed that included brief historical narratives that I wrote, copied portions of publications, and class activities and exams. Although the use of this more progressive textbook was compromised by the state Regents exam that was required in New York State at the time (that counted for 20% of the total grade for each student), which meant considerable pressure to "cover" material that would be on the exam, I did feel that I managed to present students with materials that were more engaging than the assigned textbook, as well as more honest and socially critical (Apple & Teitelbaum, 1986). What I notice as well when I go back and review these materials are my attempts to bring the study of the past into the present. To be sure, my teaching included the dusty (and numerous) facts of history that I felt needed to be presented and discussed, which I must admit I had a passion for (having at one time planned to go on for a doctoral degree in the field). However, it was often linked to my efforts to convince the many recalcitrant students in this largely working-class community that the policies, practices, events, and people that existed before they were born have relevance to their understanding of the current issues about which they were (or should be) concerned. Years later I read a passage that resonated with my thinking at this earlier time: "I would wonder what kind of present you could possibly have without knowing the stories of your past" (Mendelsohn, 2006, p. 162)—which I interpreted broadly in terms of a shared sense of humanity, or at least national identity.

During my master's degree program, I had a well-known historian as an instructor who paraphrased the famous quote by George Santayana thusly: "Those who cannot remember the past are condemned to repeat it; and those who do remember the past are condemned to repeat it." I understood and to some extent shared his cynicism, this during the time when our country was extricating itself from the War in Vietnam. However, I generally remained hopeful that I could play a role in enhancing the civic literacy of my students by providing them with opportunities not just to learn about our nation's history and its relevance to current affairs but also to critically reflect on that past and the present. (I adopted a similar approach in the sociology elective classes I taught, in which we addressed issues of race prejudice, economic inequality, women's rights, and the like.) I realized that, while we must not "suppress the nature of the danger" (Williams 1989, p. 322), hope is crucial if we are to make any progress in righting wrongs and in imagining and building alternatives worth pursuing (Apple, 2006).

I loved high school teaching. I left it because I became too interested in it—and wanted to learn more about what was taking place in schools, especially what was being taught and why, and the consequences of the choices that were made. Since then I've traveled a circuitous route in a way, but my work in teacher education and curriculum studies has always been in large part about the same thing, related to the extension and enhancement of critical civic literacy among the students with whom I am in contact, as well as among my professional colleagues, broadly speaking. It seems more important than ever to keep this goal in the forefront of public schooling.

Critical Civic Literacy

If literacy generally connotes having the ability to read, write, speaks and listen in meaningful ways, then civic literacy means being well-versed in social and political knowledge, understandings, dispositions, and skills. It means not only being able to essentially de-code and make meaning of the world around us but also to employ information and abilities for active engagement with and within civic relationships and institutions. In other words, if literacy education seeks to have people not just master but also use their skills—that is, to be literate is to read, not just know how to read—then likewise, civic literacy in our country is not just focused on learning about political structures and associations but becoming/being active democratic citizens.

Adopting a critical stance means not taking for granted what is known and in place, instead rigorously and wholeheartedly questioning the assumptions that undergird current ideas, practices, policies, and structures. It suggests a level of reflective inquiry that goes beyond techniques and strategies, beyond a consideration of doing of X better, to the ethics and goals that drive one's practices, in essence to the choice of doing X (rather than Y or Z) in the first place. As Michael Apple, Wayne Au, and Luis Armando Gandin (2009) suggest, it involves "fundamental transformations of the underlying epistemological and ideological assumptions that are made about what counts as 'official' or legitimate knowledge and who holds it" (p. 3). In addition, although not all observers might agree, I share their view that "being critical" in a democratic society includes social commitments as well, specifically "toward social transformation and a break with the comforting illusions that the ways in which our societies and their educational apparatuses are organized currently can lead to social justice" (p. 3). Critical civic literacy, then, entails more than becoming knowledgeable, skilled, and engaged in citizenship issues in the usual ways, e.g., knowing how a bill becomes a law and participating in local volunteer activities, and oftentimes including mindless rule-following (Westheimer, 2009), a kind of blind patriotism (Hamot, 2008; Kahne & Middaugh, 2006), and becoming "unquestioning followers of the capitalist system" (Lefrançois, Éthier, & Demers, 2008, p. 72). It involves interrogating the basic assumptions we have about social science knowledge and democratic citizenship, including critical inquiry of differing accounts of historical events and current affairs and the extent to which democratic participation actually exists; focusing in active ways on concerns and problems that are meaningful to students; and linking ideas, policies, and practices to larger issues of social justice.

Every period of one's life can be viewed as in some way involved with issues of civic literacy and critical reflection, from the early experiences of the pre-school age to the later senior citizen years. Indeed, a good argument can be made that unless critical literacy starts in the earliest grades (e.g., James & McVay, 2009; O'Mahony, 2009) and is consistently addressed throughout schooling, it will continue to be viewed as an afterthought or add-on to what is "really" important in the curriculum and thus what is really valued in life. Still, drawing on the work of Erik Erikson and others, many educators consider adolescence to be a prime period of life in which we are exposed to and are able to formulate conceptions of what we believe and what we can and should do with regard to social and political commitments and engagements, and it thus deserves a special place in the fostering of civic literacy (Jones, 2009). It is a crucial time in our development, or maturation, when we are better able to take account of the world beyond our immediate self and family. For many, it sets us on our path to seeking to better understand and improve our/the larger world, or, alternately, to feeling disinterested and disempowered to play any role at all in social and political change. Surely, we all agree about the crucial responsibility that schools have in promoting the former of these results. Or do we?

The Need for Civic Literacy in Our Schools

The United States was founded on the democratic ideal, what Abraham Lincoln famously described in his Gettysburg Address as a "government of the people, by the people, for the people." While since its inception this ideal has meant multiple things to different people, and while there have been notable accomplishments and notorious failures in our country's 200+ year history to live up to this ideal, one thing has been certain since the time of Thomas Jefferson, which is that education is assumed to play a crucial role in the definition, re-definition, and revitalization of democratic life. As Jefferson put it in his letters, "If a nation expects to be ignorant and free, in a state of civilization, it expects what never was and never will be. . . . Whenever the people are well-informed, they can be trusted with their own government." He considered the future of republican government in part to be "absolutely hanging on the hook [of] public education" (Coates, 1995). It is clear that for a very long time our schools have been entrusted with much of the education for democratic citizenship that is expected and considered essential for the young. As Benjamin Barber (1997) puts it, "public education . . . [is] the very foundation of our democratic civic culture. Public schools are not merely schools for the public, but schools of publicness: institutions where we learn what it means to be a public and start down the road toward common national and civic identity. They are the forges of our citizenship and the bedrock of our democracy" (p. 22). Simply put, one of the primary aims of education in the United States, seemingly as much agreed upon as any social goal, is "to prepare youth to contribute to civic life in a democracy" (Rubin, Hayes, & Benson, 2009, p. 3). Conceptualized broadly, such civic education would incorporate knowledge of politics, history, government, and current events; skills that enable communication, analysis, deliberation and action; dispositions that lead to a concern with and belief in the need for social and political change; and behaviors that involve being actively engaged in civic affairs (Levinson, 2010). It would include but go beyond a focus on how the government works, voting for political candidates to represent our individual interests, and engaging in charitable or public service projects.

How best to educate for democratic citizenship, as well as what democratic citizenship specifically means, has been a matter of debate for a long time among educators, government and business leaders, media pundits, and others. This is not the place to delve into the varied definitions, goals, and approaches, which need to be contextualized temporally as well as in terms of the varied experiences of different racial, ethnic and other groups, except to suggest that as we move into the second decade of the twenty-first century, it is clear that we need to take a closer look at current efforts to provide a meaningful and effective education for (not just about) democracy. At least three related factors can be identified that bear on this need.

First, it is important to consider where we find ourselves today with regard to civic engagement, particularly among the young. The following exchange is simply all too common:

Interviewer:	What are your feelings about government and politics?
Boy's voice:	It's boring.
Interviewer:	When you say it's boring, what's boring about it?
Boy's Voice:	The subject matter.
Girl's Voice:	Yes, very true.
Boy's Voice:	It's not just the work. It's what the work is about. We don't care about it.

(KAHNE, CHI, & MIDDAUGH, 2006, P. 388)

While certainly not all indices of civic competency and activism can or should be viewed as the result of the role of schools—that is, any suggested failure is one that many aspects of our culture can share—they do indicate a need for schools to rethink whether or not they are doing all they can to promote civic understandings and participation, especially given the historic role schools have been assumed to play in this area and particularly following the September 11, 2001, terrorist attacks (Shreiner, 2009). What we find today is that a large majority of young people are unlikely to vote, believe government can affect their lives, or even pay attention to politics at all; indeed, it appears that "American youth civic and political participation are at historic lows" (Kahne & Westheimer, 2006; Jacobsen, Frankenberg, & Winchell, 2009, p. 1). While some researchers point to an increase in voting for the 2008 presidential election and a possible increase in interest in volunteerism and service learning experiences, they still conclude that "political engagement is at an all-time low" (Jones, 2009; James & Iverson, 2009, p. 3). Former Supreme Court Justice Sandra Day O'Connor, for one, is quoted as saying that "[m]ost young people today simply do not have an adequate understanding of how our government and political system work, and they are thus not well prepared to participate as citizens" (Shreiner, 2009, p. 9). One study by the National Constitution Center found that only 38% of respondents could name the three branches of government, and yet another poll conducted two years earlier found that 59% of all Americans could name the Three Stooges (Kahne & Westheimer, 2003, p. 35). Particularly disconcerting is the seeming lack of interest among those pursuing education as a career; in one survey, 11.9% of them reported discussing politics on a regular basis, well below the already low national average of 20% (James & Iverson, 2009).

This lack of involvement is especially the case for graduates from urban schools. No doubt this gap is at least in part the result of a "civic opportunity gap," in which those who are more academically successful, White, or have parents of higher socioeconomic status receive more classroom-based civic learning opportunities and the actual knowledge, skills, and participatory experiences to become civically literate (Marri, 2009). Similarly, another researcher refers to "a profound *civic empowerment gap* between poor, some minority, and immigrant youth and adults, on the one hand, and middle-class or wealthy, white, and native-born youth and adults, on the other" (Levinson, 2010). As she notes, such a gap serves to "diminish the democratic character and quality of the United States" (p. 26). It also prevents urban students from gaining the kinds of social capital that would enhance their chances for academic success and future social mobility (Taines 2009; Jones, 2009; Jacobsen, Frankenberg, & Winchell, 2009). Just as importantly, it can lead to political identities that are based on a mistrust of "the government," which in turn reinforces a sense of powerlessness that leads to a lack of hope for a better future (Nygreen, 2008).

Clearly, there is increasing concern expressed about the level of civic knowledge and participation in our country. A good deal of this concern, however, especially from conservative groups, primarily laments "our fading heritage" and links it strictly to the inability of students to identify the three branches of the federal government, the nature of the Bill of Rights, the language of the Gettysburg Address, and so forth (Intercollegiate Studies Institute, 2008). While certainly knowledge of history and politics is crucial for young people to attain, simply adding more courses and multiple-choice assessments will do little to address the larger and more significant issue of not just the prevalent disinterest in significant historical events and important aspects of government but also the current apathy toward engaging in substantive civic activities. It is in this realm in particular that one can ask whether or not schools are doing all that they can and should. It is a vital question because meaningful participation in democratic life, not just in government per se but in what John Dewey (1916/1944) referred to as an inclusive "mode of associated living, of conjoint communicative experience" (p. 87) requires understandings, skills, and dispositions that can perhaps only be systematically developed in formal educational settings.

This general situation has not been helped any during the last decade by the second factor, which involves recent educational developments like the No Child Left Behind (NCLB) Act of 2001. I refer in particular to the legislation's strong (some might say heavy-handed) focus on reading, language arts, and mathematics, including frequent high-stakes standardized assessments of learning in those subject areas that hold directly accountable the teachers and schools involved. A related trend is the continuing overemphasis in American secondary schools on preparation for the workplace (Kliebard, 1999). Current Secretary of Education Arne Duncan is clearly not alone in suggesting that schools need to help in the effort "to educate our way [to] a better economy" (National Public Radio, 2009). Such educational policies and pronouncements serve to draw considerable attention and time (and other resources) away from social studies education in general (Au, 2009), despite the occasionally overheated rhetoric of various political and business leaders and media pundits about the need to "protect" our country's democratic heritage.

As I write this chapter, it is uncertain whether or not NCLB will be reauthorized, and if so in what form. However, it clearly has already had a substantial effect on what is taught in schools and how this teaching takes place. For many in the classroom it is the case that "real world experiences and meaningful curriculum projects are obsolete because their format does not support the test preparation regimen mandated by their school districts" (Ponder & Veldt, 2009, p. 4). Social studies education in general has become "the disappearing subject"; in a study done by the Center for Education Policy, one teacher no doubt speaks for many by stating that "[NCLB] has torn apart our social studies curriculum" (Au, 2009, p. 47). Civic education in particular gets less than half of one percent of the overall budget of the Department of Education and is increasingly "pushed to the margins of education efforts that challenge students to grapple with tough questions about society and the world" (Kahne & Westheimer, 2003, p. 35; Westheimer, 2009, p. 261). An account of one teacher educator working to address the situation in Florida notes that "civics education is being crowded out of the curriculum in many schools" (University of Florida College of Education, 2008). There is evidence as well that supplementary projects involving middle school students in activities focused on global issues have been curtailed (Teitelbaum & Brodsky, 2008). Indeed, due to NCLB and policies and legislation like it, "While we say we value a democratic society, the very institutions expected to prepare democratic citizens—our schools—have moved far from this central mission" (Kahne & Westheimer, 2003, p. 34).

The notion that schools are helping to "create a public" with a strong foundation of civic knowledge, skills and dispositions has withered in the midst of the panic for increasing reading and mathematics test scores and preparation for the workplace. Reports on education with titles that suggest a general focus on educational issues, such as recent ones from Advance Illinois (2009), The Brookings Institution (2006), and the Center on Education Policy (2009), often focus almost entirely on the teaching and learning of reading and mathematics. The increasing emphasis on high-stakes standardized tests with their expectation of "right answers," has eroded appreciation for the kinds of unsettling questions that drive critical civic literacy and the more difficult to measure results of activities to encourage civic participation.

Nevertheless, we know that our democratic way of life cannot be taken for granted or assumed to perpetuate itself without any effort on our part. Indeed, this is where the public school can play a crucial role, if it is defined as such. Perhaps it would be helpful to learn from the strategies of the proponents of the managerial new middle class (Apple, 2006) and advocate for standardized testing of youth's civic development. Indeed, several researchers have noted attempts to do so in a way that would take into account the actual participatory outcomes associated with civic education, although participation is often narrowly defined (Rubin, 2007; Jones, 2009).

Finally, the need for greater attention to civic literacy in schools comes from a consideration of the world that our young people are facing in the twenty-first century. The intensification of globalization in its many forms is transforming nation-states and local communities in significant and complicated ways (Singh, Kenway, & Apple, 2005). The most recent financial crisis has made clear what many already knew that economies are at the same time increasingly interlocked and competitive and jobs that seem to be taking place in one country can actually exist, rather easily and more cheaply, elsewhere. Climates are so intertwined that the effects of environmental despoliation in one area can have literally rippling effects across the planet. Infectious diseases and other health concerns start one place in the world and travel rapidly to continents far away. Technologies and media are ubiquitous, having the effect of bringing peoples of the world closer together on a daily basis and at the same time providing increased opportunities for privatized (and corporate) ventures. We are witnessing an unprecedented worldwide flow of immigration, in essence moving in all directions at once, which has the effect of providing greater opportunities for cross-cultural learning at the same time as exacerbating ethnic and religious conflicts. These and other complications of globalization will more than ever require an educated citizenry that can critically evaluate the complexities and defend the common good against the rapacious interests of wealthy and powerful individuals and transnational corporations. More than ever, adolescent students, about to enter not just the workplace but also adult citizenship, will need to learn and embrace the kinds of critical civic understandings and skills that can help to protect and enhance the democratic ideal and cultivate the kind of caring inclusive community that supports it. Strengthening democracy takes on added urgency during such unsettling and even volatile times when problem solvers, critical thinkers, and imaginative and innovative citizens will be needed more than ever.

In sum, we need to reverse the general erosion of civic engagement in our society and seek to encourage more direct and substantive participation in social institutions like schools. We need to contest aspects of NCLB and similar policies when they serve to seriously weaken possibilities for enhanced civic knowledge, skills, and commitments among our young people. We need to become more aware of the nature of the increasingly globalized world and how more sophisticated understandings and activism will be needed to extend democratic citizenship and social justice. Moreover, we need to develop viable curricula and instructional strategies that can be used in the classroom, to give adolescent students meaningful opportunities not just to learn about democracy but to experience for themselves the value of civic literacy and participation.

Kinds of Citizenship

The processes by which individuals come to see themselves as democratic citizens are varied, and the conceptions of democratic citizenship that guide them are different as well. This is not necessarily a bad thing; indeed, "multiple perspectives are an asset—not a hindrance—to democratic thinking, participation, and governance" (Hess, 2009, p. 77). Discussed openly and honestly, they can serve to enhance rather than weaken democratic life. What is particularly important here is a recognition that young people come to identify themselves as political subjects in wide-ranging (and rather messy) ways. In other words, a "one size fits all" approach will not adequately address the needs and interests of the diversity of students in our schools primarily because of the civic opportunity and civic empowerment gaps mentioned earlier. Given the different experiences, interests, cultural backgrounds, senses of efficacy, and other factors that exist among adolescents in our country, pedagogical strategies that "work" for one group of students will not necessarily be the case for another. As in all matters educational, there are complications and contradictions to consider. The worst approach would be to pretend that such complexity does not exist. Better to take account of this complexity to the extent possible as we seek to provide opportunities for young people to become more knowledgeable, skilled, engaged, and hopeful about the nature of our democracy, rather than feeling limited and relatively powerless to participate in political relationships and institutions.

The actual processes of determining one's political identity involve many different aspects of society; here we are concerned in particular with what happens in schools, which one could argue are "uniquely positioned to help cultivate the cognitive components that will help people solve the problems and make the decisions necessary for such democratic citizenship" (Shreiner, 2009, p. 333). What is needed first, perhaps, is to identify the conceptions of citizenship that can guide this work. Realizing that any such categorization can conceal significant differences as much as clarify similarities, the work of Joel Westheimer and Joseph Kahne (2004) is helpful in distinguishing three types of citizenship to promote critical civic literacy.

The first ideal type is the *Personally Responsible Citizen*. These are individuals who regularly vote, pay taxes on time, obey laws, give to charities, and follow current events. They may also help during times of serious need (storms and floods), contribute to clothing and food drives, give blood, and pick up litter and recycle. This kind of citizenship has a lot to do with actions at the individual level and includes primarily limited involvement in the needs of the local community, with little focus on the larger social structures and institutions of which the local is ostensibly a part. Such a conception can function comfortably within pervasive neoliberal ideology, which "prizes individual accomplishment, distrusts government, and disparages the need to work across political, ethnic, and religious differences" (Eisenhart, 2009, pp. 1–2).

The second kind of political identity is the *Participatory Citizen*. In this case, individuals are more actively involved in civic affairs, which could take place at the local, state and/or national levels. They do not just vote but they also campaign for chosen political candidates; do not just contribute to clothing and food drives but help to organize them; do not just give to charitable agencies but become actively involved on advisory boards; and do not just recycle at home but participate in neighborhood clean-up campaigns. This kind of citizenship includes greater engagement with collective efforts, joining with others in political and related activities to help shape the world in which we live.

The third category of citizenship referred to by Westheimer and Kahne is the *Justice-Oriented Citizen*. These individuals are particularly concerned with addressing systems of privilege and oppression and the root causes of social problems. They actively participate in collective strategies for change that challenge inequities related to issues of race, class, gender, and the like. While such individuals may be engaged in charity work and may volunteer for community-based organizations, they also identify with and advocate for larger social movements that seek to effect systemic change in support of the democratic ideal. They do not just help to organize clothing and food drives but also seek to address issues of hunger and homelessness in society; do not just engage in recycling but also organize with others to address the causes of environmental despoliation and climate change; and do not just vote or campaign for political candidates but actively work (and demonstrate) on behalf of policy and legislative changes that will insure the enhancement of democratic values and more equitable social conditions.

No doubt one must consider the local context when deciding what conception of citizenship is realistic to adopt in the classroom. This context will be influenced by, for example, school administrators, parents, students, and community members; local elected officials and state policies and mandates; resources available for certain educational materials and activities; and so forth. Nevertheless, an argument can be made that the first kind of citizenship, which no doubt is most prevalent, represents a welcomed but quite limited form of civic participation. Given the factors discussed earlier, as well as the disparities and divisions of our country, a more ambitious goal would seem worthwhile, one that promotes more critical civic understandings and more active support of and participation in democratic life. As such, it is the second and third categories described above that seem especially important to guide the work of schools today.

How can our schools help adolescent students, especially those from low-income and immigrant backgrounds, to feel included and empowered in areas of citizenship, rather than disengaged and passive, as seems so common today? How can we best prepare them to be participatory and justice oriented in their role as active global citizens in the twenty-first century? It is to these questions that we now turn.

Teaching for Critical Civic Literacy

As Deborah Meier (2008) suggests, parents seem to be particularly concerned with their children being well behaved in school, learning to read, and getting high test scores. Of course, these are all important ingredients of and for academic success. However, what seems to be increasingly ignored is the school's role in sustaining our democratic way of life, an effort that needs to be reborn and revitalized with each new generation in relation to broad social changes that occur. Indeed, as Meier states, "It is in schools that we learn the art of living together and where we are compelled to defend the idea of a public, not private, interest for the common good of our children." Nevertheless, "oddly enough, we have created a system for growing up in which no one takes responsibility for democracy." The result is that local citizens hardly get involved in decision making, and it is considered a significant achievement when a majority of those eligible to vote do so. Meier asks, "Can we educate children and adults for democracy if they have never experienced it? . . . Where is the time and space to make room for democracy?" (p. 23).

The most thorough approach would be for schools to become communities of learning in which the value of civic participation is made public and accessible and is realized as an integral and regular part of daily school life. In such educational settings, civic education would not be a topic but part of the very definition of the school experience; not a subject to be covered but one of the primary aims of educational practice; not a project but a curriculum theme that helps to guide teaching and learning in all grades. Schools would be less about educating "for" democracy and more about educating "through" democracy, with attention given to both the creation of "structures and processes by which life in the school is carried out" and the "curriculum that will give young people democratic experiences" (Apple & Beane, 2007, pp. 9–10). Rather than essentially ghettoizing the preparation of democratic citizens into, at best, one-hour time blocks during the afternoons in senior year government classes, it would be viewed as an essential and fundamental part of the mission-in-use of the school. Rather than an emphasis on the accumulation of factual knowledge and some future participation in civic affairs, the educational environment would be geared to engendering democratic subjectivity, with students being provided with authentic opportunities to take initiative and to be engaged (Biesta, 2007).

I am suggesting that such a holistic, integrated, and wholehearted approach to critical civic literacy is the ideal to undertake. However, of course it will not be adopted any time soon in most public schools. What are needed, then, are projects and other activities that in more limited but still significant ways can help schools to encourage adolescents to work together and to become more critically reflective and knowledgeable about and participatory in civic affairs. We need concrete curriculum materials and instructional strategies that will help to move civic education beyond a narrow focus on the different branches of government and the act of voting—and a reliance on lectures, textbook readings, and worksheets—to give students real opportunities to address social issues and problems that are consequential to them, whether in the school, local community, or at the state or national level. In essence, they need experiences in learning more about and improving the(ir) world, typically in social studies courses but quite possibly in other subject areas as well, usually in the classroom but perhaps also in after-school activities.

There are many related challenges to such a redirection, besides those that pertain to the particularities of the local context. One challenge concerns being able to offset the initial feeling of discouragement and apathy among young people toward history, politics, government, and public service; many are consumed instead with "managing daily life, finishing school, earning money, having fun, etc." and, if involved in community service at all, do so primarily to pad their college resumes (Eisenhart, 2009, p. 1). This phenomenon is completely understandable, of course, given current economic pressures, media, and commercial constructions of youth culture, and the mistrust of our political institutions especially among traditionally marginalized groups. Indeed, this is the problem in a nutshell. Another challenge involves the development of meaningful activities that take seriously adolescents' own lived experiences, skills, and interests and that do not simply privilege "the teacher's agenda" (Gustavson & Applebaum, 2005). There are many intellectual, cultural, and other differences within any class of students, as well as between schools, which include different experiences with, for example, political leaders and the police. Being aware of and sensitive to these differences when planning curricula can be a daunting task. It also means teachers willing to give over some "control" of the curriculum to students; and at the same time students departing from their typical "teacher as expert" assumptions and being willing and able (prepared) to take on more of such responsibilities. In addition, assuring the physical and emotional safety of students, that is, being sure that projects and activities engaged in are "safe" for students to pursue, must be of paramount concern. If, for example, gang-related drug use is a serious community issue (Rubin & Hayes, 2009), to what extent should students be encouraged to study and attempt to resolve the problem as part of a school-based civic learning experience? Another concern relates to the importance of political efficacy among young people and specifically the sense of hopelessness that can occur if students' efforts at civic activism are not deemed "successful." An argument can be made that feelings of efficacy are in fact crucial for later civic participation. However, at the same time, should one avoid potentially controversial issues in fear of instilling feelings of despair (Levinson, 2009; Kahne & Westheimer, 2006)? Finally, where in the curriculum is there space to pursue critical civic literacy, given the increased emphasis on reading and mathematics? This issue goes beyond standardized testing to the very courses required for graduation. For example, during the last five years in Illinois, high school graduation requirements have gone from including three years of language arts, two years of mathematics, one year of science, and two years of social studies, to four years of language arts, three years of mathematics, two years of science, and two years of social studies (Illinois General Assembly, 2009). The result is less opportunity for students to enroll in social studies and related elective courses.

Such difficulties are very real and need to be considered when seeking to introduce critical civic literacy efforts in the classroom. Depending on the context, and the extent of each of these challenges, efforts may need to be more or less limited in terms of "encouraging students to move toward human agency . . . by exercising agency through critical thinking, individual social action, and group social action" (Marri, 2009, p. 31). Still, there are many good stories to share of projects taking place in (and out of) the classroom that include rigorous study and purposeful action. Here, briefly, are a dozen of them:

- Fifth-graders who live in or near a Chicago housing project conduct research on improving conditions in their own neighborhood, specifically with regard to replacing their dilapidated and dangerous school building (Schultz, 2007).

- Students in a high school in southeastern Ohio participate as a team to interview and deliberate with teachers and others to help determine the hiring of new teachers for the school (Wood, 1998).

- High school students in a Northeastern community, in which 50% of the youths live below the poverty line, compile a scrapbook to document the ways in which their lives have been impacted by murder and drugs, to share with school, community, and state officials (Rubin, Hayes, & Benson, 2009).

- Students in a "last chance" public high school in New York City engage in an examination of Supreme Court cases dealing with issues of injustice and participate in mock retrials of these cases (Marri, 2009).

- Students in a high-poverty, urban, continuation high school in California organize a Participatory Action Research Team for Youth that establishes a vigorous political discourse among them and eventually leads them to teach a social justice class at their own school (Nygreen, 2008).

- An after-school club of 11- to 17-year-olds in a low-income Midwestern city conducts an oral history project with community elders to critically examine the recent history of their own community (Jones, 2009).

- An environmental justice class is developed by a science teacher at a high school in Boston, with students researching the problem of air quality and rising asthma rates in the surrounding neighborhood, and then organizing rallies, writing press releases, and testifying before the city council (Smith, 2008).

- A community-based youth organization in a Midwestern state provides opportunities for urban high school students to plan a Youth Summit to lobby for school funding reform, which includes having to secure school backing for the event (Taines, 2009).

- Tenth graders in an after-school engineering program for girls with strong academic records at three urban high schools in Colorado help in the construction of a playground for disabled children (Eisenhart, 2009).

- High school government students in a suburban, white, East Coast community investigate the feasibility of curbside recycling by conducting phone interviews, examining maps of population density, and analyzing projected housing growth and environmental impacts, eventually writing editorials and making public presentations on the issue (Kahne & Westheimer, 2003; Kahne & Westheimer, 2006).

- As part of a "Taking Action" curriculum design in mathematics classes, seventh graders share their analysis of data on the local costs of the U.S. war in Iraq and demonstrate to city council members that the city could channel money away from war-based efforts toward programs for the homeless and for improved park services (Applebaum, 2009).

- In an action project focusing on waste management, seventh grade students in Ontario examine hazardous wastes and their labels and then seek to change where their personal and home waste is being directed, encourage their neighbors to be mindful of littering, and reduce their own water usage (Sperling & Bencze, 2009).

These 12 examples can perhaps help us to envision what critical civic literacy projects can look like in our schools. (The publication *Rethinking Schools* is an excellent resource for other examples.) They might initially be more modest than one would like; they might not be easy to sustain; and they might not always be successful. However, without such opportunities to experience (practice) substantive research and authentic civic participation, students will know very little about what it means to be democratic in a robust way. Whether focused on school or community concerns, such projects can help students to see a purpose in what they are being taught and to experience the active role in civic affairs they can pursue after they graduate. Such curricula can include not just acquiring pertinent knowledge and participating in relevant activities but also asking basic, crucial questions concerning "what is [and is not] democratic about our . . . current state of 'democracy'?" (Tupper, 2009, p. 77). Such learning opportunities, as George Wood (1992) puts it, are guided by a vision that "is not limited to what kids learn about academics *in* school, but designed to encompass what sort of people they will be when they *leave* school" (p. 234).

Conclusion

"Democracy is not a spectator sport." Try Googling that sentence and, at least on the day that I did so, within a second you will get more than 900,000 hits. However, one should not let the overuse of this sentence obscure its central insight. Democracy requires not just a well-informed citizenry but an actively involved one as well.

I have argued in this chapter that, first, renewed efforts to promote civic literacy in schools are very much needed, given circumstances related to current levels of civic understanding and participation, educational policies that have narrowly focused attention elsewhere, and the changing, globalizing nature of the world; second, attempts to promote civic literacy should incorporate substantial components of knowledge, skills, dispositions, and experiences, as well as a sense of criticality, both in the reflective/analytical sense and the profound commitment to social justice; third, civic literacy projects should be guided by a conception of citizenship that is participatory and justice-oriented, and encourage a more collective and comprehensive approach to civic activism than the typical personally responsible forms; fourth, schools should be re-cultured to deal with issues of democratic citizenship as an integral part of school life; until that occurs, substantive and consequential critical civic literacy projects and activities of different kinds should be developed for and with students; fifth, these curricula should take as their starting (though not necessarily ending) point the varied experiences, skills, and interests of students, to engage adolescents in concerns and problems that are personally meaningful to them so they can develop their own sense of civic identity. We need to inspire adolescents to become fully realized democratic citizens; we need to give them hope that their engagement in critical analysis and civic participation can lead to an improvement of the(ir) world, even if in small ways; and we need to provide them with opportunities to experience for themselves the significant personal and social advantages to becoming more involved in the public (political) sphere. Students need practice in becoming the kind of citizens who are not content simply to vote, or to give to charity, or to know how a bill becomes a law, but who seek the skills and understandings, and the courage, to actively engage in the continuous reconstruction of democratic life. We cannot maintain a functioning democracy without such citizens, and schools can and should play a significant role in fostering them.

At the same time, although there are good examples of educational practice to share, schools alone cannot take on the responsibility for civic literacy and for building a more just and humane world. As Gert Biesta (2007) points out, "schools can neither create nor save democracy—they can only support societies in which action and subjectivity are real possibilities" (p. 470). The larger society needs to become more committed to, and one might even say obsessed with, an enhanced, thick version of democracy whereby people go beyond a mild interest in electing politicians to represent and secure their rights and instead are passionate and active in support of the dignity and rights of all individuals. Without advocacy and energy from the larger society, in multiple forms and with sufficient resources dedicated to these efforts, schools will continue to find it difficult to sustain civic education programs that substantially depart from repetition of "the dusty (and numerous) facts" of social science, the approach that leads students to announce, with a sense of resignation in their voices, that it is simply "boring" and they just "don't care about it." As such, schools will remain an untapped resource to help cultivate the informed and active citizenry that every democracy needs to survive.

Bibliography

Advance Illinois. (2009). *We can do better: Advancing public education in Illinois.* Chicago: Advance Illinois.

Apple, M.W. (2006). *Educating the "right" way: Markets, standards, God and inequality.* New York: Routledge.

Apple, M.W., Au, W., & Gandin, L.A. (2009). Mapping critical education. In M. Apple, W. Au, & L. A. Gandin (Eds.), *The Routledge international handbook of critical education* (pp. 3–19). New York: Routledge.

Apple, M.W., & Beane, J.A. (2007). The case for democratic schools. In M. W. Apple & J. A. Beane (Eds.), *Democratic schools: Lessons in powerful education* (pp. 1–29). Portsmouth, NH: Heinemann.

Apple, M.W., & Teitelbaum, K. (1986). Are teachers losing control of their skills and curriculum? *Journal of Curriculum Studies, 18*(2), 177–184.

Applebaum, P. (2009). "Taking action"–mathematics curricular organization for effective teaching and learning. *For the Learning of Mathematics, 29*(2), 39–44.

Au, W. (2009). Social studies, social justice: W(h)ither the social studies in high-stakes testing? *Teacher Education Quarterly, 36*(1), 43–58.

Barber, B. (1997). Public schooling: Education for democracy. In J. I. Goodlad & T. J. McMannon (Eds.), *The public purpose of education and schooling* (pp. 21–32). San Francisco: Jossey-Bass.

Biesta, G. (2007). Education and the democratic person: Towards a political conception of democratic education. *Teachers College Record, 109*(3), 740–769. Retrieved August 15, 2009 from http://www.tcrecord.org/PrintContent. asp?ContentID=12830

Brookings Institution, The. (2006). *How well are American students learning?* Washington, DC: The Brookings Institution.

Center on Education Policy. (2009). *Is the emphasis on "proficiency" shortchanging higher- and lower-achieving students?* Washington, DC: Center on Education Policy.

Coates, E.R. (1995). Thomas Jefferson on politics and government. In *University of Virginia Library Thomas Jefferson digital archive*. Retrieved September 19, 2009, from http://etext.virginia.edu/jefferson

Dewey, J. (1944). *Democracy and education: An introduction to the philosophy of education.* New York: Free Press. (Original work published 1916)

Eisenhart, M. (2009). Civic engagement as history in person in the lives of high school girls. Paper presented at the annual meeting of the American Educational Research Association, San Diego, CA.

Gustavson, L., & Applebaum, P. (2005). Youth cultural practices, popular culture, and classroom teaching. In J. L. Kincheloe (Ed.), *Classroom teaching: An introduction* (pp. 281–298). New York: Peter Lang.

Hamot, G. (2008). Citizenship education. In S. Mathison and E. W. Ross (Eds.), *Battleground schools* (101–110). Westport, CT: Greenwood.

Hess, D. (2009). *Controversy in the classroom: The democratic power of discussion.* New York: Routledge.

Illinois General Assembly. (2009). Illinois Compiled Statutes. Retrieved April 10, 2009, from http://www.ilga.gov/legislation/ilcs/fulltext.asp?DocName=010500050K27–22

Intercollegiate Studies Institute. (2008). *Our fading heritage: Americans fail a basic test on their history and institutions.* Retrieved September 13, 2009, from http://www.americancivicliteracy.org

Jacobsen, R., Frankenberg, E., & Winchell, S. (2009). Civic engagement and school racial context: How changing student demographics affect civic engagement outcomes. Paper presented at the annual meeting of the American Educational Research Association, San Diego, CA.

James J.H., & Iverson S.V. (2009). Civic actors, civic educators: Justice-oriented service in a pre-service teacher education program. Paper presented at the annual meeting of the American Educational Research Association, San Diego, CA.

James, J.H., & McVay, M. (2009). Critical literacy for young citizens: First graders investigate the First Thanksgiving. *Early Childhood Education Journal, 36*(4), 347–354.

Jones, D. (2009). From receivers of service to givers of service: Promoting civic engagement in youth from disadvantaged circumstances. Paper presented at the annual meeting of the American Educational Research Association, San Diego, CA.

Kahne, J., Chi, B, & Middaugh, E. (2006). Building social capital for civic and political engagement: The potential of high-school civics courses. *Canadian Journal of Education, 29*(2), 387–409.

Kahne, J., & Middaugh, E. (2006). Is patriotism good for democracy? A study of high school seniors' patriotic commitments. *Phi Delta Kappan, 87*(8), 600–607.

Kahne, J., & Westheimer, J. (2006). The limits of political efficacy: Educating citizens for a democratic society. *PS: Political Science & Politics 39*(2), 289–206.

Kahne, J., & Westheimer, J. (2003). Teaching democracy: What schools need to do. *Phi Delta Kappan, 85*(1), 34–40, 57–66.

Kliebard, H.M. (1999). *Schooled to work: Vocationalism and the American curriculum 1876-1946*. New York: Teachers College Press.

Lefrançois, D., Éthier, M.A., & Demers, S. (2008). Justice sociale et réforme scolaire au Québec: le cas du programme d'Histoire et éducation à la citoyenneté [Social justice and curricular reform in Quebec: Exploring the case of the History and Citizenship Education program]. *Revue International d'Éthique Sociétale et Gouvernementale*, *11*(1), 72–85.

Levinson, M. (2009). "You have the right to struggle": The construction of historical counternarrative as a tool for civic empowerment. Paper presented at the annual meeting of the American Educational Research Association, San Diego, CA.

Levinson, M. (2010). The civic empowerment gap: Defining the problem. In L. R. Sherrod, J. Torney-Purta, & C. A. Flanagan (Eds.), *Handbook of research and policy on civic engagement in youth*. New York: Wiley.

Marri, A.R. (2009). Closing the civic opportunity gap: Engaging urban youth in civic education. Paper presented at the annual meeting of the American Educational Research Association, San Diego, CA.

Meier, D. (2008). Educating for what? The struggle for democracy in education. *PowerPlay: A Journal of Educational Justice*, *1*(1), 20–27.

Mendelsohn, D. (2006). *The lost: A search for six of six million*. New York: Harper Perennial.

National Public Radio (2009). Duncan: "Educate our way to a better economy." Retrieved August 15, 2009 from http://www.npr.org/templates/transcript/transcript.php?storyId=100249947

Nygreen, K. (2008). Urban youth and the construction of racialized and classed political identities. In J. S. Bixby & J. L. Pace (Eds.), *Educating democratic citizens in troubled times: Qualitative studies of current efforts* (pp. 81–106). Albany, NY: SUNY Press.

O'Mahony, C. (2009). Core democratic values: Children's growth in understanding from grades three through five. Paper presented at annual meeting of the American Educational Research Association, San Diego, CA.

Ponder, J., & Veldt, M.V. (2009). Closing the loop in civic education: From teacher education, to professional development, to student learning in the elementary classroom. Paper presented at the annual meeting of the American Educational Research Association, San Diego, CA.

Rubin, B. (2007). "There's still no justice": Youth civic identity development amid distinct school and community contexts. *Teachers College Record*, *109*(2), 449–481.

Rubin, B., & Hayes, B. (2009). From "no backpacks" to "murder": Studying civic problems Across diverse contexts. Paper presented at the annual meeting of the American Educational Research Association, San Diego, CA.

Rubin, B., Hayes, B., & Benson, K. (2009). "It's the worst place to live": Urban youth and the challenge of school-based civic learning. *Theory Into Practice*, *48*(3), 213–221.

Schultz, B. (2007). "Feelin' what they feelin'": Democracy and curriculum in Cabrini Green. In M. W. Apple & J. A. Beane (Eds.), *Democratic schools: Lessons in powerful education* (pp. 62–82). Portsmouth, NH: Heinemann.

Shreiner, T.L. (2009). Framing a model of democratic thinking to inform teaching and learning in civic education. Unpublished doctoral dissertation, University of Michigan.

Singh, M., Kenway, J., & Apple, M.W. (2005). Globalizing education: Perspectives from above and below. In M. W. Apple, J. Kenway, & M. Singh (Eds.), *Globalizing education: Policies, pedagogies, & politics* (pp. 1–9). New York: Peter Lang.

Smith, G. (2008). Letter to president-elect Obama. In P. Cookson, & K. Welner (Eds.), *Fellows' education letters to the President* (n.p.). Boulder, CO: Education and the Public Interest Center, University of Colorado. Retrieved July 12, 2009 from http://epicpolicy.org/publication/Letters-to-Obama

Sperling, E., & Bencze, J.L. (2009). "Particle theory isn't everything": Engaging students in action-oriented citizenship through science education. Paper presented at the annual meeting of the American Educational Research Association, San Diego, CA.

Taines, C. (2009). Urban students' activism for educational reform and their development of social capital. Paper presented at the annual meeting of the American Educational Research Association, San Diego, CA.

Teitelbaum, K., & Brodsky, J. (2008). Teaching and learning in the age of accountability: One experience with the not-so-hidden costs. *Journal of Curriculum and Pedagogy*, *5*(1), 100–110.

Tupper, J. (2009). Unsafe waters, stolen sisters, and social studies: Troubling democracy and the meta-narrative of universal citizenship. *Teacher Education Quarterly*, *36*(1), 77–94.

University of Florida College of Education (2008). Professor heads effort to bring civics back to middle school. *Education Times*, Fall/Winter, 7.

Westheimer, J. (2009). No child left thinking: Democracy at risk in American schools and what we need to do about it. In H. S. Shapiro (Ed.), *Education and hope in troubled times: Visions of change for our children's world* (pp. 259–271). New York: Routledge.

Westheimer, J., & Kahne, J. (2004). What kind of citizen? The politics of educating for democracy. *American Educational Research Journal, 41*(2), 237–269.

Williams, R. (1989). *Resources of hope*. London: Verso.

Wood, G.H. (1992). *Schools that work: America's most innovative public education programs*. New York: Plume.

Wood, G.H. (1998). *A time to learn: The story of one high school's remarkable transformation and the people who made it happen*. New York: Plume.

This chapter originally appeared in Joseph L. DeVitis and Linda Irwin-DeVitis (eds.), *Adolescent Education: A Reader* (New York: Peter Lang, 2010).

CHAPTER THREE

Civic (Mis)education and Critical Civic Literacy

Elizabeth Yeager Washington & Ray W. Washington

Introduction

In 2010, a commitment to active critical civic literacy brought Elizabeth Washington and Ray Washington, the authors of this chapter, into the thick of a civic controversy that had erupted in the aftermath of a hotly disputed city election in Gainesville, Florida, home of the 50,000-plus student University of Florida, where Elizabeth is a professor of social studies education and Ray is a practicing attorney and writer. Our story is about how we became involved, what we accomplished, and the lessons we learned along the way.

"Critical civic literacy," as Elizabeth had been teaching her graduate social studies education students long before 2010, includes the exercising of skills of critical inquiry and analysis to help make meaning of what is happening in civic relationships and institutions in the world around us. As we ask questions and seek knowledge, we can use our understanding to challenge existing power structures.

Scholars such as Dewey (1916, 1927), Jones and Gaventa (2002), and Parker (1996, 2008) have conceptualized civic engagement as active participation in civic institutions in order to influence governance. Jones and Gaventa (2002) emphasize "the direct intervention of citizens in public activities," as well as the "accountability of the state and other responsible institutions to citizens" (p. 7). Parker (2008) uses the terms "enlightened political engagement" or "wise political action" (p. 68), explaining:

> Political engagement refers to the action or participation dimension of democratic citizenship, from voting to campaigning, boycotting, and protesting. Democratic enlightenment refers to the knowledge and commitments that inform this engagement: for example, knowledge of the ideals of democratic living, the ability to discern just from unjust laws and action…and the ability and commitment to deliberate public policy in cooperation with disagreeable others. Without democratic enlightenment, participation cannot be trusted…(and) can be worse than apathy. (p. 68)

Parker reminds us that enlightened political engagement is not easy to accomplish; in fact, it is a continuous goal toward which we work with others who hold different ideas and perspectives than ourselves.

As Ray understood from his career as a lawyer and journalist, obtaining the information we need to be active citizens requires us to be critically literate not just with regard to laws and government structures, but also with regard to media. The National Council for the Social Studies (2009) position statement on media literacy emphasizes the importance of analyzing ideology and power as we learn how media are used to position audiences and frame public opinion. Buckingham (2003) posits that media cannot be separated from the social and institutional structures in which it is situated.

As we both agreed, active critical civic literacy requires that we use what we discover, know, and understand to *critically engage* in civic life.

In the preface of this book, DeVitis emphasizes Clarence Karier's critique of Horace Mann's notion that "social harmony and consensus" are essential to civic engagement, and highlights Karier's focus on the ways in which institutions protect their vested interests. DeVitis also quotes C. Wright Mills, a public intellectual who pushed citizens and power brokers to challenge institutions to see new possibilities and to solve social problems.

Our story here is not a tale of active citizenship in an ideal world of social harmony and consensus—rather, it is a story of our personal experiment in using creative civic involvement in the contentious arena of resolving a vexing problem that could not be resolved in a harmonious way. It is a story of our attempts to utilize the concept of active civic literacy as a means of bringing clarity, rationality, and understanding to our city's civic discourse, in the face of active obstruction, obfuscation, and civic mis-education perpetrated by local media in symbiotic partnership with political operatives of a particular persuasion. It is also, more concretely, the story of how, in 2010, Gainesville became the largest city in the southeastern United States to be led by an avowedly gay mayor.

Background

Since 1995, Elizabeth has been a professor of social studies education at the University of Florida, where she has taught secondary social studies, global studies, and civics methods courses. About 7 years ago, Elizabeth started working with the Center for Civic Education, a national organization funded by Congress, as director of seminars for social studies methods professors on Constitutional issues such as the First Amendment, civil liberties, presidential power, and post-9/11 U.S. national security. In 2007, she became a Senior Fellow of the newly formed Florida Joint Center for Citizenship and has since worked on professional development for middle school teachers around Florida to teach the civics content now mandated by the Florida Legislature's Sandra Day O'Connor Civics Education Act. Elizabeth's work with the Florida Joint Center for Citizenship is an outgrowth of her involvement with the Bob Graham Center for Public Service at the University of Florida, whose mission includes enhanced citizenship and the training of current and future public and civic leaders who can identify problems and spearhead change.

The Florida Joint Center was launched by former U.S. Senator and U.S. Presidential candidate Bob Graham, a University of Florida graduate who after his retirement from the U.S. Senate in 2005 began a mission to promote the development of enlightened, responsible citizenship, and, along with former U.S. Congressman Lou Frey of Florida, joined forces in a variety of initiatives intended to strengthen civic education and improve the condition of Florida's civic health. Graham recently authored *America, The Owner's Manual: Making the Government Work for You* (2009). He has a long history of working to motivate Floridians to engage in civic life. Graham's interest in civic education was first highlighted in his 1978 dark horse candidacy for governor, built around his now trademark "Workdays" in which Graham worked at various jobs alongside Florida's diverse political constituencies. Among his "Workdays" were stints as a public high school civics teacher, a newspaper reporter, and a government bureaucrat. In that latter role, while working in a county courthouse, Graham discovered that very few government offices offered public access to restrooms. As a result of that discovery, Graham vowed that, if elected governor, he would require public offices to designate restrooms as available for public use. When Graham did become governor, he in fact issued the promised order. But here in Gainesville, creative officials implemented the order with a bit of bureaucratic ingenuity: To the doors of two restrooms that, pre-Graham, had been reserved for staff-only use, they affixed two office-style signs, one labeled "Mrs. Damen" and the other "Mr. Herren," leading many members of the public to believe the public restrooms were in fact private offices belonging to bureaucrats named Damen and Herren. The status quo, in Gainesville at least, thus was largely maintained.

Ray's experiences in Gainesville over the last 15 years have included writing a government and politics column and reporting on higher education for the *New York Times*, owning *The Gainesville Sun*, and, more recently, practicing law in Gainesville and the surrounding communities, primarily in the areas of criminal defense and civil due process indigent representation. As an undergraduate student at Duke University, Ray had studied under Professor David L. Paletz, a leading political science scholar then focusing his research on politics and the media. Under Paletz's direction, Ray authored a study analyzing how the North Carolina press in its reporting on political campaigns historically had provided ballast for continuing the racial status quo.

Shortly after graduating from Duke, Ray accepted a job as a reporter for Florida's capital newspaper, *The Tallahassee Democrat*. In that capacity, Ray met the then little-known Florida State Senator Bob Graham. He accompanied Graham on a gubernatorial campaign "Workday" in which Graham labored as a reporter for the *Madison Enterprise-Recorder*. Ray observed Graham's seemingly genuine interest in the role of the press in promoting what is now known as critical civic literacy. Ray and Graham together covered the investiture of a circuit judge who had been appointed to replace a judge convicted of racketeering. They treated the investiture ceremony as a lesson in civic education, their articles subsequently published in their competing newspapers.

Graham's decades-long focus on critical civic literacy was an indirect contributor to our decision in 2010 to set aside personal preferences for away-from-the-fray observation and explanation, and to become active participants in resolving the murky, contentious civic controversy that erupted following the 2010 Gainesville city elections, whose resolution we describe below.

The Community

From its origins as Hogtown before the Civil War until well into the 1960s, Gainesville in many ways remained an archetypal small-town, southern community, notwithstanding the arrival of the University of Florida in Gainesville in 1906. Until the end of the Depression, Florida remained the least populous of the former Confederate states. Until long after World War II, Gainesville, politically and socially, continued to reflect its small-town, southern roots, despite the transformation of the University of Florida—from an officially all-male, whites-only institution numbering only a few hundred students at the end of the war—into the educational colossus it would become. After the war, as the population of Florida burgeoned and became more urban and less southern, change came slowly to the campus (Washington, 2004a).

The GI Bill, and the formal admission of female students when the University of Florida became a co-educational institution in the late 1940s, combined with the University of Florida's unprecedented post-war growth, increased the university's enrollment from a few hundred students to over 10,000 over the span of a decade. By the mid-1950s, the first non-southerner had become president of the university—albeit an agricultural economist from rural Kansas who was selected because of his appeal to the state's political leaders as a force for maintaining the university's status quo. By the late 1950s, the first African American student was finally allowed to enroll at the University of Florida—in the law school, following a political compromise that ended years of litigation in the Florida Supreme Court. By the early 1960s, the Florida legislature had shut down the state's infamous Johns Committee—a McCarthy-style state witchhunt that for years had targeted gay professors and students at the state's public university campuses, particularly the University of Florida. By the early 1960s, the first African American students also were finally allowed to enroll at the University of Florida as undergraduates. By the mid-1960s, the university's football team had been integrated. By the late 1960s and early 1970s, as the University of Florida's enrollment grew to more than 20,000, the faculty and students had become similar to the faculties and students on large campuses across the country, and anti-Vietnam War demonstrations, student sit-ins, anti-racism protests, and abortion-rights campaigns roiled the campus (Washington, 2004b).

As the University of Florida grew, so too, eventually, did the community of Gainesville—though in the early post-war years Gainesville grew far more slowly than the university, and more slowly than Florida as a whole. As the city and the university it hosted grew, gradually the forces of change did arrive in Gainesville, and eventually they began to reshape Gainesville's political culture. In the early 1960s, the city's Reconstruction-era local newspaper, *The Gainesville Sun,* was acquired by *Cowles Media Company*—thus ending nearly a century of private southern ownership. In 1965, the newspaper won a Pulitzer Prize for editorials condemning the city's shameful slum housing in east Gainesville, the part of the city where most African American citizens resided. In 1971, *The New York Times Company* acquired *The Gainesville Sun* from *Cowles.* That year, the newspaper won another Pulitzer Prize, this time for its editorials supporting peaceful desegregation of the county's public schools (Washington, 2004c).

Today Gainesville has become more similar to university host cities and less similar to the communities that surround Gainesville—towns like Starke (dominated by the state's largest prisons, including the nearby death row prison), Palatka (whose biggest employer is the Georgia-Pacific paper mill), and Bronson (where a stone tablet carved with the Ten Commandments sits beside the county courthouse). But Gainesville, politically, can be a bubbling cauldron of widely diverse political beliefs and perspectives.

In years past, the city officially recognized United Nations Day, flying the United Nations flag over City Hall in celebration. In response, the North Central Florida Regional Militia and other groups called for the city's elected officials to be removed from office, and have organized yearly protests that at times have prompted law enforcement teams to be dispatched to City Hall.

In recent years, the city government has put into effect domestic-partner benefits for city employees, despites months of debate and protests. In 2009, the city's voters approved a referendum that included transgender people in the city's human rights ordinance. However, prior to this referendum, county voters had approved an ordinance that would have prohibited legal protections for people based on sexual orientation, had the ordinance not been later thrown out by a federal court.

In 2010 the city dominated the national news when the pastor of one of the city's non-denominational churches announced plans to conduct burnings of the Qur'an on the ninth anniversary of the September 11, 2001 attacks, designating September 11, 2010, as "International Burn a Koran Day." The plan was condemned by some, but not all, of the community's other churches.

Such is the context in which Gainesville's 2010 mayoral election controversy began.

The Election

In early 2010, a Tea Party-identified candidate named Don Marsh and his supporters organized a challenge to Gainesville City Commissioner Craig Lowe, one of several candidates to replace the outgoing mayor. Lowe had been openly gay for his entire political career, and had been elected and re-elected to the city commission without controversy. But in the run-up to the mayoral election, *The Gainesville Sun*—its paid circulation numbers in a nosedive—began publishing articles and newspaper blog installments indentifying Lowe as gay. The newspaper's rationale for reporting Lowe's sexual orientation varied; at times the reference came in articles reporting the appearance in unspecified numbers in unspecified places of anonymous bumper stickers alleging that Lowe intended to turn Gainesville into a "gay" town; at times the reference was in the context of reporting the appearance of a crude sign declaring "No Homo Mayor" on the lawn of the city's Islam-hating church, described above; at times the news peg was simply the newspaper's attempts to secure Lowe's comments about the anti-gay taunts the newspaper discovered.

The Gainesville Sun's unusual brand of campaign coverage appeared to have had the salutary effect of increasing voter turnout in the electoral contest between Lowe, a University of Florida employee and long-time elected official, and Marsh, a political newcomer who owned a window-cleaning business and railed against the liberal takeover of City Hall.

Lowe defeated Marsh in the mayoral runoff election by a 42-vote margin.

The Controversy

Although the election itself was over—the votes had been counted and recounted, and the winning candidate certified by the city's canvassing board—*The Gainesville Sun*, we soon discovered, was about to foment a manufactured controversy that would mislead voters about election laws; misinform readers about the role of courts and judges in government; and confuse the city's citizens about basic civic processes.

The first salvo against the city's civic literacy was launched the day after the election. That morning, we discovered, *The Gainesville Sun* had published the first of a string of articles, blog posts, and editorials uncritically repeating shifting allegations of election cheating and corruption that supporters of the losing candidate variously alleged to have been perpetrated by the campaign of the winning candidate, by election officials, and by voters. *The Gainesville Sun*, in the days ahead, would publish article after article repeating allegations that misconduct in the election had been so widespread that the candidate certified as the city's new mayor and scheduled to be sworn into office the following month may have been fraudulently elected. Voter fraud, not sexual orientation, now became the newspaper's focus of controversy.

Among the most troubling of the new allegations were assertions that officials in the office of the county Supervisor of Elections had fraudulently handed out multiple ballots to certain preferred voters to ensure the election of their preferred candidate and the defeat of the candidate they opposed. *The Gainesville Sun* repeatedly pounded the drum of alleged fraud, informing readers that the statutory deadline for filing an electoral challenge was approaching. The day before the deadline, the newspaper published a front-page, above-the-fold report purporting to expose a potential loophole to voter fraud. It was a Sunday, *The Gainesville Sun*'s most profitable news rack sales day. Thus began our awareness of a shameful campaign of civic mis-education, aided and abetted by the city's once-respected *New York Times*–owned newspaper, which led to our experiment in active critical civic literacy.

Civic Mis-Education, Part I

The Gainesville Sun instructed credulous readers that the results of the city's recent mayoral election were under a cloud because the Florida legislature had failed to fix a "glitch" in the state's voting laws that the newspaper had uncovered. The "glitch," the newspaper reported, theoretically could have allowed registered voters from other parts of Florida to come to Gainesville on the day of the mayoral runoff election, fraudulently declare themselves to be Gainesville residents, and illegally vote.

The article contained a one-sentence disclaimer buried inside the newspaper on a jump page acknowledging that *The Gainesville Sun* had investigated the claimed residential addresses from a list of voters who had showed up at city polling places on the day of the election offering new addresses that same day, as the law allows them to do, and had been unable to verify an instance of illegal voting. Still, the newspaper reported, the "glitch" meant that illegal voting *could* have occurred. The paper suggested that state lawmakers would do well to correct their purported oversight. In the meantime, the newspaper reminded readers that the deadline for an aggrieved voter to challenge the results of the mayoral election was only a day away.

Elizabeth's dismay upon reading the article was that of a civic educator appalled by the civic mis-education being perpetrated by a *New York Times Company*–owned newspaper that had so often promoted its participation in the nationwide "Newspapers in Education" program. That program, whose reach extended to many of Elizabeth's students when they became secondary social studies educators in Florida and around the nation, encouraged classroom teachers to use the newspaper as a tool for civic education. As Elizabeth knew, but as many readers would not know, the very premise of the newspaper's report was erroneous. The federal 2002 *Help America Vote Act* (HAVA), enacted in the aftermath of the 2000 election follies, in conjunction with other federal laws restricts state legislatures from enacting laws that hamper voting in the "glitch"-fixing manner suggested by *The Gainesville Sun*.

Ray's dismay reflected not only the chagrin of a voter, citizen, and practicing attorney in Gainesville, but also as a former journalist who a decade earlier had investigated, analyzed, and interpreted the local and Florida 2000 presidential election results for readers of *The Gainesville Sun* and the *Manchester (N.H.) Union-Leader*–owned *Sunday Journal*. Ray had been part of the media convergence in Tallahassee as Florida courts grappled with lawsuits challenging the Florida presidential election results and calling into question the national election outcome. In Tallahassee, Ray had learned firsthand of the high regard that statewide and national election experts had for the integrity and professionalism of the Alachua County Supervisor of Elections office, which avoided the electoral problems that tarnished other local elections offices in Florida that year. Gainesville elections officials, having instituted processes and procedures before the 2000 elections, had not only been exempt from the national ridicule of "hanging chads" or "butterfly ballots," but had, in the aftermath of Florida's 2000 presidential election fiasco, been widely regarded as models to be emulated across the state and nation.

Civic Mis-Education, Part II

The day after *The Gainesville Sun*'s report was published, two supporters of the losing mayoral candidate entered the Alachua County Courthouse minutes before the deadline for challenging the mayoral election, paid a $400 filing fee, and filed a lawsuit. The following day, *The Gainesville Sun*, without providing readers with clear information about the lawsuit, or analysis of the lawsuit's legal basis, published a news report headlined: "After a runoff and a recount, there is now a lawsuit." The newspaper credited its own explanatory reporting of the voting law "glitch" as the impetus for the losing candidate's supporters having filed their lawsuit.

The shape of things to come became evident to us later that week when *The Gainesville Sun* published another article about the lawsuit, this time providing no new information but stating that "despite a lawsuit challenging the results of Gainesville's mayoral election," the mayor whose election had been alleged to be fraudulent "will take office next month unless a judge intervenes." An article also called upon the judge to "object." In misreporting the basics of the workings of the judicial branch, the newspaper suggested to readers that the judge assigned to hear the lawsuit had the authority, but also the obligation, to "intervene" and to "object" to prevent the swearing-in of a candidate alleged, without proof, to have been fraudulently elected.

In that same edition, the newspaper's opinion page contained a lead editorial focused on the city's supposed electoral tarnish. "The integrity of Gainesville's elections process has been called into question, and voters need to be assured that the process is sound," announced the editorial, which asserted that because "the issue *had been raised* in connection with the recent election" of "out-of-towners flocking to Gainesville and falsely declaring themselves new residents for the specific purpose of swaying a city election," citizens could look forward to getting answers from the court.

Ray, earlier that week, had cursorily reviewed the lawsuit filed at Gainesville's civil court-house, and had discovered the unreported news that the lawsuit had nothing to do with "out-of-towners flocking to Gainesville and falsely declaring themselves new residents for the specific purpose of swaying a city election." Such allegations certainly had been the premise of the news-paper editorial that day, as it had been the premise of its breathless pre-lawsuit-deadline inves-tigation that misled readers about the existence of a so-called state election law "glitch." Ray had learned that the lawsuit, such as it was, asserted only that the plaintiffs suspected that an unknown number of unnamed voters had been voting absentee in Gainesville "for years" with-out proper legal residential qualification to do so. The plaintiffs—a Tea Party-associated local minister and a failed city commission candidate who both supported the losing candidate for mayor—had merely alleged that they were suspicious that the Supervisor of Elections may have failed to follow procedures that could have determined the correct residential addresses of some absentee voters alleged to have been registered with incorrect or outdated addresses.

To us, it seemed logical that such suspect voters, if they had in fact erroneously voted in the recent Gainesville mayoral election, were as likely to have voted for the losing candidate as for the winning candidate, given the closeness of the election. We were convinced that the lawsuit had no legal relevance to the outcome of the mayoral election, and therefore could not survive a well-pled and timely motion to dismiss. It was clear to us—contrary to *The Gainesville Sun*'s "important-dispute/legal-fight-to-settle-it" story line—that the dispute was imaginary, and that there was no possibility that anything would be settled in the courtroom.

We suspected that the plaintiffs themselves also knew this. As Ray discovered through a quick Google search, the plaintiffs appeared to have simply dug up a 2000 presidential election chal-lenge complaint they found on the Internet, cutting and pasting into their lawsuit whole sen-tences and paragraphs from the ultimately dismissed lawsuit that had challenged the results of the Palm Beach County's presidential vote and attacking the infamous "butterfly ballot." The failed Palm Beach County lawsuit had been filed in a different context, had pled different issues, and had referred to repealed statutes and outdated legal precedent. But no matter: The plaintiffs excised references to Palm Beach County, affixed their signatures, and filed their law-suit, without an attorney's review and certification.

Given *The Gainesville Sun*'s continuing erroneous and misleading news coverage, and the plaintiffs' questionable actions, we concluded that neither the plaintiffs nor the newspaper's edi-torial decision makers seemed motivated by notions of civic harmony or consensus. To the con-trary, it appeared to us that both the newspaper and the plaintiffs had become part of a peculiar institutional symbiosis antithetical to harmony and consensus. Disharmony and dispute, we con-jectured, could have a powerful appeal to news decision makers whose economic survival in a dying industry may have blinded them to traditional notions of journalistic civic responsibility. It may have also been irresistibly alluring to political partisans whose constituencies reward them most richly in times of perceived civic polarization.

But if we were right, what to do? Where, we asked ourselves, should such breakfast-table philosophizing lead us?

Active Citizenship

As Elizabeth has taught, and as Ray has long recognized in his writings and legal efforts, a critical component of "active citizenship" is the direct intervention of citizens in public activities. As residents of the city of Gainesville, we had voted in the 2010 mayoral election, and to that limited extent, we marginally had been "active citizens." But as Westheimer and Kahne (2004) have suggested, such civic involvement at best represents only the lowest of three levels of citizenship—the "personally involved citizen." The second level of citizenship, in their formulation, is practiced by the "participatory citizen," who attempts greater civic engagement. The third, and highest, level of citizenship is practiced by the "justice-oriented citizen," who addresses the root causes of social problems, attempting more intense personal involvement focused on the enhancement of democratic values.

Elizabeth occasionally has been a "participatory citizen" as a volunteer in national political campaigns and as a political blogger focused on progressive politics and social change. Ray has been a "participatory citizen" more rarely and more distantly. For example, in the late 1970s he participated in a last-ditch effort to encourage support in rural north Florida for the passage of the Equal Rights Amendment to the Constitution, giving speeches and public presentations as well as running for the Florida House of Representatives based on a platform of support for the ERA.

Although at a professional level we have been concerned with addressing the root causes of social problems, our direct, personal involvement as "justice-oriented citizens" has been rare. We do believe that "justice-oriented citizenship," as Westheimer and Kahne conceive it, requires involvement beyond the professional realm. Yet such personal involvement can be ill advised and contrary to professional responsibilities requiring circumspection and personal distance.

So, again, what to do? In the local situation we have described, we discovered that we had a unique possibility for becoming personally involved as "justice-oriented citizens" in a manner entirely consistent with our professional responsibilities. Neither of us had played a role in the political campaigns around which the post-election civic debates were now swirling, beyond educating ourselves on the issues and making our own private voting choices. Neither of us had contributed to or openly supported any of the candidates. Indeed, neither of us initially believed we had even met any of the candidates, although we would later recall that we once contracted, satisfactorily, with candidate Marsh for window cleaning services.

Ultimately, we defined our choice of how to involve ourselves as "active citizens" in terms of what we conceived to be our ultimate purpose. Our goal was not to bring about a particular political result. Rather, we wanted to contribute clarity and reason to our city's civic discourse, which had become irrational, murky, and confused, and which, we feared, would become even more damaging to the community in the 3 weeks remaining until the date set for the swearing-in of the new mayor. We decided that our first approach should be to communicate with the decision makers of the primary institutional force shaping the civic discourse—*The Gainesville Sun*—and appeal to their better angels.

When Harmony and Consensus Fail

For would-be civic actors, meaningful opportunities for influencing the media can appear quite limited. Moreover, institutional barriers to media access can be so impenetrable that influence may not seem realistic, particularly for justice-oriented citizens concerned with addressing systems of privilege and oppression and the root causes of social problems. In this assessment, such justice-oriented citizens may often be correct.

In our case, we had reason to be more hopeful. It had been nearly a decade since Ray had ended any professional affiliation with *The Gainesville Sun* and the New York Times Company. Many of the newspaper's long-time staffers were no longer there, some victims of industry-wide corporate downsizing in the face of declining circulation. But the newspaper's principal news and editorial decision makers remained there, occupying the same positions. Among these were the publisher, the executive editor, the managing editor, and the editorial page editor—the latter an acquaintance with whom Ray had continued to play poker after ending employment with the company.

Ray hoped that his access to *The Gainesville Sun*'s news decision makers might allow him to be a catalyst for our hope of transforming what had been an unfortunate episode of civic mis-education into a teachable moment for the community. He certainly did not expect the decision makers to be willing or able to expend the resources necessary to fully investigate and develop context for the stories already reported. He understood first-hand the institutional changes that had been visited upon the newspaper industry, particularly by the Internet, which had been inexorably driving down newspaper circulation for a decade. In the late 1970s, halcyon days for newspapers, Ray had been recruited and hired by the New York Times Company Vice President and New York Times Regional Newspaper Group Vice President John R. Harrison to be a company-wide roving columnist, a position Ray held throughout most of the 1980s. Harrison previously had been publisher of *The Gainesville Sun* after it had been acquired in the early 1960s by *Cowles*—in fact, Harrison had authored the progressive editorials that earned the newspaper its first Pulitzer Prize—before taking charge of the *New York Times*'s then fast-growing regional newspaper group and expanding it across the south and into California. But those days of newspaper industry growth and profitability were long gone. By 2010, many of the *New York Times* regional newspapers had been sold off, and newspapers that had not yet been sold, like *The Gainesville Sun*, were barely holding on. *The Gainesville Sun*, in fact, had seen sharp circulation declines exceeding those of most other university town newspapers, including the New York Times Company's own *The Tuscaloosa News*, Elizabeth's hometown newspaper.

On the morning *The Gainesville Sun* published the edition that mischaracterized the election-challenge lawsuit and the role of the judge in the lawsuit, Ray attended a brief meeting at the newspaper's offices in which he raised questions about the newspaper's coverage errors and mischaracterizations. He also suggested resource-efficient ways the newspaper might use its past erroneous coverage as a springboard for an analytical piece educating readers about the state's election laws and the role of the courts in election challenges.

At a minimum, we hoped to read corrections in the next day's newspaper, as theoretically required according to *The Gainesville Sun*'s policy. But no corrections appeared the next day, or on any other day. We also hoped the newspaper would publish an accurate follow-up news story about the elections lawsuit—in effect, an oblique correction. The paper remained silent. Ray then wrote a piece for the newspaper's opinion page and submitted it to his poker buddy, the editorial page editor. The piece, which he titled "Civics Negative-101," began as follows:

> As reported by *The Gainesville Sun*, two Gainesville citizens last week filed a lawsuit in circuit court in Gainesville, seeking to challenge the results of the recent Gainesville mayoral election. This citizen lawsuit is but one example of the increased civic interest and involvement generated by the 2010 Gainesville city election. Citizen action in American democratic society, most agree, is a good thing, and should be encouraged and nurtured in all branches of government, and at every governmental level, and among all political viewpoints.
>
> But professional civic educators—my wife among them—assert that citizen action is most effective for civic actors and most salutary for our democratic institutions when it is grounded in civic understanding. When grounded in civic ignorance rather than civic knowledge, civic action can have an opposite, and negative, effect.

Ray went on to discuss the basic civics errors in *The Gainesville Sun*'s news and editorial columns, to explain what the newspaper had not explained, and to call for an end to the newspaper's "brand of civic education." More silence. Ray's submission was never published.

From this experience, we concluded that justice-oriented citizenship required us now to depart from Mann's Harmony-Consensus Road and travel for a while on Conflict Highway. Together, we filed joint motions, as voices of our city's voters, to intervene in the elections lawsuit. We intended for our intervention to be a vehicle for ending *The Gainesville Sun*'s misleading, high-profile reporting and for removing the unjustified cloud that hovered over the city's duly elected mayor, whose scheduled swearing-in ceremony was now 17 days away.

"Direct Intervention in Public Activities"

As intervenors, we had availed ourselves of a legal avenue available to any citizen whose substantial interest is affected by a lawsuit. Our substantial interests as voters and as citizens of Gainesville had been affected by the taint of civic illegitimacy foisted upon our city and its elected mayor by a spurious lawsuit.

We concluded that the plaintiffs planned to let their lawsuit languish beyond the scheduled date for the new mayor's swearing-in ceremony, thus building a public perception—aided and abetted by *The Gainesville Sun*—that a judge's failure to "intervene" and dismiss the lawsuit was an indication that the suit had merit. The plaintiffs, who controlled when and if their claims would be brought before the court, had neither scheduled a hearing nor taken any action to move their lawsuit along—although they had scheduled appearances on local talk shows whose credulous hosts reinforced what had been reported in *The Gainesville Sun*.

We were soon to learn that the judge assigned to our case was newly appointed circuit judge Victor L. Hulslander, himself a proponent of civic education and the head of the Justice Teaching Program for Florida's Eighth Judicial Circuit. Florida's Justice Teaching Program had been launched in 2006 by Florida Supreme Court Chief Justice Fred Lewis, whose goal was to pair a judge or attorney with every school in the state in order to educate students about the judicial system and the role of the courts within the Constitutional framework (Justice Teaching

Program, 2011). We had heard Judge Hulslander speak at a 2006 local civic education forum and at a Justice Teaching training session he conducted in 2007, and we were hopeful that he would not only decide what was proper under the law but would do so in a way that would educate the public. In this we would not be disappointed. Within an hour of the delivery to Judge Hulslander's chambers of our motion to dismiss the lawsuit, he had set our motion for hearing.

Before our motion could be heard, the plaintiffs and their supporters had secured the services of a political operative lawyer from Orlando, where the legitimacy of that city's duly elected Democratic mayor had been clouded by two years of ultimately unsuccessful litigation. From a litigation war-room in Orlando, the plaintiffs' counsel and affiliated counsel amended the plaintiffs' lawsuit, pouring forth hundreds of pages of pleadings, legal research, and exhibits claiming to show that Gainesville's election process was corrupt or dysfunctional, and voting fraud rampant. The proceedings were reported and live-blogged by *The Gainesville Sun*, which, predictably, issued forth more creative civic mis-education, providing readers with blow-by-blow coverage in the nature of a prize fight, including a scorecard that read:

THE PLAYERS

Plaintiffs: Mason Alley, finished third in District 4 City Commission race, and Phil Courson, senior pastor at Abundant Grace Community Church; both contributed to a campaign last year for a failed amendment to repeal a city ordinance extending civil rights to transgendered people (Craig Lowe had been a major proponent of the ordinance).

Defendants: Gainesville canvassing board, a three-member board chaired by city Commissioner Thomas Hawkins that oversees city elections; Pam Carpenter, Alachua County's elections supervisor whose office conducted the election; Craig Lowe, mayor-elect and city commissioner.

Interveners: Ray Washington, an attorney; Elizabeth Washington, professor of social studies education at the University of Florida.

Other: Don Marsh, window-cleaning business owner who lost the mayoral election by 42 votes.

The suit
Alley and Courson claim they have found evidence of illegally registered voters who cast ballots in Gainesville's mayoral election and are asking the judge to void the results. The Washingtons have asked the court to dismiss the case.

Denouement

Judge Hulslander made short work of the lawsuit in a 16-page order issued May 19, the day before the new mayor was scheduled to be sworn in. We believe the order to be a masterpiece in the annals of civic education literature. The judge issued a decision that not only made clear exactly what we had been trying to get the decision makers at *The Gainesville Sun* to explain to the community, but he did so in an eloquent way. The judge fully granted our motion to dismiss the plaintiffs' baseless lawsuit, with prejudice. But his order went beyond merely granting our motion. In clear, unambiguous language, he (1) explained the election process and the laws related to it, (2) provided unqualified assurance of the soundness of the city's election process, and (3) answered questions that had been raised as a result of weeks of erroneous or misleading news and commentary published in *The Gainesville Sun.*

By quoting from or paraphrasing Judge Hulslander's order, *The Gainesville Sun* could have provided its readers with important information and context, and could have furthered this community's civic education. However, *The Gainesville Sun* did not quote a single word from the judge's order. Had the paper done so, its readers would have learned that:

- "The 'sanctity of the ballot and the integrity of the election' in this case have been maintained."
- The plaintiffs have presented "only a theory that certain suspect voters cast votes 'in technical violation of the law.'"
- The plaintiffs have "circumvented the statutory scheme and applicable criminal penalties" which puts anyone making a "'frivolous challenge' to any person's right to vote" at risk of being convicted of a first-degree misdemeanor.
- The plaintiffs have presented an "absolute lack of factual support for any claim of fraud or misconduct on the part of elections officials."

Judge Hulslander also wrote:

The Florida Supreme Court has noted that "the real parties in interest" in an election contest "are the voters." Ours is a government of, by and for the people. Our federal and state constitutions guarantee the right of the people to take an active part in the process of that government, which for most of our citizens means participation via the election process. The right to vote is the right to participate; it is also the right to speak, but more importantly the right to be heard. We must tread carefully on that right or we risk the unnecessary and unjustified muting of the public voice.

He concluded:

Even if the court assumes that all of the factual allegations provided by the Plaintiffs are true, Plaintiffs fail to state a cause that would entitle them to relief under Section 102.168. In addition, Plaintiffs fail to allege sufficient facts to support an election contest as provided by Section 102.168. Furthermore, public policy dictates that Plaintiffs should not be allowed to invalidate an entire election, and mute the voice of the real parties in interest—the voters—on a theory that a number of voters have individually failed to comply with the statutory requirements of registration or a theory that the Supervisor has failed to properly maintain the voter registration rolls for quite some time. As the Florida Supreme Court has said, "by refusing to recognize an otherwise valid exercise of the right of a citizen to vote for the sake of sacred, unyielding adherence to statutory scripture, we would in effect nullify that right."

Nonetheless, in a final act of civic mis-education, on May 20 (the day the new mayor was sworn into office) *The Gainesville Sun* published its last "election fraud" news story as a below-the-fold article that erroneously asserted:

- That Judge Hulslander "dismissed *part* of a lawsuit asking him to void Gainesville's mayoral election." (The judge in fact completely and utterly dismissed the entire lawsuit asking him to void the election.)
- That Judge Hulslander granted the plaintiffs *a right they previously did not have* to "move forward with their inquiry into the county's voter rolls." (The judge in fact restricted the plaintiffs in their future ability to use the courts to make claims calling into question the activities of the Supervisor

of Elections. He ruled that the plaintiffs—and only the plaintiffs, out of tens of thousands of Alachua County voters—had until June 1 to come forward with a specific allegation of any duty the Supervisor of Elections had failed to perform, or else be forever barred from making such claims in court.)

This is evidently where the newspaper's decision makers wished to end their long, sad lesson in civic mis-education. *The Gainesville Sun*'s decision makers determined that the conclusion to their weeks-long, uncritical coverage of shifting, unsubstantiated allegations of elections cheating, fraud, and corruption would be an article replete with quotations and paraphrases from the losing plaintiffs and their Orange County attorney. "She and her clients had not yet determined their next step," *The Gainesville Sun* reported, "though she did say they could appeal the judge's decision." These people the newspaper chose to quote were the people who—without proof or accountability—had insisted that "serious problems" existed in Alachua County's highly respected elections office, and that their purpose all along had been to ensure that those alleged problems would be corrected. *The Gainesville Sun* made no attempt to interview us, or, now, to even mention what we had stated repeatedly we were trying to accomplish. In fact, in this story, *The Gainesville Sun* made no mention of us at all, or of the fact that it was our motion to dismiss, filed as city voters, that Judge Hulslander had granted.

We pressed the paper's decision makers to provide us with an explanation of why they sanctioned the removal from the final version of the last story a link to Judge Hulslander's order. We also asked why they never corrected the erroneous assertion in the final story that Judge Hulslander dismissed only part of the lawsuit asking him to void the mayoral election. In addition, we wanted to know why they sanctioned the removal from the final version of the last story a line their reporter originally included that informed readers that because of the "partial" dismissal of the plaintiffs' lawsuit, any concerns about the standing of the new mayor are "apparently moot now." We asked why the paper failed to correct the erroneous implication that the judge had granted the plaintiffs a right they previously did not have to "move forward with their inquiry into the county's voter rolls." Lastly, we wanted to know why—when the June deadline passed without the plaintiffs having come forward with any allegations about the Supervisor of Elections—the paper's decision makers allowed that date to pass by without note in *The Gainesville Sun*. We never received answers. Instead, *The Gainesville Sun*'s three top decision makers explained to us that it was now too late for the paper to address the concerns we had repeatedly tried to bring to their attention since April 29, 2010.

Coda

Less than 24 hours after Judge Hulslander's order had been rendered, Craig Lowe was sworn in as mayor, becoming the first openly gay mayor of a southeastern U.S. city of more than 100,000. His inaugural speech included the following:

> In Gainesville there are individuals with disabilities and who are facing physical barriers to moving about in a manner that the rest of us take for granted, and they wonder, "Do I matter?" And yes, there is the transgender person who faces hostility that arises as quickly as flipping a light switch and whose plea for equality is scorned and subverted to a false fear campaign. That person wonders, "Do I matter?" And in

Gainesville there is a child from a low-income family whose mother works long hours and sends her children to school. That child lacks the physical and emotional nourishment of his or her peers. That child struggles with whether to stay in school and wonders, "Do I matter?" Each of these people and people like them wonder, "Do I matter? Is there a place for me in this city or in this world?" And our answer, Gainesville, has always been and must continue to be: In Gainesville, Florida, every person matters.

For Lowe supporters who gathered that day to see their candidate take office and hear him speak those words, free of the fog of illegitimacy that had shrouded the weeks following his election, our active critical civic literacy effort may have been considered a success. To us, not so much.

Our goal had been to contribute clarity, rationality, and understanding to our city's civic discourse. In that we had been only partially successful. Yes, the court had granted our request to dismiss a baseless lawsuit; and yes, our intervention had resulted in an order of remarkable clarity and important civic education value. But those who gathered at Lowe's swearing-in ceremony were only the smallest segment of Gainesville's citizenry. Many less civically active citizens, we believed, had no sense that the lawsuit had been baseless, or even that the lawsuit was now over. And the judge's order, for all its civic virtue, had been read by virtually no one.

Bibliography

Buckingham, D. (2003). *Media education: Literacy, learning and contemporary culture*. Cambridge: Polity Press.

Dewey, J. (1916). *Democracy and education*. New York: Macmillan.

Dewey, J. (1927). *The public and its problems*. Chicago: Swallow.

Florida Joint Center for Citizenship. (2011). About the Joint Center. Retrieved January 23, 2011, from http://www.floridacitizen.org/about.php

Graham, B. (2009). *America, the owner's manual: Making the government work for you*. Washington, DC: CQ Press.

Jones, E., & Gaventa, J. (2002). *IDS development bibliography 19: Concepts of citizenship*. Brighton, Sussex, England: Institute of Development Studies.

Justice Teaching Program. (2011). About justice teaching. Retrieved January 24, 2011, from http://www.justiceteaching.org

National Conference on Citizenship. (2006). *2006 civic health index: Broken engagement*. Retrieved January 23, 2011, from http://www.ncoc.net/index.php?tray=content&tid=top5&cid=100

National Council for the Social Studies. (2009). *NCSS position statement on media literacy*. Washington, DC: Author. Retrieved January 23, 2011, from http://www.socialstudies.org/positions/medialiteracy

Parker, W.C. (1996). "Advanced" ideas about democracy: Toward a pluralist conception of citizen education. *Teachers College Record, 98*, 104–125.

Parker, W.C. (2008). Knowing and doing in democratic citizenship education. In L.S. Levstik & C.A. Tyson (Eds.), *Handbook of research in social studies education* (pp. 65–80). New York: Routledge.

Sandra Day O'Connor Civics Education Act. (2010). Retrieved January 23, 2011, from http://www.myfloridahouse.gov/sections/Bills/billsdetail.aspx?BillId=42220

Washington, Ray. (2004a). University of Florida: The beginning of a university. *The Gainesville Sun*, July 28, 2004. Retrieved January 25, 2011, from http://www.gainesville.com/article/20040728/NEWS/40728086

Washington, Ray. (2004b). University of Florida: Postwar campus flourishes. *The Gainesville Sun*, July 28, 2004. Retrieved January 25, 2011, from http://www.gainesville.com/article/20040728/NEWS/40727128

Washington, Ray. (2004c). University of Florida: Unrest amid the boom times. *The Gainesville Sun*, July 28, 2004. Retrieved January 25, 2011, from http://www.gainesville.com/article/20040728/NEWS/40728017

Westheimer, J. & Kahne, J. (2004). What kind of citizen? The politics of educating for democracy. *American Educational Research Journal, 41*(2), 237–269.

Articles from the *Gainesville Sun*

Anti-Lowe flier stirs controversy. (Published March 1, 2010.) Retrieved January 23, 2011, from http://www.gainesville.com/article/20100301/ARTICLES/3011005

A narrow victory for Lowe triggers recount. (Published April 14, 2010.) Retrieved January 24, 2011, from http://www.gainesville.com/article/20100414/ARTICLES/4141019

Close mayoral race highlights possible quirk. (Published April 25, 2010.) Retrieved January 23, 2011, from http://www.gainesville.com/article/20100425/ARTICLES/4251003.

Marsh supporters challenging election results. (Published April 27, 2010.) Retrieved January 23, 2011, from http://www.gainesville.com/article/20100427/articles/4271014

No ruling in election suit; another hearing is Tuesday. (Published May 14, 2010.) Retrieved January 24, 2011, from http://www.gainesville.com/article/20100514/ARTICLES/100519591

Lowe's term to start unless judge objects. (Published April 29, 2010.) Retrieved January 23, 2011, from http://www.gainesville.com/article/20100429/articles/4291056.

Editorial: Voter integrity. (Published April 29, 2010.) Retrieved January 23, 2011, from http://www.gainesville.com/article/20100429/OPINION01/4291010

Judge denies suit asking for new mayoral election. (Published May 20, 2010.) Retrieved January 23, 2011, from http://www.gainesville.com/article/20100519/articles/100519282

The Judge's Ruling

A PDF of the complete text of Judge Hulslander's ruling may be found here (download): http://fellowcitizens.wordpress.com/2011/01/27/a-lesson-in-civics/

CHAPTER FOUR

In the Name of Democracy

Educational Policy and Civics Achievement in the Standards Era[1]

Lawrence C. Stedman

For over a generation, the United States has been engaged in a massive educational experiment involving standards, high-stakes testing, and accountability. From *A Nation at Risk* and Goals 2000 to national testing and No Child Left Behind (NCLB), policymakers have sought to transform schooling and improve academic achievement. With each new endeavor, civic literacy has been declared a key objective of school reform. In *A Nation at Risk*, the National Commission on Excellence in Education quoted Jefferson and emphasized that a "high level of shared education is essential to a free, democratic society" (NCEE, 1983, p. 7). As part of a "strong curriculum" (p. 70), the Commission endorsed the teaching of social studies, so students would learn "how our political system functions" and develop the "informed and committed exercise of citizenship" (p. 71). The Commission even underscored the federal government's role in "protecting constitutional and civil rights for students and school personnel" (p. 79).

In the early 1990s, the U.S. Department of Education and the Pew Charitable Trusts funded the development of national civics standards (Kendall & Marzano, 2004). *National Standards for Civics and Government* (Center for Civic Education, 1994) became the touchstone for civics reform and the basis of civics testing by the National Assessment of Educational Progress (NAEP). In Goals 2000, Congress identified social studies as a core academic subject and set "Student Achievement and Citizenship" as a vital national goal (National Education Goals Panel, 1999, p. vi). It called upon the schools to ensure that *all* students leave fourth, eighth, and twelfth grades having "competency over challenging subject matter" in diverse subjects, including civics and history, and be "prepared for responsible citizenship" (p. vi).

NCLB expanded the efforts dramatically. Although many educators are unaware of it, an entire portion of NCLB—the "Education for Democracy Act"—was devoted to civic education. It was designed to improve the teaching of civics and government and to educate students about the "history and principles of the Constitution of the United States, including the Bill of Rights" (NCLB, 2002, 115 Stat. 1662). It funded the Center for Civic Education "to provide a course of instruction" in civics and expand its "We the People" education programs (1663). NCLB also empowered the Secretary of Education to make grants to the Close Up foundation for similar work (1598–99). Congress instructed NAEP to regularly assess civics achievement (1898–99).

How well have these ventures worked? What impact have the standards movement and federal policy had on civics knowledge and understanding? How well prepared are students to participate in civic life and what are the implications for school reform and democracy?

To address these questions, I examine historical trends on the NAEP civics assessment. I focus on NAEP because it provides our best measure of long-term achievement trends and has been at the center of educational debates and federal policymaking for several decades (Stedman, 2009). The program has regularly tested large, nationally representative samples of students and used authentic materials, such as historical documents and sample ballots, in its testing.

A discussion of large-scale quantitative assessments may seem out of place in a book dedicated to philosophical and political analyses. Nevertheless, those of us interested in critical civic literacy will find much to learn from the NAEP findings. Given their role in the national policy arena, it is important to understand what they show and how they can help us make the case for progressive school reform. I have divided the paper into three parts: achievement trends, the extent of civic proficiency, and explanations of what has gone wrong.

Part I: Civics Achievement Trends

The "Great" Decline

I begin by returning to the period that launched the contemporary standards movement. In the 1970s and 1980s, concerns over a decline in excellence and an erosion of civic literacy produced a spate of reports and books on the sorry state of U.S. education. School critics assailed the decline of cultural literacy (Hirsch, 1987), the crippling of our children's future (Armbruster, 1977), and the closing of the American mind (Bloom, 1987). They maintained that society was the victim of a literacy hoax (Copperman, 1978) and that the very future of the nation was at risk (National Commission on Excellence in Education, 1983). While the SAT decline captured the headlines and public attention, many academics and commissions cited NAEP trends and findings, including those in civics.

Their case, however, was mired in hyperbole reminiscent of the 1950s conservative attacks on progressive education in such works as *Quackery in the Public Schools* (Lynd, 1953). Phrases such as "massive decline" and "unremitting fall" were typical. *A Nation at Risk* decried a "rising tide of mediocrity that threatens our very future as a Nation and a people" (NCEE, 1983, p. 5). Copperman (1978) cited NAEP data as proof of a "sharp drop-off" in science, "devastating declines" in civics, and a "deterioration of writing skills" (pp. 48, 101). Hirsch (1987) called the civics declines "alarming" (p. 7). The assault continued well into the 1990s in such provocatively titled books as *Dumbing Down Our Kids* (Sykes, 1995) and *The Decline of Intelligence in America* (Itzkoff, 1994).

The Evidence

Had there been "devastating declines" in civics knowledge as Copperman (1978) asserted? Or, a major loss of cultural literacy as Hirsch (1987) argued? To make his case, Hirsch (1987) claimed there had been a large decline in 13-year-olds' NAEP civics scores.

> The evidence for the decline of shared knowledge is not just anecdotal. In 1978 NAEP issued a report which analyzed a large quantity of data showing that our children's knowledge of American civics had dropped significantly between 1969 and 1976. The performance of thirteen-year-olds had dropped an alarming 11 percentage points. (p. 7)

Hirsch had the data wrong. While there had been a decline, it was not an "alarming" one. The civics knowledge of 13-year-olds decreased only 3 percentage points, not 11, between 1969 and 1975 (NAEP, 1978, p. 69). (The report labeled it as "citizenship" knowledge.) Their social studies drop was only 2 points (1971–1975). Such charged rhetoric and sloppy data handling has been common among those decrying the work of the public schools.

Hirsch (1987) continued: "That the drop has continued since 1976 was confirmed by preliminary results from a NAEP study conducted in late 1985" (p. 7). That study, however, dealt with 17-year-olds, not 13-year-olds, assessed history and literature, and did not include trend data (Ravitch & Finn, 1988). Thus, it provided no evidence of a further drop. Trend data, however, was available. The 1982 NAEP citizenship-social studies assessment showed there had been a 3-percentage-point *increase* in achievement among 13-year-olds from 1975 to 1981–82 (NAEP, 1983, p. 24). Whatever minor ground had been lost had been *fully* recovered. Their civics scores were rising, not declining, well before *Cultural Literacy* came out.

The focus on 13-years-olds was peculiar. There is little reason to expect such young students to know much about government and political processes. They are five years from voting and their academic study of civics comes later, in ninth grade, or as 14- or 15-year-olds. While many were taking eighth grade U.S. history, which introduces basic elements of civics, the testing had been done in the fall of 1969 and 1975, before students had gotten very far into their courses (NAEP, 1978, p. 1). With little opportunity to learn civics formally, any changes in their scores over time were likely due to outside influences rather than the work of the schools.

The situation, however, was different among 17-year-olds. Here, critics were on more solid ground. High school citizenship knowledge declined 8 percentage points from 1969 to 1976 (NAEP, 1978, p. 69). The decline was widespread, affecting all demographic groups (gender, race, and parental education), all regions of the country, and all types of communities save those in extreme rural areas where, oddly, students improved (p. 55). The declines paralleled those that showed up on the SAT and several other high school standardized tests.

What caused the decline? NAEP convened a panel of social studies educators, including R. Freeman Butts, who offered several reasons, including a decline in funding for the social studies, the expanding number of electives, and the back-to-basics push reducing time for social studies (NAEP, 1978, pp. 59–62). Yet they also observed that there had been a pedagogical shift to "intellectual process" that "for the most part has not been evaluated by current testing efforts" (p. 60). They concluded the results were "disappointing, but not surprising" (p. 59), and noted:

> The assessments spanned a turbulent era in American political history—including the Viet Nam War, cam-
> pus riots and erosion of confidence in political institutions and persons culminating in the Watergate scan-
> dal—and these events may have influenced student political knowledge and attitudes. (p. 59)

"May have influenced" was a hedge. High school students likely learned *more* about politics, international affairs, and the real workings of our government during those years, but felt less concerned about doing well on what they saw as an irrelevant multiple-choice test.

The Advisory Panel on the SAT Decline (1977) reached a similar conclusion, noting the era's
political upheavals were the only way to explain the "suddenness and concentration" of the
decline (p. 37)—half of it came in just 3 years in the early 1970s (Stedman, 1998, pp. 63, 112,
footnote 42). It, too, cited the "divisive war (which youth had to fight)" and the "corruption of
national leadership" (p. 37). It raised the specter of "burning cities" and the "political assassination (of their particular heroes)" (p. 37). Dismayed and angry, students were more interested in
changing the world than learning institutionally doled-out material or prepping for the SAT.

Strikingly, the civics decline soon halted. Like the 13-year-olds, 17-year-olds improved their
scores a bit between 1976 and 1982 (NAEP, 1978, p. 69). Their gains occurred in the "two areas
heavily dependent on knowledge about the U.S. governmental system": Structure and Function
of Government and Political Process (NAEP, 1983, p. 26). The authors of the NAEP report concluded, "Considered in light of NAEP findings in other subject areas, these results provide additional evidence of a trend toward improvement in young Americans' academic achievements"
(NAEP, 1983, p. 23). The gains from the mid-1970s to the early 1980s appeared on several other
standardized tests, including the Stanford Achievement Tests and the Iowa Test of Basic Skills
(Stedman & Kaestle, 1985, 1987).

Echoing Mark Twain, the reports of the schools' demise had been greatly exaggerated. The
declines on most tests had been minor; demographic changes in test takers accounted for much
of the score changes; and there was ample contradictory evidence as many test scores remained
stable or had even risen during the period (Stedman, 1998; Stedman & Kaestle, 1985). At the
time *A Nation at Risk* was released, whatever test score decline there had been had already ended,
and scores were on the upswing. Indeed, ITBS scores had reached all-time highs for most grades
by 1984. As Stedman and Kaestle (1985, p. 204) waggishly put it many years ago:

> The National Commission on Excellence in Education, with its dire warnings of a nation at risk in 1983,
> was about five years too late. Instead of a "rising tide of mediocrity," it should have proclaimed a rising tide
> of test scores.

The Standards Era

The die had been cast, however. Gripped by the specter of a national calamity and declining
achievement, policymakers made a massive standards push, deploying pervasive accountability
and testing systems. As part of the conservative restoration (Apple, 2000; Shor, 1992), the policies garnered widespread support, and for the past quarter of a century, this agenda has dominated schooling (Stedman, 2011).

What have been its effects on civics achievement? The staggering thing is that, in spite of
the enormous efforts, middle-school civics achievement has not improved at all since the early

1980s, and there was even a minor decline in the 1990s (Anderson et al., 1990, p. 13; Lutkus & Weiss, 2007, p. 7; Weiss et al., 2001, p. 9). More telling is what happened with high school seniors, who have formally studied both history and civics and are on the verge of graduating. Here, too, we find virtually level trends, and even some slight declines (see Figure 1).

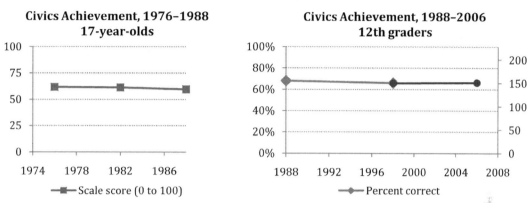

Figure 1. Data are from Anderson et al., 1990, p. 13; Weiss et al., 2001, p. 9; and Lutkus & Weiss, 2007, p. 7. NAEP placed the 1976–1988 data on a 0–100 scale; it is not percentage correct. The 1988–1998 study used percentages, while the 1998–2006 scores were on a 0–300 scale. NAEP switched from ages to grades in 1988.

These trends parallel those in other social studies areas, such as geography and history, where student achievement also has stagnated (Stedman, 2010). I examine the reasons for the flat civics achievement trends later in the paper.

Part II: The Extent of Civic Literacy

Flat trends are a major concern, but they do not tell us about the quality of students' civic literacy. To gauge that, one must look at proficiency levels and at actual test items to see what students know.

Proficiency in Civics

Proficiency has become a watchword of legislators and policymakers. Goals 2000 called for *all* students to achieve proficiency in the main NAEP assessments (NEGP, 1995, pp. 11, 36), while NCLB mandated that *all* students achieve proficiency in state assessments (NCLB, 2002, 115 Stat. 1466). Despite this emphasis and a series of major federal policy initiatives, only about one-fourth of high school seniors have achieved proficiency in civics. This is typical for the social studies (see Table 1). A third have not even reached the basic level, which reflects only "partial mastery of prerequisite knowledge and skills" and which NAEP's governing board categorically states is "not the desired goal" (Lutkus et al., 1999, p. 11). History is the worst area, where only a small fraction (13%) has achieved proficiency, and over half fall below the basic level.

TABLE 1. 12th Grade Social Studies Achievement in NAEP

Subject	Year	Below Basic	At Basic	Proficient or better
Civics	2006	34%	39%	27%
Economics	2006	21%	37%	42%
Geography	2001	29%	47%	25%
History	2006	53%	34%	13%
Average		34%	39%	27%

Note: "Proficient or better" includes students at the advanced level. Data are from the latest 12th-grade main assessments in each subject: Lutkus & Weiss, 2007, p. 1 (civics); Mead & Sandene, 2007, p. 5 (economics); Weiss, Lutkus, Hildebrant, & Johnson, 2002, p. 21 (geography); and Lee & Weiss, 2007, p. 9 (history). (Geography data do not add up to 100% due to rounding in NAEP's report.)

Congressionally mandated evaluations—themselves controversial—have questioned the way NAEP's proficiency levels are set (Cizek, 1993; Lutkus et al., 1999, pp. 12–14). Still, there are grounds for believing that even fewer students are proficient. The data do not include the 25% of students who drop out and have done more poorly in school (Stedman, 2010). The *standards* for proficiency are, ironically, weak ones. Students only have to answer 65% of the short-answer, constructed-response questions at the proficient level or 74% of the multiple-choice ones (Lutkus & Weiss, 2007, p. 31). A more reasonable standard, such as 80–90%, would mean far fewer students are actually proficient. This weak standard also means that many students deemed "proficient" still have trouble with important, even elementary, civics knowledge.

What Students Know and Do Not Know

Examining test items from the NAEP assessments bypasses the issues with the proficiency levels and gives us a concrete feel for what students know about our political institutions and processes. I focus on high school seniors, as they are about to join the electorate (or already have), and their performance reflects the culmination of 12 years of schooling, including what they have learned from courses in civics, history, and government. The items come from NAEP's civics reports and its online database (NAEP, 2010).

How should we characterize students' civic literacy? Wholesale condemnations would be unfair, as performance varies greatly depending on which items are looked at. There is civics material almost all high school students have acquired, something one would never know from reading scathing indictments of public schools and the state of civic literacy. In the 1998 trend study, for example, NAEP covered four areas of civics (Weiss et al., 2001). High school seniors did very well on items pertaining to Rights, Responsibilities, and the Law, averaging 85% (calculated from data in Weiss et al., 2001, pp. 69–70). Nearly all twelfth graders (98%) know that people accused of crimes have the right to a lawyer, to know what they are accused of (95%), and to remain silent (93%). Such knowledge, of course, may come as much from TV police dramas and reality shows as from civics classes. In addition, most students know Congress does not have the right to curtail freedom of the press or establish a national church (p. 69). These are fundamentals of U.S. democracy, so it is impressive to see how well students do on questions about them.

On the other hand, students did much worse in the other three civics areas. They averaged only 62% on the Political Institutions (Structures and Functions) and 58% on Political Processes. The worst area was Democratic Principles and the Purpose of Government, where they scored only 52%. Individual examples show the extent of the problems. Most students did not know that treaties need to be ratified by the Senate or that federal judges are nominated by the President and confirmed by the Senate (Weiss et al., 2001, p. 70). Most did not know what a referendum or a PAC is—or what bicameralism means (pp. 14, 70). Only half could identify the Declaration of Independence as the source of "We hold these truths to be self-evident . . ." (p. 14).

The 2006 assessment found similar problems. Most students do not understand the meaning of federalism or checks and balances, or how they operate (NAEP, 2010). In one telling item, only 5% of twelfth graders could "Explain three ways in which the power of the President can be checked by the legislative or the judicial branch," yet they only had to *identify* them (Lutkus & Weiss, 2007, p. 30) (see Appendix). Most could not even give one way. Even the so-called "proficient" students had difficulty—only 13% succeeded.

Several items dealt with the government's role in world affairs and showed a lack of both constitutional and historical knowledge. Half the seniors did not realize that Congress shares its foreign policy power with the President (NAEP, 2010). Over three-fourths could not explain a 1960s political cartoon depicting the domino theory (Lutkus & Weiss, 2007, p. 29). Even about half the "proficient" students failed this item. Students do better, though not that well, on factual information about the representative structure of government. A majority knows the governor is a state's chief executive (66%), the number of representatives varies with a state's population (63%), and each state has 2 senators (58%) (Weiss et al., 2001, pp. 69–70). It is surprising such basic information is not better known.

NAEP has also explored the practical side of civic literacy. In 2006, it assessed high school seniors' preparation for voting by judging their ability to read a ballot, determine which offices were up for election, and understand a public question (NAEP, 2010). Students were generally stymied—on key items, most ran into problems (60%+). Only 16% could give a pro *and* a con opinion on the public question. Furthermore, only 6% could explain two ways that citizens can effectively change laws. (See the Appendix for details on finding the percentage data for NAEP's open-ended items.)

NAEP also found that students have trouble analyzing graphs pertaining to policy issues. Over three-fifths, for example, could not read a graph comparing changes in the poverty line and AFDC benefits over time, while about 9 out of 10 could not explain charts showing trends in political party affiliation or men's and women's earnings over time (NAEP, 2010). This shows that the schools' failure to adequately teach math has consequences for civic literacy (Stedman, 2010).

Finally, students struggle in one of the most critical areas of civic literacy: constitutional issues and race relations. In 1998, while two-thirds of high school seniors could identify *Plessy* v. *Ferguson* with the separate but equal doctrine (a fraction one wishes had been larger), they did more poorly on items about *Brown* v. *Board of Education*: knowing it meant more federal authority over education (58%); that states, not federal laws or regulations, had segregated schools (40%); and the court had used the Fourteenth Amendment in its decision (36%) (NAEP, 2010). In 2006, only 61% of seniors knew that *Brown* did not end segregation, while only about half knew that it "led to a power struggle between state governments and the federal government" or why Eisenhower had to call out the troops to enforce integration in Little Rock (NAEP, 2010).

Thus, although there are some strong areas, the overall picture is on the poor side. While students are not civic illiterates, they do lack important civics knowledge and skills. One indication of that is their weak performance on test items that NAEP characterizes as "easy": from 30 to 40% of twelfth graders still do *not* know the material (NAEP, 2010).

For Better or Worse

There is, though, a question about students' motivation to perform on such low-stakes tests. Twelfth graders report not being that concerned about doing well on NAEP's writing assessment (Lutkus et al., 1999, p. 132), but they seem to take the civics one seriously. Few make off-task responses on open-ended items, and few select the off-base, sometimes humorous, options in multiple-choice items. The lack of consequences also means that the text anxiety and stereotyping threats that normally dampen performance are less of an issue. The testing burden itself is a light one. Compared to the marathon 3-hour SATs, recent civics assessments have been short ones, involving only two 25-minute blocks of items (Lutkus & Weiss, 2007, p. 3).

Three other factors suggest the data overstate how much students know. The results do not take into account guessing, which can greatly inflate the percentages correct (Cohen, 1976, p. 22). Even on items or sets of items where it looks as if a majority knows the material, most may not. Next, NAEP appears to be lenient, sometimes even lax, in its scoring of open-ended items (see Appendix). Incomplete and even flawed responses have been considered acceptable. Finally, the testing did not include dropouts, who are even less likely to know the material.

Tempered Judgments

More than a generation has passed and civic literacy remains weak. Even NAEP itself has described students as having "relatively low levels of civic knowledge," although it noted, "there is little to suggest that today's youths are less knowledgeable than their predecessors" (Weiss et al., 2001, p. 2). This is a case of damning with faint praise. Still, one's critical judgments should be tempered. Students have done well on many items and in at least one area (rights and the law). We should keep in mind that many students, especially of lower socio-economic status, attend resource-poor schools with outdated textbooks and custodial teaching. They have lacked opportunities to learn this material in school and in other ways—such as by visiting historical sites or discussing it with parents in professional and political positions. We also should remember that many of us acquired much of our civics knowledge *after* high school—reading newspapers, studying in college, and watching legislative and judicial battles.

At the same time, though, much of the material NAEP assesses is basic and comes from civics and history classes, so one would have expected high school seniors to have learned it. In addition, in spite of our optimism that such information is acquired later, national surveys of adults' knowledge show that, for the most part, civics deficiencies linger well after high school (Carpini & Keeter, 1996; Gibbon & Martin, 2008; Intercollegiate Studies Institute, 2008).

Part III: What Has Gone Wrong?

What happened? Why has there been no improvement in civics achievement in spite of a generation of sustained efforts? I offer three explanations: the first focuses on the overall record compiled under the standards movement, the second on the place of civic education within federal policies, and the third on the organizational and political structuring of schools.

Explanation 1: The Failure of the Standards Movement

It is not just civics achievement that has stagnated over the past quarter-century, but high school performance in general (Stedman, 2010). We see this not only in the social studies areas, but also in math, science, reading, and writing. Now, given how much social conditions and school populations changed, even maintaining scores could suggest resilience, but other changes have made the work of educators easier, not harder. Parental educational attainment rose dramatically, while pupil-teacher ratios and teenage birth rates declined greatly. Public school spending nearly quintupled, rising from $118 billion in 1982–1983 to over $600 billion by 2009 (National Center for Education Statistics, 2010, p. 48). Even adjusted for inflation, it more than doubled. Given these positive developments and the decades of emphasis on standards and accountability, achievement should have improved. Flat trends are an unexpected, and poor, result.

The standards movement also has fallen far short of its goal of achieving proficiency with all students. In every area that NAEP tests, most students are still not proficient (Stedman, 2010). As in civics, only about one-fourth of twelfth graders are proficient in math and writing; less than one-fifth are in science. High school students still struggle with middle-school material.

A key problem is the standards movement's press to raise test scores (Stedman, 2010). State-imposed accountability systems and "proficiency curricula" have devastated "authentic teaching and learning" (McNeil, 2000). Classrooms now focus on "dispensing packaged fragments of information sent from an upper level of the bureaucracy" (p. 5). The test and grade-driven system rewards memorization, deception, and shallow understanding (Clark-Pope, 2001). Cheating and plagiarism are serious problems as high school students take shortcuts to make the grade (Humes, 2003). The result is poorly learned and quickly forgotten material. Ironically, as Kohn (2004) observes, by over-emphasizing achievement, the standards movement has sabotaged learning. Given this, one can understand why civics achievement remains in the doldrums. Still, I believe this may not be the major reason.

Explanation 2: The Misconstruction and Marginalization of Civic Literacy

I would argue that policymakers and neoconservative school critics have not taken the schools' responsibilities toward democracy seriously. Although most federal initiatives during the standards era touted citizenship preparation, they marginalized it. Policies have largely focused on human capital development and technical training, with civic literacy redefined in economic and hegemonic terms. While civic education has received some attention, it has not played a central role in the accountability mandates. In what follows, I review several of the leading curricular and federal policy initiatives over the past generation.

Cultural Literacy and Democratic Illiteracy

Those who decried the dismal state of civics knowledge in the 1980s did not prescribe a solution equal to the problem. Hirsch (1987), for example, promoted a list of cultural literacy terms and argued that students needed only a vague familiarity with them. As he put it, "haziness is a key characteristic of literacy and cultural literacy" (p. 14). Yet students have had superficial knowledge for far too long, and their historical ignorance is problematic. They associate Lincoln with a log cabin and freeing the slaves, but need to know that he suspended the writ of *habeas corpus*, imposed martial law, and left most slaves in bondage in the Emancipation Proclamation.

The cultural literacy list perpetuated misconceptions and civic illiteracy. It included the term wetback, but not "Operation Wetback," the 1954 military-style, federally led sweep that forcibly deported tens of thousands of Mexican-Americans, including citizens. While the list had "freedom of speech," it also had "Shout fire in a crowded theater"—a phrase that has been perennially misused to restrict speech, yet is an astounding misquote. Instead of a hazy awareness, students should know that it comes from a 1919 Supreme Court decision (*Schenck* v. *U.S.*) that improperly upheld the constitutionality of the Espionage Act, one of the most egregious assaults on civil liberties in the nation's history (Dershowitz, 1989; Zinn, 1980). This World War I act—which did not make the list—provided up to 20-year prison terms for those speaking out against the draft or questioning the nation's war efforts. The federal government suppressed dissenting newspapers and magazines and, with the zealous cooperation of state and local officials, imprisoned anti-war speakers, writers, and organizers throughout the country. The phrase, by Justice Oliver Wendell Holmes, was actually "*falsely* shouting fire in a theatre and causing panic" (emphasis added), but as Zinn (1980) pointed out, even that analogy is patently wrong: the activists were better thought of as shouting "Fire!" outside of a burning theater as a warning to people not to enter. Much of the Espionage Act remains in force today. Instead of superficial cultural literacy, deep knowledge of wartime—and peacetime—threats to democracy is what matters.

The list gave short shrift to constitutional liberties and civic action. Where were such crucial Supreme Court decisions as *Miranda*, *Roe* v. *Wade*, and *Tinker* v. *Des Moines*, which defined the free speech rights of students? Where were the names of grassroots organizations that work with the poor, Latinos, and people of color such as the National Council of La Raza, United Farm Workers, and VISTA? (The NAACP was listed, but not MALDEF or the Black Panthers.) At least the song "We Shall Overcome" was included, but not such other historically important phrases as "The rich get richer" and "Workers of the world, unite!" Even the terms "grassroots" and "freedom of assembly" were missing. It was sadly clear that cultural literacy advocates had in mind a passive conception of democracy, one devoid of people's movements and struggles against oppression. Our schools' curricula, regrettably, mirror this view (Loewen, 2007).

Even had such items been included, that would not have been enough. A well-informed and engaged citizenry needs a *working* knowledge of the Bill of Rights, not vague understandings of it, and vigorous experience in public affairs, not passing familiarity with its vocabulary.

A Nation at Risk

Yes, the Commission on Excellence highlighted the Jeffersonian idea of education for democracy, but it soon blended it with a much different purpose, that "education is one of the chief engines of a society's material well-being" (NCEE, 1983, p. 21). It claimed, "The citizen is dismayed at a steady 15-year decline in industrial productivity" (p. 22) and argued the schools needed to prepare students for a hi-tech, economic future (p. 11). It wrote of "productive citizenship" (p. 81) and that the reason for "informed judgment" was "to secure gainful employment" (p. 8) and create a "strong economy" (p. 21). Instead of civic education, its recommendations centered on "more rigorous and measurable standards," stronger graduation requirements, and standardized tests "at major transition points" (NCEE, 1983, pp. 70, 73). Ignoring practical realities and the negative impact it would have on students and teachers, NCEE called for 7-hour school days and 200- to 220-day school years, and a tiered system for ranking and paying teachers (Stedman & Smith, 1983). Even in the social studies area, the Commission stressed the importance of teaching "the fundamentals of how our economic system works" and ensuring that students "grasp the difference between free and repressive societies" (p. 71).

Yet even this was done on a rhetorical level, without federal support or programs. In a staggering effrontery, it put the burden on the public to implement *and* fund the reforms. In a small-government, neoliberal posture that harkened back to John F. Kennedy's inaugural address ("Ask not what your country can do for you . . ."), the Commission wrote:

> **We recommend** that citizens across the Nation hold educators and elected officials responsible for providing the leadership necessary to achieve these reforms, and that citizens provide the fiscal support and stability required to bring about the reforms we propose. (p. 78; emphasis in original)

Goals 2000

The 1990s did not see much change in the national stature of civics. Although Goal 3 was titled "Student Achievement and Citizenship," civics and government was just one of nine subjects in which proficiency was called for. It came *after* English, math, science, and foreign languages. Its aim was "responsible citizenship" and "productive employment in our Nation's modern economy" (NEGP, 1999, p. vi). Goals 2000 made clear the inferior position of civics and other subjects by establishing a *separate* national goal for the technical subjects. Its architects clearly felt that calling for competency in the core subjects was not enough, so they also called for U.S. students to be "first in the world in mathematics and science achievement" (p. vi). Such a goal grew out of a misguided Cold War-type nationalism and a push to maintain U.S. economic hegemony. Finally, Goals 2000 set up a National Education Goals Panel to monitor progress and issue annual reports, but civics achievement was not even included until its final report in 1999. This was not the fault of the panel, but a problem with NAEP, as it had not assessed civics for an entire decade.

National Assessment of Educational Progress

Civics has had a changing role in the nation's assessment program. Originally, it held a prominent place, being one of the first subjects NAEP tested in 1969. It was then combined with social studies, but was still assessed regularly until the late 1980s. In 1988, however, Congress legislated key features of NAEP, including its testing schedule (National Assessment of Educational Progress Improvement Act of 1988, 102 Stat. 345; Stedman, 2009). Civics was not even mentioned. NAEP was required to test reading and math every two years; writing and science every four; and "history/geography and other subject areas" every six. When the NAEP program was later split in two, the long-term NAEP covered reading, math, science, and writing trends, while the main NAEP tested those and other subjects including, when it could get to it, civics.

No Child Left Behind

Civics regained prominence with NCLB. Congress funded the development of a course of civics instruction, teacher training in civics, and the "We the People" programs in public policy and constitutional issues for students. NCLB's "Education for Democracy Act," however, encompassed not just civics, but economic education, with equal funding for the National Council on Economic Education and the Center for Civic Education (NCLB, 2002, 115 Stat. 1662). Clearly, Congress was placing an understanding of the free enterprise system on an equal footing with the promotion of civics and democracy. Further diluting the effort, the Center for Civic Education was also charged with providing "materials and services to address specific problems such as the prevention of school violence and the abuse of drugs and alcohol" (NCLB, 2002, 115 Stat. 1663).

The real issue, though, is that civic literacy is not central to NCLB's mission. Instead, its focus is "stronger accountability for results" with mandated testing in reading, math, and science (U.S. Department of Education, n.d.). NCLB made national priorities clear, by relegating civics and history to second-class citizenship. The consequences were inevitable. Schools and teachers have narrowed their curricula and short-changed the time for social studies (Stedman, 2010).

NCLB's testing mandates in reading and math have had more impact on the nation's schools than has its support for civics programs. The $30 million allocated in 2002 for civic education (NCLB, 2002, § 2346, 115 Stat. 1666), which also had to cover economic education, was a miniscule amount compared to the $11.6 billion appropriated overall that year for NCLB (National Center for Education Statistics, 2004, p. 446). The "We the People" programs reach only a small fraction of the country's students. Even NCLB's military recruitment provisions, which have opened up schools to invasive and often illegal recruiting activities, have likely affected more students (Dobbs, 2005; Inouye, 2007; Medina, 2007; NCLB, 2002, § 2346, 115 Stat. 1983–1984; Stedman 2010).

The solution is not to make civics another of NCLB's required testing areas, as that would simply make harmful accountability even more intrusive. Instead, we need to understand the role NCLB plays as part of a larger neoliberal, managerial project, one that subverts democracy and sustains capitalism (Apple, 2006; Ross, 1996, 2004; Stedman, 2011). The project combines accountability with the control of labor (standardized testing, merit pay, centralized curriculum, and staff dismissals), along with choice and the market (transfer rights, vouchers, and charter schools). The project does not promote civic literacy; it even undermines democratic participation in school policy (Meier, 2004). NCLB needs to be repealed (Stedman, 2011).

Race to the Top

In contrast to earlier efforts, the recently enacted Obama-Duncan "Race to the Top" program does not even have a pretense of concern for democracy or civic literacy. The program's executive summary has only one mention of "civics," "citizenship," or "democracy," and that is under "increased learning time" where the program calls for "a longer school day, week, or year" to ensure more time in core subjects (U.S. Department of Education, 2009, p. 13). The legislation itself uses none of the terms (American Recovery and Reinvestment Act, 2009).

The program's "four core education reform areas" reveal its human capital, technocratic focus. The first is college and workplace preparation, so that students can "compete in the global economy" (U.S. Department of Education, 2009, p. 2). The second is technical, "building data systems that measure student growth and success." The third—and key—area is "rewarding, and retaining effective teachers and principals," with effectiveness measured by test scores. Finally, in a nod to equity, there is a concern for the lowest-achieving schools, but the focus is on raising scores, not confronting the prevailing problems of funding inequities, racism, and segregation.

Race to the Top is the latest element in the managerial project. It embodies key tenets of modern corporate capitalism: control and benchmarking (now of teachers as well as students), technical preparation, market competition, and a valuing of bureaucratic systems over democracy and participation (McKenna, 2009). It entrenches the noxious features of NCLB: auditing through false metrics, accountability without regard to circumstance, distrust of teachers, and a fixation on test scores instead of learning. Instead of civics, history, democracy, and individual development, Race to the Top focuses its academic efforts on preparing students for the military-industrial complex via STEM subjects: science, technology, engineering, and mathematics.

In the rules for the Race to the Top grant competition, we witness at work what Freire calls "bureaucratized minds" (Freire, 2001, pp. 42, 102, 111). The program's six selection criteria are broken into 19 areas, with points allocated to each. The focuses are disturbing, and the false precision illustrates technocratic thinking run amok. The program gives 58 points for test-based merit pay and evaluation systems—identified as "Improving teacher and principal effectiveness based on performance" (U.S. Department of Education, 2009, p. 3). It awards 65 points for expanding the power of the State and its bureaucratic control over local schools—known as "Articulating State's education reform agenda and LEAs' participation in it." It designates 47 points for data-driven instructional systems, including 24 points for a statewide longitudinal tracking system and 18 to enhance test-driven pedagogy (labeled as "Using data to improve instruction"). Apple (2006) is right that we are now immersed in what he calls the "audit culture." In such a world, critical civic literacy—let alone civics achievement—is nowhere to be found or valued.

Explanation 3: Institutional Authoritarianism

The most fundamental problem, however, is that authoritarian, bureaucratic institutions are incapable of developing critical civic literacy and preparing their charges to be active members of the polity. Over 30 years ago, the social studies panel reviewing the 1976 civics results had it right.

> The schools espouse concepts of democracy but often are run as autocratic communities where the students have little or no voice in decisions affecting them. The contrast between the "hidden curriculum" of the school—implied through teacher attitudes, administration attitudes, methods of conducting school affairs—and the concepts taught in the social studies curriculum may affect student attitudes. (NAEP, 1978, p. 61)

The standards and accountability movement has made matters worse. The schools have become more bureaucratic and less democratic. Students and teachers have even less say than they did before. Knowledge is treated as a commodity, teachers as technicians, and students as workers, not learners (Kozol, 2005). The emphasis is on compliance rather than independent thinking or creative teaching. The aim is certainly not to create a critically engaged public.

Instead of thinking of education in terms of standards and test scores, we should be discussing whose interests the current arrangements serve and how to redesign schools to develop meaningful, participatory democracy (Stedman, 2011). It is not a matter of students acquiring a potpourri of civics information and knowing how to read a ballot. As Dewey (1916, p. 101) explained, "democracy is more than a form of government; it is primarily a mode of associated living, of conjoint communicated experience." We should be educating through vibrant, *democratic* communities, where students, teachers, and families work together to solve real social problems (Allen, 2007; Apple, 1992; Apple & Beane, 2007; Dewey, 1938).

Authentic Preparation for Democracy

How civics is taught needs to be revolutionized. It should not simply deal with the static, diagrammatic structure of government. Many of us can remember learning the steps by which a bill becomes a law. What is needed, though, is not just memorizing the rules of the game, but understanding how it is played. Students should learn how a bill *actually* becomes a law, that is, the way bills are written (often by lobbyists), the influences brought to bear during the process, and the interests politicians actually represent. Equally important would be for them to learn how a bill does *not* become a law, that is, understanding how powerful interests block reforms. Both, though, are observational work, and more is needed. Paraphrasing Mao and Marx, the only way to understand the world is to try to change it (Byrne, 2004, p. 92). It is only by directly confronting institutionalized privilege that students will truly understand civics and the way our democracy operates. This is our greatest challenge—reforming our schools so they embody democratic values and truly prepare our students to join the struggle to create a just society.

Textbooks need to be overhauled. The panel reviewing the 1975–1976 citizenship-social studies results lamented "uninspiring" textbooks that present an "idealized view of the working of American democracy," one that generally ignores the "realities of the American political system" (NAEP, 1978, p. 60). Decades later, the same remains true of the nation's textbooks (Leahey, 2010; Loewen, 2007). The 1998 NAEP civics assessment plan contained excellent curricular advice about the topics vital to a proper education for democracy. These included, among many other examples, more emphasis on the gap between the goals and reality of American democracy, the skills needed by citizens for monitoring government, and the place of the United States in world affairs. (Weiss et al., 2001, p. 4)

Schools, however, focus more on perpetuating myths about democracy and American exceptionalism (Apple, 2000; Loewen, 2007). They—and federal policymakers—concentrate on producing a certain type of citizenship, labeled as "productive" or "responsible," rather than on nurturing well-informed, activist students who care about social justice and who really could be the guardians of our freedom.

These are not merely academic matters. In an increasingly corporate-controlled and nascent fascist society, we need students and adults who understand the nation's history well, have read such popular treatments as Zinn (1980) and Loewen (2007), and know the importance of people's movements in shaping democracy. We need to ensure that the Constitution is a *living* document in their lives. With weak civics knowledge, limited and distorted understanding of the country's history and civil liberties, and little experience in collaborative struggle against powerful interests, the people readily fall prey to dominant political forces.

Is it any wonder, then, that there are no massive, nationwide protests or shutdown strikes when the country contemplates going to war on false pretenses or when fundamental civil liberties are being eviscerated in the name of "homeland" security? That congressmen could do both in recent years without fearing a widespread, devastating, and career-ending electoral backlash is the true indicator of the county's lack of critical civic literacy. The politicians know that they have a docile, compliant, and ignorant populace that lacks a passionate commitment to the Constitution and doesn't fully grasp that, in times of crisis and war making, government officials routinely lie.

Assessing students' preparation for democracy should involve measuring their civics and history knowledge, but that is insufficient. NAEP has wisely expanded its canvas to probing students' understanding through constructed-response items and practical applications, such as sample ballots, but we need to go even further and gauge students' participation in politics, skills in judging diverse news and information sources, and knowledge of the corporate shaping of the political process. Civics knowledge pertaining to voting and the formal structure of government is valuable, but our electoral and political processes are corrupt and dominated by the power elite (Domhoff, 2010). At root, we need a richer and fuller conception of democracy than the one taught in civics classes and the schools—and the one envisioned by federal policymakers.

The teaching and assessment of civics, therefore, needs to deal forthrightly and extensively with the reality of capitalist democracy (Gibson, 2008), the illusion of representative democracy, and the need for participatory democracy. How well students understand those distinctions, and have the civic, historical, political, and experiential knowledge to support their judgments, is what counts. That is what critical civic literacy is all about and is the type of civics curriculum and civics achievement we should be aiming for. Anything less does a disservice to democracy.

Acknowledgments

In several places, material was adapted from two of the author's articles that appeared in *Critical Education*—see Stedman (2010, 2011). The title of the chapter was inspired by Thomas Toch's (1991) *In the Name of Excellence*, a national investigative report on the impact of school reform in the 1980s, and by Tianlong Yu's (2004) *In the Name of Morality*, a historical and political analysis of character education.

Bibliography

Advisory Panel on the Scholastic Aptitude Test Score Decline. (1977). *On further examination*. New York: College Board.

Allen, J. (2007). *Creating welcoming schools: A practical guide to creating home-school partnerships with diverse families*. New York: Teachers College Press.

American Recovery and Reinvestment Act of 2009, Pub. L. No. 111–5 (H.R. 1). (2009, February 17). 123 Stat. 115. As amended by Pub. Law 111–8 (H.R. 1105), the Omnibus Appropriations Act, 2009; Division A, Section 523; March 11, 2009; 123 Stat. 524. Retrieved from http://www2.ed.gov/policy/gen/leg/recovery/statutory/stabilization-fund.pdf

Anderson, L., Jenkins, L., Leming, J., MacDonald, W., Mullis, I., Turner, M., & Wooster, J. (1990). *The civics report card: Trends in achievement from 1976 to 1988 at ages 13 and 17; Achievement in 1988 at grades 4, 8, and 12*. Princeton, NJ: ETS.

Apple, M. (1992). Do the standards go far enough? *Journal for Research in Mathematics Education, 23*(5), 412–431.

Apple, M. (2000). *Official knowledge: Democratic education in a conservative age*. (2nd ed.). London: Routledge.

Apple, M. (2006). *Educating the "right" way: Markets, standards, god, and inequality*. (2nd ed.). New York: Routledge.

Apple, M., & Beane, J. (Eds.) (2007). *Democratic schools: Lessons in powerful education*. (2nd ed.). Portsmouth, NH: Heinemann.

Armbruster, F. (1977). *Our children's crippled future: How American education has failed*. New York: Quadrangle Books.

Bloom, A. (1987). *The closing of the American mind*. New York: Simon and Schuster.

Byrne, D. (2004). Evidence-based: What constitutes valid evidence? In A. Gray & S. Harrison (Eds.), *Governing medicine: Theory and practice* (ch. 7, pp. 81–92). Glasgow: Bell & Bain Ltd.

Carpini, M., & Keeter, S. (1996). *What Americans know about politics and why it matters*. New Haven, CT: Yale University Press.

Center for Civic Education. (1994). *National standards for civics and government*. Calabasas, CA: Author.

Center for Civic Education. (2010). We the people: The citizen and the Constitution website. Retrieved from http://new.civiced.org/programs/we-the-people

Cizek, G. (1993). *Reactions to National Academy of Education report "Setting performance standards for student achievement."* ERIC Document Reproduction No. ED 360 397. Washington, DC: National Assessment Governing Board.

Clark-Pope, D. (2001). *Doing school: How we are creating a generation of stressed out, materialistic, and miseducated students*. New Haven, CT: Yale University Press.

Cohen, J. (1976, May 8). Of guessing and knowing. [Letter to the editor]. *The New York Times*, 22.

Copperman, P. (1978). *The literacy hoax: The decline of reading, writing, and learning in the public schools and what we can do about it*. New York: William Morrow.

Dershowitz, A. (1989, January). Shouting "Fire!" *The Atlantic Monthly, 263*(1), 72. Retrieved from http://www.theatlantic.com/past/docs/issues/89jan/dershowitz.htm

Dewey, J. (1916). *Democracy and education*. New York: Macmillan Company.

Dewey, J. (1938). *Experience and education*. New York: Macmillan Company.

Dobbs, M. (2005, June 19). Schools and military face off: Privacy rights clash with required release of student information. *Washington Post*, A03.

Domhoff, W. (2010). *Who rules America? Challenges to corporate and class dominance*. (6th ed.). New York: McGraw-Hill.

Freire, P. (2001). *Pedagogy of freedom: Ethics, democracy, and civic courage*. Lanham, MD: Rowman & Littlefield.

Gibbon, P., & Martin, J. (2008). *E pluribus unum: The Bradley project on America's national identity*. Milwaukee, WI: The Lynde and Harry Bradley Foundation.

Gibson, R. (2008, August). *Chicago, Detroit, schools, and the election spectacle.* Retrieved from http://www.richgibson.com/chicago-detroit-schools-election.htm

Hirsch, E.D. (1987). *Cultural literacy.* Boston: Houghton Mifflin.

Humes, E. (2003). *School of dreams: Making the grade at a top American high school.* New York: Harcourt.

Inouye, A. (2007, July/August). Military access to public schools: Coalition against militarism in our schools halts recruiters. *Resist.* Retrieved from http://www.resistinc.org/newsletters/issues/2007/military_access.html

Intercollegiate Studies Institute. (2008). *Our fading heritage: Americans fail a basic test on their history and institutions.* Wilmington, DE: Author.

Itzkoff, S. (1994). *The decline of intelligence in America: A strategy for national renewal.* Westport, CT: Praeger.

Kendall, J., & Marzano, R. (2004). *Content knowledge: A compendium of standards and benchmarks for K–12 education.* (4th ed.). Aurora, CO: Mid-continent Research for Education and Learning.

Kohn, A. (2004). The costs of overemphasizing achievement. In S. Mathison & E.W. Ross (Eds.), *Defending public schools, Volume IV: The nature and limits of standards-based reform and assessment* (ch. 3, pp. 27–34). Westport, CT: Praeger.

Kozol, J. (2005). *The shame of the nation: The restoration of apartheid schooling in America.* New York: Three Rivers Press.

Leahey, C. (2010). *Whitewashing war: Historical myth, corporate textbooks, and possibilities for democratic education.* New York: Teachers College Press.

Lee, J., & Weiss, A. (2007). *The nation's report card: U.S. history 2006.* NCES 2007–474. Washington, DC: U.S. Government Printing Office.

Loewen, J. (2007). *Lies my teacher told me: Everything your American history textbook got wrong.* Revised edition. New York: Touchstone.

Lutkus, A., & Weiss, A. (2007). *The nation's report card: Civics 2006.* NCES 2007–476. Washington, DC: U.S. Government Printing Office.

Lutkus, A., Weiss. J., Campbell, J., Mazzeo, J., & Lazer, S. (1999). *The NAEP 1998 civics report card for the nation.* Washington, DC: U.S. Department of Education.

Lynd, A. (1953). *Quackery in the public schools.* Boston: Little, Brown and Company.

McKenna, A. (2009). *"Race to the Top": A political economy analysis.* Unpublished paper.

McNeil, L. (2000). *Contradictions of school reform: Educational costs of standardized testing.* New York: Routledge.

Mead, N. & Sandene, B. (2007). *The nation's report card: Economics 2006.* NCES 2007–475. Washington, DC: U.S. Government Printing Office.

Medina, J. (2007, September 27). Recruitment by military in schools is criticized. *The New York Times.*

Meier, D. (2004). NCLB and democracy. In D. Meier & G. Wood (Eds.), *Many children left behind* (ch. 4, pp. 66–78). Boston: The Beacon Press.

National Assessment of Educational Progress. (1978). *Changes in political knowledge and attitudes, 1969–76.* Citizenship/social studies report No. 07–CS–02. Denver: Education Commission of the States.

National Assessment of Educational Progress. (1983). *Citizenship and social studies achievement of young Americans: 1981–82 performance and changes between 1976 and 1982.* Report n. 13-CS-01. Denver: Education Commission of the States.

National Assessment of Educational Progress. (2010). *NAEP questions.* Test items from on-line database retrieved from http://nces.ed.gov/nationsreportcard/itmrls/startsearch.asp

National Assessment of Educational Progress Improvement Act of 1988, Pub. L. No. 100–297, title III, § 3401–3403, 102 Stat. 344–349 (1988). Part of the Augustus F. Hawkins-Robert T. Stafford Elementary and Secondary School Improvement Amendments of 1988, Pub. L. No. 100–297, 102 Stat. 130 (1988). [20 USC § 1221e-1, 1988 edition, Supplement V.]

National Center for Education Statistics. (2004). *Digest of education statistics 2003.* U.S. Department of Education. Washington, DC: U.S. Government Printing Office.

National Center for Education Statistics. (2010). *Digest of education statistics 2009.* U.S. Department of Education. Washington, DC: U.S. Government Printing Office.

National Commission on Excellence in Education. (1983). *A nation at risk.* Westford, MA: Murray Printing Company.

National Education Goals Panel. (1995). *The national education goals report: Building a nation of learners 1995.*

Washington, DC: U.S. Government Printing Office.

National Education Goals Panel. (1999). *The national education goals report: Building a nation of learners 1999.* Washington, DC: U.S. Government Printing Office.

No Child Left Behind Act of 2001, Pub. L. No. 107–110, 115 Stat. 1425 (2002). Retrieved from http://www2.ed.gov/policy/elsec/leg/esea02/107–110.pdf

Pellegrino, J., Jones, L., & Mitchell, K. (Eds.) (1999). *Grading the nation's report card: Evaluating NAEP and transforming the assessment of educational progress.* Washington, DC: National Academy Press.

Ravitch, D., & Finn, C. (1988). *What do our 17-year-olds know?* New York: Harper & Row.

Reese, C., Miller, K., Mazzeo, J., & Dossey, J. (1997). *NAEP 1996 mathematics report card for the nation and the states.* Washington, DC: U.S. Department of Education.

Ross, E.W. (1996). Diverting democracy: The curriculum standards movement and social studies education. *International Journal of Social Education, 11*(1), 18–39.

Ross, E.W. (2004). General editors introduction: Defending public schools, defending democracy. In D. Gabbard & E.W. Ross (Eds.), *Defending public schools, Volume 1: Education under the security state* (pp. xi–xviii). Westport, CT: Praeger.

Scheck v. *the United States*, 249 U.S. 47 (1919). Retrieved from http://supreme.justia.com/us/249/47/case.html

Shettle, C., Roey, S., Mordica, J., Perkins, R., Nord, C., Teodorovic, J., Brown, J., Lyons, M., Averett, C., & Kastberg, D. (2007). *The nation's report card: America's high school graduates.* Washington, DC: U.S. Government Printing Office.

Shor, I. (1992). *School and society in the conservative restoration.* Chicago: University of Chicago Press.

Stedman, L. (1998). An assessment of the contemporary debate over U.S. achievement. In D. Ravitch (Ed.), *Brookings papers on education policy: 1998* (pp. 53–121). Washington, DC: The Brookings Institution.

Stedman, L. (2009). *The NAEP long-term trend assessment: A review of its transformation, use, and findings.* Washington, DC: National Assessment Governing Board. http://www.nagb.org/who-we-are/20-anniversary/stedman-long-term-formatted.pdf

Stedman, L. (2010). How well does the standards movement measure up? An analysis of achievement trends and student learning, changes in curriculum and school culture, and the impact of No Child Left Behind. *Critical Education, 1*(10). Retrieved from http://m1.cust.educ.ubc.ca/journal/index.php/criticaled/issue/view133

Stedman, L. (2011). Why the standards movement failed. An educational and political diagnosis of its failure and the implications for school reform. *Critical Education, 2*(1). Retrieved from http://m1.cust.educ.ubc.ca/journal/index.php/criticaled/issue/view134

Stedman, L., & Kaestle, C. (1985). The test score decline is over: Now what? *Phi Delta Kappan, 67*(3), 204–210.

Stedman, L., & Kaestle, C. (1987). Literacy and reading performance in the United States, from 1880 to the present. *Reading Research Quarterly, XXII*(1), 8–46.

Stedman, L., & Smith, M. (1983). Recent reform proposals for American education. *Contemporary Education Review, 2*(2), 85–104.

Sykes, C. (1995). *Dumbing down our kids.* New York: St. Martin's Press.

Toch, T. (1991). *In the name of excellence: The struggle to reform the nation's schools, why it's failing, and what should be done.* New York: Oxford University Press.

U.S. Department of Education. (n.d.). *Overview: Four pillars of NCLB.* Retrieved from http://www.ed.gov/nclb/overview/intro/4pillars.html

U.S. Department of Education. (2009). *Race to the Top program executive summary.* Washington, DC: Author. Retrieved from http://www2.ed.gov/programs/racetothetop/executive-summary.pdf

Weiss, A, Lutkus, A., Grigg, W., & Niemi R., with Kulick E., Swinton S., & Jerry, L. (2001). *The next generation of citizens: NAEP assessments—1988 and 1998.* Washington, DC: U.S. Department of Education.

Weiss, A., Lutkus, A., Hildebrant, B., & Johnson, M. (2002). *The nation's report card: Geography 2001.* NCES 2002–484. Washington, DC: U.S. Department of Education.

Yu, T. (2004). *In the name of morality: Character education and political control.* New York: Peter Lang.

Zinn, H. (1980). *A people's history of the United States.* New York: Harper.

Appendix

NAEP Data Tool and the True Percentage Correct

NAEP (2010) provides a web-based tool for exploring released items. There is an important caution. In its summary tables, the percentages of "correct" responses for constructed-response items are inflated, as NAEP adds in a fraction of those who gave partial answers. The help system explains how the adjustment is made (look under "Help," then "Sort Questions"). To find the actual percentage of students who answered a question fully, select an item, click on "View Question Detail," and then "National Data." Those are the percentages I cite in the text. The "Key/Scoring Guide" link for an item gives the criteria for complete and partial responses. Another link provides "Sample Responses" with explanations of how the responses were graded.

Incomplete Knowledge and Lenient Scoring

Here are two actual student responses on a checks-and-balances item from the 2006 NAEP civics assessment (Lutkus & Weiss, 2007, p. 30; NAEP, 2010). Students were asked for three ways in which presidential power can be checked. Both responses were judged "Complete," which shows how lenient the scoring standards are. The first response has several flaws. The student offers the override as way #1, but it requires a *separate* 2/3 vote in the House *and* the Senate. As to way #2, treaties need the approval (and advisement) of the Senate, not Congress. (The constructions "Any treaty, etc." and "proposes" are also too broad.) As to way #3, the President is impeached solely by the House. The student uses the term Congress too loosely throughout. This response should have been judged partially correct rather than "complete." Still, it is a much better answer than the next one.

> Explain three ways in which the power of the President can be checked by the legislative or the judicial branch.
>
> 1) A president's veto of a law can be overridden by 2/3 of the vote of the Congress.
>
> 2) Any treaty, etc. the President proposes/enters into must be approved by Congress
>
> 3) A president may be impeached by charges brought up by congress and forced to leave office by the Senate's ruling on the charges

The second example of a "complete" response shows how little was expected (NAEP, 2010). Although the question calls for students to *explain* the ways presidential power can be checked, mere identification was all that was looked for. These "explanations" lack important details of the processes and the constitutional provisions.

1)

Congress must approve of judges the President wants to put in office.

2)

Congress can over-ride a veto.

3)

the Supreme Court can declare actions unconstitutional.

As further evidence of relaxed standards, NAEP labeled responses as "acceptable" even when students gave only *two* ways power can be checked instead of the *three* the question called for (NAEP, 2010). Even with such lenient scoring, only 5% of high school seniors gave a "complete" response, and only 16% gave an "acceptable" or "complete" one (Lutkus & Weiss, 2007, p. 30; NAEP, 2010). Most students (67%) could not identify even *one* way of checking presidential power, and that was with these generous standards (NAEP, 2010). Overall, such lenient scoring indicates that the percentage of students who truly know the civics material is likely even lower than what has been reported.

CHAPTER FIVE

Civics in the Social Studies

Critical Democratic Citizenship Education in a Corporatized Hyperreality

JOE L. KINCHELOE

Civics is central to the social studies. Picking up on many themes developed throughout *Getting Beyond the Facts*, this chapter will explore in more depth some of the basic concerns of a critical democratic civics in the social, cultural, political, and economic climate of the twenty-first century. It is amazing that so few states require civics teaching as part of the curriculum in American schools. Throughout the twentieth century, social studies educators from a variety of ideological positions spoke of the centrality of civics in any social studies program (Steinberg, 2000). But, the social fragmentation of American life since the mid-twentieth century, the depoliticization and dislocations of the postmodern condition, and educators' lack of interest in citizenship education have pushed civics to the back burner and made public life much more difficult in contemporary American society. Both students and teachers are disconnected from social and political institutions. It is in this disturbing context that democratic social studies teachers must promote a critical civics (Davis & Fernlund, 1995; Parker, 1997; Stanley, 2000).

No Neutrality Here: The Commitments of a Critical Democratic Civics

My call for a critical democratic civics is grounded in a concern with the health of democracy in the contemporary U.S. In this emergency context I want to make the commitments of a critical democratic civics education very clear. Such a curricular concept is dedicated to the creation of a politically and power-literate society whose citizens are capable of reestablishing a working democratic system. Such citizens are committed to social and economic justice and are adept knowledge workers who strive to make the world a better place to live. They possess an understanding of the context and goals of political commitment. These are not the type of citizens who band together around one political issue but are those who possess a larger understanding that frames and contextualizes their positions on a variety of issues and concerns.

The critical citizens imagined here develop a coherent system of public values and norms in light of which they are able to view contemporary affairs. Using such a critical democratic system of political meaning, they are able to criticize certain practices and embrace other public actions. In this way they can make affective investments in the pursuit of particular social and political goals worth struggling to achieve. Unapologetically, a critical democratic civics operates to protect the oppressed from exploitive power wielders, to intervene on the side of the subjugated. In this context it openly works to bring together exploited individuals who should be working together to fight oppression. Specifically, social studies educators are dedicated to a critical civics struggle to show poor Whites and non-Whites the political interests they share.

When power shifts and culture changes as much as it has over the last few decades, critical analysts maintain that changes in civic strategies and governance are necessary. Political freedom has been jeopardized by the concentration of economic power, as hierarchies have intensified and inequality has been exacerbated. In relation to their understanding power, inequality, the changing nature of work within society, the corporate control of information, and the dominant (safe) ideologies promoted in mainstream social studies and schools in general, critical democratic civics teachers generate a vision of political activism. In addition, they develop a corresponding vision of a just and practical government for a new sociopolitical era. Do not confuse—as many often do—this political activism with a form of party politics. We are referring to larger issues of democracy, not throwing our support to one political party or another. The rest of this chapter connects a critical civics education to the possibilities inherent in a new post-Cartesian politics.

A Critical New Politics for an Anti-Democratric Era

A regressive modernist view of government, like Cartesian-Newtonian thought in general, fragments our perspective and forces us to see government simply as a discrete political dynamic. Government in a more critical perspective is viewed as part of a larger political, economic, social, technological, informational, and ethical context. Perceiving this complex context allows observers to understand that a decontextualized government that sees itself functioning only in a political sphere cannot address the forces that shape it in contemporary society. The concentration of economic power by corporations over the last 20 years, for example, has dramatically changed the way governments operate. Without the benefit of this economic context and the reforms that a knowledge of it necessitates, government would soon become as superfluous as socks on a rooster. To avoid such a reality, critical civics educators argue that a new social contract is needed that explicitly addresses the ways concentrated economic power undermines political freedom. That contract would specify limits to the economic inequality that a democratic society can tolerate (Freeman & Gilbert, 1992; Reich, 1995).

American government in the twenty-first century has lost sight of the fact that when the poor fail, everyone will eventually pay for it. Thus, social justice is not merely a moral question but a pragmatic strategy for survival. Government's modernist predisposition for scientific rationalism removes political leaders and bureaucratic functionaries from the suffering of the poor and their feelings of marginalization. Governmental efficiency does not address the sense of injustice felt by the marginalized. When the marginalized speak of their hurt and their emotions, they cannot understand why no one in policymaking positions listens. Policy experts, who speak about economics with the authority of science, do not perceive the relevance of the emotional pronouncements of the dispossessed to the subject. When, for example, members of the Justice for Janitors campaign testify about their plight, government economists, operating on a different epistemological set of assumptions, see only uninformed individuals emotionally clouding the relevant issues at hand.

The economists are blind to the connection between their policies and the economic difficulties that groups like the janitors must face daily. Operating outside the rationalistic discourse of positivistic political economics, the janitors, their neighbors, and their families' recognize the experts' blindness—their "rational irrationality."

A central feature of the dominant power bloc's ability to dominate those who fall outside its boundaries involves its ability to use scientific rationality over human emotions. The understanding of this epistemological dynamic, this rational irrationality, is, of course, a central feature of a critical social studies curriculum. In the governmental context, this understanding grounds a critical vision of government; it opens the possibility of developing new forms of thinking that help us transcend the limitations of rationalism. This new form of thinking would help critical civics students see through corporate attempts to mystify them about the politics of self-interest. Corporate leaders and their political allies have been able to convince many individuals that democratic political and economic change is not in their best interest. Whereas conservatives attempt to mystify Americans, especially those from the working class, about democratic reform, liberals tend to focus their reforms on the techniques of government, in the process avoiding fundamental questions of power and its equitable distribution. A prerequisite for the creation of a renewed public sphere, a critical civics is an exposure and disruption of existing power relations.

That path is difficult, there is no doubt. But those committed to a critical vision of government have no choice; they must take the path of maximum resistance, the path that contributes to the nurturance and cultivation of democracy. Such critical citizens must make sure that government collects a fair share of taxes from corporations, enforces laws regulating corporate pollution, protects American jobs from exploitive use of foreign labor, provides health care and health insurance for those who need it, and helps the unemployed find good work. Critical civics educators and their allies in other social spheres understand that a democratic government has numerous means of helping establish a more equal social order.

Contrary to the well-publicized pronouncements of right-wing commentators, the use of such mechanisms will not constitute an attempt to "legislate equality." What such spokespersons fail to realize is that leveling access and weeding out impediments to social mobility is merely an effort to address a flagrantly unfair system. Policies such as these do not constitute a move to provide special advantage but are designed merely to lessen many of the disadvantages poor and other marginalized peoples face daily. A critically grounded government can adjust fiscal policy, taxation, support of research and development, and regulation of collective bargaining, to mention only a few strategies for democracy (Gee, Hull, & Lankshear, 1996; Kallick, 1996).

Advocates of a critical civics are well aware of the potential for governmental tyranny. They know that governmental promises have often turned into nightmares and that public institutions often regulate individuals far more than they contribute to their emancipation. In order to address such political dysfunction, critical civics educators must understand the unexamined belief structures on which it rests. In this regard, we can begin to rethink government, both in its organization and its function. In our critical vision, government works hard to establish and maintain an economic democracy with as little bureaucracy and personal regulation as possible. No one here is advocating some form of blind faith in our reliance on big government, as calls for egalitarian reforms are often represented by right-wing operatives.

We know too much about the pathology of bureaucracy to fall into that trap. In the public conversation about American politics, it is rarely noted that the growth of government in the twentieth century did not take place in a social and historical vacuum. Governmental growth was a response to the growth of corporate power in the industrial era and the unprecedented problems such expansion caused. Small-business owners and farmers were unable to compete with emerging megafirms; monopolies tortured consumers with price fixing; labor lost the power to bargain effectively with its corporate bosses; and intoxicated by their growing power, megacompanies lost interest in consumer and worker health and safety. Such dynamics reflect the indifference of uncontested power wielders.

A New Civics, a New Politics in a Critical Democratic Social Studies

The creation of a powerful government as a countervailing force to corporate power was a logical move in the 1930s. And in the power-balancing act created in the Fordist compromise that responded to that need, big government achieved some modest successes in mitigating the impact of disparate wealth. But, of course, big government became, like other hierarchies of administration, more and more bureaucratic in its organizational culture, a situation which resulted in rational irrationalities. When the public became sufficiently fed up with the dysfunctionality of government bureaucracy in the 1970s, corporate leaders took advantage of the impulse and manipulated it to their own ends. Instead of calling for a reform of government bureaucracy and inefficiency in its role as countervailing force to corporate power, corporate leaders and their allies convinced many Americans that neither government nor its countervailing power function were needed. Thus, reference to the all-too-real problem of bureaucratic pathology became a front for a much larger corporate agenda: the end of government interference in its affairs and the termination of attempts to mitigate the growing disparity of wealth (Bowles, Gordon, & Weisskopf, 1990; Wirth, 1983; Ferguson, 1984).

For social studies educators who promote the critical vision of government, the question thus becomes this: How can we create the political power to counter the expanding domination of corporations without the bureaucratic side effects the organizational structure of such an entity tends to produce? In many ways, this may be the most important political question of our era. The concern with bureaucratic government should induce us to strengthen the democratic nature of the state, not destroy it. Maybe, government has something to learn from the more progressive aspects of post-Fordism's organizational strategies. If government understood these features, it would move away from mass-produced administration to a more flexible and decentralized state. Public services in this model would abandon centralized and standardized forms of delivery and focus attention on differentiated, contextually relevant goals. The counterbureaucratic critical governmental vision would embrace a true notion of localism, not the pseudolocalism of post-Fordist megacorporations that paint a "ma-and-pa" facade on their franchises. Indeed, the critical vision holds that government would be big enough to thwart the oppression of corporations but smart enough to perform its tasks humanely.

Many argue that the time has come for a progressive government to relegate many of its functions to other, nongovernmental organizations. However, that proposal is dangerous and must be addressed very carefully. Critical educators and cultural workers need to study this question carefully before dismissing or including the proposal in their critical vision of government. Liberalism has undoubtedly been too single-minded in its reliance on government and, in the process, has ignored the reformist possibilities of other social sectors. Leaders of the women's movement understood this dynamic when they urged women to politicize the personal; democratizing power in personal relationships was not the province of government.

Addressing such personal issues was the concern of men and women and groups in what might be termed "civil society." Women therefore did not push for passage of laws legally forcing men to change diapers and wash dishes. Instead, they sought a variety of social influences, including small groups that aided those who wanted change and educational groups that called attention to problematic forms of masculinity and patriarchal structures. In this context, such civil society efforts would be supported by governmental actions requiring equal pay for equal work, preventing sexual harassment in the workplaces, and increasing educational opportunities for girls in school (Murray, 1992; Gee, Hull, & Lankshear, 1996; Kallick, 1996).

The lesson to be learned from this example is that a socially concerned government is needed but is not to be relied upon to carry out all aspects of social action. Thus, critical civics educators must carefully distinguish between rhetoric that advocates action in civil society for the purpose of shutting down government's role of countering excessive corporate power and discourse that envisions a creative and progressive synergy between government and civil groups. Obviously, the point made here is that civil organizations, such as unions, can play an important role in the quest for social and economic justice, egalitarian institutions, and a critical democratic social studies education.

The possibilities raised by government, education, unions, and other civil organizations working together for such goals are exciting. I have no problem with including an active civil society working with the help of state agencies in our critical civics. If carefully planned, the civil agencies could help rebuild civil life by aiding the poor, extending health care, constructing affordable housing, cleaning up the environment, and helping with education for work. Part of this careful planning would involve the engagement of government support for these supplemental social actions from the civil sector.

The role of civil organizations becomes especially vital given the social, economic, and political changes wrought internationally by the globalized economy and its multinational corporations. The same forces that undermine the well-being of Americans are insidiously operating throughout the world. Americans, either with or without the help of government, must connect their democratic and justice-related interests with people with similar concerns in other countries. Working together, unions, educational organizations, and other civil groups can demand specific standards of behavior from multinational corporations. As we know, the post-Fordist economy pays no allegiance to national boundaries, and as a result, transgovernmental organizations are needed to police the transgressions. Critical civics educators can connect with and help construct these transgovernmental organizations, so they and their students can learn and benefit from the knowledge gained in the effort to monitor and limit the irresponsible behavior of the multinational mega corporations (Moberg, December 16, 1996; Kallick, 1996; Rifkin, 1995; Greider, 1992).

The Fading Public Political Domain: Addressing the Dissolution of American Democracy

Electoral politics in the first decade of the twenty-first century is a sham in the ways it attempts to hide the way government actually works from citizens. Of course, this circumstance holds dramatic implications for social studies in general and critical civics education in particular. The sacred values that Americans have associated with democracy are crumbling, as power shifts from the many to the few. Government now responds less to popular will and more to narrow financial interests and influential elites. New alignments of power interests decimate the democratic expectations of a public that grows increasingly jaded and cynical. Interestingly, despite the dramatic breakdown in democracy over the last decades of the twentieth century, the form and veneer of democratic government has stayed the same.

The only change in the format of American electoral politics over the last 30 years has been that more money is spent by and for candidates than ever before. Amazingly, the way American government and civics are taught in elementary and secondary social studies, despite such dramatic changes in the function of democracy, is indistinguishable from such classes of the 1950s. "Now, class, the three branches of government are the executive, legislative, and judicial branches; a bill becomes law by . . ." Such decontextualized teaching conveys a misleading impression of how government works in contemporary America.

A critical civics asks questions left unexplored in most government classes: Why do some groups shape the government's process of decision making while others have little voice? Why, critical civics educators ask, do monied interests consistently gain government support for their needs while the vast majority of people are ignored? In building a construct of the world that helps social studies students place themselves socially, critical civics educators describe an American democracy that is a struggle for power, not between citizens but between organized economic interests. How can unorganized working people, weak unions, or small civil organizations compete with corporations or coalitions of corporations that employ teams of lawyers and lobbyists, fund political parties, political action committees, and even TV shows? (*The McLaughlin Group*, for example, is a corporate-friendly weekly news program funded by General Electric.) The impact of such investments places corporate concerns on the government's front burner, moving the individual needs of citizens off the stove.

The public perception that monied interests control government through bribery misses the subtle way influence is typically peddled. Corporate money employs lawyers and lobbyists with connections. Their job is often to build relationships between corporate leaders with particular needs and government functionaries. Indeed, many of the lawyers and lobbyists are former— many of them high-ranking—governmental officials. Their job is to put the corporate leaders in touch with the government operatives who can help them. Such real-life issues are rarely addressed in mainstream social studies classes. What a disservice this does students who want to make civic contributions.

What do the corporate financiers get for their purchased influence? Generally speaking, the answer involves the passage of legislation tailored to maximize the financial well-being of corporate management, and this pay-off is often referred to as corporate welfare, or welfare for the rich. In 1993, the federal government, for instance, provided $104 billion in direct payments and tax breaks to American multinational corporations. The Sunkist food company received almost $18 million for the promotion of its orange juice. Farming conglomerates collectively received over $29 billion that same year. McDonald's received $456,000 to tout its Chicken McNuggets. Mining, timber, pharmaceutical, and many other types of corporations are annual beneficiaries of such government handouts.

Another bargain corporations get for their money is velvet-glove treatment for corporate or white-collar crime. 62% of *Fortune* 500 corporations have been involved in one or more significant illegalities; 42% have been found guilty of two or more corrupt activities; 15% have been convicted in five or more cases (Greider, 1992). Corporate influence allows major offending companies to avoid the penalties most working Americans would suffer. Ordinary Americans who are criminals are prohibited from engaging in politics; corporate convicts continue to play dominating roles in the political process. No wonder Senator John McCain's modest proposals for campaign reform in the 2000 Republican primary struck such a nerve with individuals familiar with these power driven realities.

Corporate lawyers have slyly won legal rulings that consider corporations as organizations the same as people under the law. This means that corporations as a legal entity, not individual corporate leaders, are liable for corporate criminal activity. Since you cannot imprison a corporation and corporate leaders are shielded from prosecution, corporations literally get away with murder and continue to operate with little more than a slap on the wrist. The million-dollar-plus salaries corporations pay their lawyers are lucrative financial investments, since their legal henchmen use their expertise to pervert legislation designed to protect labor unions and workers so as to serve corporate objectives. In fact, laws passed several decades ago to protect the interests of the weakest members of American society are now used daily to undermine the needs of the poor and protect corporations from legal penalties for their sociopathic actions.

Such disparity of treatment insults the concept of equal protection under the law, since it pounds another nail into the coffin of democracy. Without a civic faith in the connections between the governed and the government, the country will descend into a civil chaos that produces more Tim McVeighs, White militias, and violent antigovernment movements of all stripes. The role of the critical civics educator is to reveal these injustices and threats to democracy but also to channel the outrage and cynicism of citizens into democratically affirming and socially responsible actions (Greider, 1992; Bowles, Gordon, & Weisskopf, 1990; Rifkin, 1995; Schwartz, 1994).

The Need for a Critical Global Civics:
Privatization around the World

The decline of democracy and the decline of government in general is exacerbated by the globalization of the economy and the evolution of powerful national corporations into superpowerful multinational corporations. The multinationals are so powerful that they have subverted the capacity of governments to protect their citizens. Leaders of multinational corporations are now able to bypass established political institutions, among them tax laws, commercial regulations, employment policies, and environmental statutes. Nation-states no longer have the power to regulate their democratic economic spheres as they did even 20 years ago. Given the powerful role of megacorporations, national governments grow more and more reluctant to protect their domestic markets. So far, no governmental strategy has been developed to respond to the profound changes wrought by the power reconfigurations of globalization. Asian, African, and Latin American governments are collapsing, as multinational corporations vie with indigenous people's movements and informal economics to fill the political and economic vacuums created.

The hand of government grows weaker as the invisible hand of the market strengthens in this era of globalization and privatization. Private corporations are better suited to the new electronic world, the privatization argument goes, than traditional governments. Not being connected to any specific geographical place, they can cope with the supersonic pace of global market forces. With their post-Fordist dynamic flexibility, they can move markets quickly from one continent to another, in the process, shaping the commercial and political priorities of all countries they encounter. Thus, governments are adrift and on the retreat in the face of the march of privatization. A critical civics must attend to this expanding crisis of government and carefully delineate a new, globally conscious, justice-directed, democratic, and creative mission for the nation-state. Without a critical vision of government for the new globalized world, privatization is likely to create untenable conditions in the short run for the poor and working people and, in the long run, for everyone (Barnet & Cavanagh, 1994; Aronowitz & DiFazio, 1994; Rifkin, 1995).

The wealthy can protect themselves to a large degree from the deterioration of the public space by withdrawing into their secure and self-sufficient fortresses. Working people and the poor, however, must suffer the brunt of such deterioration because they have no place to which they can retreat. Without an interruption in the march of privatization and the decline of government, more and more individuals will find themselves unemployed or underemployed, sinking ever deeper into an intractable underclass. They will engage in an informal economy to survive, bartering and trading for food. Many will turn to theft, crime, drug dealing, and prostitution to get by.

At one level, talk of privatization may be misleading, since it implies a boundary between the public sector and the private sector that has faded away in the last few years. Because of the overwhelming influence corporations exert on national, state, and local governments, it is hard to delineate exactly where the public ends and the private begins. This blurring of the private and public that comes under the umbrella of privatization is seen in the new business-operated schools with curricula, of course, that discourage questioning the path of the new privatized world and its sacred icons of deregulation, consumerism, competition, and individualization or, more accurately, customization. The highest expression of the communications revolution is the privatized battering of eyes and ears with inducements to consume.

So pervasive and compelling are these advertisements that six-year-olds know more about beer than democracy. Using the neoclassical language of the free market and privatization, the power derived from controlling the global media empire, and their inordinate influence on governments domestic and foreign, megacorporations are becoming the emperors of the twenty-first century (Reich, 1995; Rifkin, 1995; Gee, Hull, & Lankshear, 1996; Barnet & Cavanagh, 1994). If not the emperors, corporations are at least the most important civics teachers of the twenty-first century.

Ford Motor Company's economy, for example, is already bigger than that of Saudi Arabia or Norway. The yearly sales of Philip Mortis are larger than New Zealand's annual gross domestic product. Such statistics are interesting but mean little if they are not accompanied by the understanding that the balance of power in global politics has moved from public territorial governments to nomadic private companies. The national state is being supplanted by the meta-state—a coalition of multinational corporations and their allies in national governments, international trade organizations, and education. These multinational corporation-led coalitions are the first secular organizations to plan and operate on a global level. Amazingly, little of the planning and organizational work of the corporate meta-state deals with the questions raised here concerning the deteriorating public space, the growing disparity of wealth, and the teaching of civics.

It seems of little importance to the new emperors that the profit needs of the multinationals are forcing governments to nullify protective labor codes and other securities for poor and working people. In this new context, employers in nations around the world are enabled to pay lower wages and to import cheap, undocumented workers. Thus, the disparity of wealth grows both between rich and poor countries and within rich and poor countries. In light of globalization's creation of the meta-state, there no longer exists a discrete entity called the U.S. workplace; we now have a global workplace. Such issues are central to the ability of civic educators and their students to make sense of the forces that shape the political economy in general and civic consciousness in particular. These understandings are central to the critical civics curriculum (Smart, 1992; Aronowitz & DiFazio, 1994).

Left without a Clue:
The Emergence of a New Form of Government

Often, when I observe middle school civics teachers lecturing their students about how a bill becomes law, never referring to lobbyists and economic power wielders' role in the process, I wonder about the future of participatory democracy. If students are to learn how power actually operates and how governing takes place in a privatized twenty-first century, they will have to unlearn the fairy-tale civics lessons they learn in many schools. To help these students, workers and other people around the world understand the merging role of these multinational corporations, it may be appropriate to characterize such organizations as a new form of government-corporate government. That designation removes megacompanies from the shadowy realm in which they operate and exposes their function for precisely what it is. Along with their allies in public government, the media, and education, corporations form a private governmental system.

Such a system, via its technopower, regulates its worldwide empire more effectively than any previous form of governance. This ultimate privatization, or rule by private government, holds far more power over people's lives than "public government," because it dictates terms of employment and controls people's livelihood. As this corporate governmental system shapes individuals' ability to make a living, it exacts a degree of subservience that public government could never equal. Corporate governments' ability to punish economically is a more powerful tool of domination than the laws deployed by public government. Dismissal from one's job can take place without warning and can be just as personally devastating as a prison term or even capital punishment. When the effects of dismissal from a job are studied, we find that getting fired often causes the untimely death of a worker—a form of death penalty by the economic government.

The social understanding we have of our governmental system has been skewed by the corporate government's ability to blame socioeconomic problems on the public government. Often, workers, who themselves have been laid off by corporate downsizing or deindustrialization, speak of getting "government off our backs," blaming the corporate action on public government. They often vote for candidates who promise to reduce the size of government and get government out of business affairs, not knowing that they are helping exacerbate the tyranny of an unregulated corporate government. Using this "get government off our backs" mantra, corporations, since the late 1970s, have steadily gained the power to govern and, as a result, make more money. Attempts to make life better for working people become more and more difficult as citizens and elected officials continue to turn power over to the corporate emperors. Despite the picture painted by business leaders and their political allies, public government experienced a decline in power over the last decades of the twentieth century. By the first decade of the twenty-first century, fewer decisions that shape our lives are made through the traditional political process.

An important development that has served to strengthen this corporate government involves the defection of middle- and high-ranking government officials to corporate payrolls. From different presidential administrations, members of the Treasury Department, including legislative counsel and assistant secretaries, Energy Department lawyers, the chair of the Joint Chiefs of Staff, and even former attorney generals of the United States now work for big business. Their job is to influence the decisions their former departments make in a manner that benefits their corporate bosses, and there is no doubt that corporations get what they pay for in this respect. With these functionaries in place and buoyed by the heady freedom of action provided by deregulation, the corporate government is a post-Fordist version of the old urban political machine. Differing in scale and power—there are hundreds of corporate "private" political machines in operation—the corporate government is less attentive to its constituency than the old party machine, since it teaches, leads, and dictates without the accountability sometimes forced on the machines by elections.

This politics of corporatism, armed with IRS technopower, claims, like other governments, to look out for various constituencies in need of protection. It is not public government, corporate government maintains, that speaks for workers but the humane corporation; in other words, your corporation, my McDonald's, "do it all for you." In addition to the broad category of citizens, corporations speak for consumers, stock holders, the world of business in general, and Americans and their interests around the planet. Policies that are beneficial for us, corporate spokespeople maintain, are good for the masses. When particular groups oppose the needs of the corporate government, the myth tells us, they are hurting millions of Americans. Corporate welfare for the rich, for example, is justified on the basis that its real beneficiaries are the "little guys" that such funding allows the corporate government to help.

Because of their unparalleled access to the public via control of the various media, corporations provide appealing' and simplistic explanations for complex socioeconomic problems. Do answers such as "big government," a "failure of personal responsibility," the "waning of the work ethic," "rock and rap music," "schools not teaching values," and "welfare loafers" sound familiar? These are the "correct answers" to the civics tests provided by omnipresent corporate civics teachers. What we need, in addition to less public government, corporate government's philosophers conclude, is a positivist intelligentsia that issues indisputable edicts based on management science, neoclassical economics, evolutionary biology, and behavioral theory. By the way, from the perspective of corporate government's educational experts, such an intelligentsia can make use of these disciplines to build a good philosophy of privatized civics education. A critical civics appreciates the fatal limitations of such a pedagogy of regulation.

In light of the power and tyrannical behavior of corporate government, those Americans who have placed such great faith in "the new day of freedom coming," when the public government is to be rendered sufficiently insignificant, are in for profound disappointment. Although their freedom to shop at Wal-Mart may well remain intact in the future, a wide variety of traditional political freedoms, such as having a voice in the making of political policies, will have vanished. The protections citizens enjoy from public government were guaranteed by the Constitution, but no similar document exists to limit corporate government. Indeed, there are no institutions to provide checks and balances in the privatization of government. Unless critical citizens act, nothing will impede the penetration of market values into all phases of human life from romantic relationships to corporate education. In this context, the term "free market" is used as a signifier designed to disguise the coercive process that devalues people and their well-being, as corporate leaders pursue policies that ultimately enhance their profit margins (Reich, 1995; Greider, 1992; Schwartz, 1994).

Nowhere to Run:
The Corruption of American Political Parties

When push comes to shove in contemporary American politics, neither political party, Republican or Democrat, is willing to challenge corporate government. Both are far too invested in it, too ensnared in its tentacles to resist it. Most important, both parties are too addicted to corporate money to stray too far away. Thus, Americans find themselves in a peculiar situation: Their two major political parties operate in the grasp of the corporate government. Corporate leaders and their political allies in the public government and the media perpetuate the myth that the views expressed by the Republicans and Democrats represent the full spectrum of political opinion. Thus, it is easy to dismiss opinions such as the ones presented here; in the pseudo-universe of civic perspectives, they simply do not exist.

The way to understand the difference between the Republicans and Democrats is to look at their corporate clients, or, as some analysts describe them, their investors. Ideological differences do not divide contemporary political parties; the needs of their clients do. At most, parties serve as mediating agencies between different corporations and not between individuals with differing political viewpoints. In fact, many of the most important issues of American politics involve conflicts between these investors and their Republican and Democratic gladiators. Such corporate control of the political agenda degrades the democratic process and the parties that claim to operate on particular civic principles. At the same time, it undermines the interests of citizens and all those who fall outside the inner circle of corporate management. Republicans have been comfortable with corporate coziness for decades. Often involved with commerce, Republicans have found it easy to view voters as consumers. Their job as politicians, they came to believe, was to identify what voters think and feel and to then adjust their political advertising to those thoughts and feelings. Since Republicans represented the monied interests, no one was particularly surprised when Republicans provided increasing support to the corporate government.

The Democratic Party's sellout was a different matter. Known and identified at one time as the party of average people, the Democrats have grown closer and closer to corporations and their money. By the close of the 1980s, the Democrats were, in reality, the party of corporate lawyers. Such political operatives rotate in and out of private and government jobs and have replaced the old networks of local party leaders, who decades ago formed the basis of the party. When political analysts argue that Democratic liberalism is dead, they are unwittingly referring to the fact that liberal operatives made a devil's pact with corporate money: They could not take corporate money and defy the rule of the free market. Liberals have few ideas because they, like the Republicans, have laid down their arms in deference to neoclassical economics and corporate rule.

The Democrats have particularly courted high-tech corporate moneylenders, winning friends in Silicon Valley and other high-tech corridors. One of the starkest examples of the Democrat's corporate coitus involved their support of corporate raider Frank Lorenzo's attempt to crush the labor unions at Eastern Airlines. Hiring a host of Democratic Party lawyers and influence peddlers to negate the influence of the machinists', pilots', and flight attendants' unions, Lorenzo fought these unions with the help of Democratic "friends of labor." Lorenzo was forced into mediation and eventually lost the airline, but the support generated in the Democratic Party for such a flagrant enemy of labor held profound implications (Cooper, 1996; Greider, 1992; Reich, 1995).

That forces in the Democratic Party could support Lorenzo illustrated the power of the corporate government in the most unlikely places. With the victory of Bill Clinton in the wake of these capitulations, it comes as no surprise that the New Democrats have consistently supported the freedom of multinational corporations to move, regardless of the consequences for workers in America and around the world. In his two administrations, Clinton never promoted workers' interests to the point that his party's Wall Street supporters might balk. Indeed, it never struck Clinton as a problem that average worker wages were 13% lower by the end of the 1990s than they were in 1973. The Democratic collaborators of the first decade of the twenty-first century are cavalier about the fact that one of three contemporary workers is unemployed, underemployed, or stuck in the peripheral workforce with no benefits or protections. No wonder so many

Americans, working-class Americans in particular, are fed up with both political parties. So far has the Democratic Party strayed from its New Deal concern for the well-being of the poor that only about one in ten Americans identifies it as the party of the average person. How do critical civics educators tell their economically marginalized students that, in the existing political configuration, they have no one to represent their needs?

The corporate government fears the anger that permeates the electorate. Such discontent could lead to an abrupt seismic shift in the political landscape that could express itself in a frightening fascist extremism or, more positively, in a progressive politics that transcends senile liberalism and Social Darwinist conservatism. Many critical analysts have recently advocated formation of an American Labor Party, maybe one that, at least in the short run, would not run a slate of candidates but would campaign for public awareness of the political dynamics discussed here. Many union leaders have endorsed that idea, hoping to devise a way to respond to the corporate government's wildly successful efforts to divide workers around issues of gun control, race, and abortion.

We keep giving the Democratic Party money, union leaders complain, and they kick us down. A little time passes, they continue, and we reward them with more money. A labor party could learn from the ridiculous behavior of the existing political parties that spend hundreds of millions of dollars on vacuous TV advertisements but virtually nothing on grassroots organizing. If political money were spent on developing methods of responding to people rather than manipulating them, citizens would soon understand that the purpose of the party was not simply to win elections but to serve their civic needs. The present operations of the Republicans and the Democrats make it hard for Americans to imagine such a political reality (Bacon, 1996; Pollin, 1996; Kallick, 1996; Cooper, 1996).

The political dysfunctions described here call for new forms of action, new types of civic education. So far, few Americans have objected to forms of education that overtly promote partisan corporate interests. Even traditional high school economics, as previously argued, has been pressured by business leaders to redesign itself as free enterprise economics, characterized by crass celebrations of neoclassical economics and an unregulated market. Business-operated vocational programs teach future workers little more than compliance to management demands and positive (passive) attitudes. To argue for a critical civics that provides another perspective on what might be democratic is in part an effort to balance a curriculum dominated by the ideologies and economic interests of the corporate government. Since public government no longer works like the model taught in school, critical democratic social studies educators teach an alternative civics that helps future citizens understand the demands of citizenship along the postmodern divide. The corporate government has used its power to saturate the society with what many label as a hegemonic picture of the world. A hegemonic portrait attempts to win citizens' consent to a way of seeing their lives and reality that works to the advantage of those in positions of power.

Despite the fact that the corporate-taught privatized civics is a form of indoctrination, the critical civics proposed here refuses to indoctrinate its perspectives. It does not pass off its belief structures as truth. Despite this protest, many will view such an overtly political form of civics as a manifestation of indoctrination. Such a charge confuses the development of a civic vision with the pedagogy that is used in conjunction with it. Critical social studies educators who teach a critical civics, argue that they can admit their own political commitments while teaching their students to act on the democratic principles of learning to make their own choices and acting on their own beliefs. A major difference separates a corporate privatized civics from the critical civics education presented here. Critical civics teachers always alert their students to the fact that a particular view of the political world is being provided.

Also, students in a critical civics class understand that they are free to agree or disagree with the critical perspective. Their success in the class does not hinge on their acceptance of the point of view of the teacher. They are asked simply to understand the perspective and engage with it in a profound way. Education, especially civics education, is never neutral. Indeed, when we attempt to remain neutral, like many churches in Nazi Germany, we support the prevailing power structure. Recognition of the political implications of thinking suggests that teachers should take a position and make it understandable to their students. However (and critical social studies teachers are very clear about this), teachers' political commitments do not grant them the right to impose these positions on their students. It is important to emphasize this point: It is not the critical civics teachers described here who are guilty of indoctrination; it is the "neutral" corporate civics teachers who never tell their students that they are providing them with a point of view.

Such information producers/teachers simply pass off a view of the superiority of a corporate government (not even using such a term) as the truth. When such corporate advocates promote the notion that all words and deeds that oppose the dominant political ideology of the day are forms of educational indoctrination, they forget how everyday experience is constructed in a sociopolitical context marked by an inequitable distribution of power. To refuse to name the structural sources of human suffering and exploitation or the forces that subvert democracy is not a neutral position, In fact, such a stance subjectively supports oppression and the power relations that sustain it. The mainstream argument that any oppositional way of seeing represents an imposition of one's views on somebody else is similar to the nineteenth-century ruling-class idea that raising one's voice, struggling politically, or engaging in social criticism violated a gentlemanly code of civility (Giroux, 1988). Who's indoctrinating whom? In the name of neutrality, the corporatist mainstream promotes particular forms of decontextualized thinking. Here lies the irony of civic objectivity.

As part of their objective lessons on contemporary government, corporate civics pass along what critical social studies educators view as "an anti-democratic map of political reality." The power of this oppressive map of civic reality is difficult to overestimate (Reich, 1995). A misleading map of reality is being promoted when individuals are induced to buy into a worldview that proposes that public government will not allow businesses and corporations the freedom to act in ways that would improve the lives of workers and consumers; when any growth of public government is seen as bad and any growth of corporations is good; when non-Whites and women are portrayed as having all the advantages and, because of affirmative action, are thriving while White men are suffering; when unions are described as outdated and as doing nothing but impeding the efficient operations of corporations; and when education that teaches the necessity of an unregulated market and worker compliance to management is viewed as nonpolitical, but a critical civics education is seen as political. The success of such promotion has left us with a lack of civic knowledge that undermines our ability to make sense of the macrostructures of which we are a part. Critical civics helps social studies students make sense of the larger social context and of their place in it, because it teaches them the hidden rules and assumptions that permeate the invisible social organism.

In a book on vocational education, *How Do We Tell the Workers? The Socioeconomic Foundations of Work and Vocational Education*, I wrote about how a corporate-directed form of vocational education taught workers a civic education grounded on passivity and acceptance of a corporate view of the workplace. Present forms of vocational education, unfortunately, too often avoid the issues raised by a critical civics. When young women are educated for office work, for example, technical knowledge about office equipment and material processing takes precedence.

Issues of social relations, the role of the work in the larger structure of the corporation, safety, worker rights, pay, unions, or the personal effects of new technology are not deemed a part of the vocational curriculum. A vocational program built around an awareness of our critical civics would promote a metaconsciousness of the purposes of vocational education and school in general. With the rise of corporate government and its social and educational influence, an awareness of the objectives of a vocational program becomes more and more important. Students need to understand whose interests are being served by the curriculum, as well as the way the program views their own personal role in the enterprise. Questions concerning this massive corporate power and its ability to quash inquiry into the actual results of vocational programs are infrequently asked in the enterprise of vocational education.

If having power involves learning to act in one's own behalf, few vocational students study power. Corporate government attempts to train its workers to be passive in civics but active in the pursuit of corporate values. It is fascinating to observe this post-Fordist schizophrenia in operation, as future workers are encouraged ad nauseam to use their minds, take chances, show initiative, ask questions, and break away from the chains of tradition—but not in relation to questions of worker rights and justice. Corporate leaders covertly induce workers, worker-trainees, and vocational students to do just the opposite in these domains.

In the corporate mind-set, the idea of empowered worker-citizens who ask questions of democracy and insist on good work is not a pleasant thought. In order to keep such a civic empowerment process from occurring, corporations monitor vocational programs and spend millions of dollars on TV and other media to promote countermessages. Even without the conscious hegemonic messages promoted by corporations, TV as a communications medium seems to undermine the interest of younger viewers in the political sphere. This has added to the depoliticization process. Political participation has remained relatively stable among citizens who came of age before TV, but it has fallen precipitously among younger people. Research on younger workers indicates that political reporting seems remote and nonsensical to them, and, as a result, they quickly lose interest in it.

If TV has taught these viewers to be hip and cynical about the mediated world it presents, then such hip cynicism reaches its apex in young viewers' perspectives toward the political domain). Such perspectives position them as remote and impotent in relation to the political cosmos. Citizenship thus becomes a concept that simply fails to connect with everyday life. No one profits from such civic alienation more than corporate government. This circumstance enables it to continue its transference of power from the public to the private with minimal interference. As corporations colonize the concept of empowerment, the term's connection with the political sphere is frayed. Empowerment in this corporate discourse becomes a privatized notion, revolving around the freedom to consume and to work within wider boundaries of creativity. Just as long as the empowered creative work contributes to an increase in productivity and short-term profit margins, workers can be as empowered as they want to be. In the lexicon of the post-Fordist corporate government: Enjoy the benefits of the Brave New Empowered World! A critical civics in this bizarre dimension becomes far more difficult to teach, but far more necessary.

Critical civics in a vocational educational setting is both a pedagogy and a political vision that struggles to provide vocational students and workers with an understanding of the social, economic, political, philosophical, and ethical context in which labor and schooling for it takes place. A critical civics for workers attempts to counter the confusion created by corporate messages and the crazy-quilt media civics taught on TV. In a hyperreality marked by confusion and a loss of meaning, critical civics attempts to make sense of the socioeconomic and political world. In order to accomplish this difficult feat, the invisible must be made visible. For example, a central feature of any critical vocational teacher's civics curriculum would involve the recognition of the market's influence on vocational education.

Indeed, this observation may form the basis of any critical civics program for future workers. This understanding can serve as a springboard to an analysis of the impact of twenty-first-century global economics on the work lives of vocational students. In this context, teachers induce students to question the ways public and corporate governmental decisions shape their work futures: Will students be able to gain steady, long-terms jobs? Will they be able to achieve economic security? Will they have access to career advancement and financial mobility? Will the attainment of good work be possible? How as worker-citizens can they help shape political and economic policies to benefit themselves and their fellow workers around the world (Valli, 1988; Reich, 1995; Schwartz, 1994; Lakes, 1994; Simon, Dippo, & Schenke, 1991).

Dirtying Our Hands: Engaging in Political Work

With these understandings of the insidiousness of corporate civics in mind, critical civics demands that students be introduced to the messy everyday world of politics. As unpleasant and distasteful as the media has convinced us to consider this realm, work within it is noble, patriotic, and necessary. Critical civic work in this realm means reaching across racial, class, and gender boundaries and forming alliances with people who are in some way different from oneself in the pursuit of common goals. Such critical civics work involves humbly engaging in dialogue about values and visions and their application in the complexity and ambiguity of everyday life. The work of critical citizenship requires a fidelity to the principles of social and economic justice and a commitment to marginalized individuals that is so strong it can overcome the divisive issues that separate us from one another. Middle- and upper-middle-class "experts" must refrain at all costs from "leading" such a movement and speaking for their lower-status allies. Such agents must develop the ability to work with exploited people in a way that is permeated with a genuine humility.

For all the cynicism that the political and economic events of the last several decades have generated in all of us, we can make a difference. Nothing shocks the unresponsive Congress as much as seeing several of their colleagues defeated in their reelection bids by a popular movement of organized people. Just because public government now takes a back seat to corporate government does not mean that the situation is irreversible. The monied interests have always feared movements that speak in terms of democracy and egalitarianism. Critical democratic social studies educators must confront these contemporary monied interests that have subverted the notion of a government by the people and build coalitions of friends of democracy. Such friends might include a united worldwide labor movement, indigenous peoples movements, environmental movements, women's movements, and ethnic justice movements, all of which can interrupt the smooth operations of the international corporate government. The future of democracy in the U.S. and around the world is intimately connected with the success of our critical civics.

Bibliography

Aronowitz, S., & DiFazio, W. (1994). The politics of science wars. In A. Ross (Ed.), *Science wars.* Durham, NC: Duke University Press.

Bacon, D. (1996, April 1). For a labor economy. *The Nation*, 262 (13), 14.

Barnet, R. & Cavanagh, J. (1994). *Global Dreams: Imperial corporations and the new world order.* New York: Simon and Schuster.

Bowles, S., Gordon, D., & Weisskopf, T. (1984). *Beyond the wasteland: A Democratic Alternative to Economic Decline.* New York: Doubleday.

Cooper, M. (1996, May 27). Class war @Silicon Valley: Disposable works in the new economy. *The Nation*, 262 (21), 11–16.

Davis, J., & Fernlund, P. (1995). Civics: If not, why not? *The Social Studies*, 86 (2), 56–59.

Ferguson, K. (1984). *The feminist case against bureaucracy.* Philadelphia: Temple University Press.

Freeman, R., & Gilbert, D. (1992). Business, ethics and society: A critical agenda. *Business and Society*, 31 (1), 9–17.

Gee, J., Hull, G., & Lankshear, C. (1996). *The new work order: Behind the language of the new capitalism.* Boulder, CO: Westview.

Giroux, H. (1988). *Teachers as intellectuals: Toward a critical pedagogy of learning.* Boston: Bergin & Garvey.

Greider, W. (1992). Who will tell the people? The betrayal of American democracy. New York: Touchstone.

Kallick, D. (1996, November 11). Left turn ahead. *The Nation*, 263 (15), 22–24.

Lakes, R. (1994). Critical education for work. In R. Lakes (Ed.), *Critical education for work.* Norwood, NJ: Albex.

Moberg, D. (1996, December 16). Labor as neighbor. *The Nation*, 263 (20), 18–21.

Murray, R. (1992). Fordism and post-Fordism. In C. Jenks (Ed.), *The post-modern reader.* New York: St. Martin's Press.

Parker, W. (1997). Democracy and difference. *Theory and Research in Social Education*, 23 (4), 302–331.

Pollin, R. (1996, September 30). Economics with a human face. *The Nation*, 263 (9), 21–23.

Reich, D. (1995). *Opposing the system.* New York: Crown Publishers.

Rifkin, J. (1995). *The end of work: The decline of the global labor force and the dawn of the post-market era.* New York: Tarchner/Putnam.

Schwartz, B. (1994). *The costs of living: How market freedom* erodes *the best things in life.* New York: W. W. Norton.

Simon, R., Dippo, D., & Schenke, A. (1991). *Learning work: A critical pedagogy of work education.* Westport, CT: Bergin & Garvey.

Smart, B. (1992). *Modern conditions, postmodern controversies.* New York: Routledge.

Stanley, W. (2000). Curriculum and the social order. In D. Hursh & E. W. Ross (Eds.), *Democratic social education: Social studies for social change.* New York: Falmer.

Steinberg, S. (2000). The new civics: Teaching for critical empowerment. In D. Hursh & E. W. Ross (Eds.), *Democratic social education: Social studies for social change.* New York: Falmer.

Valli, L. (1988). Gender identity and the technology of office education. In L. Weis (Ed.), *Class, race, and gender in American education.* Albany: State University of New York Press.

Wirth, A. (1983). *Productive work—in industry and schools.* Lanham, MD: University Press of America.

CHAPTER SIX

Politics and Patriotism in Education

JOEL WESTHEIMER

In November of 2001, less than two months after the terrorist attacks on the World Trade Center, Nebraska's state board of education approved a patriotism bill specifying content for the high school social studies curriculum in accordance with the state's 1949 statute—the Nebraska Americanism law. Social studies, the bill read, should include "instruction in . . . the superiority of the U.S. form of government, the dangers of communism and similar ideologies, the duties of citizenship, and appropriate patriotic exercises." The board further specified that middle school instruction "should instill a love of country" and that the social studies curriculum should include "exploits and deeds of American heroes, singing patriotic songs, memorizing the 'Star Spangled Banner' and 'America,' and reverence for the flag."[1] Nebraska was not alone. Within a few months, more than two dozen state legislatures introduced new bills or resurrected old ones aimed at either encouraging or mandating patriotic exercises for all students in schools. Seventeen states enacted new pledge laws or amended policies in the 2002–03 legislative sessions alone.[2] Since then more than a dozen additional states have signed on as well. Twenty-five states now require the pledge to be recited daily during the school day, and 35 require time to be set aside in school for the pledge.

The federal role in encouraging patriotic passion has been significant as well. On 12 October 2001, the White House, in collaboration with the politically conservative private group Celebration U.S.A., called on the nation's 52 million schoolchildren to take part in a mass recitation of the Pledge of Allegiance. Four days later, the U.S. House of Representatives passed a resolution (404–0) urging schools to display the words "God Bless America" in an effort to reinforce national pride. In 2002, six months before the Iraq War, the federal government announced a new set of history and civic education initiatives aimed squarely at cementing national identity and pride. These initiatives, President George W. Bush declared, would "improve students' knowledge of American history, increase their civic involvement, and deepen their love for our great country." To engender a sense of patriotism in young Americans, we must, Bush emphasized, teach them that "America is a force for good in the world, bringing hope and freedom to other people."[3] And the 2005 federal budget allocates $120 million to grants that support the teaching of "traditional American History." In addition, a campaign by the National Endowment for the Humanities seeks to fund the celebration of traditional "American heroes."

The drive to engage students in patriotic instruction shows no sign of abating and, in fact, may be taking on new fervor. These efforts share at least two characteristics. First, as I detail below, the form of patriotism being pursued by many school boards, city and state legislatures, and the federal government is often monolithic, reflecting an "America-right-or-wrong" stance—what philosopher Martha Nussbaum warns is "perilously close to jingoism."[4] Many educators have condemned these developments as a legislative assault on democratic values in the school curriculum. Second, few of these initiatives included teachers or local school administrators in their conception or development. The direction has come from on high—from the U.S. Department of Education, from local and state boards of education, and from politicians.

But the grassroots response has been far more complex. At the level of the classroom and the school, the efforts of individual teachers, students, principals, and community organizations paint a broad array of curricular responses to the calls for patriotic education.

Many teachers and administrators have implemented mandatory policies, shunned controversy, and reinforced the America-is-righteous-in-her-cause message, just as the Bush Administration and politically conservative commentators have wanted. However, terrorism, war, and the threat of fundamentalist intolerance have sparked other educators' commitments to teaching for democratic citizenship, the kind of citizenship that recognizes ambiguity and conflict, that sees human conditions and aspirations as complex and contested, and that embraces debate and deliberation as a cornerstone of patriotism and civic education. In the nation's classrooms, patriotism is politically contested terrain.

What Is Patriotism?

It has often been said that the Inuit have many words to describe snow because one would be wholly inadequate to capture accurately the variety of frozen precipitation. Like snow, patriotism is a more nuanced idea than is immediately apparent. Political scientists, sociologists, and educators would do well to expand the roster of words used to describe the many attitudes, beliefs, and actions that are now called "patriotism." So before we can talk about the politics of patriotism in schools, it makes sense to get clear on at least a few definitions.

Although it is beyond the scope of this article to delve deeply into the many forms of patriotic attitudes and actions, two umbrella categories of patriotism are worth brief exploration. Each is relevant to debates over curriculum and school policy, and each represents political positions that have implications for what students learn about patriotism, civic engagement, and democracy. I will be calling these two manifestations of patriotism *authoritarian* and *democratic*, and their distinctive characteristics are displayed in Table 1.

TABLE 1.
The Politics of Patriotism

	Authoritarian Patriotism	Democratic Patriotism
Ideology	Belief that one's country is inherently superior to others.	Belief that a nation's ideals are worthy of admiration and respect.
	Primary allegiance to land, birthright, legal citizenship, and government's cause.	Primary allegiance to set of principles that underlie democracy.
	Nonquestioning loyalty.	Questioning, critical, deliberative.
	Follow leaders reflexively, support them unconditionally.	Care for the people of society based on particular principles (e.g., liberty, justice).
	Blind to shortcomings and social discord within nation.	Outspoken in condemnation of shortcomings, especially within nation.
	Conformist; dissent seen as dangerous and destabilizing.	Respectful, even encouraging, of dissent.
Slogans	My country, right or wrong.	Dissent is patriotic.
	America: love it or leave it.	You have the right to NOT remain silent.
Historical Example	McCarthy Era House Un-American Activities Committee (HUAC) proceedings, which reinforced the idea that dissenting views are anti-American and unpatriotic.	The fiercely patriotic testimony of Paul Robeson, Pete Seeger, and others before HUAC, admonishing the committee for straying from American principles of democracy and justice.
Contemporary Example	Equating opposition to the war in Iraq with "hatred" of America or support for terrorism.	Reinforcing American principles of equality, justice, tolerance, and civil liberties, especially during national times of crisis.

Authoritarian Patriotism

In a democracy, political scientist Douglas Lummis argues, patriotism reflects the love that brings a people together rather than the misguided love of institutions that dominate them. "Authoritarian patriotism," he notes, "is a resigning of one's will, right of choice, and need to understand to the authority; its emotional base is gratitude for having been liberated from the burden of democratic responsibility."[5] Authoritarian patriotism asks for unquestioning loyalty to a cause determined by a centralized leader or leading group. In his 1966 book, *Freedom and Order*, historian Henry Steele Commager observed, "Men in authority will always think that criticism of their policies is dangerous. They will always equate their policies with patriotism, and find criticism subversive."[6] Authoritarian patriotism demands allegiance to the government's cause and therefore opposes dissent.

To say that authoritarian patriotism comes only from the ruling authority would be too simplistic, however. The social psychology of authoritarian patriotism (especially in a democracy) depends on a deliberate and complicit populace. Following September 11, an abundance of American flags and bumper stickers suddenly sprouted in virtually every city, suburb, town, and rural district in the country. While the flags signaled understandable solidarity in a time of crisis, other public expressions of national pride carried more worrisome messages. Fiercely nationalistic and jingoistic sentiments could be seen and heard on bumper stickers, news broadcasts, and television, as well as in politics. Schools were no exception, and students soon witnessed adults showcasing authoritarian responses to issues of enormous democratic importance.

For example, in 2004 more than 10,000 high schools, community colleges, and public libraries were mailed a free video called "Patriotism and You" by the Washington, D.C.–based group Committee for Citizen Awareness. The group boasts that the video has now been seen by 30 million children and adults nationwide. Teacher Bill Priest of Rock Bridge, Maryland, showed the video to his class as "an example of propaganda of a sort."[7] Statements such as "Patriotism is respecting authority" and "We should manifest a unity of philosophy, especially in times of war" pervade the video. Priest wondered why nobody in the film talks about the right to express patriotic dissent. As this video and dozens of other recent initiatives that aim to teach patriotism illustrate, the primary characteristic of authoritarian patriotism is disdain for views that deviate from an official "patriotic" stance. And proponents of an authoritarian kind of patriotism have looked to the schools to help deliver a unified message and have sought to punish educators who allow or offer dissenting perspectives.

Democratic Patriotism

In a National Public Radio show titled "Teaching Patriotism in Time of War," social historian Howard Zinn described eloquently a possible counterstance to authoritarian patriotism. "Patriotism," he said, "means being true and loyal—not to the government, but to the principles which underlie democracy."[8] Democratic patriotism aims to remain true to these principles. A few historical examples illustrate this position.

In 1950, Sen. Margaret Chase Smith (R-Me.) was the first member of Congress to publicly confront Sen. Joseph McCarthy (R-Wis.). She prepared a Declaration of Conscience urging her fellow senators to protect individual liberties and the ideals of freedom and democracy on which the United States was founded. As she presented the declaration, Sen. Smith said the following: "Those of us who shout the loudest about Americanism are all too frequently those who…ignore some of the basic principles of Americanism—the right to criticize, the right to hold unpopular beliefs, the right to protest, the right of independent thought."[9]

Many educators, policy makers, and ordinary citizens have embraced a vision of patriotism that reflects these ideals about democracy and the duties of democratic citizens. When he sang Woody Guthrie's "This Land Is Your Land," Pete Seeger expressed many patriotic sentiments about the United States, but when he appeared before McCarthy's House Un-American Activities Committee (HUAC), he noted: "I have never done anything of any conspiratorial nature, and I resent very much and very deeply the implication…that in some way because my opinions may be different from yours…I am any less of an American than anybody else. I love my country very deeply."[10]

African American actor, performer, and All-American football player Paul Robeson addressed HUAC in even starker terms: "You gentlemen…are the non-patriots, and you are the un-Americans, and you ought to be ashamed of yourselves."[11]

More recently, some citizens agreed with former Attorney General John Ashcroft's admonition that anyone who criticizes the government is giving "ammunition to America's enemies" (a notably authoritarian patriotic position). Others saw things differently: dissent is important, and, as a popular march placard indicates, in a democratic nation, "Dissent Is Patriotic."

Another look into history reveals a democratic vision of patriotism as well. Although millions of schoolchildren recite the Pledge of Allegiance every day, far fewer know much about its author. Francis Bellamy, author of the original 1892 pledge (which did not contain any reference to "God"), was highly critical of many trends of late-19th-century American life, most notably unrestrained capitalism and growing individualism. He wanted America to reflect basic democratic values, such as equality of opportunity, and he worked openly to have his country live up to its democratic ideals.

Was Bellamy patriotic? Of course, but his was not patriotism of the authoritarian kind. Indeed, many of America's national icons shared a democratic vision of patriotism. For instance, Emma Lazarus wrote the poem that became the inscription on the base of the Statue of Liberty: "Give me your tired, your poor / Your huddled masses yearning to breathe free." Katherine Lee Bates, an English professor and poet at Wellesley College, wrote the lyrics to "America the Beautiful," including the words "America! America! God mend thine every flaw!" Bellamy, Lazarus, Bates, and many like-minded reformers throughout America's history asserted their patriotism by strongly proclaiming their beliefs in democratic values such as free speech, civil liberties, greater participation in politics, and social and economic equality.[12]

Caring about the substantive values that underlie American democracy is the hallmark of democratic patriotism. This does not mean that democratic patriots leave no room for symbolic displays of support and solidarity. Few would argue with the power of symbols. And the authors and composers mentioned above created the very symbols of American patriotism on which proponents of authoritarian patriotism rely. But democratic patriotism seeks to ensure that "liberty and justice for all" serves not only as a slogan for America but also as a guiding principle for policies, programs, and laws that affect Americans. To be a democratic patriot, then, one must be committed not only to the nation, its symbols, and its political leaders, but also to each of its citizens and their welfare. "This land is your land, this land is my land," "Life, liberty, and the pursuit of happiness," "Crown thy good with brotherhood"—for democratic patriots, these visions represent the ideal America, one worth working toward openly, reflectively, and passionately.

Increasing Authoritarian Patriotism in Schools

I have already detailed several district, state, and federal campaigns to promote one particular view of American history, one narrow view of U.S. involvement in the wars in Iraq and Afghanistan, and so on. There are others. Hundreds of schools, for example, now use the Library of Congress' new "Courage, Patriotism, Community" website. Advertised widely among educators, this website was founded "in celebration of the American spirit" and includes "patriotic melodies" and "stories from the Veterans History Project."[13] Despite a few prominently posted questions—such as "Does patriotism mean displaying the flag or practicing dissent or both?"—there is little material on the site that lends anything but a prowar, America-can-do-no-wrong vision of patriotism. Similarly, the Fordham Foundation produced a set of resources for teaching patriotism called *Terrorists, Despots, and Democracy: What Our Children Need to Know*, which, under the guise of teaching "indisputable facts," presents storybook tales of "good" and "evil" in the world. But the smaller stories—those taking place in the nation's classrooms and individual schools—might portray more tangible causes for concern.

In New Mexico, five teachers were recently suspended or disciplined for promoting discussion among students about the Iraq War and for expressing, among a range of views, antiwar sentiments. One teacher refused to remove art posters created by students that reflected their views on the war and was suspended without pay. Alan Cooper, a teacher from Albuquerque, was suspended for refusing to remove student-designed posters that his principal labeled "not sufficiently pro-war." Two other teachers, Rio Grande High School's Carmelita Roybal and Albuquerque High School's Ken Tabish, posted signs about the war, at least one of which opposed military action. And a teacher at Highland Hills School was placed on administrative leave because she refused to remove a flier from her wall advertising a peace rally. Roybal and Tabish were suspended, and all of the teachers in these cases were docked two to four days' pay by the Albuquerque Public Schools. Each of these schools posts military recruitment posters and photographs of soldiers in Iraq.[14]

In West Virginia, high school student Katie Sierra was suspended for wearing a T-shirt with a rewritten version of the pledge on it: "I pledge the grievance to the flag," it began. And it ended, "With liberty and justice for some, not all." Some of her classmates at Sissonville High School told reporters that they intended to give Katie a taste of "West Virginia justice." The school's principal, Forrest Mann, suspended Katie for three days and forbade her to wear the controversial shirt, saying that her behavior was "disrupting school activity." Indeed, at least one of Katie's classmates felt that the shirt disrupted her studies, writing that Katie's actions "greatly saddened me and brought tears to my eyes. I watched as a young lady was permitted to walk down the hallways of Sissonville High School wearing a T-shirt that spoke against American patriotism." No students were disciplined for wearing shirts emblazoned with the American flag.[15]

In Broomfield, Colorado, 17-year-old David Dial was suspended for posting fliers advertising an "International Student Anti-War Day of Action." He noted that it was "just a peaceful protest against the war in Iraq," adding that his suspension was hypocritical given the fanfare at the school surrounding new curricula that promoted student civic and political involvement.[16]

But perhaps two of the most interesting cases involve the Patriot Act. In the first case, a Florida teacher handed out to his students copies of a quotation: "They that can give up essential liberty to obtain a little temporary safety deserve neither liberty nor safety." He asked students to interpret this statement in light of current events. (The class had previously studied the circumstances surrounding the internment of Japanese Americans during World War II.) After discussing the implications of the quotation, the teacher asked the class whether anyone knew who wrote it. When none guessed correctly, he showed them an overhead slide that included the name and a drawing of its author: Benjamin Franklin. They then discussed the intentions of the nation's Founders, constitutional protections, and so on. This teacher was supported by parents but was disciplined by the principal for straying from the mandated civics curriculum standards. A letter of reprimand remains in his personnel file.

The second case might be apocryphal, but this story (and many others like it) has been circulating among teachers, professors of education, and concerned parents. I have been unable to find solid documentation, but I include it here to demonstrate the degree to which these stories invoke teachers' and the public's sense that, in the current climate of intimidation, dissent in the context of civic education is subject to repression and regulation.

The story goes roughly thus: A New York State high school teacher was reprimanded for having his students examine historical comparisons of crisis times in U.S. history. He introduced students to the Alien and Sedition Acts of 1798 and the Sedition Act of 1918. The earlier acts allowed President John Adams to arrest, imprison, and deport "dangerous" immigrants on suspicion of "treasonable or secret machinations against the government" and to suppress freedom of the press. The more recent act restricted criticism of the government, the Constitution, and the military. Pairing these acts with the text of today's Patriot Act, the teacher asked students to assess the three time periods and argue for the justice or injustice of each law. Several parents complained that he was not encouraging patriotism, and the principal instructed the teacher to discontinue the lesson.

Patriotism as a Substitute for Politics

Much of the rationale behind the cases of teachers being reprimanded in schools rests on the idea that patriotism, especially where public schools are concerned, should remain above partisan politics. Dissent, rather than being viewed as an essential component of democratic deliberation, is seen as a threat to patriotism. Indeed, in this view, "politics" is something unseemly and best left to mudslinging candidates for public office: being political is tantamount to devaluing the public good for personal or party gain. Education, in this way of thinking, should not advance "politics" but rather should reinforce some unified notion of truth that supports—without dissent—officially accepted positions.

For example, Sen. Lamar Alexander (R-Tenn.), a former U.S. secretary of education under President Reagan, introduced the American History and Civics Education Act in March 2003 to teach "the key persons, the key events, the key ideas, and the key documents that shape [our] democratic heritage."[17] According to Sen. Alexander, this legislation would put civics back in its "rightful place in our schools, so our children can grow up learning what it means to be an American."[18]

These efforts by the Congress and by conservative members of the Bush Administration have been applauded by those who view education primarily as a means of conveying to American youths and young adults a monolithic set of important historical facts combined with a sense of civic unity, duty, and national pride. Reaching back to a 1950s-style understanding of the American past and the workings of American society, Sen. Alexander and like-minded politicians suggest that Americans, despite diverse backgrounds and cultures, all share a unified American creed or a common set of beliefs and that these beliefs are easily identifiable. Explicitly borrowing from consensus historian Richard Hofstadter, Sen. Alexander believes that "it has been our fate as a nation not to have ideologies but to be one."[19]

Telling students that history has one interpretation (and that interpretation is that the U.S. is pretty much always right and moral and just in its actions) reflects an approach to teaching love of country that too easily succumbs to authoritarianism. Yet teaching this one unified creed—especially in the wake of the September 11 attacks—is rarely viewed as being political. "Being political" is an accusation most often reserved for exploring views that are unpopular—

the kind of views, not surprisingly, that come from critical, reflective, and democratic forms of patriotic teaching.

In many schools throughout the U.S., this tendency to cast patriotism and politics as opposites runs especially deep. So strong are the anti-politics politics of schooling that even mundane efforts at teaching for democratic understandings, efforts that aim to encourage discussion around controversial topics, for example, are often deemed indoctrination. After a teacher allowed students at a school assembly to recite an antiwar poem they had written, one parent argued in a parents' forum, "We live in the USA, so singing a patriotic song isn't inappropriate. But politics has no place in the school."[20]

Similarly, after the National Education Association developed lesson plans about the events of September 11, politicians, policy makers, and some parents worried that the curriculum—titled "Tolerance in Times of Trial"—did not paint a positive enough picture of U.S. involvement in world affairs. Conservative political commentator and talk show host Laura Ingraham attacked the curriculum as indoctrination, warning that the lessons encouraged students to "discuss instances of American intolerance." Curricular materials developed by the Los Angeles-based Center for Civic Education that included discussion of controversial issues in multiculturalism, diversity, and protection of the environment drew similar criticism. And we are already seeing evidence of attacks on curriculum that examines the social, economic, and political implications of Hurricane Katrina.[21]

Politics Is Not a Dirty Word

But politics is not a four-letter word. Patriotism, if it is to reflect democratic ideals, needs politics. In a lecture on citizenship in the 21st century, Harry Boyte, co-director of the University of Minnesota's Center for Democracy and Citizenship, argued that politics is the way people with different values and from different backgrounds can "work together to solve problems and create common things of value."[22] In this view, politics is the process by which citizens with varied interests and opinions negotiate differences and clarify places where values conflict. Boyte cited *In Defense of Politics* by Bernard Crick in calling politics "a great and civilizing activity." For Boyte, accepting the importance of politics is to strive for deliberation and a plurality of views rather than a unified perspective on history, foreign policy, or domestic affairs. For those seeking to instill democratic patriotism, "being political" means embracing the kind of controversy and ideological sparring that is the engine of progress in a democracy and that gives education social meaning. The idea that "bringing politics into it" (now said disdainfully) is a pedagogically questionable act is, perhaps, the biggest threat to engaging students in discussions about what it means to be patriotic in a democratic nation.

It is precisely this aspect of politics with which educators wrestle. While many, like Boyte, see education as an opportunity to teach the critical and deliberative skills that are consistent with democratic patriotism and enable students to participate effectively in contentious public debates, others are uncomfortable with approaches to teaching that encourage dissent and critique of current policies. For example, the events of the Iraq War and the ongoing "reconstruction" have led policy makers and educators who favor authoritarian patriotism to prefer celebrating what President Bush has repeatedly called "the rightness of our cause."

The classroom dramas described above illustrate the intensity with which battles over controversial issues in the classroom can be waged. Yet there are dozens, perhaps hundreds, of curricular efforts that deliberately engage "politics" as a healthy embodiment of the diversity of opinions, motivations, and goals that make up democratic patriotism.

Teaching Democratic Patriotism

Many valuable debates about patriotism do not take as their starting point the question "Should patriotic instruction be apolitical or political, obedient or critical?" Rather, they begin with questions such as "Whose politics do these education programs reflect and why?" or "Which citizens benefit from particular policies and programs and which do not?" Such approaches aim toward democratic patriotism.

Initiatives that emphasize a vision of democratic patriotism tend to come from nongovernmental education organizations, small groups of curriculum writers, and individual teachers rather than from textbook companies or district, state, and federal education departments. As Operation Iraqi Freedom began in March 2003, Oregon teacher Sandra Childs asked students to consider the relationship between patriotism and the First Amendment, using the words of Sen. John McCain (R-Ariz.) as a starting point: "The time for debate is over." A school in Chicago reorganized its interdisciplinary curriculum around the theme of competing national concerns for civil liberties and safety. Some efforts encompass an entire school as the vision is infused into nearly every aspect of the curriculum, extracurricular activities, and even the physical space. I briefly describe two such programs here, but I encourage readers to search out others.[23]

El Puente Academy for Peace and Justice. The El Puente Academy for Peace and Justice is located in Brooklyn's Williamsburg neighborhood.[24] It was established in 1993 by El Puente ("The Bridge"), a community organization, in partnership with the New York City Board of Education. The academy is academically successful (a 90% graduation rate in an area where schools usually see 50% of their students graduate in four years). But what makes the school especially compelling is its firm commitment to reverse the cycles of poverty and violence for all community residents. It teaches "love of country" by teaching caring for the country's inhabitants. The curriculum, organization, and staff embody a living vision of democratic patriotism at work.

One of the concerns of both El Puente, the organization, and El Puente, the academy, is the health of the community. Williamsburg and nearby Bushwick are called the "lead belt" and the "asthma belt" by public health researchers. As Héctor Calderón, El Puente's principal, declares, "Williamsburg reads like a 'Who's Who of Environmental Hazards.'"[25] Students at El Puente study these toxic presences not only because they are concerned about the health of the natural environment, but also because these hazards directly affect the health of the community. Science and math classes survey the community in order to chart levels of asthma and provide extra services to those families affected by the disease. One year, students and staff became intrigued when they found that Puerto Ricans had a higher incidence of asthma than Dominicans. They wondered if Dominicans had natural remedies not used by Puerto Ricans. Their report became the first by a community organization to be published in a medical journal. Another group of students successfully battled against a proposed 55-story incinerator that was to be built in the neighborhood (which is already burdened with a low-level nuclear waste disposal plant, a nuclear power plant, and an underground oil spill). While math and science classes measured and graphed levels of toxicity, a humanities class produced a documentary on their findings.

That all men (and women) are created equal is indeed a truth that is self-evident to these urban students. That all members of their community are entitled to a healthy life—as well as liberty and the pursuit of happiness—is also self-evident in the academy curriculum. For El Puente students, patriotism means love of American ideals, whether that entails supporting current social and economic policies or critiquing them.

La Escuela Fratney Two-Way Bilingual Elementary School. A spiral notebook always accessible in Bob Peterson's elementary class is labeled "Questions That We Have." Peterson is one of many teachers at La Escuela Fratney, which opened in Milwaukee in 1988 and is Wisconsin's only two-way bilingual elementary school. All of its 380 students begin their schooling in their dominant language (English or Spanish) and by grade 3, they have begun reading in a second language. Rita Tenorio, teacher and co-founder of Fratney, explains that the school's mission includes preparing students "to play a conscious and active role in society," thereby enabling them to be active citizens who can participate in democratic forums for change and social betterment.

Peterson, who is founding editor of *Rethinking Schools* and the 1995 Wisconsin Elementary Teacher of the Year, placed the notebook prominently at the front of the classroom on 12 September 2001, after a fifth-grader pointed out the window and asked, "What would you do if terrorists were outside our school and tried to bomb us?" Peterson's notebook, relatively ordinary in ordinary times, appeared extraordinary at a time when unreflective patriotic gestures commonly associated with authoritarian patriotism abounded. Recall President Bush's admonition to both the world and to U.S. citizens that "you are either with us or you are with the terrorists" or White House Press Secretary Ari Fleischer's dire warning to Americans to "watch what they say and watch what they do."[26] It was in these times that Escuela Fratney teachers felt especially compelled to teach the kind of patriotic commitments that reflected such American ideals as freedom of speech, social justice, equality, and the importance of tolerating dissenting opinions.

Using a curriculum Peterson developed for Rethinking Schools focused on 9/11, terrorism, and democracy, teachers at Escuela Fratney encouraged students to ask tough questions, to explore many varied news sources, and to share their fears, hopes, and dreams about America. For example, after reading a poem by Lucille Clifton titled "We and They," students responded through stories, poems, and discussion. One student wrote her own poem, "We Are from America," about what ordinary citizens of the United States think about ordinary citizens of Afghanistan and vice versa: "We are from America / they are from Afghanistan / We are rich to them / they are poor to us," and so on. Another class discussed the history and meaning of the Pledge of Allegiance. Through exercises like these students learn a kind of patriotism that gives space to thoughtful reflection and that honors the ideals of democracy on which the United States was founded. Ironically, Peterson's curriculum may do more to teach students "traditional" history and the Founding Fathers' ideals than those lessons suggested by Lamar Alexander and his colleagues. The curriculum won the Clarke Center's national competition for innovative ways to teach 9/11 in the classroom (elementary division). Classroom activities and assignments at La Escuela demonstrate that teaching a commitment to these ideals is not facile. La Escuela Fratney puts its mission into practice by encouraging teaching that makes clear the connections between students' lives and the outside world, between their communities and the larger national community, and between the concerns of our nation and the global concerns of all nations.

Conclusion

There is evidence that many students are learning the lessons of authoritarian patriotism well. A poll of California high school students found that 43% of seniors, having completed courses in U.S. history and U.S. government, either agreed with or were neutral toward the statement "It is un-American to criticize this country." Another poll shows that a majority of students nationwide have some ideals consistent with democratic patriotism (and this is probably due in no small part to the efforts of individual teachers and administrators), but a sizable minority (28%) believe that those who attend a protest against U.S. military involvement in Iraq are "unpatriotic."[27]

In a climate of increasingly authoritarian patriotism, dissent grows ever more scarce. But a democratic public is best served by a democratic form of patriotism. To ensure the strength of our democratic institutions and to foster a democratic patriotism that is loyal to the American ideals of equality, compassion, and justice, adults must struggle with difficult policy debates in all available democratic arenas. Trying to forge a national consensus in any other way or on any other grounds (especially through attempts at authoritarian patriotism) is what leads to troubled waters. And students need to learn about these contentious debates with which adults struggle and prepare to take up their parts in them. To serve the public interest in democracy and to reinforce a democratic kind of patriotism, educators will need to embrace rather than deny controversy.

Langston Hughes, in his 1936 poem "Let America Be America Again," speaks of the gap between a rhetorical patriotism rooted only in symbolic gestures and love of the American ideals of liberty and equality:

> O, let my land be a land where Liberty Is crowned with no false patriotic wreath, But opportunity is real, and life is free, Equality is in the air we breathe.

That's the best kind of patriotism we can hope for.

Notes

1. Nebraska State Board of Education, "Board Minutes," 1–2 November 2001 (revised following 7 December 2001 meeting).
2. Jennifer Piscatelli, "Pledge of Allegiance," *State Notes: Character and Civic Education*, Education Commission of the States, August 2003.
3. "President Introduces History and Civic Education Initiatives," remarks of the President on Teaching American History and Civic Education Initiative, 17 September 2002, www.whitehouse.gov.
4. Martha Nussbaum, *For Love of Country: Debating the Limits of Patriotism* (Cambridge, MA: Beacon Press, 2002), p. 29.
5. C. Douglas Lummis, *Radical Democracy* (Ithaca, NY: Cornell University Press, 1996), p. 37.
6. Henry Steele Commager, *Freedom and Order: A Commentary on the American Political Scene* (New York: George Braziller, 1966), p. 117.
7. See http://archive.columbiatribune.com/2005/feb/20050201news003.asp.

8. NPR, "Citizen Student: Teaching Patriotism in Time of War," 6 February 2003.

9. Cited in Nat Hentoff, "The Patriotism Enforcers: Miseducating the Young on Freedom," *Village Voice*, 2–8 January 2002.

10. U.S. House of Representatives, Committee on Un-American Activities, Investigation of Communist Activities, New York Area (Entertainment): Hearings, 84th Congress, 18 August 1955. Available at http://historymatters.gmu.edu/d/6457.

11. U.S. House of Representatives, Committee on Un-American Activities, Investigation of the Unauthorized Use of U.S. Passports, 84th Congress, Part 3, 12 June 1956, in Eric Bentley, ed., *Thirty Years of Treason: Excerpts from Hearings Before the House Committee on Un-American Activities, 1938–1968* (New York: Viking Press, 1971), p. 770.

12. Many of the examples cited here can be found in Peter Dreier and Dick Flacks, "Patriotism and Progressivism," *Peace Review*, December 2003, p. 399.

13. See www.loc.gov/today/pr/2003/03–095.html.

14. *Freedom Under Fire: Dissent in Post-9/11 America* (New York: American Civil Liberties Union, 2003); and Kathleen Kennedy Manzo, "Teachers Grapple with Wartime Role," *Education Week*, 20 March 2003, p. 27.

15. "W. Va. Student Suspended for Starting Anti-War Club: School Says Fliers Disrupted Educational Environment," *Student Press Law Center Report*, Winter 2002, p. 7.

16. Chris Frates, "High School Junior Suspended After Posting Anti-War Fliers," *Denver Post*, 28 February 2003.

17. National Coalition for History, "Senator Alexander's 'American History and Civics Education' Bill Passes Senate," *Washington Update*, 27 June 2003.

18. "Senator Alexander's American History and Civics Bill Passes Senate Unanimously," press release, Sen. Alexander's office, 20 June 2003.

19. Hofstadter is quoted by Sen. Alexander in "Remarks of Senator Lamar Alexander on the Introduction of His Bill: The American History and Civics Education Act," 4 March 2003.

20. "Beware Leftists in Our Schools!!!," anonymous parent posting, Southern Maryland Online chat forum, 2003, http://forums.somd.com.

21. See, for example, Bree Picower's curriculum, "An Unnatural Disaster," which asks students to consider the many interlocking causes of the extensive damage of Katrina and its aftermath, especially for the African American population of New Orleans (www.nycore.org); and "Washin' Away," Ian McFeat's mock-trial activity for Rethinking Schools (www.rethinkingschools.org) that asks students to explore the roles various people and contexts played in the Katrina tragedy. For contrast, see the MindOH Foundation's Hurricane Katrina resources that include, for example, "Thinking It Through: Why Do Bad Things Happen to Good People?" This activity opens with "Life is not always fair. Bad things happen to good people....We may be able to make educated guesses about Mother Nature's weather patterns, but . . ." (www.mindohfoundation. org/hurricanekatrina.htm).

22. Harry C. Boyte, "A Different Kind of Politics: John Dewey and the Meaning of Citizenship in the 21st Century," Dewey Lecture, University of Michigan, Ann Arbor, 1 November 2002, p. 11.

23. Some resources for getting started in seeking such programs include Rethinking Schools (www.rethinkingschools.org); Educators for Social Responsibility (www.esrnational.org); *New York Times* lessons (www.nytimes. com/learning); American Social History Project: Center for Media and Learning (www.historymatters.gmu.edu); and Teaching for Change (www. teachingforchange.org).

24. Karen Suurtamm, project director for Democratic Dialogue (www. democraticdialogue.com), did the lion's share of research for and writing of the descriptions of El Puente Academy and La Escuela Fratney Elementary School.

25. Catherine Capellaro, "When Small Is Beautiful: An Interview with Héctor Calderón," *Rethinking Schools*, Summer 2005.

26. Bill Carter and Felicity Barringer, "In Patriotic Time, Dissent Is Muted," *New York Times*, 28 September 2001.

27. Dennis Gilbert, "Hamilton College Patriotism Poll: Eleven Key Findings," 20 March 2003, Question 17, Appendix, p. 7. Available at www. hamilton.edu/levitt/surveys/patriotism/patriotismreport.pdf.

This chapter originally appeared in *Phi Delta Kappan*, Vol. 87, No. 8 (April, 2006). Published here with permission of Phi Delta Kappa International.

CHAPTER SEVEN

Is Patriotism Good for Democracy?

A Study of High School Seniors' Patriotic Commitments

JOSEPH KAHNE & ELLEN MIDDAUGH

Is patriotism good for democracy? Or does a commitment to patriotism threaten democracy? Educators do not agree on this issue. Chester Finn (former assistant secretary of education in the Reagan Administration) argues that, since September 11, "American education has generally made a mess of a teaching opportunity" by focusing on "tolerance and multiculturalism, not civics and patriotism."[1] In an essay titled "Patriotism Revisited," he worries that "it's become a compulsion to pull down America rather than celebrate and defend it."[2] This view aligns with William Damon's perspective that "too many students today learn all about what is wrong with our society without gaining any knowledge of our society's great moral successes. To establish a sound cognitive and affective foundation for citizenship education," Damon writes, "schools need to begin with the positive, to emphasize reasons for caring enough about our democratic society to participate in it and to improve it. Schools need to foster a sympathetic understanding informed by all the facts and energized by a spirit of patriotism."[3]

Other educators see a problem related to patriotism that is very different from the one described by Finn and Damon. Rather than worrying that there is excessive criticism of the U.S. in schools and a lack of patriotism among youths, they point to pressure, exerted in the name of patriotism, on individual citizens and groups to refrain from criticizing the actions and policies of the U.S. government. In addition, they note a growing set of global problems that require international cooperation.[4] These considerations lead some to flat out reject patriotic sentiments in favor of commitments to global citizenship and principles of international human rights.[5]

Is there a problem or not? And if there is a problem, which problem is it? Are schools turning students into critics of the U.S. who can't appreciate the country's strengths? Or is the opposite occurring? Is the push for patriotism in response to 9/11 leading students toward patriotic commitments at the expense of critical analysis and an appreciation of the need to protect human rights and democratic principles? Unfortunately, we have little data to draw on when thinking about these issues. Schools systematically monitor the number of 11th-graders who know the difference between equilateral and right triangles, but we often rely on journalists' interviews with three or four students to assess what high school students think about patriotism and democracy.

For this reason, we decided to take a systematic look at high school seniors' views on patriotism and its relationship to democracy. In doing so, we are hoping to reframe the discussion. "Is patriotism good or bad?" The answer is not one or the other but "It depends." The values, priorities, and behaviors associated with patriotism can vary dramatically. Some forms of patriotism are profoundly democratic, and other forms can undermine democratic ideals. It is therefore very important that we clarify the factors responsible for these different outcomes.

In sorting through the ways to make these distinctions, we found it very helpful to consider the two standards provided by John Dewey for a "democratically constituted society": 1) "How numerous and varied are the interests that are consciously shared?" and 2) "How full and free is the interplay with other modes of association?"[6] In other words, a democratic society requires that citizens recognize their common interests and that they fully and openly discuss their differing perspectives on issues related to these common priorities.

The implications for a democratic vision of patriotism are substantial. Patriotic commitments in a democratic society should be motivated by and reinforce recognition of the variety of interests that citizens have in common. In addition, these patriotic commitments should not constrain what Dewey called "free and full interplay" and what we might call informed debate and discussion that considers a wide range of views.

What does this mean for students and for schools? We believe that schools should work to promote a democratic vision of patriotism that is based on Dewey's two standards. In the following sections, drawing on the work of the Harwood Institute and on studies by Robert Schatz, Ervin Staub, and Howard Lavine, we discuss a set of criteria that can help us determine the degree to which students' patriotic commitments align with the needs of a democratic society, as envisioned by Dewey. Specifically, we focus on three dimensions of patriotic belief: commitment to country, attitudes toward critique of country, and active involvement. Then, using this framework as a guide, we share findings from our study of the patriotic commitments of California's high school seniors.

Commitment to Country: An Uncertain Support for Democracy

It is common to define patriots simply as those who love their country.[7] Why would such a commitment be controversial? Individuals love their families more than they love strangers. They also tend to feel a stronger sense of connection to the town they are from than to a town they have never visited. Shouldn't we expect most individuals to love their country—and to love it more than they love other countries?

Frankly, this isn't the point. The important question is not whether it is common or "natural" to love one's country—the question is whether such commitments are desirable. After all, jealousy is also a rather common or "natural" emotion, but that doesn't make it a virtue. Indeed, in some cases, one could argue that patriotism is a vice. The term's etymology—loyalty to the fatherland—has nothing to do with a commitment to democracy. Both fascist states and democracies desire loyalty.

To say this is not to deny the potential of patriotic commitments to serve as a support for a democratic society. In line with Dewey's framework, patriotic commitments can support democratic goals by developing a sense of shared interests and a commitment to act. More specifically, patriotic commitments may lead individuals to better balance their own interests with those of the broader society by helping them integrate societal interests into their own sense of what's important.[8] In addition, patriotic commitments (especially when informed by recognition of shared interests) may motivate citizens to actively engage in the civic and political life of the community—a key need in a democracy. Finally, if one's love of country is based in part on recognition of the desirability of life in a democratic society, such patriotic commitments can help citizens identify with the nation's democratic ideals. "The American trick," Benjamin Barber writes, "was to use the fierce attachments of patriotic sentiment to bond a people to high ideals…to be an American was also to be enmeshed in a unique story of freedom."[9] In short, there are democratic visions of patriotism: ones that focus on loyalty to democratic principles and practices and that emphasize lateral connections to other citizens rather than hierarchical commitments to the nation.

Unfortunately, some forms of patriotism that emphasize shared interests fail to meet Dewey's second criterion for a democratic society—full and free interplay. Indeed, the emphasis on shared interests can become problematic if not balanced by engagement with a broad range of groups and perspectives. R. Freeman Butts explains it this way: "At its best, patriotism binds the diverse elements of American society into an integrated whole, fostering mutual acceptance of citizens as a common political order. At its worst, patriotism can degenerate into a nationalistic chauvinism."[10]

Thus patriotic commitments are an uncertain support for democracy. The key question is not whether one is a patriot. It is the form of one's patriotic commitments that turns out to be of prime importance.

In order to assess the role schools in a democracy should play with respect to patriotic aims, it is therefore necessary to clarify some other dimensions of patriotic beliefs. We do so below.

Attitudes toward Critique: Blind and Constructive Patriots

Among those who study and theorize about patriotism, the question of whether patriotic commitments foster democracy often highlights a crucial distinction between blind and constructive patriotism.

Blind patriotism. Blind patriots adopt a stance of unquestioning endorsement of their country—denying the value of critique and analysis and generally emphasizing allegiance and symbolic behaviors.[11] Studies also indicate that blind patriots frequently engage in nationalism—asserting their nation's superiority and supporting their nation's dominance over others.[12] Blind patriotic commitments are well captured by comments like "My country—love it or leave it" and by notions that it is "unpatriotic" to criticize one's own country. This form of patriotism is inconsistent with educational and democratic institutions because its intolerance of criticism signifies a lack of "free and full interplay." This perspective obscures the value of reasoned debate and fails to recognize analysis and critique as engines of improvement. Thus, while some forms of patriotism might broaden citizens' concerns to include the whole nation rather than just themselves, their family, and friends, blind or nationalistic patriotic commitments can narrow one's concerns in dangerous and antidemocratic ways.

Constructive patriotism. Rather than embrace blind or uncritical forms of patriotism, constructive patriots applaud some actions by the state and criticize others in an effort to promote positive change and consistency with the nation's ideals.[13] For example, imperialistic actions, though often advantageous for the imperialist nation's citizens, should be rejected as inconsistent with democratic values. Rather than view critique or debate as unpatriotic (as a blind patriot might), constructive patriots consider a wide range of perspectives and enact what Ervin Staub calls "critical loyalty."[14]

From the standpoint of democracy, this orientation is essential. The point is not to downplay the value of civic knowledge or the promise of America's democratic commitments to equality and justice; rather, it is to help students use their love of country as a motivation to critically assess what is needed to make it better.

Active Patriotism

If we are interested in determining whether patriotism is good for democracy, there is one more distinction to make—whether a patriotic commitment to one's country requires active participation. While both blind and constructive patriots love their country, neither type is necessarily actively engaged in civic or political life. Both blind and constructive patriots can discuss their perspectives in coffee shops and bars, for example, without acting in any way that substantively supports the nation. Such behavior differs markedly from the kind of active engagement a participatory democracy requires.

Active patriots, whether blind or constructive in their orientation, are those who take it upon themselves to engage in democratic and civic life in an effort to support and sustain what they feel is best about the country and to change features they believe need improvement. Their actions may begin with, but will move beyond, voting. Their forms of engagement may include PTA meetings or political protests. Active patriots may volunteer with the elderly or work on a campaign. Their love of country and their desire for it to thrive are demonstrated by their deeds.[15]

Patriotism among High School Seniors

Drawing on these criteria for a democratic vision of patriotism, we now attend to students' perspectives. Specifically, we describe findings from the California Survey of Civic Education—a survey of high school seniors we developed to inventory students' civic commitments and capacities as well as the opportunities schools have provided to foster them. The survey is part of a broader school change initiative called "Educating for Democracy: California Campaign for the Civic Mission of Schools."[16]

In the spring of 2005, we gave the survey to 2,366 high school seniors from a very diverse set of 12 California high schools. We assessed students' commitments and capacities in the spring of their senior year because at that time they were completing their state-funded public schooling and they had reached or were reaching voting age—becoming eligible to assume the full responsibilities of citizenship. One component of the survey measured the different kinds of patriotic commitments we discuss in this article.[17] In an effort to probe more deeply, we also conducted 10 focus groups with 50 students from five of these high schools. Though the survey is clearly an early step in the effort to understand patriotic outcomes, our hope is that it will help move the conversation forward by providing useful indicators of student commitments and their relationship to a democratic vision of patriotism.[18]

Commitment to country. In our focus groups, students frequently expressed strong patriotic commitments. As one student told us, "I definitely love America. I don't think we're a bad country. We try to help people—of course we have our flaws, and sometimes our reasons for doing that are sketchy, but I think overall we try to do our best and help. We have so many rights, and I can't imagine living anywhere else."

Seventy-three percent of the seniors we surveyed agreed, for example, that "the United States is a great country," while only 10% disagreed (the remaining 17% were neutral). And their level of agreement declined only slightly—to 68%—when the statement became "I have a great love for the United States" (with only 12% disagreeing).[19] Thus, while we will argue that high school students' vision of patriotism should be developed to better align with the responsibilities of democratic citizenship, it seems clear that there is little reason to worry that students are being turned into critics who focus on the country's shortcomings and fail to appreciate its strengths. For the most part, California's adolescents endorse patriotic sentiments.[20]

Constructive patriotism. In focus groups, many students also expressed a clear sense that patriots sometimes offer critiques in an effort to improve the country. One said, for example, "I think a lot of people get confused and say being patriotic means that you think America is perfect. I think being patriotic is trying to make a difference in your country because you care so much about it. Whether you're Republican or Democrat doesn't matter, it's just that you want to make it a better country."

Some students also distinguished between supporting the country's principles and supporting its particular practices and policies. As one young woman explained, "I like the moral ideas that America has. I don't like how they are going about it."

Our survey results were consistent with these sentiments. For example, 68% agreed with the statement (with only 11% disagreeing) "I oppose some U.S. policies because I care about my country and want to improve it." Similarly, 69% agreed that "if you love America, you should notice its problems and work to correct them." (Only 12% disagreed.)

Active patriotism. As discussed above, patriotic citizens in a democracy must do more than express their love for the country or talk about ways it could improve. For democracy to work, citizens must also be willing to act. Less than half of the students we surveyed, however, shared this belief. Indeed, in response to the statement "To be truly patriotic, one has to be involved in the civic and political life of the community," only 41% agreed. This response is similar to what the Harwood Institute found when it first asked this question of adults in 2002. These findings also mirror findings of numerous other studies of both youths and adults. Participation in many forms of civic and political engagement has declined markedly over the course of the past several decades. To a significant degree, we seem to be a nation of spectators. The risk this tendency poses to democracy is substantial.[21]

Blind patriotism. Our survey indicates that, for many students, commitments to patriotism are associated with antidemocratic orientations that emphasize blind or uncritical support for the country. For example, more high school seniors agreed (43%) than disagreed (29%) with the statement "I support U.S. policies because they are the policies of my country." In fact, even when we asked students more pointedly whether they thought "it is un-American to criticize this country," 22% agreed and 21% were neutral. Thus 43% of the high school seniors in our sample, having completed required courses in U.S. history and in U.S. government, failed to reject this patently antidemocratic stance.

These findings do not demonstrate that California's high school seniors are blind patriots, but they do indicate that patriotic sentiments rather than analysis may often guide assessments of the nation's policies and practices—as well as responses to critiques by others.

A democratic vision of patriotism. Unfortunately, while the majority of students in our sample endorsed statements associated with love of country, few of these high school seniors endorsed all three of our other indicators of democratic patriotism. Indeed, only 16% expressed that they were committed patriots, endorsed active and constructive patriotism, and rejected blind patriotism.[22] We would not expect every student to consistently support these four criteria for a democratic vision of patriotism, but 16% is hardly impressive. If patriotic education consistent with the demands of democracy is a goal for our schools, it appears that we are coming up quite short.

Two Problems in Need of Attention

While there are clearly limits to what this survey can tell us, it does provide some guidance. First, it appears that some of the most impassioned remarks related to schools and patriotism overstate the case. Schools are neither turning students into critics of the United States who cannot appreciate its virtues, nor are they failing to help students recognize the role critique can play as a means to make society better. At the same time, the fact that only 16% of the diverse group of students we surveyed in California expressed consistent support for a democratic vision of patriotism is cause for concern. We have identified two problems, in particular, that deserve our attention.

Problem 1. Passive patriots. Many students fail to appreciate the importance of civic participation. Only 41% of students surveyed believed that loving one's country requires being civically or politically active. This finding parallels other studies that highlight young people's increasingly passive conceptions of "good citizenship."[23]

Fortunately, recent research is beginning to provide a clearer sense of curricular approaches that promote commitment to active engagement. These include instruction in history and government that emphasizes the importance of informed civic engagement, as well as such strategies as service learning, discussing social problems, and the use of simulations. Creating a school climate that allows students to participate in meaningful aspects of school governance, to be active in after-school clubs, and to openly discuss controversial issues in the classroom also appears efficacious.[24] Of course, given the current emphasis on No Child Left Behind and related standards, whether schools will choose to focus on such priorities and will do so effectively is far from clear.

Interestingly, one argument for patriotism is that a commitment to one's country will lead to active engagement. Indeed, we see evidence from our survey that supports this claim. Fifty-four percent of those who say they love their country endorse the value of civic and political engagement, while only 34% who do not agree that they love their country endorse the value of civic and political engagement. This finding would seem to back up the proposition that a sense of patriotic commitment motivates citizens to be more active.

Problem 2. Patriotic commitments sometimes lead to blind patriotism. While committed patriots may be more civically and politically active, patriotic commitments do not appear to help with the problem of blind patriotism—indeed, at times they appear to contribute to it. Our survey indicates that those who say they love their country are three times more likely than those who do not (28% vs. 9%) to endorse the idea that it is "un-American to criticize the country." In short, love of one's country seems to be distracting some students from recognizing the need for critique in a democracy.

Reflecting a similar pattern, the value of critique is endorsed by high school seniors when it is framed as a way to make the country better. For example, 68% agreed with the statement "I oppose some U.S. policies because I care about my country and want to improve it" (only 11% disagreed). But when a conflict is implied between patriotism and critique of the country, comfort with critique drops markedly. In fact, more students agreed (42%) than disagreed (38%) with the statement "There is too much criticism of the U.S. in the world. We, its citizens, should not criticize it."

Thus, for a significant number of students, invoking notions of patriotism appears to lead them to want to stifle critique. This finding makes the need for educators to strengthen students' understandings of both patriotism and democracy quite clear. To do so they must ground commitments to patriotism in appreciation of our country's democratic ideals and practices rather than in a sense of blind loyalty.

Unfortunately, there is little evidence that policy makers are considering such issues. Margaret Nash, who recently examined how state education policies attend to patriotism, found that many states include patriotism among their list of goals, but often without specifying how to promote patriotism or what exactly this goal entails. To the extent that they do specify a means of fostering patriotism, however, Nash found that reciting the Pledge of Allegiance is the most common strategy.[25] Indeed, following 9/11, when the interest in patriotism surged, 17 states either enacted new pledge laws for schools or amended current policies.[26] As former Sen. S. I. Hayakawa (R-Calif.) once commented, "Patriotic societies seem to think that the way to educate children in a democracy is to stage bigger and better flag saluting."[27]

This tendency isn't surprising. The pledge is our nation's most explicit patriotic exercise, and the practice has long been integrated into the school day. Unfortunately, reciting the pledge is inadequate. The problem is not that saying the pledge is a symbolic act. Symbols have a place in society. The problem is that symbols can complement, but not substitute for, substance.

What Educators Can Do

Educators can do a great deal to foster understandings of patriotism that support democratic values and practices. Rather than "teaching" students to love their country, teachers need to help students build an explicit connection between their "love of country" and democratic ideals—ideals that include the role of informed analysis and, at times, critique; the importance of action; and the danger of blind loyalty to the state.

Clearly, countless opportunities exist, especially in literature, history, and government courses. Teachers can deepen students' love of country by explaining the value of democratic ideals. We should teach about key instances in which the implications of patriotic commitments were debated and about the actions of critics who, in support of our ideals, worked to change the country. We should teach about the sacrifices patriotic citizens have made and consider our debt to them. We also need students to learn about those who may have used the rhetoric of patriotism to constrain liberty and stifle dissent. True to the demands of democracy, this curriculum will engage controversial issues and will require debate, discussion, and analysis. Even when broad democratic principles are agreed upon, not all will agree about the implications of such principles in particular instances. This curriculum should examine the past and should also rely on current events. To support students' recognition of the need for participation in a democracy, opportunities for action may also be included. Our goal here is not to lay out a particular curriculum—though we do believe that such a curriculum should be developed. Our point is that attention to patriotism and democracy should become sustained and coherent components of the broader school curriculum—just like other important learning objectives. Right now, with only 16% of students consistently endorsing commitments associated with a democratic vision of patriotism, it appears that we have much work to do.

This effort deserves the attention of teachers and principals and of those in district, state, and federal offices that shape curricular priorities. Students' patriotic commitments can develop in ways that meaningfully support and enhance our democratic society. Alternatively, some kinds of patriotic commitments can undermine our most precious values. Citizens do not instinctively or organically develop understandings of patriotism that align with democratic ideals. Educators have a role to play—helping students to think carefully about forms of patriotism that support our democracy and forms that do not.

Notes

1. Chester E. Finn, Jr., "Teaching Patriotism: An Educational Resource for Americans," *National Review Online*, 6 December 2001, www.nationalreview.com/comment/comment-finnprint120601.html.
2. Chester E. Finn, "Patriotism Revisited," Center for Education Reform, 1 October 2001, http://edreform.com/index.cfm?fuseAction=document&documentID=208&sectionID=69NEWSYEAR=2001
3. William Damon, "What Schools Should Do to Prepare Students for Democracy," paper presented at a meeting on "Youth and Civic Engagement," sponsored by the Center for Information and Research on Learning and Citizenship, Washington, D.C., March 2005.
4. Michael Apple, "Patriotism, Pedagogy, and Freedom: On the Educational Meanings of September 11th," *Teachers College Record*, December 2002, pp. 1760–72; Chris Coryn, James Beale, and Krista Myers, "Response to September 11: Anxiety, Patriotism, and Prejudice in the Aftermath of Terror," *Current Research in Social*

Psychology, March 2004, pp. 1–23; and M. Samuel Haque, "Patriotism Versus Imperialism," *Peace Review*, vol. 15, 2003, pp. 451–56.

5. Patrick G. Coy, Gregory M. Maney, and Lynne M. Woehrle, "Contesting Patriotism," *Peace Review*, vol. 15, 2003, pp. 463–70; and Martha Nussbaum and Joshua Cohen, eds., *For Love of Country: Debating the Limits of Patriotism* (Boston: Beacon Press, 1996).

6. John Dewey, *Democracy and Education* (New York: Free Press, 1916), pp. 87, 83.

7. Igor Primoratz, *Patriotism* (Amherst, NY: Humanity Books, 2002).

8. Stephen Nathanson, "In Defense of 'Moderate Patriotism,'" *Ethics*, vol. 99, 1989, p. 535.

9. Benjamin W. Barber, "Constitutional Faith," in Nussbaum and Cohen, p. 32.

10. R. Freeman Butts, *Civitas: A Framework for Civic Education* (Calabasas, CA.: Center for Civic Education, 1991), p. 31.

11. Robert T. Schatz, Ervin Staub, and Howard Lavine, "On the Varieties of National Attachment: Blind Versus Constitutional Patriotism," *Political Psychology*, March 1999, pp. 151–74.

12. Seymour Feshbach, "Attachment Processes in Political Ideology: Patriotism and Nationalism," in Jacob Gerwitz and William Kurtines, eds., *Intersections with Attachment* (Hillsdale, NJ: Lawrence Erlbaum Associates, 1991), pp. 207–26.

13. Schatz, Staub, and Lavine, p. 153.

14. Ervin Staub, *The Roots of Evil: The Origins of Genocide and Other Group Violence* (New York: Cambridge University Press,1989).

15. Harwood Institute, *Post-September 11th Patriotism, Civic Involvement and Expectations for the 2002 Election Season* (Bethesda, MD: Harwood Institute for Public Innovation, 2002).

16. For information on the campaign, see www.cms-ca.org/index.html. For a report summarizing findings from our broader study, see www. cms-ca.org/civic_survey_final.pdf.

17. Participating schools were selected from various geographic areas to provide a portrait of current conditions representing a range of factors including student race, ethnicity, and academic performance levels. The indicator of general patriotism was adapted from items used in the civic education study by the International Association for the Evaluation of Educational Achievement. (Information on the study is available at www.wam.umd.edu/~jtpurta/studentQ.htm.) The measures of blind and constructive patriotism were modified from Schatz, Staub, and Lavine, op. cit. The indicator of active patriotism was developed by the Harwood Institute (www.theharwoodinstitute.org). All items within the scales for constructive patriotism, blind patriotism, active patriotism, and general patriotism were entered into a factor analysis and emerged as four distinct scales. Please contact the authors at jkahne@mills.edu for more details on the measures used in this study.

18. There are numerous ways to deepen the knowledge base in this area. We are currently undertaking a study, for example, that looks at the ways particular classroom contexts and opportunities influence patriotic commitments.

19. Students, we should point out, were not uniformly positive. Only 28% agreed, for example, that "people in government care about what people like me and my family need."

20. Consistent with this finding, 30% of students in a national study reported that the most common theme in their U.S. history and social studies classes had been "great American heroes and the virtues of the American system of government," while only 11% said the most common theme was "problems facing the country today." See Peter Levine and Mark H. Lopez, *Themes Emphasized in Social Studies and Civics Classes: New Evidence* (Washington, D.C.: Center for Information and Research on Civic Learning and Engagement, 2004).

21. Stephen Macedo et al., *Democracy at Risk: How Political Choices Undermine Citizen Participation, and What We Can Do About It* (Washington, D.C.: Brookings Institution, 2005).

22. We judged an individual to be endorsing committed patriotism and constructive patriotism if his or her average response on the items measuring those criteria was greater than 3 and if his or her average response on the items measuring uncritical patriotism was less than 3 (on a 5-point scale on which 3 represented neutral). Only one item measured an individual's commitment to active patriotism, so in that instance, a 4, which signified agreement, was required to be considered an endorsement. Had we used 4 as our standard for endorsing all given forms of patriotism, the percentage of students endorsing a democratic vision of patriotism would have been even lower.

23. Macedo et al., op. cit.

24. Cynthia Gibson and Peter Levine, *The Civic Mission of Schools* (New York: Carnegie Corporation of New York and the Center for Information and Research on Civic Learning, 2003).

25. Margaret Nash, "How to Be Thankful for Being Free: Searching for a Convergence of Discourses on Teaching Patriotism, Citizenship, and United States History," *Teachers College Record*, vol. 107, 2005, pp. 214–40.

26. Jennifer Piscatelli, "Pledge of Allegiance," Education Commission of the States, 2003, www.ecs.org/clearing-house/47/20/4720.htm.

27. Samuel Ichiye Hayakawa in quotegarden.com/patriotism.html.

This chapter originally appeared in *Phi Delta Kappan*, Vol. 87, No. 8 (April, 2006). Published here with permission of Phi Delta Kappa International.

CHAPTER EIGHT

Democracy's Promise and the Politics of Worldliness

Implications for Public Intellectuals

HENRY A. GIROUX

In the United States, a war is not only being waged abroad, but also at home. Young people increasingly find themselves out of work, warehoused in substandard schools, or under the jurisdiction of the criminal justice system; people of color are being incarcerated at alarming rates and immigrants are increasingly treated as criminals or threats to national security. However, these groups are not the only targets. Universities are accused of being soft on terrorism; dissident artists are increasingly branded as un-American because of their critiques of the Bush administration; homophobia has become the poster-ideology of the Republican Party; and a full-fledged assault on women's reproductive rights is being championed by Bush's evangelical supporters—most evident in Bush's two recent Supreme Court appointments. An incessant assault on critical thinking itself and a rising bigotry have undercut the possibility for providing a language in which vital social institutions can be defended as a public good. Moreover, as visions of social equity recede unfettered from public memory, brutality, self-interest, and greed combined with retrograde social policies make "security" and "safety" top domestic priorities. As the spaces for producing engaged citizens are either commercialized or militarized, the crushing effects of domination spread out to all aspects of society, and war increasingly becomes the primary organizing principle of politics.[1]

Unfortunately, the university offers no escape and little resistance. Instead, the humanistic knowledge and values of academia are being excised as higher education becomes increasingly corporatized and stripped of its democratic functions. The appeal to excellence by university leadership functions as a corporate logo, hyping efficiency while denuding critical thought and scholarship of any intellectual and political substance. In the corporate university, academics are now expected to be academic entrepreneurs whose value largely depends on the grant money they attract, rather than the quality of education they offer to students.[2] As the university is annexed by defense, corporate, and national security interests, critical scholarship is replaced by knowledge for either weapons research or commercial profits; just as the private intellectual now replaces the public intellectual, and the public relations intellectual supplants the engaged intellectual in the wider culture. In addition, faculty are increasingly downsized and turned into an army of part-time workers who are overworked and underpaid, just as graduate students are reduced to wage slavery as they take over many undergraduate teaching functions.

It is important to note that such attacks on higher education in the U.S. come not only from a market-based ideology that would reduce education to training and redefine schools as investment opportunities; they also come from conservative Christian organizations such as the American Family Association (AFA), as well as conservative politicians, and right-wing think tanks. These groups have also launched an insidious attack on peace studies, women's studies, Middle Eastern studies, critical pedagogy, and any field that challenges the "orthodoxy of the doctrinaire right-wingers" and is critical of the aims and policies of the Bush administration.[3] This is the same administration that alludes to gay married couples as "terrorists," while saying nothing about U.S. involvement in the torture and abuse at Abu Ghraib prison (or any of the other secret prisons run by the Central Intelligence Agency [CIA]) or the U.S. policy of "extraordinary rendition" that allows the CIA to kidnap people and send them to authoritarian countries to be tortured.[4]

The frontal nature of such attacks against both dissent and critical education can also be seen in attempts by conservative legislators in Ohio and a number of other states to pass bills such as the Academic Bill of Rights, which argues that academics should be hired on the basis of their conservative ideology not only in order to balance out faculties dominated by left-wing professors, but also to control what conservative students are taught, allegedly immunizing them against ideas that might challenge or offend their ideological comfort zones. Professors who address critical issues in their classrooms, push the borders of critical inquiry, and encourage students to question authority are condemned for teaching propaganda. For instance, the governor of Colorado called for the firing of Professor Ward Churchill because of an essay he wrote shortly after 9/11 in which he condemned U.S. foreign policy. Senator Rick Santorum introduced legislation that would have cut federal funding to universities that allowed faculty and students to criticize Israel. Additionally, U.S. Congressman Anthony Weiner from New York called for the firing of Joseph Massad, a Columbia University professor, who has been critical of Israeli policies against Palestinians. Under the guise of patriotic correctness, conservatives want to fire prominent academics such as Churchill and Massad because of their opposition to U.S. foreign policy while completely ignoring the quality of their intellectual scholarship. Of course, such attacks are not limited to academics. *New York Times* columnist Thomas Friedman called upon the State Department to draw up a blacklist of those critics he calls "excuse makers," which included those who believe that U.S. actions are at the root cause of violence. According to Friedman, "These excuse makers are just one notch less despicable than the terrorists and also deserve to be exposed."[5] Challenging the current conservative wisdom—that is, holding views at odds with official orthodoxy—has now become the grounds for being labeled un-American, dismissed from one's job, or put on a government blacklist.

Higher education has also been attacked by right-wing ideologues such as Lynne Cheney and David Horowitz, who view it as the "weak link" in the war against terror and a potential fifth column.[6] Horowitz, in particular, acts as the figurehead for various well-funded and orchestrated conservative student groups such as the Young Americans for Freedom and College Republicans, which perform the groundwork for his "Academic Bill of Rights" policy efforts that seek out juicy but rare instances of "political bias" in college classrooms.[7] These efforts have resulted in considerable sums of public money being devoted to hearings in multiple state legislatures, most recently in Pennsylvania, in addition to helping impose, as the *Chronicle of Higher Education* put it, a "chilly climate" of self-policing of academic freedom and pedagogy.[8] At the University of California, Los Angeles, the Bruin Alumni Association has posted on its Web site an article called "The Dirty Thirty" that targets the university's "most radical professors" and states as its mission the task of exposing and combating "an exploding crisis of political radicalism on campus."[9] The Bruin Alumni Association does more than promote a "McCarthy-like kind of smear," intolerance, and anti-intellectualism through a vapid appeal for "balance"; it also offers $100 prizes to students willing to provide information on their teachers' political views.[10] Rather than genuinely protest pedagogical demagoguery, such tactics not only inject a climate of fear and suspicion in the classroom, they also discredit the spirit of critical inquiry and legitimize a deadening conformity. Within this discourse, education becomes the measure by which critical thought and social responsibility can be escaped.

In spite of their present embattled status and the inroads made by corporate power, the defense industries, and the neoconservative Right, universities and colleges remain uniquely placed to prepare students to both understand and influence the larger educational forces that shape their lives. As Edward Said observed, "It is still very fortunately the case, however, that the American university remains the one public space available to real alternative intellectual practices: no institution like it on such a scale exists anywhere else in the world today."[11] Such institutions—by virtue of their privileged position, division of labor, and alleged dedication to freedom and democracy—also have an obligation to draw upon those traditions and resources capable of providing a critical, liberal, and humanistic education to all students in order to prepare them not only for a society in which information and power have taken on new and potent dimensions, but also for confronting the rise of a disturbing number of anti-democratic tendencies in the most powerful country in the world and elsewhere across the globe.

Part of such a challenge means that educators, artists, students, and others need to rethink and affirm the important presuppositions that higher education is integral to fostering the imperatives of an inclusive democracy and that the crisis of higher education must be understood as part of the wider crisis of politics, power, and culture. Jacques Derrida argued that democracy contains a promise of what is to come and that it is precisely in the tension between the dream and the reality of democracy that a space of agency, critique, and education opens up and signals both the normative and political character of democracy.[12] But, as Derrida is well aware, democracy also demands a pedagogical intervention organized around the need to create the conditions for educating citizens who have the knowledge and skills to participate in public life, question institutional authority, and engage the contradiction between the reality and promise of a global democracy. For Derrida, democracy must not only contain the structure of a promise, but it must also be nurtured in those public spaces in which "the unconditional freedom to question" becomes central to any viable definition of individual and social agency.[13] At stake here is the recognition that if democracy is to become vital, then it is imperative to create citizens who are critical, interrogate authority, hold existing institutions accountable for their actions, and are able to assume public responsibility through the very process of governing.[14] In Derrida's perspective, the university "should thus be a place in which nothing is beyond question, not even the current and determined figure of democracy, and not even the traditional idea of critique."[15] The role of the university in this instance, and particularly the humanities, should be to create a culture of questioning and resistance aimed at those ideologies, institutions, social practices, and "powers that limit democracy to come."[16] Derrida's views on higher education and democracy raise important questions not only about the purpose of higher education, but also what it means for academics to address what the sociologist Zygmunt Bauman calls taking "responsibility for our responsibility."[17]

Part of the struggle for viewing the university as a democratic public sphere and a site of struggle against the growing forces of militarism, corporatism, neoconservatism, and the religious fundamentalism of the Christian Right demands a new understanding of what it means to be a public intellectual, which in turn suggests a new language for politics itself. Central to such a challenge is the necessity to define intellectual practice "as part of an intricate web of morality, rigor and responsibility" that enables academics to speak with conviction, enter the public sphere in order to address important social problems, and demonstrate alternative models for what it means to bridge the gap between higher education and the broader society.[18] This is a notion of intellectual practice that refuses both the instrumentality and privileged isolation of the academy while affirming a broader vision of learning that links knowledge to the power of self-definition and the capacities of administrators, academics, students, and artists to expand the scope of democratic freedoms, particularly as they address the crisis of the social as part and parcel of the crisis of democracy itself. This is the kind of intellectual practice that is attentive to the suffering of others and "will not allow conscience to look away or fall asleep."[19]

Cornel West has argued that we need to analyze those dark forces shutting down democracy, but "we also need to be very clear about the vision that lures us toward hope and the sources of that vision."[20] In taking up this challenge, I want to examine Said's notion of worldliness and analyze its implications for both the nature of what it means to be a public intellectual and what it would mean to make the pedagogical more political. Said is particularly relevant here because his work embodies both a particular kind of politics and a specific notion of how intellectuals should engage public life. For Said, worldliness connected texts, knowledge, representations, and intellectual practice to the world. He wrote:

> Worldliness—by which I mean at a more precise cultural level that all texts and all representations were in the world and subject to its numerous heterogeneous realities—assured contamination and involvement, since in all cases the history and presence of various other groups and individuals made it impossible for anyone to be free of the conditions of material existence.[21]

Few intellectuals have done more within the last four decades to offer a politics of worldliness designed to confront the crisis of democracy under the reign of neoliberalism, neocolonialism, and the emerging fundamentalisms throughout the world than Said, one of the most widely known, influential, and controversial public intellectuals of the latter part of the twentieth century.

In what follows, I want to connect the promise of democracy to Said's notion of worldliness and how it shaped both his important consideration of academics as oppositional public intellectuals and his related emphasis on cultural pedagogy and cultural politics.[22] From the time of his own political awakening after the 1967 Arab-Israeli war, Said increasingly became a border crosser, moving between his Arab past and his New York present, mediating his fierce defense of Palestinian rights and the demands of a university position. His academic post gave him the freedom to write and teach, while at the same time, represent an institutional power that sought to depoliticize the politics of knowledge or, to use Said's terms, to "impose silence and the normalized quiet of unseen power."[23] Said embraced the idea of the "traveler" as an important metaphor for engaged intellectuals. As Stephen Howe points out, for Said,

> It was an image which depended not on power, but on motion, on daring to go into different worlds, use different languages, and "understand a multiplicity of disguises, masks, and rhetorics. Travelers must suspend the claim of customary routine in order to live in new rhythms and rituals . . . the traveler crosses over, traverses territory, and abandons fixed positions all the time.[24]

And as an intellectual and traveler, Said embodied the notion of always "being quite not right," evident by his principled critique of all forms of certainties and dogmas and his refusal to be silent in the face of human suffering.

Said's view of the engaged public intellectual, particularly his admonition to intellectuals to function within institutions, in part, as exiles, "whose place it is publicly to raise embarrassing questions, to confront orthodoxy and dogma (rather than to produce them), to refuse to be easily co-opted by governments or corporations,"[25] offered a model of social engagement that redefined the role of the oppositional and public intellectual. This politically charged notion of the oppositional intellectual as homeless—in exile, and living on the border, occupying an unsutured, shifting, and fractured social space in which critique, difference, and a utopian potentiality can endure—provided the conceptual framework for generations of educators fighting against the deadly instrumentalism and reactionary ideologies that shaped dominant educational models at the time.[26] Said provided many of us both in and out of the academy with a critical vocabulary for extending the meaning of politics and critical awareness. In part, he did this by illuminating the seductions of what he called the cult of professionalism with its specialized languages, its neutralizing of ideology and politics through a bogus claim to objectivism, and its sham elitism and expertise rooted in all the obvious gendered, racial, and class-specific hierarchies. He was almost ruthless in his critique of a narrow ethic of professionalism with its "quasi religious quietism" and its self-inflicted amnesia about serious socio-political issues.[27]

For Said, the cult of professionalism separated culture, language, and knowledge from power and in doing so avoided the vocabulary for understanding and questioning how dominant authority worked through and on institutions, social relations, and individuals. Rooted in narrow specialisms and thoroughly secure in their professed status as experts, many full-time academics retreated into narrow modes of scholarship that displayed little interest in how power was used in institutions and social life to include and exclude, provide the narratives of the past and present, and secure the authority to define the future.[28] Said was particularly critical of those intellectuals who deny the possibility of linking understanding and critique to the ability to intervene in public life. He was insistent that many intellectuals had become prisoners of their own specialisms, insularity from public life, and distorted sense of professionalism. As such, they not only undermined the space of the university as a democratic public sphere but exhibited a slightly disguised disdain for those oppositional intellectuals dedicated to locating the energy of resistance in their own teaching and cultural work. Said argued, instead, against the insularity of such positions, one that has a tendency to ignore questions of intervention and degenerate into scholasticism, formalism, or career opportunism. We can get a glimpse of how this discourse plays out politically in a *New York Times* op-ed article in which Stanley Fish urged academics "to just do their jobs, to keep their intellectual work within the ivory tower, and to avoid crossing," as he put it, "the boundary between academic work and partisan advocacy." Oddly reversing one of Marx's most important ideas, Fish argues, "Our job is not to change the world, but to interpret it."[29] This is also a far cry from John Dewey's call to link education to the creation of an articulate public. In opposition to Fish's retreat from understanding education as a moral and political practice rather than a merely contemplative one, Said's view of education links knowledge and learning to the performative and worldly space of action and engagement, energizing people to not only think critically about the world around them but to also use their capacities as social agents to intervene in the larger social order and confront the myriad forms of symbolic, institutional, and material relations of power that shape their lives. In my view, it is precisely this connection between pedagogy and agency, knowledge and power, thought and action that must be mobilized in order to confront the current crisis of authoritarianism looming so large in the U.S. and elsewhere around the globe today.

Said was especially critical of those intellectuals who slipped into a kind of professional somnambulism in which matters of theory had less to do with a conscious challenge to politics, power, and injustice than with either a deadening scholasticism or a kind of arcane cleverness—a sort of narcotic performance in fashionable irony—which, as he suggested, neither threatened anyone nor opposed anything. He was especially ill at ease with what he called the "special private languages of criticism and professionalism" and thought "it was much more important . . . that people write in order to be understood than write in order to be misunderstood."[30] He was extremely disheartened by the academic turn in literary theory and cultural studies toward a depoliticized postmodernism in the 1980s, and he viewed such a turn as an unacceptable retreat from one of the primary obligations of politics and intellectuals, "to reduce the violence and hatred that have so often marked human social interaction."[31] He was extremely critical of a kind of religious model of criticism, which amounted to an "elaboration on elaboration" on sacred texts rather than a critical commentary on the power and authority that made such texts possible.[32]

Refusing to separate learning from social change, he constantly insisted that we fail theory when we do not firmly grasp what we mean by the political. To Said, theorizing politics of and for the twenty-first century was one of the most challenging issues facing the academy. He urged us to enter into a dialogue with ourselves, colleagues, and students about politics and the knowledge we seek to produce together, and to connect such knowledge to broader public spheres and issues. He argued that the role of engaged intellectuals was not to consolidate authority but to understand, interpret, and question it.[33] According to Said, social criticism had to be coupled with a vibrant self-criticism, the rejection "of the seductive persuasions of certainty," and the willingness to take up critical positions without becoming dogmatic or intractable.[34] Moreover, he insisted that critical intellectuals pluralize the sites of resistance and social change.

Accepting the demands of worldliness, for Said, implied giving voice to complex and controversial ideas in the public sphere, recognizing human injury beyond the privileged space of the academy, and using theory as a form of criticism to redress injustice.[35] Worldliness required not being afraid of controversy, making connections that were otherwise hidden, deflating the claims of triumphalism, and bridging intellectual rigor and clarity, on the one hand, and civic courage and political commitment on the other. Worldliness as a pedagogical construct meant using theory as a resource, recognizing the worldly space of criticism as the democratic underpinning of publicness, and defining critical literacy not merely as a competency, but as an act of interpretation linked to the possibility of intervention in the world. Worldliness pointed to a kind of border literacy in the plural in which people learned to read and write from multiple positions of agency; it was also indebted to the recognition forcibly stated by German political theorist Hannah Arendt that "Without a politically guaranteed public realm, freedom lacks the worldly space to make its appearance."[36]

What is particularly important about Said's work is his recognition that intellectuals have a special responsibility to promote a state of wakefulness by moving beyond the language of pointless denunciations. As such, he refused to view the oppressed as doomed actors or power as simply a crushing form of oppression. For Said, individuals and collectivities had to be regarded as potential agents and not simply as victims or ineffectual dreamers. It is this legacy of critique and possibility, of resistance and agency, that infuses his work with concrete hope and offers a wealth of resources to people in and out of the academy who struggle on multiple fronts against the rising forces of authoritarianism.

So much of what Said wrote and did with his life offers both a model and inspiration for what it means to take back politics, social agency, collective struggle, and the ability to define the future. Said recognized with great insight that academics, students, and other cultural workers had important roles to play in arousing and educating the public to think and act as active citizens in an inclusive democratic society. Most importantly, he called upon such groups to put aside their petty squabbling over identities and differences and to join together collectively in order to become part of what he called a fully awakened, worldly coalition that would be actively opposed to those forces at home and abroad who are pushing us into the age of totalitarianism without anyone even complaining or, for that matter, even noticing.[37] Near the end of his life, Said argued that the U.S. government was in the hands of a cabal, a junta "dominated by a group of military-minded neoconservatives," that posed a grave threat to world peace and global democracy—a sentiment now being echoed by Seymour Hersh, Robert Kennedy Jr., and Gore Vidal.[38]

Both Said and Derrida insisted rightly that democracy demands the most concrete urgency. Of course, urgency is not only a response to the crisis of the present, increasingly shaped by the footprint of an emerging authoritarianism wielded through the anonymous presence of neo-liberal capitalism and a number of other anti-democratic tendencies, but also connected to the future that we make available to the next generation of young people. How much longer can we allow the promise of democracy to be tainted by its reality?

Making pedagogy and education central to the political tasks of reclaiming public space, rekindling the importance of public connectedness, and infusing civic life with the importance of a democratic worldly vision is at the heart of opposing the new authoritarianism. Arendt recognized that any viable democratic politics must address the totality of public life, refusing to withdraw from such a challenge in the face of totalitarian violence that legitimated itself through appeals to safety, fear, and the threat of terrorism.[39] She writes: "Terror becomes total when it becomes independent of all opposition; it rules supreme when nobody any longer stands in its way. If lawfulness is the essence of non-tyrannical government and lawlessness is the essence of tyranny, then terror is the essence of totalitarian domination."[40] The promise of a better world cannot be found in modes of authority that lack a vision of social justice, renounce the promise of democracy, and reject the dream of a better world, offering instead the pale assurance of protection from the nightmare of an all-embracing terrorism. Against this stripped down legitimation of authority is the promise of public spheres that in their diverse forms, sites, and content offer pedagogical and political possibilities for strengthening the social bonds of democracy, new spaces from which to cultivate both the capacity for critical modes of individual and social agency and the crucial opportunities to form alliances to collectively struggle for a biopolitics that expands the scope of vision, operations of democracy, and the range of democratic institutions—that is, a biopolitics that fights against the terrors of totalitarianism. In a complex and rapidly changing global world, public intellectuals are confronted with the important task of taking back control over the conditions of intellectual production in a variety of venues and forms in which the educational force of the culture takes root and holds a powerful grip over the stories, images, and sounds that shape people's lives throughout the globe. Such sites constitute what I call "new spheres of public pedagogy" and represent crucial locations for a cultural politics designed to wrest the arena of public debate within the field of global power away from those market forces that endlessly commodify intellectual autonomy and critical thought while appropriating or undercutting any viable work done through the collective action of critical intellectuals. Such spheres are about more than legal rights guaranteeing freedom of speech; they are also sites that demand a certain kind of citizen informed by particular forms of education, a citizen whose education provides the essential conditions for democratic public spheres to flourish.

Cornelius Castoriadis, the great philosopher of democracy, argues that if public space is not to be experienced as a private affair, but as a vibrant sphere in which people experience and learn how to participate in and shape public life, it must be shaped through an education that provides the decisive traits of courage, responsibility, and shame, all of which connect the fate of each individual to the fate of others, the planet, and global democracy.[41] Artists, cultural workers, youth, and educators need to create new discourses of understanding and criticism, but also offer up a vision of hope that creates the conditions for multiple collective and global struggles that refuse to use politics as an act of war or markets as the measure of democracy. Democracy's promise demands more justice, not more ritual. Democracy is a site of struggle whose outcome is always uncertain but whose future should never remain in doubt.

Notes

1. Michael Hardt and Antonio Negri, *Multitude: War and Democracy in the Age of Empire* (New York: Penguin Press, 2004).
2. See Henry A. Giroux and Susan Searls Giroux, *Take Back Higher Education* (New York: Palgrave, 2005).
3. Con Lehane, "An Interview with Noam Chomsky," *Thought and Action* (Fall 2005), 94.
4. Jane Mayer, "Outsourcing Torture," *The New Yorker* (Febuary 14, 2005).
5. Thomas Friedman, "Giving the Hatemongers No Place to Hide, *New York Times* (July 22, 2005).

6.   This charge comes from a report issued by the conservative group, American Council of Trustees and Alumni (ACTA), founded by Lynne Cheney (spouse of Vice President Dick Cheney) and Joseph Lieberman (Democratic senator). See Jerry L. Martin and Anne D. Neal, *Defending Civilization: How Our Universities Are Failing America and What Can Be Done About It* (February 2002). Online: www.goacta.org. ACTA also posted on its Web site a list of 115 statements made by allegedly "un-American Professors."

7.   Horowitz's book trades in racist accusations, the ongoing claim that almost anyone who criticizes the Bush administration hates America, and accuses critics of the Iraq war of getting Americans killed in Iraq. His latest book, *The Professors: The 101 Most Dangerous Academics in America* (New York: Regnery, 2006), purports to name and expose those left-wing professors who hate America and the military, and give comfort to terrorists.

8.   See "Forum: A Chilly Climate on the Campuses," *Chronicle of Higher Education* (September 9, 2005), B7–B13.

9.   See "The Dirty Thirty": www.uclaprofs.com/articles/dirtythirty.html.

10. Piper Fogg, "Independent Alumni Group Offers $100 Bounties to UCLA Students Who Ferret Out Classroom Bias," *Chronicle of Higher Education* (January 19, 2005).

11. Edward Said, *Humanism and Democratic Criticism* (New York: Columbia University Press, 2004), 72–73.

12. Jacques Derrida, "The Future of the Profession or the Unconditional University," *Derrida Downunder*, Laurence Simmons and Heather Worth, eds. (Palmerston North, New Zealand: Dunmore Press, 2001), 253.

13. Ibid., 233.

14. Cornelius Castoriadis, "Democracy as Procedure and Democracy as Regime," *Constellations* 4:1 (1997), 10.

15. Derrida, 253.

16. Ibid.

17. Cited in Madeline Bunting, "Passion and Pessimism," *The Guardian* (April 5, 2003).

18. Arundhati Roy, *Power Politics* (Cambridge, MA: South End Press, 2001), 6.

19. Said, 143.

20. Cornel West, "Finding Hope in Dark Times," *Tikkun* 19:4 (2004), 18.

21. Said, 48–49.

22. See Henry A. Giroux, *Against the New Authoritarianism* (Winnipeg: Arbeiter Ring, 2005).

23. Edward Said, "The Public Role of Writers and Intellectuals," *The Nation* (October 1, 2001), 31.

24. Stephen Howe, "Edward Said: The Traveler and the Exile," *Open Democracy* (October 2, 2003).

25. Edward Said, *Representations of the Intellectual: The 1993 Reith Lectures* (New York: Pantheon Books, 1994), 8–9.

26. See Henry A. Giroux, *Border Crossings: Cultural Workers and the Politics of Education* (New York: Routledge, 2005).

27. Abdirahman Hussein, Edward Said: *Criticism and Society* (New York: Verso, 2004), 302.

28. Stanley Aronowitz, *How Class Works: Power and Social Movement* (New Haven, CT: Yale University Press, 2003), 53.

29. Stanley Fish, "Why We Built the Ivory Tower," *New York Times* (May 21, 2004). See also Robert Ivie, "A Presumption of Academic Freedom," *The Review of Education, Pedagogy, and Cultural Studies* 27 (2005), 4.

30. Gauri Viswanathan, ed., *Power, Politics, and Culture: Interviews with Edward Said* (New York: Vintage, 2001), 176.

31. Hannah Arendt, *Between Past and Future: Eight Exercises in Political Thought* (New York: Penguin, 1977), 149.

32. Edward Said, "The Public Role of Writers and Intellectuals," *The Nation* (October 1, 2001), 31.

33. Edward Said, "On Defiance and Taking Positions," *Reflections on Exile and Other Essays* (Cambridge, MA: Harvard University Press, 2001), 501.

34. Hussein, 297.

35. See Giroux, *Border Crossings*.

36. Arendt, 149.

37. Edward Said, *Culture and Resistance: Interviews with David Barsamian* (Cambridge, MA: South End Press, 2003), 167.

38. Ibid.

39. Hannah Arendt, Totalitarianism: *Part Three of the Origins of Totalitarianism* (New York: Harcourt, 1976), 162.

40. Ibid.

41. See, especially, Cornelius Castoriadis, "The Greek Polis and the Creation of Democracy," *Philosophy, Politics, Autonomy: Essays in Political Philosophy* (New York: Oxford University Press, 1991), 81–123.

This chapter originally appeared in *Afterimage: The Journal of Media Arts and Cultural Criticism*, Vol. 33, No. 6 (May/June, 2006). Published here with permission of Visual Studies Workshop.

CHAPTER NINE

A New Paradigm for Citizenship Education

The Personal-Political Approach

Elizabeth E. Heilman

Educating students with the capacity for critical judgment and the willingness and ability to make their communities, their nation, and indeed the world better, more just and livable through active citizenship is widely acknowledged to be profoundly important. At the same time, we have a preponderance of evidence that citizenship education is failing. Few students are able to make reasoned critical judgments about how power functions and the ways in which governments, corporations, or media purveyors impinge on liberty and justice for all. Indeed, most students lack even the most basic understanding about the branches and functioning of government. Fewer still take action for change. If we were to imagine what our society would be like if critical citizenship were ordinary instead of rare, the gap between possibility and reality suggests that citizenship education has been a colossal failure. It's common to blame teachers and schools in which standardized testing and rote learning predominates. I think, however, that the fundamental nature of citizenship education has been misperceived. We have been doing it all wrong. The focus of most citizenship education has been misconceived, and the monumental difficulty of fostering the qualities of critical citizenship has not been adequately understood.

A Focus on the Political-Personal Instead of Politics

Citizenship education has typically been focused on policy and politics; I'm calling for a focus on the political-personal. A citizenship education for politics focuses on the public sphere and prepares one to participate in a current social order. It focuses on what we know, how we make claims, and what we do. From this perspective, healthy institutions and legitimate processes help to create good lives and a good society. Citizenship education for politics relies on insights from political science and from liberal democratic deliberative theory and students learn about criteria for justice and liberty, the reasons for government and its branches and functions, current social issues, the qualities of different cultures, and the sort of actions a citizen can take both alone and with others within the system as ways to improve the system. Democratic society is presented as real and realized, and our citizens have to live up to what our democracies have become.

A citizenship education for the political-personal relies on insights from radical democracy and poststructuralism, and much more broadly on psychology, ethics, life span development, spiritual traditions, and indeed the whole social cloth. It undoes the boundaries between the seemingly separate disciplines, and spheres of the public, the economic, the private, and the personal, and it even aims to undo the seemingly separate boundaries within the self. From this perspective the democratic polity relies on the quality of *our* political-personal imaginations and the quality of the relationships, communities and polities that our imaginations lead us to enact. It focuses on who we are, how we imagine, how we've become, why we act, and in what ways we might quest for another imaginary, another self and a better, more just, more free, more peaceful world reflective of our imaginaries. Democratic society is presented as a temporary fiction that is never realized, and our democracies have to live up to what we have and will become.

Much of the literature dealing with the development of participatory and justice-oriented citizens employs sociological and political theory and, as such, describes the *process* of change but not the development of those *people* effecting change. While research is done on how organizations affect change, little research explores why people come to participate and continue to do so. While many schools and universities help students think about social issues and even organize social action projects that involve students, few focus in a serious way on the dispositions and ways of thinking that might lead students to make critical judgments and develop projects on their own. Democracies require critically minded, active citizens for both ordinary and extraordinary forms of good. It was active critical citizens who led the movements to extend suffrage, created handicapped rights, desegregated schools and challenged immoral foreign policies and wars; and it is was active citizens who were responsible for making sure that the rug you buy wasn't made by child labor. However, citizenship education has not been concerned with how "real" active citizens actually develop and whether there are common experiences and traits which lead some people to become citizens who can see injustice, deconstruct discourses that justify it and encourage passivity, and instead take action and effect change.

Most educators who support active critical citizenship believe that citizenship education is best learned through direct experiences with social action by teachers and students (Berman, 1993). However, the vast majority of existing citizenship education curricula and practices do not focus on educating to become active citizens who change and improve society but instead emphasize gaining knowledge of democratic processes, the reasons for government and its branches and functions, and, to some degree, current social issues (Boyle-Baise, 2003; Grant & Vansledright, 1996; Gibson & Levine, 2003; Hahn, 1998; Thornton, 2005; Westheimer & Kahne, 2004). This approach educates "responsible citizens" who maintain society unchanged. Westheimer and Kahne (2004) argue that there are three types of citizens and label them as: 1) the personally responsible citizen, who obeys laws, contributes to good causes, recycles, gives blood, etc. 2) the participatory citizen, who volunteers for community work, joins community or social groups, helps organize programs to help others, etc. and 3) the justice-oriented citizen, who critically assesses the causes of social problems and works actively to alleviate them. We mostly educate students to be "good" but not great, and to be responsible, but not heroic citizens, and to join or follow rather than to lead.

The dominant discourse of citizenship education is rational, structural and institutional. Kenneth Strike (1982), Amy Gutman (1995), Diana Hess (2004), and Eamonn Callan (1997), among others, all primarily want to develop rationally deliberative citizens for "justice as reasonableness" (Callan p. 8) who think and act within existing structures rather than as emotionally and socially engaged citizens who pursue justice through social action, whether inside or beyond existing structures. Citizenship education has been disembodied in these kinds of approaches and has been removed from real time and place and the immediate motivations of individuals. As a result, the ability to use these theories as avenues for personal and social change are minimized (Heilman, 2005). Instead, this study locates citizenship in "the political" (Mouffe, 2005) rather than in politics and assumes a poststructural, personal, and hermeneutic interpretation rather than structural and organizational positions on social change and citizenship (Berman, 1993; Heilman, 2003; Richardson, 2008; Segall & Gaudelli, 2007). In place of a citizenship education for *politics*, a citizenship education that explicitly aims to foster active citizens is political-personal and is for *life*. It asks: How do I integrate active citizenship into my identity? How do I construct my own ideas about power and social change? When, where, and how can I become disposed to act and effect change? What or who inspires me? This is an education in personal development as well as in deep civic criticality and searches towards something new, a better world. Most simply stated, citizenship has been approached as a straightforward topic of study and a set of skills and disputations to obtain rather than as a difficult aspect of identity and a way of seeing how the world is to develop. While there has been work that distinguishes types of citizenship education, it distinguishes among political orientations and degrees of criticality but does not differ in the object of study. In other words, debates in the field have explored orientations towards the subject but have not questioned its substance.

A citizenship education for the political-personal relies on insights from radical democracy, poststructuralism, social psychology, psychoanalytic theory, and cultural studies, i.e., it depends much more broadly on the whole social cloth. Structuralism is a way of thinking about dominant structures across disciplines as diverse as linguistics, psychology, and political science and is generally characterized by a focus on breaking down processes into basic components on the assumption that there are identifiable units in institutions as well as in cultural meaning. This has tended to produce scholarship, and ultimately textbooks, with a linear understanding of power, which makes macro-level generalizations and does not explore micro-level processes. Contrary to structuralism, poststructuralism rejects tidy scientific sorting and controverts structuralism's linear and functional views of the transmission of power and meaning. Citizenship education has been a largely structural academic enterprise in which individual experience and the contradictions of knowledge and cultural production are not adequately explored.

Poststructuralism is useful in a political-personal approach to citizenship education because it focuses on processes of identity and knowledge production and conceptualizes both identity and knowledge as sites of power in which only some identity choices are valued; and limited experiences count as knowledge. Poststructuralist perspectives challenge the notion of transcendent universalizing truths and focus on the role language plays in mediating the relationship between power and knowledge. As such, poststructuralism undoes the boundaries between the seemingly separate disciplines and spheres of the public, the economic, the private, and the personal; and it even aims to undo the seemingly separate boundaries within the self. A personal-political citizenship education posits that bringing about change at the micro- level in the home and in the community and at the macro-level in politics and economics involves "engaging in deconstruction, experimentation and especially narrative-generation: building the possibilities for new stories, explanations and connections with experience, which challenge dominant and taken-for-granted realities." (Coleman, 2002, p. 23).

From this perspective, the realization of justice and the quality of democratic life rely most centrally on the quality of personal political imaginations and the quality of the relationships, communities and policies that our imaginations lead us to enact. It focuses on who we are, how we imagine, how we've become, why we act, and in what ways we might quest for another imaginary, another self and a better, more just, more free, more peaceful world—one that is reflective of our imaginaries. Democratic society is presented as a temporary fiction that is never realized, and our democracies have to live up to what we can image and what we can become.

Poststructuralist theories emphasize that self is not a static entity but instead is multiple, fluid, and perpetually engaged in the act of becoming (or unbecoming). This shift in identity theory began with Freud (1940), who first shattered the Kantian and Cartesian notion of a unitary, integrated, sovereign, autonomous self by introducing the "unconscious," thus first giving rise to the notion of a "split subject." Diverse theories that continued to unseat modernist structuralist ideas of identity include pragmatism (Dewey, 1896; Peirce, 1955), symbolic interactionism (Mead, 1934), social constructionism (Gergen, 1985), and sociocultural theory (Vygotsky, 1962; Wertsch, 1991). Postmodern theories of identity include feminist, postcolonial, and poststructuralist theory (Lacan, 1977; Butler, 1991; Bhabha, 1994; Hall, 1996; Derrida, 1978; Althusser, 1971; among others). In the constructivist and poststructuralist views, there is no such thing as a pre-constituted identity. Rather, identities are projects, joint (conscious or unconscious) performances by both contingent selves and by determining structures that produce a coherent, stable, and unified sense of self (subjectivity) out of the default splitting that may then serve as a more secure grounding for a way of being in the world.

A political-personal citizenship education would focus on helping students learn about how they have come to understand concepts such as liberty, justice, power, and democracy through the use of deconstructive tools. They would develop a personal understanding of the cultural narratives they use and discard as they make sense of how national and global politics functions, how rights and goods are distributed, and how they, as citizens, should respond in the moment to a civic issue or choice. This is not quite the distinction Chantal Mouffe (2000) makes but it is related. She describes "politics" as "the ensemble of practices, discourses and institutions which seek to establish a certain order and organize human coexistence in conditions that are always potentially conflictual because they are affected by the dimension of 'the political' while 'the political' is the realm of conflict itself" (p. 95). This captures the immediacy of actual conflict and is something that happens among people rather than in the formal political realm. The personal-political entails all claims and meanings, not just claims in formal policy conflict.

Instead of Studying Structures of Government and Finished Events, Explore Contestments

Personal-political citizenship education, then, focuses on the political rather than on politics. This is especially important because the social imagination required to maintain a stable democratic society is very different from that that required to make a better one. Politics aims to manage the political. Change comes from the antagonism of the political. Our collective willingness to participate in a law-based society with defined memberships, rights, laws, and polices creates stability; and, for the most part, government sponsors citizenship education for orderly, reasonable, political participation in this society. Yet, the ethical and political claim to worthiness enacted in this fixity and stability actually relies on its profound opposites: critique, ambiguity, emotion, radical imaginative flux, deep criticality, disorder and destruction—in an open, uncertain quest for our future. It is always our individual and collective political-personal willingness to challenge stability that creates more just and free lives and societies. Yet, history and civics education rarely focuses on power struggles, *processes* of change, the uncertainty of the people involved, and the contingency of the entire enterprise. There was no historical inevitability to our heroes or villains; our present national and global circumstances could easily be radically differrent. An education focusing on the political-personal is always oriented towards the multiple possibilities embodied in "real" space and time and not on the theoretical citizenship of democracy on textbook page 56. We are the subject; citizenship is not a school subject.

When I emphasize the importance of narrative and personal interpretations, I want to be clear that I am not devaluing what's typically called content knowledge. Critical citizenship education requires that students have a much deeper and more sophisticated understanding of history, government, and economics than is currently the case. Knowledge matters. However, even strong AP test scores suggesting a comparatively critical understanding of history and economics is often not serving to inform students' understanding of the world as it unfolds around them; and it is not serving to suggest possibilities for civic action that they may take. Thus, I am hoping that a personal-political approach to citizenship education will enable students and future citizens to integrate their content knowledge of history, economics and "social studies" into the more personal narratives that inform their understanding and actions in the world around them. This means that as we teach history, for example, it's important to draw explicit connections to current political situations; as current events are taught, connections need to be drawn back to past historical events. For example, the American foreign-policy decision not to allow Jewish refugees to enter the United States prior to World War II can be connected to current treatments of refugees from places such as Haiti, Sudan, and Afghanistan. It means as well that students would consider the range of immediate civic choices open to others in the past and to them right now if they believe more refugees should be accepted. A solid contextual historical understanding of economic policy in the middle of the twentieth century has immediate applicability for critiquing current policy, and students should be able to make these very immediate connections. As Susan George (1999) writes:

> In 1945 or 1950, if you had seriously proposed any of the ideas and policies in today's standard neo-liberal toolkit, you would have been laughed off the stage at or sent off to the insane asylum. At least in the Western

countries, at that time, everyone was a Keynesian, a social democrat or a social-Christian democrat or some shade of Marxist. The idea that the market should be allowed to make major social and political decisions; the idea that the State should voluntarily reduce its role in the economy, or that corporations should be given total freedom, that trade unions should be curbed and citizens given much less rather than more social protection—such ideas were utterly foreign to the spirit of the time. Even if someone actually agreed with these ideas, he or she would have hesitated to take such a position in public and would have had a hard time finding an audience.

Social Studies education is widely justified as citizenship education, yet often the subject matter floats disconnected form current issues and from students' lives. Students are forced to make connections on their own. But they often can't.

Howard Gardner has described how Harvard graduate students in physics were able to pass tests suggesting that they understood a wide range of physical phenomena. Yet when asked to offer in an informal narrative explanation for phenomena such as gravity or the causes for the different seasons, they failed to activate their scientific content knowledge and instead offered utterly inaccurate popular cultural misconceptions about those phenomena. The same thing happens when students need to be able to use what they've learned in history, geography, government, or economics in order to interpret an immediate reality. In interviews Gardner observes:

> There's a famous example of Harvard graduates being asked, as they received their diploma, why the earth is warmer in the summer than in the winter. Out of 25 students, nearly all gave exactly the same answer that a 5-year-old would: the earth is closer to the sun in summer than in the winter. The fact is, it has nothing to do with that; it has to do with the tilt of the earth on its axis, which is either away or toward the sun, depending on what time of the year it is in a particular location. (Brandt, 1993)

In reference to the academic disciplines Gardner (1996) details

> In math, you have "rigidly applied algorithms," [and] in the areas of the curriculum which involve humanistic thinking, social-scientific thinking, and the arts, what we have are scripts or stereotypes—these are familiar patterns of events which we learn to expect...So in the *The Unschooled Mind*, I go through all the disciplines and show that no matter which discipline we are looking at, students are filled with misconceptions, scripts and stereotypes, formulas which they've memorized but can't use, and it's very, very discouraging.

It is difficult for students to translate their school learning into actionable knowledge, and it is very difficult for them to think beyond popular cultural narratives. This calls into question our understanding of what it means to know something. For the sake of active critical citizenship, we are aiming for a kind of knowledge that facilitates a sophisticated critical reading of the present world and promotes the capacity to take action in the actual world to foster liberty and justice for all. If educators began with the goal of actionable political-personal understanding, our civic education would be very different indeed.

Reconsidering Scale, Positioning and Emotion for a More Personal-Political Civic Education

In calling for personal-political citizenship education with a more explicit focus on students' personal understandings, I am aware that educators do not adequately understand or reflect on the position from which students learn subjects such as civics and history; and further, based on what we do know, such pedagogy is in need of much more research and radical revision. While there seems to be a considerable social and policy-level anxiety that students might not really understand and make future use of mathematics or science, there is little concern and thus little policy or research on the problem that students do not really understand and make future use of what is taught in history, economics, and government classes. The ill-informed future scientist seems to be a national emergency but not the ill-informed citizen.

History has often been traditionally taught as a narrative on a large scale, featuring major historical figures and events. The position students are in as they read many textbook presentations of history is one of emotional remove. This position provides comparatively little detail about human emotion and experience and the texture of day-to-day life. Many historians argue that this is simply bad history because students are not privy to the inevitable human drama and the human personalities from which history is hewn. Without close and complex knowledge, students often don't come to understand how momentous historical turning points might have turned out otherwise. Human beings, cultures, and intergroup relations are complex and contingent. Students should thus be learning history from more intimate perspectives—both in order to gain richer understanding of particular historical moments and personalities, and also because students seem to find more intimate presentations interesting, and, importantly, more personally relevant.

That circumstance has led to a moderate increase in the use of material which features the perspectives of ordinary people (including youth) as well as the increased use of historical fiction and narrative histories. A problem teachers face is deciding between the presentation of history from a far remove which covers a lot of time and ground versus a more intimate presentation of history in which students become able to understand the lives and the reasoning of historical figures. Yet the ways in which students understand history and use of such history to inform citizenship are not well understood. To what extent is it necessary to be able to understand and relate to particular historical figures in order to be able to understand the history of that time and use that understanding to inform the present? While materials about youth in history and narrative presentations of history are becoming more commonplace in classrooms, there is little research on the civic effectiveness of different types of materials and pedagogical approaches.

In addition to the matter of the civic effectiveness of a personal or a more removed position when learning about history or current events there is the question of the moral and emotional orientation of the learner. Students often position themselves within an event as a potential historical actor. This means that students might relate to either victims or oppressors, they might relate to ordinary people or major political figures, or they might learn history and current issues without a sympathetic association with any figures or groups of people. Further, when learning about American history, students not uncommonly learn history from the standpoint of either the dominant culture or the government and, as result, some feel guilty for policies such as slavery, the Trail of Tears, and the wars in Iraq and Afghanistan. This guilty reaction seems to be more common among dominant-culture middle-class students. How does their guilt about such learning affect political citizenship? Does it make students shut down emotionally or make them lean towards justifying bad policies? For minority students and economically marginalized students or students who may associate with or empathize with any negative history, one possible emotional response that teachers notice is sadness. What are the civic implications of this? Associating with people in history who have been dehumanized, displaced, or killed can inspire feelings of fear, anger, sadness and even contempt among students. Those emotions are often both powerful and unpleasant and may cause students to turn away from learning history and from becoming political actors addressing injustice in their communities. The question of how certain materials tend to inspire emotional responses and how materials and educational experiences position students who are learning history, and how students voluntarily position themselves while learning history is important but hasn't been adequately understood.

Psychoanalytic perspectives suggest that some historical topics are inherently traumatic if understood and taught properly. History entails difficult, tragic, and sometimes frightening knowledge and the resulting psychological challenges of imagining not just that which is different but also catastrophic and threatening. As Shoshanna Felman (1992) explains, such education is personal and psychological, and thus cannot be understood merely as the transmission of passive knowledge. Felman even suggests that "if teaching does not hit upon some sort of a crisis, if it does not encounter either the vulnerability or the explosiveness of a (explicit or implicit) critical and unpredictable dimension, it has perhaps not truly taught " (53). Alice Pitt and Deborah Britzman (2003) describe student reactions to "difficult knowledge," i. e., the traumatic effects such new knowledge can present for students (p. 759). The difficulty, Britzman and Pitt (2003) explicate, is not a matter of conceptually difficult understanding, but rather learning that requires students to "encounter the self through the otherness of knowledge" (p. 755). Engaging difficult, tragic, and frightening knowledge potentially requires the repositioning of both the psychological and political reorientation because so much of global experience and national history is inherently disturbing and controversial, and because so much of it makes very personal ethical and political demands upon us. Or it should. (See Chapter 36 of this text for an additional focus on the concept of "difficult knowledge.")

Teach Cultural Studies to Deconstruct Cultural Narratives, Identities and Discourses

A personal-political approach to citizenship education also requires serious attention to political learning from media and popular culture. Traditional theories of democracy provide traditional mechanisms to prevent corruption and oppression in the political realm, for example, formal separations of powers; but they provide only a free press, open public spheres, and public education to prevent corruption and oppression of the political-personal through cultural power. Present "democracies" are largely capitalist and comparatively hegemonic societies, which means that our imaginings of things such as freedom, rights, and a good society occur as we live our lives in spaces that are deeply penetrated by the technologies of cultural persuasion. It is naïve to hope as Habermas (2006) does for the "the independence of a public sphere that operates as an intermediary system between state and society" as part of the "bedrock of liberal democracies." It is hard to believe that media and the "public sphere" can provide "…a realm of our social life in which something approaching public opinion can be formed" and that citizens can "confer in an unrestricted fashion…about matters of general interest" (Habermas 1974: 49) given the seductive, somnambulant appeal of illiberal, hegemonic, and colonial myths told and retold and remade in new forms in our media. Thinking carefully, paying attention, and listening are always hard to do. But information spaces and places have become less public, less critical—and more homogenous, more omnipresent, and less conducive to democratic contemplation and deliberation—than perhaps ever before.

Students who have any chance of becoming critical citizens need high-level critical media and cultural studies educations to respond to high-level media hegemony; they need to be able to deconstruct the cultural spaces, products, and messages they personally encounter every day. This requires formal instruction. The study of the novel was introduced to the school curriculum in the Progressive Era on the argument that novels were both influential and ubiquitous, and so students needed the skills to understand them. The argument remains compelling. The skills needed for critical analysis of cultural products are much greater yet largely absent from school. The information landscape has been dramatically transformed in recent decades by deregulation, technological change, and a wave of massive mergers and acquisitions. Enormous media and communications conglomerates—particularly AT&T, AOL Time Warner, Walt Disney, Viacom, News Corporation, and Vivendi—are horizontally and vertically integrated with other information industries, including book and magazine publishing, cable and network television, radio, movie studios, music companies, as well as theme parks and sports teams. Those conglomerates saturate the world's production and distribution of information and culture (Warf, 2007). The spaces that are open and public and the quality of the public sphere have declined because of the reach and the semiotic guerilla tactics of modern technologized society and mass media. We require an education equal to all of this.

An individual's seemingly logical civic deliberations are often reflections of the wider discourses and mythos available in society; and these seemingly logical ideas are tied down with emotion-laden, media-driven interpretations of words, myths, and stories. Citizenship education commonly features debates in which students present and justify arguments for their civic opinions and policy stances. However, students hardly ever learn to explore the narrative, cultural, psychological and emotional undersides of "opinion." For example, a student's belief in an argument for "tighter restriction on immigration from Africa" may really stem from an image of a Black person and feelings about the word "black" as dark, bad, dirty, and evil; notions of dark thoughts, black moods, and shady behavior might arise. It might be influenced by the colonial story of the naïve savage. *They aren't civilized. They are kind of savage and violent. A lot of them don't even wear real clothes.* It might be influenced by repressed sexual desire for the sexualized black male body that has been presented on film and television. *Hot black men, black athletes in tight pants. Khloe Kardashian married hot Lamar Joseph Odom. Kim Kardashian was with that Reggie Bush, NFL New Orleans Saints running back. I would like to do what they do.* An argument for "more open immigration from Africa" might be influenced by the Christian story compelling a desire to save a heathen soul. This is how Global Youth Ministry describes interacting with Africans.

Imagine ministering in the midst of Africa. You are surrounded by people whose culture is very different from yours, but they are eager to meet you and hear what you have to say. The adult leaders and youth surround you, their eyes as big as saucers. They are waiting for you to tell them what you came so far to say…the story of a Savior who loves them. Ministry in Africa is unique among mission fields. The culture is different; the weather is different; the people of course, are different. But nevertheless, you will be able to communicate the love of Christ to eager learners. (2011)

It sounds good. An opinion might be influenced by a Marxist solidarity story compelling a desire to free the colonial subject. *I just watched* Motorcycle Diaries. *We are a single mixed race, from Mexico to the Strait of Magellan So, trying to free myself from any nationality load, I raise a toast for Peru and for America united! I want to be like Che Guevara.* It might be influenced by wanting to be like Angelina Jolie. *Angelina Jolie is so pretty and she was on a talk show asking for more open immigration. She has that pretty African baby girl. I kind of would like to have one too. I would like to do what she does.* These are all narrative personal-political musings with heavy cultural-emotional payloads; and they have enormous civic implications.

Thus, a "civic argument" might not be an argument at all. It might be a swim through a powerful subterranean ocean of received stories, hackneyed explanations, cultural tropes, appealing images, fears, shames, and desires. My thoughts about the other might really be my thoughts about myself. My thoughts about my choices might really simply express the way my culture encourages me to feel about myself in relationship to those choices.

In place of a citizenship education for politics, a citizenship education for the political-personal would bring all of this to the surface. Informed by cultural studies, poststructuralism, and psychoanalytic theory would be an education in which we understand our "logic" and our very being to be inevitably affected by the discursive terrain in which we think and feel. In this education, we would ask: How have we come to construct our identities? What are the life choices and beliefs our culture makes available to us, and what does it make inescapable? When, where and how are we disposed to make certain choices and have certain emotions towards them? What received stories, hackneyed explanations, cultural tropes, appealing images, fears, shames, and desires shape my views of the political and economic world? Those questions highlight the personal-political; they are "here," and not in "distant" politics.

This is an education in deep criticality in which students explicitly learn how to read, deconstruct, and recursively reconstruct their identity and their world and quest towards something other. Students learning in this way would study and deconstruct both their own narratives' interpretations and narratives common in political discourse, such as the following offered by Susan George (2007):

> The market solution is always preferable to state regulation. Private enterprise surpasses the public sector on criteria of efficiency, quality, availability, and price. Free trade will ultimately serve the entire population of any country better than protectionism. It is normal and desirable that healthcare and education be profit-making activities. Higher defense spending and tax cuts for the rich guarantee security and prosperity. Inequality is inbuilt in any society and probably genetic if not racial. If people are poor, they have only themselves to blame. Hard work will always be rewarded. A free society cannot exist in the absence of market freedom. It follows that capitalism and democracy are mutually supportive. The United States, by virtue of its history, its ideals, and its superior democratic system should use its economic and military might to intervene in the affairs of the rest of world. (p. 53).

As we make ordinary choices as citizens in any particular circumstance, or more broadly, as we live and imagine a life plan, we make reference to socially given narratives, characters, archetypes, important objects, and images. We use the kinds of plots, genres, and narrative conventions (the verbs, adjectives, sentences) available to us. They often seem neutral, but they are indeed not neutral. The most important educative technique for radical democracy is to be able to move from the center to the margin and thus to have the ability to create space around hegemonic constructions, mythos, and discourses.

Teach a Sophisticated Understanding of the Relationships between Language and Power

I argue that, as citizens make what seem to be neutral, ordinary choices and what seem to be bigger and more obviously political choices, there are all sorts of possible harm that we can do to ourselves and to others by using language and imagery we believe to be neutral and not power-laden. Our culture and our language inevitably contain violence and dehumanization. The tools we think with contain violence. If we want a less violent society, we have to construct new tools, new language, new plots, and new myths to create new thoughts and new feelings. One way to think about violence is that it involves changing something into that which it does not want to experience or to be. At its most extreme, one changes a live person into a dead one. But you can also damage somebody by dehumanizing her in speech. Cultural dehumanization is a precursor to oppression and certainly to genocide. If I call you a nigger or a kike, I actually can create you as something you are not. Since theorists have agreed that although there is "real" materiality, we make sense of that materiality only as we use it in action and speech; i.e., a damaging social construction is a form of "real" violence.

As Laclau and Mouffe argue, speech acts are no less "real" than physical acts, since both are given "reality" by their interpretation within what Foucault (1989) calls a "discursive formation." When I say or think "Mary the nigger," I create her as the nigger. We don't have to actively invoke representations behind words. Instead, we can hardly escape them. Certain representations are unavoidable inheritances. There are different significations for words. But, if you try to change the meaning too much, you can reach the point of antagonism, and you can't be understood.

This is one of the most basic problems of those seeking justice and making new and different claims; and so it is a key challenge for critical citizenship education. This is one of the reasons political architects from John Dewey to Chairman Mao have made new words when they want to make a new idea. There is no escape from the violence in our language and in our world. There is no escape from the violence in our heads. We simply cannot think of a Black person without the nigger in our head. We can't quite think of a blond woman without Barbie. We can't think of a Jew without Shakespeare's greedy Shylock, or think of "scientist" without thinking of a man (and not a woman) in a lab coat. When you expect to meet a blond Jewish scientist, Barbie, Shylock and the iconic "scientist" are in your thoughts to some degree as well. As Laclau and Mouffe explain, "If language is a

system of differences, antagonism is the failure of difference"; thus, antagonism cannot really be grasped within language "since language only exists as an attempt to fix that which antagonism subverts" (1985, p. 125).

The boundaries and centers of meaning exist, but they are not fixed. They change across communities of meaning-makers and over time. A hopeful approach to antagonistic representations that are past even the zone of contentment is to populate the edges—the boundaries—with a plurality of outliers, conceptualizations, images, claims, feelings, or stories. In this way, commonsense meaning is nudged and can be a source for news offering choice and action. What seemed strange can even become the new commonsense. Claims for recognition, for new social meaning, can be both a first-order "good" and contribute to a material good. Students, and more broadly, citizens, can learn to write new stories, new literatures, and splitertaures that subvert stories and choices. For example, in order to promote women's suffrage, the representation of a woman was discursively dislodged enough to change policy. Then, when social policy and the practices around us had changed over time, the representation changed further, and the idea of a woman voting became the new commonsense. Helping citizens to deconstruct and reconstruct social meaning is not a trivial enterprise. It is at the heart of social justice work and it is actually very difficult. It requires an explicit education and distinctive conceptual tools.

Teach the Conceptual Tools of Cultural Studies

Right now these tools are not available in a form that teachers can readily use and understand. Indeed, even graduate students can struggle with them. The conceptual tools include the concepts of hegemony, discourse, binary, hegemonic representation, hegemonic ideal, myth, place, and quest. A number of different thinkers use some of these terms in similar ways—and, to some extent, in contradictory ways—so I shall offer some possible workable definitions. At the most macro-level the overarching structuralist concept is **hegemony**. According to its originator, Antonio Gramsci, this term denotes the permeation throughout society of an entire system of values, attitudes, beliefs, and practices that have the effect of supporting unequal power relations. hegemonic society employs "discourses" as the "organizing principles" of everyday life. A discourse is a system of signs and signifiers, which means the words and images (signs) that they connote (signifiers) establish the boundaries for making sense of the world. A discourse is a whole way of speaking and thinking. When discourses are internalized, they are hegemonic. When they come to be felt as "commonsense," they create a culture and social structure that actually favors those with power, but this appears as the natural, or neutral, order of things. There is generally a dominant discourse in society—for example, in the USA, I could say it is neo-liberalism—as well as sub-discourses such as progressive discourse, consumer discourse, environmental discourse, medical discourse, academic discourse, and sports discourse. One way to understand and break down a discourse is to begin to notice its important oppositions or binary structures of meaning and value. These **binaries** could include, for example, pass/fail, health/illness, black/white, public/private, and male/female. With deconstructive analysis, one can ask how these terms are positioned within a field so that one of each pair always appears to be the normal, the right, and the only one in a situation. When you ask questions such as: "Why does passing and failing matter? How is passing like failing and failing like passing?" an opposition that seems true becomes instead a zone of exploration in which the basic orthodoxies of the discourse can be contested.

A **hegemonic representation** is smaller than a discourse. A hegemonic representation is usually more of a noun; it is a particular concept like scientist, immigrant, Jew, blond, nigger, or good professional, and it is held up within discourses and their binaries. Hegemonic representations are attempts to dominate the field of discursivity, "to arrest the flow of difference to construct a center." A **hegemonic ideal** is in effect and has a powerful influence when a certain idea, group, or type "naturally" seems better or right and everyone knows what it is; a **hegemonic representation** is a more general term, and it is in effect when everyone comes up with a similar image and interpretation in response to a simple word like blond or scientist or family. Hegemonic ideals and representations are those to which most people give "spontaneous consent" to the "general direction imposed on social life by the dominant fundamental group" (Gramsci, 1978, p. 12). An important point here is that you don't personally have to feel you believe in for it to affect you and be operating as a truth. You can tell it is hegemonic when you have to recognize it because it is ubiquitous. So, if I were to ask students to describe what society considers the ideal man, ideal family, or typical immigrant, and they all came up with something similar, it is a hegemonic construct. For example, consider the "ideal" family construct. What is the ideal family like? In the USA, it is the two-child nuclear family that is commonly seen on television and in magazine stories, and in advertisements for vacations, new cars, and cereal, among other products. The boy is about two or three years older than his sister. As a university professor, I have frequently asked American preservice teacher college students to "draw a typical family," and those characteristic are what is most commonly depicted (often along with a medium-sized dog).

If I ask students to think of the ideal immigrant, can they? Does the question seem odd? Does thinking about the typical immigrant seem easier? This is an important point. It is also useful to be able to distinguish hegemonic ideals from other hegemonic representations. Hegemonic representations don't exist on a flat plane. They serve different purposes, and some are more important in terms of their capacity to motivate action or stimulate feeling. Lacan refers to **privileged signifiers** that fix the meaning of a signifying chain although other theorists use related ideas and terms. As Laclau and Mouffe point out, "Any discourse is constituted as an attempt to dominate the field of discursivity, to arrest the flow of differences, to construct a centre. We will call the privileged discursive points of this partial fixation, *nodal points*" (1985, p. 112). So a hegemonic representation of the "ideal family" can help fix the meaning of ideal mother, ideal father, and more broadly of woman and man. "Nodal points" can even vary from one context to the next, but in any given instance they are more central and can draw other meanings to them, thus organizing the social-discursive field. Discourses do not simply describe the social world; they categorize it, they establish order and value, and they bring some things into sight while hiding others. The less important, or less hegemonic, representations in discourses are either very homogenous or very heterogeneous. "Pen" has a rather homogenous meaning. I think it means approximately the same thing to many people. "Paper" is more heterogeneous; it means very different things to different people, but in some discourses nobody cares. "Paper" has a different meaning in academic discourses than in medical discourse; and "the body" is a nodal point in medical discourse but not in academic discourse.

I think of what Roland Barthes calls a **myth** as the story that goes with hegemonic ideals. In "On Myth," Barthes explains that we have "myths of order" that are necessary for social control and cohesion. We use them to interpret action, objects and scenes and to suggest choices. They organize understanding over time. They have a plot. In this way, because they occur over time and are historical, they are four-dimensional. For Barthes (1973), myth is a "second-order semiological system" made from "a material which has already been worked on so as to make it suitable for communication" (p. 2). Myth is a linguistic system constituted of hierarchies of symbols, of signs built on signs. The original signifiers of the semiotic construction constitute a crowded terrain of disparate referents, a landscape that interlaces language, history and geography and recedes as the symbols that denote them become a part of a detached mythic architecture (p. 4). Barthes suggests that the semiotic structure of mythic discourse—the process by which language is reified and distorted—is eminently suited to a containing social paradigm, in which the central symbols of the State are removed from political contestation. He calls myth "depoliticized speech" because the awareness that we are making claims that could and should be contested disappears.

Hegemonic ideals and myths connect feeling, judgment, and socialization. Mythic interpretation consists, in part, in the ways in which people are culturally encouraged to have certain emotions towards a story or a concept. We are generally proud to fulfill an ideal or a myth and ashamed to not do so. You should be proud of your country. You are moved because it is so fair and inclusive. We want to be considered inclusive. It feels nice to be proud and to be moved. So, it is not just the case that we can dispassionately argue, as Habermas suggested, and as most citizenship educators aim toward.

We have tended to teach students not to notice difference and to attend to commonality, to move away from the edges, to homogenize and smooth out difference, and to promote harmony to reduce violence—and this is exactly wrong. We need instead to teach students about how difference is constructed and not to minimize it. We need to hone their ability to see just how much difference we act on but not always with full consciousness.

Discourses pin people down, and we can come to understand that flat positionality. Yet, literally, discourse means "running back and forth." It suggests movement. We can read literature that "*strays away* from the canon" and explore art forms that are "*out there*." We can have a "*breakthrough*" in understanding. We can open up spaces within metanarratives—the different stories of what an urban black man is. We can reveal space between the nodes and the non-nodes. The periphery makes the center possible. Who am I? What contradictions and tensions do I embody? Who am I marked as? Who am I told to be? What do I condemn or even despise in myself? Who benefits from my inscriptions? What is the borderland of efficacy for an idea? What motivates me in a new way to make me feel I can act? What do I come to see is worth fighting to change? Who do I now think I can work with? With whom do I recognize solidarity? We reconstitute ourselves and our relations as a way to change the world. That kind of education accepts alterity. We read and we can't know. It is ok to become strangers to ourselves and our past. Ideas and identities can be places we move into—to and from various boundaries and then perhaps stay as temporary resting spots. That kind of education can open up spaces in which the inevitable is not inevitable.

Focus on Quest and the Necessity of Unsettlement

To govern our lives and policies in this way requires that we face and address the paradox of stability and flux. Our collective willingness to participate in law-based society creates stability and we educate for this. But, at the same time, we have to see stability as problematic. An institution built on a principle such as "good" or "just" is not coequal with goodness or justice. As Derrida explains, in the case of justice, when we make a judgment that simply follows the rules or the law, it is "right" but not just. For a decision to be just, the judgment cannot be automatic. Experience and feeling can't be removed. One must experience undecidabilty. "A decision would only come into being in a space that exceeds the calculable program that would destroy all responsibly by transforming it into a programmeable effect of determinate causes" (Derrida, 1988, p. 116). The situation should be creatively imagined, and the judgment must become like the first judgment of this kind. Indeed the experience of the judgment should be a novel, self-authored experience. This is to "re-institute" it, to create a new judgment. When one programmatically follows a code, he or she is merely a "calculating machine." Now, to do this all of the time is not practical, of course. What I am pointing out is that there is a difference between law and justice that we must be acutely aware of. We need to be mindful of the difference, not the law. We need to teach our children about the floating foundational concept of "justice" and to notice the difference between how it floats and where it lands, and not to respect the fixed law.

This Derridean critique of unreflective calculation is actually quite similar to John Stuart Mill's third argument for the need for "liberty of thought and expression," which also suggests that we need a citizenship education in which all ideas are subject to scrutiny. Mill (1869/2009) explains, "First, if any opinion is compelled to silence, that opinion may, for aught we can certainly know, be true. To deny this is to assume our own infallibility. Secondly, though the silenced opinion be an error, it may, and very commonly does, contain a portion of truth; and since the general or prevailing opinion on any subject is rarely or never the whole truth, it is only by the collision of adverse opinions that the remainder of the truth has any chance of being supplied." And then Mill warns that without criticality we are in danger of becoming Derrida's calculating machines. He explains, "Thirdly, even if the received opinion be not only true, but the whole truth; unless it is suffered to be, and actually is, vigorously and earnestly contested, it will, by most of those who receive it, be held in the manner of a prejudice, with little comprehension or feeling of its rational grounds." (p. 64)

What is less difficult for people to accept is that all *ideas* can be contested. We don't take ideas so personally. What is more difficult to consider is that all feelings, all futures, all identities, all inspirational myths, our grandmother, all discourses, your belief that your recipe can't be improved, my version of my family's history, your story of your marriage, her way to approach child rearing, can and should all be undone and floated around with the tools and playfulness of poststructuralisms and mined for hegemonic ideals and representations, nodes, myths, and fixing constricting constructions of place. Your grandmother and your church are "subjects" of social constructions and reconstruction. Philosophically, if we sign up to displace the myth that colonization is good, we also have to be willing to displace the myth colonization is bad, that autonomy for marginalized cultures is good. A piety in poststructuralism has been to only use our methods to critique what seems to us to be bad. This is placing authority before exploration, hardness before softness. With an attitude of authority, the desire not to oppress marginal cultures can result in a new orthodoxy of culture that itself is an authority. It is fine to have these authoritative cultures if they are understood to be fixed points one has arrived at rather than fixed points one stays within. As I have argued, there are indeed loose foundations in a democracy. We land on a foundation, however temporary, in order to function. It is not the case that everything goes.

But it is the case that everything can be discussed. Every idea, every culture, every supposed truth should be examined.

The point here is that floating, questing, explorations of personal-political citizenship education aim not for replacement, which is hegemonic, but displacement. We aim to create distance and form the further-away space you can move back to your center. After you critically explore fundamentalism, you can be a fundamentalist. We can choose something as a temporary truth claim, as a culture we can want to live in, and as a person we want to be. But it has to be a choice. We can't take our culture or our selves too personally. Any cultural or discursive fixity needs to be a point you understand as a point on a field you can go to and away from. Furthermore, everyone needs to be a stranger or an outsider at some time because to consider destinations is to be in flux, to be a democratic spirit is to experience undecidability and to live for a while away from current memberships as epistemological, political, and cultural outsiders. Conversely, nobody ever travels forever. We all have arrivals. We all claim space and a home and a truth we can live with.

Our democratic governments are concerned with respecting cultural diversity and other forms of different identities. Yet, this creates a tension. How do we reconcile respect for who people are with who they might become? How do you reconcile respect for cultures as they are with what they might become? You simply can't. There, finally, is a choice between honoring fixity or honoring flux, between a definitive way of being and new options, between officially supported forms of diversity and support for diversity as a principle, between authoritative ways and experimental ways, between stability and change, between staying and quest. The deep poststructuralist position and the radical democratic position is in favor of flux, options, diversity as a principle not a condition, experiment, change, and quest.

In the spirit of pragmatism, in nations with hard choices to make, there are all sorts of very real reasons to leave some practices untouched and to allow some cultural groups less scrutiny than radical democratic theory suggests. There are reasons sometimes to foster unity and patriotism, to center people at home, to circle around an idea. But I think, at the same time, that we need to accept the full radicalism of democracy and to see these choices as merely pragmatic. It is helpful to consider our authority, our current laws, our celebrated practices, our nationalist parades, our moving patriotic songs, as pragmatic choices and practices that uphold certainty and can foster some goodness for a while. Yet we have to remember that this authority is temporary and requires scrutiny because solid authority violates democratic principles. As Derrida (1978) observes, it is possible to remain faithful to a double intention "to preserve as an instrument something whose truth value"(p. 284) is criticized. Both matter. We need instruments and we need to consider a "both/and/other" approach to theory and policy choices that allow for multiple epistemologies, multiple philosophies, and multiple futures. It is our willingness to challenge stability and to quest that create more just and free lives and worlds.

Bibliography

Althusser, L. (1971). Ideology and the ideological state apparatuses (Notes towards an investigation) (B. Brewster, Trans.). In *Lenin and philosophy and other essays* (pp. 127–186). New York: Monthly Review Press.

Barthes, R. (1973) *Mythologies*, Paladin, London

Berman, S. (1993). Introduction. In S. Berman & P. La Farge (Eds.). *Promising practices in teaching social responsibility* (pp. 1–12). Albany: State University of New York Press.

Bhabha, H. (1994). *The location of culture*. New York: Routledge.

Boyd-Barrett, Oliver, and Chris Newbold. Eds. (1995). Eds. *Approaches to Media: A Reader*. London: Hodder Arnold.

Boyle-Baise, M. (2003). Doing democracy in social studies methods. *Theory and Research in Social Education*, 31.1: 51–71.

Brandt, R. (1993). On Teaching for Understanding: A Conversation with Howard *Gardner. Educational Leadership*, 50 (7).

Butler, J. (1991). *Gender trouble: Feminism and the subversion of identity*. London: Routledge.

Callan, E. (1997). *Creating citizens*: Political education and liberal democracy. Oxford: Oxford University Press.

Coleman G. (2002). Gender, power and post-structuralism in corporate citizenship: A personal perspective on theory and change, *Journal of Corporate Citizenship*. 5, 17–25

Derrida, J. (1978). Structure, sign and play in the discourse of the human sciences. In *Writing and difference* (pp. 278–93). Chicago: University of Chicago Press.

Derrida, J. (1988). *Limited Inc*. Evanston, IL: Northwestern University Press.

Dewey, J. (1896). The reflex arc concept in psychology. *Psychological Review, 3*.

Foucault, M. (1989) *The Archaeology of Knowledge*, London: Routledge.

Felman, S. (1992). Education and crisis, or the vicissitudes of teaching In S. Felman and Dori Laub. *Testimony: Crises of Witnessing in Literature, Psychoanalysis and History*. pp. 1–56. New York: Routledge.

Freud, S. (1940). *An outline of psycho-analysis*. trans. James Strachey (1969). New York: W.W. Norton & Company Inc.

Gardner, H. (Writer), & DiNozzi, R. (Producer/Director). (1996). *MI: Intelligence, understanding and the mind* [Motion picture]. Los Angeles: Into the Classroom Media.

George, S. (1999) *The Lugano Report: On Preserving Capitalism in the 21st Century*. London: Pluto Press.

George, S. (2007). Manufacturing "common sense" or cultural hegemony for beginners. In. A. Vanaik (ed.) *The Masks of Empire*, pp. 45–73. New Delhi: Tulika.

Gergen, K. (1985). The social constructionist movement. *American Psychologist, 40*, 266–275.

Gibson, C., & Levine, P. (2003). *The civic mission of schools*. New York and Washington, D.C.: The Carnegie Corporation of New York and the Center for Information and Research on Civic Learning.

Global Youth Ministries. (2011). About missions abroad. Retrieved March 30, 2011 from http://www.globalyouth-ministry.org/missions_about.html

Gramsci, A. (1978). *Selections from the Prison Notebooks of Antonio Gramsci*. (Trans and Ed). Q. Hoare and N. Smith. New York: International Publishers.

Grant, S.G., & Vansledright, B. (1996). The dubious connection: Citizenship education and the social studies. *Social Studies*, 87(2), 56–59.

Gutmann, A. (1995). Civic education and social diversity. *Ethics*, 105 (13), 557–579.

Habermas, Jurgen. (1974). The public sphere: An encyclopedia article (1964), *New German Critique* 3 (Autumn): 49–55.

Habermas, J. (1989). *The structural transformation of the public sphere*. Cambridge: Polity.

Habermas, (2006). Political communication in media society: Does democracy still enjoy an epistemic dimension? The impact of normative theory on empirical research, *Communication Theory*, 16 (4), 411–426.

Hahn, C. (1998). *Becoming political: Comparative perspectives on citizenship education*. Albany: State University of New York Press.

Hall, S. (1996). The work of representation. In S. Hall (Ed.) *Representation: cultural representations and signifying practices*. London: Sage

Heilman, E. (2003). Critical theory as a personal project: From early idealism to academic realism. *Educational Theory*, 53 (2), 247–274.

Heilman, E. (2005). Escaping the bind between utopia and dystopia: Eutopic critical pedagogy of identity and embodied practice. In Gur-Ze'ev, I. (Ed). *Critical pedagogy and critical theory today*. (pp. 114–142). New York: Kluwer Academic Press.

Hess, D. (2004). Controversies about controversial issues in democratic education. *PS:Political Science & Politics*, 37, 257–261.

Kahne, J., & Westheimer, J. (2006). Teaching democracy: What schools need to do. In E.W. Ross (Ed). *The social studies curriculum: Purposes, problems, and possibilities* (pp. 297–318). Albany: State University of New York Press.

Lacan, J. (1977). *Ecrits. A selection.* New York: WW Norton & Company.

Laclau, E. (1990). *New reflections on the revolution of our time.* London: Verso.

Laclau, E., and Mouffe, C. (1985). *Hegemony and socialist strategy: Towards a radical democratic politics.* London: Verso.

Mead, G. H. (1934) *Mind, Self and Society.* Chicago: University of Chicago Press.

Mill, J.S. (1869, 2009). *On Liberty.* New York: Nuvision Publishers.

Mouffe, C. (2000). *The democratic paradox.* London: Verso.

Mouffe, C. (2005). *On the political.* New York: Routledge.

Oldfield, A. (1990). *Citizenship and community: Civic republicanism and the modern world.* London: Routledge.

Peirce, C. S. (1955). *Philosophical writings of Pierce.* New York: Dover Publications.

Pitt, A., & Britzman, D. P. (2003). Speculations on qualities of difficult knowledge in teaching and learning: an experiment in psychoanalytic research. *Qualitative Studies in Education*, 16 (6), 755–776.

Richardson, G. (2008). Within the liminal space: Re-positioning global citizenship education as politics of encounter, disruption and transcendence (pp. 127–138). In George Richardson & Ali Abdi (Eds.). *De-colonizing democratic education: Transcultural dialogues.* Rotterdam, Netherlands: Sense Publishers.

Segall, A., & Gaudelli, W. (2007). Reflecting socially on social issues in a social studies methods course. *Teaching Education*, 18 (1), 77–92.

Strike, K. (1982). *Educational policy and the just society.* Chicago: University of Illinois Press.

Thornton, S.J. (2005). Enactment of curriculum that matters. In S.J. Thornton, *Teaching social studies that matters: Curriculum for active learning* (pp. 104–108). New York: Teachers College Press.

Vygotsky, L. (1962). *Thought and language* (E. Hanfmann & G. Vakar, Trans.). Cambridge, MA: MIT Press.

Warf, B. (2007). Oligopolization of global media and telecommunications and its implications for democracy. *Ethics, Place and Environment* 10, 89–105.

Westheimer, J., &. Kahne, J. (2004). What kind of citizen? The politics of educating for democracy. *American Educational Research Journal* 41 (2), 237–69.

Wertsch, J. V. (1991). *Voices of the mind: A sociocultural approach to mediated action.* Cambridge, MA: Harvard University Press.

CHAPTER TEN

Critical Civic Literacy and the Building of Community for a Globalized World

BARRY M. FRANKLIN & STEVEN CAMICIA

I.

Earlier this year we published an essay in which we considered how we might reconstitute the notion of community to establish a suitable lens for exploring curriculum reform under conditions of globalization. We argued that a central purpose of this notion throughout the twentieth century and now into the twenty-first on the part of educational reformers has been regulative, namely as a framework for interpreting the role of the curriculum as a unifying element in national settings. For much of this period, we went on to argue, that regulation was intended to build a sense of collective belonging and common purpose that we defined in terms of the notion of community (Camicia & Franklin, 2010).

We concluded our essay by questioning the continuing value of a notion of community for talking about the kind of collective belonging that is now required and that schools should promote in today's globalized world. The problem for us was that the notion of community is a nebulous term with multiple meanings that are not necessarily consistent. It is in fact what is called a floating or empty signifier—a term without a single or specific referent (Burgos, 2003; Laclau, 1994). We noted in this vein that the term community has been used in American educational discourse throughout our history to promote inclusion and democracy as well as being employed as an exclusionary notion for intents that are decidedly anti-democratic and authoritarian.

Our goal for this essay is in part historical and is directed toward describing how these two different intents have emerged in twentieth-century educational thinking and played themselves out in actual curriculum practice. The essay is also policy oriented and considers how we might frame an understanding of community for the globalized world in which we live. Our intent in this essay is threefold. First, we will situate historically the emergence of those ideas within our social and educational discourse that during the years around the turn of the twentieth century came together to shape what we might think of as a notion of community.

Second, we will consider how those ideas took shape over the course of the century within the fields of curriculum and social studies education to become what we currently think of as a formal notion of civic literacy. And third, we will examine how in the contemporary period this notion of civic literacy has affected our efforts to formulate a notion of community that fits the demands of globalization.

II.

From the earliest days of the Republic, Americans have viewed education in general and public schooling in particular as vehicles for teaching what we are now calling civic literacy. Spurring this role for the schools was the interplay of four factors. The first was the institutionalization and development of public schooling into an organized structure of common schools and then high schools to educate the nation's growing school population. The second was the expansion and diversification of this enrollment as a result of the influx into the American population of large numbers of immigrants whose backgrounds were different from the Northern and Western Europeans who dominated earlier migrations. During the first half of the nineteenth century, this movement was spearheaded by the arrival of Catholics, largely from Ireland. Adding to that number in the second half of the century were other groups, including Catholics and Jews from Eastern and Southern Europe. Increasing this diversity even further was the limited access to schools provided, albeit in segregated settings, to former African slaves. The third factor was the transformation of America from a largely rural and agrarian society to an urban industrialized one. The fourth factor was the demand for new knowledge to explain and control the effects of this growth and diversity.

For many but not all Americans, these factors represented a challenge to the political, economic, and cultural life of the nation. A host of informal and quasi-formal educational institutions that appeared during the early days of settlement required increasing organization to create a formal system of schooling for transforming British subjects into American citizens. Rendering this work more complicated, and injecting it with myriad forms of conflict over the next two centuries, was the need to create more elaborate institutional structures that could provide for a growing and more diverse school population of immigrants and former slaves in the midst of the market revolution, rapid industrialization, and growing urbanization (Howe, 2007; Kaestle, 1983; Ravitch, 2001; Reuben, 2005; Reese, 2005; Sellers, 1991; Tyack, 1974; Wiebe, 1967; Zimmerman, 2002). And paralleling these structural requirements were the efforts within the emerging fields of education, psychology, and sociology for such new regulative discourses to explain and rationalize these changes as those provided by the notion of community (Franklin, 1986; Popkewitz, 2008).

Early twentieth century American intellectuals developed two discourses to account for these changes and to point to different and conflicting notions of civic literacy. For one group of these thinkers—Edward A. Ross and Edward L. Thorndike in the fields of sociology and psychology respectively, as well as such educators as David Snedden and Ross L. Finney—the changes that we have described were troubling and in effect threatening to the established social order. These individuals were native-born Americans and for the most part products of Eastern and Midwestern small, rural towns. They were the descendents of those who originally came to America from Northern and Western Europe and were Protestant in religion. As these individuals saw it, American democracy was embodied in the values and attitudes of the rural town. They saw the growing diversity of the population, particularly the presence of large numbers of Eastern and Southern Europeans, as a danger to what they believed was a homogeneous American culture reflecting the lives and culture of the native-born, Protestant inhabitants of small rural towns.

It was the small size and the deep, face-to-face personal relationships that were possible in these restricted settings that seemed to provide for the feelings of intimacy and like-mindedness to form what they believed was a homogeneous culture and a democratic polity. The arrival of increasing numbers of Eastern and Southern European immigrants and African Americans represented a challenge to this supposed unity and uniformity (Franklin, 1986, 2010). The notion of community was the term that they often used to describe the discursive field embodying these concerns and aspirations (Camicia & Franklin, 2010).

These intellectuals were never all that certain that immigrants could acquire the knowledge and attitudes that they believed American citizens required. They held for the most part to a hereditarian understanding of human characteristics and saw this seeming incapacity for acquiring the outlook of democratic citizenship as rooted in the inherent makeup of these populations. Holding to that viewpoint, they framed a two-prong solution to the dilemmas that they perceived diversity posed to the nation. If at all possible, they favored keeping these immigrants from entering the country and supported policies of immigration restriction. Believing in effect that these individuals were inherently incapable of adjusting to the demands of American citizenship, they advocated immigration regulations that would restrict their entry into the country. When those policies failed over time, they turned to regulative institutions, particularly the public schools, to socialize this immigrant population with the knowledge, values, and dispositions that they identified as constituting American citizenship. As Ross noted in his 1920 *Principles of Sociology*, society required institutions to "nationalize" its diverse populations with correct ideas and attitudes. "The Tsars relied on the blue-domed Orthodox church in every peasant village to Russify their heterogeneous subjects, while we Americans rely for unity on the 'little red school house'" (1920, 409).

The central task of the schools for these thinkers was to build a sense of community by instilling immigrants and others who were thought to be less able with what they saw as American beliefs, attitudes, and standards of behavior. It was to be largely a process of imposition, reflecting their belief in an emerging behavioral psychology, in which these children would be virtually conditioned to adhere to proper beliefs and standards of behavior. University of Minnesota educational sociologist Ross L. Finney was one of the clearest exponents of this view:

> Ours are the schools of a democracy, which all the children attend. At least half of them never had an original idea of any general nature, and never will. But they must behave as if they had sound ideas. Whether these ideas are original or not matters not in the least. It is better to be right than to be original. What the duller half of the population needs, therefore, is to have their reflexes conditioned into behavior that is socially suitable. And the wholesale memorizing of catchwords—provided that they are sound ones—is the only

practical means of establishing bonds in the duller intellects between the finds of social scientists and the corresponding behavior of the masses. Instead of trying to teach dullards to think for themselves, the intellectual leaders must think for them, and drill the result memoriter into their synapses. For the dullards it is that or nothing. (1928, 395)

Those who subscribed to this position often doubted that education could resolve their concerns (Franklin, 1986, 2010). Their beliefs have ebbed and flowed over the course of this century, and despite the more accepting view of immigration in reaction to the rise of fascism and American participation in World War II, they espouse a brand of civic literacy embedded with a suspicious if not outright hostile view toward certain immigrant groups. The notion of community to which they subscribed was one that acted to exclude immigrants from the life of the nation.

III.

There was another group of intellectuals—John Dewey, George Herbert Mead, and Charles Horton Cooley—who despite similar backgrounds to the thinkers we have just considered introduced a very different discourse for talking about a notion of community and the place of immigrants and blacks in American society. For these individuals, diversity was a source of strength for the America of their day. They did not fear those whom they considered outsiders but rather welcomed them as a source of rich ideas and innovative practices that would enrich society. Their understanding of community was one that was built on the mutual adjustment of all segments of society to a commonly agreed-on set of values, attitudes, and standards of behavior reflecting the diverse cultural practices of the population. The resulting like-mindedness was not one that would subordinate one set of beliefs to others but rather would incorporate these various cultural practices into a common and shared community. Securing this adjustment and mutuality was the task of a democratic brand of social control that was to be entrusted to a host of social institutions including the schools (Franklin, 1986, 2010).

Dewey was, as it turns out, the most important spokesperson for this understanding of community. As he saw it, the arrival of immigrants and others in the midst of a society that was becoming increasingly urban and industrialized did have the effect of undermining an older brand of intimate, face-to-face relationships and the sense of identity that it had infused throughout the dominant population. The result in Dewey's words was a "Great Society" that lacked an important element of his more desirable "Great Community," namely the reciprocal interplay and mutual adjustment among group members in shaping an agreed-upon set of common purposes (Dewey, 1927, 147). Individuals, according to Dewey, did not live in isolation from each other but rather were joined together in society. Society was democratic, he went on to say, to the extent that majority and minority opinion could be shaped into a unified whole. The relationship that emerged was a reciprocal one with shared goals to which all its members were committed. Such an outcome did not require the kind of homogeneity that Ross and others sought. Rather what was required was the bringing together of the various members of society to form a shared and mutual accord that was built out of the give and take of the group and the resulting ultimate agreement (Franklin, 2010).

Despite developing a theory of community, Dewey is sometimes criticized for not having provided an explicit description of the community that he envisioned and how it might be realized. There were, however, individuals and groups during the interwar years that offered a more concrete view of civic literacy (Benson, Harkavy, & Puckett, 2007). One such individual was Leonard Covello, an Italian immigrant and principal of New York City's Benjamin Franklin High School from 1934 to 1956. A proponent of the intercultural education movement of the 1930s and 1940s, Covello saw his school as a vehicle for connecting his students and their families to the East Harlem community that the school served and to American society more broadly. His efforts included using the curriculum to explore a host of problems that the community faced in the areas of health, parent education, recreation, housing, and sanitation, and bringing together students and community members to attempt to resolve them.

The school, in other words, became a place for bringing together diverse viewpoints about a host of community problems. To enhance this effort, Covello established a number of committees within the school to bring about citizen participation. One such group was the Community Advisory Council, which was composed of a number of subcommittees that addressed such problems as health, citizenship, parent education, race, and guidance. Another group were the street units that were physically located outside the school in storefronts in surrounding neighborhoods that served as venues to bring together residents, business owners, parents, teachers, and students to work together to improve the neighborhood surrounding the school. These street units sponsored a community garden, provided meeting space for community groups, and established educational programs, employment services, and citizenship training for Italian- and Spanish-speaking immigrants (Banks, 2004; Montalto, 1981; Johanek & Puckett, 2007).

A decade later the schools of Holtville, Alabama, undertook a similar effort to link their educational program to the problems that the surrounding community faced. One such dilemma was the declining productivity of the region's farms. Holtville students undertook a study of the problem and were able to identify a number of ways of increasing yields through crop rotation and diversified farming, which they communicated to local farmers. They also learned about the use of check dams to control soil erosion and communicated this information to local farmers. Another problem that students in Holtville addressed was that of nutrition. After studying the diet of local residents, the students suggested a number of ways that farmers could improve the nutrition of local residents, including the production of more diversified crops and the establishment of an area refrigeration facility so that fresh produce and meat could be readily available throughout the year (Franklin, 1988).

IV.

The last half of the twentieth century, and now the twenty-first, have seen a number of important social, political, and economic transformations that have altered the discursive terrain in which discussions of civic literacy can and should take place. These are in effect changes that have introduced increased tension and conflict over issues of civic participation. They include battles over the national and universal nature of citizenship, struggles surrounding race, gender, disability, and sexual orientation as they affect aspirations for equal treatment and social justice, and the economic dislocations associated with globalization. Also included are developments in social science knowledge—especially those associated with a widening acceptance of postmodern and poststructural explanatory categories—that have affected our understanding of these transformations and their resulting conflicts (Dean, 1994; Olssen, Codd, & O'Neill, 2004; Popkewitz, 2008; Wagner, 1994).

These changes have created new demands upon civic education to be responsive to, in particular, the asymmetrical power relations within and between democratic communities, both locally and globally. This has led to critical orientations to civic literacy in local, national, and global communities, orientations that prepare students to solve shared problems while accounting for the power imbalances within and between communities (Banks et al., 2005). In what follows, we describe multiple views related to critical civic literacy that attempt to understand how curriculum can help students participate democratically and justly in increasingly multicultural and global communities. In particular, we examine strands related to multicultural education, democratic education, and post-colonial theory. We believe that these three lenses are productive in understanding new directions in critical civic literacy and different visions of community.

Critical civic literacy complements these approaches by adding the lenses of power and positionality to learning activities, discussions, and civic action. Post-structural theorists such as Foucault (1990), Derrida (1976), Lather (1992), and Butler (1997) have provided productive lenses to understand how power functions within education and society. The degree to which a citizen can speak is largely a function of how knowledge and power operate within classrooms and the community at large (Anyon, 2005; Apple & Franklin, 2004; Camicia, 2008; Pinar, 1998). This implies that the degree to which students' voices are recognized is related to the positionalities that they bring into their classrooms. Identities such as those related to race, ethnicity, gender, sexual orientation, language, and class, combine to create overlapping forms of oppression (Collins, 2000). When teachers ignore these forms of oppression, the dominant voices of a society perpetuate their oppressions in classrooms.

Critical democratic and civic literacy depend upon representation of all groups within the curriculum. This representation is only possible if the power inequities of the larger community are examined within the classroom. Philosophers of democratic theory have long held that the legitimacy of decisions in a democracy are proportional to the degree to which all who are affected by policies take part in the deliberation of such policies (Camicia, 2010; Habermas, 1996; Young, 2000). Critical civic literacy opens space within the curriculum by providing students with opportunities to explicitly examine how power and knowledge are connected in the deliberation of public issues.

Up to this point, we have mentioned critical civic literacy in relation to lenses that are largely contained between stakeholders and groups within local and national geopolitical boundaries. Postcolonial and global education theorists help frame the way that power asymmetries are produced, reproduced, and deconstructed on a global scale (Camicia & Bayon, in press; Merryfield & Subedi, 2001; Willinsky, 1998). Although these literatures are vast, they are used by some in critical civic literacy to help students identify the ways that dominant cultures and nations have used representation and misrepresentation as tools of domination. Rather than focusing exclusively on local and national communities, global education uses postcolonial lenses to conceive of a global or cosmopolitan community. The themes found in intergroup, multicultural, post-structural, and democratic education are extended to a global public. Students learn how local and national narratives serve to enhance the knowledge and power relationship on a global level that serves to keep dominant nations in positions of domination.

An elementary school that Camicia is now researching in California illustrates an attempt to implement critical civic literacy in a way similar to what we have proposed so far. The majority of the students at the school are recent immigrants from Mexico, Central America, and South America. The school is a dual-language—Spanish and English—immersion school. Students speak and learn in Spanish half of the day and English during the other half of the day. In alignment with the framework that we provided above, the school curriculum decenters English as the dominant language in the curriculum and empowers Spanish-speaking students in a society that uses English to reinforce oppressive power asymmetries in relation to many immigrant students and their families. Both Spanish learners and English learners are language learners in the curriculum.

As a further illustration, a white, male, sixth-grade teacher, whom we call Mr. Hanford, provides a decolonizing curriculum in his classroom that connects the school with the larger community. He accomplishes this by providing opportunities for students to examine issues relevant to their lives such as power asymmetries related to immigration policy, same-sex marriage policy, and school funding. In an inquiry-based format, students gather data such as immigration policy statements and statistics, voter pamphlet texts, and campaign literature to perform discourse analysis related to themes having a direct impact on their lives. Specifically, Mr. Hanford helps students identify the ways that representation, misrepresentation, and text within public conversations serve to reify socially constructed hierarchies of oppression. These examinations often have a global and historical perspective that emphasizes power asymmetries. Finally, Mr. Hanford helps students and their families identify laws and public services aimed at solving issues of social injustice within their community. This is empowering to undocumented students and creates strong bonds among the school, students, their families, and the larger community.

The historical and contemporary strands of civic literacy that we examine are illustrations of how a shift in the meanings, discourses, and discursive fields related to civic literacy is closely connected to the meaning of community. This connection works both ways; understandings of community shape the civic literacy curriculum. In the first part of this essay we identified two conflicting discourses about community that early twentieth-century American intellectuals, including educators invoked in their efforts for addressing and rationalizing the political, social, and economic transformations that the national community was then experiencing. The focus of their attention in dealing with these changes was the increasing diversity of the population in the wake of a growing immigration from Eastern and Southern Europe and the migration of African Americans from the rural South to the urban North. One such civic republican discourse was exclusionary, perceived diversity as a threat, and sought to contain it in the name of like-mindedness and homogeneity. The notion of community was that of a finished project in which future generations and marginalized notions of community needed to assimilate to this finished project.

The other discourse of civic literacy was inclusionary, saw diversity as making a positive contribution to the nation, and sought to develop a shared and common culture reflecting those differences. Of the two discourses of civic literacy that we examine here, it has been the more inclusionary one, reflecting largely the views of Dewey, that has come to dominate our contemporary educational discourse. The notion of community in this inclusionary version of civic literacy is that community is an unfinished project. Dominant perspectives are subject to change, contingent, and responsive to issues of social justice.

In the second part of our essay we explored how what was essentially a Deweyan formulation of the idea of community has come under multiple intellectual influences. The most important of those influences for new and responsive notions of community are those that arise from postmodern and poststructural thinkers, because they examine power asymmetries in the deliberation and engagement of community issues. This shift in the discursive field has shaped the notion of critical civic literacy into one that we can use to guide the curriculum and pedagogical decisions that are required of contemporary educators in the twenty-first century.

The different orientations to civic literacy that characterize our current thinking about community implies different scopes, qualities, and relationships within and between communities. While visions of a global community have been a part of discourses of civic education for a long time, the consideration of this topic in the United States has tended to focus on local and national communities. This restricted viewpoint has been the one that we saw in the first half of this essay as characterizing discussions of community during the early to mid years of the twentieth century. In the remainder of the essay, we went on to explore the shift in meanings, discourses, and the discursive field toward a new vision of community as agonistic pluralism that recognizes that democracy and communities are always unfinished projects. Conflict can be productive in bringing about socially just outcomes for communities with diverse perspectives and interests (Mouffe, 2000). Rather than search for completeness in our notion of community, this perspective views community and related critical civic literacy as best when they are responsive to a shifting field of power relations. This new vision emphasizes that identity and geopolitical belonging affect the relative power of voices in the public sphere. This attention to power asymmetries on local, national, and global levels has challenged traditional republican models of civic education with critical civic literacy.

We conclude that, as a response to the complexity involved with critical civic literacy, more work needs to be done with incorporating theorists such as Butler and Derrida, who point to a postmodern ethics of recognition within communities. This recognition can only be accomplished when democratic alliances are formed with attention to the relative privilege of some voices over others. This ethic implies a critical civic literacy for current and future students who are faced with shared global issues such as resource depletion, climate change, oppressive debt structures, and human migration. In the face of accelerating globalization, market pressures, standardization, and accountability, citizens of local, national, and global communities can form alliances that create communities that are responsive on many levels and driven by demands for social justice.

Bibliography

Anyon, J. (2005). *Radical possibilities: Public policy, urban education, and a new social movement.* New York: Routledge.
Apple, M.W., & Franklin, B.M. (2004). Curricular history and social control. In M.W. Apple, *Ideology and curricu-*

lum (3rd ed., pp. 59–76). New York: RoutledgeFalmer.

Banks, C.A.M. (2004). Intercultural and intergroup education, 1929–1959. In J.A. Banks (Ed.), *Handbook of research on multicultural education* (2nd ed., pp. 753–769) San Francisco, CA: Jossey-Bass.

Banks, C.A.M. (2005). *Improving multicultural education: Lessons from the intergroup education movement.* New York: Teachers College Press.

Banks, J.A., Banks, C.A.M., Cortés, C.E., Hahn, C.L., Merryfield, M.M., Moodley, K.A., et al. (2005). *Democracy and diversity: Principles and concepts for educating citizens in a global age.* Seattle, WA: Center for Multicultural Education, University of Washington.

Benson, L., Harkavy, I., & Puckett, J.L. (2007). *Dewey's dream: Universities and democracies in an age of education reform— Civil society, public schools, and democratic citizenship.* Philadelphia: Temple University Press.

Burgos, R. (2003). Partnership as a floating and empty signifier within educational policies: The Mexican case. In B.M. Franklin, M. Bloch, & T. Popkewitz (Eds.), *Educational partnerships and the state: The paradoxes of governing schools, children, and familes* (pp. 57–79). New York: Palgrave Macmillan.

Butler, J. (1997). *Excitable speech: A politics of the performative.* New York: Routledge.

Camicia, S.P. (2008). Deciding what is a controversial issue: A case study of social studies curriculum controversy. *Theory and Research in Social Education, 36*(4), 290–307.

Camicia, S.P. (2010). Deliberation of controversial public school curriculum: Developing processes and outcomes that increase legitimacy and social justice. *Journal of Public Deliberation, 6*(2), 1–20.

Camicia, S.P., & Franklin, B.M. (2010). Curriculum reform in a globalised world: The discourses of cosmopolitanism and community. *London Review of Education, 8*(2), 93–104.

Camicia, S.P., & Bayon, A. (in press). Democratic education curriculum development between the colonizer and the colonized: Complexities, contradictions, obstacles, and possibilities of global alliances. In T. C. Mason & R. J. Helfenbein (Eds.), *Ethics and international curriculum work: The challenges of culture and context.*

Collins, P.H. (2000). *Black feminist thought: Knowledge, consciousness, and the politics of empowerment.* New York: Routledge.

Dean, M. (1994). *Critical and effective histories: Foucault's methods and historical sociology.* New York: Routledge.

Derrida, J. (1976). *Of grammatology* (G.C. Spivak, Trans.). Baltimore: The Johns Hopkins University Press.

Dewey, J. (1927). *The public and its problems.* New York: Henry Holt.

Finney, R.L. (1928). *A sociological philosophy of education.* New York: Macmillan.

Foucault, M. (1990). *The history of sexuality: Volume I: An introduction* (R. Hurley, Trans.). New York: Vintage Books.

Franklin, B.M. (1986). *Building the American community: The school curriculum and the search for social control.* London: Falmer Press.

Franklin, B.M. (1988). Education for an urban America: Ralph Tyler and the curriculum field. In I. Goodson (Ed.), *Inernational perspectives in curriculum history* (pp. 277–296). New York: Routledge.

Franklin, B.M. (2010). *Curriculum, community, and urban school reform.* New York: Palgrave Macmillan.

Gay, G. (2000). *Culturally responsive teaching: Theory, research, and practice.* New York: Teachers College Press.

Habermas, J. (1996). *Between facts and norms: Contributions to a discourse theory of law and democracy* (W. Rehg, Trans.). Cambridge, MA: MIT Press.

Howe, D.W. (2007). *What hath God wrought: The transformation of America, 1815–1848.* New York: Oxford University Press.

Johanek, M.C., & Pucket, J.L. (2007). *Leonard Covello and the making of Benjamin Franklin High School: Education as if citizesnship mattered.* Philadelphia: Temple University Press.

Kaestle, C.F. (1983). *Pillars of the republic: Common schools and American society.* New York: Hill and Wang.

Laclau, E. (1994). Why do empty signifiers matter to politics? In J. Weeks (Ed.), *The lesser evil and the greater good: The theory and politics of social diversity* (pp. 167–178). London: Oram Press.

Ladson-Billings, G. (1994). *The dreamkeepers: Successful teachers of African American children.* San Francisco, CA: Jossey-Bass.

Lather, P.A. (1992). Post-critical pedagogies: A feminist reading. *Feminisms and critical pedagogy* (pp. 120–137). New York: Routledge.

Merryfield, M.M., & Subedi, B. (2001). Decolonizing the mind for world-centered global education. In E.W. Ross

(Ed.), *The social studies curriculum: Purposes, problems, and possibilities* (pp. 277–290). Albany: State University of New York Press.

Moll, L.C., & González, N. (2004). Engaging life: A funds-of-knowledge approach to multicultural education. In J.A. Banks & C.A.M. Banks (Eds.), *Handbook of research on multicultural education* (2nd ed., pp. 699–715). San Francisco, CA: Jossey-Bass.

Montalto, N.V. (1981). Multicultural education in the New York City public schools, 1919–1941. In D. Ravitch & R.K. Goodenow (Eds.), *Educating an urban people: The New York City experience* (pp. 67–83). New York: Teachers College Press.

Mouffe, C. (2000). *The democratic paradox.* London: Verso.

Olssen, M., Codd, J., & O'Neill, A.-M. (2004). *Education policy: Globalization, citizenship and democracy.* London: Sage Publications.

Pinar, W.F. (Ed.). (1998). *Queer theory in education.* Mahwah, NJ: Lawrence Erlbaum Associates.

Popkewitz, T.S. (2008). *Cosmopolitanism and the age of school reform: Science, education, and making society by making the child.* New York: Routledge.

Ravitch, D. (2001). Education and democracy. In D. Ravitch & J.P. Viteritti (Eds.), *Making good citizens* (pp. 15–29). New Haven, CT: Yale University Press.

Reese, W.J. (2005). *America's public schools: From the common school to "No Child Left Behind."* Baltimore: The Johns Hopkins University Press.

Reuben, J.A. (2005). Patriotic purposes: Public schools and the education of citizens. In S. Fuhrman & M. Lazerson (Eds.), *The public schools* (pp. 1–24). New York: Oxford University Press.

Ross, E.A. (1920). *Principles of sociology.* New York: The Century Company.

Sellers, C. (1991). *The market revolution: Jacksonian America, 1815–1846.* New York: Oxford University Press.

Tyack, D. (1974). *The one best system: A history of American urban education.* Cambridge, MA: Harvard University Press.

Wagner, P. (1994). *A sociology of modernity: Liberty and discipline.* London: Routledge.

Wiebe, R. (1967). *The search for order, 1877–1920.* New York: Hill and Wang.

Willinsky, J. (1998). *Learning to divide the world: Education at empire's end.* Minneapolis: University of Minnesota Press.

Young, I.M. (2000). *Inclusion and democracy.* New York: Oxford University Press.

Zimmerman, J. (2002). *Whose America? Culture wars in the public schools.* Cambridge, MA: Harvard University Press.

CHAPTER ELEVEN

Critical Civic Engagement from Inside an Australian School and Its Community Put at a Disadvantage [1]

JOHN SMYTH

Introduction: The Nature of the Paper

It is important that I say something about what kind of essay this is from the outset. It is different, not only because of where I am situated, in Australia, but also because of the way I want to provide a different 'take' on critical civics literacy. I am not so much concerned about the loss of social capital or the absence of civic knowledge and competency among young people, pressing though these might be, nor with how to craft, implement, and teach a better civics program and transport it to a service learning context. Rather, my intention is much more grandiose in that I want to attempt to provide some insights from a case study analysis of what critical civics literacy might look like when viewed from the 'underside' of a school and a community officially labeled as being 'disadvantaged.' I want to look at this official government designation and an intervention initiative that occurred as a result of it, as well as at an insurgent response from within the community. (For an extended critique of Australian governments' attempts at 'social inclusion,' see Smyth, 2010.) In the process, I want to get up close to and inside the experiences of the participants in the school and community setting, and to understand these from their vantage point. In that respect, this is an essay about the capacity of a community to become involved in community organizing in speaking back to a place-based government intervention, with a view to supplanting it with an alternative that has a more democratic intent. In that regard, this is a paper about trying to get inside and understand what living critical civic competency and activism might actually mean.

Dispensing with a Key Definitional Issue

As Teitelbaum (Chapter 2 in this book) explains, critical civic literacy involves the ability to not only 'decode and make meaning of the world around us but also to employ information and abilities for active engagement with and within civic relationships and institutions,' in other words, 'becoming/being active democratic citizens.' Invoking Apple, Wu, & Gandin (2009), Teitelbaum concurs that adopting a critical stance requires a questioning of fundamental assumptions, policies, practices, and structures in ways that challenge 'the underlying epistemological and ideological assumptions that are made about what counts as "official" or legitimate knowledge and who holds it.' This entails developing what Bartolome (2007) calls political and ideological clarity, where:

> "Political clarity" refers to the ongoing process by which individuals achieve ever-deepening consciousness of the sociopolitical and economic realities that shape their lives and their capacity to transform such material and symbolic conditions…[while] "Ideological clarity" refers to the process by which individuals struggle to identify and compare their own explanations for the existing socioeconomic and political hierarchy with the dominant society's. (p. 264)

I argue here that both of these are crucial.

Brookfield (2005) describes the kind of critical reflection involved in critical civic literacy as being 'the learning tasks of critical theory' (p. 39), and he envisages the critical intellectual work as entailing seven key elements: 'learning to challenge ideology, contest hegemony, unmask power, overcome alienation, pursue liberation, reclaim reason, and practice democracy' (p. 65).

Something about the Specific Context, the Case, Its Times and Circumstances

In 2001 the State of Victoria, Australia, embarked on an adventurous program designed to redress the imbalance of an uneven playing field for groups in society who for a variety of reasons were being increasingly excluded, silenced, marginalized, and left behind socially and economically despite relatively prosperous times. As part of the broader government agenda to build more cohesive communities and reduce inequalities, it introduced a place-based intervention referred to as *Neighbourhood Renewal: Growing Victoria Together*. The well-meaning intent and purpose of the program was to provide ways of involving residents to a much greater extent than had previously been the case in identifying problems and having a say in how external assistance might be best targeted and applied to the alleviation of disadvantage and inequality. On the surface, this appeared to be a dramatic departure from previous heavy-handed, top-down bureaucratic, and all-knowing approaches that rode roughshod over the lives, experiences, and aspirations of the people who were supposed to be the beneficiaries. The espoused intent in the first 10 communities in which this intervention was initiated, was to:

- 'empower local communities to shape their own futures…'
- 'working together…government and community resources will be harnessed and better co-ordinated…'
- 'changes will be made around people and the places they live, work and play, to better connect government programs to real community needs' (Department of Human Services, 2002).

Neighbourhood Renewal, as it was known, was envisaged as a way of connecting 'bottom up' involvement by residents with 'top down' processes of government at local, regional, state and federal levels.

Eight years later, in a community I will call Olympic Estate, community surveys indicate residents believe there to have been 'a 23 per cent increase in perceived levels of safety, a 28 per cent increase in perceived levels of community participation, and a 26 percent increase in perceived levels of belonging…with a remarkable 84 per cent improvement in pre-school enrolments' (Department of Human Services, 2009, p. 4). Clearly, on these kind of indicators something was changing in this community that looked at a surface level as if the community felt it was being treated differently.

Going back to the 1950s, Olympic Estate was a community that was predominantly a public welfare housing area that had a reputation for having significant problems and toward which there were serious negative attitudes by the wider town of which it was a part. There was a significant stigma associated with being seen to live in Olympic Estate. In the 1990s it was regarded as an area in significant decline and something of a basket case. It seemed that there was a remarkable turnaround occurring in this community including in its school as a result of the new initiative.

Much has, therefore, been achieved over the eight years of the renewal intervention in Olympic Estate, including the demolition of two schools and the construction of a new state-of-the-art facility. What has been achieved ought not to be ignored or diminished, but it is also clear that much remains to be done especially around the way the school, the community, and the various government departments and other agencies relate to one another and work to benefit the community.

Genuine Community Voice

The larger framing issue that is central to what has occurred in Olympic Estate is community voice, and eight years on it is still the elephant in the room. While there have been various points at which the community feels it has been consulted, there remain significant issues around which the community feels it has been slighted, ignored, marginalized, and silenced—one of the most contentious being the move from the concept design to the bricks-and-mortar realization of the school-community hub, as the school is now called.

If we think about civic literacy, or civic engagement, as being the practical embodiment—to use Milner's (2002) words—of 'how informed citizens make democracy work,' then having a living, working exemplar of democracy in a school-community partnership learning facility ought to be a crucial and indispensable element. With this in mind, and having worked extensively in a previous research project in Olympic Estate from 2002 to 2009, myself and colleagues were invited to design an action research project with the objective of producing 'sustainable and successful school-community-partnerships, which aim to enhance health, development and learning outcomes for children, young people and the broader community' (from the RQP).

There are various registers or genres in which community voice can be given expression. To borrow from Westheimer & Kahne (2004), in response to the question 'What kind of citizen do we need to support an effective democratic society?' they provide a threefold typology: 'the *personally responsible citizen*; the *participatory citizen*; and the *justice-oriented citizen*' (p. 239). Each of these has a qualitatively different emphasis that may give us a window into how and in what ways community voice might be given expression and how that occurred (or not) in the case of Olympic Estate.

The *personally responsible citizen* is one who 'acts responsibly in his or her community,' is willing to 'help those less fortunate,' and displays all the qualities of 'honesty, integrity, self-discipline, and hard work' (p. 241). While these are eminently laudable and admirable qualities, they are nevertheless ones that in many respects represent dominant societal views about what it means to be a 'good citizen,' and to that extent they may rest somewhat uneasily with people who lead more colourful lives or who at some point have fallen afoul of the law. Indeed, it might just be the case, as was pointed out to us in Olympic Estate, that people here don't see themselves as citizens so much as 'residents.' This distinction is not just a matter of semantic quibbling. Being a citizen implies a set of relationships, rights, obligations, and responsibilities that are qualitatively quite different from what it means to be a resident or have residency—which have connotations much more to do with one's place of abode, habitation and permanency of place. When a person shifts from a state of homelessness, is resettled because of family fragmentation or breakdown, employment, insufficient educational qualifications, or a collapse of the labour market, then having security of residency is crucial. In these circumstances, to be able to say you have 'a place' is fundamental to re-defining one's identity and may have little to do with altruism or civic mindedness that come much further up the needs hierarchy.

The *participatory citizen*, in contrast, is one who has some sense of and 'actively participate[s] in the civic and social life of the community' (Westheimer & Kahne 2004, p. 241). These are people who have a sense that it is important to participate beyond what is legally required or morally expected by being actively involved in activities that have some benefit to making the community and society a better place. Again, there is a kind of Judaeo-Christian ethic operating here that may or may not resonate with communities who themselves have been 'done to' by the forces of globalization, de-industrialization, and the operations of the welfare industry. It could be, for example, that people from contexts that have *put them* at a disadvantage, regard collective activity more as a circuit breaker for cycles of despair and isolation and as ways of connecting with others in contexts of family dysfunction and breakdown. In other words, they may affiliate for much less loftier and altruistic reasons than those being suggested by Westheimer & Kahne (2004). There may be much more pragmatic reasons having to do with the need for otherwise absent extended relationships.

Finally, the *justice-oriented citizen* is the one who is supposedly animated by the need for and 'opportunities to analyze and understand the interplay of social, economic and political forces' and in engaging with these to explicitly attend to 'matters of injustice and to the importance of pursuing social justice' (Westheimer & Kahne, 2004, p. 242). According to Westheimer & Kahne (2004), this is 'the perspective that is least commonly pursued' (p. 242). Now, this may well be the case in largely middle-class settings where there is little motivation to upset the advantaging status quo, but in the kind of communities I am speaking of it may actually be the case that those who experience the greatest injustice are also the most astute analysts of how they got to be in that situation in the first place, what it means to experience injustice, how power operates, what material conditions exist to sustain and maintain inequality, and what needs to be done to change that. What I am suggesting, therefore, is that the view of the justice-oriented citizen being constructed by Westheimer & Kahne is a very partial one that is being imposed from a largely middle-class perspective. What it assumes a priori is a deficit view of the capacity and willingness of the people most affected, to be informed about and activist in respect to changing their situations. To suggest otherwise is at best demeaning, and at worst arrogant.

The kind of typology being advanced by Westheimer & Kahne (2004), while seemingly helpful in some ways, may not in the end be that useful when absent from an actual context that enables us to gauge its efficacy. Let me proceed to take the next step of providing something of that context in the case of Olympic Estate.

Community-Centred Action Research

We commenced a community-centred action research process in Olympic Estate in July 2009. What this entailed was a structured process intended to provide both a forum through which ideas and discussion could surface in a non-threatening way (so much as that can ever be possible), as well as a means by which we could get up close to and understand how people in the community and the school were thinking about a partnership they had become involved in. Our approach was one that was heavily skewed in the direction of actively listening to what people had to say. We didn't have an agenda beyond hearing what people had to say, we didn't come in with a package of 'solutions' to their problems, and all we had was a desire to provide a process that might help them to find a way to move from paralysis and despondency, to positive action. We crashed headlong into both of these challenges early on in the project, even to the point where the project had to take an enforced, 6-month 'pause' because of heightened tensions. We also had no blueprint as to how this was all going to work, beyond our gut feeling, a little bit of accumulated wisdom, and a small bank of goodwill from having worked in and been connected to this community for several years. Our overall positioning was one of listening, reflecting back, helping people to identify obstacles, and finally working with them to develop what we called 'local solutions.'

Our action research approach to community engagement (Smyth & Harrison, 2009) had five phases to it:

1. Listen/Talk

What this amounted to was us as facilitators/researchers actively creating public forums or spaces with an unstructured agenda in which people could speak openly about topics and issues that would otherwise have been impossible or engage in discussions that would have been closed down. Formal meetings with representational constituencies, all of whom had axes to grind, were typical of how genuine public debate was being stifled in Olympic Estate. Open and honest forums had ceased to exist in this community, and their absence was a source of much anguish. We found that once we could engender a degree of trust around being seen to be honest brokers, then people were prepared to discuss and reveal things that—once made public—were able to be acted upon. An example of the way we did this was through organizing a *Community Listening Forum*, which occurred on October 29, 2009, attended by 45 people, in which the aim was to hear what the community thought about the school-community learning partnership. The broad themes from the unstructured small group and reporting-back discussions took the form of responses to a number of tentative questions about the nature of the partnership:

- What does the partnership exist for?
- Do I feel a part of the partnership?
- What works well in the partnership?
- What could work better?
- How could the partnership work for the *whole* of this community?

If there was a single word to characterize this phase, it was 'dialogue.'

2. Collect/Research

Having opened up some dialogic space with the school and community during the *Listen/Talk* phase, particularly through our initiation of the *Community Listening Forum*, we embarked on a round of ethnographic interviews. These interview conversations provided a more detailed way into the broader themes from the *Community Listening Forum*. It was also a way for the most marginalized or silenced viewpoints to be heard. During November 2009 we undertook 28 of these ethnographic interviews with a total of 65 people (made up of 39 residents, 4 community leaders, 5 agency employees, 5 representatives of government departments, and a focus group of 12 students).

3. Reflect/Refine

Having done a good deal of listening, this was the point at which the research team retreated from the site and engaged in some 'sense making' around what had been learned from phases 1 and 2. This was considered to be an important precursor to reflecting ideas back to the community as a possible basis for any action they might want to take in relation to the working of the school-community learning partnership. What guided our reflections and the refining of the issues was the extent to which people believed the partnership had been working as they expected it to.

4. Interrupt/Suggest

Given that this was not a project that presumed to have 'answers' or 'solutions' to other people's problems, we reconnected with the school and the community by having a dialogue around some 'emergent issues' that we presented in a discussion paper in respect of which we conducted a workshop. There were to be two forums—(i) a *Partners' Forum* (made up of all of the partners in the learning partnership), and (ii) *School/Community Governance Forum* (the wider community and school at large). The former occurred on November 20 and was attended by 7 people (3 from the school and 4 from the two community partners in the project), while the latter forum was postponed and eventually abandoned due to the withdrawal of one of the community partners from the learning partnership and the project going into recess while the withdrawal of the partner was sorted out by the partnership consortium.

Without going into detail about what we heard through our 'listenings,' the essence of the 'reflections' we took back were as follows:

- There was a widespread view that the learning partnership was not truly representative of the wider community. The way it was succinctly put to us was that the partnership was dominated by 'the school' upon whose grounds and in whose facility the learning partnership was physically located.
- The governance structure (through which broader policy decisions were made) was seen to be too heavily dominated by 'outsiders' who did not have a day-to-day connectedness to the workings of the learning partnership. The effect of that was that people who had a diminished commitment were allowed too much space in which to run with their private agendas effectively paralysing and sidelining local voices and local issues.
- It was felt that there had been a very significant drift from the original vision of a shared school/community facility and its replacement by outright competition for the use of the facilities.

5. Act/Celebrate

This final phase (in the first cycle) of our action research process was designed to be a culminating element in which the kind of grassroots issues indicated above and which had been allowed to surface, would be listened to, and not be subject to retributive actions, that would enable the community to ponder and debate alternatives and ways to implement them. Coming out of the previous Interrupt/Suggest phase, this involved the following:

- A commitment to radically re-work the governance structure through abandoning an unrepresentative committee (of more than 16 different constituencies) that had operated according to vested interests, and its replacement by a smaller committee (of four) that more closely reflected the immediate interests of the school/community facility and partnership. This occurred in the period up to February 2010, and the potential was created for a broadening of the basis for decision making to include more members from the community, at the expense of outside 'experts.'
- A strong desire to revisit and, if necessary, dramatically revise the vision of the partnership. This occurred at a re-constituted *Community Governance Forum* convened by the research team on July 14, 2010 (after the six-month enforced project 'pause') that was attended by 17 people widely inclusive of the composition of the school and community. A particularly apposite comment made by one community member about this being a "word of mouth community" led to the idea that the re-visioning should be initiated through a "Bring a Friend" Forum—scheduled to occur at the time of writing on August 30, 2010 (but which did not subsequently occur because of community exhaustion). The intention here was to democratize even further the basis of discussions.

By this point in the project we had returned to our original action research starting point with the members of Olympic Estate and its school of *Listen/Talk*. From here we were about to enter another round of *Collect/Research* (more interviews), *Reflect/Refine* (making sense), *Interrupt/Suggest* (reflecting back alternatives), and *Act/Celebrate* (try something out and see what happens).

From this brief snapshot overview of the project, the question to turn to now is: *In what way does what has occurred reveal anything of Critical Civic Engagement?* It is important to ask this question at this stage, and several answers emerge:

This is a community that clearly shows indications of being able to think beyond the immediacy of issues as they affect themselves directly as individuals, in the sense that they understand how power works. They formed an early, politically savvy realization that even the most well-meaning 'outsiders' were not without private agendas, and, at worst, some outsiders were blatantly using this context for their own personal advancement or for bolstering the associated reputations and images of their bureaucratic/political masters—at the expense of grassroots ownership.

There was also a sense that something very fundamental was being tested out here. This was a 'disadvantaged' community that had been provided with a fabulous, state-of-the art facility that offered the children a totally different set of opportunities and life choices than had been afforded their parents. In a sense, then, they could be expected to display a modicum of 'gratefullness' for this, and in turn, appreciative deference to the providers, to the point of acquiescence. In other words, for this community to not allow those who had been so generous to bask at least momentarily in the reflected glow of their beneficence, could be seen to be a little churlish.

Part of this also had to do with the community being able to see beyond the surface immediacy of the bricks-and-mortar of the facility, and the ability of the community to consider the essence of the relationships that existed and their exploitative nature. When relationships came into the frame, what this tested out was the preparedness of outsiders to genuinely believe that the people of this community, who were demonstrably 'disadvantaged' on all measure of outside indicators, could possibly have the capacity to make decisions in their own best interests—especially when such decisions might even run the risk that the facility might be damaged or spoiled as a consequence. What was being sorely tested out in this instance was whether the notion of democracy could be extended to people who to all appearances were in the situation they were in because of 'poor lifestyle choices'—clearly a form of deficit labelling.

If we take Apple, Au, and Gandin's (2009) notion of 'critical' as entailing a capacity to 'expose how relations of power and inequality…are manifest and are challenged' (p. 3), then the instance of Olympic Estate and our engagement with it does display some of the hallmarks of their more robust definition of the critical as involving a 'thorough-going reconstruction of what education is for, how it should be carried out…and who should be empowered to engage in it' (p. 3).

In the case provided here, I have delved a little into something that goes considerably beyond what occurs in classrooms, to the way in which a community is prepared to assert what it sees as its democratic right to organize its school and its partnership with the community in other than a benign, acquiescent, or deferential way. It could be argued that the broader message to students here, albeit in an indirect way, is that while their parents may not have been significant beneficiaries of education, their offspring should not be so reticent in learning what it means to be obdurate in confronting the forces of domination and reproduction. Indeed, it would probably not be an exaggeration to say that this proud community displayed a degree of indignation and activism, when provided with the opportunity, in challenging the status quo that was cemented in place by a dominant but well-meaning professionalism that was orchestrating their lives.

While the community of Olympic Estate would certainly not put it in these terms, there are some signs of the nascent beginnings of what Apple et al. (2009), invoking Fraser (1997), refer to as an exposure of 'the relations of exploitation and domination' (p. 3) and the '*politics of redistribution* (exploitative economic processes and dynamics) and the *politics of recognition* (cultural struggles against domination and struggle over identity' (p. 3; emphases mine).

It seems that in respect to matters having to do with citizen democracy and political issues, what the residents of Olympic Estate were struggling with in their action research encounter with us was a school and a community that existed in some kind of parallel universe. There seemed to be no cross-over between the school and the community in which the students could be witnesses to, learn about, or be involved in the political struggles being engaged in by their parents and the wider community. It was as if these two things had been hermetically sealed lest the school be contaminated by the struggles of the community. Perhaps this is something of an over-interpretation, but it certainly seemed that the school existed in a reality in which community politics were not seen as breaching the classroom door—even though there were matters that regularly collapsed in upon and were a major pre-occupation of the principal, often in quite dramatic ways.

This kind of separation and keeping students at arms length from learning about and being involved in what it means to participate in the democratic politics of their community is not a natural or inalienable state of affairs. Quite the contrary. There are many examples of schools similar to Olympic Community College where this has not been the case and where the struggles of the community are overtly used by the school to allow students to directly experience what it means to confront advantage and injustice. Two that readily come to mind—one with which I have had a close experience in Australia, the case of *Plainsville School* (Smyth & McInerney, 2007a; Smyth & McInerney, 2007b), and the other, *Emily Carr School*, in Canada (McMahon & Portelli, 2004; Vibert, Portelli, Shields, & LaRocque, 2002; discussed in Smyth, 2008). Maybe rather than regarding critical civics in the layered way envisaged by Westheimer & Kahne (2004), we can advance matters by more sensibly pursuing an approach of 'teaching for social justice' of the kind discussed by Stovall (2010), which he describes as:

> the day-to-day processes and actions utilized in classrooms and communities centred in critical analysis, action and reflection (praxis) among all educational stakeholders (students, families, teachers, administrators, community organizations, community members) with the goal of creating tangible change in their communities, cities, states, nation, and the larger world. (p. 38)

Conceptualized as an approach that taps into the 'underutilized expertise of students, parents, families with academic skills to address their conditions' (p. 38), such processes are deeply connected to the issues of people's lives by providing 'a tangible example of what justice looks like in a [school] and in our communities' (p. 39).

Implications for a *Community Organizing Approach* to Critical Civic Engagement

What this chapter has highlighted is that critical civic engagement in the sense of knowing 'how to actively participate in and initiate change in your community and the greater society' (Urban Agenda, n.d.) involves the capacity to create an agenda as 'an avenue to gather support and raise awareness both for the community members and elected officials about what's happening in the community' (Urban Agenda, n.d.). The chapter has also revealed some underlying problems and tensions within a well-meaning, place-based intervention intended to improve people's lives, around an absence of opportunity for community activism, particularly in respect of young people being aware of and having a voice in what is happening in and to their community.

Where the finger accusingly points in this chapter is to the fact that in communities *put at a disadvantage*, there is an imperative to work across a dual front or boundary—community activism and school reform/change. Without this, the effort will have as much effect as the sound of one hand clapping! To invoke Gold, Simon, Mundell, and Brown (2004), there is an incontrovertible and compelling case for "Bringing Community Organizing into the School Reform Picture." To put it at its sharpest, there can be no improvement in student learning in the most disadvantaged schools unless there is school and community activism to force governments at all levels to provide the conditions for improving learning at the same time as improving the material and relational conditions of people's lives in the wider community (Smyth, Angus, Down, & McInerney, 2008; Smyth, Down, & McInerney, 2010).

Community organizing is an approach that had its beginnings in the 1930s through to the 1960s, in the work of of Chicago community organizer and activist Saul Alinksky (1989a, 1989b). Some of Alinsky's ideas have been picked up recently and used in the United States by groups who place themselves broadly under the label of 'community organizing for school reform' (Shirley, 1997, 2002, 2009; Warren, 2001, 2004, 2005; Warren et al., 2009; Mediratta et al., 2001, 2002, 2003, 2008; Gold et al., 2002, 2004, 2005; Zachary & olatoye, 2001). While this movement is a helpful step in a sorely needed direction, it is not always clear exactly how some of this literature connects to Alinsky's ideas and philosophy, and there is a tendency sometimes to drift from the essence of Alinsky's ideas. With that in mind, and in the context of the particular case discussed earlier in this chapter, it may be useful to briefly revisit some of Alinksy's key ideas.

A colourful, flamboyant, even slightly outrageous figure, Alinsky was not at all uncomfortable wearing the label ascribed to him by one of his biographers, Sanford Horwitt (1989), in *Let Them Call Me Rebel*. Because he was not a scholar in the conventional sense, but rather a community activist and organizer of others to agitate for change, it is not always easy to coherently draw out Alinsky's key ideas, but four of them are readily apparent, and below I summarise these as I have explored them in more depth elsewhere (Smyth, 2006, 2009) especially around the central notion in Alinsky of 'relational solidarity' (Smyth, Angus, Down, & McInerney, 2009, pp. 57–62).

1. Relational Immediacy

Residents and parents of young people in low-income communities are most likely to 'buy into' reform processes, whether that be of schools or the wider community, when they can see it is likely to result in tangible and immediate benefits to their own life chances and those of their children. As Warren (2005) put it, they 'are more likely to begin their engagement in community and public life with the issues and institutions that most immediately affect them' (p. 158). The fundamental basis of community organizing is 'face-to-face relationships' (p. 158), or as Avila (2006) calls it, 'conversations around questions that matter' (p. 7). In other words, it is about making connections between people around the issues that concern and worry them in their everyday lives. When we step back and be analytical for a moment, what is really occurring here is a 'relational-organizing' approach in which: 'Change starts through conversations…[and] concerns [and] agenda for action emerge from these conversations and relationships' (p. 160), for example, around immediate concerns for 'safety' (p. 160). Although the language may sound somewhat off-putting because of its tones of indulgence and selfishness, Avila (2008) refers to this aspect of the Alinsky tradition as 'self-interest,' or, as she put it:

> what people really care about and which is important enough for them to want to get deeply involved [in] over a long period of time. (p. 5)

The dual intent of the community organizing approach is to both engage people around issues that hold passion for them, while at the same time changing long-term power relationships. It is 'the art of building relationships while still aiming to build collective power…' (Avila, 2006, p. 4). There is bound to be a level of discomfort in this, as Avila (2006) says, if 'we are to be real with each other, to show our vulnerabilities, our real passion, fears, pain and anger to each other' (p. 6). The challenge, she says, is 'to put all this into a societal context, to create spaces where we can learn, reflect, and act together to create change, to restructure power relations' (p. 6). Actions, therefore, grow 'authentically from…interests and ideas' and have the imprimatur of 'enthusiastic support,' rather than being 'imposed from outside' (Warren, 2005, p. 160). When this occurs, what is really happening is a process of building 'social capital and relational power' (p. 163). What gets spawned through this way of operating are 'initiatives that are strongly rooted in local conditions, interests and values' in which 'educators, parents and community members are committed and enthusiastic' (p. 167). The effect of this kind of participation is that it 'creates a sense of ownership of the change process and a commitment to making it a success' (p. 167).

2. Investment in Indigenous Leadership

Alinsky (1989a) argued that 'native leadership' is crucial to the wider re-workings of power implicit in this approach, and it involves 'those persons whom the local people define and look up to as leaders' (p. 64). He argued that 'most attempts at community organizing have foundered on the rock of native leadership' (p. 65). Allowing and enabling local people to own and develop leadership is central to Alinsky's 'Iron Rule: never do for others what they can do for themselves' (Cortes, 1993, p. 300). In other words, outsiders cannot speak for others, and the best they can do is engage them in ways that teach them 'how to speak, act, and to engage in politics for themselves' (Cortes, 1993, p. 300). Implicit in this indigenous or native approach to leadership is what Warren (2005) refers to as a strong commitment 'to engage and train leaders to take public action for the improvement of their communities' (p. 159)—where leadership training is taken to have a loose and generative rather than a prescriptive meaning. What this means, practically speaking, is regarding community members as 'change agents' rather than 'clients' (p. 163). In other words, 'not as recipients of services, but as public actors and change agents, capable of being leaders of their community' (p. 164), that is, shifting from a situation of 'seeing children, their families and their communities as problems to be fixed, toward an appreciation of their potential strengths and contributions' (p. 166).

What is being advocated is a process of investing ordinary people with power founded on a 'willingness to collaborate and compromise' (Warren, 2005, p. 160). This means moving away from traditional, hierarchical notions of management toward a collaborative model of fostering leadership. Warren (2005) says that 'By paying more explicit attention to questions of power,' what is created is 'relational power' that generates an internal capacity for cultural change. This is a view of leadership that requires an investment in careful and 'patient work' (p. 167), that moves beyond mere involvement of isolated individuals, to one of having a 'collective [view of] leadership' (p. 165) in which power relations are radically transformed.

3. Interdependency

Alinsky (1989a) also argued that power and change lay in numbers, and that power came from being able to organize large numbers of people to act on their own behalf. His single most important article of faith was

> a belief in people, a complete commitment to the belief that if people have power, the opportunity to act, in the long run they will, most of the time, reach the right decisions. (p. xiv)

Alinsky was sanguine enough to realize that collectives of people could not operate alone and that there was a crucial need for dialogue with outsiders. His point is that there needs to be continuous 'dialogue between experts and [an] engaged community' (Warren, 2005, p. 167). Unlike the currently prevalent thin or diminished view of accountability, what we have here is 'accountability to an organized informal constituency' (p. 167). If we follow the lines of effect here, and connect them for our purposes to the instance of schools, then reforming communities in this way produces parent and community partnerships that 'build capacity for change' (p. 166) in schools in quite explicit ways.

4. Painting a Bigger Picture

The idea that school reform might be more constructively based on 'build[ing] relational power beyond the school' (Warren, 2005, p. 162), and that it is political work, is part of a wider set of understandings that to gain power it is necessary to have 'a broader agenda [of] addressing the needs of low-income families' (p. 162), which in effect means attending to the 'broader structural issues' (p. 159) that make things the way they are. In other words, ensuring that there is a broad-based organization and constituency that has 'a vision of education reform linked to the strengthening of civil society' (p. 168). The larger frame is, therefore, a deeply held conviction that problems in low-income communities are 'the result of fundamentally unequal power relationships in our society' (p. 167).

In conclusion, the argument and example analysed in this chapter provides us with some optimism that critical civic engagement has a chance of being brought into existence—if there is an insistence on ideas like those of community organizer and social activist Saul Alinsky. Maybe we need to heed the words of another Aylinsky-ite who urged us to get into 'the habit of relating' (Gecan, 2004).

Note

1. I wish to express my gratitude to my collaborators in the research project upon which this chapter is based, Tim Harrison and Peter McInerney. The ideas in this paper have improved immensely from the dialogue and fied-

work with both of these close colleagues over a long time. Sincere appreciation as well to the members of the school and community of Olympic Estate (my pseudonym), and to the Victorian Department of Education and Early Childhood Development for its support.

Bibliography

Alinsky, S. (1989a). *Rules for radicals: A pragmatic primer for realistic radicals*. New York: Vintage.

Alinsky, S. (1989b). *Reville for radicals*. New York: Vintage Books.

Apple, M., Au, W., & Gandin, L. (2009). Mapping critical education. In M. Apple, W. Au, & L. Gandin (Eds.), *The Routledge International handbook of critical education* (pp. 3–19). New York: Routledge.

Avila, M. (2006). *Transforming society by transforming academic culture*. Unpublished manuscript, Occidental College, Los Angeles, CA.

Avila, M. (2008, April). *How community organizing can build reciprocal academic civic engagement: Stories and voices from an evolving model at Occidental College*. Paper presented at Portland State College.

Bartolome, L. (2007). Critical pedagogy and teacher education: Radicalizing prospective teachers. In P. McLaren & J. Kincheloe (Eds.), *Critical pedagogy: Where are we now?* (pp. 263–286). New York: Peter Lang Publishing.

Brookfield, S. (2005). *The power of critical theory for adult learning and teaching*. Maidenhead: Open University Press/McGraw-Hill.

Cortes, E. (1993). Reweaving the fabric: The iron rule and the IAF strategy for power and politics. In H. Cisneros (Ed.), *Interwoven destinies: Cities and the nation* (pp. 294–319). New York: W.W. Norton.

Department of Human Services. (2002, December). *Neighbourhood renewal: Evaluation framework 2002–2003*. Melbourne: Department of Human Services, Victoria.

Department of Human Services. (2009). *[Olympic Estate]: The journey continues. The year 8 report on the [Olympic Estate] community renewal 2001–09*.

Fraser, N. (1997). *Justice interruptus: Critical reflections on the "postsocialist" condition*. New York and London: Routledge.

Gecan, M. (2004). *Going public: An organizer's guide to citizen action*. New York: Anchor Books.

Gold, E., Simon, E., Mundell, L., & Brown, C. (2004). Bringing community organizing into the school reform picture. *Nonprofit and Voluntary Sector Quarterly*, *33*(3; suppl.), 54–76s.

Gold, E., Simon, E., with Brown, C. (2005). A new conception of parent engagement: Community organizing for school reform. In F. English (Ed.), *Sage handbook of educational leadership: Advances in theory, research and practice* (pp. 237–268). Thousand Oaks, CA: Sage Publishing.

Gold, E., & Simon, E., with Brown, C. (2002). *Successful community organizing for school reform. Strong neighbourhoods strong schools. The indicators project on education organizing*. Chicago: Cross City Campaign for Urban School Reform.

Horwitt, S. (1989). *Let them call me a rebel: Saul Alinsky, his life and legacy*. New York: Knopf.

McMahon, B., & Portelli, J. (2004). Engagement for what? Beyond popular discourses of student engagement. *Leadership and Policy in Schools*, *3*(1), 59–76.

Mediratta, K., Fruchter, N., et al. (2001). *Mapping the field or organizing for school improvement: A report on education organizing*. New York: Institute for Education and Social Policy, New York University.

Mediratta, K., Fruchter, N., & Lewis, A. (2002). *Organizing for school reform: How communities are finding their voices and reclaiming their public schools. A report*. New York: Institute for Education and Social Policy, New York University.

Mediratta, K., & Karp, J. (2003). *Parent power and urban school reform: The story of mothers on the move*. New York: Institute for Education and Social Policy, New York University.

Mediratta, K., Shaha, S., McAlister, S., Fruchter, N., Mokhtar, C., & Lockwood, D. (2008). *Organized communities, stronger schools. A preview of research findings*. Providence, RI: Annenberg Institute for School Reform at Brown University.

Milner, H. (2002). *Civic literacy: How informed citizens make democracy work*. Hanover, NH: University Press of New England.

Shirley, D. (1997). *Community organizing for urban school reform.* Austin: University of Texas Press.

Shirley, D. (2002). *Valley interfaith and school reform.* Austin: University of Texas Press.

Shirley, D. (2009). Community organizing and educational change: A reconnaissance. *Journal of Educational Change,* *10*(2,3), 229–237.

Smyth, J. (2006). Schools and communities put at a disadvantage: Relational power, resistance, boundary work and capacity building in educational identity formation. *Learning Communities: International Journal of Learning in Social Contexts, 3,* 7–39.

Smyth, J. (2008). Listening to student voice in the democratisation of schooling. In E. Samier, with Stanley, G. (Ed.), *Political approaches to educational administration and leadership* (pp. 240–251). London and New York: Routledge.

Smyth, J. (2009). Critically engaged community capacity building and the 'community organizing' approach in disadvantaged contexts. *Critical Studies in Education, 50*(1), 9–22.

Smyth, J. (2010). Speaking back to educational policy: Why social inclusion will not work for disadvantaged Australian schools. *Critical Studies in Education, 51*(2), 113–128.

Smyth, J., Angus, L., Down, B., & McInerney, P. (2008). *Critically engaged learning: Connecting to young lives.* New York: Peter Lang.

Smyth, J., Angus, L., Down, B., & McInerney, P. (2009). *Activist and socially critical school and community renewal: social justice in exploitative times.* Rotterdam, The Netherlands: Sense Publishers.

Smyth, J., Down, B., & McInerney, P. (2010). *'Hanging in with kids' in tough times: Engagement in contexts of educational disadvantage in the relational school.* New York: Peter Lang.

Smyth, J., & Harrison, T. (2009). *Action research project at the Olympic Estate learning hub. Research proposal to the Department of Education and Early Childhood Development.*

Smyth, J., & McInerney, P. (2007a). 'Living on the edge': A case of school reform working for disadvantaged adolescents. *Teachers College Record, 109*(5), 1123–1170.

Smyth, J., & McInerney, P. (2007b). *Teachers in the middle: Reclaiming the wasteland of the adolescent years of schooling.* New York: Peter Lang.

Stovall, D. (2010). Teaching, organizing, and justice: Tapping the resources of K–12 classroom teaching and community organizing for solidarity, praxis and survival. In R. Verma (Ed.), *Be the change: Teacher, activist, global citizen* (pp. 37–51). New York: Peter Lang.

Teitelbaum, K. (2010). Critical civic literacy in schools: Adolescents seeking to understand and improve the(ir) world. In J. DeVitis & L. Irwin-DeVitis (Eds.), *Adolescent education: A reader.* New York: Peter Lang.

Urban Agenda. (n.d.). What is civic literacy? Accessed August 27, 2010, from http://www.urbanagenda.wayne.edu/whatiscl.htm

Vibert, A., Portelli, J., Shields, C., & LaRocque, L. (2002). Critical practice in elementary schools: Voice, community, and a curriculum for life. *Journal of Educational Change, 3*(2), 93–116.

Warren, M. (2001). *Dry bones rattling: Community building to revitalize American democracy.* Princeton, NJ: Princeton University Press.

Warren, M. (2004). *Linking community development and school improvement. A report prepared for the Ford Foundation.* Accessed June 3, 2008, from: http://www.lsna.net/display.aspx?pointer=2515

Warren, M. (2005). Communities and schools: A new view of urban school reform. *Harvard Educational Review, 75*(2), 133–173.

Warren, M., Hong, S., Rubin, C., & Uy, P. (2009). Beyond the bake sale: A community-based relational approach to parent engagement in schools. *Teachers College Record, 111*(9), 2209–2254.

Westheimer, J., & Kahne, J. (2004). What kind of citizen? The politics of educating for democracy. *American Educational Research Journal, 41*(2), 237–269.

Zachary, E., & olatoye, s. (2001). *A case study: Community organizing for school improvement in the South Bronx.* New York: Institute for Education and Social Policy, New York University.

CHAPTER TWELVE

Social Control and the Pursuit of Dangerous Citizenship

E. Wayne Ross & Kevin D. Vinson

> Yes, citizenship—above all in a society like ours, of such authoritarian and racially, sexually, and class-based discriminatory traditions—is really an invention, a political production. In this sense, one who suffers any [or all] of the discriminations…does not enjoy the full exercise of citizenship as a peaceful and recognized right. On the contrary, it is a right to be reached and whose conquest makes democracy grow substantively. Citizenship implies freedom…Citizenship is not obtained by chance: It is a construction that, never finished, demands we fight for it. It demands commitment, political clarity, coherence, decision. For this reason a democratic education cannot be realized apart from an education of and for citizenship.
>
> —Paulo Freire, 1998, p. 90

The nature of citizenship and the meanings of citizenship education are complex, as are their multiple and contradictory implications for contemporary schooling and everyday life. The issues citizenship education presents are critical and inexorably linked to the present and future status of public schooling and the maintenance, strengthening, and expansion of individual and democratic rights.

In his classic book *Democracy and Education* (1916), John Dewey opens with a discussion of the way in which all societies use education as a means of social control. Dewey argues that education as a social process and function has no definite meaning until we define the kind of society we have in mind. In other words, there is no "objective" answer to questions about the means and ends of citizenship education, because those purposes are not things that can be discovered.

In *Normative Discourse*, Paul Taylor (1961) succinctly states a maxim that has the potential to transform our approach to the civics, citizenship education and the whole of the social studies curriculum: "We must decide what ought to be the case. We cannot discover what ought to be the case by investigating what is the case" (p. 278). We—educators and citizens—must decide what ought to be the purpose of citizenship education. That means asking what kind of society, what kind of world we want to live in and then taking action to make it a reality. And, in particular, in what sense of democracy do we want this to be a democratic society? In order to construct meaning for civics and citizenship education, we must engage these questions not as merely abstract or rhetorical, but in relation to our lived experiences and our professional practice as educators.

Not surprisingly then civics and citizenship education—which is generally accepted as the primary purpose the social studies education—has always been a highly contested curricular area. The tapestry of topics, methods, and aims we know as social studies education has always contained threads of social reconstructionism (Hursh & Ross, 2000). Social reconstructionists such as George S. Counts, Harold Rugg, and later Theodore Brameld argued that teachers should work toward social change by teaching students to practice democratic principles, collective responsibility, and social and economic justice. Dewey advocated the democratic reconstruction of society and aspects of his philosophy inform the work of some aspects of citizenship education. The traditional patterns of social studies teaching, curriculum, and teacher education, however, reflect little of the social reconstructionist vision of the future, and current practices in these areas are more often focused on implementing standardized curriculum and responding to high-stakes tests than developing and working toward a vision of a socially just world (Gabbard & Ross, 2008; Mathison & Ross, 2008; Vinson & Ross, 2003). Indeed, the self-described social studies "contrarians" who advocate the "transmission" of "facts" and reject pluralism in favor of nationalism and monoculturalism (e.g., Leming, Ellington, & Porter-Magee, 2003) seem to be have the upper hand in most schools and classrooms, despite spirited resistance (Ross & Marker, 2005a; 2005b; 2005c).

Undoubtedly, good intentions undergird citizenship education programs such as Quigley & Bahmueller, 1991; Center for Civic Education, 1994; and National Council for the Social Studies, 1994. And yet, as Vinson (2006) points out, too often their oppressive possibilities overwhelm and subsume their potential for anti-oppression and anti-oppressive education, especially as states, the national government, and professional education associations continue their drive to standardize, to impose a singular theory and practice of curriculum, instruction, and assessment.

The Mexican American studies program at Tucson (AZ) High Magnet School, provides a vivid example of the oppressive and anti-oppressive possibilities of civics and citizenship education (as well as an illustration of how education functions as normative social control). In response to a 1974 desegregation order, Tucson schools established an African American studies program and later added Mexican American studies to the curriculum. The Mexican American studies program includes course work about historical and contemporary Mexican American contributions, social justice, and stereotypes. Students examine U.S. history from a Chicano perspective, reading highly acclaimed works such as Rodolfo Acuña's *Occupied America: A History of Chicanos* in addition to classics such as Paulo Freire's *Pedagogy of the Oppressed* (Lacey, 2011; Reinhart, 2011). Studies conducted by the Tucson schools have shown that Mexican American students in the program scored higher on statewide tests (AIMS), were twice as likely to graduate from high school, and three times as likely to go on to college as Mexican American students that do not participate (Reinhart, 2011).

Early in 2010, Arizona passed anti-immigration legislation, which was widely condemned as undermining basic notions of fairness by politicians and commentators on the left and right as well as by religious, business, and law-enforcement leaders (Nichols, 2010). Less well known was the passage of another law, written by Arizona schools chief Tom Horne, which targeted Latino and other students in the state's public schools. HB 2281 banned schools from teaching ethnic studies. And in January 2011, Horne, now the state's attorney general, declared the Mexican American studies program in Tucson schools "illegal" stating it violated the law's four provisions, which prohibit any classes or courses that:

1. Promote the overthrow of the United States government;

2. Promote resentment toward a race or class of people;

3. Are designed primarily for pupils of a particular ethnic group; or

4. Advocate ethnic solidarity instead of the treatment of pupils as individuals. (Horne, 2010; House Bill 2281, 2010)

Despite the solid curriculum and academic success of the program, Horne described the program as "propagandizing and brainwashing," less about educating than about creating future activists. If the program is not immediately scrapped, Horne said the Tucson school district would lose ten percent of its funding, which amounts to $15 million.

The *New York Times* reported that students asked teachers if they were now considered terrorist since Horne described them as wanting to overthrow the government. If not terrorists, the state of Arizona has declared these students, and their teachers, enemies of the state—dangerous citizens—for studying the history of the U.S. from a Chicano perspective, a perspective that makes it impossible to ignore the historical and contemporary manifestations of racism, imperialism, as well as social, economic, and political inequalities. Indeed, what Horne and the Arizona legislature have done is make it illegal for students in Arizona to examine the key elements of capitalism: social relations; people in their struggle with nature to produce and reproduce life and its means, to seek rational knowledge in order to survive, and for freedom (Gibson & Ross, 2009).

We believe educators must pursue, as obviously some already do, an agenda dedicated to the creation of a citizenship education that struggles against and disrupts inequalities and oppression (DeLeon & Ross, 2010; Ross & Queen, 2010). Classroom practice must work toward a citizenship education committed to exploring and affecting the contingencies of understanding and action and the possibilities of eradicating exploitation, marginalization, powerlessness, cultural imperialism, and violence in both schools and society. Freire, as illustrated in the quotation that opens this chapter, like Dewey, teaches us that citizenship education is essential to democratic education, and that democratic education is essential to a free and democratic society. Students must know that birth, nationality, documents, and platitudes are not enough. They must understand that the promises of citizenship (freedom), the fulfillment of its virtues, are unfinished, and that they remain an ongoing, dynamic struggle. And they must come to act in a variety of creative and ethical ways, for the expansion and realization of freedom and democracy, the root of contemporary notions of citizenship, is in their hands, and it demands of them no less than the ultimate in democratic and anti-oppressive human reflection and human activity.

Contemporary conditions demand an anti-oppressive citizenship education, one that takes seriously social and economic inequalities and oppression that result from neoliberal capitalism (Ross & Gibson, 2007; Gibson & Ross, 2009) and that builds upon the anti-oppressive possibilities of established and officially sanctioned approaches. Some new and potentially exciting directions and alternatives exist, however, within the recent scholarship surrounding Freirean and neo-Freirean pedagogy, democratic education, and cultural studies.

The pedagogical power "dangerous citizenship," which we explore in the balance of this chapter, resides in its capacity to encourage students and educators to challenge the implications of their own education/instruction, to envision an education that is free and democratic to the core, and to interrogate and uncover their own well-intentioned complicity in the conditions within which various cultural texts and practices appear, especially to the extent that oppressive conditions create oppressive cultural practices, and vice versa.

Controlling Images: Surveillance, Spectacle, and Social Control

Increasingly today conceptualizations of public schooling rest upon the influence of dominant and dominating *images* rather than on more authentic understandings of the complex realities of classroom life (Vinson & Ross, 2003; Vinson, Ross, & Welsh, 2010).

We create our interpretations of what is, what was, and what should be based on what is presented within the mainstream news media and what we see in the movies and on television. This especially holds true in the ever more powerful contemporary social, cultural, political, economic, and pedagogical settings of standards-based educational reform, where the omnipresence of high-stakes standardized testing constitutes a regime in which both the cultural knowledge and the behavior of students, teachers, administrators, parents, classrooms, schools, and districts are (in)validated and disciplined.

This "hegemony of the image" mirrors and is mirrored by several developments in contemporary society, particularly within the realms of technology and globalization. It is, for instance, consistent with the advent of 24/7 access to video monitors and cameras, in terms both of *seeing* and of *being seen*. This emerges, for example, in the proliferation of web cams, around-the-clock broadcast and cable (and satellite and Internet) television, state-sponsored privacy-monitoring, the multiplication of media outlets, and the explosion of "reality" television programs.

Image, Surveillance, and Spectacle

Critical social theory and the sociological study of political order have both discovered that images are a basic component of the social construction of reality and operate fundamentally to control human behavior and shape human thought within institutional contexts (Vinson & Ross, 2003).

Images are generated and located both physically and ideologically within the complex social and cultural totality of advanced state capitalism.

- *Images also tend to reinforce existing power and exchange relations* on the level of human cognition and the structure of political power within advanced capitalism. Images are generally created by those who own and control the means of communications, particularly mass communications, or who are otherwise able to seize control of the processes of reality construction in society.

- *Image has a dialectical relationship with power:* power creates and elevates images to hegemonic status and is bolstered by them, while images simultaneously create and are created by power. While the relationship between image and power is mutually reinforcing, this is not to say that image never contradicts power or that competing images never vie for predominance in the social and cultural totality. Hegemonic images are images that achieve a significant measure of control over human behavior and cognition, and are also controlled and manipulated by powerful social groups.

Understanding the social reality of image under advanced state capitalism requires the study of the contexts in which images are produced, how they shape behavior, and the social, political, and economic interests they serve. This means that the study of images associated with schooling and education must focus attention on the relationship between the learning and the social and cultural patterns of the global totality of capitalism.

Central to the global totality of advanced capitalism is the role of the state as the primary agent of social control through its activities in planning, reality definition, and the maintenance of social control through direct coercion. In the era of state capitalism, the essential role of the state is to mitigate the conflicts and contradictions that threaten the stability of this socio-historical formation.

The core functions of the state under advanced capitalism include the enforcement of those norms and patterns that mitigate conflict, crisis, and contradiction, which occurs partially through the discipline of individuals, groups, and organizations that pose a potential challenge to existing power and exchange relations.

Discipline and enforcement occur under advanced state capitalism largely through the vehicles of *surveillance* and *spectacle*.

Surveillance and Social Control—The Few Observe the Many

In his study of the birth of the prison, Michel Foucault identified the process of *surveillance* as a basic means by which power is exercised and social control is maintained in contemporary society. Foucault clearly views power not as an entity but as a network that operates within institutional contexts. While *Discipline and Punish: The Birth of the Prison* (1979) is primarily concerned with the incipient social organization of the prison as a modern form of punishment, Foucault is ultimately interested in discipline and enforcement as social processes situated in a broader socio-historical environment. The social organization of the prison becomes a means for understanding the structure of discipline and enforcement in society and the exercise of power through surveillance.

An important point of departure in Foucault's discussion of surveillance is Jeremy Bentham's design of the modern prison, the Panopticon, which is physically structured in a manner that enables the warders to observe continuously the behavior of the prisoners. The Panopticon is a social and cultural totality that physically permits the "hierarchical observation" of the many by the few, and socially and culturally supports the right of the few to make "normalizing judgments" about the behavior of the many. (Part of Foucault's point as well was that the prisoners could not see the guard, enabling the "automaticity" of power, where even the possibility that someone might be watching was disciplinary. In effect, the prisoners would discipline themselves.)

For Foucault, surveillance resolves the problem of political order in the modern world because technology and cultural norms encourage the procurement of "the instantaneous view of a great multitude" (p. 478) for a small number of observers, or even a single individual. Foucault argues that community and public life in civil society are no longer significant mediators of human behavior in advanced societies.

We are left, on the one hand, with individuals, whose selves, goals, and purposes are highly privatized and isolated, and, on the other hand, the state, which has become increasingly dominant among social institutions.

As a consequence, social relations can be regulated only in the form of surveillance by the state and its collusion with large-scale organizations, which provide technological support for a social system that is based on the observation of the many by the few.

Spectacle and Social Control—The Many Observe the Few

In *The Society of the Spectacle*, Guy Debord (1995/1967) maintains that the whole of life of those societies in which modern conditions of production prevail presents itself as an immense accumulation of spectacles. All that once was directly lived has become mere representation. (pp. 12–13)

For Debord, the society of the spectacle defines a societal totality in which reality is replaced by image; life becomes advertised life. The images generated by information systems, marketing, advertising, and public relations obtain and pursue a reality unto themselves. They are distinct from, not merged with, the lived experience of humans.

The society of the spectacle is a form of alienation in which "being" is collapsed into "appearing," in which the image becomes a distorted and disconnected form of communication that mediates all social relationships. For Debord, the spectacle is not merely a collection of images. Instead, "it is a social relationship between people mediated by images" (p. 12).

Economically, Debord notes that earlier stages of the economy's domination of society included a downgrading of *being* into *having*. The present stage of social development, however, entails a shift in emphasis from *having* to *appearing*, consider for example how Facebook, YouTube, Twitter, FourSquare, etc. illustrate this shift.

Politically, the spectacle is an endless discourse "upon itself in an uninterrupted monologue of self-praise. The spectacle is the self-portrait of power in the age of power's totalitarian rule over the conditions of existence."

The spectacle's division of society into those who wield power and those who passively observe or contemplate the spectacle "is inseparable from the modern State, which, as the product of the social division of labor and the organ of class rule, is the general form of all social division." This view is not unlike what Chomsky (2002) has called "spectator democracy" (see also, Ross, 2006).

For Debord, the spectacle maintains its own regime of control and discipline, differentiated from surveillance and the panopticon, based on the *observation of the few by the many*. It controls by isolating and fragmenting, distorting communication, alienating human action, and restructuring communication to ensure one-way, instantaneous messaging. It operates to mitigate community and dialog and, thus, to control image, conflict, and change. Those who control images have the ability to mystify being and hierarchical power relations within the spectacle.

Social Control and the Merging of Surveillance and Spectacle

Both Foucault and Debord articulated libertarian and anti-statist visions of power, authority, and control in contemporary society. Both are centrally concerned with the role of the state and the mechanisms it uses to ensure direct and ideological social control in a society characterized by a loss of community and the structures of civil society that mediate relationships among people.

Foucault's studies envisioned a Panopticon of surveillance, or the *observation of the many by the few*. Debord's studies envisioned society as a collection of spectacles where appearance is more important than being and where the *many observe the few* (a status Foucault confined to antiquity).

High-stakes testing provides one case in which the merger of surveillance and spectacle can be understood, and which can itself be understood as surveillance and spectacle. One example of the operation of surveillance is the hierarchical observation of the behavior and performance of institutions, programs, staff, and students when tests are administered. An example of spectacle occurs in the presentation and reporting of school and system performances via media reports of standardized test scores to public education's many constituencies. Both surveillance and spectacle elevate image above authenticity and operate as vehicles of social control, political domination, and cultural conformity.

Dangerous Citizenship

So what to do? Against these problematics we propose an admittedly idiosyncratic notion, "dangerous citizenship."

As we see it, the practice of citizenship, critical citizenship, or social justice-oriented citizenship, requires that people, as individuals and collectively, take on actions and behaviors that bring with them certain necessary dangers; it transcends traditional maneuvers such as voting and signing petitions, etc. For in some ways citizenship today, from this perspective, requires a praxis-inspired mindset of *opposition and resistance*, an acceptance of a certain strategic and tactical stance. Of course, the implication here is that dangerous citizenship is dangerous to an oppressive and socially unjust status quo, to existing hierarchical structures of power.

As we construe it, as pedagogy, dangerous citizenship embodies three fundamental, conjoined, and crucial generalities: *political participation, critical awareness*, and *intentional action*. In terms of schooling, surveillance, and spectacle, its underlying aims rest upon the imperatives of resistance, meaning, disruption, and disorder.

Political participation implies partaking in the "traditional" rights and responsibilities of democratic citizenship. It does not intend, however, and should not be read to intend any sort of complacency or comfort relative to the dominant status quo. In fact, political participation might ironically insinuate *non*-participation. At its most simplistic political participation suggests such activities as (1) acting on the feasibilities of the freedoms of speech, assembly, religion, the press, and so on; and (2) undermining the actions of corporate-state government relative to, for example, abusing personal privacy and to contradicting the principles of justice, freedom, and equality (e.g., consider marches, demonstrations, petitions, etc.).

The second key component, *critical awareness,* builds on such constructs as Paulo Freire's (1970) *conscientização.* Overall, its point and purpose is to enable the range of interested stake-holders to see (1) how things are; (2) that things can be different; and (3) how things might or should be. It is grounded, in part, within Freire's conception of "reading the world" and Marx's construction of "class consciousness" among other critical views (see Lukács, 1967).

The third and easily most complicated factor, *intentional action,* clearly could connote a range of useful activities. In our usage, however, and within the confines of the spectacle, intentional action refers most directly to those behaviors designed to instigate human connection, the true engagement with everyday life, meaningful experience, communication, and change. They seek, that is, a forceful combat against the mechanisms of image, passivity, commodification, and separation.

Among these behaviors we advance the Situationist International's techniques of dérive and détournement in the closing sections of this chapter. However, de Certeau's (1984) understanding of *la perruque* (e.g., "the workers own work disguised as work for his employer") and sabotage (DeLeon, 2010) also easily fit under the heading of dangerous citizenship, as would certain aspects and practices of post-left or insurrectionary anarchism. Regarding the latter see the myriad examples of dangerous citizenship (and/or politically inspired art) in the book *The Interventionists: User's Manual for the Creative Disruption of Everyday Life* (Thompson & Sholette, 2004), which includes interviews, commentary, and images of the work of William Pope.L, subRosa, The Yes Men, The Biotic Baking Brigade, The Surveillance Camera Players, Ruben Ortiz-Torres, and many other dangerous citizens.

Dérive and Détournement as Insurrectionist Pedagogy

Guy Debord and other members of the Situationist International (SI) advocated techniques not yet extensively explored for their conceivable and critical pedagogical significance, yet of special interest given their promise vis-à-vis the controlling and enforcing propensities of standards-based education and its companion, high-stakes testing.[1]

The first, the dérive, literally "drifting," implies "a mode of experimental behavior linked to the conditions of urban society: it is a technique of transient passage through varied ambiances" (Situationist International, 1981, p. 45). According to Debord:

> In a dérive one or more persons during a certain period drop their usual motives for movement and action, their relations, their work and leisure activities, and let themselves be drawn by the attractions of the terrain and the encounters they find there. The element of chance is less determinant than one might think: from the dérive point of view cities have a psychogeographical relief, with constant currents, fixed points and vortexes which strongly discourage entry into or exit from certain zones. (Debord, 1981, p. 50)

For the SI, "psychogeography" referred to "the study of the specific effects of the geographical environment, consciously organized or not, on the emotions and behavior of individuals" (Situationist International, p. 45).

On the second technique, détournement, literally "diversion," the SI wrote:

Short for: détournement of preexisting aesthetic elements. The integration of present or past artistic production into a superior construction of a milieu. (Situationist International, pp. 45–46)

Détournement involves a quotation, or more generally a re-use, that "adapts" the original element to a new context, the theft of aesthetic artifacts from their contexts and their diversion into contexts of one's own device. In short, a détournement is a variation on a previous media work, in which the newly created one has a meaning that is antagonistic or antithetical to the original.

Examples of détournement can be found scattered across the landscape of popular culture. For example, culture jamming in the form of conceptual artist Barbara Kruger's black and white photographs with overlaid captions such as "I shop therefore I am" and *Adbusters'* subvertisements aim to disrupt and subvert corporate advertising. Punk rocker Frank Discussion is known for his "interventions" where he "detourns physical events by intervening with an out-of-place element in the physical world, a tactic expressed as simply as placing disparate items in unsuspecting people's shopping carts, thereby raising the action beyond the level of mere prank to a conscious tactic used to undermine society and to express a unified critique of it" (Museum of Learning, 2011). In the early 1980s, Discussion and his band, Feederz, detourned an image of Ronald Reagan for the cover of their album *Let Them Eat Jellybeans*. More recently Jello Biafra and the Guantanamo School of Medicine followed suit by adapting the Barack Obama "Hope" poster for the cover of their album *Audacity of Hype*.[2]

Together *dérive* and *détournement* sprang from Debord and his colleagues' "dreams of a reinvented world" a world of experiment and play. According to Marcus (1989):

These means were two: [jointly] the "dérive," a drift down city streets in search of signs of attraction or repulsion, and "détournement," the theft of aesthetic artifacts from their contexts and their diversion into contexts of one's own device . . .

[Ideally] to practice détournement—to write new speech balloons for newspaper comic strips, or for that matter old masters, to insist simultaneously on a "devaluation" of art and its "reinvestment" in a new kind of social speech, a "communication containing its own criticism," a technique that could not mystify because its very form was a demystification—and to pursue the dérive—to give yourself up to the promises of the city, and then to find them wanting—to drift through the city, allowing its signs to divert, to "detourn," your steps, and then to divert those signs yourself, forcing them to give up routes that never existed before—there would be no end to it. It would be to begin to live a truly modern way of life, made out of pavement and pictures, words and weather: a way of life anyone could understand and anyone could use. (pp. 168, 170)

Dérive and Détournement in Schools—Examples

As techniques of resistance aimed toward the enforcement elements of standards-based education and high-stakes testing (as controlling images, within the setting of surveillance-spectacle), what might dérive and détournement mean? What might they look like? How might they be applied? And how might they work?

Applied to schooling and high-stakes testing, the dérive, the more difficult of the two, demands first a re-understanding of the geographical shifts brought on by changes in gaze-based technologies and advanced state capitalism. It requires further a consideration of the architectural evolution induced by surveillance-spectacle and its effects.

In each instance, note that images dominate and that surveillance and spectacle converge or coexist. This means, in that dérive is a social act, that students and teachers would move communally, cooperatively, drifting, as it were, through buildings but also through cyberspace, virtual space, hyperspace, through the various architectures of contemporary schooling, as they were attracted or repelled, as their emotions and behaviors were piqued.

These drifters would, for instance, freely enter or exit testing sites (both physical and virtual) as they were encouraged or discouraged to do so, and they would seek simply to experience, to disrupt, and to play. They would surf websites, confronting relevant images, come and go, utilize monitors and web cams for "travel," compelled toward or away from various zones, from, say, "official" image bases, from control, and from the enforcing effects of standardization schemes.

Conceivably, albeit in the extreme, they could drift in and out of—even hack into—testing locales and interrupt them, create with them, toy with them. They could, moreover, enter and exit classrooms, schools, central offices, government domains, and media positions where high-stakes testing is enacted and where, in the end, controlling images are most oppressively enacted. All as a means of resistance.

Consider too the lessons to be learned by civic educators from Wikileaks—the non-profit media organization that enables independent sources to leak information, including state secrets (e.g., Afghan War Diary; Iraq War Logs; and hundreds of thousands of U.S. State Department cables), to journalists.

Wikileaks is not the one-off creation of a solitary genius; it is the product of decades of collaborative work by people engaged in applying computer hacking to political causes, in particular, to the principle that information-hoarding is evil. (Ludlow, 2010)

Wikileaks, and hacktivist culture in general, are based upon the "hacker ethics" of (1) all information should be free; and (2) mistrust of authority and the promotion of decentralization (Levy, 1984), two ideas that must be seriously engaged with in any educational endeavor that claims to promote democracy and freedom.

With respect to détournement, the implications for resistance are perhaps clearer, especially within the contexts of image, surveillance, and spectacle.

Consider, for example, this plausible newspaper headline:

PRESIDENT OBAMA, SECRETARY DUNCAN ANNOUNCE "RACE TO THE TOP"
Plan Emphasizes Paying Teachers Based on Student Test Scores

In and of itself, this seems (or may seem to some) innocuous, even positive, in that the administration will be devoting billions of dollars to schools, seeking to ensure that data collection tells us whether improvements are actually happening, and tying student achievement to assessments of teachers. Suppose, however, that as a mode of resistance the headline is juxtaposed next to a poster illustrating what we know about the history of paying teachers for student performance, which is that pay for performance gains are mostly illusions:

- In England, when payment-for-results was finally dropped in the 1890s, the overwhelming judgment was that it was unsound policy. Cynics referred to schools as "grant factories" and children as "grant-earning units."

- Payment-by-results appeared briefly in Canada in 1876, causing conservatives to rejoice because it made teachers and students work harder to avoid failure. The Canadian experience showed that test scores could be increased quickly, so long as the subject matter could be narrowed and measured. But, as in England, the system caused teachers to focus their energies on students who were most likely to succeed, helping them cram for examinations while ignoring the others. In 1883, a public outcry ended the experiment abruptly.

- Nearly a century later in the U.S., a "performance contracting" experiment in Arkansas produced only scandal and the lack of results ultimately doomed performance contracting, and it was declared a failure. Like the earlier English and Canadian experiments, performance contracting once again showed how financial incentives failed to produce expected gains, while at the same time generating damaging educational effects.

As a second example, imagine this newspaper headline:

HALF OF STATE'S PUBLIC SCHOOLS DON'T MAKE THE GRADE IN READING AND MATH
Schools rated poorly could lose students or be closed[3]

Suppose, further, an accompanying chart with the names of schools or districts in one column and mean standardized test scores in a second column, perhaps with pass-fail cutoff scores indicated.

Now consider recent (mind-boggling but true) news reports that within a particular state funding has been provided to equip school system administrators with smart phones at a cost of thousands of dollars, while because of budget cuts at the school level parents have been asked to donate supplies, including toilet paper, as a means to save money that might otherwise have to be diverted from instruction. (According to some reports, some schools actually have engaged in a system of bartering donated supplies, again, including toilet paper, in order to obtain necessary educational material.) Now, re-imagine the image. The headline:

HALF OF STATE'S PUBLIC SCHOOLS DON'T MAKE THE GRADE IN READING AND MATH

The chart? Column One: names of schools or districts. Column Two: number of rolls of donated toilet paper (with appropriately arbitrary pass-fail levels reported). As with the first case, both meaning and significance have been changed.

At the heart of détournement rests the notion that in all instances either the image is altered to "fit" the context, or the context is altered to "fit" the image. Such processes—or pedagogical strategies—enable students, teachers, and others to confront and combat the enforcing/enforcement properties of high-stakes testing *as* image.

What they require, though, are access to and facility with those technologies that make such enforcement possible, as well as an understanding—a *critical consciousness*—of controlling images, surveillance, and spectacle. Joined with dérive and Foucauldian analyses, détournement provides an untapped mode of situated and critical resistance, *praxis*.

Summary and Conclusions

The predominance of image must be understood within the prevailing context of surveillance and spectacle, a context that reinforces and is in turn reinforced by the presence of dominant and dominating images. Within this setting the mechanisms and technologies of seeing and being seen struggle against those of *not* seeing and *not* being seen according to a multiple and complex interplay among desire, possibility, existence, and necessity.

Contemporary schooling as a contested site moves within and across these borders. Its participants engage in oppression *and* resistance, a disciplinary drama in which they are positioned simultaneously as both the many observed by the few and the few observed by the many. Standardization regimes coerce educational stakeholders toward a privileged image supported by and supportive of the interests of the most wealthy and powerful among us, all in the name—the *appearance*—of democracy, achievement, and economic opportunity. And, not surprisingly, the "copy" frequently *is* more "real" than the "original."

Within the convergence of surveillance and spectacle standards-based education and high-stakes testing function as a mechanisms of enforcement, proceeding as a matter both of control *by* images and control *of* images.

Certain dominant images, established and maintained by elite educational managers, force a disciplinary and antidemocratic conformity on the part of (among others) teachers, students, and schools toward the interests of the same wealthy and powerful minority who sanction the contents, policies, procedures, and consequences of standardized and education and high-stakes testing in the first place. Those who control images produce images that control—power produces (and maintains and reinforces) images, images produce (and maintain and reinforce) power—all in their own power-laden interests. These are contexts that demand dangerous citizenship.

We offer the practices of dérive and détournement not as absolutes or final statements on what dangerous citizenship is or could be, but as quotidian and incremental praxis, a tentative set of steps toward reestablishing the place of living and authenticity as against alienation, passivity, antidemocracy, conformity, and injustice. For in the end, standardized education and high-stakes testing is not the whole story, but merely a piece of the bigger story, one in which we and our children are author and character, subject and object, player and played on. Perhaps this is our true test. If so, then the stakes are high indeed.

Notes

1. The published works of Guy Debord and other members of the Situationist International are widely available online. The Bureau of Public Secrets (http://bopsecrets.org) and the library at nothingness.org (http://library.nothingness.org/articles/SI/all/) are excellent resources.
2. For additional examples of détournement see Ross (2010).
3. The Pittsburgh *Post-Gazette* ran this headline on August 13, 2003: "Half of Pa. public schools don't make the grade in math and reading—Under new U.S. law, schools rated poorly could lose students." Retrieved from http://www.post-gazette.com/localnews/20030813schoolreport0813p1.asp

Bibliography

Center for Civic Education. (1991). *CIVITAS: A framework for civic education*. Calabasas, CA: Author and National Council for the Social Studies.

Center for Civic Education. (1994). *National standards for civics and government*. Calabasas, CA: Author.

Chomsky, N. (2002). *Media control: The role of the media in contemporary politics*. New York: Seven Stories Press.

Debord, G. (1995). *The society of the spectacle* (D. Nicholson-Smith, Trans.). New York: Zone Books. (Original work published 1967)

Debord, G. (1981). The theory of dérive. In K. Knabb (Ed.), *Situationist International anthology*. Berkeley, CA: Bureau of Public Secrets.

De Certeau, M. (1984). *The practice of everyday life*. Berkeley, CA: University of California Press.

DeLeon, A. (2010). Anarchism, sabotage and the spirit of revolt: Injecting the social studies with anarchist potentialities. In A. DeLeon & E. W. Ross (Eds.), *Critical theories, radical pedagogies, and social education: Toward new perspectives for social studies education*. Rotterdam: Sense Publishers.

DeLeon, A., & Ross, E. W. (Eds.). (2010). *Critical theories, radical pedagogies, and social education: New perspectives for social studies education*. Rotterdam: Sense Publishers.

Dewey, J. (1916). *Democracy and education*. New York: Free Press.

Foucault, M. (1979). *Discipline and punish: The birth of the prison* (A. Sheridan, Trans.). New York: Vintage Books. (Original work published 1975)

Freire, P. (1998). *Teachers as cultural workers: Letters to those who dare teach* (D. Macedo, D. Koike, & A. Oliveira, Trans.). Boulder, CO: Westview Press.

Freire, P. (1970). *Pedagogy of the oppressed*. New York: Continuum.

Gabbard, D. A., & Ross, E. W. (2008). *Education under the security state*. New York: Teachers College Press.

Gibson, R., & Ross, E. W. (2009). The education agenda is a war agenda: Connecting reason to power and power to resistance. *Workplace: A Journal for Academic Labor, 16*, 31–52. Retrieved from http://m1.cust.educ.ubc.ca/journal/index.php/workplace/article/view/47

Horne, T. (2010, December 30). *Finding by the state superintendent of public instruction of violation by Tucson unified school district pursuant to a.r.s. § 15–112(b)*. Retrieved from http://www.azcentral.com/ic/pdf/horne-findings-ethnic-studies.doc

House Bill 2281. (2010). Amending title 15, chapter 1, article 1, Arizona Revised Statutes relating to school curriculum. Retrieved from http://www.azleg.gov/legtext/49leg/2r/bills/hb2281s.pdf

Hursh, D. W., & Ross, E. W (Eds.). (2000). *Democratic social education: Social studies for social change*. New York: Falmer.

Lacey, M. (2011, January 7). Rift in Arizona as Latino class is found illegal. *The New York Times*. Retrieved from http://www.nytimes.com/2011/01/08/us/08ethnic.html?_r=1

Leming, J. S., Ellington, L., & Porter-Magee, K. (2003). *Where did social studies go wrong?* Washington, DC: Thomas B. Fordham Foundation.

Levy, S. (1984). *Hackers: Heroes of the computer revolution*. Garden City, NY: Anchor.

Ludlow, P. (2010, October 4). Wikileaks and hacktivist culture. *The Nation*. Retrieved from http://www.thenation.com/article/154780/wikileaks-and-hacktivist-culture

Lukács, G. (1967). *History and class consciousness*. London: Merlin Press. (Original work published 1920) Retrieved from http://www.marxists.org/archive/lukacs/works/history/lukacs3.htm

Marcus, G. (1989). *Lipstick traces: The secret history of the twentieth century*. Cambridge, MA: Harvard University Press.

Mathison, S., & Ross, E. W. (Eds.). (2008). *The nature and limit of standards based reform and assessment*. New York: Teachers College Press.

Museum of Learning. (2011). Frank Discussion. Retrieved from http://www.museumstuff.com/learn/topics/Frank_Discussion

National Council for the Social Studies Curriculum Standards Task Force. (1994). *Expectations of excellence: Curriculum standards for social studies*. Washington, DC: National Council for the Social Studies.

Nichols, J. (2010, April 23). Arizona law is not "merely cruel," it is "immoral." *The Nation*. Retrieved from http://www.thenation.com/blog/arizona-law-not-merely-cruel-it-immoral

Reinhart, M. K. (2011, January 3). Tom Horne: Tucson Unified School District runs afoul of ethnic studies law. *The Arizona Republic*. Retrieved from http://www.azcentral.com/news/election/azelections/articles/2011/01/03/20110103arizona-ethnic-studies-tucson-tom-horne.html

Ross, E. W. (2010). *Education for dangerous citizenship: War, surveillance, spectacle, and the education agenda*. Educational Leadership and Policy Studies Distinguished Lecture, University of Texas, San Antonio, November. Retrieved from http://www.ewayneross.net/E._Wayne_Ross/Talking_Heads_files/SA%20Talk.ppt

Ross, E. W. (2006). Remaking the social studies curriculum. In E. W. Ross (Ed.), *The social studies curriculum: Purposes, problems, and possibilities* (3rd Ed., pp. 319–332). Albany: State University of New York Press.

Ross, E. W., & Gibson, G. (Eds.). (2007). *Neoliberalism and education reform*. Cresskill, NJ: Hampton Press.

Ross, E. W., & Marker, P. M. (2005a). (If social studies is wrong) I don't want to be right. *Theory and Research in Education, 33*(1), 142–151.

Ross, E. W., & Marker, P. M. (Eds.). (2005b). Social studies: Wrong, right, or left? A critical analysis of the Fordham Foundation's "Where did social studies go wrong?" (Part II). *The Social Studies, 96*(5).

Ross, E. W., & Marker, P. M. (Eds.). (2005c). Social studies: Wrong, right, or left? A critical analysis of the Fordham Foundation's "Where did social studies go wrong?" *The Social Studies, 96*(4).

Ross, E. W., & Queen, G. (2010). Globalization, class, and the social studies curriculum. In D. Kelsh, D. Hill, & S. Macrine (Eds.), *Class in education: Knowledge, pedagogy, subjectivity* (pp. 153–174). New York: Routledge.

Situationist International. (1981). Definitions. In K. Knabb (Ed.), *Situationist International anthology*. Berkeley, CA: Bureau of Public Secrets.

Taylor, P. (1961). *Normative discourse*. Englewood Cliffs, NJ: Prentice-Hall.

Thompson, N., & Sholette, G. (2004). *The interventionists: User's manual for the creative disruption of everyday life*. North Adams, MA: MASS MoCA.

Vinson, K. D. (2006). Oppression, anti-oppression and citizenship education. In E. W. Ross (Ed.), *The social studies curriculum: Purposes, problems, and possibilities* (pp. 51–75). Albany: State University of New York Press.

Vinson, K. D., & Ross, E. W. (2003). *Image and education*. New York: Peter Lang.

Vinson, K. D., Ross, E. W., & Welsh, J. F. (2010). *Controlling images: Surveillance, spectacle and high-stakes testing as social control*. In K. J. Saltman & D. A. Gabbard (Eds.), Education as enforcement (2nd ed.). New York: Routledge.

CHAPTER THIRTEEN

The Work of the Criticalist

Critical Civic Literacy and Intervention in Social Class Processes

AARON M. KUNTZ

In this chapter I articulate my concern that social class has been reduced to an economic marker in discussions on education, with particular consequences for teachers, students, and community members alike. This static representation of class finds meaning in the broader social context of what Michael Apple (2006) terms *conservative modernization*; a contemporary sensibility that simultaneously emphasizes logics of economic determinism and American individualism. More than yet another conceptual model for reading our contemporary world, conservative modernization impacts our own hopes and dreams, the very possibilities we find viable given our present circumstances. In short, the contemporary problem of class extends far beyond deterministic correlations of employment and educational attainment, say, or household income levels and degree acquisition. Class analysis involves perceptions of key civic terms such as *freedom*, *agency*, and *justice*. Looking beyond class as marker or place on a standard hierarchal scale requires the skill of critical civic literacy, an active approach to interpreting, engaging, and intervening within the world in which we live. As I detail below, initially, critical civic literacy may imply learning to labor reflectively within the class processes that shape our identities. In this reflection, we may be able to give voice to the practical consciousness that values this labor against normalizing contexts and social structures. Ultimately, critical class consciousness must allow for the possibility of a complex dissolution of class as we know it in the critical work of opening contradictory assumptions onto the repetitive processes that structure our daily lives.

To begin, I critique commonsensical representations of class and class analysis—those interpretive means of presenting class as static positioning. In everyday discourses class signifies a place individuals reside within, hope to move out of, and fear falling into; often, class is seen as an attribute owned or added onto an identity. These representations of class have particular consequences, most notably a reductive effect on thoughts for how social change might occur and on what level change is even possible. I then align critical civic literacy with what

Kincheloe and McLaren (2005) term the "criticalist," a particular approach to the social world that emphasizes critique as intervention in normalizing institutions such as education. Next, I present these consequences as extending from our contemporary era of conservative moderniza- tion, a particular assertion of "common sense" that gives legitimacy to the class-as-position under- standing. Finally, I end by pointing to critical civic literacy as a means for intervening in the logics of conservative modernization and the importance of understanding class-as-process, particu- larly in relation to education. I do this by returning to the notion of the criticalist and consid- ering its impact on a small project with teachers at a local elementary school. In this way, I hope to present the active critique of critical civic literacy as more than a theoretical approach: criti- cal civic literacy presents real, material means for intervention and productive action on both micro and macro levels of context.

Reducing Class

As Michael Apple (2006) has noted, "too many people have either ignored or given up on the power of class analysis" (p. 233). "Class" and "class analysis" remain important elements of civic literacy, though both the term and interpretive frame have come to lack a critical sensibility. Van Galen (2010) notes a "silence about class in public and academic discourse (p. 253), while Reay (2006) critiques the ongoing conflation of class with race, gender, etc., in both academic work and mainstream discourse, resulting in class being "everywhere and nowhere" at the same time (p. 290). In this way, if class is discussed in contemporary discussions concerning education, it is subsumed within larger discussions of inequity, a placeholder-term simply invoked with lit- tle explanatory or critical power. Thus, when class *is* presented as an analytic frame, it makes good sense to examine the consequences of its use. How might normative conceptions of class enable particular interpretations of the world and constrain others? In short, what do particular asser- tions of what class is and how it operates reveal about corresponding interpretations of the world?

As noted in the work of Gibson-Graham, Resnick, and Wolff (2000), when class is invoked in contemporary discussions it most often is rendered as a place or position in relation to a legit- imizing series of economic markers. Here, we have the positioning of the self or others above or below the poverty line, for example, or the middle class as located within specific parameters of household income. This presents class as a hierarchal ordering mechanism, a means through which to identify oneself in relation to others. It also presents class as a static, unchanging marker—individuals move up and down the class hierarchy, but the measuring stick of class never changes.

A similar hierarchal model of class often invoked in contemporary discussions regarding edu- cation relies on the notion of class-as-possession. Inherent in this understanding of class is the deficit-model of students bringing with them particular knowledge deficiencies when entering the classroom. In this sense, students in lower classes (and the schools they subsequently attend) do not possess particular knowledges or dispositions to succeed within the educational (and eco- nomic) system. As a consequence, were students to simply *possess more* they might rise within a class-defined hierarchy. Similarly, the schools such students attend are ranked as low perform- ing, while others, to which they are compared, are high performing.

What links these two prevalent perspectives is their portrayal of class as a standard hierarchy defined by objective, static measures. As a consequence, individuals never escape interpreting their placement in relation to others along the class hierarchy. As Gibson-Graham, Resnick, and Wolff (2000) assert, "no dimension of social existence escapes the anxious and invidious ordering that is the hallmark of the hierarchical conception of class. Everything can be read as a class marker, and anything and anyone can be placed in a class" (p. 3). Class as ordered placement, then, integrates into our understandings of ourselves and constitutes our identities in relation to others.

Of course, class calls forth more than monetary acquisition. The assertion of a class hierarchy implies that anyone may (freely) take actions to move up the hierarchy, thus (freely) altering his/her own class status. Consequently, *freedom*, a key component upon which our democratic society rests, becomes an economic measurement of activity—the ability (imagined or otherwise) to operate within and among a neutrally classed system. Yet, as Apple (2006) claims, "Any definition of freedom based on economic independence must by its very nature draw a line between those classes of people who have it (economic independence) and those who do not" (p. 12). As Apple's comments indicate, the freedom to rise within an economic hierarchy presumes an economic independence that not all people, or groups of people, share. In this sense, agency is construed as the ability to be upwardly mobile, to attain and actively utilize one's own economic independence.

In addition, as presently constructed, movement within the class hierarchy most often emphasizes the individual as moving into and out of particular class positions. In this sense, mobility is interpreted as individual, not class-based, movement. The consequences of such individualistic interpretations of class articulate in conceptions of change within the individual (in relation to his/her class), not the larger social order. Change occurs within the individual, not the social structures in which the individual is immersed. In his ethnography *Learning to Labor*, Paul Willis (1977) makes this point explicitly:

> The logic of class or group interests is different from the logic of individual interests. To the *individual* working class person mobility in this society may mean something. Some working class individuals do "make it" and any particular individual may hope to be one of them. To the class or group at its own proper level, however, mobility means nothing at all. The only true mobility at this level would be the destruction of the whole class society. (p. 128; emphasis in original)

Understanding class as an objective place or position requires a simultaneous assumption of change at the level of the individual; any other conception of change requires the invention of a new working system. As a consequence, intervention in hierarchical presentations of class is necessarily limited; individuals might hope to actualize their freedom to "make it" out of their class, but the very system that relegates them to particularly classed positions never changes. Freedom is thus defined at the individual level, and according to the parameters of an objectively rendered hierarchy. To imagine the locus of change as extending beyond the individual is to consider a more radical change—alterations to the very system that make class (in its present incarnation) visible and known. Yet this larger-order change rarely finds traction in a culture that emphasizes both unquestioned class division and individually based freedoms. This intersection of fixed class position and individual-level of change finds additional meaning in a cultural mythos of American individualism, the results of which are found throughout education today.

The Criticalist

I take one of the foundations of critical civic literacy to be an active engagement with matters of government generally, and the generation of a working democracy more specifically. Education, of course, plays a key role in developing (or not) a critical citizenry. Unfortunately, as Michael Apple (2006) notes, "most of our existing models of education tend to ratify or at least not actively interrupt many of the inequalities that so deeply characterize this society" (p. 5). In this sense, our educational systems often fail to promote the skills necessary for critical engagement with civic matters. This is to say that contemporary notions of civic literacy in education emphasize *managing* our social contexts rather than intervening within them. This is particularly evident in issues of class wherein class analysis emphasizes describing the various class positions (e.g., working class, the middle class) as discrete categories through which individuals pass based on their ability to negotiate the "neutral" frame of capitalism. In this way, educational curricula often make little attempt to change the capitalistic system that produces class inequity, emphasizing instead the skills with which one works within capitalism itself. Critical civic literacy, on the other hand, seeks to counter traditional representations of class through refusing the passive representations that predominate our contemporary culture in favor of recognizing class as produced, an ongoing social construction that requires strategies of intervention. More than description, critical social analysis enables daily practices that intervene in social inequity, that work to change the very processes through which capitalism is enacted. Thus, these strategies of intervention become the work of the criticalist.

Kincheloe and McLaren's (2005) *criticalist* does not simply describe but intervenes in particular social injustices: "'critical' must be connected to an attempt to confront the injustice of a particular society or public sphere within the society" (p. 305). Because unjust social structures are not static, but are continually reproduced through our everyday meaning making and interaction, critique becomes emancipatory action by exposing the contradictions inherent in contemporary social formations. When these seemingly static structures are questioned, they may no longer be accepted by the dominant culture as commonsensical or natural (Kincheloe & McLaren, 2005, p. 306). In this way, the criticalist employs analyses that expose, for example, the contradiction within a cultural rationale that purports to offer all individuals equal access to education, regardless of background and discrimination, even as it upholds the development of an educational marketplace through the use of school vouchers, magnet schools, and charter schools that reproduce social inequities by ostensibly offering all consumers a right to buy without ensuring their purchasing power. A market (in this case, an educational market) is introduced as a neutral entity wherein all participants are governed by the same rules, regardless of an unequal distribution of resources. As a consequence, the logic of market neutrality (and necessity) is ratified by developing models of education and educational systems.

Importantly, the criticalist foregrounds class as an entry point for intervention, questioning contemporary views that claim various social processes (such as race, class, gender, and sexuality) are equally weighted in critical discussions regarding social injustice. As Kincheloe and McLaren (2005) note, embedding class within other forms of inequality "reduces capitalist exploitation and relations of capitalist production to one set of relations, among others, that systematically denies the totality of capitalism that is constitutive of the process of racialized class relations" (p 321). In civic literacy, class can be no longer subsumed within social processes that would allow for conceptions of democracy outside of its formation within capitalism. This logic has often resulted in the conflation of democracy with capitalism, or freedom with the unencumbered marketplace. In Kincheloe and McLaren's view, class remains a radical element, what Marx noted as a form of universal exploitation whose elimination requires the simultaneous eradication of all types of oppression (see Marx, 1978). The criticalist, through foregrounding class analysis, is politically engaged and emancipatorily minded.

The perspective of the criticalist resonates well with conceptions of critical civic literacy. If we take *civic literacy* to connote both socio-political knowledge and the ability to engage those skills as an active citizen, then *critical civic literacy* encourages the interrogation of assumptions that govern the contemporary status quo. Both the terms "literacy" and "critical" imply an active stance, with the former encouraging the application of knowledge and the latter an ongoing historicizing and questioning of existing world views (see, for example, Teitelbaum, Chapter 2 in this volume). Overlaying this notion of critical civic literacy with Kincheloe and McLaren's (2005) notion of the criticalist adds a third dimension, that of seeking to intervene in class processes and actively working to alter the systematic reproduction of social injustices. Here then, the criticalist employs the skills of critical civic literacy to historicize contemporary presentations of class with the aim of altering institutions that make class known. The most visible of these institutions is education (Louis Althusser famously noted that education had replaced the church as the most dominant ideological state apparatus).

Importantly, this amalgam of critical civic literacy and the criticalist requires a reflective positioning, one that proves capable of moving beyond static representations of our social world toward recognizing and engaging in an overlapping array of social processes, systems that often contradict and confront one another, yet as often remain hidden through the overarching norms of the commonsensical, or the status quo. Teaching about class often involves recognizing the parameters of class hierarchy without questioning the very production of class and an ordered hierarchy. Employing the skills of critical civic literacy, the criticalist works to move beyond static representations of class, to recognize our interpretations of class as historically situated and resulting in particularly classed ways of knowing and moving within the world. In this way class is seen to impact our perceptions of, and movements within, our social world. Class analysis, consequently, makes possible new interpretations, new practices within our daily lives.

The Logic of Conservative Modernization

Conservative modernization makes possible a hyper-individualization that occludes interpretations of individuals as constituted through an array of socio-cultural processes. It is through the values of conservative modernization that class, if recognized at all, is rendered as static object, a fixed hierarchical sequence of categories that one seeks to progress through in the hope of attaining progressive economic mobility.

Michael Apple (2006) explains conservative modernization as "a new hegemonic bloc . . . a very creative articulation of themes that resonate deeply with the experiences, fears, hopes, and dreams of people as they go about their daily lives . . . integrated . . . within economically dominant forms of understanding, and within a problematic sense of 'tradition'" (pp. 27–28). In this sense, conservative modernization contributes to a developing sense of who we are and what we might become, a particular frame that makes possible select ways of operating within the world; it entails both discursively aligned and materially manifest practices. Conservative modernization exists as an ongoing series of social processes that privilege conservative educational practices and overly simplistic renderings of the world in which we live. Such processes "sustain the dominant power structure and exacerbate social inequalities, under the guise of rhetoric that espouses 'freedom' and purports the values of meritocracy" (Gildersleeve, Kuntz, Pasque, & Carducci, 2010, p. 88).

Without the skills inherent in critical civic literacy, conservative modernization would continue unchecked. As a way of interpreting and acting within the world, conservative modernization operates according to the very rationalities that it produces—defining freedom, for example, as the ability of individuals to operate unencumbered within a global market even as it foregrounds the importance of economic ideals that remain unattainable for many. Within education, specifically, conservative modernization manifests in a sequence of accountability measures aimed at assessing individual teacher activities within individual classrooms, in individual schools. Students, in turn, are measured against standardized norms and objectively situated standards that have little use for local contexts of schooling. In short, students, teachers, and schools are accounted for and classed, each positioned within a pre-defined marketplace of success.

Inherent in conservative modernization is the simplification of otherwise dynamic social processes, a simplification that implicates how we come to understand class as static rather than process-based, for example. This simplification remains the extension of a hegemonic means of engaging with the world. Indeed, neoliberalism, a contributing element of conservative modernization, develops according to an overarching model of economic determinism, one that contributes to a sense of hyper-individualism, with the individual known and understood through an ongoing relation to the economic market. This hyper-individualism finds meaning in the ongoing mythos of the great American individual who can overcome any obstacles—be they the speed bumps of class positioning or poor schooling—toward financial success.

Of course, we should remain wary of the overt simplification of complex social processes. As Couldry (2010) writes, "the point of hegemonic terms is to treat as similar, things that are very different, that is why such strategies must be opposed by name, in a reverse strategy of simplification" (p. 6). Conservative modernization operates under logics of simplification—employing economically determinant ways of knowing, for example—that must be both problematized and countered. More simply stated, conservative modernization calls for a strategic response that employs a sense of critical civic literacy, one that is politically engaged and rejects a status-quo view of class as a static category through which agential individuals pass in their ongoing process of economic mobility.

Critical Civic Literacy and Class as Process

This strategic response is only attainable through critical reflection, a means through which to understand ourselves as other than we commonly are. One way to critically engage with conservative modernization generally and simplistic renditions of class more specifically is to consider class as a historical social process, one that never fully accounts for individual or collective identities, nor for the daily practices through which we live our lives. Class-as-process counters cause-and-effect thinking that typifies the logic of conservative modernization. Examples of cause-and-effect thinking might be found in deficit models of education and class: if I had more money, I would move out of this class; if my students came with more knowledge—were not as deficient—my teaching scores would improve.

A critical interpretation of class is strictly anti-essentialist, countering cause-and-effect logic with the claim that "every cause is itself an effect and vice versa" (Resnick & Wolff, 1987, p. 3). Resnick and Wolff (1987; 2002) articulate a critical perspective on class processes, locating the possibility for social change through contradiction. They write: "All entities in society change as the direct consequence of the complex contradictions that constitute their existence. To exist at all . . . is to be overdetermined, contradictory, changing, and hence in a state of process" (1987, p. 7). As a consequence, social analysis is not meant to find the key determining cause that explains or justifies contemporary circumstance (Resnick & Wolff, 2002, p. 9). Instead, social analysis is an intervention into the (re)production of contemporary class processes; it involves critical work. Class process thus becomes a site for critical inquiry, an entry point for analysis that is a relation, a process, and not a thing. In order to both recognize and instigate progressive change, one engages in criticism.

As Resnick and Wolff go on to note, *criticism* is "the specification of differences between [one's] own and other theories" (1987, p. 5). This criticism is made possible because we all participate in multiple class processes, each with multiple sets of interests; contradiction becomes inevitable. Yet, it seems fair to ask at this point how one incorporates a critical perspective into an educational system bent on simplification of social context, one that refuses the possibility of contradiction within the very processes and practices it maintains.

One potential way to make manifest the skills of critical civic literacy is to encourage discussions of possibility in the daily practices of education on all levels. As an open-ended term, *possibility* assumes the element of change, refusing the static representation of any context. The era of conservative modernization, on the contrary, empties contemporary context of possibility, requiring its abstraction to some future time and place beyond the immediate context of people's lives. As Gibson-Graham, Resnick, and Wolff (2000) note, the particular effects of our contemporary context include:

> resignation (at least where revolutionary possibility is concerned), the tendency to focus on pain and injury rather than hope and possibility, blaming and moralizing rather than envisioning and acting. . . . Revolutionary possibility is relegated to the future and the present becomes barren of real possibility. It is therefore also empty of the kinds of emotions (like creative excitement, pleasure, hope, surprise, pride and satisfaction, daily enjoyment) that are associated with present possibilities. (p. 15)

In order to counter the projection of possibility to some unknowable future, the criticalist might employ the skills of critical civic literacy to emphasize possibilities inherent in present circumstances, the inability of the present to be fully accounted for our defining. As noted above, a key element of critical work is to establish social inequities such as class as historically produced and, consequently, never fully formed. This critical work, in turn, gives us "different ways to make sense and take action" (Gibson-Graham, Resnick, & Wolff, 2000, p. 2). It allows for connections of class to areas where it has been excluded, activities that have been deemed "non-economic." The final section of this chapter presents an overview of a small project at a local elementary school that sought to recognize the possibility inherent in teachers' work, their labor within multiple class processes.

The Creative Pedagogy Project

Much has been written on the labor of teaching, as well as the multiple consequences of our contemporary fixation on teacher accountability and devotion to testing as a means for defining student, teacher, and school success. Specifically, this project's teachers at a small elementary school in Alabama can be said to develop a series of work practices whose ends are appropriated into an accountability system, one that interprets and places value on their labor based on student scores on an array of tests. Beginning last year, I worked with these teachers on an action-research project named the Creative Pedagogy Project aimed at critically engaging with such circumstances.

The teachers I encountered through the project remained frustrated by the ease with which their efforts and identities were appropriated into a developing and technocratic accountability system—one in which student test scores, for example, were cast into a globalized, neoconservative arena. The goal of the project, frankly, was to find creative ways for teachers to better manage their exploitative circumstances, to allow them to locate a degree of agency in otherwise overly structured circumstances. In this sense, the project sought to create a collaborative space in which critical reflection was possible, a space where we could interpret work practices and identities that extend beyond fixed representation, as intersecting and intervening in multiple social processes. The school's principal, recognizing that there were a number of young, energetic teachers at the school who were becoming frustrated with external constraints, coordinated substitute teachers so we could meet together once a month to work on our project. I'm not sure the project raised any participants' class consciousness, though I do think it provided an opportunity for what might be termed productive failure. We have yet to change the system of accountability that so dominates these teachers' lives, though we have worked to locate the contradictions and gaps inherent in such normative processes, key activities necessary for the work of critical civic literacy. In short, we have challenged the overly simplistic rendering of teacher pedagogy and labor that is representative of our era of conservative modernization.

Each teacher in our group recognized the labor she produced in the classroom as well as the frustration when such labor was appropriated and distributed within a rigid system of accountability. These teachers also noted that the values and assumptions that governed the accountability system contradicted their own, as well as the personal pedagogical goals they carried with them every time they entered the classroom. In this sense, the teachers had already located criticisms of their present circumstance, yet they found little means to respond to their exploitation. As a group, we worked to locate the gaps, the interstices in the accountability system where they might articulate and employ pedagogical practices more in line with their own assumptions about the need for individual and systemic change. In this sense, we followed what Raymond Williams (1977) termed *practical consciousness*, or the "experiences to which the fixed forms do not speak at all" (p. 130); that which extends where official knowledge falls short. As Horner (2000) notes, "official consciousness," in our project's contexts of testing and accountability data, "both interferes with and substitutes for the articulation of practical consciousness" (p. 216). So, through articulating the practical consciousness of their work, teachers develop a critical class consciousness—developing skills of critical civic literacy—that allows them to see the lived process of their labor and its inherent commodification. Here we draw from Horner's (2000) notion that the degree to which academic or community-related work seems authentic depends on "whether the worker is able to learn to use the occasion of the work to learn, grow, and contribute to society, or at least to see herself doing so (p. 160). On a practical level, teachers developed collaboratively a series of in-class activities meant to address their own individual goals as well as system-wide standards. Obviously, this project aimed to create spaces for critical collaborative work as much as a series of productive in-class activities; the process of collaboration remained as important as the product itself.

An alternative, more cynical reading of this project may point to the notion that teachers were asked to engage in additional labor, above and beyond that appropriated by the accountability system in which they were immersed. Though enabled through their principal, teachers labored to create dynamic projects capable of meeting the goals of two seemingly contradictory value systems. Thus, in order to manage the contradictions inherent in their labor system, these teachers had to increase their labor and production, especially if we consider their reflective work an element of labor.

Yet their participation in the project allowed them to see the systems in which they were immersed differently, to recognize them as less than all-encompassing. They collaborated to develop the self-reflective and intervention skills necessary for critical civic literacy. Further, this project points to the necessity of not over-simplifying processes of labor within educational systems. In this instance, teachers claimed portions of their pedagogical labor as their own, not ceding the full meaning of their classroom practices to the system of accountability. So, in the end, this ongoing project might be read as a failure, not creating an alternative class structure as scholars such as Resnick and Wolff hope will occur in social institutions such as education. Yet I hope that it was at least a productive failure, one that created the space for critical civic literacy to develop. We sought to create a critical process, to ourselves become criticalists.

Conclusion

A developing indifference to class analysis is indicative, I believe, of increasingly simplistic interpretations of class in our times. This leads to the perspective that class is everywhere and understood, when it is circulated as a static attribute or identity, rather than a process so intrinsic to our everyday lives that we have difficulty imagining education otherwise. This reductive understanding of class comes at a time when globalization has increased economic disparity at local and national levels, when unfettered capitalism is mistakenly equated with democratic ideals worldwide, and more and more groups of people—both domestically and abroad—lack the basic resources necessary for daily survival. In short, we seem to have lost the skill of class analysis at the very time when it is most needed, when interventions in class processes might bring about productive change in the name of social justice. In this vein, Stephanie Jones (2006) emphasizes the importance of class analysis given our contemporary socio-political contexts, writing, "Social class analyses are crucial, given the economic and political era in which we find ourselves, where neo-liberal global capitalism continues to devalue and dehumanize human labour—and the human beings who labour" (p. 302). In this way, critical class analyses go a long way toward recognizing and considering the effects of human activities and identities that otherwise might go unnoticed or remain illegitimate in the eyes of an economic system that fails to value their presence and/or production. Within education, this might consist of teachers who actively work to encounter students, families, and their own work activities beyond the structured accountability measures in which they are defined. Such activities most often escape notice as they exist outside legitimized spheres of educational work.

A key component to critical work, the work of the criticalist, is the ability to reflect on daily practices as an extension of overlapping, historically situated, social processes. Unfortunately, particularly within the arena of education, there is little time and space for such reflective acts. Educational activity is all too often reduced to the work of the technocrat—employing and assessing various accountability measures, standards, and prescribed learning outcomes. This produces what Van Manen terms "hopeless hope." As Van Manen (1990) writes, "the language by way of which teachers are encouraged to interpret themselves and reflect on their living with children is thoroughly imbued by hope, and it is almost exclusively a language of doing—it lacks being" (p. 122). Consequently, hope, or the belief in possibility, remains relegated to some future position, never directly impacting present circumstances. The simple aim of projects such as the Creative Pedagogy Project is to provide a space for developing critical skills, and to link critical thinking in a collaborative fashion.

Bibliography

Apple, M. (2006). *Educating the "right" way: Markets, standards, God, and inequality* (2nd ed.). New York: Routledge.

Couldry, N. (2010). *Why voice matters: Culture and politics after neoliberalism*. Thousand Oaks, CA: Sage.

Gibson-Graham, J. K., Resnick, S., & Wolff, R. (2000). Introduction: Class in a poststructuralist frame. In J.K. Gibson-Graham, S. Resnick, & R. Wolff (Eds.), *Class and it others* (pp. 1–22). Minneapolis: University of Minnesota Press.

Gildersleeve, R., Kuntz, A., Pasque, P., & Carducci, R. (2010). The role of critical inquiry in (re)constructing the public agenda in higher education: Confronting the conservative modernization of the academy. *The Review of Higher Education, 34*(1), 85–121.

Horner, B. (2000). *Terms of work in composition: A materialist critique*. Albany: State University of New York Press.

Jones, S. (2006). Lessons from Dorothy Allison: Teacher education, social class and critical literacy. *Changing English, 13*(3). 293–305.

Kincheloe, J., & McLaren, P. (2005). Rethinking critical theory and qualitative research. In N. Denzin & Y. Lincoln (Eds.), *The Sage handbook of qualitative research* (3rd ed., pp. 303–342). London: Sage.

Marx, K. (1978). Economic and philosophical manuscripts of 1844. In R. Tucker (Ed.), *The Marx-Engels reader* (pp. 70–91). New York: Norton.

Reay, D. (2006). The zombie stalking English schools: Social class and educational inequality. *British Journal of Educational Studies, 54*, 288–307.

Resnick, S., & Wolff, R. (1987). *Knowledge and class: A Marxian critique of political economy*. Chicago: University of Chicago Press.

Resnick, S., & Wolff, R. (2002). *Class theory and history: Capitalism and communism in the USSR*. New York: Routledge.

Van Galen, J. (2010). Class, identity, and teacher education. *Urban Review*, *43*(4).

Van Manen, M. (1990). *Researching lived experience: Human science for an action sensitive pedagogy*. London, Ontario: Althouse Press.

Williams, R. (1977) *Marxism and literature*. Oxford: Oxford University Press.

Willis, P. (1977). *Learning to labor: How working class kids get working class jobs*. New York: Columbia University Press.

CHAPTER FOURTEEN

Mediating Education and Promoting a Progressive Civics Curriculum

Pedagogies of Philosophy, Dissent, and Democracy

AARON COOLEY

> We have frequently printed the word Democracy, yet I cannot too often repeat that it is a word the real gist of which still sleeps, quite unawakened, notwithstanding the resonance and the many angry tempests out of which its syllables have come, from pen or tongue. It is a great word, whose history, I suppose, remains unwritten, because that history has yet to be enacted.
> —WALT WHITMAN, DEMOCRATIC VISTAS

Introduction

Democracy, it would seem, should engender greater equality among its citizens (Putnam & Putnam, 1993). Unfortunately, equality in terms of economic outcomes and political power (Ross, 2006) continues to be a struggle to attain. This is in spite of the possibly naïve assumption that the majority of the nation's population would at the very least want to collectively advance its own interests. How can this be, especially given the tremendous amount of information now made available through technology? Quite simply, the media in all its diverse outlets filters and manipulates how people see political issues. Sadly, progressives and egalitarians are confronted with the fact that people often actively support governmental and educational policies that are misleading and that go against their own economic and political interests (Marginson, 2006; Shapiro, 2002). This chapter addresses some of the foundational issues in understanding how traditional civics education and the media often advance a social and political agenda that furthers inequality and undercuts the capacity of young people to develop critical civic literacy.

The first part of the chapter briefly discusses the work of John Dewey and Cornel West. The purpose of this section is to underscore a vital tradition in American thought that has receded from the mainstream of political theory, but that should be central to revitalizing civic education. Their interrelated work stresses the importance of democratic engagement to confront the powerful forces that seek to control and dictate the terms of social and political life for the masses. Both Dewey and West see the media and education as key territories that must be retaken if the interests of the majority are to be repositioned above elites that continue to skew foreign and domestic policy in their interest under the façade of freedom and individual rights.

The following section moves to the important and indicative case of how civics courses deal with the ever-present issue of immigration. This is an area where media and educational systems contribute to misunderstanding in the public arena. This misunderstanding of the facts and events through texts and curricula leads to further misguided policies and their support by the public. To establish this exemplar, a widely used textbook on civics and economics will be discussed with attention devoted to what is mentioned and what is left out from the text. Further, this part will show how both of these aspects of the textbook fail to deliver the needed emphasis to attain critical civic literacy.

The penultimate section discusses what alternatives might exist in attempting to create and promote a progressive civics curriculum that changes the fundamental assertions of the traditional curriculum and avoids the inherent biases of the present system. These alterations will work around the media filters and assist students in developing the qualities and characteristics that are needed to pragmatically dissent from prevailing viewpoints in their schools and communities. The major theorists put to work in this section are Kwame Anthony Appiah and Peter Singer.

The final section addresses the type of political strategy required to put this new civics orientation into action. Here, the work is speculative and honest about the chances of this change given the present political moment and the overriding historical considerations. However, the overwhelming importance of reorienting society toward greater egalitarianism demands that every effort be put into fighting the growth of inequality through dissent and democratic education.

Dewey and West on Democracy and Dissent

A long-suggested means of intervention in social inequality is education and, in the modern era, public schooling (Benson, Harkavy, & Puckett, 2007). The importance of linking education to political change continues to be a source of debate. However, it is a nearly universally held position that schools should play a role in how we teach subsequent generations about the aims and ideals of a democratic republic (see Biesta 2007; Freedman 2007; Garrison 2008; Noddings 2008). Additionally, this democratic training should include how to dissent from prevailing views and see through corporate and governmental propaganda promoted by the media as news.

Hence, this section of the essay proceeds by analyzing the work of John Dewey and Cornel West as offering both a more progressive and pragmatic path forward to overcome elite mechanisms of control. Here, it pays to begin with Dewey's thought on how the project of democracy is a continual effort toward positive action and policy along with the need to fight misinformation and intentional deception by the government and powerful elites.

Dewey contended that the misleading of the masses was happening in new ways and

> has put at the disposal of dictators means of controlling opinion and sentiment of a potency which reduces to a mere shadow all previous agencies at the command of despotic rulers. For negative censorship it has substituted means of propaganda of ideas and alleged information on a scale that reaches every individual, reiterated day after day by every organ of publicity and communication…for the first time in human history, totalitarian states exist claiming to rest upon the active consent of the governed. (Dewey, 2008, p. 156)

What is crucial about this section is the critical attitude that one can see Dewey taking toward hollow assertions of freedom and democracy that can be spoon-fed to a largely unaware public and even more forcefully transmitted through civics curricula in school. Dewey's understanding of how citizens are able to contribute to a democratic community requires a commitment to an engagement with the issues of the day and a willingness to dissent from the majority if one feels that the majority is taking an unjust position.

Dewey is also quite sure that the economic environment of his day was prioritizing the needs of the elites over the majority of citizens. Further, he sees the developing influence of big business as an imperiling crisis for the possibilities of political change. Dewey states:

> Politics in general is an echo, except when it is an accomplice, of the interests of big business.…As long as politics is the shadow cast on society by big business, the attenuation of the shadow will not change the substance. The only remedy is new political action based on social interests and realities. (Dewey, 1985, p. 163)

Dewey's words gain more resonance in the present, where big business has only magnified its place in the political arena and the Supreme Court has given corporations an even larger megaphone for political speech via the *Citizens United* ruling. Yet, the temptation to characterize Dewey as pessimistic about the possibilities of positive social change, because of this corporate influence, would be wrong. He is simply attending to the weakness of political actions through discourses that only allow certain ends. Again, the shadow metaphor demonstrates that democracy can serve to confine and oppress in ways that are much more subtle than outright totalitarianism, but that are, nonetheless, insidious in their ability to stunt the potential for social progress through dissent and democratic education.

Dewey continues this attack on the conventional ways of contributing to political change by taking on the established structure of the entrenched political parties for what they brazenly and nakedly claim to be—the handmaidens of "big business." He states: "The old parties…they have surrendered abjectly to domination by big business interests and become their errand boys. No wonder people have become indifferent and careless about political issues" (Dewey, 1984, p. 442). Clearly, Dewey has sympathy for the apathy that all too often reigns in the hearts of citizens when they are exposed to the power politics that exclude them from a profitable dialogue on the issues of economic and social inequality. However, he does not go so far as to assert the even more radical position that this is in fact an inherent part of the system that is meant to frustrate citizens to a point of political acquiescence and compliance, thereby allowing the elites to subdue the masses' potential for political action by non-aggressive means of propaganda via the ubiquitous media. Next, it is crucial to turn to the work of Cornel West for his assessment of the contemporary political and democratic context.

In *Democracy Matters* (2004), West makes clear that the contested concept of democracy must be defended even against those who self-righteously claim to uphold its legacy. He states: "We must not allow our elected officials—many beholden to unaccountable corporate elites—to bastardize and pulverize the precious word *democracy* as they fail to respect and act on genuine democratic ideals" (p. 3). In this section, the deep Deweyan roots of West's thought, in connecting the political to the economic spheres of public life, come to the fore. Concepts such as democracy are meaningless unless their constituent elements are fulfilled through an active process that more equally distributes a minimal level of power, opportunities, and goods to all members of society.

West does not stop there and identifies trends that are preventing the attainment of a more ethically conscious democracy that cuts through media misinformation and reenergizes democratic education. He warns: "The greatest threats come in the form of the rise of three dominating antidemocratic dogmas" (West, 2004, p. 3). West names the heads of this political Cerberus as free-market fundamentalism, militarism, and authoritarianism. Any of these elements alone contributes to an environment that impedes positive social progress. In coordination, they degrade opportunities for people to realize that democratic action is possible, that they should be grateful that things are not worse, and that they should take what they are getting from their democracy. West (2004) wants to rethink Socrates's view of democracy and contends that he was about half right in understanding the human predicament: "We must out-Socratize Socrates by revealing the limits of the great Socratic tradition. My own philosophy of democracy that emerges from the nightside of American democracy is rooted in the guttural cries and silent tears of oppressed peoples" (p. 213). West's extension of the Socratic pose to all members of a society is a fundamental element of a new perspective on civics that values each member of society equally and, further, is willing to acknowledge past horrors with compassion. It goes without saying that this complex process does not lend itself to the media's style and prevailing narrative.

Each of these philosophers extends the common understanding of democracy and the underlying elements of reforming civic education for critical civic literacy. The attitudes that adults express are often reflected and/or neglected in what students are supposed to learn about civic issues in school and of course through the media. Immigration serves as an appropriate exemplar of this phenomenon. A look at North Carolina's civics textbook and its treatment of immigration follows to fill in the educational and media functions that narrow the possibilities for dissent and the development of critical civic literacy.

Traditional Civic Lessons on Immigration

In moving from these recent examples of public attitudes toward immigration, this section will look at what the public school civics curriculum and its texts[1] discuss about immigration and its role in the state and country. This section will use North Carolina's primary civics text and its accompanying curriculum, because of the state's more recent encounters with immigration issues as compared to the border states of the Southwest.

The analysis of this text centers on its descriptions of immigration and related concerns, which ultimately reflect the present civics curriculum as being intellectually impoverished and as having a right-leaning political bias that has ties to the media and corporate conglomerates.

By extension, it does not strain credulity to think that these civic lessons have an impact on students' developing civic and political attitudes. This is problematic, as what is being taught does not encourage an inclusive, tolerant, and democratic attitude but instead, at best, gives students a deluded notion of the immigrant experience that is only reinforced in media representations and newstainment from cable networks.

Before moving to the passages that speak directly to the most recent wave of immigration, two preliminary points about the text must be made: (1) there is only a limited discussion of the first immigrants to North America who became the founders of the United States; and (2) there is no mention that dissent is an important part of civics and citizenship, especially in relation to immigrant issues. The first point speaks to the fact that the first immigrants are considered to be patriots, and raising the "illegality" of their immigration would be unpatriotic at worst and revisionist history at best. This is not particularly surprising (as Howard Zinn was not usually consulted by textbook authors from major corporate publishers), but nonetheless it is worthy of documentation. The second point buttresses the first, in that the historical points made throughout the text regarding immigration do not allow for other positions to be taken on the issues at hand. Here again, at best, there is a "bump out" or text box that may ask a question that is a modest counterpoint to the narrative of the text, but these questions are not true dissent from the orthodox positions and are not even close to an alternative narrative. Without such examples it would be difficult for students to fight against the overwhelming tide in the media pushing a dominant political narrative on the issue. With these points made, attention can be turned to the text and curriculum.

Motivation is a key issue in understanding why people emigrate to another country. Yet, the answers suggested by the text are simplistic and are not explanatory. The text states: "Despite immigration limits, approximately 5 to 6 million aliens are living in the United States illegally. Some were refused permission to immigrate; others never applied for permission because they feared a long, slow process or being turned down" (Remy, Patrick, Saffell, Clayton, & Whitaker, 2003, p. 16). Here there is no discussion of NAFTA, no mention of the inequalities in the home countries of immigrants, and certainly no analogies to the first patriotic immigrants who founded the country on land that was already inhabited.

Next, the text quickly moves to how this problem of illegal immigration arose. Why is it that the United States with its powerful government cannot do something fairly basic such as keeping out non-citizens? Again, the answers the text gives do not speak to the complexity of the situation. Although an extended discussion may not be appropriate for this forum, something more than what follows must be warranted:

> Illegal aliens come to the United States in a variety of ways. A few enter the country as temporary visitors but never leave. Others risk capture and arrest by illegally crossing our borders with Mexico and Canada. Other illegal aliens are foreigners who have stayed in the United States after their permits have expired. (Remy et al., 2003, p. 17)

In this instance, one begins to see an overriding problem with the text and its curriculum in that there is a massive chasm between what the government should be doing and what it does. There is no follow-up paragraph about why America's borders are porous. There is no mention of why people can so easily be referred to as "illegals" or "aliens." This lack of awareness and the concomitant problem of facts not matching reality smack of old fashioned cognitive dissonance. The language of the text and its curriculum proceed forward blissfully uninterested in any facts, interpretations, or thoughts that would complicate its mainstream narrative.

The text then jumps back to the rationale for immigrants coming to the United States at all costs. In the next passage, the text makes what are the strangest and most distasteful comments yet:

> Whatever the method, the reason is usually the same. "I came for work and for a better life," explained one Mexican immigrant; yet illegal aliens often have a difficult time in the United States. Many have no friends or family here, no place to live, and no sure way to earn money. It is against the law to hire illegal aliens, and those who do find work usually receive little pay and no benefits. Every day they live with the fear that government officials will discover and deport them—send them back to their own country. (Remy et al., 2003, p. 17)

In generosity to the authors, it could be that these comments about the plight of the immigrants are meant to instill a sense of compassion and social sympathy. However, considering the context of the passage and the overall tenor of the textbook, the passage seems quite sinister and obviously at odds with the facts (again the dramatic cognitive dissonance), as many immigrants come to the United States with their families and friends or to reconnect with their families and friends. Further, the prime motivation for most immigrants, as for most immigrants throughout history, has been for work, so the comment that they cannot find jobs is absurd, especially considering that, in some quarters, immigrants are bashed for taking away "Americans' jobs." This is not to mention the last assertion about housing, which again does not match reality, as many banks have begun giving home loans to immigrants to the outrage of anti-immigrant factions.

A variation of the right-leaning political attitudes to immigration in the text comes from further discussion about unity in the national population. Here, the text comes out with a tough English-language-first position. Unsurprisingly, there is no mention of the other languages that were spoken in the United States throughout the history of the country. The passage also showcases a typical milquetoast counter opinion, which is easy to identify even when wedged between the opinions that matter:

> A second significant source [of unity] is a single language, English, which is generally accepted as the primary means of communication in education, government, and business. Americans are free to speak any language. However, the community of citizens in the United States is strengthened by the common and public use of one language, which can be used by diverse groups of Americans to communicate freely with one another. (Remy et al., 2003, p. 23)

This small freedom to speak any language is quickly rebuffed as not adding to national strength and therefore should be minimized.

Another strange item must be mentioned about the text. Out of the blue and with no introduction, there is a Spanish-language glossary from pages 889 to 899 that mirrors the standard glossary that precedes it. This seems to sadly represent a civic attitude of passive acknowledgment of the need for students whose first language is not English to improve their scores on the state tests. It is unfortunate that this is the best the schools can do. No other context or assistance is noted in the text—it is just the glossary. This is the civics curriculum at its worst.

In the second part of the text, there is a shift to economics from civics. There is a noticeable change in the language used to describe the government and its actions. The government goes from providing positive activities for its citizens to generally being a hindrance to the business growth of free markets. What is unaccounted for in this ratcheting up of the right-leaning rhetoric is a discussion of why free markets always like immigrants. The answer, of course, is cheaper labor, but this is not touched on in the following section on labor:

> Labor is a resource that may vary in size over time. Historically, such factors as population growth, immigration, education, war, and disease have had a dramatic impact on both the quantity and the quality of labor. (Remy et al., 2003, p. 425)

Immigration is mentioned, but it is hidden in between[2] other categories and no mention is made of why immigration is important to the United States economy. It is these dramatic omissions and decontextualized ideas that make this civics text and curriculum so unhelpful to the development of critical civic literacy in students. Further, it is amazing to note that there is no substantial discussion of the fact that there are many "illegal aliens" taking this civics course in which their status is overlooked. With these types of courses and their accompanying texts, it is no wonder that our country continues to have a paltry civic culture, which is reflected in all areas of public life from low voter turnout to low-information voters who have little knowledge about issues such as immigration.

Toward a Progressive Civics Curriculum That Encourages Dissent and Supports Democratic Education

So, if the present civics curriculum and the texts that are used throughout the country are insufficient in creating the type of critical civic attitudes in our nation's young people that are desired by educators, what might work better and from what perspective could this progressive civics curriculum emerge? Here, it seems, a composite view is needed that seeks to alter the presently held meaning of the central term in this analysis—civics. At present, the civic perspective taught in schools neglects the interconnections of our common human community. It is a profound negligence of our educational system to have students inculcated into a civic life that excludes so many of the world's people. A key to this revision is expanding the meaning of civics to encompass a global attitude to the rights and responsibilities people have in their social lives. This expansion returns to classical roots through the words of Diogenes: "I am a citizen of the world." This fundamental reorientation of civics toward cosmopolitanism could substantially improve the ways in which students in America's schools come to understand their rights and responsibilities to other individuals. Doing this requires dissent from prevailing nationalistic attitudes as well as efforts at democratic education to overcome media spin on a panoply of social, economic, and political issues.

A key guide in this reorientation is the work of Kwame Anthony Appiah and his volume, *Cosmopolitanism: Ethics in a World of Strangers*. His view merits attention in trying to rethink the present civics curriculum, especially how to transform it into a new progressive (and cosmopolitan) civics curriculum. Appiah presents the challenge of bringing the citizen into the broader and more compassionate social world:

> Only in the past couple of centuries, as every human community has gradually been drawn into a single web of trade and a global network of information, have we come to a point where each of us can realistically imagine contacting any other of our six billion conspecifics and sending that person something worth having: a radio, an antibiotic, a good idea. Unfortunately, we could also send, through negligence as easily as malice, things that will cause harm: a virus, an airbourne pollutant, a bad idea. And the possibilities of good and ill are multiplied beyond all measure when it comes to policies carried out by governments in our name. (Appiah, 2006, p. xii–xiii)

From this central tension, Appiah moves to understanding how individual countries can gravitate to more socially sympathetic attitudes to other countries and thereby increase their own cosmopolitan attitudes that attend to inequality as matters of ethics and not cost/benefit analysis. He asserts:

> In thinking about trade policies, immigration policies, and aid policies, in deciding which industries to subsidize at home, which governments to support and arm abroad, politicians in the world's richest countries naturally respond most to the needs of those who elected them. But they should be responding to their citizens' aspirations as well. (Appiah, 2006, p. 173)

Next, Appiah claims a hero of the present right-leaning civics text, Adam Smith, and uses him in a way about which Smith would probably be happier. He states:

> If we accept the cosmopolitan challenge, we will tell our representatives that we want them to remember those strangers. Not because we are moved by their suffering—we may or may not be—but because we are responsive to what Adam Smith called "reason, principle, conscience, the inhabitant of the breast." The people of the richest nations can do better. This is a demand of simple morality. But it is one that will resonate more widely if we make our civilization more cosmopolitan. (Appiah, 2006, p. 174)

Appiah's call for greater cosmopolitan attitudes among the world's citizenry cannot be misunderstood as being directed fully at the United States. However, by size of economy and military force, it is inevitable that the United States could use a great deal of cosmopolitanization to improve the lives of people around the world. As such, it is appropriate to situate this process into the American educational system through an alteration of its present civics curriculum.

So, a basis for this progressive civics curriculum finds its foundation in a cosmopolitan attitude, but, as one delves deeper, one must have an ethical commitment to support cosmopolitan action. Here it is important to turn to Peter Singer, as he provides a solid foundation for ethical conduct in a cosmopolitan civic context. Singer states:

> Ethics appears to have developed from the behavior and feelings of social mammals. It became distinct from anything we can observe in our closest nonhuman relatives when we started using our reasoning abilities to justify our behavior to other members of our group. If the group to which we must justify ourselves is the tribe, or the nation, then our morality is likely to be tribal, or nationalistic. If, however, the revolution in communications has created a global audience, then we might feel a need to justify our behavior to the whole world. This change creates the material basis for a new ethic that will serve the interests of all those who live on this planet in a way that, despite much rhetoric, no previous ethic has done. (Singer, 2004, p. 12)

Hence, if one could reframe civics toward a cosmopolitan attitude, the education students receive in civics courses would have a much different tenor, and students' relations to each other and other individuals around the globe might become more ethical. Singer's global ethical project must be connected to independent national critical civic literacy projects, or both will fall short. While Singer would certainly support this effort, one can imagine that there would be considerable resistance from education departments and ministries around the globe to this sort of project. Of course, it would seem most likely that the countries with the most to lose would be the most resistant to the extension of progressive civic attitudes to other populations, but this should not mean giving up this crucial territory for social and political advancement.

Singer makes this point clear, and one can easily imagine what such prescriptions would suggest for our present field of analysis—immigration. Singer pleads:

> All it would take to put the world on track to eliminate global poverty much faster than the Millennium Summit target would be the modest sum of 1 percent of annual income—if everyone who can afford it were to give it. That, as much as anything, tells us how far we still are from having an ethics that is not based on national boundaries, but on the idea of one world. (Singer, 2004, p. 195)

Clearly, Singer is realistic, but he is also optimistic about what the likelihood of such a fundamental political shift would be and what social will it would take to accomplish it.

What is also clear is that transnational companies, international courts, and trade agreements are presently serving as a de facto governance structure of the world. What is unfortunate is that there have not been better efforts to demonstrate the connections between the disparate countries of the world and their diverse populations. The integration of cosmopolitan prose into civic education should serve as a key element in reframing and filling the present civic void in this country—one that dramatically impacts the rest of the world.

As has been seen through the lens of attitudes to immigration, America's present civic mindedness reflects a nationalism that is ethically impoverished, not to mention outdated, in the present world of unprecedented wealth. For Singer, this global ethical dilemma is a central problem of the future of humanity:

> Now the twenty-first century faces the task of developing a suitable form of government for that single world. It is a daunting moral and intellectual challenge, but one we cannot refuse to take up. The future of the world depends on how well we meet it. (Singer, 2004, p. 200–201)

A Political Strategy toward a Progressive Civics Curriculum

The conversion of an idea into policy is the toughest part of any practically geared inquiry. This is certainly true in this case, as my assertion that a progressive civics curriculum is needed in America's public schools is unlikely to come to pass without a considerable change in the attitudes of the nation's educational policymakers. To convince everyone, from national political candidates to school board officials, of the need to rethink something as tried and true as America's civics curriculums will require a genuine and sincere effort. This effort would rely on a strong demonstration of the need to revitalize our common democratic institutions by stressing the importance of dissent and pushing back against the misinformation of the media. That being said, one must also have citizens and immigrants alike demand different policies from these very same policymakers and news organizations. The burden of cosmopolitanism is that everyone must think of strangers near and far as fellow citizens and treat them as such. This is a burden we must seek to shoulder.

Notes

1. It is my view that the text and the curriculum (embodied in North Carolina Standard Course of Study) are synonymous as the text has the principles of the curriculum throughout it, which are linked to every chapter and learning outcome. With the requisite state-mandated tests, there is presumably little room for civic lessons outside the scope of the text and the curriculum.
2. This placing of somewhat countering opinions in between the main points only seems to make the counter-comments even less important.

Bibliography

Appiah, K.A. (2006). *Cosmopolitanism: Ethics in a world of strangers*. New York: W.W. Norton.

Benson, L., Harkavy, I., & Puckett, J. (2007). *Dewey's dream: Universities and democracies in an age of education reform: civil society, public schools, and democratic citizenship*. Philadelphia: Temple University Press.

Biesta, G. (2007). Education and the democratic person: Towards a political conception of democratic education. *Teachers College Record, 109*, 740–769.

Dewey, J. (1899). *The school and society*. Chicago: University of Chicago Press.

Dewey, J. (1929). *Impressions of Soviet Russia and the revolutionary world, Mexico–China–Turkey*. New York: New Republic.

Dewey, J. (1948). *Reconstruction in philosophy*. New York: H. Holt and Company. (Original work published 1920)

Dewey, J. (1957). *The public and its problems*. Denver: A. Swallow. (Original work published 1927)

Dewey, J. (1966). *Democracy and education: An introduction to the philosophy of education*. New York: The Free Press. (Original work published 1916)

Dewey, J. (1968). *Problems of men*. New York: Greenwood Press. (Original work published 1946)

Dewey, J. (1984). *The later works, 1925–1953 (Volume 5: 1929–1930)*. Carbondale: Southern Illinois University Press.

Dewey, J. (1985). *The later works, 1925–1953 (Volume 6: 1931–1932)*. Carbondale: Southern Illinois University Press.

Dewey, J. (1996). *The collected works of John Dewey, 1882–1953: The electronic edition*. Charlottesville, VA: InteLex Corp.

Dewey, J. (2008). *The later works, 1925–1953 (Volume 13: 1938–1939)*. Carbondale: Southern Illinois University Press.

Freedman, E. (2007). Is teaching for social justice undemocratic? *Harvard Educational Review, 77*, 442–473.

Garrison, W. (2008). Democracy and education: Empowering students to make sense of their world. *Phi Delta Kappan, 89*, 347–348.

Marginson, S. (2006). Engaging democratic education in the neoliberal age. *Educational Theory, 56*, 205–219.

Margolis, J. (2002). *Reinventing pragmatism: American philosophy at the end of the twentieth century*. Ithaca, NY: Cornell University Press.

Noddings, N. (2002). *Starting at home: Caring and social policy*. Berkeley: University of California Press.

Noddings, N. (2008). Schooling for democracy. *Phi Delta Kappan, 90*, 34–37.

Putnam, H., & Putnam, R. (1993). Education for democracy. *Educational Theory, 43*, 361–376.

Remy, R., Patrick, J., Saffell, D., Clayton, G., & Whitaker, G. (2003). *Civics today: Citizenship, economics, and you*. New York: Glencoe McGraw-Hill.

Ross, M. (2006). Is democracy good for the poor? *American Journal of Political Science, 50,* 860–874.

Shapiro, I. (2002). Why the poor don't soak the rich: Notes on democracy and distribution. *Daedalus, 130,* 118–128.

Singer, P. (2004). *One world: The ethics of globalization.* (2nd ed.). New Haven, CT: Yale University Press.

West, C. (1989). *The American evasion of philosophy: A genealogy of pragmatism.* Madison: University of Wisconsin Press.

West, C. (2004). *Democracy matters: Winning the fight against imperialism.* New York: The Penguin Press.

CHAPTER FIFTEEN

Negotiating a Parallel Curriculum

Making Space for Critical Civic Literacy in the Social Studies Classroom

CHRISTOPHER LEAHEY

Good citizenship cannot be indoctrinated. Our superpatriots favor indoctrination, and they would reduce to a narrow catechism the rich heritage that is America. But we teachers know that indoctrination alienates discerning students, and the degree to which it "takes" robs students of the ability to think critically and to adjust to the realities, the diversities, and the inevitable changes of life.

Let me repeat: Good citizenship cannot be indoctrinated. Good citizenship is a by-product of an intelligent understanding of the range and complexities of life and of society.

Besides, good citizenship is not good enough. Every person is more than a citizen of a national state; he is more than a mere political animal. He is a human being, and a human being has more than a political nature. He has a social nature, an economic nature, an artistic nature, a moral nature. The objective of the social studies is to make more than good citizens; it is to make well-rounded, decent, and civilized human beings. If properly taught, all subjects contribute to these ends, but by their very nature the social studies and humanities should contribute the most.

(CARLETON, 1955)

These are the opening lines of political science professor William G. Carleton's speech delivered to the student body of Mississippi State College for Women in April of 1955. In this speech, Carleton urged the student body to develop their intellect and resist the pressures to conform created by big business, big government, the mass media and the "mass standards increasingly applied to education ..." (p. 1367). He argued that democracy starts with the individual and the community, and that liberty was "the ability to make personal choices in significant life situations" (p. 1366). These liberties, he warned, could be threatened by groups who hold more power and act in undemocratic ways "to trample on the individual rights of members of other groups and impair liberty" (p. 1366). The best way to safeguard liberty and democracy, he reasoned, was to embrace a social studies that provided "perspective, balance, and critical judgment," supporting students in "meeting…problems as they arise, and adjusting them in light of [the] cultural past and of changed conditions" (p. 1368).

While Carleton's words were spoken some 55 years ago, his concerns about cultivating a critical citizenry possessing the skills and disposition to understand their individual political, social, and economic interests is particularly germane in today's prevailing climate of standardization and accountability. This essay explores the meaning of critical civic literacy; the constraints core curricular standards, accountability mechanisms, and high-stakes testing place on democratic education and critical civic literacy; and how social studies teachers can negotiate a parallel curriculum that supports a form of democratic education that empowers students to use history as a medium to critically analyze the past and present, and work toward a more equitable future.

Democracy and Critical Civic Literacy

At the heart of democratic education is the classical notion that education is a prerequisite for personal freedom. In the classical world, a proper education provided students with the ability to think critically about the most pressing issues of the day, deliberate their cause and meaning, and speak eloquently about the possible solutions (Martin, 1996). For those privileged Athenians who had access to the academy, education was not only training of the mind, but also training for public life. Classic liberal education emphasized the wholeness between thought and action, it recognized learning and knowledge was not limited to predetermined, fixed ends; instead, learning was the ongoing application of reason and judgment to deliberate and solve problems in an ever-changing world (Reid, 1999).

Deliberation and Democracy

If we accept the idea that a liberal education is designed to support students in developing reason and judgment to work collectively to solve problems, we can understand education as a social practice. As such, the primary mission of a liberal education and social studies in particular, is to train students to become intelligent, active, citizens capable of working together to solve problems. Dewey (1991) explains that a democratic society is one that "makes provisions for participation in its good of all members on equal terms and which secures flexible readjustment of its institutions through the interaction of the different forms of associated life …" (p. 99). This interaction assumes the existence of a citizenry that possesses the ability to evaluate and even challenge the forces that shape their lives. At the heart of democratic political life is political judgment emanating from activity and discourse with those that share similar *and* divergent interests. This requires each citizen to be prepared to engage their fellow citizens in a critique of the status quo, as well as a discourse of what may be possible, and the best ways to pursue new possibilities. Barber (1998) puts it best when he asserts that "Democratic political judgment can be exercised only by citizens interacting with one another in the context of mutual deliberation and decision-making on the way to willing common actions" (p. 25).

To fully appreciate the nature of democratic deliberation it is necessary to view deliberation as a dynamic, continuous process. Gutmann and Thompson (1996) assert that "deliberation continues through stages, as officials present their proposals, citizens respond, officials revise, citizens react, and the stages recur" (p. 143). Embedded within these recurring stages are the principles of reciprocity, publicity, and accountability. Reciprocity, Gutmann and Thompson explain, requires public policy decisions to be made under terms of equality, where policy decisions must be justified in a way that opposing parties will find acceptable. The principle of publicity demands that officials provide reasons for policy decisions, and that all relevant information be made available to the public. The third principle, the principle of accountability, calls for public officials to openly justify their decisions and "give reasons that can be accepted by all those bound by laws and policies they justify" (Gutmann & Thompson, 1996, p. 129).

The contours of deliberative politics can be found in many areas of contemporary life ranging from the design of the social studies curriculum to debates about how best to provide adequate health insurance to American citizens to the ongoing debate surrounding stem-cell research. The current debate over government funding of stem-cell research is fascinating, as it involves religious values, ethical concerns about new medical treatments, and questions regarding the government's role in supporting or stifling cutting-edge medical research. The debate over stem-cell research can be traced to the 1960s when Canadian scientists Ernest McCulloch and James E. Till explored stem cells in the bone marrow of mice in research at the University of Toronto. As new discoveries were made in both the sources of self-renewing stem cells (e.g., human embryos, umbilical cords) and the possible uses of such cells (e.g., treating cancers, repairing damaged organs and tissue), various Christian religious organizations objected to destroying human embryos to develop new stem-cell lines. This came to a head in 2001, when President George Bush limited government funding to supporting existing stem-cell lines, but not supporting new lines of research involving human embryos (Wikipedia, 2010). This decision generated a lively discussion about the promise of stem-cell research as well as the ethical problems associated with tampering with and/or destroying human embryos. Between 2005 and 2007, Congress passed a series of laws expanding federally funded stem-cell research that were later vetoed by President Bush. Presently, the Obama administration does not allow federal funds to be used to support the development of new lines, although public funds can be used to support stem-cell lines created and developed by private organizations. Federal restrictions notwithstanding, the issues regarding the government's role in supporting stem-cell research is far from being resolved. The last decade has been marked by breakthroughs in locating new sources of stem cells such as human skin, hair, and amniotic fluid, as well as processes to harvest cells without destroying the embryo (Swaminathan, 2007; Wade, 2005; Weiss, 2005). These developments are likely to sustain this complex deliberation for the next several decades, and as we move forward the arguments for and against government support of new stem-cell lines will fuel more deliberative politics about the relationship between science, religion, and government.

Defining Critical Civic Literacy

Whereas deliberative politics is a dynamic process that requires citizens and stakeholders to engage in a dialogue with their elected officials, a critical approach to civic literacy necessarily involves using a deliberative approach to examining the world and the forces that influence our daily lives. At the heart of critical civic literacy is the notion that students must be taught to question the constructs and categories offered in schools, the corporate media, and dominant cultural groups. Critical civic literacy rejects the notion that knowledge can be directly transmitted from curriculum to teacher, from teacher to student in politically neutral, encapsulated forms. Rather, a critical approach to civic literacy insists that students become active participants in constructing their own knowledge and worldviews and use education as a tool to interrogate and confront the forces that both shape and limit their lives. Giroux (1987) explains, "At its best, a theory of critical literacy needs to develop pedagogical practices in which the battle to make sense of one's life reaffirms and furthers the need for teachers and students to recover their own voices so they can retell their own histories and in so doing 'check and criticize the history [they] are told against they one [they] have lived'" (p. 15).

A critical approach also allows for the examination of how social injustices and unequal power relationships adversely influence the policies and decisions that affect our lives. Wolk (2003) offers this definition of critical literacy:

> Critical literacy is about how we see and interact with the world; it is about having, as a regular part of one's life, the skills and desire to evaluate society and the world. That critique is especially focused on issues of power: Who has it and who is denied it; how it is used and how it is abused. More specifically, that critique revolves around issues of race, culture, gender, media, and the environment in the hope of creating a more just, humane, democratic, and equal world. (Wolk, 2003, p. 101)

If we return to the example of stem-cell research, a critical approach not only considers whether or not federal funds should be set aside to support research, but might also ask "Who benefits from such restrictions?" "What are the consequences of allowing private corporations to take the lead in conducting stem-cell research, maintaining cell lines, and developing therapies?" "Are these restrictions likely to make stem-cell therapies more or less accessible for lower-class citizens, the millions of uninsured Americans, or racial and ethnic minorities?" These types of questions indicate a willingness to engage in a dialogue that acknowledges the larger social context in which policies are made. It also underscores the reality that we do not live in a world where power and goods are distributed equally, and such iniquities are often reproduced through government, public policy, and in schools. A robust form of critical civic literacy encourages citizens to do more than react to those public policies placed on the agenda for deliberation. It takes a proactive approach that sees students as having the capacity to use their understanding of the world to identify problematic policies, raise awareness, and work together to place those policies on the agenda and to have them satisfactorily resolved.

While cultivating the habits of mind that support students in thoughtful analysis of public policy and the skills of deliberation is a worthwhile goal in the social studies classroom, deliberation is not an end in and of itself. All too often students experience a false deliberation that is decontextualized, disconnected from daily problems, and confined to the classroom. To offer only analysis, debate, and vibrant classroom discussion without a practical application or purposeful political action is to stop short of preparing students for active citizenship. Action is the essential product of democratic education. In *The Public and Its Problems*, Dewey (1927) declared that the public does not actually exist until the disorganized citizenry is activated by what it perceives as a problematic government or economic policy. Private citizens become public when they choose to set aside narrow self-interest and the distractions of popular culture and work together to address or challenge those policies that appear to be unjust or threatening. This work allows private citizens to become public citizens who work together to solve problems, pursue goals, and find common ground about future action

Implicit within the deliberative tradition is the notion that citizens must possess the ability to understand their interests, use reason and logic to evaluate the policies that shape their lives, and to organize to challenge those policies that appear detrimental or dangerous or to promote policies that improve people's lives (Bohman, 2000; Mathews, 1996). We can see these movements throughout the United States. In upstate New York, the Sierra Club's Gas Drilling Task force mobilized to raise awareness and oppose corporate hydrofracking, the high-pressure injection of unspecified chemicals, sand, and water into the ground to create fissures in the shale, releasing natural gas (Sierra Club, 2010). The Gulf Coast Civic Works Project is a student group gathering support for a federal bill to support the creation of 100,000 jobs to rebuild infrastructure destroyed in Hurricane Katrina and restore estuaries, wetlands, and fisheries spoiled by British Petroleum's oil spill (Gulf Coast Civic Works Project). A group of Arizona high school teachers, citing infringements on free speech and equal protection, have recently filed a lawsuit against the State of Arizona for prohibiting ethnic studies from being taught in public classrooms (Change.org). In each of these cases citizens are working together to address problems or perceived inequities. As social studies educators, it is our responsibility to create spaces for students to use reason, personal values, and life experiences to examine public policy, form positions, and act.

Critical Civic Literacy in the Age of Accountability

Producing students who possess the desire to work toward developing their own voices and the skills to effectively deliberate public policy and to recreate their world is a goal worth achieving. Dewey reasoned that "if our schools turned out their pupils in the attitude of mind which is conducive to good judgment in any department of affairs in which the pupils are placed, they have done more than if they sent out their pupils merely possessed of vast stores of information, or high degrees of skills in specialized branches" (Dewey, 1991, p. 101). Active citizens, capable of using judgment to engage in public deliberation, and working to improve the world are not born, however. Rather, they must be created, and the prevailing climate of standards-based reform undermines the development of such a citizenry. Specifically, the use of standardized test results as the primary indicator of student achievement (and teacher efficacy) and the narrowing of the school curriculum has placed considerable constraints on teaching students to become thoughtful citizens who possess the skills to advocate for themselves and their fellow citizens.

The New Cult of Education Efficiency

While the use of standardized tests and curriculum can be traced back to the military tests and the application of the principles of scientific management to the classroom (Gould, 1996; Callahan, 1962), the passage of the No Child Left Behind Act (NCLB) fundamentally changed the role high-stakes tests would play in defining educational achievement in America. Although it was not the first time curricular standards or high-stakes tests were used in schools, it marked the first time the federal and state governments used test scores as the primary yardstick to measure education quality and student achievement. The passage of NCLB marked a new era in education in which new technologies in recording, retrieving, sharing, and storing test data would be used to provide federal and state officials a framework to monitor schools. This framework is presently used on a national level as part of a new data-driven culture of test-driven school reform. Test grades have evolved to be more than a measure of what students learn in class; they are now a part of a larger bureaucratic system that uses test grades to evaluate programs, teacher effectiveness, and school quality.

The implementation of top-down accountability is an ongoing, all-encompassing ritual. Starting at the top and working down, NCLB requires all schools to be making "Adequate Yearly Progress" (AYP) toward a set of target test scores that every public school in America is to meet by 2014. To make AYP, students must earn test scores that the individual states deem "Proficient," an abstract and arbitrary level of achievement set by state officials who can (and do) lower cut scores to demonstrate improvement or raise cut scores to avoid criticism for lowering standards and expectations (see Ravitch, 2010; Berliner & Nichols, 2007). Schools that fail to reach academic targets (as evidenced by test scores) are required by law to allow students to transfer to other public, private, or charter schools within the district. Schools that continuously fail to make AYP may be restructured, have their administrators fired, or in extreme cases, be closed.

The Obama administration has recently added an additional layer of top-down bureaucratic reform to America's public schools. "Race to the Top" (RTTT) legislation is a $4 billion competitive federal program that calls for, among other things, lifting statutory limits on charter schools and using standardized test results to determine teacher effectiveness as well as a factor in retention, dismissal, and tenure decisions. This has created a new collaboration among states, the federal government, and teacher unions. In New York State, a winner of a Race to the Top grant, the Board of Regents, New York State Department of Education (NYSED), and New York State Union of Teachers designed a "performance-based" teacher evaluation system. This new system will assign teachers an effectiveness score out of a possible 100 points. Forty percent of this score will be based on student test scores, while the other sixty percent will be developed at the local level. These composite scores will be used to assign New York State's teachers one of four categories: "highly effective," "effective," "developing," or "ineffective" (NYSED, 2010).

In addition to these reforms, the nation is moving toward developing and implementing a common curriculum in English language arts and mathematics. This common core curriculum will be implemented in all schools throughout the country. It is suggested that a common core curriculum will strengthen the American education system in a variety of ways: it will eliminate the need for teachers to guess what will be on the assessments; it will make it easier for a students who change schools to continue with the same curricula; it will allow for teacher education programs to better prepare prospective teachers; and, lastly, it will foster disciplinary collaboration within schools and across the nation (American Educator, 2010). While these are laudable goals, a common core curriculum may make it impossible for teachers to design lessons and activities to meet the diverse needs of the student populations and communities they serve. If a common core curriculum is implemented in social studies one might wonder who should be granted the authority to determine the content, scope of study, and assessment design for every student in the nation. Furthermore, Wraga (2010) points out that the language of the core curricula in English language arts and mathematics fails to acknowledge schools' traditional mission to prepare students for active, intelligent citizenship in favor of preparing students for college-level work and to successfully compete in the new global economy.

Throughout the last decade education officials and teachers working at the local level have experienced a significant erosion in their power to operate schools, develop and implement curricula, and assess students. NCLB, the emphasis on standardized testing, the recent move toward evaluating teachers with test scores, and the call for a common core curriculum have taken many of the most important decisions out of the hands of the professionals who work directly with students.

Teaching in a Standardized Environment

While the stated goal of standards-based learning and the development of core curricula is to raise student achievement through carefully monitoring student, teacher, and school performance as evidenced by test scores, standards-based learning is an educational program founded on a set of assumptions about curriculum, learning, and evaluation that make critical democratic education challenging, if not impossible. The first assumption is that local education officials do not have the capacity to develop curricular materials or design assessment programs that fit the unique needs of the communities they serve. Deborah Meier (2004) asserts that federal legislation that relies on standardized exams as the key component for measuring learning is likely "to dumb down decades of efforts to provide all children with what was once offered only to the rich—a genuinely challenging and engaging program of study" (p. 71). Rather than allowing local educators to make important decisions about curriculum, assessment, and instruction that meet the distinctive needs of the students schools serve, standards-based education imposes a rigid bureaucratic system where the curriculum and instruction is narrowed to reflect the content and types of activities likely to appear on the exam. This irrational quest for accountability becomes "a totalizing discourse" that redefines critical thinking as the ability to correctly answer standardized test questions, dictates what can and cannot be said in faculty meetings, and determines which staff members are and are not deemed quality educators (Lipman, 2004, para. 29).

By allowing federal and state officials to define curriculum and assessment, test scores take on a second meaning: they not only serve as the primary method of measuring what students learn, but they also enforce compliance with the sanctioned state curriculum and ensure that teachers make it a priority to teach the skills and content featured on standardized exams. Most standardized tests, however, feature simple multiple-choice questions, scripted writing assignments, and use grading scales and 5-point rubrics to measure student achievement. Sacks (1999) questions the use of timed exams as an appropriate device for measuring the wide variety of learning styles and modalities students present in the classroom. He argues that the administration of timed, mass-produced tests undervalues important cognitive skills like deliberation, critical thinking, and problem-solving while rewarding those students who possess the skills to excel at completing "fast-paced, logical, and reflexive tasks" (Sacks, 1999, p. 219).

The second assumption of standards-based reform is that scientific principles should guide educational reform. Frederick Winslow Taylor, the father of scientific management, explains that

"The development of a science…involves the establishment of many rules, laws, and formulae which replace the judgment of the individual workman and can be effectively used only after having been systematically recorded, indexed, etc." (Taylor, 1947). Preparing teachers for working in a standards-based environment requires imparting a set of skills, activities, and techniques to effectively and efficiently deliver the predetermined concepts found within the curriculum. Authentic pedagogical practices, critical analysis, and personal experience are not valued within this system, as they cannot be measured by the limited technology of the test. Rather, producing highly effective teachers is reduced to training prospective educators to efficiently deliver the content in a way that will result in students attaining a high degree of recall that will translate into high scores on tests administered at the end of the academic year. This, it is believed, is the key to putting American students on a level of academic achievement comparable to their international peers.

Teaching within this system makes creativity, intellectual curiosity, dialogue, and even hope unnecessary elements for a well-run classroom operated by a highly trained teacher. It denies teachers and students the right to be treated as human beings whose experiences and ideas inform the way they see the world. Instead, the world of standards-based learning prizes predictability and conformity, and educating the masses is a technical problem that can be overcome by carefully delineating the curriculum, aligning classroom instruction, and designing resources around the test. In a data-driven world of standards-based learning, a well-organized curricula has the potential to integrate classroom instruction and assessment. Curricular experts (Jacobs, 1997; Hale, 2007) have called for replacing district-based curriculum committees with pseudo-scientific procedures that can be used to analyze curricular implementation, classroom instruction, and student assessment, the primary goal being the development of curriculum maps that indicate the appropriate amount of time allotted for the topic, concept, and skills within a unit of instruction for each course offered within a district. Building curriculum maps for each grade level allows district-level administrators to use test data to evaluate the larger educational program and determine strengths and weaknesses within and across disciplines and align classroom instruction with state standards.

In addition to placing new demands on streamlining curriculum and instruction, the implementation of standards-based learning initiatives measured by high-stakes testing has also ushered in a new body of literature defining quality classroom instruction and what is means to be an effective teacher. Marzano et al.'s *A Handbook for Classroom Instruction That Works* (1999) offers practical strategies for summarizing and recording notes, identifying similarities and differences, setting objectives, generating and testing hypotheses, designing homework, and using graphic organizers to visually represent received "knowledge" (Marzano et al., 2001). More recently, Lemov's popular book, *Teach Like a Champion* (2010) contains 49 techniques of successful classroom teachers. While he offers sound advice for designing lessons and units of instruction, many of these techniques blend classroom instruction with discipline and control (e.g., Technique #2: Demanding students who provide incorrect answers repeat the correct response when it is given; Technique #28: Teaching students a routine of how to correctly enter the classroom; Technique #34: Training students to give non-verbal seat signals when they need to use the bathroom or sharpen a pencil). These types of techniques implicitly degrade teachers and students by treating quality instruction not as a humanistic endeavor of learning and discovery, but as a series of rules and procedures that can be applied and implemented by any teacher in any context to satisfy the idols of raising test scores and preparing students for college-level work.

While these volumes are valuable resources for classroom teachers working within a standards-based environment, there is a common thread that is undeniably problematic for those of us interested in critical civic literacy. The content of each of these books and the standards movement by and large are organized around teachers imparting information and skills that will support students in meeting predetermined curricular objectives and performing well on high-stakes paper and pencil exams. Wexler (1989) describes this quest for predictability and efficiency as a form of "scientism" where the construction of knowledge rooted in personal experience and guided by reason is replaced with the sterile transmission of predetermined sets of information and skills. The problem is that young people and teachers are compelled to passively accept these preordained concepts and skills as the ends of education while neglecting personal experience, local history, or community-based resources. This makes critical inquiry and reflection incompatible with the nation's larger mission to raise test scores. For instance, Morrell (2008) describes a powerful critical media literacy project where Los Angeles students worked with local media professionals and UCLA staff to create 5-minute documentaries on their community and schools. He explains that this project was conducted in a summer seminar, as it could not fit within the parameters of the traditional schedule and articulated curricular disciplines (Morrrell, 2008).

In addition to divesting local officials of control over the curriculum and reducing the art of teaching to a set of procedures, standards-based learning necessarily distills the complex acts of teaching and learning to information that can be quantified, compared, and generalized as reliable measures of student achievement. Wayne Au (2009) explains that this process of quantification necessarily involves reducing students and complex social conditions to numerical values:

> The reduction to a numerical score is a key requirement of systems of testing, because it enables the perpetuation of the means-end rationality associated with social efficiency. In the process of the quantification of student knowledge and understanding, students themselves are necessarily quantified as a number. This quantification lies at the heart of the measurement itself, which turns people and real social conditions into easily measurable and comparable numbers and categories. (Au, 2009, p. 40)

While standards-based reform initiatives reduce instruction, learning, and children to numerical values for internal evaluation, Vinson and Ross (2001) further argue that standards-based educational reform also creates a new form of discipline in which test scores serve as the subject of bureaucratic surveillance, intruding on schools, classrooms, and students, measuring the degree to which the official curriculum has been faithfully carried out. The reporting of these test scores creates a spectacle (another form of discipline) by which the public is provided limited, de-contextualized information (i.e., test scores) to evaluate school quality and make facile comparisons within and across school districts (Vinson & Ross, 2001).

Assailing the Unthinkable

Where a democratic system of education might be anchored in inquiry-based learning, problem solving, the development of judgment, and the fostering of dialogue, a standards-based approach prizes simplicity, speed, and efficiency. Behind this "cult of efficiency" (Callahan,

1962) lies a discourse of power, where an externally defined and ideologically charged program of compliance dictates the selection of content, organization of curriculum, and development of assessment, creating an artificial "academic" world that bears little resemblance to the complex world in which we actually live. Nonetheless, these representations have been imported within schools via the curriculum, textbook, and test, and educators are measured by the degree to which they faithfully carry out the appropriate rituals to attain the specified results. The outcome is the creation of an instrumentalist literacy that "prevent(s) the development of critical thinking that enables one to 'read the world' critically and to understand the reasons and linkages behind the facts" (Macedo, 2006, p. 16). In the end, one might be concerned that a highly educated student may master the state or national curriculum, but have little understanding or knowledge of the forces that shape her life or the world in which she lives.

By making test results the primary indication of student achievement and teacher effectiveness, standards-based learning systems also reinforce the boundaries of academic disciplines. Test-driven reform demands that classroom instruction and a teacher's pedagogy be subordinate to the content and structure of the exam. Learning and understanding become a high-paced ritual of instruction and assessment, where teachers serve as disciplinary tour guides, responding to the pressure to "cover" the vast number of content objectives that may or may not appear on the next exam. Standards-based classroom instruction is driven by a fairly (although not completely) predictable set of content objectives that will be used to measure students' ability to perform well on multiple-choice questions and scripted writing assignments. In an attempt to prepare students for this exam, teachers rely on textbooks written in a format reflecting the content and structure of the state curriculum. From year to year, the items and tasks will change only in content, creating what I have described as a "curricular shell-game" (Leahey, 2010) encouraging teachers and administrators to analyze past exams to predict content of upcoming exams, and guide curricular organization and classroom instruction to maximize student performance on future exams.

In addition to narrowing the curriculum and creating pressure to teach to the test, standards-based learning in social studies distorts the past through a process of simplification where sterilized textbooks serve as the primary narrative of the past, rendered as an a-political string of figures, events, and concepts presented without a sense of perspective in text without footnotes (Loewen, 1996). While textbooks necessarily obstruct teachers' efforts to gain free, unfettered access to the past, "Standardized testing confines legitimate 'interaction' to test driven teaching and learning. It reduces meaningful 'intercourse' to that which is officially and formally sanctioned" (Vinson, Gibson, & Ross, 2004). This framework of curriculum-textbook-test makes it difficult to approach studying the past as problematic, asking questions of the historical record, and drawing lessons that can be connected to contemporary events. For instance, studying ancient Greece from a critical perspective with implications for today might require students to examine various city-states, their political policies, and their stance toward colonization. Students might closely read Pericles's Funeral Oration and note its function in perpetuating the Peloponnesian wars. A critically oriented study of Athens would include an examination of the relationship between power and truth, social class and political privilege, as well as gender and inequality. Students might explore Plato's *Republic* as a foundational text about the relationship among citizens, authority, and rulers. By contrast, the standards-based approach found in New

York State's core curriculum merely requires students to associate Athens with direct democracy and Sparta with militarism, identify Athenian cultural achievements, and connect Alexander the Great with the diffusion of Hellenistic culture (NYSED, 1999, p. 95).

The result of this narrowing of the curriculum is that the exploration of alternative perspectives, the critical analysis of primary documents, or the investigation of Greek ideals and institutions become unnecessary (and sometimes unwelcome) detours in the quest to cover all of the content that may appear on the next exam. Approaching history education in this fashion makes drawing parallels between the past and present nearly impossible. The standardized curricula, tests, and texts will not reward teachers and students who draw connections between the disastrous results between Athens's imperial ambitions and the United States's present military predicament. The organization of the curriculum and test sublimate the recitation of discrete bits of information while making such connections impossible, or unthinkable. Describing the "thinkable" and "unthinkable," French sociologist Pierre Bourdieu (1971) asserts that one role schools play is to "ensure the consensus of various groups on a minimal definition of the legitimate and illegitimate, of which objects deserve discussion and which not, of what must be known and what can be ignored, of what can and what must be admired" (Bourdieu, 1971, p. 1255). Corporate publishing houses, political elites, and bureaucratic leaders have the power and authority to regulate the process of curriculum development, textbook design, and test content. Within the boundaries of the standardized system of learning, the classroom teacher's primary function is to uncritically introduce, rehearse, and reinforce those messages embedded within the state curriculum, printed in textbook narratives, and likely to be featured on the exam. Indeed, the uncritical acceptance and endorsement of these messages is the *sine qua non* of high-quality teaching in the present standards-based system that prevails throughout the United States of America.

Making Space for Critical Civic Literacy

Many classroom teachers are presently faced with negotiating a way to implement critical civic literacy while resisting the call to standardize their instruction and assessment. Kincheloe (2008) explains that critically oriented teachers engage in a form of praxis by examining the relationship between theory and practice and acknowledging multiple forms of knowledge that allow teachers to "perform our jobs in more informed, practical, ethical, democratic, politically just, self-aware, and purposeful ways" (p. 117). Rather than abandoning critical civic literacy, progressive teachers can negotiate a parallel curriculum that makes critical civic literacy a vital part of classroom study. The first step in developing social studies curriculum centered on critical civic literacy is to reorient the way we think about the past. We must acknowledge that the past can never be fully known and that our knowledge of the past is predicated on asymmetries of power that influence the historical archive and what is left from those who have gone before us. Trouillot (1995) explains that "the making of the archives involves a number of selective operations: selection of producers, selection of evidence, selection of themes, selection of procedures—which means, at best, the differential ranking and, at worst, the exclusion of some producers, some evidence, some themes, some procedures" (p. 53). These asymmetries of power also influence access to the historical archive, what is considered worthy of narration, who sets the boundaries of permissible discourse, and which voices are included and which are silenced. Within our schools, teachers can actively question why history is presented as a list of concepts, figures, and achievements. One might also ask why some concepts or figures are included in the curriculum and textbook and why others are not. (I have yet to encounter a textbook that includes Ernesto "Che" Guevara.) Actively questioning these taken-for-granted assumptions provides new opportunities to achieve a deeper understanding of our profession as well as possibilities to improve it.

When we consider that what we know about the past is wholly dependent on a series of choices that draw our attention to one of many ways to tell a story while silencing others, the calls for student proficiency and even mastery of American history or world history appear hopelessly incompatible with the complex nature of historical production and the limited nature of understanding the past through the use of the curriculum, textbook, primary and secondary resources, popular film, and literature. Complexity and power embedded within historical production requires critical classroom teachers to approach history education modestly, seeking tentative answers to questions, acknowledging the limitations of what can and cannot be known about the past while simultaneously attending to how power and privilege influence various historical productions. An inquiry-oriented approach means that there can be no one textbook, only texts that offer incomplete fragments of the past. Approaching history in this manner may be best described as "following the threads" (Selwyn, 2009) as opposed to "mastering the curriculum." Selwyn (2009) explains that this form of inquiry draws upon student interest, provides time and resources for in-depth investigation, allows opportunities to draw upon multiple disciplines, requires students to take an authentic approach to investigating the past, and provides choices for how the information is communicated and assessed (pp. 13–14).

Negotiating a Parallel Curriculum

While many teachers may appreciate and even desire to take a critical approach to history education, there are few who make the leap from theory to practice. Although the current policy of standards-based learning does not allow individual teachers to write the curriculum or control the design and content of the test, teachers can and do directly influence the way students interact with the formal curriculum, the selection of materials, the way in which texts are used, classroom interaction, and the ways in which students are assessed. Perhaps the most common way critical civic literacy is used in schools is as a supplement to the social studies curriculum. Hess (2009) relates how the discussion of controversial issues can be used in the classroom to prepare students to participate in political engagement, instill respect and tolerance for diverse perspectives, and forge relationships between social groups that have significant differences in political orientations. In her work on social studies teaching methods, Schmidt (2007) describes ways in which community-based social justice projects can be used to exceed the expectations found in most curriculum standards. She describes a variety of projects that include the use of photography, websites, and historical archives to capture community-based problems as well as the poverty, racism, and sexism linked to unjust social policies (Schmidt, 2007). While these concepts and activities are valuable ways to introduce students to critical literacy, they are limited to fit within the constraints of time and space created by the dominant framework of the curriculum, textbook, and test.

A second way critical civic literacy has been implemented into the social studies classroom is by generating themes and organizing instruction around these themes. Teachers who work directly with students can also engage in this type of negotiating. Sleeter (2005), in her study of classroom teachers working to implement multicultural curricula under the constraints of what she calls the "standards-textbook-test trilogy," offers a road map to "un-standardizing the curriculum" (p. 146). She suggests classroom teachers use Wiggins and McTighe's (1998) backward design that starts with teachers reflecting on the essential ideas students are to learn, what they believe is valuable to teach, and what they view as the best way for students to demonstrate their learning (Sleeter, 2005). From there Sleeter suggests that teachers actively organize the curriculum, select resources, and develop assessment strategies around big ideas they find to be both meaningful and engaging. Using Sleeter's work as a guide, I have implemented critical civic literacy within my ninth-grade world history class. At the beginning of the year we construct definitions for concepts such as equality, hegemony, power, and oppression. As we work our way through the world history curriculum, we apply these concepts to a variety of legal documents starting with Hammurabi's Code to the Twelve Tables of Rome, the Justinian Code, the Magna Carta, and the Declaration of the Rights of Man and of the Citizen. Operationalizing the curriculum in this way empowers students to engage in critical investigation and see history not as an isolated set of facts, but as a series of struggles toward equality and freedom.

A third and perhaps most radical way to implement critical civic literacy is to either tacitly or explicitly abandon the standardized curriculum for what Shor (1992) describes as an "agenda for empowerment." This "agenda for empowerment" questions conventional wisdom (e.g., "Why does the government force children to go to school?"), allows students to actively participate in directing their own learning, and reestablishes the relationship between experience, emotion, and thinking (Shor, 1992, p. 11). This can be done to highlight important critical issues that may include multicultural education, social justice, environmental degradation, militarism, and issues of equity (Au, Bigelow, & Karp, 2007). For instance, in the run-up to the 2003 U.S. invasion of Iraq, I designated classroom instruction to study the political, economic, and historical antecedents to the conflict, the social differences between Western and Middle Eastern culture, and the mainstream media's treatment of the conflict. This was a choice I made in response to the questions students raised about the conflict as well as their concerns for relatives who were serving in the armed services (Leahey, 2004). I intentionally chose to set aside the state curriculum and make the crisis an event to be actively studied and analyzed. This allowed me to make time and space for assisting students (and acknowledging their humanity) with their questions and concerns, and treat history not as the settled past, but as a force that continuously shapes the present state of affairs between the United States and Iraq as well as our own lived experiences.

Conclusion

What is at stake is more than international comparisons of students on standardized exams. What is at stake is the kind of experiences, skills, and cognitive dispositions we want our students to possess and draw upon as they become the citizens of tomorrow. The prevailing system of top-down, standards-based reform that values conformity, uncritical acceptance of official directives, and the celebration of technical literacy is bound to produce students who lack the skills and perhaps even the desire to address the complex problems of social decay, environmental degradation, corporate power, and economic decline that currently confronts the United States of America. What classroom educators interested in critical civic literacy need is not more efficient methods to teach the standardized curriculum, but more ideas and concepts to create spaces in which we can examine our lives, acknowledge lived experiences, and engage in critical inquiry. These are the prerequisite steps toward preparing our students for political engagement and pursuing a more just, safe, and equitable world.

Bibliography

American Educator. (2010). Common core curriculum: An idea whose time has come. *American Educator, 34*(4), p. 2.

Au, W. (2009). *Unequal by design: High-stakes testing and the standardization of inequality.* New York: Routledge.

Au, W., Bigelow, B., & Karp, S. (Eds.). (2007). *Rethinking our classrooms: Teaching for equity and justice* (Vol. 1). Milwaukee, WI: Rethinking Schools.

Barber, B. (1998). *A passion for democracy.* Princeton, NJ: Princeton University Press.

Berliner, D.C., & Nichols, S. (2007). *Collateral damage: How high-stakes testing corrupts America's schools.* Cambridge, MA: Harvard Education Press.

Bohman, J. (2000). *Public deliberation: Pluralism, complexity, and democracy.* Cambridge, MA: MIT Press.

Bourdieu, P. (1971, October 15). The thinkable and unthinkable. *Times Literary Supplement,* 1255–1256.

Callahan, R. (1962). *Education and the cult of efficiency.* Chicago: University of Chicago Press.

Carleton, W.G. (1955, July 17). Citizenship and the social studies: Not scientific precision but wisdom is the goal. *Vital Speeches of the Day, 21*(19), 1363–1369.

Change.org. (2010, October 25). *Arizona teachers sue against ethnic studies ban.* Retrieved December 5, 2010, from http://immigration.change.org/blog/view/arizona _teachers_sue_against_ethnic_studies_ban

Dewey, J. (1991). *How we think.* New York: Prometheus Books. (Original work published 1916)

Dewey, J. (1927). *The public and its problems.* New York: Swallow Press.

Dewey, J. (1944). *Democracy and education.* New York: The Free Press.

Giroux, H. (1987). Literacy and the pedagogy of political empowerment. In P. Friere & D. Macedo (Eds.), *Literacy: Reading the word and reading the world* (pp. 1–28). South Hadley, MA: Bergin and Garvey Publishers.

Gould, S.J. (1996). *The mismeasure of man.* New York: W.W. Norton and Company.

Gulf Coast Civic Works Project. (n.d.). Retrieved December 5, 2010, from http://www.solvingpoverty.com/

Gutmann, A., & Thompson, D. (1996). *Democracy and disagreement.* Cambridge, MA: Harvard University Press.

Hale, J. (2007). *A guide to curriculum mapping: Planning, implementing, and sustaining the process.* New York: Corwin Press.

Hess, D. (2009). *Controversy in the classroom: The democratic power of discussion.* New York: Routledge.

Jacobs, H.H. (1997). *Mapping the big picture: Integrating curriculum and assessment K–12.* Alexandria, VA: Association for Supervision and Curriculum Development.

Kincheloe, J. (2008). *Critical pedagogy.* New York: Peter Lang.

Kliebard, H. (1995). *The struggle for the American curriculum, 1893–1958*. New York: Routledge.

Leahey, C. (2010). *Whitewashing war: Historical myth, corporate textbooks, and the possibilities for democratic education*. New York: Teachers College Press.

Leahey, C. (2004). Examining media coverage: A classroom study of Iraq war news. *Social Education, 68*(4), 280–285.

Lemov, D. (2010). *Teach like a champion: 49 techniques that put students on the path to college*. San Francisco, CA: Jossey-Bass.

Lipman, P. (2004). Education accountability and repression of democracy post-9/11. *Journal for Critical Education Policy Studies, 2*(1). Retrieved December 2, 2010, from http://www.jceps.com/?pageID=article&articleID=23

Loewen, J. (1996). *Lies my teacher told me*. New York: Touchstone/Simon and Schuster.

Macedo, D. (2006). *Literacies of power: What Americans are not allowed to know*. Boulder, CO: Westview Press.

Martin, T.R. (1996). *Ancient Greece: From prehistoric to Hellenistic times*. New Haven, CT: Yale University Press.

Marzano, R. J., Norford, J. S., Paynter, D., Pickering, D., & Gaddy, B. (1999). *A handbook for classroom instruction that works*. Alexandria, VA: Association for Supervision and Curriculum Development.

Matthews, D. (1996). Reviewing and previewing civics. In W. Parker (Ed.), *Educating the democratic mind* (pp. 265–286). Albany: State University of New York Press.

Meier, D. (2004). NCLB and democracy. In D. Meier & G. Wood (Eds.), *Many children left behind: How the No Child Left Behind Act is damaging our children and our schools* (pp. 66–78). Boston: Beacon Press.

Morrell, E. (2008). *Critical literacy and urban youth*. New York: Routledge.

New York State Education Department. (1999). *Global history and geography core curriculum*. Albany: State University of New York Press.

New York State Education Department. (2010). Questions and answers related to implementation of the new comprehensive teacher and principal evaluation law (Education law §3012-c as added by Chapter 103 of the Laws of 2010). Retrieved December 1, 2010, from http://www.p12.nysed.gov/memos/performeval/qa083110.html

Ravitch, D. (2010). *The death and life of the great American school system: How testing and choice are undermining education*. New York: Basic Books.

Reid, W. (1999). *Curriculum as institution and practice: Essays in the deliberative tradition*. Mahwah, NJ: Lawrence Erlbaum Associates.

Sacks, P. (1999). *Standardized minds: The high price of America's testing culture and what we can do to change it*. Cambridge, MA: Perseus.

Schmidt, L. (2007). *Social studies that sticks: How to bring content and concepts to life*. Portsmouth, NH: Heinemann.

Selwyn, D. (2009). *Following the threads: Bringing inquiry research into the classroom*. New York: Peter Lang.

Shor, I. (1992). *Empowering education: Critical teaching for social change*. Chicago: University of Chicago Press.

Sierra Club. (2010). Stop the rush on New York State gas drilling. Retrieved December 5, 2010, from http://newyork.sierraclub.org/gas_drilling.html

Sleeter, C. (2005). *Un-standardizing curriculum: Multicultural teaching in the standards-based classroom*. New York: Teachers College Press.

Swaminathan, N. (2007, January 7). New source of stem-cells: Amniotic fluid. *Scientific American*. Retrieved July 3, 2010, from http:// www.scientific american.com/article.cfm?id=new-source-of-stem-cells

Taylor, F.W. (1947). *The principles of scientific management*. New York: W.W. Norton.

Trouillot, M. (1995). *Silencing the past: Power and the production of history*. Boston: Beacon Press.

Vinson, K., Gibson, R., & Ross, E.W. (2004). Pursuing authentic teaching in an age of standardization. In K. Kesson & E.W. Ross (Eds.), *Defending public schools: Teaching for a democratic society* (Vol. 2, pp. 79–95). Westport, CT: Praeger.

Vinson, K.D., & Ross, E.W. (2001). Education and the new disciplinarity: Surveillance, spectacle, and the case of SBER. *Cultural Logic, 4*(1). Retrieved December 2, 2010, from http://eserver.org/clogic/4–1/4–1.html

Wade, N. (2005, August 18). Furrier mice yield stem-cell discovery. *The New York Times* (online). Retrieved August 10, 2010, from http://www.nytimes.com/2005/08/18/science/18cell.html

Weiss, R. (2005, August 22). Skin cells converted to stem cells. *Washington Post* (online). Retrieved November 1, 2010, from http://www.washingtonpost.com/wpdyn/content/article/2005/08/21/AR2005082101180.html

Wexler, P. (1989). Curriculum in the closed society. In H.A. Giroux & P. McLaren (Eds.), *Critical pedagogy, the state, and cultural struggle* (pp. 92–104). Albany: State University of New York Press.

Wiggins, G. & McTighe, J. (1998). *Understanding by design*. Alexandria, VA: Association for Supervision and Curriculum Development.

Wikipedia. (2010). Stem cell controversy. Retrieved December, 1, 2010, from http://en.wikipedia.org/wiki/Stem_cell_controversy

Wolk, S. (2003). Teaching for critical literacy in the social studies. *The Social Studies, 94*(3), 101–106.

Wraga, W. (2010, August 18). Dangerous blind spots in the common core standards. *Education Week*. Retrieved November 31, 2010, from http://www.edweek.org/ew/articles/2010/08/18/01wraga.h30.html?tkn= UXTFLys0bd4Q6Uzl%2F%2B80Ppm%2FvJvW4gF6dlGA&intc=es

CHAPTER SIXTEEN

A Core Curriculum for Civic Literacy?

DONALD LAZERE

What role should collegiate liberal education play in a renewal of education for civic literacy? I propose a core curriculum based on the disciplines of critical thinking and argumentative rhetoric, along the lines of courses that I have taught for many years as part of English and humanities general education and breadth requirements. This immodest proposal necessitates no less than a re-definition of humanistic studies that centrally includes critical thinking about, and analysis of, public rhetoric at the local, national, and international levels. Far from being a radical proposal, this is a conservative one in returning to something more like the eighteenth-century rhetoric-based curriculum in American education, before the diaspora of studies in literature, composition, forensics, and other humanistic fields. Such a curriculum would, as Michael Halloran (1982) describes the eighteenth-century model, "address students as political beings, as members of a body politic in which they have a responsibility to form judgments and influence the judgments of others on public issues" (p. 108).

A 1980 report of the Rockefeller Foundation Commission on the Humanities, *The Humanities in American Life*, concluded:

> The humanities lead beyond "functional" literacy and basic skills to critical judgment and discrimination, enabling citizens to view political issues from an informed perspective . . . (12). High schools should concentrate on an articulated sequence of courses in English, history, and foreign languages. Courses in these disciplines should not divorce skills and methods from knowledge of content and cultural context. . . . English courses need to emphasize the connections between expression, logic, and the critical use of textual and historical evidence. (44)

Another historical artifact that I want to resurrect is a 1975 resolution by the National Council of Teachers of English:

> Resolved, that the National Council of Teachers of English support the efforts of English and related subjects to train students in a new literacy encompassing not only the decoding of print but the critical reading, listening, viewing, and thinking skills necessary to enable students to cope with the sophisticated persuasion techniques found in political statements, advertising, entertainment, and news.

Multiple impediments within and beyond the academic world in succeeding decades have prevented commonsense recommendations like these from being centrally incorporated in most undergraduate curricula (a topic that I pursued in "Bringing"). Few would dispute, however, that the social needs these statements addressed have become ever more acute over that period.

We have all by necessity been thinking a lot lately about one particular branch of civic literacy: economic knowledge. How many high school, college, or graduate students and teachers could pass a test on elementary understanding of the global economy, monetary versus fiscal policy, or arcane terms like derivatives, hedge funds, equity funds, sub-prime mortgages, and credit default swaps? How many among us understand how or why our personal economic fates—including our mortgages, retirement pensions, and universities' funding and endowments—are captive to booms and busts in the stock market and the occult realm of national and international high finance? In the prophetic words of the "corporate cosmology" revealed by the arch-capitalist Arthur Jensen in Paddy Chayefsky's 1976 film *Network*, "The totality of life on this planet" is now determined by "one vast and immane, interwoven, interacting, multi-variate, multinational dominion of dollars" (130).

What a tragic gulf lies between most citizens' understanding of these economic forces and their power over each of our daily lives and livelihoods. And what an enormous hole there is both in K–12 and college curricula in the absence of instruction in basic knowledge and critical understanding of these forces as an integral part of general education. One of the shameful aspects of No Child Left Behind and Race to the Top was their virtual exclusion of civic education. The last decade has seen an outpouring of books and reports, from both the political right and left, deploring young (and older) Americans' civic ignorance. Among the more constructive efforts, David Mindich in his book *Tuned Out: Why Americans Under 40 Don't Follow the News*, has made the highly sensible proposal of requiring a section in college entrance exams on civic literacy and current events. I would stipulate that this section should supplement, not preempt, sections on history, both emphasizing, in the Rockefeller Commission's words, "critical judgment and discrimination, enabling citizens to view political issues from an informed perspective."

It is encouraging that several national organizations have recently been formed, such as the Campaign for the Civic Mission of Schools, the Carnegie Foundation Political Engagement project Campus Compact and its Research University Civic Engagement Network, the Center for Information and Research on Civic Learning and Engagement, and the Association of American Colleges and Universities' program Core Commitments: Fostering Personal and Social Responsibility on College and University Campuses. These organizations have published important interdisciplinary books such as Colby et al., *Educating for Democracy* (2006), and Jacoby et al., *Civic Engagement in Higher Education* (2009). Many local campus programs have also been exemplary.[1] Addressing these issues in *The Assault on Reason*, Al Gore (2009) praised the American Political Science Association for starting a Task Force on Civic Education. That should prompt similar task forces in other professional associations, along with a unifying, umbrella organization, a National Commission on

Civic Education. Indeed, what is lacking is any kind of national coordination of organizations and curricular projects. Coordination is needed among various academic disciplines, as well as among programs for civic education at the secondary and postsecondary levels. We can hope for support in all these efforts from the Obama administration in the U.S. Department of Education or NEH. I am compiling a reference list on these topics, and I welcome all further ideas and leads.

Unfortunately, the very term "core curriculum" has become a culture-war wedge issue, with conservatives pre-empting it in the cause of Eurocentric tradition and American patriotism, thus provoking intransigent opposition from progressive champions of cultural pluralism and students' freedom to decide on their own studies. Surely, however, it is time for ideological adversaries to seek common ground in a curriculum that itself addresses issues of ideological partisanship and seeks to incorporate, if not overcome, them. Although my proposed curriculum leans to the left, I expect that conservatives would endorse parts of it and suggest reasonable modifications for others. One would hope for sponsorship in such efforts by both conservative and liberal foundations. In his recent *The Making of Americans*, E.D. Hirsch (2009) refines his notion of cultural literacy to champion a common national core of subject matter for citizenship. He denies favoring rote memorization of dry facts, but argues that critical thinking or rhetorical instruction can only be effectively taught in application to a base of essential factual knowledge. He opposes the kind of decontextualized standard tests imposed under No Child Left Behind but supports a standardized national curriculum that would facilitate tests based directly on the factual content in courses all students have taken, incorporating critical analysis and argumentation, and determined with input from diverse community constituencies.

I quite agree with Hirsch in relation to political literacy, and I admire his denial that he and his version of cultural literacy are politically conservative. In *Cultural Literacy* (1987) he endorsed "radicalism in politics, but conservatism in literate knowledge" (p. 22). Now he adds, "Practical improvement of our public education will require intellectual clarity and a depolarization of this issue. Left and right must get together on the principle of common content" (p. 177).

Any notion of national standards for curriculum or testing in secondary education, even if not required, sets off similar partisan hot-buttons, with conservatives fearing the tyranny of the liberal elite and defending the Jeffersonian tradition of local control, and liberals fearful of national conservative pressure groups imposing their own version of political correctness. In a depressing object lesson here, a panel of distinguished historians including Gary Nash and Joyce Appleby produced an excellent set of national standards for high school history that applied critical thinking and argumentative skills to historical knowledge. These standards, published in 1994, became the victim of a Republican culture-wars offensive. They were bizarrely made the subject of a full Senate vote, which was railroaded through with almost no senators having read them and overwhelmingly defeated (Nash, 1979). This fiasco set the cause of national standards back for over a decade, but bipartisan suggestions for its revival appear in recent works of Hirsch (2009), Diane Ravitch (2010), Martha Nussbaum (2010), Mike Rose (2006), Gerald Graff and Cathy Birkenstein (2008), and the National Governors' Association Common Core State Standards Initiative (2010). In *Not for Profit: Why Democracy Needs the Humanities* (2010), Nussbaum writes:

> If a nation wants to promote . . . democracy dedicated to "life, liberty and the pursuit of happiness" to each and every person, what abilities will it need to produce in its citizens? At least the following seem crucial: The ability to think well about political issues affecting the nation, to examine, reflect, argue, and debate, deferring to neither tradition nor authority. . . . (p. 25)

Critical Thinking, Cognitive Development, and Civic Literacy

The topics of study in my proposed curriculum are framed within the disciplines of critical thinking and cognitive development. A historical detour is necessary here. In 1980, Chancellor Glenn Dumke announced the requirement of formal instruction in critical thinking throughout the 19 California State University campuses, serving some 300,000 students. The announcement read:

> Instruction in critical thinking is to be designed to achieve an understanding of the relationship of language to logic, which should lead to the ability to analyze, criticize, and advocate ideas, to reason inductively and deductively, and to reach factual or judgmental conclusions based on sound inferences drawn from unambiguous statements of knowledge or belief. The minimal competence to be expected at the successful conclusion of instruction in critical thinking should be the ability to distinguish fact from judgment, belief from knowledge, and skills in elementary inductive and deductive processes, including an understanding of the formal and informal fallacies of language and thought.

Similar requirements were soon adopted by community colleges and secondary schools throughout California and elsewhere. Here is the list of "Basic Critical Thinking Skills" in the California State Department of Education's Model Curriculum for Grades 8–12 in 1984.

1. **Identify similarities and differences**
   The ability to identify similarities and differences among two or more objects, living things, ideas, events, or situations at the same or different points in time. Implies the ability to organize information into defined categories.
2. **Identify central issues or problems**
   The ability to identify the main idea or point of a passage, argument, or political cartoon, for example. At the higher levels, students are expected to identify central issues in complex political arguments. Implies ability to identify major components of an argument, such as reasons and conclusions.
3. **Distinguish fact from opinion**
   The ability to determine the difference between observation and inference.
4. **Recognize stereotypes and clichés**
   The ability to identify fixed or conventional notions about a person, group, or idea.
5. **Recognize bias, emotional factors, propaganda, and semantic slanting**
   The ability to identify partialities and prejudices in written and graphic materials. Includes the ability to determine credibility of sources (gauge reliability, expertise, and objectivity).
6. **Recognize different value orientations and ideologies**
   Values which form the common core of American citizenship . . . will receive primary emphasis here.
7. **Determine which information is relevant**
   The ability to make distinctions between verifiable and unverifiable, relevant and nonrelevant, and essential and incidental information.
8. **Recognize the adequacy of data**
   The ability to decide whether the information provided is sufficient in terms of quality and quantity to justify a conclusion, decision, generalization, or plausible hypothesis.
9. **Check consistency**
   The ability to determine whether given statements or symbols are consistent. For example, the ability to determine whether the different points or issues in a political argument have logical connec-

tions or agree with the central issue.
10. **Formulate appropriate questions**
   The ability to formulate appropriate and thought-provoking questions that will lead to a deeper and clearer understanding of the issues at hand.
11. **Predict probable consequences**
   The ability to predict probable consequences of an event or series of events.
12. **Identify unstated assumptions**
   The ability to identify what is taken for granted, though not explicitly stated, in an argument.

The fields of developmental psychology, sociolinguistics, and composition theory have provided supplements to such criteria with other skills of analysis and synthesis that distinguish advanced stages in reading, writing, and reasoning (sometimes termed "higher order reasoning," or in sociolinguist Basil Bernstein's [1975] terms, "elaborated codes"). These include the abilities to reason back and forth among the concrete and the abstract, the personal and the impersonal, the local and the global, cause and effect, the literal and the hypothetical or figurative, and among the past, present, and future; also, the abilities to retain and apply material previously studied and to sustain an extended line of exposition or argument in reading, writing, and speaking.

Some scholars make a further distinction, between critical thinking skills, related to formal or informal logic, and dispositions that foster or impede critical thinking within the broader context of psychological, cultural, social, and political influences. Dispositions that foster critical thinking include facility in perceiving irony, ambiguity, and multiplicity of meanings or points of view; the development of open-mindedness, autonomous thought, and reciprocity (Piaget's [1976] term for ability to empathize with other individuals, social groups, nationalities, ideologies, etc.). Dispositions that act as impediments to critical thinking include defense mechanisms (such as absolutism or primary certitude, denial, and projection), culturally conditioned assumptions, authoritarianism, egocentrism and ethnocentrism, rationalization, compartmentalization, stereotyping and prejudice.

Many of these critical thinking skills and dispositions coincide with ideas that were generated, beginning in the 1930s, by the International Society for General Semantics, the Institute for Propaganda Analysis (which flourished from 1937 to 1942), and the journal *et cetera*, still published by the re-named Institute of General Semantics. A GS approach to rhetorical analysis was implicit in Dumke's reference to "an understanding of the formal and informal fallacies of language and thought"—suggesting questions of denotation and connotation, deception and lying—as well as in the skills in the California guidelines distinguishing fact from opinion and identifying stereotypes, "partialities and prejudices in written and graphic materials," bias, propaganda, semantic slanting, different value orientations and ideologies, and ambiguity and multiplicity of meanings or points of view.

Many critical thinking skills and dispositions, such as the abilities "to identify central issues in complex political arguments" and "identify partialities and prejudices," provide a warrant for the application to studies in political criticism in the above NCTE resolution and Commission on the Humanities Report, as well as of Frankfurt School, Freirean, and other Marxist, feminist, multicultural, and postcolonialist theories critiquing authoritarianism and conformity, ethnocentrism, and Orwellian-Marcusean one-dimensional language. The references to value orientations, ideologies, and multiple viewpoints further warrant a cultural studies perspective examining ideological implications and subject positions in a wide range of cultural practices and texts, as in James Berlin's (1996) social-epistemic rhetoric: "the study and critique of signifying practices in their relation to subject formation within the framework of economic, social, and political conditions" (p. 77).

Some of us in English at the Cal State universities were active in developing critical thinking courses in the eighties, but the movement never got a foothold in English studies nationally, and even in California such courses withered away as Philosophy and Speech won the turf wars. The main research centers, such as the Center for Critical Thinking at Sonoma State University and the Centre for Reasoning, Argumentation and Rhetoric at the University of Windsor, have been philosophy-centered, as is the Association for Informal Logic and Critical Thinking. But even in the American Philosophical Association, studies in critical thinking have been marginal, and courses in critical thinking and argumentative rhetoric—which to my mind should be the master academic disciplines—have withered away, whether in Philosophy, English, or Speech-Communication.

We have missed many opportunities, then, to apply a framework of critical thinking, cognitive development, and civic literacy not only in undergraduate instruction but to scholarly theory and research. A wealth of such opportunities was suggested in the following passage in a 1987 article by Stanley Aronowitz (a Frankfurt School disciple) titled "Mass Culture and the Eclipse of Reason: The Implications for Pedagogy," whose title alludes to Max Horkheimer's *Eclipse of Reason*:

> Research suggests a correlation of television watching (and consumption of mass culture in general) to a tendency toward literalness in thought. . . . Put succinctly, children of all social classes . . . seem unable to penetrate beyond the surfaces of things to reach down to those aspects of the object that may not be visible to the senses. . . . The problem of abstraction becomes a major barrier to analysis because students seem enslaved to the concrete. Finally, teachers notice that many have trouble making connections between two objects or sets of concepts that are not related to each other in an obvious manner. . . . The critical project of learning involves understanding that things are often not what they seem to be and that abstract concepts such as "society," "capitalism," "history," and other categories not available to the senses are nonetheless real. This whole critical project now seems in eclipse. (pp. 769–770)

Aronowitz's "children . . . seem unable to penetrate beyond the surfaces of things" jumps out as an allusion to Thoreau: "I perceive that we inhabitants of New England live this mean life that we do because our vision does not penetrate the surface of things. We think that that is which appears to be" (1967, p. 177). The allusion, along with "connections between two objects or sets of concepts that are not related to each other in an obvious manner," connects to the whole realm of Romantic and Transcendentalist, neo-platonic poetic theory. That section of Thoreau's "Where I Lived, And What I Lived For" brilliantly embodies the operations of the poetic and intellectual mind in precisely those activities that Aronowitz enumerates as being incapacitated by mass culture, e.g., "The intellect is a cleaver; it discerns and rifts its way into the secret of things" (p. 178). I have found that several class periods in close reading of Thoreau's chapter go a long way toward restoring those capacities in students, while reading it in tandem with "Civil Disobedience" connects with Thoreau's protest against mass acceptance of false appearances of rectitude in slavery and the Mexican-American War. The kind of research cited by Aronowitz could also be applied in advanced scholarship to empirical research on the cognitive and ideological patterns of college (or high school) students in response to political texts, news broadcasts, and other mass-cultural products. Such research could further include evaluation of the effectiveness of various pedagogical approaches to humanities and other courses, fostering critical thinking and cognitive-moral development in these realms.

The Core Curriculum

Finally, then, let's go back to the drawing board to envision how the preceding principles might be embodied in a sequence of undergraduate courses, which would follow an English course in First-Year Writing, perhaps an introductory public speaking course, and one (either in English, Speech-Communication, Rhetoric, or Philosophy) in Critical Thinking and Argumentative Rhetoric. Each could incorporate further argumentative writing and speaking, and they would, ideally, complement rather than replace basic courses in history, government, economics, and literature. I devised most of this sequence for chapters in my textbook *Reading and Writing for Civic Literacy* (2005), but my own and others' frustrating conclusion from teaching it was that no single book or course is anywhere near adequate to cover this subject matter that most students are so unfamiliar with from their previous education, so that each chapter could easily become the basis for a course in itself.

My curriculum is, of course, a platonic ideal rather than a model that has much chance of being implemented anywhere in the near future. In that sense, though, it at least dramatizes the distance between any such concept of a cogent curriculum and the present realities; it implicitly indicates all the forces that stand in the way of implementing curricular reform, and it perhaps might help us envision avenues of action toward overcoming those forces. A prime obstacle, or challenge, would be the drastic shift in professional values needed toward rewarding faculty commitment to core-level course-planning, teaching, and scholarship keyed to this level rather than specialized research and publication—a shift that might require a generation of re-gearing graduate studies.

Course One: Thinking Critically about Political and Economic Rhetoric

Political Semantics. Survey of semantic issues in defining terms like left wing, right wing, liberal, conservative, radical, moderate, freedom, democracy, patriotism, capitalism, socialism, communism, Marxism, and fascism. Analysis of their denotative complexity and the ways in which they are oversimplified or connotatively slanted in public usage. Objectively defining ideological differences between the political left and right, along with the range of positions within both. Relativity of political viewpoints—e.g., the *New York Times* is to the left of Fox News but to the right of the *Nation*; the Democratic Party is to the left of the Republicans but to the right of European social-democratic parties. Contingency of political beliefs and biases on everyone's relative subject position on a spectrum from far left to far right, nationally and internationally. The need to identify one's own subjectivity in order to progress toward objectivity.

Evaluating political and economic arguments: application of principles of analyzing argumentative rhetoric to "reading the news" in a diversity of journalistic and scholarly sources and ideological viewpoints—newspapers, journals of opinion, books, web journals, etc.—on current political and economic controversies. Locating and evaluating partisan sources across the political spectrum. Predictable patterns of partisan rhetoric.

Course Two: Thinking Critically about Mass Society and Mass Communication

Survey of theoretical perspectives on and literary depictions of modern mass society and culture. Debates over elitism and populism. Academic versus popular discourse. Liberal and conservative theories of highbrow, lowbrow, and middlebrow culture, and their modifications in recent cultural studies and postmodernist theory. Mass communication and social control. Cognitive effects of mass communication, especially on reading, writing, and political consciousness.

Do the media give people what they want or do people want what the media give them? Are news media objective, and should they be? The debate over political bias in media. Diverse influences in media: employees (editors, producers, writers, newscasters, performers); owners and advertisers; external pressure groups; audiences. Levels of literacy in productions and audiences. Ideology in entertainment: images in media (present and past) of corporations, the rich, poor, and middle class, labor, professions, gender roles, minorities, gays, foreigners, other parts of the world, Americans' presence abroad, and war. How the Internet and the decline of print media have reshaped media issues. Possible alternatives to present media, especially those in decline.

Course Three: Deception Detection: Propaganda Analysis

Study of problems in defining and evaluating propaganda. Possible biases in government, media, education, and research resulting from special interests, conflict of interest, and special pleading. Survey of varieties and sources of propaganda in contemporary society, including government and the military; corporate and other special-interest lobbying, advertising, public relations, and subsidized research. The anatomy of deception: patterns of propagandistic argument in public discourse; how to lie with economic statistics. Critical consumer education: reading the fine print in contracts such as those for student loans, credit cards, rental agreements and mortgages; health and environmental issues in consumer products; the hidden facts of the production, marketing, and nutritional value of food.

Course Four: Civic Literacy and Service Learning

Connecting these academic studies with arenas of participatory research, public service, community or national activism, work in government or community organizations, journalism, and so on. The challenge that I see here is overcoming the tendency for service learning to become isolated from, or even hostile toward, academic civic literacy, through focusing exclusively on local community issues, diverse constituencies, and ideological pluralism, at the expense of studying broader, common ideological and rhetorical issues. See Cushman (1999) for a good model of connecting the two realms, as well as the two excellent recent collections edited by Kahn and Lee (2010) and by Ackerman and Coogan (2010).

Possible Objections

Q: "Aren't these courses outside the scope of humanities professors' professional preparation and expertise, and don't they get into issues that are the proper realm of the social sciences?"

A: Well, this shouldn't be the case. The issues addressed in this curriculum do not involve information at the level of specialized scholarship but at the level of the public sphere—political speeches and arguments, journalistic and entertainment media, etc.—information that is, or should be, within the grasp of every American citizen to understand, and of every English or other humanistic teacher to teach, armed only with the rhetorical tools of our trade.

Q: "What you are proposing is that college humanities courses take on the impossible burden of remediation for the failures of the entire American education system in civic literacy."

A: You betcha. It's a dirty job, but someone has to do it, and I don't see any disciplines that might be more likely candidates jumping into the breach, especially disciplines whose courses are conventional general education and breadth requirements. (Many Speech, Journalism, and Communication departments offer courses in media criticism or political communication, but mostly for upper-division major students.) An ideal solution would be for these courses to be offered as interdisciplinary core courses, in which English faculties would collaborate with those in the social sciences, communication, and so on. If civic education at the secondary and introductory college level ever picks up the slack that it should, college studies can phase out. Michael Halloran was incisive as always in his paper at the 2010 Rhetoric Society of America conference, advocating linkage between K–12 and postsecondary rhetorical education. Recapitulating the history of classical rhetorical pedagogy, he observed, "There's more than a bit of irony here: we devote scholarship to treatises from the past that were meant for students at what we would recognize as the elementary and secondary levels, but we give little if any attention to how the principles behind those treatises might be relevant in schooling at the elementary and secondary levels today" ("The Third C," p. 3). He also recapitulated the schism in 1914 between NCTE and teachers of public speaking who founded a series of organizations eventuating in NCA, organizations that regrettably did not include strong K–12 sections as NCTE always has. He praised the recent Common Core State Standards Initiative of the National Governors' Association, which emphasized "college and career readiness standards," but he recommended adding a third C—"readiness for citizenship," in which study of political rhetoric would be central (5). He concluded by advocating that "the Rhetoric Society of America might strive in some official way to add citizenship to the agenda of education reform in our elementary and secondary schools" (p. 7).

Q: "Mightn't your proposals just be a Trojan Horse for dragging in the academic left's same old agenda and biases?"

A: These courses could be conceived in their specifics and taught by teachers with varying ideological viewpoints—or best of all, through team teaching by leftist and conservative instructors. In principle, this framework would "teach the conflicts," not through advocacy or the monologic perspective of any teacher's own beliefs, but through enabling students to identify and evaluate a full range of opposing ideological perspectives (including those of the instructor), their points of opposition, and the partisan patterns and biases of their rhetoric. (I have found it easy to grade students on the basis of their skill in articulating these points, without regard to my or their own political viewpoint.) To be sure, this conception itself runs up against the near impossibility for anyone even to define terms and points of opposition between, say, the left and right, with complete objectivity and without injecting value judgments. This problem itself, however, can become a meta-pedagogical subject of study within these courses as well as in advanced scholarly inquiry—one of many ways in which such courses can serve to bridge the gap between scholarship and teaching.

Note

1. My long-time mentor from Berkeley graduate school, Charles Muscatine, was a champion of coherent liberal arts programs with a civic emphasis, even within large universities. He was, not coincidentally, one of the authors of *The Humanities in American Life*, cited above. Less than a year before his death in 2010 at 89, he published *Fixing College Education*, whose viewpoint resembles mine here and which surveyed such curricula around the country, mainly at four-year liberal arts colleges. Similar surveys appear in the collections edited by Colby (2006) and Jacoby (2009).

Bibliography

Ackerman, J.M., & Coogan, D.J. (Eds.). (2010). *The public work of rhetoric: Citizen-scholars and civic engagement.* Columbia: University of South Carolina Press.

Aronowitz, S. (1987). Mass culture and the eclipse of reason: The implications for pedagogy. In D. Lazare (Ed.), *American media and mass culture: Left perspectives.* Berkeley: University of California Press.

Berlin, J. (1996). *Rhetorics, poetics, and cultures: Refiguring college English studies.* Urbana, IL: NCTE.

Bernstein, B. (1975). *Codes, class, and control.* New York: Schocken.

California State Department of Education. (1984). *Curriculum guidelines, grades 8–12.* Sacramento: State Board of Education.

Chayefsky, P. (1976). *Network.* New York: Pocket Books.

Colby, A., Beaumont, E., Ehrlich, T., & Corngold, J. (2006). *Educating for democracy: Preparing undergraduates for responsible political engagement.* San Francisco, CA: Jossey-Bass.

Commission on the Humanities. (1980). *The humanities in American life.* Berkeley and Los Angeles: University of California Press.

Cushman, E. (1999). The public intellectual, service learning, and activist research. *College English, 61,* 328–336.

Dumke, C.G. (1980). *Executive order 338.* Long Beach: California State University.

Gore, A. (2007). *The assault on reason.* New York: Penguin.

Graff, G., & Birkenstein, C. (2008, May–June). A progressive case for educational standardization. *Academe Online.*

Halloran, S.M. (1982). Rhetoric in the American college curriculum: The decline of public discourse. *Pre/Text, 3,* 93–109.

Halloran, S.M. (2010). The third C of education reform: Citizenship. RSA conference paper.

Hirsch, E.D., Jr. (1987). *Cultural literacy: What every American needs to know.* New York: Houghton Mifflin.

Hirsch, E.D., Jr. (2009). *The making of Americans: Democracy and our schools.* New Haven, CT: Yale UP.

Jacoby, B., et al. (2009). *Civic engagement in higher education: Concepts and practices.* San Francisco, CA: Jossey-Bass.

Kahn, S., & Lee, J. (Eds.). (2010). *Activism and rhetoric: Theories and contexts for political engagement.* New York: Routledge.

Lazere, D. (2010, February 5). A core curriculum for civic literacy. *Chronicle of Higher Education,* B4–5.

Lazere, D. (2005). *Reading and writing for civic literacy: The critical citizen's guide to argumentative rhetoric.* Boulder: Paradigm Publishers. [Brief edition, 2009.]

Lazere, D. (Forthcoming). Bringing concord out of educational discord by teaching political controversy. *Proceedings of 2010 Rhetoric Society of America Conference.*

Mindich, D. (2005). *Tuned out: Why Americans under 40 don't follow the news.* New York: Oxford University Press.

Muscatine, C. (2009). *Fixing college education; A new curriculum for the twenty-first century.* Charlottesville: University of Virginia Press.

Nash, G.B. (1997). *History on trial: Culture wars and the teaching of the past.* New York: Knopf.

National Council of Teachers of English. (1975). Resolutions on language. Urbana, IL: NCTE.

National Governors Association. (2010). Common core state standards initiative. http://www.corestandards.org/

Nussbaum, M.C. (2010). *Not for profit: Why democracy needs the humanities.* Princeton, NJ: Princeton University Press.

Piaget, J. (1976). The transition from egocentricity to reciprocity: The development in children of the idea of the homeland and of relations with other countries. In S. Campbell (Ed.), *Piaget sampler.* New York: Wiley.

Ravitch, D. (2010). *The death and life of the great American school system.* New York: Basic Books.

Rose, M. (2006). *An open language: Selected writing on literacy, learning, and opportunity.* New York: Bedford/St. Martin's.

Thoreau, H.D. (1967). *Walden and other writings.* Ed. Joseph Wood Krutch. New York: Bantam.

CHAPTER SEVENTEEN

Critical Civic Literacy and the Arts

NEIL HOUSER

I thoroughly enjoy curriculum development, lesson-planning, and the act of teaching, but I detest the grading of papers and assigning of grades. Nor do I believe I am alone in these preferences. For many educators the most rewarding aspects of teaching, beyond the growth we observe and relationships we build, involve imaginative activity and the creative impulse. As humans we strive to understand, to solve problems, to build and improve. Human impulses to imagine and create can lead to movement, action, and the unfolding of innate possibilities, and within this unfolding are the seeds of hope.

At its core, civic literacy involves critical understanding of the explicit and implicit arrangements by which humans regulate their own activities and through which they are regulated by others. Scholarly analyses often assess the impact of broad economic and political structures on the body politic. Although structural analyses are important, it is also necessary to examine the influence of formal systems on individual lives, including personal thoughts, feelings, actions, and identities. This is necessary not only because larger systems affect personal lives, but because personal actions impact the larger system. As social psychologist John Hewitt (1994) observes:

> Only individuals *act*. Everything else—society, culture, social structure, power, groups, organizations—is ultimately dependent on the acts of individuals. Yet, individuals can act only because they acquire the capacity to do so as members of a society, which is the source of their knowledge, language, skills, orientations, and motives. Individuals are born into and (influenced) by a society that already exists and that will persist long after they are dead; yet the same society owes its existence and continuity to the conduct of its members. (p. 4)

This suggests that changing the norms of a society ultimately requires changing the actions of its individual members. This can also be a source of hope, for it implies that incremental changes in the perspectives of individuals can lead to cumulative changes in the structure of society.

However it is approached, critical civic literacy requires a deep appreciation of the value of diversity (Baldwin, 1988; Capra, 1996; Houser, 2009; Nieto, 2000), of the historical processes by which societal norms change and evolve (Foucault, 1997; Takaki, 1989; Zinn, 1995), and of the function of personal reflection and action in social transformation (Freire, 1970). The basic idea is for citizens to become deeply and critically conscious of the world in which they live with an eye toward establishing and maintaining more just and equitable societal conditions.[1]

The arts are more difficult to define. Like other complex constructions, there are few universally agreed upon definitions. Within the Western tradition alone, art has been variously described as "human creativity" (Neufeldt & Sparks, 1995, p. 33), "human effort to imitate, supplement, alter, or counteract the work of nature" (Morris, 1970, p. 74), and "the conscious production or arrangement of sounds, colors, forms, movements, or other elements in a manner that affects the sense of beauty" (Morris, 1970, p. 74). Similarly, aesthetics has been characterized both as "the philosophy of art and beauty" (Neufeldt & Sparks, 1995, p. 10) and as "pertaining to the criticism of taste" (Morris, 1970, p. 21). Along with varying descriptions, different views on the purposes, processes, and relationships of the arts have also been deliberated for generations. Debates continue over questions of form and content, form and function, process and product, art and craft, high art and low art, and so forth.

Although universal definitions are not available, it may be useful to provide a working assumption. For the purposes of this paper I will consider the arts *imaginative activity utilizing various media for expression and critique*. In addition to this basic supposition, three further characteristics are also relevant to the aims of critical civic literacy. First, the arts tend to be rooted in everyday aesthetic experience. Second, the arts have the capacity to generate emotion. Third, the arts draw upon active and intentional impulses such as imagining, creating, and actualizing human potential.

How Can the Arts Contribute to Critical Civic Literacy?

One characteristic of the arts is that they are rooted in everyday aesthetic experience According to Dewey (1934):

> The intelligent mechanic engaged in his job, interested in doing well and finding satisfaction in his handiwork, caring for his materials and tools with genuine affection, is artistically engaged….Craftsmanship [that is] artistic in the final sense must be "loving"; it must care deeply for the subject matter upon which skill is exercised. (pp. 5, 47–48).[2]

Acknowledging variations among individuals and cultures, Dewey insisted that aesthetic experience is a natural aspect of living one's life. This view is supported by numerous others (e.g., Anzaldúa, 1999; Duncum, 1999; Getlein, 2005). For example, Getlein (2005) observes that current divisions between "art" and "craft" are a relatively recent European invention that did not occur until the beginning of the 16th century. Prior to this time it made little difference whether aesthetic works were designed to serve a function or intended for contemplation alone. Nor is it difficult to ascertain why these changes occurred. New distinctions in the arts coincided with the rise of the middle class and emergence of the mercantile system as entrepreneurs sought to establish themselves in European society. Among other things, these efforts reinforced deepening divisions in race, class, gender, and power.

Examples of aesthetics in everyday life are all around us. They are reflected in the selection of our clothing, the arrangement of our living spaces, and the preparation of our bodies for public display. Everyday aesthetics can also be observed in the historical foundations and contemporary manifestations of virtually every major social institution. They can be seen, for example, in ancient traditions of hospitality involving the breaking of bread under a roof, before a hearth, or around a campfire. Such traditions combine social interaction (gathering in community), aesthetics (song, poetry, storytelling, carefully prepared food served in elaborately decorated vessels), security (the unspoken promise of sustenance and protection within the host's care), and sustainability (tacit recognition that what is offered to a stranger today can be expected from another tomorrow). Hospitality traditions are virtually universal and, as I recently experienced in Tanzania, many ancient practices continue today (Figures 1 and 2).

Because the arts are grounded in everyday experience, they can be used to deconstruct problematic hierarchies while affirming important social and cultural connections. Since hierarchies are interlocking (McIntosh, 1989), questioning inequality in one area can increase critical awareness in other areas. For example, distinctions between "art" and "craft" are often associated with alleged differences between "high culture" and "low culture" in general. In the musical arts, many have historically assumed that symphonies and concertos, with audiences who passively sit and listen, represent higher musical quality than genres such as country music or blues, with audiences who stand, dance, sing along, or otherwise physically participate in the process. In recent years such claims have received increased scrutiny, including the racist and classist assumptions embedded within them. Another way to deconstruct problematic hierarchies might be to show students how their own arts have been both demeaned and exploited (Dretzin & Rushkoff, 1999). Over the years, youth-spawned musical genres such as rock and roll, hip-hop, and punk rock have been simultaneously vilified by the mainstream and appropriated by opportunistic corporations intent on repackaging and selling them back to those from whom they were taken. Unfortunately, this marketing involves hidden costs. As Berger (1972) explains, publicity is "a language in itself which is always being used to make the same general proposal…that we transform ourselves, or our lives, by buying something more" (p. 131). Demystifying such constructions can help affirm students' worth while making them less vulnerable to hegemonic exploitation (Gramsci, 2000).

Another important characteristic of the arts is their capacity to evoke emotion. Eisner (1991) argues that the arts can provide empathetic understanding of the human condition that may not be expressed through more scientific or didactic means of communication:

> Different forms of representation provide different kinds of meaning. What one is able to convey about a society through a literal or quantitative form of sociology is not the same as what is sayable through a novel.…What all of the arts have in common is their capacity to generate emotion, to stimulate and to express the "feel" of a situation, individual, or object.…Feeling is a part of all human encounters and all situations and objects. When the feeling tone is incongruous with the content described, understanding is diminished. (1991, pp. 552, 554)[3]

Clearly, feeling has much to do with social understanding. Without feeling there would be no basis for concern about others. Indeed, without feeling it would be impossible to care about obstacles, and without caring about obstacles there would be no reason to imagine better alternatives (Greene, 1988). Because the arts express emotion, they can help us *feel* people and life. This was a primary concern of the Romantic Movement. After more than a century of exacting rational analysis, there was a feeling by many that the spirit of the whole had been lost in endless microscopic examination of the parts. The Romantics desired not merely to analyze life but to feel it, and they proceeded to investigate the entire spectrum of human emotion. With today's heightened emphasis on specialization and proficiency, many are again advocating approaches that embrace our capacity to feel the "largeness of life" (Palmer, 1998, p. 5).

Again, there are numerous examples of the power of the arts to generate emotion. Classic cases in the musical arts range from the serene contemplation of the medieval Gregorian plainchant to the turgid, disjunctive power of Ludwig van Beethoven. Contemporary examples include the joy and spontaneity of Louis Armstrong, the weighty reflections of Memphis Slim, the hard-hitting commentary of Bob Dylan, and the raw energy of Jimi Hendrix. Equally compelling examples prevail in the visual arts. Quiet solitude is communicated in Edward Hopper's (1930) *Early Sunday Morning*, eerie premonition marks Giorgio De Chirico's (1914) *Mystery and Melancholy of a Street*, and racking pain of body and soul are met with dignity and defiance in Frida Kahlo's (1944) *The Broken Column*. It would be difficult indeed for statistical summaries to communicate feelings such as these.[4]

As a specific example, consider Edvard Munch's (1893) disturbing *Scream*, which shattered the silence of the pre–World War European landscape (Figure 3). Among other things, Munch's work expresses the anxiety and turmoil of the social malaise arising on an increasingly nationalistic European continent. A despairing individual stands on a bridge emitting a wailing scream. In the background, two silhouettes heighten the psychological trauma. What could be worse than screaming and not being heard? Munch's reply: Being heard by a society that does not care. Even more haunting is *Death Seizing a Woman* (1934), part of Käthe Kollwitz's chilling account of the victims of war during Hitler's reign (Figure 4). In Kollwitz's case, the message is unnervingly personal. Death, which eventually claims us all, hunches over a woman's shoulder, but the panic she experiences is not for herself alone. Greater still is the terror she feels for her child to whom she desperately clings unwilling to abandon to cope with life on her own. Much of Kollwitz's work addresses the sanctioned violence of war, which others have called institutionalized terrorism.

A different problem involves fatalistic feelings that can lead to depression, despair, and personal and societal paralysis, leaving existing structures in place and unopposed. Feelings of inevitability can leave the impression that what presently exists is inevitably there—is *just the way things are* (Greene, 1988). Such sentiments are captured in George Tooker's (1956) *Government Bureau*, in which a faceless public awaits despondent bureaucrats who in turn await the end of the day (Figure 5). Such feelings are heightened in Simon and Garfunkel's (1965) *Sounds of Silence*, where no one "dares disturb the sound of silence" and "silence like a cancer grows . . ."

Yet another characteristic of the arts is their tendency to draw upon active impulses such as imagining, creating, and actualizing potential. At their core, artistic processes are generative in nature (Dewey, 1934; Eisner, 1991; Greene, 1995). Aristotle claimed that a fundamental human trait is our tendency toward the realization of innate potential. He argued that humans have a basic orientation toward development and actualization. Since the arts are based on similar impulses, they are capable of reflecting and generating physical, social, and psychological movement. For example, in the visual arts, 19th-century impressionists imagined alternative representations of light, movement, and color. Similarly, music can be seen as sound in time (Greenberg, 2007), performing arts unfold in time, and poetry can envision change over time—as Robert Frost (1960) famously demonstrates in "The Road Not Taken."

Because the arts utilize active impulses, they are capable of supporting personal growth and societal transformation, and because they can foster structural change, they have the further capacity of generating hope.[5] Indeed, action and hope are intimately related. Cornell West (1993) explains that many African Americans whose ancestors arrived on the continent in chains have historically associated movement with hope. A small movement can be a prelude to a larger movement, which can lead to greater movement still. The critical moment, the vital line of demarcation, is between moving and not moving. Without the initial impulse and tentative first step, nothing else can follow. This simple yet profound realization has been essential in the ongoing struggle for freedom (Greene, 1988).

An initial step in developing critical consciousness is to recognize the existence and nature of oppressive conditions (Freire, 1970; Greene, 1988). Having identified challenges to personal growth and social transformation (e.g., interlocking hierarchies; simultaneous vilification and appropriation of minority cultures; commodification of basic human needs; reductionistic analyses that disconnect people from the largeness of life; anxiety and malaise associated with unchecked extremism; fatalistic assumptions leading to social paralysis), it may be possible to consciously resist their influences and to imagine and enact viable alternatives.

One way to support social transformation is to identify and resist oppressive relationships. An example is illustrated in Getlein's (2005) *Living with art* in a photograph entitled *Africa looks back*. The setting is a tribal masquerade, which traditionally involves ritualized routines conducted by masked dancers. Masquerades are meaningful events, often calling on the spirits of ancestors to assist in times of need. Because they are poignant to tribal societies, African masquerades are frequently visited by Western tourists and scholars. In this case, Getlein has located an unusual participant. Rather than representing an animal or spirit as is usually the case, this dancer wears an intricately carved mask depicting a European anthropologist. With pencil and notebook in hand, this solemn intruder records the natural habits of those who have gathered to study *him*, thus turning the tables on the cultural invaders (Freire, 1970; Spivak, 1995).

Other forms of resistance utilize humor. Such is the case with the Theater of the Absurd, an existentialist genre of dramatic literature that emerged in France during the first half of the twentieth century. Like the philosophical tradition to which it is linked, the Theater of the Absurd is intended to communicate a sense of bewilderment, anxiety, and wonder in the face of inexplicable conditions. Like a Charlie Chaplin film, commonplace details of life are presented in all their absurdity, but what is most absurd is the fact that no one seems to notice. The objective is for the audience to notice that nobody notices and to begin registering tentative parallels between the theatrical situation and the absurdity of their own lives. Through humorous participation in the absurdity of others, the process of critical reflection begins.

Although classic examples of Theater of the Absurd (such as Samuel Beckett's *Endgame*, 1957) are largely a thing of the past, the spirit of the absurd remains active in popular culture today. Increasing numbers of Americans seem to be experiencing a sort of general malaise as government officials thumb their noses at the electorate, multinational corporations export "American jobs," exploitive environmental policies and profit-driven wars are given euphemistic labels like "Clear Skies Initiative" and "Operation Iraqi Freedom," and efforts to privatize the public good are veiled behind self-serving policies such as "No Child Left Behind." Tapping this absurdity are a variety of media sources such as the tragicomic films of Michael Moore, the animated series *South Park*, and the long-running cartoon program *The Simpsons*.

An excellent contemporary example of Theater of the Absurd is Jon Stewart's *The Daily Show*, which presents "news stories" from around the world featuring "on the spot" reporting by highly trained "experts" and special "consultants." Mock reporting of Washington and Middle East politics, Supreme Court deliberations, school mandates, religious debacles, the Afghan War, Mexican immigration, and the outsourcing of American jobs provides a forum in which politicians, businessmen, and especially the media are lampooned with impunity. Dubbing actual clips from the sermons of televangelists, the speeches of high-ranking military personnel, and the comments of prominent politicians, *Daily Show* "senior specialists" report from unlikely locations, such as the eye of the Hurricane (Katrina), press bases on Mars (during the landing of the Mars Exploration Rover), and the inner chambers of the White House presidential suite. With perfectly straight faces, the *Daily Show's* "journalistic experts" provide unflinchingly objective reporting and up-to-the-minute commentary on the events of the day. Of course, as "embedded reporters," they are duty-bound to honor, protect, and defend the views of their informants. Few seem to notice that the *Daily Show's* "remote locations" are actually remote corners of the studio rigged with green-screened backdrops. Nor is it remarkable to anyone (except the audience) that Monday's "Senior Palestinian Analyst" is Tuesday's "Senior Hurricane Expert," Wednesday's "Senior Child Molestation Expert," and Thursday's "Senior Papal Vacancy Expert." While audience members chortle and interviewees squirm, the *Daily Show's* crack reporters remain unflappable. As "seasoned professionals" they are objective, embedded, and oblivious to the absurdity of the entire affair.

In addition to identifying and resisting oppressive conditions, the arts can also assist in the realization of new possibilities, including alternative structural relationships. Social transformation requires changed consciousness related to existing political and economic arrangements. One way to begin changing public consciousness is to acknowledge the contributions of those who have been previously excluded from the official histories of societies and nations. This was exactly what Judy Chicago (1979) sought to accomplish with her gigantic installation *The Dinner Party*. In this 48-foot triangular construction, Chicago and her colleagues created places for 39 prominent women in history and mythology whom, they believed, had been written out of the historical record.

Numerous other contributions are also available via the arts. A powerful example includes the musical collaborations of Mississippi Slim, Big Bill Broonzy, and Sonny Boy Williamson, faithfully recorded with the artists' conversations in *Blues in the Mississippi Night* (Lomax, 1990). One composition begins as follows:

> You got to cry a little, die a little.
> Chorus:
> O life is like that,

Well, that's what you've got to do,
Well, and if you don't understand,
Peoples, I'm sorry for you.

Sometimes you'll be held up, sometimes held down,
Well, and sometimes your best friends don't even want you around,
You know…(chorus)

There's some things you've got to keep, some things you gotta repeat,
People, happiness, well, is never complete,
You know…(chorus)

Sometimes you'll be helpless, sometimes you'll be restless,
Well, keep on strugglin,' so long as you're not breathless.

At first we see a classic blues theme: life is associated with pain. Upon closer inspection, additional nuances begin to appear. In order to be *fully* alive, it is necessary to *understand* the pain. But there is still more. In order to truly *live*, it is necessary to *die* ("and if you don't understand, Peoples, I'm sorry for you"). This profound observation stands in sharp contrast to dominant themes in contemporary Western society such as the association of virtue with fearlessness and the assumption that ignoring a problem will somehow make it go away. Far from avoiding difficult realities, these works *embrace* the complexities of life. Coping with the blues is part of what it means to live in the first place.

Another important contribution to the consciousness of society is reflected in the borderland poetry of Gloria Anzaldua (1999). Anzaldua grew up in southern Texas, just north of the Rio Grande, a land originally inhabited by Indians, eventually occupied by Spaniards, and ultimately "annexed" by the United States government:

The U.S.-Mexican border *es una herida abierta* where the Third World grates against the first and bleeds. And before a scab forms it hemorrhages again, the lifeblood of two worlds merging to form a third country—a border culture. Borders are set up to define the places that are safe and unsafe, to distinguish *us* from *them*. A border is a dividing line, a narrow strip along a steep edge. A borderland is a vague and undetermined place created by the emotional residue of an unnatural boundary. It is in a constant state of transition. The prohibited and forbidden are its inhabitants. *Los atravesados* live here: the squint-eyed, the perverse, the queer, the troublesome, the mongrel, the mulato, the half-breed, the half dead; in short, those who cross over, pass over, or go through the confines of the "normal." (p. 25)

While borderlands can be places of painful displacement, they can also be places of profound possibility. For those who are able to reclaim the right to follow their instincts in the face of strong opposition, the borderlands can be powerful sites of reflection and growth:

She is getting too close to the mouth of the abyss. She is teetering on the edge, trying to balance while she makes up her mind whether to jump in or to find a safer way down. That's why she makes herself sick—to postpone having to jump blindfolded into the abyss of her own being and there in the depths confront her face, the face underneath the mask….I am tired of fighting. I surrender. I give up, let go, let the walls fall. And in descending to the depths I realize that down is up, and I rise from and into the deep. And once again I recognize that the internal tension of oppositions can propel (if it doesn't tear apart)…an agent of transformation, able to modify and shape primordial energy. (Anzaldua, 1999, pp. 96–97)

Although borders are set up to "define the places that are safe and unsafe, to distinguish *us* from *them*," Anzaldua asserts that the people of the borderlands, like the spaces they inhabit, are complex, evolving, and amorphous. They are irreducible and can never be completely circumscribed or eliminated. In the end, Anzaldua defiantly claims her right—as *Chicana*, as *tejana*, as a *"new mestiza"*—never to yield to the constructions of others. For her, it is not in *spite* of the borderlands that she can claim this right, but *because* of the borderlands that such an act may be possible at all.

Yet another example of how the arts can contribute to structural transformation involves John Steinbeck's (1939) *The Grapes of Wrath*. This epic novel provides a richly contextualized portrayal of the plight of a family of Oklahoma sharecroppers during the Great Depression/Dust Bowl era. Utilizing vivid metaphor, nuanced detail, and keen sensitivity to the conditions of poor white Americans, Steinbeck provides a stark contrast between the human needs of working-class families, the mechanistic efficiency of the existing economic system, and the greed and fear of those who profit from conditions they cannot help but know to be unjust.

Forced to flee before the bulldozers arrive, the Joads, like other families, head for the promise of a new life in California. However, rather than finding better opportunities, they encounter new forms of greed, rejection, and unexamined privilege. Demonstrating remarkable courage and a tenacious desire to preserve the family, the Joads come to realize that only through collective resistance can groups of ordinary people hope to change their material conditions, and only through alternative activities can they begin to transform the system itself.

Maxine Greene (1988) argues that the plight of the Joads represents a sort of collaborative existentialist project, a critical coming to consciousness that could only have unfolded as the result of a shared search for—and opposition to—the social and historical causes of oppression. Many displaced victims in society have been able to sense, but never fully articulate, the nature of the conditions they face (Freire, 1970). This was the case with Steinbeck's petulant Muley Graves, who confronted the hapless drivers of the bug-like tractors, owned by the nameless, faceless companies:

> Well, the guy that come aroun' talked nice as pie. "You got to get off. It ain't my fault." "Well," I says, "whose fault is it? I'll go an' I'll nut the fella." "It's the Shawnee Lan' an' Cattle Company. I jus' got orders." "Who's the Shawnee Lan' an' Cattle Company?" "It ain't nobody. It's a company." Got a fella crazy. There wasn't nobody you could lay for. Lot a the folks jus' got tired out lookin' for somepin to be mad at—but not me. I'm mad at all of it. I'm stayin. (Steinbeck, 1939, p. 61)

Others, however, eventually begin to unravel the conditions that ensnare them. Steinbeck's protagonist, young Tom Joad, recently released from prison, has managed to survive through keen observation, keeping his nose out of the business of others, and simply "puttin' one foot in front a the other" (p. 223). Joining his family in the move to California, Tom notes the searching reflection of the strange Reverend Casy and the dogged tenacity with which Ma tirelessly resists the disintegration of the family. Recognizing the fruits of Casy's relentless "figgerin,'" Joad gradually begins to perceive the powerful mechanisms by which the "Okies" are kept subservient first in Oklahoma and finally in California. In the end, Tom must choose between maintaining a philosophy of personal survival ("I know—I know. But—I ruther not. I ruther jus'—lay one foot down in front a the other," p. 227) and continuing the work of Reverend Casy, who has concluded that only through critical reflection and collective resistance can working-class people transform the conditions of their own domination.

Lacking institutional power, it is difficult to cast either Casy or Tom as a classic "oppressor." Yet, as uncritical participants in the structures of society, they unwittingly collaborate in the domination of others as well as themselves. It is only as Casy continues to "figger" and as Tom eventually joins in that they are able to identify the underlying problems, to recognize their own complicity, and to consciously select alternative paths. In the end, even social critique is not enough; critical reflection is needed as well.

Finally, novelist Daniel Quinn (1992, 1996, 1997) demonstrates how the arts can promote an appreciation of social and biological diversity, a deeper sense of historical consciousness, and a clearer understanding of the critical relationships between personal action and social transformation. With remarkable protagonists and compelling story-lines, Quinn's work explores the subtle processes by which ancient farmers of the agricultural revolution, once a tiny fraction of the human community, gradually expanded and unconsciously imposed their ways of life upon all with whom they came in contact. Initial efforts to accommodate a growing population—the inevitable result of an expanding food supply—led to increasingly aggressive actions to acquire additional resources. In turn, these additional resources led to the development of increasingly narrow and controlling agricultural practices. Like other totalitarian entities, this new and growing "culture" utilized specific mechanisms to eliminate its competition, including the annihilation of alternative perspectives and life-styles. What began as a novel way of life gradually evolved into a dominant worldview based on principles of acquisition, expansion, consumption, and control.

After thousands of years of accelerating expansion, this acquisitive worldview is now prevalent on every continent—north, south, east, and west. While other cultural distinctions may persist, there are few remaining humans who have failed to adopt the basic premises of totalitarian agriculture. With time and repetition, an approach antithetical to cultural diversity and ecological sustainability has become not merely the *prevalent* way of life, but the *only* (acceptable) way of life, passed from generation to generation through mechanisms of social transmission and cultural assimilation. The irony, according to Quinn, is that the destruction of alternative cultural perspectives has left us with only "one right way" to live, and such uniformity is the single greatest threat to the community of life.

It would be difficult to imagine a more disturbing thesis. Each of us—male and female, young and old—is part of a larger culture that is inexorably destroying the world, and the supreme irony is that we simply cannot see that this is the case. Yet, in the end, Quinn's argument is neither decrepit nor morose. Rather than advocating an impossible "return to the past" or the sacrificing of happiness on the altar of survival, his ultimate message is one of hope. By revealing how we have constructed the myths that constrain us, Quinn points to the existence of real alternatives. His greatest contribution is in demonstrating that it is genuinely possible for things to be otherwise. Although Quinn's facts are solid and his arguments logical, the real power of his work is in the artistic virtue with which it is rendered. Readers are drawn into narratives from which there is no escape, and many—including myself—have been profoundly moved.

A Personal Account

Having asserted that the arts are grounded in everyday experience and that critical reflection is a vital aspect of civic literacy, it seems fitting to end with an acknowledgment of my own use of the arts as a means of striving to develop a more critical understanding of myself and society.

This admittedly feels awkward, not unlike those moments many have experienced when a student or peer becomes too personal, too emotional, within the confines of the academic institution. We intuitively recognize that the setting is wrong (Gee, 1989) and may squirm with discomfort until the ordeal is over. I am certainly aware of these norms, yet it does not make sense to maintain an impersonal discourse when the very essence of the arts is their capacity to express human emotion.

As a child I was thin with red hair and freckles, used hand-me-down clothes, and wore an outdated haircut. I was too shy to act in school plays, was unable to carry a tune, and failed miserably when my parents attempted to teach me to play the piano. However, a modest ability to draw recognizable objects elicited positive attention in school and eventually led to a bachelor's degree in art. During high school and college I had also become increasingly involved in organized sports, and through combined activities in arts and athletics I had gradually changed both my physical stature and my overall self-image.

After graduating from college I returned to California, was married, and began a series of odd jobs, working in a psychiatric hospital, an art supplies store, as a vacuum salesman, and as a sales clerk in a "head shop" (specializing in posters, tee-shirts, and drug paraphernalia). With college athletics and accolades behind me, my self-esteem was again beginning to flag. As a football player, much of my identity had been associated with my physical abilities and my attitude toward competition. Over the years I had developed an increasingly narrow view of masculinity focused on fierce competition, a willingness to win at all costs, and a physical image requiring hours in the weight room to develop and maintain. Now, with regular training a thing of the past, I was painfully conscious of my diminishing stature, and I mentally flinched every time someone observed that I was no longer as big or athletic as I once had been. Recognizing the truth in these claims, I doubled my efforts in the weight room, began studying karate, and became increasingly obsessive about my diet. In the meantime my job prospects were disappointing, I was spending little time at home, and my personal relationships were beginning to suffer.

I was eventually employed as a prison guard (euphemistically called "group counselor") in a large urban juvenile hall. Although open-minded and willing to learn, I was wholly unprepared for what I encountered. Within the culture of the juvenile hall, kindness was typically viewed as a weakness among prisoners and staff alike. With a constant emphasis on safety and security (a fellow guard was stabbed in the eye with a pencil just prior to my hiring, and failure to secure one's keys was grounds for instant dismissal), I woke twisted in my sheets night after night. In the meantime, the macho culture of the institution (a standard among guards was the ability to "body slam" the largest ward without having to call for back-up) furthered my already narrow perspectives on masculinity. Yet, even as I continued my athletic endeavors, I was distinctly aware that something was wrong. Tensions at home, a new son to care for, and the obvious warehousing of the youth at work simply could not be ignored. As a college athlete I had always thought I knew who I was, but who was I now? What was my relationship to my wife and son, what were my obligations to my peers and the youth, what did I owe the juvenile institution, and what did this mean for my future activities?

About this time two important events occurred. The first was that I began working with a new unit supervisor who approached his work from a different perspective. Although physically capable and culturally savvy, Ed refused to condone the abuses embedded within the system. With Ed's support, I began taking greater psychological risks at work. Utilizing my interpersonal skills and artistic interests, I gradually developed healthier relationships not only with my peers but also with the youth. Among other things, we began working on group art projects, including an eight-foot tall castle with copper roofs and a working drawbridge (Figure 6). Although I was never able to completely extricate myself from the impact of the organization, simply knowing an alternative approach was possible made a marked impact on my growth.

The second event was that I began pursuing a master's degree in art at the local university. Although many details have faded from memory, I distinctly recall my first semester in graduate school. I remember feeling overwhelmed and inadequate the first night of class as students bandied about the names of theories and theorists as if they were second nature. I remember feeling embarrassed the second week of class when, asked to present our own work, I brought a wood-burned etching of a panther climbing a ledge. During the critique one of my peers observed that the panther's hindquarters appeared more human than feline. Mortified, I heard nothing else the remainder of the evening.

The third week's assignment was to compose a work of art involving time and change. Determined not to be humiliated again, all week long I pondered how to create a profound, witty, and artistic work that would satisfy the requirements. I became increasingly concerned as the night of class drew close and I still had not arrived at a solution. Finally, nearing desperation, a thought occurred as we sat down to eat the night before class. I was familiar with the ideas of found art (featuring works that are "found" rather than created) and ephemeral art (featuring the fleeting and the momentary rather than the permanent), and I shrewdly began to contemplate the fried chicken resting on my plate. This chicken had certainly undergone a metamorphosis involving time and change. Even disregarding the embryonic phases of its life, it was possible to observe change in the most recent stages of its existence, the transition from flesh to bone. I further considered what might happen to the bones after they were discarded. Would they be devoured by wild animals? Would they dry and bleach in the sun? Would they decompose in the earth over a period time, eventually contributing to the cycle of life? Surely such thoughts as these would satisfy the demands of this week's assignment.

The next evening I nervously packed my materials, including a clear drinking glass in which I intended (for reasons I no longer remember) to display the chicken bones submerged in water. On the way to class I worried that my project might not be seen as sufficiently artistic or sophisticated. All the way across town I worried that I might have outsmarted myself. I was aware of the risk I was taking, hoping a highly competitive group of graduate students would take my project seriously. It was one thing for a famous artist like Marcel Duchamp (1917) to present a urinal as a fountain, but what right had I to attempt such a thing? Mercifully, I never learned the answer to this question. Prior to our presentations, one of my peers publicly observed that "something smelled like chicken." Others heartily agreed, and again I was mortified. The chicken bones remained concealed until break when I was able to discreetly dispose of them in the men's room.

Eventually, like other graduate students, I began to learn the specialized discourse of my field and gained greater facility with a whole new realm of ideas and skills. I was particularly interested in works that focused on social critique and psychological analysis. I noted Honoré Daumier's satirical commentaries on poverty and war (*Third Class Carriage*, 1864), Francisco Goya's excoriation of the Spanish government (*The Third of May—1808*, 1814; *Saturno*, 1819–1823), and the critical works of artists like Munch and Kollwitz.

One artist in particular who caught my attention was Edward Kienholz. Like me, Kienholz had worked at a number of odd jobs, including a "mental hospital." He had even served a stint as a vacuum salesman. Dissatisfied with his experiences, Kienholz eventually began using his art as a means of expressing his social concerns. I was struck by many of his works, but none so much as a piece entitled *The State Hospital* (Figure 7). Based on vivid personal experience, *The State Hospital* (1966) depicts two identical figures, lying on filthy mattresses, strapped to institutional bunk beds presumably for their own protection. Their bodies are emaciated. Yellowed skin is roughly rendered with waxy lumps of resin. A bare bulb dangles from the ceiling, a bed pan is carelessly placed out of reach, and the smell of disinfectant permeates the room. However, the most haunting aspect, in my opinion, is an elliptical neon thought-bubble emanating from the head of the bottom figure and encircling the identical figure lying on the top. This element speaks directly to the issue of critical consciousness. It is tempting to rationalize our actions when making difficult decisions, such as committing others against their will to a hospital, to jail, or to death. One way to assuage our conscience is to convince ourselves that the other is not fully conscious, not fully aware, perhaps not even fully human. Kienholz's thought bubble dispels notions. The figure on the bottom is keenly aware of every detail of his situation, for the figure on top is none other than himself.

As my graduate studies proceeded, I eventually began to explore my own circumstances as well. In time, this became the basis of my master's show, which drew hundreds of visitors, received article-length coverage in several newspapers, and led to a personal interview on the evening news. One piece included in the show was an assemblage entitled *The Insult that Made a Man Out of 'Mac'* (Figure 8). The work consisted of a full-sized closet constructed of wood with two well-sculpted torsos suspended from hooks. Upon close inspection it became evident that the torsos, male and female, were nothing more than empty cavities. The papier maché openings for the arms and legs transitioned into functional sleeves, and embedded zippers began at the sternum and ended at the throat. The figures were appendages, accessories, hollow physical shells awaiting people yet to "exist."

Posted on the inside of the closet door was a blown-up copy of an advertisement I had read countless times as a child. It was a page from a comic book with a personal message from Charles Atlas, the original body builder, explaining to countless boys like me how he could "make a man out of 'mac.'" Becoming the "man" Charles had promised took considerably longer than the few short weeks suggested by his advertisement, and it was many years further before I began to question the ramifications of such remarkably simple recipes for success.

The problem with such formulas is that they narrow the ways we are able to define ourselves as men and as women, as citizens of a nation and citizens of a world. They offer uniform standards to a society in desperate need of understanding its diversity. As my personal options gradually narrowed, so did my ability to question and complicate the broader structures of my society. Conversely, as I began to challenge the structures that limited my growth, I was better able to integrate the various aspects of the person I am and to appreciate the complex ways in which others construct their identities as well. I am still physical and competitive in many ways, and this will doubtlessly remain part of my identity; however, these are no longer rigid parameters that constrain my perception of what it means to be a man.

It seems ironic that a medium used to manipulate identity could also serve as a means of personal resistance and social transformation. Yet this is precisely what has occurred. Countless messages via television and radio and magazines and the Internet have been discovered to be exactly what they are: manipulative uses of the arts to consolidate power and profit at the expense of individual persons and the public at large. Fortunately, others have used the arts to expose these abuses, to reclaim and expand stolen identities, and to restore the richness of our democratic society to those to whom it rightfully belongs. The arts alone cannot ensure the development of a literate citizenry, but they can most assuredly assist in the process.

Appendix A: Illustrations

Figures 1 (left) and 2 (right). Hospitality received in the home of Mama YiYi, right, in a Massai village in northern Tanzania. 2008.

Figure 3 (left). Edvard Munch. 1895. *The Scream.* Lithograph.
Figure 4 (right). Käthe Kollwitz. 1934/35. *Death Seizing a Woman.* Lithograph.

Figure 5 (left). George Tooker. 1956. *Government Bureau.* Tempera on wood.
Figure 6 (right). Award-winning Castle, Fresno County Fair. 1982. Ceramic, papier mache, copper glaze.

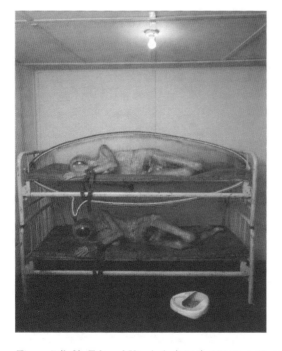

Figure 7 (left). Edward Kienholz (1966). *The State Hospital.* Mixed media tableau.
Figure 8 (right). Neil Houser (1983). *The Insult that Made a Man Out of 'Mac.'* Mixed media assemblage.

Notes

1. Here I refer broadly to the notion of a "global" or "cosmopolitan" citizen. The term "critical" does not merely imply negativity. My frame of reference is the art or film critic who seeks to illuminate virtues as well as liabilities.
2. This opposes the Western canon, which views "art" as aloof, ideal, and remote (Berger, 1972).
3. The arts evoke emotion because they are *im*mediate, or at least *less* mediated by rational thought than are other forms of communication. As experience-based forms of expression, the arts appeal more or less directly to the senses (Eisner, 1991; Gaztambide-Fernandez, 2002; van Halen-Faber & Diamond, 2002).
4. Children's literature can also be quite valuable. I have addressed its uses extensively elsewhere (Houser, 2001).
5. Transforming social "reality" is not a mysterious or unobtainable objective. Not only is structural social transformation possible, it is inevitable, and there are identifiable mechanisms by which the process occurs (Hewitt, 1991; Mead, 1934; Wertsch, 1991). The question is not whether humans transform their environments but in what direction, for what purposes, and with what degree of clarity and control regarding the causes and consequences of our actions (Greene, 1988).

Bibliography

Anzaldua, G. (1999). *Borderlands: La frontera*. San Francisco: Aunt Lute.

Baldwin, J. (1988). A talk to teachers. In R. Simonson & S. Walker (Eds.), *The Graywolf annual five: Multicultural literacy* (pp. 3–12). St. Paul, MN: Graywolf Press.

Beckett, S. (1958). *Endgame*. New York: Grove Press.

Berger, J. (1972). *Ways of seeing*. London: Penguin Books.

Bowers, C.A. (2001). Toward an eco-justice pedagogy. *Educational Studies*, *32*(4), 401–415.

Capra, F. (1996). *The web of life*. New York: Anchor Books.

Devall, B., & Sessions, G. (1985). *Deep ecology*. Layton, UT: Peregrine Smith.

Dewey, J. (1934). *Art as experience*. New York: Perigee.

Dretzin, R., & Rushkoff, D. (1999). *The merchants of cool*. Frontline: The Public Broadcasting System.

Duncum, P. (1999). A case for an art education of everyday aesthetic experiences. *Studies in Art Education*, *40*(4), 295–311.

Eisner, E.W. (1991). Art, music, and literature within the social studies. In J.P. Shaver (Ed.), *Handbook of research on teaching and learning*. New York: Macmillan.

Foucault, M. (1997). *Society must be defended*. New York: Picador.

Freire, P. (1970). *The pedagogy of the oppressed*. New York: Continuum.

Freire, P., & Macedo, D. (1987). *Literacy: Reading the word and the world*. Westport, CT: Bergin & Garvey.

Frost, R. (1960). *A pocket book of Robert Frost's poems*. New York: Washington Square Press.

Gaztambide-Fernandez, R.A. (2002). (De) constructing art as a model/(Re) constructing art as a possibility. In T.S. Poetter, C. Haerr, M. Hayes, C. Higgins, & K.W. Baptist (Eds.), *In(Ex)clusion: (Re)visioning the democratic ideal*. Second Annual Curriculum and Pedagogy Conference, University of Victoria, B.C., October 2001.

Gee, J.P. (1989). What is literacy? *Journal of Education*, *171*(1), 18–25.

Getlein, M. (2005). *Living with Art*. New York: McGraw-Hill.

Giroux, H.A. (1985, May). Teachers as transformative intellectuals. *Social Education*, 376–379.

Gramsci, A. (2000). Hegemony, intellectuals, and the state. In J. Storey (Ed.), *Cultural theory and popular culture: A reader*. Athens: University of Georgia Press.

Greenberg, R. (2007). *Understanding the Fundamentals of Music*. Chantilly, VA: The Teaching Company.

Greene, M. (1988). *The dialectic of freedom*. New York: Teachers College Press.

Greene, M. (1995). *Releasing the imagination*. San Francisco, CA: Jossey-Bass.

Habermas, J. (1984*). Communication and the evolution of society*. London: Heinemann.

Hewitt, J.P. (1994). *Self and society: A symbolic interactionist social psychology*. Boston: Allyn & Bacon.

Houser, N.O. (2001). Literature as art, literature as text: Exploring the power and possibility of a critical, literacy-based approach to citizenship education. *Equity and Excellence in Education, 34*(2), 62–74.

Houser, N.O. (2009). Ecological democracy: An environmental approach to citizenship education. *Theory and Research in Social Education, 37*(2), 192–214.

Lomax, A. (1990). *Blues in the Mississippi night.* Salem, MA: Rykodisc.

McIntosh, P. (1989). White privilege: Unpacking the invisible knapsack. *Peace and Freedom,* July-August, 10–12.

Mead, G.H. (1934). *Mind, self, and society.* Chicago: University of Chicago Press.

Morris, W. (1970). *The American Heritage dictionary of the English language.* Boston: Houghton Mifflin.

Neufeldt, V., & Sparks, A.N. (1995). *Webster's new world dictionary.* New York: Simon & Schuster.

Nieto, S. (2000). *Affirming diversity.* New York: Longman.

Palmer, P.J. (1998). *The courage to teach.* San Francisco, CA: Jossey-Bass.

Quinn, D. (1992). *Ishmael.* New York: Bantam.

Quinn, D. (1996). *The story of B.* New York: Bantam.

Quinn, D. (1997). *My Ishmael.* New York: Bantam.

Spivak, G. (1995). Can the subaltern speak? In B. Ashcroft, G. Griffiths, & H. Tiffin (Eds.), *The postcolonial studies reader.* London and New York: Routledge.

Steinbeck, J. (1939). *The grapes of wrath.* New York: Penguin.

Takaki, R. (1989). *Strangers from a different shore: A history of Asian Americans.* New York: Penguin.

Todorov, T. (1984). *Mikhail Bakhtin: The dialogical principal.* Minneapolis: University of Minnesota Press.

van Halen-Faber, C., & Diamond, P.C.T. (2002). Doing an arts-based dissertation inquiry. In T.S. Poetter, C. Haerr, M. Hayes, C. Higgins, & K.W. Baptist (Eds.), *In(Ex)clusion: (Re)visioning the democratic ideal.* Second Annual Curriculum and Pedagogy Conference, University of Victoria, B.C., October 2001.

Warren, K. (1990). The power and promise of ecological feminism. *Environmental Ethics, 12*(2), 125–146.

Wertsch, J. V. (1991). *Voices of the mind: A sociocultural approach to mediated action.* Cambridge, MA: Harvard University Press.

West, C. (1993). The new cultural politics of differences. In C. McCarthy & W. Crinchlow (Eds.), *Race identity and representation in education* (pp. 11–23). New York: Routledge.

Zinn, H. (1995). *A peoples' history of the United States.* New York: HarperCollins.

CHAPTER EIGHTEEN

Lessons in Conversation

Why Critical Civic Engagement Requires Talking about Religion, and What That Means for Public Schools [1]

ROBERT KUNZMAN

This essay considers the role religion should play in an education for critical civic literacy in U.S. public schools. As suggested by the chapter title, my focus here is primarily on helping students learn to talk about issues of civic controversy: to explore and understand unfamiliar ethical perspectives that inform conflicting viewpoints, and to deliberate respectfully about the implications for our lives together. While it's true that "democracy isn't all talk," as Jeffrey Stout acknowledges, it's hard to imagine a just society without it: "The democratic practice of giving and asking for ethical reasons…is where the life of democracy principally resides."[2]

In other words, we must be willing and able to explain to others why we advocate certain laws or policies, and open to hearing the reasons that others have for believing otherwise. Some of these reasons will likely stem from religious sources. The efficacy of such "talk" relies on a groundwork of mutual understanding, respect, and goodwill. Public schools, I contend, need to cultivate a commitment to, and capacity for, such talk in their students.

Religion, according to philosopher Richard Rorty, is a conversation-stopper. [3] When citizens point to religious scripture or the will of God as the reason for their political positions, Rorty contends, there's nothing left to talk about—they've entered the realm of incommensurable criteria, with no way to judge among claims. And even if they were to try to keep the conversation going, the presence of religious language and dogma would almost certainly derail it, leaving a pileup of suspicion, mistrust, and ill will.

The only reasonable alternative, many theorists say, is to keep religion out of our political conversations and decisions about public policy.[4] Religious convictions are private matters and should remain so; to preserve this distinction, these theorists advocate a procedural approach to deliberation that follows certain rules about what counts as acceptable reasons—namely, reasons that draw from secular sources that we can purportedly all share, secular and religious citizens alike. This debate over the role of religion in public life has been a primary focus of liberal political theory over the past forty years.[5]

Anyone who pays attention to public discourse in the United States, however, will note that "religion talk" is still very much a part of the civic conversation, for better or worse. The influence of organizations such as the Moral Majority or Christian Coalition waxes and wanes across the decades, and one may certainly question their tactics and motivations. But many everyday Americans without overt political agendas would find it nonsensical to deliberate about civic commitments while ignoring their religious ones. As Nicholas Wolterstorff explains, "It belongs to the *religious conviction*s of a good many religious people in our society that *they ought to bas*e their decisions concerning fundamental issues of justice *on* their religious convictions. They do not view it as an option whether or not to do so.…Their religion is not, for them, about *something othe*r than their social and political existence; it is *also* about their social and political existence."[6]

Furthermore, it is important to recognize that it's not only conservative religious ideology and organizations that influence citizens' perspectives. Many supporters of environmental protection, progressive taxation, and assistance to the poor, for instance, draw their motivation from religious sources; and while organizations on the Christian Right may garner more headlines, its progressive counterparts such as Sojourners and the National Council of Churches also seek to influence the civic views of the populace. The same ideological diversity can be found within other religious traditions as well.

Simply put, anyone seeking to engage thoughtfully and critically with the ideals and realities of democratic citizenship must have an appreciation for the role religion plays in the lives of many citizens. This is particularly true in U.S. society, where more than 80% of citizens claim a religious affiliation, and survey data support Wolterstorff's contention that (at least on some issues) citizens draw heavily from their religious convictions when forming positions on public policy.[7]

If public schools are to prepare students for active democratic citizenship, they ignore the reality of this religion-infused milieu at our peril. It is my contention that we need to help students learn how to keep the civic conversation going even when religion is part of the mix.[8] But this doesn't mean accepting the status quo of religious talk in the public square, which too often resembles a series of indignant soliloquies delivered with self-righteous certainty; instead, a critical civic literacy should instill in students a desire and ability to engage respectfully and productively with religious diversity.

Such an educational goal is a daunting challenge, to be sure. Respectful civic dialogue would be complicated enough if we pursued the more procedural approach of mainstream deliberative theory that sharply limits the use of religious reasons. But recognizing the centrality of religion in the convictions of many citizens means that keeping the civic conversation going becomes less about procedure and more of a dispositional commitment, one that relies on a groundwork of skills and virtues that I call "civic multilingualism."

Religion as Part of the Broader Ethical Domain

Before unpacking the idea of civic multilingualism, however, an important conceptual point is in order, one that widens our scope beyond formal religion and into the broader ethical realm. Citizens' positions about public policy—the shape of our civic life together—are informed by our values. But these values are typically more than just a sense of right and wrong; they emerge from our particular vision of the good life. This may not be a singular model (many believe that good lives can take a variety of forms), but most of us have a sense of what we value and why.[9] This realm of consideration—not just "what is it good to do?" but "who is it good to be?"—is what the ancient Greek philosophers called *ethics*.[10]

Clearly, our ethical perspectives are not always informed by religion; these fundamental conceptions of value and purpose can be shaped by a variety of cultural sources and personal experiences. Regardless of their source, they orient us toward a particular conception of what it means to live well, and this in turn informs our perspective on how society should be structured to enable such lives.

With this in mind, then, the focus for this chapter extends to the broader ethical realm, including but stretching beyond formal religion. This clarification accomplishes two things: one, it sidesteps the endless legal and philosophical arguments about what exactly constitutes a religion; and two, it acknowledges that plenty of citizens draw from ethical sources other than religion when forming and expressing their views on civic matters.

Principles of Civic Multilingualism

In recent years, the call has increased for American students to study foreign languages. In an interconnected, global society, the argument goes, Americans must be able to communicate effectively with a diversity of peoples and cultures, whether for purposes of commerce, research, or national security. I contend that another form of fluency is increasingly needed in today's world—the ability to converse across different ethical perspectives in search of understanding, compromise, and common ground. At home and abroad, this may in fact represent the greatest social challenge of the twenty-first century.

Civic conversation need not entail an abandonment of our ethical convictions, religious or otherwise. In fact, religious communities and their distinctive languages of justice have contributed powerfully to pivotal democratic movements in U.S. history, such as the abolition of slavery and the Civil Rights Movement. And despite the many, well-publicized ways that religious talk and religious interest groups can trouble our democracy, social science research consistently suggests that religious Americans are more civically active—such as belonging to community organizations, solving community problems, and participating in local political life—than their secular counterparts.[11]

The goal of civic multilingualism is that citizens in our diverse democracy will bring with them to the public square their own ethical languages, their own ways of seeing and ordering the world, but also have the capacity to communicate respectfully and effectively with those holding conflicting perspectives. So how can public schools help foster civic multilingualism in their students? In what follows I explain three vital facets of this approach: imaginative engagement, realm recognition, and civic humility.

Imaginative Engagement

Gaining proficiency in a language obviously entails learning vocabulary, grammatical rules, and other propositional knowledge. But to truly understand a language, to gain genuine fluency, speakers must understand the cultural context in which it is spoken. In the same way, understanding of unfamiliar ethical perspectives requires an ongoing exercise of imaginative engagement, an appreciation for not only *what* others believe, but *why* they believe it and the significance of such convictions in the lives of those who hold them. This imaginative engagement involves a more substantive exploration than is typically found in state standards frameworks and textbooks. It requires a variety of angles and exposure to the subject, drawing on a range of media: literature, art, film, guest speakers, historical documents, and so on.[12]

Such a variety of sources can help students recognize that diversity exists within religious and other ethical traditions as well. The potential value of this recognition should not be overlooked, as it can help outsiders to avoid viewing a particular religion in monolithic (and frequently negative) terms, and hopefully be more willing to investigate the particularities of a particular insider's claims or perspectives. In addition, for students who share that particular religious tradition, the recognition of internal diversity may provide a greater sense of intellectual or ideological freedom, an openness that says, "My fellow Muslim (or Christian, Jew, etc.) looks at this issue differently—perhaps I should reconsider my view." Or just as meaningful would be the observation, "Others from my faith tradition believe differently—even though I disagree, I should refrain from demonizing my opponents."[13] The possibility of such educationally powerful conclusions should impel us to provide a rich and nuanced exposure to, and engagement with, religious diversity.

It's also important to help students understand that developing this sort of substantive appreciation for unfamiliar ethical perspectives doesn't require approval or endorsement of those perspectives. We demonstrate civic respect toward others not by agreeing with them, but by striving mightily to understand what they value and why. Such insight doesn't guarantee fruitful deliberations, of course, but it's hard to imagine how a deep-seated ignorance of our fellow citizens and their priorities could lead us to fair and respectful decisions about the shape of our public life together.

Realm Recognition

Perhaps the most crucial element of civic multilingualism is a recognition of the difference between the private and public realms, and what that distinction means for our disagreements with fellow citizens. Simply put, students need to understand that citizens in a diverse democracy cannot expect—nor should they seek—a society that is a mirror image of their private ethical convictions.

Realm recognition can be defended on both principled and practical grounds. Most religious adherents in the United States do not seek a theocracy, where religious leaders run the government and religious law supplants civil law. For some religious traditions, such an arrangement might be rejected on theological grounds, emerging either from a belief that political power corrupts faith or from a respect for individual freedom and will. On a practical level, a lack of distinction between private and public poses as many risks for the religious believer as anyone else, since there is no guarantee that her religion would retain power—and even if it did, internal disagreements might one day result in her being labeled a heretic and thus an enemy of the state. Democracy is the imperfect compromise that seeks room for disagreement among ethical traditions, in part by preserving a civic realm distinct from private beliefs.

The remaining—and unavoidably complicated—question, of course, is how the two realms should relate to one another. While people will undeniably live the bulk of their lives in the nonpolitical realms guided by their private visions of the good life, mutual respect requires a different sort of conversation when we're deciding how we will live *together*. This distinction between public and private realms, and the need to communicate differently in them, is not about the prohibition of religious perspectives in public deliberation. Rather, it's a recognition that different contexts require different approaches, and that when we're advocating for decisions that will affect the lives of others, we should exercise what Christopher Eberle calls "conscientious engagement"—striving to frame our deeply held convictions in ways that will resonate with our conversational partners.[14]

Civic Humility

Genuine conversation—public or private—requires an openness to the ideas and perspectives of others, an acknowledgment that we are not infallible in our interpretations or arguments. At the same time, however, many of our deeply held identities and commitments will be private ones (religious or otherwise) that are, necessarily and quite appropriately, close-minded and not readily open to revision. What matters most to us about who we are and what we believe is not continually "up for grabs."

This might seem to present a dead end for efforts toward a critical civic literacy that seeks to question tradition, structures, and received wisdom of all kinds. But civic humility remains a tenable virtue because of the principle of realm recognition. We can adopt a provisional stance toward our civic positions without needing to extend this fallibilism to core ethical convictions themselves.

Put another way, civic multilingualism doesn't ask us to reconsider the essence of our private ethical language or how we live out those convictions in our private world.[15] Rather, civic humility requires us to acknowledge that our application of private beliefs to civic life together will often be a matter of reasonable disagreement.

Teachers should encourage this type of open-minded civic humility, while emphasizing to students that this obligation applies to their role as citizens in the political realm, the arena where our ethical convictions inform policy or laws that affect fellow citizens who may not share those convictions. In so doing, they make clear that the distinction between the private and broader civic realm provides room for those who believe in absolute or singular truth, as long as they recognize that civic obligations require all of us to seek compromise and accommodation in the public realm with other reasonable perspectives.

Fostering Conversational Virtues

Civic multilingualism involves a range of conversational virtues that emerge from a commitment to the principles of imaginative engagement, realm recognition, and civic humility. Teachers can help cultivate civic multilingualism by encouraging the development of these communicative virtues.

One such virtue is a willingness to identify the strength of opposing arguments, not simply pinpoint weaknesses. This form of charitable interpretation asks the question, "What is the strongest case that can be made for this position?" Conversely, students should be urged to acknowledge the shortcomings of their own position. Such interpretive generosity not only moves students toward fairer and more accurate evaluations, it establishes a tone of goodwill and reciprocity toward one's dialogical partners.

Teachers can help students recognize the complexity of issues by taking care not to frame public controversies as inherently two-sided; even within such highly polarized issues as abortion or gay marriage, identifying a basic "pro" and "con" dichotomy heightens the risk of caricature and oversimplification. Again, the internal diversity of religious traditions often deserves particular emphasis with complex social controversies. In addition, teachers can help avoid misrepresentation by emphasizing the twin virtues of what Uma Narayan calls methodological humility (wherein I acknowledge that I may be missing something) and methodological caution (wherein I take great care in translation to reduce the chance I will misinterpret). These are especially important when considering the experiences and perspectives of people experiencing oppression, Narayan emphasizes; it is far too easy to assume understanding we don't have.[16]

These various practices of interpretive generosity, combined with ongoing efforts toward imaginative engagement, should enable what is perhaps *the* central civic virtue: recognizing reasonable disagreement. When considering the goals of civic literacy, what's crucial is that students learn how to recognize the reasonableness of other perspectives, not that they change their minds to agree with those perspectives. In other words, teachers can help their students understand that "reasonable doesn't necessarily equal right." At the same time, however, our acknowledgment of the reasonableness of our fellow citizens should impel us toward compromise and accommodation with them whenever possible.

Of course, it's also possible that students will move beyond reasonable disagreement and begin to modify their own views on the proper shape of our public life together, and the appropriate public policies to support that vision. Again, this need not imply a shift in core beliefs (although it certainly could); the experience of civic discourse may help students see how their core ethical premises can actually lead to different conclusions about policy implications.

Perhaps it goes without saying, but the skills of civic multilingualism will not emerge spontaneously in most classrooms (as Benjamin Barber contends, citizens are not born—they have to be made), and neither can they be developed in a brief unit on democratic engagement. Teachers need to be intentional and relentless in their focus on modeling and encouraging such practices in their students, creating a classroom culture where these types of conversational virtues become second nature.[17]

The Fruits of Civic Multilingualism: Civic Friendship

Taken together, these practices can help cultivate the powerful dynamic of civic friendship. As Danielle Allen explains, civic friendship is not about emotional fondness, but emerges from a faithful commitment to a relationship marked by ongoing communication and political restraint. "No political order can meet the requirement that every collaborative decision be a perfect bargain for all parties," Allen points out. Civic friends trust that conversation will continue despite political loss, and that opportunities for compromise and accommodation will be sought even by the victors. Restraint is a virtue that ultimately rewards all participants, Allen contends. By contrast, "if we always act according to our own unrestrained self-interests, we will corrode the trust that supports political bonds."[18]

Public schools hold significant possibilities for learning and practicing the virtues of civic friendship. As Walter Parker observes, they can be places full of diverse strangers who wrestle with academic challenges and social disagreements.[19] Schools also have the potential to be places where the power of conversation is reinforced by an institutional culture of respect, where cultural norms convey the message that actions and words cohere.[20]

While the foundation of trust in civic friendship emerges from a relationship marked more by conflict than affection, it's worth noting that conventional friendships can also serve as means of navigating ethical disagreement. In their extensive study of religion in contemporary America, Robert Putnam and David Campbell describe what they term the Aunt Susan Principle. "Most Americans," they report, "are intimately acquainted with people of other faiths." They may not know much about the details of the person's religion, but they know that they like and trust that person. That leads them to a more positive assessment of that religion than they would otherwise have.[21]

While Aunt Susan automatically gets the benefit of the doubt by virtue of our personal relationship with her, perhaps this principle can also extend to our civic interlocutors as well. When we build and benefit from relationships of democratic trust in the face of disagreement, we may find ourselves more willing to extend interpretive goodwill toward our fellow citizens who hold beliefs different from our own.

The Civic Rationale for Religion in the Curriculum

Making a case for the exploration of religion and other ethical perspectives in the public school curriculum requires an appreciation for the many concerns, legitimate and otherwise, of the stakeholders in public education. Certainly, the controversy generated by political philosophers about the role of religion in civic deliberation pales in comparison to our social disagreements over religion's role in public schools! Lawsuits pertaining to religious practices and observances (prayer, holidays, etc.) appear regularly, and disagreements over formal curricular matters are not far behind. Observing that the "vast majority" of citizen complaints to present-day school boards focus on religious issues, historian Jonathan Zimmerman argues that the inclusion of differing religious perspectives in America's textbooks and curricula has proven to be far more complicated and contested than even the inclusion of racial and ethnic minorities.[22]

The incendiary potential of religion's presence in the public school curriculum should not lead us to avoid engagement, but it should prompt great caution and care in how we go about it. In this matter, my approach differs sharply with Nel Noddings, one of the foremost advocates for including the study of religion in the public school classroom. Noddings asserts that public schools should have students address questions such as, "Is there a God (or gods)?…Must I believe everything that my religious denomination teaches?…Should we reject the notions of hell and damnation as incompatible with the belief in God's goodness?" Noddings asserts that "to 'educate' without addressing these questions is to engage in educational malpractice."[23]

From a personal perspective, I agree with Noddings that it is immensely valuable for all of us to contemplate such questions, and to explore the rich range of responses that human culture has developed across time and place. But I think Noddings is mistaken in both her rationale and methodology for exploring religion in public schools. If we believe that public schools should be the place where the general public learns how to *be* a public, then it will not serve our purposes if curricular attention to religious matters drives families away from public schools.

Noddings unintentionally illustrates this danger in her own examples of how teachers can prompt students to explore theological issues such as the problem of evil and the existence of hell. Her analysis and interpretations draw from a limited array of sources, and her conclusions that Christian interpretations of evil are inherently "handicapped" and that it is "logically incompatible" to believe in both hell and an all-good God certainly do not represent the full range of philosophical work on these complex questions.[24] In another instance, Noddings relates approvingly how a committed theist rejects the biblical miracle stories, which she sees as "charming nonsense."[25] The problems inherent in having students evaluate the "strong" and "weak" points, the "insights" and the "nonsense" of religion, as Noddings portrays them, are immense.[26] Noddings characterizes religious commitment as something readily—and unproblematically—subject to customization and revision, and the theological topics she urges teachers to explore are rife with opportunities for oversimplification and misrepresentation.

Noddings asserts that "fundamentalist students should be welcomed in our public schools," acknowledging that "our democracy depends on bringing our children together, not alienating them." But her approach to religious matters would almost certainly alienate a great many students and families, and this works against our civic purposes. Our democracy must persuade, rather than compel, its citizens to be generous listeners, tolerant neighbors, and willing to compromise in the face of reasonable disagreement; this becomes a much more difficult task when families perceive that such a vision of citizenship also requires their children to question their deepest sense of who they are and what they believe. A different approach is needed.

If our schools are to survive as places where religious diversity is broadly welcomed in the conversation, we ought to promote a civic rationale based on the need to grapple with issues of deep public disagreement. With the focus shifted to the civic implications for our lives together—rather than on the question of religious truth itself—the vital role of critical thinking and the need for fallibilism may be less problematic for many religious adherents. The need to prepare students to talk respectfully about matters of deep civic disagreement provides a far stronger rationale for the inclusion of religion in the public school curriculum.

Democracy as Penultimate Commitment

Civic multilingualism is about becoming fluent—or at least conversant—in a language that provides room for expression of our values and commitments, but in a way that acknowledges and honors the reality of reasonable disagreement in the public square. To the extent that a critical civic literacy seeks to foster critical thinking, interrogation of traditional structures, and the questioning of received wisdom, a potential tension exists with many religious traditions. We can navigate this tension by viewing civic multilingualism as a penultimate commitment of sorts. As Stout explains:

> Democracy involves substantive normative commitments, but does not presume to settle in advance the ranking of our highest values. Nor does it claim to save humanity from sin and death. It takes for granted that reasonable people will differ in their conceptions of piety, in their grounds for hope, in their ultimate concerns, and in their speculations about salvation. Yet it holds that people who differ on such matters can still exchange reasons with one another intelligibly, cooperate in crafting political arrangements that promote justice and decency in their relations with one another, and do both of these things without compromising their integrity. Cooperating democratic citizens tend also to be individuals who care about matters higher than politics, and expect not to get their way on each issue that comes before the public for deliberation.[27]

If we wish to become a more reasonable people, as Stout describes, then our public schools have a formidable but vital task before them. Our challenge as educators is how to foster a critical civic literacy that finds value in a broader public that connects all of us while also recognizing that it is our narrower communities and private identities that sustain us in ways at least as powerful and important.

No, democracy isn't all talk, but learning how to talk about the issues that matter most deeply to us, to consider their implications for our civic life together, is a central task of preparation for engaged, critical citizenship. No deliberative procedure, no dialogical formula, can adequately encompass the complexity that ethical pluralism creates for democratic citizens. Instead, we must rely on the cultivation of civic virtues such as interpretive generosity and reasonable disagreement to help keep the conversation going. In this way, we can hope to shape a public life together marked by understanding and respect.

Notes

1. Many thanks to Keith Barton and James Damico for their helpful comments on an earlier draft of this chapter.
2. Jeffrey Stout, *Democracy and Tradition* (Princeton, NJ: Princeton University Press, 2004), 6.
3. Richard Rorty, "Religion as a Conversation-stopper," in *Philosophy and Social Hope* (London: Penguin Books, 1999), 168–74.
4. Throughout this essay, I use the terms political and civic to denote the public realms of society, where we interact and coexist with citizens who may not share the private beliefs and commitments found in families, religious communities, etc. In political theory scholarship, the term political refers more narrowly to the involvement of government and state power.
5. In 1971, John Rawls's *A Theory of Justice* argued for keeping private, comprehensive doctrines (such as those informed by religion) out of public deliberations, in favor of "public reason" that citizens could share in com-

mon. Political theorists have been taking sides on this argument ever since.

6. Robert Audi and Nicholas Wolterstorff, *Religion in the Public Square: The Place of Religious Convictions in Political Debate* (Lanham, MD: Rowman & Littlefield, 1997), 105.

7. Robert D. Putnam and David E. Campbell, *American Grace: How Religion Divides and Unites Us* (New York: Simon & Schuster, 2010), 7–10, 369–418; "2010 Annual Religion and Public Life Survey," a poll conducted by the Pew Forum on Religion and Public Life, July–August 2010.

8. As Jeffrey Stout contends, "It is foolhardy to suppose that anything like the Rawlsian program of restraint or what Rorty calls the Jeffersonian compromise will succeed in a country with our religious and political history. So the practical question is not whether religious reasons will be expressed in public settings, but by whom, in what manner, and to what ends" (*Democracy and Tradition*, 299).

9. Charles Taylor describes this as an ethical framework, the "commitments and identifications which provide the frame or horizon within which I can try to determine from case to case what is good, or valuable, or what ought to be done, or what I endorse or oppose" ("Two Theories of Modernity," *The Responsive Community* 6, no. 3 [1996]: 24). If we claim to know where we stand on matters of importance to us, we have an ethical framework.

10. Bernard Williams, *Ethics and the Limits of Philosophy* (Cambridge, MA: Harvard University Press, 1985).

11. Putnam and Campbell, *American Grace*, 443–492; Paul J. Weithman, *Religion and the Obligations of Citizenship* (Cambridge, UK: Cambridge University Press, 2002), 36–66; Christian Smith and David Sikkink, "Is Private School Privatizing?" *First Things* 92 (April 1999): 16–20.

12. For a more detailed explanation of this idea of imaginative engagement, see Robert Kunzman, *Grappling with the Good: Talking about Religion and Morality in Public Schools* (Albany: State University of New York Press, 2006), 59–78.

13. My thanks to Keith Barton for drawing my attention more fully to the civic and educational value of ideological diversity within a religious tradition.

14. Eberle contrasts conscientious engagement with the procedural model of deliberation described earlier that restricts the kinds of reasons and languages we use in civic dialogue (Christopher J. Eberle, *Religious Convictions in Liberal Politics* [Cambridge, UK: Cambridge University Press, 2002], 104–108).

15. Some (such as Nel Noddings, whose views I critique in a later section of this chapter) disagree with this deliberate limitation on critical analysis. They argue that a good education should provide opportunities and encouragement for students to question everything about their world. I have no quarrel with providing space and opportunity for students to do this, but public schools in a pluralistic democracy must tread lightly here, or they risk alienating parents who feel such an approach intrudes on their childrearing domain.

16. Uma Narayan, "Working Together across Difference: Some Considerations on Emotions and Political Practice," *Hypatia* 3, no. 2 (1988): 31–47.

17. That being said, it's also important to acknowledge that this vision for civic multilingualism runs counter to the dominant ethos in current K–12 policy, where easy-to-quantify skills and knowledge serve as the barometer for educational success. The more that teachers can interweave this kind of civic conversation with the development of the skills and knowledge mandated by academic standards frameworks, the more acceptable it may seem to those unable or unwilling to acknowledge its vital importance in creating capable democratic citizens.

18. Danielle S. Allen, *Talking to Strangers: Anxieties of Citizenship since Brown v. Board of Education* (Chicago: University of Chicago Press, 2004), 138.

19. Walter Parker, "Listening to Strangers: Classroom Discussion in Democratic Education," *Teachers College Record* 112, no. 1 (2010): 2815–2832.

20. Of course, the opposite also holds true, and arguably is more descriptive of much institutional schooling—curricular emphases of respect, communication, and interpretive goodwill mean little when the broader school environment lacks these qualities.

21. Putnam and Campbell, *American Grace*, 526. I suspect the Aunt Susan Principle applies similarly to ethical commitments beyond formal religion. Knowing that their likeable colleague is gay, or their trusted neighbors are lesbians, probably moves people toward greater tolerance and acceptance of homosexuality as well.

22. Jonathan Zimmerman, *Whose America? Culture Wars in the Public Schools* (Cambridge, MA: Harvard University

Press, 2002), 7–8.

23. Nel Noddings, *Critical Lessons: What Our Schools Should Teach* (Cambridge, UK: Cambridge University Press, 2006), 250.

24. Noddings, *Critical Lessons*, 265, 270. For an example of a philosophically sophisticated alternative interpretation of these questions, see Robert Merrihew Adams, *Finite and Infinite Goods: A Framework for Ethics* (New York: Oxford University Press, 1999).

25. Nel Noddings, "Dialogue Between Believers and Unbelievers," *Religious Education* 92, no. 2 (1997): 247.

26. Nel Noddings, *Educating for Intelligent Belief or Unbelief* (New York: Teachers College Press, 1993), 18–40.

27. Stout, *Democracy and Tradition,* 298.

CHAPTER NINETEEN

Attempted Cultural Baptism

The Bible Literacy Project's Impact on Civic Engagement

PAMELA K. SMITH & DIANNE SMITH

Introduction

In this post-era of "compassionate conservatism" (Spring, 2005), many participants in diverse educational arenas have encountered a problematic theoretical and ideological moment in terms of religious beliefs that are presented as natural and true for all people in all situations at all times. The political frame that has dominated this nation for the past 20 years or more suggests using religion as a means of social and political control of both the body and the mind, thus making the private more public and the public supported more heavily by privatized interests.

This political frame is represented in what has been a largely non-interrogated movement promoted as the Bible Literacy Project. As of 2010, 490 schools in 43 states had decided that the curriculum developed by this group should be included in their high schools' curriculum requirements (Bible Literacy Project, 2010). Many questions arise for educators who take seriously what constitutes definitions of "truth" and how we, as critical educators, come to decide what forms of knowledge will be promoted within schools. In this sense, we also have to call into question who has designed the Bible Literacy curriculum, what their stated and unstated histories have been, and what interest groups may underpin the supporters' and creators' thinking.

In addition, it is imperative that consideration be given as to how this curriculum may promote the kind of thinking that silences discourse in public schools and legitimates students' refusal to consider alternative points of view that fall outside the dominant ideology that pervades the last quarter century. In classrooms at all levels, it is not uncommon for teachers and professors to run into brick walls as they try to promote issues affecting non-dominant groups whose religions, sexual orientations, gendered presentations, etc., do not fall within the purview of such a prescriptive curriculum. Indeed, the first question to be asked is: Which Bible will be used as the primary text in this course, given that the promoters state in the teacher's guide for the course that the "Bible" will be studied (Bible Literacy Project, 2006, p. T3)? At this juncture in time, any Bible can be used, and that which is selected is left to the teacher's discretion. In a culture which fears non-Judeo-Christian religious ideas, the King James Bible is a likely contender for consideration. The Project has tried to avoid criticism of this point by writing its own book, *The Bible and Its Influence*, which was designed to be read along with the Bible (Bible Literacy Project, 2010). Questions that arise from study of the texts that deal with issues of faith are to be directed to the students' own religious/faith leaders. Another concern emerges at this point: what if the student comes from a family background that does not follow any denominational or religious affiliation? In that case, the dominant views presented by a Bible Literacy Project trained teacher will become the "answer."

Therefore, in this chapter, we will begin with an investigation of religion's inclusion in the public school curriculum, survey who wrote the initial curriculum for this group, study who sits on the Bible Literacy Project's Board of Directors and what their ideological backgrounds and interests indicate, and then critically interrogate what is, indeed, included in the curriculum. Finally, we will conclude with recommendations for further study and comments regarding how this movement relates to civic engagement in truly democratic public spheres.

Discussion

In the early years of the educational system in the United States, religion was assumed to hold a pivotal role in determining curricular inclusions and exclusions. For example, the Massachusetts School Law of 1647 (Spring, 2008) specifically stated that communities with 50 or more families must hire a teacher, and those with 100 or more households must build a grammar school where students could study Greek, Latin, and grammar for civic and religious instruction. Ignorance of classical educational codes and inability to read were deemed to be sources whereby Satan's influence could draw young people into the ways of evil.

One cannot suggest that Calvinism was the sole religion to weave its ideas into the schools. Two hundred years after the passage of the New England school laws, Horace Mann and proponents of the Common Schools Movement argued that teachers' primary purposes were to transmit moral virtue, as defined by Judeo-Christian traditions (Spring, 2008). The influx of immigrants, both those who chose to enter by traditional legal means and those whose national designation was altered by territorial acquisition and/or forced immigration through enslavement (e.g., the Louisiana Purchase; the Mexican Cession, which was a result of the Treaty of Guadalupe Hidalgo that ended the Mexican-American War; and the slavery of Africans), made schools an arena for acculturation in which Eurocentric values, including Protestantism, could be promulgated. As Goodlad (2004) has noted, Christianity, rules for civic engagement, and communal living were distinctly interwoven into one belief system.

In an age of political correctness, religion and diversity has led to a return to what was originally thought to be inherent to this country's makeup—a repeated call for the separation of church and state. One could argue that religion's being taught implicitly in school may not have occurred during some years, but the hidden curriculum has kept it intact within the curriculum during that debate.

After much legal wrangling, it has been accepted that teaching the Bible is not necessarily considered to be a First Amendment violation. As the Bible Literacy Project promoters (2010) write:

> Academic study of the Bible in public schools is legal in all 50 states of the union. In 1963, the Supreme Court ruled that public schools may not require *devotional* use of the Bible. In that same decision, however, the Supreme Court explicitly acknowledged that academic study of the Bible in public schools is constitutional as part of a good education.

In 1999, the Bible Literacy Project worked with the First Amendment Center to develop and co-publish *The Bible & Public Schools: A First Amendment Guide,* which established how such study could occur (Bible Literacy Project, 2010).

The promotion of religious ideology in public schools has been an issue in previous eras, and laws have been passed to curtail its promotion. Currently, the textbook co-published by the Bible Literacy Project and the First Amendment Center meets the standards for Bible literacy courses in Alabama, Florida, Georgia, Oklahoma, South Carolina, Tennessee, and Texas (Bible Literacy Project, 2010). When looking at a map of states teaching the Bible Literacy Project in their schools, it seems that deception may be afoot. It appears that this movement has been approved in all but five of the states in the union. In fact, in five states in the union (Nevada, Utah, Wyoming, Montana, and Iowa), the Project has not been put into place in school curricula. However, when one checks on a map by clicking one's mouse on states that have not agreed to the Project, a message appears which points out that the first school district to adopt the curriculum will receive a free set of textbooks (Bible Literacy Project, 2010). This is clearly a marketing device. Additionally, the Project has not been unilaterally adopted by the other 45 states of the union. Thus, it is used in some districts but not all.

Study of the Bible is always a matter of contention because of the nature of the debate. Kevin McGuire (2008) writes extensively of U.S. Supreme Court actions that have been taken to control the pervasion of particular religious ideology into public school classrooms. His conclusion is that though the Court may rule on issues from prayer to religious teaching in the classroom, no guarantee exists that states will comply with any ruling. Indeed, it seems that the states have found ways through which to bypass the Court's rulings, beginning with violations of the First Amendment's Establishment Clause (McGuire, 2008). By arguing that the Bible Literacy Project is intended to provide a backdrop for more effective teaching of Western literature, art, music, history, and other subjects, and by suggesting that these same core subjects in the high school curriculum cannot be truly understood without a working knowledge of both the Old and New Testaments, proponents have found a way to insert the Bible back into the schools.

At the same time, in an effort to bring the Bible directly back into the mainstream curriculum, proponents of the Bible Literacy Project argue that in order for students to "make it" through school, they need to study the Bible directly. Thus, literacy is reduced, yet again, to a non-interrogated form of indoctrination and memorization, akin to E.D. Hirsch's (1988) attempts to define cultural literacy.

However, the Bible Literacy Project appears to be geared toward a two-pronged attack upon non-secular, diverse educational practices: first, the Bible would be taught as a course in public schools through a canned package developed by directors of the Project; and second, at a time when U.S. domination of public space is in global jeopardy, the doors to the Eurocentric traditions within this country can be walled up against outsiders by teaching the art, literature, and cultural heritages that make up this nation in an "as is" fashion.

This second element is significant because it privileges the dominant culture at its highest standard at a time when minority cultures and differing worldviews are becoming part of this country's landscape. The Bible Literacy Project's teacher's edition states:

> There are many important rationales for bringing high-quality academic instruction about the Bible to all American schoolchildren. Students of all faiths (and none) need to know about the Bible to engage their American heritage in key areas of language, arts, and literature, as well as history, law, and politics. Why should any student, regardless of faith tradition, be denied the tools to understand some of the most inspiring rhetoric in American history? (p. T5)

In a sense, what is said here implies that students from different faiths, or none, are culturally deficient and need to be remediated so that they can fully be acculturated into current U.S. society.

As we begin to think about religious teachings in public schools today, we would argue that they are often rooted in the very sort of cultural deficit theory manifested in the Massachusetts Bay School Law of 1647. According to the *Bible Literacy Report: What Do American Teens Need to Know and What Do They Know?* (Wachlin & Johnson, 2005), "data" is represented to show that "substantial minorities [sic] lack even the most working knowledge of the Bible. Almost one of ten teens believes that Moses is one the twelve Apostles" (p. 6). Material such as this leads to the assumption that parents/guardians of non-dominant group students either lack necessary knowledge of the Bible so that they can teach what is right and true to their students, or they are simply unconcerned with doing so. In effect, then, this sort of thinking mirrors that of the early colonists of this "America" who took religious teaching as a civic responsibility. Fines were levied in the 1600s when knowledge of the dominant group was judged to have been taught insufficiently. We would argue that fines are levied in different ways today when schools lacking resources for teaching materials demanded by standardized tests are also called upon to support the moral values of the neoconservative Christian movement.

Spring (2005) suggests that most social problems, i.e., poverty, crime, and threats to democratic society, are typically conceived to result from failings in personal character and values. Spring furthers this thought with a linkage to the No Child Left Behind (NCLB) legislation which has now been replaced with the even more fractious "Race to the Top" that emerged from the Obama administration. Both give the U.S. Department of Education a distinct role in ensuring that school prayer be allowed (Spring, 2005, p. 5). This section of NCLB, then, would appear to sanction a return to religion in the schools and a denial of the separation of church and state.

Efforts to move Bible literacy into the mainstream curriculum are definitely on the rise. In 2007, the Georgia State Board of Education voted to add two academic Bible courses to a list of state-funded courses (Duffy, 2007). The two courses, though elective, would have taught high school students the history and literature of both the Old and New Testaments of the Bible. Perhaps an occurrence that is more indicative of the pervasive nature of Bible literacy as a curricular phenomenon is that several privately developed curricula "are employed in 460 districts in at least 37 states" (Van Biema, 2007, p. 2).

During an economic period in this nation when school districts suffer constraints in elective offerings and when standardized testing determines whether students graduate from high school, critical educators have to ask how it is that time will be available to teach the Bible. Congruently, it is necessary to ask why money and personnel are available for Bible literacy courses when band, art, foreign languages, and other subjects have been cut because of lack of funds. This is a problematic issue for all levels of education.

It is also problematic for students who come from diverse backgrounds reflecting religious teachings that are not based upon a Eurocentric Christian tradition. In a diverse nation, public schools are touted as bastions of democratic thought, not as protectors of Christian ideology. Divergent religious and nonreligious ideologies come into play. If Bible literacy takes precedence over respect for cultural diversity, further marginalization of non-Eurocentric groups will occur (Kaminer, 1999).

Given the Bible Literacy Project's successful movement into many public schools' curricula, it is important to scrutinize the originators and leaders of the Project so that their sociopolitical ideologies can be made transparent, thus providing potential purchasers of the material with a clearer view of what lies behind the movement. First, we will begin with Marie Wachlin (1993), and then we will look at the interests and past actions of the Bible Literacy Project's board members so that we can unearth any agendas underpinning their work.

According to a question-and-answer column published by Sotille (2005) in the *Willamette Week Online*, Wachlin, a former high school English teacher at Benson High School in Portland, Oregon, is an adjunct professor at Concordia University, a Christian institution located in the Northeast sector of the city. Concordia University has numerous sites throughout the country, with courses offered both onsite and online. The school is strongly imbued with Lutheran theology. Wachlin did her doctoral dissertation at Concordia-Portland, during which time she conducted a survey investigation of 41 teachers who polled their students on knowledge of the Bible (Wachlin, 1993). Wachlin argues that if students are to understand the humanities, they need to be able to have a working knowledge of Biblical figures and stories. At the same time, she contends that "with the Koran, it's just not a part of our culture as much. You want to teach what's pertinent" (Sotille, 2005). Wachlin, who identifies herself as a Christian, exhibits a narrow world view that would marginalize the life experiences and definitions of the humanities that move beyond Western cultural domination.

The Board of Directors of the Bible Literacy Project consists of Mark Berner, Kevin J. "Seamus" Hasson, Pamela Scurry, Richard R. Vietor, and Chuck Stetson (Bible Literacy Project, 2010). Only Vietor and Scurry are not directly tied to religious interests. Vietor is President of R.R. Vietor L.L.C, a consulting firm for healthcare companies, and Scurry owns Wicker Garden's Children, a children's store located on Madison Avenue in New York City. She is a wife and mother of two.

Mark Berner is involved in work that is directed toward creating a series of initiatives "focusing on renewing the moral, intellectual, and spiritual foundations of public culture" (Bible Literacy Project, 2008). How those foundations are defined is not included on his website, but Berner has also been a businessman in the oil industry, has managed hedge funds focused on troubled assets, and has served on unnamed charitable boards.

Kevin J. "Seamus" Hasson is a graduate of the University of Notre Dame Law School, as well as having taken a Master's degree in theology from the same university. He focuses his work on religious liberty and has established an interfaith public interest law firm which is devoted to ensuring religious free expression for all persons. In this regard, he can negotiate the First Amendment issues of free speech and separation of church and state which are central to the discussion and activities of the Bible Literacy Project.

Chuck Stetson is Chairman of the Board for the Project. He also has served as Chairman of the Board for the National Rifle Association. It is significant that Stetson is closely associated with Charles Colson, who was involved in the Watergate fiasco that brought down the presidency of Richard M. Nixon. Colson underwent a religious conversion of a fundamentalist nature following his fall from grace during the Nixon era and established Prison Fellowship Ministries, an evangelical organization focused upon prison populations (Plotz, 2000).

The Bible Literacy Project is prepared for challenges to its curricular content. Indeed, in the teachers' edition to the text, which was written by followers of the movement, *The Bible and Its Influence: Teacher's Edition* (Schippe & Stetson, 2007), the authors state:

> The primary task now is to move beyond words, to action: To muster support for a Bible literacy curriculum for public schools that is fair, balanced, rigorous, and constitutional, accompanied by a textbook which will harm no child's faith while leaving every teen knowledgeable about the Bible. This Bible course has been reviewed by leading Bible literacy scholars, faith leaders, and educators to ensure its fairness and accuracy. The Beckett Fund for Religious Liberty has agreed to defend, free of charge, any school district sued for using our Bible curriculum in a manner consistent with *The Bible and the Public Schools: A First Amendment Guide*. This applies to districts in which the teacher has taken the online training course. (p. T9)

Given that one of the Bible Literacy Project Board Members, Kevin J. "Seamus" Hasson, heads the Beckett Fund for Religious Liberty, a somewhat convenient truth appears. Essentially, money is to be made from this project in that the student textbook itself is listed at $66.11 on Amazon.com (it has been reduced from $73.45), and it can be purchased on the Bible Literacy Project's website for $50. The teacher's edition is $75. The online training for teachers is sponsored by Concordia University, where Marie Wachlin did her Ph.D. and where she has worked as an adjunct professor (Bible Literacy Project, 2008). Teachers are required to complete four online workshops through Concordia at $200 each, or teachers can take courses for continuing education credit at $800 or for graduate credit at $1,620 (Bible Literacy Project, 2010). Multiplying these numbers times those previously mentioned in this chapter indicates that a significant amount of money is being accrued by proponents and purveyors of the Bible Literacy Project for instructing students in our "free" democratic public schools.

Conclusion

The fundamental question begins with what is taught in traditional high school curricula in this society and how it is Eurocentrically biased. If Wachlin and Johnson (2005) found a need for high school students to have a higher level of awareness of Biblical events and figures, it might reflect the curricular emphasis placed upon U.S. and English literature, which are the two dominant literary forms taught in secondary schools in the country. This, too, is problematic, because as this society becomes increasingly diverse, the curricula remain in a perennialist coffin that is protected by the moneyed elite who fund protection of a culture which they claim as theirs alone.

When societies are in a state of change, and global populations face an imperative to understand one another to avoid annihilation of the planet, the Bible Literacy Project seems to attempt to closet, cloak, and cover public school students in many states with an extremely truncated world view. Though it contends that it uses three versions of the Bible (The King James Version, The New Revised Standard Version, and the Jewish Bible, the Tanakh), others have been omitted. For example, the Catholic Bible is different, i.e., it contains more books which are controversial to ultraconservative Christian groups. In addition, if students need to learn religion so that they can better understand culture, would it not have been better to have developed courses in comparative religions that included elements of the Bibles, the Torah, the Quran, the Book of Mormon, the Book of Tao, and so many other religious texts, including those written, spoken, and painted or drawn? This would include non-written but narrative structures that have informed cultures in South America, Africa, Australia, the Far East, and other parts of the world which offer different faith structures, including those rooted within an earth-based system. Why, then, have 43 states to date implemented the Bible Literacy Project without careful interrogation of this system?

Perhaps it is the globalized, market-based ideology which has led our culture to live in fear of "the other." Fear in U.S. society has been in a liquid form (Bauman, 2006) since the events of September 11, 2001, if not before. When we cannot locate the specific enemy, the boundaries of fear spread like uncensored tentacles of creeping doubt, and aggressive behavior against the perceived "other" results.

Currently, the United States faces an economic crisis that is second (at the moment) only to the Great Depression of the 1930s. The U.S. government is deeply indebted to China; depends upon outsourced labor from India for IT services; relies on oil from Venezuela, Russia, and Saudi Arabia; and lacks a sustainable economy to protect natural environs. Perhaps citizens' fear of the "other" has increased as the United States rapidly moves toward potential status as a Third World country while fighting two wars in a part of the world that celebrates a religion which is foreign to many, but not all, of the people living in America. Congruently, as China increases its economic growth, religious structures which have fortified that society, while being suppressed during times of transition, are removed from the discourse of faith in this country.

In a related sense, we are ultimately compelled to ask: Could it be that the Bible Literacy Project has been developed as a means of circumventing previous legislation related to First Amendment issues, while also bringing a second level of ethnic indoctrination into place? And what might that indoctrination be? It is a non-interrogated view of the Western tradition that tells students and teachers that anything that is different is deficient, dangerous, and deviant.

Bibliography

Bauman, Z. (2006). *Liquid fear*. Cambridge, MA: Polity Press.

The Bible Literacy Project (2006). *The Bible and its influence: Introduction to the teacher's edition.* Retrieved October 19, 2007, from http://www.bibleliteracy.org

Bible Literacy Project (2008). *Bible literacy project: An educated person is familiar with the Bible.* Retrieved October 17,

2008, from http://www.bibleliteracy.org/site

Bible Literacy Project (2010). *Bible literacy project: An educated person is familiar with the Bible*. Retrieved September, 19, 2010, from http://www.bibleliteracy.org/site

Duffy, K. (2007, March 8). State education board to vote on Bible classes. *The Atlanta Journal-Constitution*. Retrieved March 9, 2007, from www.ajc.com/metro/stories/ 2007/03/08/metboe0308a.html

Goodlad, J. (2004). *Education for everyone: Agenda for education in a democracy*. San Francisco: Jossey-Bass.

Hirsch, E.D. (1988). *Cultural literacy: What every American needs to know*. New York: First Vintage Books.

Kaminer, W. (1999). *Sleeping with extraterrestrials: The rise of irrationalism and perils of piety*. New York: Pantheon Books.

McGuire, K. (2008). Public schools, religious establishments, and the U.S. Supreme Court: An examination of policy compliance. *American Politics Research*. Retrieved October 17, 2008, from http://www.unc.edu/~/kmcguire /papers/prayer.pdf

No Child Left Behind Act of 2001 (2002). Public Law 107–110, 115 Stat. 1425.

Plotz, D. (2008, March 10). Charles Colson: How a Watergate crook became America's greatest Christian conservative. *Slate*. Retrieved October 17, 2008, from http://www.slate.com/id/77067

Schippe, C., & Stetson, C. (2007). *The Bible and its influence: Teacher's edition*. Fairfax, VA: BLP Publishing.

Schoollaw1642html (2007). *Massachusetts bay school law (1642)*. Retrieved August 1, 2007, from http://personal.pitnet.net/primarysources/schoollaw1642.html

Sotille, M. (2005, October 19). Marie Wachlin: Portland prof instructs public school teachers how to teach the Bible in class. *Willamette Week Online*. Vol. 31, No. 50. Retrieved on October 17, 2008, from http://wweek.com/editorial/3150/6840/

Spring, J. (2005). *Poltical agendas for educators: From the religious right to the green party*. Mahwah, NJ: Lawrence Erlbaum.

Spring, J. (2008). *The American school: From the Puritans to No Child Left Behind*. Boston: McGraw Hill.

Van Biema, D. (2007, March 27). The case for teaching the Bible. *Time*. Retrieved April 2, 2007, from www.time.com/time/printout/0,8816,1601845,00.html

Wachlin, M. (1993). *The place of Bible literature in public high school English classes*. (Doctoral Dissertation, University of Oregon). Ann Arbor, MI: University Microfilms International.

Wachlin, M., & Johnson, B.R. (2005). *Bible literacy report: What do American teens need to know and what do they know?* Fairfax, VA: Bible Literacy Project.

CHAPTER TWENTY

The Usefulness of Pragmatic Interpretation in Civic Education

ANDREW NUNN MCKNIGHT

What follows is a survey of four prominent pragmatist philosophers' views concerning how we conceptualize truth, position method, and determine the social use of historical analysis in civic education. These positions could be useful in helping educators and students find useful language, order their encounters, and critically interpret and engage our world. Although much of what follows is familiar philosophical territory, and many of the arguments presented are not explicitly new, this piece aims to portray the stated objective from a different angle. It tries to fuse the pragmatic conception of truth with the study of history, along with references to sites for communicative action and social problem solving, in order to build toward a more ethical and mutual society via critical civic inquiry.

Introduction

Much of the history of human experience has entailed a groping for certainty: certainty concerning the nature of our existence, and certainty in the nature of our experiences as representing a shared reality rather than solipsistic perception and isolated conception. The other side of what John Dewey (1929) terms the "quest for certainty" resides in our inability to exactly control the paths our lives take. It is from this uncertainty that we create belief systems that grant at least illusory surety concerning the nature of our experience, the historical antecedents of our experience, and the potential context of possible future experience. Dewey, attempting a philosophical explanation of this phenomenon states, "We *believe* in the absence of knowledge or complete assurance. Hence the quest for certainty has always been an effort to transcend belief" (26). This presents two potential aporias. First, belief at once affirms its subject, and then, in turn, negates the affirmation by acknowledging the possibility of its falseness. Unchecked, this may lead to a default relativism for students concerning the import of differing opinions—a reclining to a position that all are equally valid regardless of evidence or argument. Second, it also makes assumptions about one context relative to matters in a potentially changing context, thus creating confusion regarding social continuity or fluidity. Can we assist students toward something better than mere belief about history and its legacy in the present, i.e., something closer to a truth? What is at aim here is to foster the development of better belief, or perhaps, put another way, hypothesis rather than opinion. To ground such a field of analysis for students, let us explore a useable conception of truth.

Locating Pragmatic Truth and the Complications of Action

Truth is slippery as retrospect, as a wholly accurate expression of our memories or interpretation of texts. However, we can possibly help students arrive at subjective, yet verifiable, determinations of truth and falsehood concerning the past and present direction. Of course, this requires a rather malleable definition of truth which we will now explore.

William James (1995) states, "Truth is what we say about them [new contexts], . . . it must both lean on old truth and grasp new facts; and its success . . . in doing this, is a matter for the individual's appreciation." (25). In this sense, pragmatic truth takes an albeit relative, situational, and *a posteriori* tone, but nonetheless possible objective of social use-value as its impetus. The *fact* made relevant is done so because it aims toward the subjective end of being potentially beneficial. As James states, "*the true is the name of what ever proves itself to be good in the way of belief, and good, too, for definite assignable reasons*"(30). Thus, our inquiry into the past and present, interpretation of data, and the scope of action should yield present benefit. For instance, we might search for useful truths about education with our students, i.e., those matters that prove to be good, such as tolerance and respect for the assignable reasons of peace.

The method of determining truth, although typically malleable, begins and ends with experience and investigative process, respectively. According to James, the pragmatist

> turns away from abstraction and insufficiency, from verbal solutions, from bad *a priori* reasons, from fixed principles, closed systems, and pretended absolutes and origins. He [sic][1] turns toward concreteness and adequacy, toward facts, toward action, and toward power. That means the empiricist temper regnant, and the rationalist temper sincerely given up. It means the open air and possibilities of nature, as against dogma, artificiality and the pretense of finality in truth. (20)

Jamesian pragmatism finds its genesis in direct contradiction to philosophical traditions that would posit truth as an eternally rational determinism. James' departure from the determinist's fixed positions of immutability lies in the recognition of the ambiguous and polysemic. He criticizes the determinist position concerning the scope of possible investigative freedom as too confining. Freedom, under these conditions, assumes that we can definitively determine, and work within, the parameters in which we have choice. Thus, for the determinist, as James (1951) would have it, "bondage to the highest is identical with true freedom" (40). The rational determinist teacher denies an ambiguous past, present, or future, and thus denies chance concerning potential ethical manifestations, their affect, and circumstantial import. Under this rational prescription, they deny the potential for equivocation in action or result; for if there can be either/or determinations, our ethical intentions should render actions that correspond directly to *good* real-world manifestations, i.e., good reasoning should lead to just consequences.

In contrast, James' pragmatic version of freedom finds its truth not in predetermined nomological relationships, but in its use, its process, and benefit in each instance. He states, "if determinism is to escape pessimism, it must leave off looking at the goods and ills of life in a simple objective way, and regard them as materials, indifferent in themselves, for the production of consciousness, scientific and ethical, in us" (52). However, James was careful to point out that, while absolute determinism is impossible and ineffectual, pure indeterminism denies us the possibility of knowledge. His version of indeterminism

> says that the parts have a certain amount of loose play on one another, so that the laying down of one of them does not necessarily determine what the other shall be. . . . [It] denies the world to be one unbending unit of fact. It says there is a certain ultimate pluralism in it. . . . Actualities seem to float in a wider sea of possibilities from out of which they are chosen; and *somewhere*, indeterminism says, such possibilities exist, and form a part of truth. (41)

As scientific pragmatism finds its value in the physical result, socially directed pragmatism finds its value in its cultural manifestation. The possible parameter for scientific value might be utility or theoretical explanation of observable physical phenomena. For historical inquiry, this should be cultural relevance, i.e., connection to the lives of knowing subjects, and should be based on the basic *a priori* premise that its value be of ethical benefit. This benefit may be, for our purposes here, defined as mutual societal benefit, i.e., a better shared ethical existence for the sake of various ideological abstractions such as freedom, happiness, contentment, imagination, creativity, etc. It is an attempt to move toward ethical benefit in a pluralistic and ever-changing social context.

The grimmer side of indeterminism, however, is that we can never truly know the outcome of our actions. Our analysis and ethical ruminations of our "understanding backwards" does not pay us the same chances of verification for our "living forwards" (171). The best we can do is to look at how past and present contexts inform ethical action through what James terms "the free-will theory of popular sense based on the judgement of regret, [which] represents that world as vulnerable, and liable to be injured by certain of its parts if they act wrong" (59–60).

Pragmatic verification resides in the connections that are provided by documentation, rational ordering, ideological and methodological consensus, and consensus of interpretation. Initial verification comes from experience that influences perception and conception—observation and forming ideas and beliefs, respectively—regarding something physically extant or conceptually palpable. When students inquire about a text like a social contract, we may address its potential application by what we identify its social use-value to be: a system of rights, responsibilities, laws, etc. The use-value of the social contract, and its specific problem-solving potential, is verified communally through discourse and through consensual communicative action.

James notes that "all human thinking gets discursified; we exchange ideas; we lend and borrow verifications, get them from one another by means of social intercourse" (166). Pragmatic verification thus is always rendered contingent by its subject-specific process, away from any hope of becoming a reified method to follow and acquire universal instruction on how to perceive, experience, analyze and act. It involves a vicissitudinous process of intersubjective interpretation. However, consensual agreement concerning practical and social use-value can be discerned from statements that are false in most occurrences. The acts of directed inquiry and communication, and the subsequent forming of fact, are bound in the process of active social projection, or as Dewey (1929) puts it: "the maintenance and diffusion of intellectual values, of ethical excellencies, the esthetically admirable, as well as the maintenance of order and decorum in human relations are dependent on what men do"(31).

In similar fashion, James (1951) asserts that verification, or a pragmatic conception of truth, "happens to an idea. It *becomes* true, is *made* true by events. Its verity is in fact an event, a process" (161). So we are always examining an event from individual experience and through discourse with others, only to arrive at useable truths through consensus which relies on our ability to draw parallels among experiences for students. The social contract may remain potentially useful from experience and in the constant verification of interpretation. Perhaps this is why James evokes the thoughts of Kierkegaard that "we live forwards, . . . but we understand backwards"(171). Given this, intentions of actions derived from experience, and the resulting consequences, are often contradictory. Students should come to take the position that, as James states, "judgement and belief regarding actions to be performed can never attain more than a precarious probability" (6). In concert, Dewey (1929) states, "[And] doing is always subject to peril, to the danger of frustration" (33). The point largely unavoidable concerning what we can or cannot know, and what we may be able to predict, is that action is inevitable. The discernment of truth, its corresponding ethical implications, becomes the stuff of some cultural manifestation, whether we act purposefully or not. The peril is real, but we must act, so we should attempt to locate and move toward "whatever is judged to be honorable, admirable, [and] approvable" (Dewey, 32) through intersubjective interpretation of our circumstances. We next will set the historical ground from which pragmatic civic education may bare fruit followed by a discussion of how such inquiry and action may take shape among multiple actors.

Toward a Theory of History, Inquiry, and Change

Problems of memory and retentiveness of what we are able to discern concerning the causes of our inherited circumstances are relativized by the act of communal interpretation, which will be discussed in terms of mechanics in the next section. According to George Santayana (1954), this communicative diversity exists in the "flux" of our inherited circumstances and individual memories as acted upon by some conscious ideals not realized and more "spontaneous variations" (82) in the greater milieu. The conservative act of retentiveness, the critical recall of those unrequited ethical aspirations, perhaps tied to the more universal application of tenets found within the social contract, becomes, for Santayana, the meaning of historical progress:

> Progress, far from consisting in change, depends on retentiveness. When change is absolute there remains
> no being to improve and no direction is set for possible improvement: and when experience is not retained,

as among savages,[2] infancy is perpetual. . . . [There is] no progress unless some ideal at the beginning is transmitted to the end and reaches a better expression there; without this stability at the core no common standard exists and all comparisons of value with value must be external and arbitrary. (82–83)

The idea of retentiveness does not deny the import of circumstance or memory. It represents a method of examining the inherited aspects of events that placed us in our current circumstance, with ideals and unrequited ethical baggage.

Rather than attempt rootless changes or blind shifts in the social order, Santayana posits that the present mode of life, and all of its various cultural contradictions, holds the experiential data from which we can seek ethical resolution. At first glance, this may seem conservative and unimaginative. However, the "core" of an ideal, as described by Santayana, rather than interpreted as a determined conservatism, assumes the radical ethical expression of our memories and historical situation as containing unrequited aspirations. For Santayana, "civilisation is cumulative. . . . ethical evolution is accordingly infinite. . . . [and its] character is more determinated at every step" (83–84). Put another way, there may be ways in which our present circumstance can be altered through more rationally complex and beneficial forms of social life. But, what implication does this hold for the individual, the group, students and their inquiry into the past and the logical consistency of the present? The atavistic tendency of memory and the process which Santayana terms *reason* must somehow be joined to address two tasks: an attempt at verification, i.e., to ferret out that which isn't false within our idealized intentions, and to formulate actions that, *mutatis mutandis,* may lead to higher degrees of ethical satisfaction.

On the subject of the former, verification, Santayana's philosophy helps to illuminate one of the many pragmatic approaches to the problems surrounding memory and its relation to our conceptions of what constitutes history. But like most pragmatic conceptions of verification, it problematizes the use of memory as a point of departure for progressive ethical action. Concerning interpretation of historical events, he states:

History is nothing but assisted and recorded memory. . . . [And] in order to sift evidence we must rely on some witness, and we must trust experience before we proceed to expand it. . . . [and] the picture we frame of the past changes continually and grows every day less similar to the experience which it purports to describe. (394)

From this ambiguity, we see how precarious a consummate historical view becomes when all we may possess is interpretation and its contingent referent experience. Therefore, if any veracity is to be extracted from an interpretation, it must be connected to other aspects. The interpretation is relative to being "corroborated by another memory" (395). This is what constitutes evidence— its connection to other memories that support the former in consensus rather than question it through contradiction. For Santayana, the facts are "reached by inference, and their reality may be wisely assumed so long as the principle by which they are inferred, when it is applied in the present, finds complete and constant verification" (399). The extent to which facts possess validity is the extent to which they agree with their circumstance.

However, as circumstances change, and by the very application of rational analysis, so to0 does the ability to find evidential corroborations change. Eternal constancy in interpretation is impossible, for as Santayana states,

> Each time the tale is retold it suffers a variation which is not challenged, since it is memory itself that has varied. The change is discoverable only if some record of the narrative in its former guise, or some physical memorial of the event related, survives to be confronted with the modified version. (396)

We reach a topical but ephemeral formalization of fact when we, with other knowing subjects, negotiate a consensus concerning our respective memories. The connections and correlations we are able to draw concerning the former, through powers of discourse and reason, become the projection of further inquiry. This, if pursuing a pragmatic historiography, represents discursive activity as the bulk of classroom deliberations—the dialogical process of communicating and interpreting the form and function of subjective facts and then making decisions regarding action.

The truth in the classroom, at its most bare, becomes what is decided upon as the best of our interpretations, and how these correspond to our vague idyllic vision of possible futures, as it is necessarily reflected in our empirical references. This is largely the role of reason in constituting what might be termed knowledge rather than just raw information or emotion. This reasonable attempt at classification may also be the point at which memory departs into something we call "history." In support of this notion, Santayana states that "history, which is derived from memory, is superior to it for while it merely extends memory artificially it shows a higher logical development than memory has and is riper for ideal uses" (407). However, rather than depict a social end in itself,

> history proves to be an imperfect field for the exercise of reason; it is a provisional discipline; its value, with the mind's progress, would empty into higher activities. The function of history is to lend materials to politics and to poetry. (406)

History then becomes a synthesis of purposeful memory and ethical import to present concerns—political so far as they are useful and beneficial. So the unfulfilled embedded ideals of the past, like aspirational intentions of a social contract, provide the seed-ground for present ethical deliberation, or as Santayana suggests, "the historian, in estimating what has been hitherto achieved, needs to make himself the spokesman for all past aspirations" (406). Yet these ideals become problematized by their historical location in past context, and thus for Santayana, "history is always written wrong, and so always needs to be rewritten" to be reconciled to the contingency of present epistemological modes and social conditions (397).

What is comforting, however, is the belief that on the sliding scale of facts and falsehoods, we may, in pedagogical spaces with exercise of reason and constant self-reflection and reinterpretation of our experiences, deem which social courses are potentially more beneficial than others. There remains, imperfect as the process may be, a critical importance for our students to develop a critical consciousness for civic investigation that places them in the map of our present. It is similarly paramount that there be an impetus toward reparative action, i.e., ethical social problem solving, concerning issues of democracy and lingering historically rooted contradictions regarding the intentions of social contracts. Upon reflecting about Santayana and the importance of purposeful remembrance in the pursuit of beneficial social use-value, I am reminded of a passage in Carl Sandburg's (1992) poem "I am the People, the Mob." He states:

When I, the People, learn to remember, when I, the People, use the lessons of yesterday and no longer forget who robbed me last year, who played me for a fool—then there will be no speaker in all the world say the name: "The People," with any fleck of a sneer in his voice or any far-off smile of derision. The mob—the crowd—the mass—will arrive then. (172)

Starting Social Inquiry as a Process

Where shall we begin, and how shall we frame our inquiries regarding civic education? Dewey (1938) gives us a potential structure in *Logic: The Theory of Inquiry* with what he terms "the determination of a problem-solution" (108). Pursuant, and via our perennial example of the social use-value of any given social contract, we must first establish if the construct to be examined is determinate, that it has form and concepts that can be observed—it is "located *somewhere*" (109), as Dewey would have it. The observable constituents in the case are the document itself and the various institutions and initiatives they reflect and are supported by. This would lead us to examine governmental structures and social arrangements that arise out of their influence.

One social use-value question we may ask, one problem that might have a solution, is are the protections given in a social contract successful in promoting a social environment that is beneficial to its constituents, e.g., in defending them against intrusions into the free expression of their social lives or economic endeavors? This notion, for Dewey, begins as, "an idea" and "a possibility" (109). It gives shape to what Dewey proffers as the definition of inquiry, namely, "the controlled or directed transformation of an indeterminate situation into one that it is so determinate in its constituent distinctions and relations as to convert the original situation into a unified whole" (104–105). All is done in the name of what Dewey calls "warranted assertability" (7), which entails the establishment of "progressively stable beliefs" (10) within a system of inquiry that is self-critical, where "inquiry is a continuing process in every field. . . . [and] the 'settlement' of a particular situation by a particular inquiry is no guarantee that *that* settled conclusion will always remain settled" (8). In our example, new and perhaps better forms of social inquiry will affect our conclusions, as will shifts in the social landscape. We have now established the staging ground for our rational ordering and subsequent judgment. For Dewey, this starts as "subject-matter" (119), or the matter the process of inquiry is directed toward, and ends, such as whether it can exist in a context that is "progressive and temporal" (118), as "content . . . on account of its *representative* character, content of propositions" (119). Here the method and the content find praxiological synthesis and can become the fodder for judgment and action. What follows looks at a method of interpretation for students (plural) once this problem has been set and enters the individual student's senses as an object of perception. We will now turn to Josiah Royce's conception of interpretation.

Perceiving, Conceiving, and Interpreting about Social Use-Value with and for Others

This brings us to an advocation of interpretation, and an examination of the dynamics of consensual action. Josiah Royce (Fisch 1951) views the terms *perception* and *conception*, mentioned previously, not as mutually opposed parts of out cognition, but synthetic in their process (214). What is ignored by having perception and conception as separate ends of analysis is the communicative act by which this dialectical synthesis is rendered as public discourse. Perception and conception are largely individual-specific noetic devices. Societal relevance demands a projection of these insights into the common social space and, in our case, a pedagogical space. Thus, the presence of another knowing subject makes all communication an *interpretative* act, for its intention is to reach some sort of commonness of understanding among knowing subjects though intersubjective discursive inquiry. Interpretation is therefore a public affair.

However, this consensus is not to be thought of as absolute; for as Royce asserts, "our neighbor's perceptions, in their immediate presence, we can never quite certainly share" (215). Instead, we aim for the probability of mutual interpretation with regard to meaning about a given object (action, person not present, physical entity, emotion, text, artifact, etc.), as a knowing subject, with another subject to whom the interpretation is addressed, and upon whose consensus we rely as the verification of our own interpretation. The historical interpretative task depends on a consensus of the present actors. For the purpose of this discussion, the specific instances to be discursified and potentially agreed upon, are the records of the past and our own memories. Royce states,

> For what we all mean by past time is a realm of events whose historical sense, whose records, whose lessons, we may now interpret, in so far as our memory and the documents furnish us the evidences for such interpretation. We may also observe that what we mean by future time is a realm of events which we view as more or less under the control of the present will of voluntary agents, so that it is worth while to give to ourselves, or to our fellows, counsel regarding this future. And so, wherever the world's processes are recorded, wherever the record are preserved, and wherever they influence in any way the future course of events, we may say that . . . the present potentially interprets the past to the future, and continues to do so *ad infinitum*. (219)

To tersely paraphrase the preceding statement, we work with what we have in evidence and memory in social relation with those around us in an "infinite series of mutual interpretation" (221). This creates what Royce calls a "community of interpretation" (222), with the preeminent right of the individual being the "will to interpret" (223).

Royce's interpretative method, however, does not eliminate the temporal aporia of only being able to examine the physical remnants (textual and physical) and memories of the past, and of not knowing how our actions affect the present, and thus, the future. In all fairness, he does not try to do so. Royce allows for a democratization of interpretation, which could be argued as a universally ethical intention. But it still points to a vague future bound in hope, and "a common ideal future event at which we aim" (224), as the somewhat hazy vision of a more just life. The communal interpretative act is thus not as rooted in verification as we may wish; and the ambiguity, which may be insurmountable, still weighs heavy on our ability to act toward a more ethical future. However, the prerogative to interpret in itself apportions a larger demonstration of democratic participation and possible communal action, which certainly opens the field for a wider range of possible futures with more profound levels of individuals expressing themselves within a group context.

Royce's method allows us to look at a problem (to perceive the evidential artifacts of reseg-regation of schools, for instance) and introduce it to students so they must see it—palpable in terms of statistical data, but also of experience, either provided via narrative texts or owned by the students. Students can then begin to order the experience and form a conception of its whole, its historical shape and context. From individual conception we create the active communicative content for dialogue about why schools are more segregated now than thirty years ago (Orfield, 2001). Using the intentions of a social contract as a benchmark, students also might delve into the complicated history of how race was variously defined at different times and in different places, how these constructs have led to persistent inequity and discrimination in housing, and how these inequities in housing have led to segregation that, in turn, causes inequity in educational quality (Galtster 1991, Feagin 1999). The obvious desired outcome would be to then determine what educational and social actions would have to be implemented to remedy this inherited problem. In the classroom, one might imagine students engaged in a conversation about the complex historical origins of social contracts and how different voices have given it different meanings and scopes over time. This renders interpretations concerning the aforementioned problematic, but knowable. It means we can understand the basic premises operated upon by those with power to do so in the past, however faulty or unethical their reasons may have been, that led to Jim Crow laws and their impact on how whites and people of color were educated (or not). The application of pragmatic strains of inquiry, even differently comprehended within a group of students may still end with a general consensus about the effect of past decisions. It is hoped that when an idea like the social contract is applied universally and without the prejudice of manifest difference imposed by bigotry we might make strides toward the negation of its past application. This movement toward action will be touched upon in the next, and final section, of this essay.

Conclusion: Dewey, Experience, and Action

The societal connection of experience to interpretation and action involves inquiries into narratives, that is, to actual written texts or to objects that necessarily elicit interpretations. From these examinations we draw inferences, then connections, and finally cultural judgments. The penultimate expression of a pragmatic civic education emerges when we begin to ask questions of how these texts relate to lived experiences, and to what degree these experiences reflect an ethical or unethical existence. The final expression of pragmatic inquiry concerns the transition from interpretation to ethical action in the present activities of the individuals still implicated in the content and inferences of the texts, artifacts, and cultural formations. To discern something as imperative, as a fact, requires experience, reason, and the communal verification of interpretation. From this we may say that we have knowledge about something in our past or present. This knowledge is subject to constant verification and modification within the very context of its ability to be experienced; it "is not something separate and self-sufficing," as Dewey (1940) posits, "but is involved in the process by which life is sustained and evolved" (87). It is a lived knowledge that flows with us, is modified by us, and, in turn, alters our perspectives and thus necessitates a system of dialectical change in its interpretation and lived experience.

So out of this philosophical abstractness, what would a lived experience look like in the potentially contrived and artificial laboratory of the K-12 classroom? This is a question that I feel cannot be adequately addressed in enough detail in this essay so as to depict a complete encounter in terms of curriculum and performance. However, in the context of our discussion of social contracts, perhaps we may explore some examples. As asked previously, what should we expect a social contract to do, taking into account its historical origins, and how might this be applied according to democratic principles in the present? Additionally, does the aforementioned context in which the social contract was written resemble at all present conditions in terms of technology or cultural values? As an example, the current debate about health care exists in terms of both ideological and practical considerations. Ideologically, we must ask questions about the intent of the social contract when written and how this applies to our various conceptions concerning democracy and rights. For instance, what is the function of democracy that is more beneficial than other social arrangements, and how do we determine what is a right and what is a want? Does a social contract that gives as one of its charges, as the United States Constitution does, "to promote the general welfare" extend to universal health coverage over two hundred years after the writing of the document? Does the existence of technology that could give everyone within the jurisdiction of the social contract health care fall under the purview of the general welfare, within our present sociohistorical context? Also, does this term apply to needs or wants, e.g., a perceived need such as health care or a want such as a more general access to luxury goods? Or, is there such a degree of disconnect between current conditions and the intention of the social contract to render it irreparably incongruous? If the latter is the case, would we require a new contract or additions that would incorporate facets of a newfound need or desire? In terms of our possible actions in regard to these questions, the decision leads to a new set of benefits, complications, and problems—and, indeed, a new set of questions. The pedagogical task is to mediate these inquiries and dialogues, to separate out what is verifiable and what is false, to iron out logical and ethical inconsistencies in philosophy, and to plot courses of action as if the students had the power to implement them.

Dewey offers the following conviction concerning the pursuit of past events and our experience as they may be used to provide examples toward future conditions:

> We do not merely have to repeat the past, or wait for accidents to force change upon us. We *use* our past experiences to construct new and better ones in the future. The very fact of experience thus includes the process by which it directs itself in its own betterment. (95)

The *sine qua non* of this notion of possible societal betterment lies in, and is itself much of the substance of, our inquiry's intention: the constant and dialectically reflexive pursuit of the ethical through democratic discursive activity. The pedagogical task is to engage in the process of inquiry as a democratic process, one that has us encounter truths, within a shifting social landscape, toward democratic ends, i.e., ends that afford a better social experience. While we cannot know the result of communicative acts in the classroom or in the larger society as finalities, our "prior experience supplies the conditions which evoke ideas and which thought has to take account" (Dewey 1929, 167). It is these experiences either lived or introduced through education that furnish the stuff of consciousness, dialogue, and action—the method of thoughtful rational discussion of constantly transforming ideas and ideals as they shift in import to students' experiences, needs, and desires.

For students, recognizing the transitory nature of ideals as matters "experimental [and] not abstractly rational" (167) is paramount to avoiding lapses into deterministic adherences. Dewey (1938) states,

> *The idea that any knowledge in particular can be instituted* apart from its being the consummation of inquiry, and that knowledge in general can be defined apart from this connection is, moreover, one of the sources of confusion in logical theory. For the different varieties of realism, idealism and dualism have their diverse conceptions of what "knowledge" really is. In consequence, logical theory is rendered subservient to metaphysical and epistemological preconceptions, so that interpretation of logical forms varies with underlying metaphysical assumptions. (8)

The "consummation of inquiry" here is the critical process by which we avoid having students lean too heavily on a fixed view of history or of cozy myths or ideologies about an idealized past in which events unfolded in ways we might have wanted. In contrast, through a pragmatically guided process of inquiry, ideals generated from experience may guide us in our problem-solving abilities and provide the fodder for more complex and ethical social choices. However, as with the aforementioned myths and ideologies, they should not be seen as permanent solutions or ends-in-advance. For our present actions change the forms of all past ideals. This, for students, creates a new dynamic consciousness or, more simply put, a way of seeing oneself in history as an actor and a new way of looking at our world. It creates a dialectic between the past and its better aspirations concerning the nature of our future as something to be sought in the constant discursive transaction of interpretations. Our experience and cultural memory form the *potential* of creating greater degrees of freedom. However, this is likely to occur only through augmented levels of rational democratic investigation, communication, and participation while avoiding, as alluded to previously (and as Dewey [1940] cautioned), "falling into a paralyzing worship of super-empirical authority or into an offensive 'rationalization' of things as they are" (102). The pedagogical task is to foster the idea that knowledge and intelligence are engendered by continuing to engage in the process of knowing about our social conditions. Civic progress, then, relies on communicating and acting upon our best practical and ethical intentions toward a new and better set of circumstances—one that in turn will need investigating, *ad infinitum*.

Notes

1. The reader is asked to infer a lack of intentional gender bias in my use of these older texts.
2. This is an unfortunate phrase, but given the context it may be interpreted to signify human activity before individuals had yet to live together in organized association with organized structures of knowledge and language.

Bibliography

Dewey, John. 1929. *The Quest for Certainty.* New York: G.P. Putnam.
Dewey, John. 1938. *Logic: The Theory of Inquiry.* New York: Henry Holt and Co.

Dewey, John. 1940. *Reconstructions in Philosophy*. Boston: Beacon Press.

Feagin, Joe R. 1999. "Excluding Blacks and Others From Housing: The Foundation of White Racism." *Cityscape: A Journal of Policy Development and Research* 4 (3), 79–91.

Fisch, Max H. (Ed.) 1951. *Classic American Philosophers*. New York: Appleton-Century-Crofts.

Galster, George C. 1991. Housing Discrimination and Urban Poverty of African-Americans. *Journal of Housing Research* 2 (2), 87–119.

James, William. 1995. *Pragmatism*. New York: Dover Publications.

James, William. 1951. *Essays in Pragmatism*, New York: Hafner Publishing Company.

Orfield, Gary. 2001. Schools more Separate: Consequences of a Decade of Resegreation. Cambridge, MA: The Civil Rights Project, Harvard University: http://www.civilrightsproject.harvard.edu/research/deseg/Schools_More_Separate.pdf (accessed May 4, 2005).

Sandburg, Carl. 1992. *Chicago Poems*. Chicago: University of Illinois Press, 1992.

Santayana, George. 1954. *Life of Reason*. New York: Scribners.

CHAPTER TWENTY-ONE

Political Liberalism and Civic Education

BARRY L. BULL

The intention of this chapter is to offer a conception of the purposes and to a lesser extent the content and instructional approach of civic education when it is understood from an important perspective that has roots in a long tradition of political philosophy, one that has historically and systematically influenced the structure and operation of government in the United States and around the world, the tradition that political philosophers call political liberalism. Although I will explain in some detail what this tradition involves, it is important at the outset to distinguish this philosophy from the ordinary meaning of liberalism as it is currently used in American politics. Liberalism as a political philosophy takes the establishment and protection of citizens' *liberty* to be the central purpose of government, and not, for example, economic development, the advancement of civilization, or even democratic decision making. As a result, many of those who label themselves in common parlance as liberal and conservative in the United States and elsewhere can be seen to be operating in the tradition of liberalism as it is understood by political theorists.

This chapter first unpacks the meaning of political liberalism, especially as it is represented in the work of John Rawls. Second, the chapter considers the implications of this philosophy for the purpose of civic education. Finally, the chapter discusses the possible content and instructional procedures relevant to achieving that purpose.

The Nature of Political Liberalism

John Rawls was probably the world's most influential political philosopher during the last half of the 20th century. In 1971, he published *A Theory of Justice* (see Rawls, 1971, for the original and Rawls, 1999a, for the revised edition), in which he attempted to revitalize the tradition of social contract theory that was first articulated by Thomas Hobbes and John Locke in the 17th century, the latter of whom influenced the American founders, especially Thomas Jefferson, in the 18th. The basic idea of this tradition was that the only legitimate form of government was one to which all citizens had good reason to consent, and Locke argued that the social contract would necessarily provide protections for basic personal and political liberties of citizens. In the Declaration of Independence, Jefferson charged that the English King George III had violated these liberties of the American colonists, and therefore the colonies were justified in revolting against English rule. Moreover, the Bill of Rights of the Constitution of the United States can be understood as protecting certain basic liberties—freedom of religion and expression, for example—on the grounds that they are elements of the social contract that place legitimate constraints on the power of any justifiable government.

During the late 18th and 19th centuries, however, the social contract approach became the object of serious philosophical criticism, especially because the existence of an original agreement among all citizens was historically implausible and because such an agreement failed to acknowledge the fundamentally social, rather than individual, nature of human decision making, especially about political affairs. In light of this criticism, British philosophers, in particular Jeremy Bentham and John Stuart Mill, suggested that the legitimate justification of government lay not with whether citizens actually consented to it but with whether it and its policies were designed to maximize the happiness of its citizens and actually had that effect. This approach to political theory was called utilitarianism, and it came to dominate Anglo-American political philosophy in the late 19th and early 20th centuries, providing the moral foundation of, for example, economic criteria for choosing and judging government action on the grounds that expanding economic productivity is a means to maximizing happiness.

Despite the efforts of John Stuart Mill to argue that utilitarianism is compatible with a wide range of individual liberties because individuals are often the best judges of what makes them happy and thus that government policies should enable them to exercise their own judgments about the particular personal and social arrangements that are appropriate, Anglo-American philosophers became troubled about the potential of this doctrine to override and sometimes to neglect individual liberties altogether in the interests of increasing total happiness, especially given the early 20th-century experience with a variety of totalitarian regimes. Beginning in the mid-20th century, John Rawls attempted to construct a version of political theory that placed a priority on individual personhood as opposed to collective happiness, a doctrine that he labeled Justice as Fairness. This doctrine drew upon the social contract tradition, but it represented the social contract as a hypothetical agreement developed in a fair decision-making situation into which citizens could enter in their imaginations at any time to determine the principles that would regulate their political relationships rather than an actual historical agreement.

Although the details of Rawls's social contract argument are beyond the scope of this chapter, he argued that the parties to the agreement would select principles of justice that would guarantee basic personal and political liberties, equal opportunities to compete for the society's various positions on the basis of citizens' qualifications for those positions, and a distribution of the society's material resources that would maximize the income of the society's least advantaged citizens (Rawls, 1971). Only once these principles are satisfied could a society consider the efficiency of its social relationships, as would be required under utilitarianism, and, even then, it did not have a moral obligation based on social justice to choose the most efficient arrangements.

Now, Rawls's specific theory of justice is important (and controversial) in itself, but it will not be the focus of this chapter. Instead, I will focus on Rawls's later characterization of the kind of society that could adopt either his specific theory or one of several alternative theories, all of which he came to label politically liberal societies. These societies' citizens develop an agreement on political principles that does not require them to agree in their comprehensive conceptions of the good, which involve their commitments about the most worthwhile and fulfilling lives for themselves, including perhaps beliefs about the religious or metaphysical nature of the universe and humans' place in it. Thus, politically liberal societies develop an agreement about justice that citizens who hold many different reasonable conceptions of the good can accept. According to Rawls, such reasonable citizens have a desire to cooperate fairly for mutual advantage when others do so. They also recognize the burdens and limitations of judgment, which imply that reason alone cannot definitively determine the ultimate truth or falsity of all matters that may enter into one's conception of the good so that, although they are committed to their own conceptions of the good, they can recognize many others' conceptions as reasonable. Thus, according to Rawls, citizens potentially can agree on basic principles of justice for regulating relationships among themselves that will enable them and others with such reasonable conceptions, despite their differences in belief, to embrace and pursue their aspirations to live a life guided by their own specific conceptions of the good.

On Rawls's view, such an agreement is both political and liberal. It is political in that it is a pragmatic agreement for cooperation among those with varying comprehensive views of what ultimately makes life worth living, views that lead the parties to the agreement to hold different final ends and thus different fundamental justifications for the agreement. Thus, one party might justify the agreement as being consistent with the fulfillment of her religious duties, and another as being consistent with the wholly secular obligations to others implied by her conception of the good, for example. Thus, these justifications are based on very different ultimate personal commitments, but the agreement does not require all to accept the same ultimate commitments. In this way, the agreement is also liberal in that it is consistent with many different specific configurations of belief. It thus leaves to citizens, acting either individually or in groups of the likeminded, the final determination of their own conceptions of the good. It therefore is predicated on a wide freedom of conscience about the particular conceptions of the good that citizens find worthy.

For this reason, Rawls characterizes the agreement about the principles of justice in a politically liberal society as in the end an overlapping consensus among reasonable citizens with different comprehensive conceptions of the good. That is, one citizen's conception of the good allows him to accept political principles of justice that are justified on different grounds by the conceptions of the good held by other citizens in the society. In this way, citizens' conceptions of the good, even though they are different, can be understood as overlapping one another sufficiently to generate a society-wide agreement about political justice. Thus, citizens in such a society reach a moral agreement about the appropriate political arrangements of their society, even though they disagree about the non-political moral goals they pursue in their individual lives or their private associations. However, Rawls came to recognize that the principles he argued for in *A Theory of Justice* were not the only ones that could provide for an overlapping consensus. To be sure, liberty of conscience, basic political liberties, and equal recognition of the personhood of all seem to be necessary for such a consensus, but the precise principles and priorities laid out in his earlier work do not seem to be the only possible way to achieve those political necessities. Rawls continued to argue that the conception of justice provided in *A Theory of Justice* was the most egalitarian of the politically liberal schemes, but it was not the only one. Thus, political liberalism can be understood as embracing a family of related but not identical conceptions of justice.

Of course, not all conceptions of the good are compatible with an overlapping consensus about justice. Some conceptions, for example, might deny freedom of conscience to apostates or might fail to recognize the equal personhood of some members of society—women or the members of particular racial or ethnic groups, for example. Thus, those who hold such conceptions of the good could not fully and in good conscience enter into an agreement about justice with those who are excluded from or victimized by their conceptions. However, Rawls speculates that even those with such conceptions would be willing to abide by a political agreement that falls short of the systematic enforcement of their preferred ends if such an agreement turns out to be the most effective way to advance their conceptions in a society of others who conceive the good differently. Rawls labels such an agreement a *modus vivendi* and further speculates that by living under such an agreement citizens can come to modify their conceptions of the good to permit the emergence of a genuinely conscientious overlapping consensus about social justice. In this way, Rawls views politically liberal societies as the culmination of a developmental political process (Rawls, 1993).

To make the emergence of politically liberal societies possible, Rawls acknowledges that he must make certain assumptions about human beings. In particular, he assumes that people have two moral powers—namely, the capacities for a conception of the good and a sense of justice. The capacity for a conception of the good implies that people have the ability to establish ends for their lives and to arrange their activities to achieve those ends. The capacity for a sense of justice implies that people have the ability to establish and follow moral rules for their political relationships with others that they themselves accept as regulative of their activities, particularly when others agree to and follow the same rules. It is important to recognize that these two powers do not automatically guarantee the emergence of a politically liberal regime. For, first, it is possible for one's conception of the good to be determined by the collective or despotic authority of others—families, churches, or governments, for example—rather than by the exercise of the conscience and judgment of each citizen. Second, the specific content of one's sense of justice can also be determined by sources entirely external to the individual. Thus, these two powers are just as compatible with authoritarian regimes as they are with politically liberal regimes. Moreover, these two powers are not necessarily consistent with each other in that it is possible for one's personal ends to conflict with the rules dictated by one's sense of justice. Despite these possibilities, these two moral powers do make the emergence of a politically liberal regime feasible when individual conscience is free to determine the content of both the good and the just. In this way, political liberalism can be understood as a form of reflective equilibrium, to use Rawls's term, between citizens' self-determined conceptions of the good and their sense of justice. Of course, others can and undoubtedly do have an important role in citizens' thinking about the good and the just. For example, others can provide a range of alternative possibilities for one's conception of the good. And others' self-defined interests and their circumstances form an important context for judging the rules of justice that would secure their cooperation. However, what political liberalism forbids is that these social contributors to citizens' thinking about these matters are the final arbiters, regardless of individuals' own judgments about them. Thus, the specific formulation of one's conception of the good and one's sense of justice is simultaneously a social and individual enterprise in a politically liberal society.

Implications for and Purposes of Civic Education

Although Rawls has written very little about it, this characterization of political liberalism suggests a number of different purposes for the civic education that such a regime might undertake, if any. For example, civic education might seek to shape citizens' conceptions of the good or their sense of justice. In the former case, a society might determine the range of available conceptions of the good that are compatible with the current overlapping consensus about justice and then seek to restrict citizens' choices only to the conceptions so determined. In the latter, a society might initially seek to socialize citizens to accept the moral rules of justice included in the prevailing overlapping consensus, which in turn would make it unlikely that citizens would select conceptions of the good that conflict with justice. Or, indeed, it might do both simultaneously. Using these approaches, a society could try to induce the coherence of its citizens' sense of justice with their conceptions of the good, which seems to be important or perhaps necessary for the stability of such a society, especially given the possibility that they might conflict. Moreover, these approaches do not require the government to determine the details of their citizens' conceptions of the good in specific cases; that is, they would permit citizens to exercise their own judgment about their conceptions of the good, at least within a permissible range of alternatives. However, there are serious objections to either of these approaches to civic education, objections based on the nature of political liberalism itself, for the first strategy assumes that the content of various conceptions of the good can be completely known in advance and is static. Moreover, both assume that the content of the overlapping consensus is itself permanent and unchanging.

Whatever the precise configuration of rules about justice that emerges in a specific politically liberal society, considerable freedom of conscience for citizens about their conceptions of the good will figure in the overlapping consensus, as we have already noted. After all, making their own judgments about the good is central to being able to lead lives that citizens deem to be worthwhile, especially given the inevitable diversity of their talents, circumstances, and proclivities and, in light of that diversity, the limitations of human reason to determine a single good for all. Of course, the strategy of developing an approved list of officially authorized conceptions of the good does provide for a degree of freedom for citizens to make judgments among the conceptions included in that authoritative list, but it runs into two related difficulties. First, that list inevitably assumes that citizens' talents and proclivities and their social circumstances in the future will remain the same as they have been in the past so that novel conceptions of the good will not be needed. Second, it assumes that conceptions of the good that are currently inconsistent with the overlapping consensus about justice will forever remain so, which further assumes both that the overlapping consensus is static and that conceptions of the good cannot be modified to be consistent with it. However, the conceptions of the good that were seen as fulfilling by one generation can be experienced as restrictive by the next as new possibilities for the development of talent emerge. And, as Rawls came to realize and as we have already noted, there are many conceptions of justice that are compatible with the basic requirements of political liberalism; in his later work, he refers to political liberalism as being compatible with a "family" of conceptions of justice (Rawls, 1999b, p. 133). Thus there can be different conceptions of justice within a single politically liberal society and different kinds of politically liberal societies, depending upon which ones dominate their citizens' thinking. Moreover, a politically liberal society can come to change its dominant conception of justice over time and with experience. That is, a conception of justice that citizens judge to be adequate at one time can come to seem inadequate at a later time because, for example, it does not take into account the emerging threats to justice or the emerging configurations of talent and circumstance experienced by its citizens. Because fulfilling conceptions of the good and adequate conceptions of justice can change in a politically liberal society, any authoritative list of conceptions of the good will inevitably prove unsatisfactory, especially for the young who are most likely to experience the possibilities for change most fully. Thus, a civic education that attempts to limit young citizens' conceptions of the good to such a list is likely to become unstable in the long run because it is incapable of accommodating itself to the possibilities for change that its citizens experience. Thus, the freedom that a politically liberal society must recognize is not only the freedom to make judgments among the currently available conceptions of the good but also the freedom to modify the available conceptions.

These observations also reveal the inadequacy on politically liberal grounds of a civic education that socializes the society's citizens to a particular prevailing conception of justice, even if that conception is consistent with the requirements of political liberalism. Unlike the previous approach, such an education would not directly constrain citizens' judgments about their conceptions of the good. However, because there are alternative conceptions of justice that are fully compatible with political liberalism, such a civic education would effectively prohibit a society from changing its conception of justice from one politically liberal conception to another. And as we have noted, a politically liberal society's conception of justice can come to seem inadequate to its citizens, not because it violates the fundamental premises of political liberalism, but because it fails to accommodate what citizens come to see as important threats to justice, the full range of alternative conceptions of the good that its citizens find fulfilling, or both. Socialization to a conception of justice effectively denies to citizens, again especially to the young, the freedom to make judgments about justice based on their experience and their assessment of future possibilities for the society and themselves. Here, too, such a civic education can, therefore, be a source of social instability because the prevailing rules of social justice are at odds with citizens' evolving sense of justice. Thus, the freedom that a politically liberal society must recognize includes the freedom to make judgments about the adequacy of the society's conception of justice and subsequently to develop modifications in that conception.

Therefore, even in a fully politically liberal society, where the prevailing agreement about justice represents a genuinely overlapping consensus among its citizens' conceptions of the good rather than a mere *modus vivendi*, the civic education system cannot be predicated on the immutability of the available conceptions of the good or the conception of justice in that society, thereby placing either one beyond the experience and the judgments of the society's citizens. Admittedly, a society that abides by these constraints upon its civic education system does run certain risks of instability, namely, the risks that the citizens' conceptions of the good or of justice might evolve in ways that are inconsistent with political liberalism But it avoids other potential sources of instability that undermine the very liberties that are the foundation of the political order, namely, the freedom to determine one's own conception of the good and to decide with others the society's conception of justice according to the dictates of conscience.

Moreover, these constraints on civic education also apply in societies that are in the process of becoming fully politically liberal, that is, societies in which an overlapping consensus about justice has not yet completely emerged. The second approach to civic education is clearly ruled out for such developing politically liberal societies because, on the one hand, there is no prevailing conception of justice to which to socialize citizens and, on the other hand, because of the multiplicity of such conceptions that are consistent with political liberalism. However, it might seem that the first approach is a promising way to accelerate progress toward an overlapping consensus. The political authorities in such a society could survey the available conceptions of the good, determine which of them is consistent with political liberalism, and then limit the conceptions of the good that young citizens might develop to those included in the resulting authoritative list. This approach might seem to guarantee that future citizens would all have a conception that is compatible with political liberalism, which would in turn make it more likely that an overlapping consensus about justice would emerge. However, this possibility is more apparent than real. For in determining the authoritative list of conceptions, political authorities would need to refer to a specific conception of justice in making their judgments, and by assumption no such conception is available in this society. As a result, either they must abandon this approach because the required conception of justice does not yet exist, or they must predict the agreement about justice that they deem likely to emerge in the society. Because of the many conceptions of justice that are compatible with political liberalism, such a prediction would inevitably reflect the officials' own prejudices and preferences about justice, especially because they cannot know with certainty the novel social circumstances that might arise in the society and citizens' judgments about them. Even if this approach to civic education were to succeed in producing a future overlapping consensus about justice, which itself is doubtful, that consensus would reflect the biases of government officials rather than the free judgment of citizens, no matter how sincere the officials have tried to be in their efforts to construct the list. However, this constrained agreement about justice is not what political liberalism requires.

In the face of the problems with these two most apparent approaches, it might seem that civic education in a politically liberal society is to be avoided, and some critics of liberalism have maintained that it makes civic education impossible or at best extremely limited (e.g., Callan, 1997). Certainly, civic education in such a society cannot include, as has been shown, a demand that citizens restrict their conceptions of the good to a particular list or that they adopt a specific conception of justice. However, at least one other possibility for the purpose of such an education remains. Rather than civic education seeking to impose direct constraints on the outcomes of the political process—that is, citizens' conceptions of the good or justice—it is perhaps more appropriate to understand civic education for this kind of society as aiming to involve its citizens in the political process from which those outcomes, at least in part, emerge, namely, the process of developing and maintaining an overlapping consensus.

Recall that for Rawls an overlapping consensus has two important characteristics. First, it consists of a family of conceptions of justice that can be accepted as justified under the many different reasonable conceptions of the good that are held by the citizens of a politically liberal society; in fact, this multiple justification of justice is what makes the agreement about it overlapping. Thus, on the one hand, the overlapping consensus is not a single set of beliefs about justice but rather a set of specific doctrines about it that are compatible with one another and with the conceptions of the good to which citizens are also committed. Thus, while individual citizens or associations may be committed to a single conception of justice, the overlapping consensus is not limited to a single conception but includes many such conceptions that are reasonably consistent with each other. Moreover, although a single conception of justice may be dominant in a society, that conception is not identical to the overlapping consensus, which embraces a variety of somewhat different but compatible ways of thinking about justice. This characteristic in significant part is what makes a civic education that aims at the socialization of citizens to a particular conception of justice inappropriate for a politically liberal society. Second, the overlapping consensus is recognized by its participants as imposing genuine and important moral constraints on their conceptions of the good. That is, citizens view the overlapping consensus as having a moral status that is partially independent of the commitments they make as a result of their particular conceptions of the good. It is, therefore, not as if the participants in an overlapping consensus believe that it is justified only to the extent that it fully achieves the outcomes implied by their conceptions of the good. Rather, the overlapping consensus is understood to place moral limitations on the content of and the changes that may be entertained in citizens' conceptions of the good that they adopt as individuals and as members of associations.

This complex nature of an overlapping consensus places important limitations on the education that a society should undertake in order to enable its citizens to participate in that consensus. For such a consensus clearly depends on citizens having their own conceptions of the good, that is, of the lives they judge to be worth living and in terms of which they can make judgments about the justifications of the consensus. However, such conceptions do not provide the only criterion for a justification of the overlapping consensus, for they also are committed to a scheme of cooperation that enables them and other citizens to hold and pursue their reasonable conceptions of the good, a commitment that places constraints on the conceptions of the good that they themselves may embrace. As a result, citizens of a politically liberal society both place a high moral value on such social cooperation and recognize a variety of conceptions of the good as reasonably consistent with such cooperation, even though those conceptions are not identical to the ones to which they are committed. Therefore, they also come to embrace a particular conception of justice that is a member of the family of such conceptions that are consistent with their own conceptions of the good and their commitment to social cooperation for mutual advantage among the citizens of a politically liberal regime. In fact, this conception of justice can be understood as specifying the particular moral rules for their own judgments and actions that their commitment to social cooperation implies and the public justifications that they provide for them, given the circumstances that prevail in their society. Thus, the civic education required must, first, enable all citizens to develop and modify their own particular conceptions of the good according to their constitution, conscience, and experience. Second, it must enable citizens to respect the reasonable conceptions of the good embraced by others. Third, it must make it possible for citizens to understand the advantages of social cooperation for themselves and others. Finally, that education must enable citizens to develop and modify conceptions of justice that reflect the moral importance they assign to their own conceptions of the good, the respect they have for others, and the social cooperation they value. The overarching purpose of civic education in a politically liberal society is to enable citizens to participate in an evolving overlapping consensus. In effect, these four characteristics provide criteria for whether the civic education undertaken by a society is genuinely compatible with the emergence and maintenance of an overlapping consensus:

1. Civic education is consistent with citizens developing their own commitments to a wide variety of reasonable conceptions of the good.
2. Civic education enables citizens to respect others' reasonable conceptions of the good.
3. Civic education enables citizens to recognize the value of social cooperation for the achievement of their own and others' reasonable conceptions of the good.
4. Civic education enables citizens to develop conceptions of justice coherent with their own conceptions of the good, their respect for others, and their commitment to social cooperation.

Content and Procedures of Civic Education for Children

It should be clear that civic education in a politically liberal society is a lifelong undertaking, one that continuously influences the attitudes, judgments, and actions of both adults and children. For the full range of institutions and practices of the society are critical in maintaining the environment that shapes these characteristics of citizens. However, in contemporary society, it is conventional to distinguish educational practices for the young from those for adults. Moreover, the civic education of children poses especially important issues for political liberalism in that such an education can undermine the liberal character of such a society by, on the one hand, excessively centralizing control over the education of children and, on the other hand, excessively delegating the education of children to parents and other local adults, both of which can socialize children in a way that prevents the adults that children become from being sufficiently their own persons. In light of these problems, I will focus in this section on the content and procedures of civic education of children only, recognizing that this characterization provides an inevitably incomplete account of civic education.

In previous work, I have rather artificially divided the education of children for civic purposes into two distinct categories—education for personal liberty and education for democracy (Bull, 2008). Education for personal liberty enables children to make judgments about their own developing conceptions of the good by exposing them to the conceptions available in their own communities and beyond in such a way that those conceptions become genuine possibilities for their lives and so that they make critical judgments about and among them taking into account their own talents and proclivities. This aspect of education not only enables children to develop conceptions that they find personally worthy but also to respect other conceptions because they appreciate them as meaningful possibilities for themselves. Thus, education for personal liberty meets the first two criteria for civic education—developing self-defined conceptions of the good and respect for others' conceptions. In this section I will emphasize, however, education for democracy, because that education more intuitively represents what is recognized as the social functions of civic education that respond specifically to the last two criteria—recognizing the value of social cooperation and developing conceptions of justice.

The public education system of a politically liberal society can be understood as, in part, a set of government institutions and practices that enable and promote the continual emergence of a reflective overlapping consensus. From this perspective, civic education in public schools is the element of the public education system that undertakes and accomplishes this task for the young. This education is not adequately conceived as simply a vehicle for informing the young about adults' current civic beliefs, for such information is at most only one element of what children need to learn to participate in the development of an overlapping consensus. Nor is such civic education adequately conceived as the enforcement on the young of an authoritative and determinate civic doctrine, for no such doctrine is characteristic of an overlapping consensus because its principles are subject to constant reconsideration and modification. Finally, an adequate civic education is certainly not instruction in a particular comprehensive system of belief, even one with specific civic content or purposes, for such instruction confuses public with private morality.

Against this background, the curriculum of civic education aims, first, to enable children to learn about the current state of the overlapping consensus—the civic principles of their society and how they derive from widely held intuitions about the relationships and obligations among citizens. Second, such a curriculum must enable children to learn about the meaning and consequences of those principles—how they have been interpreted in the society, the institutions and social practices in which they are instantiated, and the outcomes of those policies and practices, both intended and otherwise. Third, the curriculum must enable children to reflect on the relationship between, on the one hand, those principles and their consequences, and, on the other, the overlapping consensus and their developing conceptions of the good. If the curriculum succeeds in achieving these aims of helping children to understand the origin, meaning, public consequences, and personal implications of the society's civic principles, children should emerge from the public school system with the ability to take part as adult citizens in the evolution of the overlapping consensus by means of a process of reflective equilibrium between their conceptions of the good and of justice. However, not only must citizens have this ability, but they also must be inclined to make use of it. Finally, an adequate civic education curriculum must, in addition, enable children to see and to appreciate the public purpose and personal meaning of what after all is an intellectually and morally demanding undertaking.

Undoubtedly, many particular configurations of curricular content can enable public schools to achieve these aims of civic education, and the content appropriate to them may vary from one locality to the other, depending on the diverse initial socialization and circumstances of children and the varying histories of the wider societies in which they grow up. In other words, one cannot deduce a specific account of the content or structure of the curriculum from these general aims; they provide only general criteria for constructing and evaluating particular proposals for the curriculum. Moreover, much of the school curriculum that has not traditionally been understood as part of civic education may make an indirect contribution to accomplishing these aims. Language instruction and logical training, for example, provide children with skills that facilitate the requisite learning. In light of these observations, therefore, I analyze only some general aspects of the school curriculum that are relevant to the specifically civic content appropriate to achieving these aims.

As I have suggested previously, an education for personal liberty involves teaching children to understand and to appreciate at least some of the many cultures in their nation that, on the one hand, enable children to consider for themselves conceptions of the good as alternatives to those available in their families and neighborhood communities. Therefore, it expands their freedom to become their own persons rather than persons determined entirely by their immediate social environment. On the other hand, such teaching simultaneously strengthens the entire system of personal liberty by helping children to appreciate others' cultures as real possibilities for their own lives, not just as alien curiosities to be benevolently or perhaps grudgingly tolerated. In addition, teaching about a nation's cultures also makes an important contribution to civic education for an overlapping consensus but for reasons at odds with those often cited in the civic education literature, namely, to facilitate democratic deliberation by helping children understand, anticipate, and negotiate the disagreements that they are likely to encounter in democratic societies (Gutmann & Thompson, 1996). After all, teaching about other cultures in their society can also enable children to understand the commonalities as well as the divergences in belief among the members of those cultures. In this way, such teaching can provide children with an understanding of elements of citizens' beliefs that contribute to the current overlapping consensus about political principles and of the various private moral commitments from which it derives. Thus, the content of an adequate civic education emphasizes whatever commonality of belief that may exist or be possible across cultural differences in addition to the differences themselves.

Combined with instruction that emphasizes our diversity to foster and strengthen personal liberty, the content of the school curriculum, therefore, provides a robust conception of multiculturalism in the society, a conception that expresses both what may unify a nation's citizens and what may divide them. On this view, in teaching children about religion, for example, public schools should not simply endorse an abstract political principle of toleration of others' beliefs while leaving the beliefs to be tolerated unexplored and unexamined. Instead, they should sympathetically and honestly investigate the substantive doctrines of various accessible religions and nonreligious philosophies, including the ways the commitments to toleration and various other public values are understood and justified within them. In an important sense, such cultural learning makes accessible to children knowledge of the habits of thought and the social practices on which a society's overlapping consensus is built and an appreciation of the potential for constructive change implicit in that reality. This robust multicultural education is an element of civic education that provides the foundation for children's recognizing the value of social cooperation for the pursuit of their own developing conceptions of the good and those of others whom they have grown to respect.

Next, the content of history also has a special relevance to civic education for an overlapping consensus. For learning about history presents the opportunity to consider at a remove in time and place the relationships between nations' cultures, their civic ideals, the policies adopted to achieve those ideals, and those policies' results. Especially when the nations or communities under study are politically liberal societies, the study of history can also reveal the tensions among those four factors and the way the societies have adapted their ideals, policies, and practices in light of those tensions. And when the nation or community under study is one's own, history reveals to children the changing nature of the overlapping consensus and the reasons in the national or community experience for the changes that have taken place in its civic aspirations and ideals. These lessons are crucial for children's gaining an accurate understanding of the nature of an overlapping consensus and for providing them with an appropriate perspective on the tentative justifiability of one's own nation's or community's current political principles and policies. Without such a perspective, children might come to regard their nation's or community's commitments to be either absolute or entirely culturally relative. Either of these assumptions actively discourages children from taking the reformulation of a nation's overlapping consensus seriously, for on the first there is seemingly no need to do so, and on the second there is no point in expending one's energy on a matter that is immune from conscious influence. However, the historical education that has just been described is an important corrective to such assumptions. For, first, it is obvious that learning about the changes that have taken place in a nation's or a community's civic ideals and their policy interpretations contradicts the assumption that they are immutable or infallible. But also learning that those changes can be seen as rational, if sometimes mistaken, responses to experience also corrects the assumption that those ideals and policies are nothing but an expression of the majority's untutored cultural preferences.

As one possible example, the history curriculum in schools might consider the social, economic, and religious controversies involved in the debate over slavery before and during the U.S. Civil War and the evolving policy proposals and public policies to which they led. Such a study of the evolving overlapping consensus during this time, the changing public policies in which it was instantiated, the social and economic consequences of those policies, and the various private and public reactions to those consequences can illustrate to children both the tentative nature of civic ideals and the patterns of reasoning employed by citizens at the time to reconcile their private moralities, aspirations, and experiences with those of their fellow citizens.

Admittedly, this curriculum involves a particularly intellectualized view of history, for it entails the perspective that human reason and understanding play a significant role in shaping the national ideals and the events that flow from them. For that reason, it will not be easy for children to master. Nonetheless, it reveals just how profoundly cerebral the task of civic education for an overlapping consensus is. In this way, this perspective on the study of history provides the foundations for children's developing sense of justice, for it enables them to recognize how social ideals evolve from the perceptions, values, and experience of a nation's citizens and particularly those of their own country.

This quality of the curriculum is equally on display in another crucial and related aspect of its content. Now, an overlapping consensus is the reasonable confluence of popular belief about abstract principles of government and the obligations of citizenship, not merely shared opinions or intuitions about what should be done in particular circumstances. For children to view the rights and duties of citizens as resulting from such principles, the civic education curriculum must also include a philosophical element, in its widest sense. The purpose of this element is to enable children to view their own and others' actions as instances of the application of, to use Immanuel Kant's phrase, maxims of action (Kant 1785/1985). Understanding people's actions as following such general rules implicates and develops children's capacity to abstract from particular actions and to see patterns in them. It may also be one of humans' fundamental logical and moral capacities. Be that as it may, in developing this capacity, one must avoid enforcing Kant's metaphysical doctrines about such maxims—such as, that the only genuinely moral maxims are universal and unconditional—because public education is not to indoctrinate children to accept controversial metaphysical positions. Nevertheless, it is possible to teach children this way of viewing human actions without any particular metaphysical accompaniment. In doing so, one enables children to analyze the actions of governments and their citizens as flowing from general principles, which they can then formulate, reflect on, and perhaps criticize, reinterpret, or reformulate on the basis of their and others' experience and their own developing conceptions of the good. Indeed, these philosophical abilities can be developed in part in the context of the cultural and history curriculum, as it has been conceived earlier. Children can be invited and encouraged to conceptualize, for example, the principles of government and their rationales that may have emerged from the commitments and circumstances of various social groups during the Civil War era. They can be asked and assisted to understand how these principles changed during the debates over slavery and in response to the events and experiences that they precipitated.

On such a model, children can be enabled to understand current policies and policy outcomes as deriving from both the current overlapping consensus and the tensions that it and its policy consequences create among groups with various cultural orientations and aspirations. For example, they can be invited to consider the phenomena of globalization not only as sources of economic threat and opportunity but also as forces of cultural exchange and challenge that have ramifications for a nation's self-understanding and individuals' and communities' own views of themselves. These abilities to comprehend and to respond to the circumstances of social change are crucial to children's eventual participation in the process of reflective equilibrium as I, following Rawls, have conceived it, for they make it possible to see actions, practices, and policies as serving principles. This philosophical education also contributes to children's developing conceptions of justice in that it enables them to understand how the proclivities and practices of the citizens of a society can be captured in principles of justice for that society.

This characterization of the content of the civic education curriculum as involving multicultural, historical, and philosophical elements is, no doubt, incomplete. But it demonstrates the kind of analysis necessary for formulating such a curriculum. However, there is one central element of civic education to which the content I have outlined does not necessarily speak, namely, children's motivation to involve themselves in the reflective process through which an overlapping consensus emerges. Achieving this aim, I believe, is less a matter of curricular content than of the instructional procedures through which that content is presented and learned.

Perhaps the key to such motivation is to enable children to explore the connection between the formulation of and adherence to civic principles, on the one hand, and their emerging conceptions of the good, on the other. By this I do not mean what consequences the principles have for the selfish interests of children, because conceptions of the good, which are substantially based in culture, are not inherently or even usually self-directed. Rather, what I do mean is what consequences these principles have for children's own self-defined interests, which are not necessarily limited to interests in themselves. Nor do I mean that such an exploration should focus only on the teleological consequences of the principles, for children's emerging personal conceptions undoubtedly have deontological as well as teleological components. In short, this exploration involves the connection between the civic principles and what children are coming to believe is right and good.

To accomplish this exploration, it seems necessary to encourage children to assess from their own perspectives the principles that they are discovering in the overlapping consensus. In other words, the teaching about cultures, history, and principles must at some point make room for and facilitate children's reaching their own judgments about the nature and justification of the content of the current overlapping consensus. In part, this means that children must be encouraged to be active and independent in the search for the civic meaning of current governmental and social policies and practices. They must not only be encouraged to formulate hypotheses about such matters, but they must also be encouraged to take seriously the hypotheses of others, including adults and other children. For what they are ultimately seeking is not only their own private interpretations but also an understanding of civic principles that can stand up to public scrutiny. Equally important, they must be encouraged to formulate their own judgments about the adequacy of these principles, judgments based in part on what is publicly known about the principles' content and consequences and in part on what their emerging conceptions of the good make of that content and those consequences. These observations about this aspect of civic education imply a civic education classroom in which children are mutually engaged in the search for the formulation and meaning of their civic ideals and that is respectful of the judgments that children form about them.

In an important sense, this motivational element completes and makes personally meaningful the civic education of children that meets the criteria of valuing social cooperation and developing a sense of justice. For the multicultural, historical, and philosophical content of civic education are compatible with an impersonal understanding of social cooperation and justice in which those two features are understood only as abstract possibilities for one's own and other societies. However, this motivational element connects these abstract outcomes of civic education to children's own developing conceptions of the good in a way that, if successful, enables social cooperation and the principles of justice on which it is based simultaneously to facilitate one's pursuit of a personally meaningful conception of the good and to influence one's judgment about socially constructive conceptions of the good.

The Civic Relevance of Political Liberalism

The purpose of this chapter has been primarily to demonstrate the meaning and implications of a tradition of political thought that has been important in the development of political arrangements and institutions, including those in the United States, as that tradition has been continued and extended in the work of John Rawls. As I believe I have shown, this tradition has clear ramifications for the purposes and conduct of civic education for children. It also offers a different vision of that education than a variety of other traditions that have been important in the recent conversation about politics and civic education—namely, utilitarianianism, democratic theory (e.g., Gutmann, 1999), nationalism, communitarianism (e.g., Strike, 1994), and comprehensive liberalism (e.g., Callan, 1997). In this concluding section, I will not provide a detailed and systematic argument for the superiority of this approach but instead will indicate a few of its attractions.

Foremost, this approach to civic education supports the personal and political liberties of the adults whom children become because it emphasizes and develops the judgment of children. In part it does so by ensuring that children's conceptions of the good involve their own reflective judgments about the lives that they find worthwhile, given their talents, circumstances, and proclivities. But it also ensures that the conceptions of justice that they develop and embrace equally involve their considered judgments about their relationships with others, rather than the imposition on them of externally determined political doctrines. Of course, knowledge about one's own and other societies and their histories and serious conversations with others are important elements in the formulation of children's thinking about justice, but the final determination of their judgment on this subject and the ultimate responsibility for it lies with the developing children themselves.

To be sure, this process of self-formation in the prevailing social context brings with it a number of risks and uncertainties, especially with regard to the ultimate outcomes of the process. But it ensures to the maximum extent possible that those outcomes will be meaningful and acceptable to the adults whom children become, both as individuals and as members of the various associations of civil society. And it equally ensures that those outcomes will be the result of constructive and civil engagement with others to whom the results are of the highest importance.

Of course, this civic education makes profound and sometimes difficult intellectual and social demands on children. For it requires them to think seriously about the history and current state of their society and to develop serious normative judgments about these matters. At the same time, it requires children to confront critically the judgments of others, both children and adults. But it also ensures that children's developing judgments are the result of reflection, not just the internalization of others' thinking or the acceptance of prevailing social convention.

As a result, such civic education opens children up to others in a way that competing approaches do not, most obviously to the other citizens of their own society but potentially to citizens of other societies as well. For the overlapping consensus in which they come to participate involves issues about appropriate moral relationships with both (Rawls, 1999b).

Bibliography

Bull, B.L. (2008). *Social justice in education: An introduction*. New York: Palgrave Macmillan.

Callan, E. (1997). *Creating citizens: Political education and liberal democracy*. New York: Clarendon Press.

Gutmann, A. (1999). *Democratic education* (rev. ed.). Princeton, NJ: Princeton University Press.

Gutmann, A., & Thompson, J. (1996). *Democracy and disagreement*. Cambridge, MA: Belknap Press.

Kant, I. (1985). *Foundations of the metaphysics of morals* (Lewis White Beck, Trans.). New York: Macmillan. (Original work published 1785)

Rawls, J. (1971). *A theory of justice*. Cambridge, MA: Belknap Press of Harvard University Press.

Rawls, J. (1993). *Political liberalism*. New York: Columbia University Press.

Rawls, J. (1999a). *A theory of justice* (rev. ed.). Cambridge, MA: Belknap Press of Harvard University Press.

Rawls, J. (1999b). *The law of peoples, with the idea of public reason revisited*. Cambridge, MA: Harvard University Press.

Strike, K.A. (1994). Community, the missing element of school reform: Why schools should be more like congregations than banks. *American Journal of Education, 110*(3), 215–232.

CHAPTER TWENTY-TWO

Rethinking the State

Responding to the Educational, Economic, and Environmental Crises

DAVID HURSH

Given the multiple crises we face—an economic recession followed by, at best, a jobless recovery, schools that fail to adequately educate students to contribute to society, and global climate change—it would be reasonable to ask the question of whether we need to rethink how we live together and, in particular, whether our form of governance enables us to solve our problems. In particular, I suggest, we need to question whether neoliberalism, the current form of governance, with its emphasis on individualism, competition, free markets, and privatization, not only does not alleviate the crises but also is a primary source of them. In fact, I will argue that neoliberalism fails to achieve both its stated economic goals and exacerbates our educational and environmental problems.

I will argue that we need to replace neoliberalism with a form of social democracy that can rein in reckless, unregulated markets and enable us to work together to find solutions to our common problems. Moreover, not only do we need to rethink the form of governance in the United States—what is often referred to as the nature of the state (Held, 2009; Held & Brown, 2010; Jessop, 2009)—but also we need to rethink the relationship between countries. No nation is an island. The U.S. economic crises have impacted other countries, and the deficits in Portugal, Spain, Greece, and Ireland have impacted the European Union as a whole and other countries generally. Environmental crises—such as climate change, air pollution, and water shortages—can no longer be solved at the level of individual nations (Judt, 2010; Orr, 2009; Sachs, 2008). Instead, we will need to think how nations can work together to solve shared problems.

Neoliberal ideals have dominated the global economic system for so long that many people may no longer recall the system it replaced. Therefore, I will begin this chapter by describing the main tenets of neoliberalism and comparing it to social democracy, the governing system that achieved dominance in most Western nations in the 1930s and remained so until the early 1970s. I will then critique the central tenets of neoliberalism—its faith in unregulated markets, the minimal state, and privatization—as either unattainable or harmful. Then, I will specifically examine the consequences of neoliberalism for the economy, education, and the environment and conclude with suggestions for what we need to consider in rethinking the state.

The Rise of Neoliberalism and the Decline of Social Democracy.

Neoliberal theory began to be promulgated in the 1940s by economists in Europe, most notably by Hayek (1944, 1960), and in the United States most notably by Milton Friedman (1952, 1962, 1995) and other members of the Mont Pelerin Society. They described themselves as neoliberals "because of their fundamental commitment to human freedom" and to the "free market principles of neo-classical economics" (Harvey, 2005). However, neoliberal theory was not put into widespread practice until the late 1970s and early 1980s when Ronald Reagan became president of the United States and Margaret Thatcher prime minister of Britain.

While the United States holds primary responsibility for elaborating neoliberal theory through Milton Friedman and his followers at the University of Chicago, and installing it in the United States and through military and political pressure and persuasion in other countries, the term is little known and less understood by most citizens. Contrary to what the label might suggest, neoliberalism is not a new form of social democratic liberalism that builds on the policies of Franklin Delano Roosevelt's New Deal or Lyndon Johnson's Great Society. Rather, neoliberalism builds on the original or classical version of liberalism, which began in the 17th century and remained dominant until the 20th.

Liberalism first emerged in the 1600s as the philosophical and political rationale for opposing the authority of the church and monarchy. In place of obedience to the church and crown, liberal social philosophers, including Locke (1960), Hobbes (1968), and Voltaire (2000), put forward the "principles of civil rights, rights of property, a limited conception of state power and a broadly negative conception of freedom" (Olssen, Codd, & O'Neill, 2004, p. 80). Liberalism reconceptualized the relationship between the individual and the secular and sacred state, aiming to free individuals from state interference and portraying individuals as pursuing their self-interest, which, coincidently, also served societal interests and promoted social progress.

In time, liberalism revolutionized societies in Europe and North America. The ways in which people conceptualized and talked about individuals and society and the kinds of social practices that could be carried out were transformed. Representative governments and the rule of law replaced the monarchy. Societies industrialized and, overall, their wealth grew.

However, liberalization came with a cost—increased wealth for a few and increased poverty for many. One need only think of the society described by Victorian writers such as Charles Dickens in which those who could not pay their bills ended up in the poorhouse. Consequently, workers began to organize and demand better working conditions, and the general public called for laws to protect women and children from excessive labor and their families from poverty. Cities and states passed legislation in relation to education, employment, health, and other issues with the increasing acknowledgment that local and state governments must be involved in social and economic affairs by providing the conditions for all people to realize their capacities.

The Great Depression of the 1930s further exposed the shortcomings of classical liberalism. In the United States, Roosevelt responded by implementing Keynesian economic theories, in which the state used spending, tax, and welfare policies to rebuild the country and to fund the military effort in World War II. The United States emerged from the war victorious, and Keynesian economics and social democratic liberalism were to remain dominant up to the 1970s.

During the period immediately following the war, workers, women, and people of color fought to not only improve their economic conditions but also to extend their personal and political rights for education, housing, health, workplace safety and to vote (Bowles & Gintis, 1986, pp. 57–59). These efforts resulted in improved working and living conditions and, not insignificantly, increased wages that fueled economic growth.

However, with increased wages, corporations' profits began to decline, and neoliberalism arose in part as a means to reduce the economic demands of workers and to cut taxes and governmental spending on social services. While neoliberalism is presented as a natural or neutral evolution of the economy, it primarily serves to restore corporate power and the wealth of the privileged. Harvey (2005) writes that neoliberalism is

> a benevolent mask of wonderful sounding words like freedom, liberty, choice and rights, to hide the grim realities of the restoration or reconstitution of naked class power, locally as well as transnationally, but more particularly in the main financial centers of global capitalism. (p. 119)

An example of the way in which neoliberalism is presented as all things wonderful is the writing of Thomas Friedman, who has numerous best-selling books, including *The World Is Flat: A Brief History of the Twenty-First Century* (2005) and who writes a weekly opinion column for the *New York Times*. In *The Lexus and the Olive Tree* (1999), Friedman asserts that we have no choice but to pursue free-market capitalism, which is the term many U.S. politicians and commentators substitute for neoliberalism:

> The driving force behind globalization is free-market capitalism—the more you let market forces rule and the more you open up your economy to free trade and competition, the more efficient your economy will be. Globalization means the spread of free-market capitalism to virtually every corner of the world. Therefore, globalization also has its own set of economic rules—rules that revolve around opening, deregulating and privatizing your economy, in order to make it more competitive and attractive to foreign investment. (9)

Friedman adds that it is only free-market capitalism that will ensure "economic growth, maintain a low rate of inflation and price stability, [and reduce] the size of the state bureaucracy" (105), all apparently desirable outcomes. Under neoliberalism, government should be limited to providing for internal security and national defense.

Further, with the diminishment of the state, the individual becomes responsible for his or her own self. As Margaret Thatcher famously said, "There is no such thing as society...there are individual men and women, and there are families. And no government can do anything except through people, and people must look after themselves first" (Thatcher, 1993, pp. 626–627). Lemke (2002) adds how, under neoliberalism, the individual is conceived as an autonomous entrepreneur who can always take care of his or her own needs. Neoliberalism seeks

> to unite a responsible and moral individual and an economic-rational individual. It aspires to construct responsible subjects whose moral quality is based on the fact that that they rationally assess the costs and benefits of a certain act as opposed to other alternative acts. (p. 59)

For neoliberals, those who do not succeed are held to have made bad choices. Personal responsibility means nothing is society's fault. People have only themselves to blame. Moreover, the market becomes central within such a conception of the individual:

> Every social transaction is conceptualized as entrepreneurial, to be carried out purely for personal gain. The market introduces competition as the structuring mechanism through which resources and status are allocated efficiently and fairly. The "invisible hand" of the market is thought to be the most efficient way of sorting out which competing individuals get what. (Olssen et al., 2004, pp. 137–138)

Neoliberalism, write Leitner, Sheppard, Sziarto and Maringanti (2007), replaces the common good and the concern for public welfare with the entrepreneurial individual aiming to succeed within competitive markets. Neoliberal policies favor

> supply-side innovation and competitiveness; decentralization, devolution, and attrition of political governance, deregulation and privatization of industry, land and public services [including schools]; and replacing welfare with "workfarist" social policies.…A neoliberal subjectivity has emerged that normalizes the logic of individualism and entrepreneurialism, equating individual freedom with self-interested choices, making individuals responsible for their own well-being, and redefining citizens as consumers and clients. (pp. 1–2)

The Failures of Neoliberalism

However, I want to argue that neoliberalism not only fails to meet its stated goals of increasing economic growth, but that it fails as a response to the current economic, educational, and environmental crises. As I will show, neoliberalism fails for several reasons, but a primary one is that many of our problems cannot be solved through individual actions. We live in a world in which actions that seem justified on an individual level can be counterproductive when taken by many individuals. For example, while individuals may benefit by diverting water from a river for their own use, if too many individuals do the same, they can dry up the river. Using coal to produce electricity may be beneficial because coal is cheap, but the carbon dioxide from too many coal-powered plants increases global warming. Instead, we need to examine the collective effects of our actions and how to use societal organizations to affect our behaviors (Orr, 2009).

Furthermore, neoliberalism fails to achieve its stated economic goal of increasing economic growth at a rate equal to or faster than under the previous social democratic policies. The United States and most of the other nations around the globe are mired in the worst economic recession since the Great Depression of the 1930s. Millions have lost their jobs and/or their homes. Because people earn and spend less, individual states, such as New York, California, and Texas (Davey, 2011), have more citizens who need social supports while the states simultaneously receive less tax revenue. Consequently, states are facing large deficits and, therefore, are cutting funding for education and social services, laying off employees, and reducing retiree pensions—all of which are likely to exacerbate the crisis.

This recession occurs within a longer-term decline in economic growth and follows several other financial crises. Neoliberal economic policies have not resulted in the economic growth that Friedman and other neoliberal economists claimed. Increases in the Gross National Product have been less than those under earlier Keynesian economic policies (Harvey, 2005). At the global level, the gap between the rich and the poor has widened, and while two countries—India and China—have increased the size of their middle class, in much of the developing world more people live in poverty (Jomo & Baudot, 2007). In the United States, income levels have remained stagnant for the last several decades. Between 1969 and 1999, U.S. census data show that household incomes in the "middle fifth increased by an average of only $315 a year, less than 1 percent annually after inflation." Since 1999, those meager gains have almost been eliminated as the median household income fell from $52,547, after adjusting for inflation, to just $49,534 in 2009. Furthermore, the poverty rate for 2009, the most recent year reported, was 14.3%, the highest poverty rate since 1994, and higher than the annual rate for almost every year since the mid-1960s (*Too Much*, 2010).

Moreover, the current economic recession largely results from neoliberals' irrational faith that markets can regulate themselves. Earlier Keynesian economic policies advocated that the state had to regulate corporate behavior, whether it was in breaking up monopolies, ensuring that industries were safe, or passing laws, such as the Glass-Steagal Banking Act of 1933 that created the Federal Deposit Insurance Corporation, which protected individuals' deposits and limited the kinds of loans in which institutions could engage. Instead, the Glass-Steagal Act was repealed during the Clinton administration, permitting banks to create derivatives and other misleading practices (Johnson & Kwak, 2010, p. 120) that, for a time, covered up banks' toxic loans. Then the banking system began to collapse under its own greed. The federal government, fearing that the further collapse of the largest banks and financial institutions would result in an economic depression worse than anything we have imagined, stepped in to provide emergency funding. Most of the financial institutions have recovered and have returned to making record profits and granting record salaries and bonuses to the corporate elite (Greider, 2010).

However, the federal government provided less assistance to bailing out the states, and state budgets are being balanced on the backs of public services workers whose jobs are being eliminated or, if they still have a position, their salaries frozen and pensions cut. It remains to be seen whether most families will regain the jobs, salaries, and home equity that they lost during the depth of the recession. Just as importantly, few rules have been put in place to block financial institutions from again pursuing the same risky behaviors.

In education, neoliberal theories have become increasingly dominant, beginning under the Reagan administration with the publication of the report *A Nation at Risk* in 1982, and culminating in Obama's Race to the Top program. Over almost three decades, public education policies have increasingly embodied the central neoliberal tenets of markets, competition, privatization, and quantification.

A Nation at Risk called for educational reforms as a response to the economic recession caused not, as the report claimed, by other countries' superior educational systems, but by neoliberal federal economic policies that sought to increase unemployment as a means of reducing inflationary pressures and restoring corporate profits. *A Nation at Risk*, as have several subsequent education policies and proposals, sought to shift the blame for the nation's economic problems away from neoliberal policies that have reduced employment and wages, and onto schools. Moreover, the report reflected a renewed and more sophisticated effort to reform education along economic lines, preparing students to compete in the global workplace, promoting curriculum and pedagogy deemed efficient, and assessing results through standardized tests.

Having successfully argued for efficiency and standardized testing, it became easier for education reformers to argue that teachers and students need to be assessed and held accountable through high-stakes standardized tests. Consequently, beginning in the late 1980s, states began establishing requirements that students pass one or more standardized tests to pass from one grade to the next to graduate from high school. Some states, such as Texas, require passing exams in Math and Reading (yes, they mean reading, not literacy), while New York requires passing five tests, one each in English, science, and math, and two in history. As I have documented elsewhere (Hursh, 2007a, 2007b, 2008), high-stakes standardized testing has resulted in teaching to the test, narrowing the curriculum to what is likely to be covered in the test, and eliminating subjects not tested, such as social studies, the arts, and science. None of this seems to have resulted in students learning more. In fact, even with the increased emphasis on math and literacy during the decade of the 1990s, the average score on the NAEP exam failed to rise as quickly as it had during the 1960s, and the achievement gap between white students and students of color remained much the same.

Most recently, Obama's educational initiative, Race to the Top (RTTT), exemplifies the neoliberal agenda of markets, competition, privatization, and accountability through standardized tests scores. RTTT requires that states compete for federal funding by agreeing to change state laws regarding how many charter schools are allowed in the state and authorizing that teacher pay can be based in part on students' scores on standardized exams. Because most states are facing serious economic crises requiring them to reduce educational funding, many states entered the RTTT competition in a desperate attempt to gain additional funding. For example, New York State raised the limit on the number of charter schools from 200 to 460 and removed legal prohibitions on using students' test scores to decide teacher pay. However, only 15 states received RTTT funding; and, in New York, half of the funding goes directly to the State Education Department. Except for the five largest urban school districts, most districts will be lucky to receive enough funding to hire an additional administrator, who will need to design and implement the RTTT mandates regarding assessment and salaries. The RTTT funding provides no additional funding to run current programs. Worse yet, for those states not "winning" the race, they will have passed sweeping legislation creating radical changes in their education systems without receiving any of the funding to implement it. Moreover, RTTT demonstrates that, in a climate of financial desperation, extortion works.

Lastly, neoliberalism, with its emphasis on markets, individual choice, and economic growth, contributes to our environmental crises of resource depletion, in which the world will face oil and food shortages and increasing global warming. David Orr (2009), professor of environmental studies and politics at Oberlin College, adopts the phrase "the long emergency" from William Howard Kunstler (2005) to argue that even the most optimistic scenarios regarding global warming indicate that its impact on the environment will be catastrophic. Because of nature's positive feedback loops (such as how the warming atmosphere increases melting of the permafrost, thereby releasing increased amounts of methane gas, which adds to global warming), even if we were to immediately eliminate producing greenhouse gases, the effects from our past activities will be with us for centuries (see Archer, 2009). Writes Orr (2009):

Even if we stop emitting heat-trapping gases quickly; we will still experience centuries of bigger storms, large and more frequent floods, massive heat waves, and prolonged drought, along with rising sea levels, disappearing species, changing diseases, decline of oceans, and radically altered ecosystems. (pp. xii–xiii)

Neoliberal policies not only undermine our efforts to respond to these environmental crises, they cause and exacerbate them. The central aim of neoliberalism is to generate new markets, expand the economy, and increase profits. Its central measure of success is whether the Gross Domestic Product is expanding and corporate profits are increasing. Furthermore, its means of achieving these goals is through individual competition in markets that operate on the basis of profit seeking.

Neoliberalism, then, intentionally marginalizes any consideration of values other than profits. In this way environmental conditions are externalized from economic and political decisions, as are questions regarding the general welfare of society. Problems are to be solved, if they are to be faced at all, through the magic of the marketplace. Deliberation over our values and societal goals are replaced by voting with our dollars.

In response, I want to argue that we need to rethink the purpose of society and how we make decisions. Tony Judt, in *Ill Fares the Land* (2010), laments the way in which neoliberalism has shredded the very fabric of society. He begins the book:

Something is profoundly wrong with the way we live today. For thirty years we have made a virtue out of the pursuit of material self-interest, indeed, this very pursuit now constitutes whatever remains of our sense of collective purpose. We know what things cost but have no idea what they are worth. We no longer ask of a judicial ruling or a legislative act: Is it good? Is it fair? Is it just? Is it right? Will it help bring about a better society or a better world? Those used to be *the* political questions, even if they invited no easy answers. We must learn once again to pose them. (p. 1; emphasis in original)

Judt lays out the rationale for ending the neoliberal experiment and replacing it with social democracy, which some European countries have embraced and the United States partially embraced during the late 1960s with the War on Poverty and the Civil Rights Movement. Judt "suggest(s) that the government can play an enhanced role in our lives without threatening our liberties—and to argue that, since the state is going to be with us for the foreseeable future, we would do well to think about what sort of a state we want" (p. 5).

If we are to adequately respond to the problems we face regarding social and economic inequality, global warming, and resources depletion, we will need to rethink our economic principles so that, rather than focusing on growth and increasing the Gross Domestic Product, we instead focus on improving the quality of our lives and our local communities. Bill McKibben, in *Deep Economy: The Wealth of Communities and the Durable Future* (2007), argues that we need to ask: How do we measure people's quality of life and how do we develop economies that work toward improving the well-being of everyone? What would a different economic system look like?

Similarly, David Harvey critiques the neoliberal conception of the individual, freedom, and nature. He suggests that, for neoliberals, the individual exists outside of space and time. For neoliberals the individual is merely *homo economicus*, making rational choices in terms of one's own economic future and prospects. Such an individual does not need to concern herself about her relationship with other people or to nature.

Instead, Harvey (2009) argues that we need to place the individual within the context of existing socio-ecological dialectic, from which (no matter how much we wish otherwise), we cannot escape. He writes that individuals cannot

> be considered as isolated from and outside of the socio-ecological dialectic and ongoing activities of place formation and re-formation. Their positionality in relation to nature, production systems, social relations, technologies, and mental conceptions, as these impinge upon everyday life, is perpetually shifting, as are the contexts of their feelings, sensitivities, and practical arrangements. If, in short, the geographical theory I am proposing is correct, then the whole question of what constitutes an "individual" has to be reconceptualized in radically different ways than that of neoliberal theory. (pp. 255–256)

Harvey's notion of freedom, then, differs from the neoliberal notion of "freedom from." Instead, he sees freedom as relational, not just in relation to other people but also in relation to nature. Nature both places limits on us and, as we interact with nature, we affect those limits. Therefore, he wants to examine the ongoing relationship humans have with nature. "Human beings," he notes, " are part of nature. The only difference from other organisms…is that human beings can engage in this process consciously, knowledgeably, and reflexively" (p. 238).

Harvey further argues that all political and social projects are ecological in nature. For example, in examining the creation and use of technology, we explore how technology transforms nature, but also how technology transforms our relationship to one another and the nature of our activities. Likewise, Harvey requires us to examine the ways in which we produce goods and services and their effect on nature and the built environment; the daily process in which individual and social groups reproduce themselves and their social relations, including consuming, living, reproducing, and communication; social relations, such as network hierarchies and institutional arrangements; and, finally, mental conceptions, or "the whole inherited arsenal of language, concepts, and stored symbolic, cultural, religious, ethical, scientific, and ideological meanings and aesthetic and moral judgments" (p. 239).

All of these interact with one another and are created as a dialectical outcome between individuals and their environment. Harvey continues:

> Any conception of alternatives [to the existing conditions] has to answer the question of what kind of daily life, what kind of relation to nature, which social relations, what production processes, and what kinds of mental conceptions and technologies will be adequate to meet human wants, needs, and desires. (247)

Rather than understanding freedom in the neoliberal sense in which the individual is free to pursue his or her own economic interests, freedom can only be understood as action within relationships, whether with humans or nature. This is not so different than Dewey's (1938) notion of freedom in which "The only freedom of enduring importance is freedom of intelligence, that is to say, freedom of observation and of judgment exercised in behalf of purposes that are intrinsically worth while" (61). Further, Dewey argued, "there can be no greater mistake…than to treat freedom as an end in itself" (63). Freedom is not the ability to do as one pleases; rather it is action within the continuum of experience—and it is the continuum, the relationships, that matters.

The differences between neoliberalism and social democracy reflect two contrasting conceptions of the role of the state and the individual in society. Neoliberalism emphasizes developing the entrepreneurial individual within a minimal state, and the commodification of everything, including nature. Schooling emphasizes efficiently producing economically productive individuals. Consequently, education and other social services are to be privatized and efficiency increased by submitting schooling to the pressures of the market. Achieving efficiency requires developing quantitative measures, so students and teacher are assessed through standardized test scores. Further, tests and other assessments can be used to shape the behavior of individuals to ensure that goals are achieved.

In contrast, David Orr (2009) asks:

> How do we reimagine and remake the human presence on earth in ways that work over the long haul? Such questions are the heart of what theologian Thomas Berry [1999] calls "the Great Work" of our age. This effort is nothing less than the effort to harmonize the human enterprise with how the world works as a physical system and how it ought to work as a moral system. (p. 3)

We need to rethink the state so that we build a social democracy that focuses on the relationship that the individual develops with others and nature. The state, rather than pretending to be neutral, plays a role as it supports and is supported by individuals and groups in creating cultures, technologies, social relations, production processes, and mental conceptions adequate to meet human wants, needs, and desires. One role for the state (which is, after all, made up of citizens) is to respond to the different conceptions throughout society of how we are to live together in some way.

What those arrangements are to look like are part of the political and social project in which neither the process nor the outcome can be predetermined. Rather, like Dewey's conception of means-ends (1938), the process and the product are equally important. Therefore, I do not have the ability to lay out in this chapter how a social democratic state and the relations between states should be organized, except to say that those structures need to be developed through a democratic collaborative process.

Further, we need to get better at communicating to one another how we want to live and relate to one another, what kind of relation we want with nature, and in what kinds of work and technology we want to engage. The world is not preordained, and another world is possible. We need to engage with one another in creating and sustaining that world.

Bibliography

Archer, D. (2009). *The long thaw: How humans are changing the next 100,000 years of earth's climate.* Princeton, NJ: Princeton University Press.

Berry, T. (1999). *The great work.* New York: Bell Tower.

Bowles, S., & Gintis, H. (1986). *Democracy and capitalism: Property, community and the contradictions of modern thought.* New York: Basic Books.

Davey, M. (2011, January 17). Budget worries push governors to same mind-set. *New York Times*, A-1.

Dewey, John. 1938. *Experience and education.* New York: Collier Books.

Friedman, M. (1952). *Essays on positive economics.* Chicago: University of Chicago Press.

Friedman, M. (1962). *Capitalism and freedom.* Chicago: University of Chicago Press.

Friedman, M. (1995, June 23). *Public schools: Make them private.* Cato briefing paper from *Washington Post*. Briefing paper no. 23. Retrieved from www.cato.org/pubs/briefs/bp-023.html

Friedman, T. (1999). *The Lexus and the olive tree.* New York: Farrar, Straus & Giroux.

Friedman, T.L. (2005). *The world is flat: A brief history of the twenty-first century.* New York: Farrar, Straus & Giroux.

Greider, W. (2010, June 30). Battling the banksters. *The Nation.* www.thenation.com/article/36905/battling-banksters

Harvey, D. (2005). *The new imperialism.* New York: Oxford University Press.

Harvey, D. (2007). *A brief history of neoliberalism.* Oxford: Oxford University Press.

Harvey, D. (2009). *Cosmopolitanism and the geographies of freedom.* New York: Columbia University Press.

Hayek, F.A. (1944). *The road to serfdom.* Chicago: University of Chicago Press.

Hayek, F.A. (1960). *The constitution of liberty.* Chicago: Henry Regnery.

Held, D. (2009). Restructuring global governance: Cosmopolitanism, democracy and the global order. *Millennium–Journal of International Studies, 37*(3), 535.

Held, D., & Brown, G. (2010). *Cosmpolitanism.* Cambridge, UK: Polity Press.

Hobbes, T. (1968). *Leviathan* (C.B. Macpherson, Ed.). London: Penguin. (Original work published 1651)

Hursh, D. (2007a). Assessing the impact of No Child Left Behind and other neoliberal reforms in education *American Educational Research Journal, 44*(3), 493–518.

Hursh, D. (2007b). Exacerbating inequality: The failed promise of the No Child Left Behind Act. *Race Ethnicity and Education, 10*(3), 295–308.

Hursh, D. (2008). *High-stakes testing and the decline of teaching and learning: The real crisis in education.* Lanham, MD: Rowman and Littlefield.

Jessop, B. (2009). Avoiding traps, rescaling states, governing Europe. In *Leviathan undone? Towards a political economy of scale.* Vancouver: University of British Columbia Press.

Johnson, S., & Kwak, J. (2010). *13 bankers: The Wall Street takeover and the next financial meltdown.* New York: Pantheon.

Jomo, K.S., & Baudot, J. (2007). Preface. In K.S. Jomo & J. Baudot (Eds.), *Flat world, big gaps: Economic liberalization, globalization, poverty, and inequality* (pp. xvii–xxvii). New York: Zed Books.

Judt, T. (2010). *Ill fares the land.* New York: Penguin Press.

Kunstler, J.H. (2005). *The long emergency: Surviving the end of oil, climate change, and other converging catastrophes of the twenty-first century.* New York: Grove Press.

Leitner, H., Sheppard, E.S., Sziarto, K., & Maringanti, A. (2007). Contesting urban futures: Decentering neoliberalism. In H. Leitner, E.S. Sheppard, & J. Peck (Eds.), *Contesting neoliberalism: Urban frontiers.* New York: Guilford Press.

Lemke, T. (2002). Foucault, governmentality, and critique. *Rethinking Marxism, 14*(3), 49–64.

Locke, J. (1960). *Two treatises on government* (P. Laslett, Ed.). Cambridge: Cambridge University Press. (Original work published 1690)

Martinez, B. (2010, May 29). Charter-school advocates raise cap. *Wall Street Journal.* http://online.wsj.com/article/SB10001424052748704596504575272942716879192.html

McKibben, B. (2007). *Deep economy: The wealth of communities and the durable future.* New York: Times Books.

Olssen, M., Codd, J., & O'Neill, A.M. (2004). *Education policy: Globalization, citizenship and democracy.* Thousand Oaks, CA: Sage.

Orr, D. (2009). *Down to the wire: Confronting climate collapse.* Oxford: Oxford University Press.

Sachs, J. (2008). *Common wealth: Economics for a crowded planet.* New York: Penguin Group USA.

Thatcher, M. (1993). *The Downing Street years.* London: HarperCollins.

Too Much. (September 20, 2010). *Too Much: An Online Weekly of Excess and Inequality.* Accessed September 20, 2010, at http://www.toomuchonline.org/tmweekly.html

Voltaire, F. (2000). *Treatise on tolerance* (B. Masters, Trans.; S. Harvey, Ed.). Cambridge: Cambridge University Press. (Original work published 1763)

CHAPTER TWENTY-THREE

Democracy

A Critical Red Ideal

JASON M. PRICE

> Education for a democracy has provided a deeply treasured language for shaping our children's schooling and a litmus test for judging their purposes and practices....Democratic schooling has been the basis of struggle. . . .
>
> —LINDA MCNEIL, 2002

> Surely it is time to re-open public discussion about the aims of education and ensure that our current policies and practices are consistent with the core qualities of democracy; democracy not narrowly defined as a form of government but as Dewey characterised it—as a way of life, as an ethical conception and hence always about the democracy still to come.
>
> —ROGER SIMON IN PORTELLI & SOLOMON, 2001

Introduction

My overarching purpose in this paper is to trouble popular notions of democracy and in the process generate questions that raise doubts about the validity and value of popular conceptions of the meaning and practices of democracy. I will also suggest some core qualities of democracy for the readers' consideration that I use in my work as an educational researcher, pre-service and post-graduate teacher education instructor, and practicum supervisor to evaluate educational philosophies, policies, curriculum, pedagogy, cocurricular activities, decision making and discipline in schools.

Is democracy a way of life, a way of organising the political, social, and economic life of communities that is defined by a generalised participative dialogic process that is directed towards the nurturance of peace, and social, economic and ecological justice? In this paper I will be comparing and contrasting, this ideal, what I refer to as critical red democracy,[1] with the popular view and practice of democracy. I have written this political paper as an intervention in the world (Freire, 2004), an intervention directed towards reclaiming and reasserting an ideal of democracy I believe worth struggling for. According to my understanding of democracy, which has been composed, coloured and shaded by my firsthand experiences of "Fourth World" "democracies"(Bobiwash, 2001) and my mixed Haudenosaunee and working-class Scot/Irish heritage, the core distinguishing content qualities of a democratic community are: generalised and empowered dialogue, ecological justice, peace, equity, anti-racism, cooperation and sharing, freedom from hunger and freedom to shelter and clothe oneself

Specifically, I will examine multiple constructions of democracy in popular and academic discourse. I argue that continued attempts to clarify the meaning(s) of democracy, to analyse the academic and popular discourse on democracy, and to examine diverse, historic, and contemporary examples of indigenous democracy is crucial if we hope to reclaim a substantive democracy and counter the popular flawed logic that voting and free markets define as democracy.

Aboriginal ways of knowing guide my thinking. My purpose here is anti-colonial, and disruptive, yet hopeful, playful and constructive. I am, of course, keenly interested in issues related to the continuing and seemingly inexorable power of the social, economic and political minority to name, rename, define, redefine, populate and depopulate the world and the word. The philosophy of hope and possibility guiding this intervention paper springs from the discursive and redemptive moral and intellectual power of Fourth World people's knowledge, practices, and institutions (Gunn, 1986; Graveline, 1998; Maracle, 1988; Said, 1985). Ironically, this paper is also situated within an approach to social science research Walter Mignolo (2002) conceives of as "critical cosmopolitanism." Mignolo portrays efforts to explore contextualised democratic experiences that respect diversity in order to avoid the dread homogeneity of a "new universalism," as crucial. Mignolo suggests these inclusive democracy stories from below are an empowered counternarrative to globalisation from above, and that these local histories must be given a prominent hearing in critical dialogues exploring and analyzing democracy.

The Rhetoric and Reality of Democracy

I am deeply concerned that in popular and academic usage democracy has become reduced to being dangerously associated first and foremost with elections and specific procedures with the result of demeaning and degrading the importance of content as a distinguishing feature of democracy. Like Chantal Mouffe (2002) I can't help but draw a connection between reduced political engagement as evidenced by the alarming absence of voting and political participation by our youth and marginalised members of our society, and the lack of meaningful substantive choice and visions of democracy in popular discourse. I am also concerned by the blurring of the demarcated policy lines that once served to differentiate the major political parties in Canada, the United Kingdom, and the United States apart from one another that in effect left marginalised populations with little or no representation or choice. In contrast to popular and academic charges of apathy against these groups, my explanation is anti-pathy. That along with a decline of the content and meaningful alternatives in democracy, has come an understandable interpretation by our youth and so many other "citizens" that voting and other forms of formal political participation does not matter. That democracy is an elite dominated process and procedure show, where the outcomes are often predictable and often only marginally important to their lives. Many people do not see their visions of their own and collective futures and pasts represented in many self proclaimed democracies. Is it not rational, moral, and even pragmatic for "democratic citizens" to resent a system that neglects their needs, and hopes, and that goes on in an inexorable way as if every life system and life support system of our earth is not in decline? For many citizens even the ideal of democracy embodied by these governments is not worth struggling for, not even worth a drive to the local school to cast a ballot.

I am surprised more educators are not alarmed by the demeaned usage of the term *democracy* in both the popular media and academic discourse. Democracy is being regularly used fast and loose as a verb, an adverb, an adjective, and a noun in both popular and academic usage. It is most often used to describe a process of elections and procedure of leadership selection and representative decision-making, to describe states that utilise some form of universal suffrage, and that conform to a large extent to neoliberal economic policies. Perhaps, as a symptom of the "war against terrorism" it is also presented as something citizen armies must fight for, something that Western nations can bring to or impose on "others," or even a gift one enlightened people can give to "others."

Democracy is also held up as an end in itself that individual citizens create together and preserve by casting their vote, or it is portrayed as fragile, and under constant threat from within by unpatriotic and apathetic citizens and from beyond its borders by "terrorists," undemocratic regimes and "backward" civilizations. Ironically it is also portrayed as a political-economic system that makes nations strong and free, but can also make them weak in times of crisis, and so according to its defenders needs well defined limits. It is also frequently portrayed as a system of governance that can only be built upon and sustained by free markets, private property, increased consumption and productivity, and the over-arching pursuit of profit. Unfortunately, democracy is often presented as a system of government to be uncritically appreciated. Likewise, it is seen as a system of governance that depends on elections, laws and institutional force and coercion to protect and preserve it.

Democracy is ubiquitously constructed as a system of governance the world owes to the enlightened elite few of ancient and modern Europe and North America; therefore, we hear the common catchphrase "Western democracy." Democracy is portrayed with folktale regularity in the academy, popular culture and letters as moving from the centre to the periphery. From "cultural" centres of "civilization" like Athens, Paris, Washington, and London democracy is described as radiating out to the outer world like the rays of a purifying white light. According to these accounts democracy is not associated with non-European or non-Western peoples,[2] and importantly with the way of life and governance of many different people historically and today, in theory and in practice.

The popular view of democracy as primarily a process rings hollow in my ears and in my heart. It conflicts and contrasts with, and is contradicted by critical democratic theories and practices of democracy, and by the world and the word of many Fourth World or Original peoples. I can't help but marvel at the brazen audacity of some Western nations, who use "democracy" as a semantic Trojan horse to hide the psychotic[3] corporate captains of transnational capital inside.

Behind this cloak of decency, of self-proclaimed "democracy," most industrialised "democratic" nations pursue their historic and continuing war for market expansion, oppression and domination. Arguably the result has been the commoditisation of Third- and Fourth-world suffering, human-to-human alienation, the decline of local communities,[4] and the continued conquest of the peoples of the Fourth World and exploitation of the land, air, and water and all living beings (Bobiwash, 2001; Chomsky, in Hill, 2001). Within these same "democratic" nations, disparities of opportunity, treatment, and personal wealth have arguably reached new levels, or remain disturbingly inequitable. Industrial and military pollution, prisons overpopulated with Black, Aboriginal and the poor, homelessness, poor underfed children without adequate health care or educational opportunities, union busting, layoffs, executive compensation, and rampant corporate malfeasance all speak to the undemocratic content of self-declared democratic nations. In short, inequity and injustice, and environmental destruction and devastation continue at an alarming pace within these self-declared democracies throughout the world. Despite these realities Freedom House, a high profile non-government organisation created to monitor "freedom" and "democracy" by the likes of early supporters such as Eleanor Roosevelt and Wendell Wilkie, endorses 112 nations as electoral democracies and very generously anoints 89 nations as maintaining the content of democracy as they construct it.[5]

The Language Game: What Is Democracy?

Is "democracy" a language game? There is no consensus on "democracy" and what it means. The Oxford English dictionary defines the term simply as "government by the people." "Democracy" is often used to describe the process, procedures and content of group decision making, leaders and approaches to leadership with a stress on process and a neglect of content. According to Bertolo (1997) the term *democracy* which was coined by its enemies

> is inappropriate as *kratos* means domination or force exercised by one part of society over another, while legitimate authority is *arkhe*. It would thus be more correct to speak of demarchy than democracy and maybe *acracy* than anarchy. (Bertolo, 1997, ft. 22)

Democracy could be said to be an empty vehicle to be filled with meaning through reflection, dialogue and experience. Michael Apple (2002) characterises democracy as a contested concept and that the "use automatically presupposes ongoing dialogue with other competing meanings" (Apple, 2002, p. 14).

Dewey (1938) was one of the first twentieth century non-Original peoples to argue that democracy is a way of life.[6] He also quipped that different democracies can represent different people and suggested we could differentiate democracies by asking the following telling questions: which people's interest are served and represented, why and how (Dewey, 1937)? Miles Horton co-founder of the Highlander Folk School[7] tells us in *The Long Haul* (1990) that he could never define democracy because "it's a growing idea." Rousseau (1978) proposed that democracy was the social expression of the intrinsically egalitarian nature of humankind. In contrast, according to Marx, democracy was a capitalist construction and was simply a transitory phase in world history, waiting to be supplanted by socialism (Muhlberger & Payne, 1993).

The meaning of democracy, it would seem, then, could be said to be socially constructed and contextual. One could also argue that democracy is constantly under reconstruction. There are competing definitions and expectations of democracy. Some definitions of democracy are epistemically privileged and others are contained. Macedo argues that democracy is a pervasive literalism that disguises our social, economic, and political realities (Macedo, 2003). Fotopoulos (1997) states today's democracy is a "flagrant distortion of the intended meaning." He passionately argues that democracy should be participatory and dedicated to realising social justice.

Noam Chomsky (1987) also speaks of "the complicit…inherent hypocrisy of contemporary democracy." Chomsky (1987), in his book *On Power and Ideology*, offers one of many of his definitions of democracy that he seems to develop extemporaneously and sprinkle like rough gems throughout his writing and interviews.

> Democracy…refers to a system of government in which elite elements based in the business community control the state by virtue of their dominance of private society, while the population observes quietly. So understood democracy is a system of elite decision and public ratification, as in the United States itself. Corresponding popular involvement in the formation of public policy is considered a serious threat. (p. 6)

Castoriadis (1996) makes a distinction between democracy as a "regime" and as a "procedure." Democracy has also been described as possessing content, as well as being both a destination and a journey. There are arguably also different aspects and degrees of democracy. Democracy is also described paradoxically as being about liberation and control.

Watson and Barber (1988) comment on the contradictory nature of democracy, noting that it is "most often the product of wisdom and blood, of reason and violence." Democracy is often described as messy and noisy, and as being "deeply rooted in talk" (Watson & Barber, 1988, p. xvii), and Montesquieu (1752/1914) told us this is because where there is "orderly silence" there is "tyranny"(pp. 140–141).

Democracy then is not a zero-sum equation. For some it exists as part of their daily life and is associated with social justice, and for others it is simply a process. For some an ideal to struggle towards, and for others still, it seems to represent a somewhat abstract and demeaned, yet integral part of their national mythology or story—a democracy story or myth that often serves as the rhetorical wellspring of their pride in their nation or communities. Thus, for many adults and children democracy is a vague distant notion, a label defined by their own nation's practices, institutions and history, and not to be applied to "others." Democracy is most often described as difficult to achieve but worth struggling for. De Tocqueville (1835) described democracy as a levelling process for wearing down hierarchy. Democracy could then be also described as being about hope and commitment, power, possibility and promise.

Democracy is most often defined in academic discourse by process, rather than by content.[8] There is no shortage of political scientists, philosophers, economists, and educationists attempting to define, analyze, compare and contrast definitions of democracy. Many of their definitions are stipulative or conversely ambiguous and persuasive. Many attempts to define democracy also seem complicated by the differences between how it exists in theory and how it exists in practice; and further, by how it existed in "classical" Greece, and how it exists in contemporary nations, societies, communities, and organisations around the world today.

Unsurprisingly, many academic writers and researchers on democracy seem to take great relish in describing the "Classical Athenian democracy" as both a model and an ideal. In their starry-eyed retelling, Athens sounds a lot like what many hard liberal commentators would like to realise for their nations, with its "ideals"[9] of political participation, strong sense of community, the sovereignty of the people, and equality of all citizens under the law (Ober & Hedrick, 1996). This classical Athenian ideal, so beloved of Western writers on democracy, stands in stark contrast to the practice of individualistic capitalist power politics in modern representative democracies (and in complimentary shading to the Haudenosaunee conception of democracy which I will introduce later), which stress the procedural nature of representative democratic governance over the participatory and community based ideals of Athens. Attempts to expand the criteria for democracy demonstrate that it makes some sense to talk about *degrees* of democracy based on content and process rather than neatly dividing states or organisations into categories of democracies and non-democracies. Arguably, it makes sense to think that classrooms, pedagogies, and pedagogues, schools, and theories may come in different degrees of democracy. What do we learn if we begin to look at education and schools in this way? However what is the highest degree, or ideal we should use to judge our schools, organisations, leaders and governments? Who names it? Who are the custodians of the democratic ideal(s) in our society?

A Critical Red Conception of Democracy

For me an organisation, community, or nation can only be said to be truly democratic when it realises the process related ideals of generalised participation in decision-making and the content goal of peace, as defined as the presence of social, economic, and environmental justice. I refer to this democracy as critical red democracy. Goodman (1992) articulated a similar expanded notion of democracy, which he refers to as "critical democracy." His theory of critical participatory democracy, like Paulo Freire's (2004), is dependent upon the dialogic process, which brings the voices of the oppressed and marginalised to the table at the moment of decision-making as subjects and honouring their words in the world. However, it is the core qualities related to social, economic, and environmental justice that distinguish a critical democracy.

> Critical democracy also implies moral commitment to promote the "public good" over any individual's right to accumulate privilege and power. In this sense, it suggests strong values for equality and social justice. As a result critical democracy presupposes that social arrangements will be developed within a socio-historical context. When groups of people have suffered historically from economic, social, and/or psychological oppression, there are accepted responsibilities to alter current social arrangements to redress previous inequalities, whether these are based upon class, race, religion, ethnic, heritage, gender, or sexual preference. Critical democracy also suggests the extension of this responsibility beyond the borders of any particular state; that is, it recognises the interdependence of all life forms on this planet, and therefore implies a commitment to the welfare of all people and other living species that inhabit the earth. (Goodman, 1992, pp. 7–8)

Goodman and others who write in support of critical democracy are following a long and distinguished tradition in many Fourth-World communities today and going back thousands of years in others. For example, the Huadenosaunee democracy could serve as an ideal of democracy that could supplant the classical Greek ideal, or the popular view of democracy. Of course, the

Haudenosaunee democracy is just one example of many possible diverse sources of democratic inspiration and example for establishing contextualised or localised approaches to democracy as a way of life and governance. Exploring, celebrating, and struggling towards the Haudenosaunee ideals of democracy might possibly have a contagious and expansive effect on the participation of youth and non-dominant and marginalised groups in organisations and local, regional, national, and international civic and political society.

Critical Red Democracy: An Alternative Radical Grand Narrative

Before contact and to the present day the Haudenosaunee democratic ideal was of a participatory democracy with an equitable distribution of economic, political, and social power, an inclusive social, economic, political, and environmental democracy, with an ideal trinity of protection, provision, and participation for its entire people. A "confederation" of distinct peoples who arguably achieved and continue to practice a freedom from wants and fear, and a freedom to speak, think and act that was the envy of many "enlightened" people who encounter(ed) them.[10] Many more people and thinkers on democracy were first introduced to the Haudenosaunee through the eyes and words of writers like Rousseau (1978), Thomas More (1516/1929), Karl Marx and Frederick Engels (1884/1942) and Benjamin Franklin (in Johansen, 1982). From the rich and varied primary source records it is clear the Haudenosaunee achieved a remarkable level of inter-tribal peace, prosperity and "social justice."[11] Agriculturists, democrats, diplomats, keen observers of mother earth and her teachings, the women and men of the Haudenosaunee were sometimes romanticised in early colonial accounts, yet not nearly as often as they fell to the colonial strategies of discipline, assimilation and ultimately attempted extermination.

As rigorously documented in the histories of the Haudenosaunee by Johansen (1990) and Oromo peoples of Ethiopia by Legasse (2000), there is mounting evidence to challenge Western claims to historical precedence or superiority in the procedure and organisation of representational democracy. Similarly, Spring (2001) also recently argued "from evidence" of a strong historic respect for human rights in Muslim, Hindu, and Confucian "civilisations," and the ongoing and inexorable interchange of ideas between the West and the "others." Spring unfortunately fails to take into account the "asymmetrical power relations" (McLaren & Giroux, 1997; Young, 1990) between nations, civilisations, cultures, and individuals that has resulted in an "inequitable global flow" of credit and claim to democracy, and its core qualities.

The continuing and historic contributions of Fourth-World peoples to the conceptualisation, approach, procedure, and content of a range of democratic ideals, warrants broader public, academic, and intellectual recognition, nurturance, and critical celebration in our governments, academies, workplaces, schools, classrooms, texts, and discussions. The Haudenosaunee see values as shared principles that guide a good mind, good decisions and the good life. First among the democratic values is the importance of the participation of all members of the group and their thinking in decision making. Thinking is to be done collectively, with all decisions made by consensus. All people and points of view must be heard and respected including the interests of the coming seven generations and maintaining respect for the past seven generations.

For a discussion of the highly convincing evidence on the influence of the Haudenosaunee on the constitution of the United States the reader should refer to the well researched and engaging works of Grinde (1977), Johansen (1982, 1998), Bagley & Ruckman (1983), and Calloway (1995).The influence of Aboriginal "civilizations" on a progressive "democratic' spectrum of writers and thinkers, including Utopians, anarchists, syndicalists, feminists, suffragettes, guild socialists, Marxists, environmentalists and Federalists to name but a few sects of, or approaches to, democracy is richly detailed in primary sources. However, this "influence" is often neglected or ignored in the mainstream secondary literature on democracy and in the media (Johansen, 1998).

I hope that a short exploration of the example of the living Haudenosaunee democratic ideal, and its historic and continuing potential for influence on the practice, organisation, and philosophy of democracy will help the reader transcend the endemic cultural democratic myopia that serves to essentialise and mythologise democracy as a European legacy to the world, a legacy that erroneously ties democracy as a regime and process to Western "representative democracies" and their predatory transnational military-industrial-liberal economies. I recognise that my efforts to use Haudenosaunee democracy as a comparative ideal (based on historic and living experience) will be resisted by some readers. As Forbes states, the imperial "denial" of "Native American intellectual influences" is a "cardinal act of faith in European superiority" (1990). I am preparing myself for a baptism in Eurohegemonic fire. Even the stodgy national newspaper of "multicultural Canada," *The Globe and Mail* can be counted on to guard the Eurocanon by questioning the existence of the Haudenosaunee Peacemaker Deganiwidah and their long history of democracy, because "most experts don't think they really existed" (17 August 2002). I can't help but remain mindful that while the "Noble Savage" was "idealised" and even idolised by the great white fathers of democracy, they were "being slaughtered to make silence and way for progress" (Grinde, 1990, p. 48)

Haudenosaunee democratic tradition is a living ideal of democracy supportive of the transformative praxis of critical pedagogues and a source of philosophic inspiration and practical foundation for a redemptive democratisation of educational philosophy (Grande,2004). Haudenosaunee democracy is inspired by inclusion, voice and participation, and founded upon a vision of peace, as the presence of economic and social justice, and the importance of reverence for, and the need to uphold a respectful custodianship of the air, water, land, and all animal life. A democracy that makes all decisions based on their possible benefits and consequences for the "coming faces" of seven generations, a democracy where even the voices of unborn children are heard and answered in peace, protection, provision, and participation. Although conscious of the problems of portraying the Haudenosaunee nation, history, and people in monolithic terms, an overview of the ideals of the Haudenosaunee democracy or way of life offers a valuable illustration of an alternative approach to democracy, as both a process founded on voice and expressed through a content stressing peace and social, environmental and economic justice.

The Peacemaker (Deganiwidah), the founder of the Haudenosaunee nation (AD 1100), carried withnin the message of Kaianeraserakowa (The Great Law of Peace).The Huron Peacemaker came to the Haudenosaunee with his message of Skennen (Peace), Kariwiio (The Good Word), and Kasatensera (Strength),which contains the principles of peace, equality, respect, love, and justice. All members of the Haudenosaunee are expected to be responsible to every other member past, present and future. This responsibility is to all members no matter their age or status. Responsibility and duty begins with service to the family, creation, clan, nation, and the

Confederacy. Because each individual is a reflection of the group and creation they are asked to value and care for themselves without being egotistical and possessive or acquisitive. In fact, all labour and the results of all labour must be shared. Reality for the Haudenosaunee is also a collective ideal, with reality represented as a shared conception achieved only when a shared perception by all members (Johansen,1998, p. 171). This shared or communal sense of reality is referred to as *Ethno niiohtonha k ne onkwa Nikon:ra* (Now our minds are on one path). All gifts of the creator including special talents or abilities must be used to the benefit of the collective. The Haudenosaunee are also responsible for being observant, like the Far Seeing Eagle atop the Great Tree of Peace. They must be alert to changes in the environment and dangers on the horizon that may affect their neighbours, community, any relation (all people) and Mother Earth or themselves. One way to be observant is to listen carefully, a skill honoured as greatly as the power to speak.

One of the best ways to understand the Haudenosaunee is to look at what is being right minded among the Haudenosaunee. One of the most admired qualities of the right-minded individual is their desire to share and be generous with others. The right-minded Haudenosaunee is respectful of every person, creature and thing and is prepared at all times to offer their labour and ideas in cooperation with others. They honour others before themselves and give their love freely to all people. They offer hospitality to all people and living spirits in need and out of kindness to every person of the Four Colours and from the Four Sacred Directions. The right minded live in peace with all people and leave only the faintest prints on the earth where they have trod to mark their passing. They must live in balance and harmony with nature, at all times considering the impact of their actions on the earth and all living beings including the sun, moon, earth, winds, and rain, and the living spirit in animals, plants, water, winds, and even minerals (Six Nations, 2003). The righteous Haudenosaunee give thanks for all that they receive from the creator and others and is not covetous or insincere in their appreciation for even the humblest gift of other living being and living spirits.

Conclusions

Discussions of democracy are rich in practical and theoretical possibilities for policy makers and public educators struggling daily to provide our children democracy in education, and an education for democracy. Dialogue on democracy helps us get our moral heads straight, to identify the sources of doubt, the ambiguities, contradictions, controversies, failures and successes, constraints and possibilities.

The grand narrative song of "Western democracy" dominates, demeans, and degrades our understanding of the possibility and true nature of democracy. And so it has been the goal of this paper to focus critical red light on democracy on the word and the world, to journey along with the reader from Doxa to Logos, from the workhouse to the Longhouse.

Will we find the "quasi religious" path or inspiration in democracy that Stanford ecologist Paul Erlich (1986) theorises that we must locate to work our way out of our destructive way of life which threatens to irreparably poison our air, water and land, and threaten human and animal and plant survival? The biophilia, or literally love of life, that Harvard Biologist E. O. Wilson

(1984) theorises that we must uncover and nurture within ourselves and our society if we and our Mother Earth are to survive? Can we start by raising the bar on what it means for an institution, state, or education system to be considered democratic? By adopting an ideal that stresses a substantive content of economic, social, and ecological justice, as well as procedures, that favour direct generalised participation and dialogue over elite representation and cooperation over competition, we may just survive. The only thing worth struggling for as educators, as people, are ideals, but we must first make sure the ideals are worth struggling for. Is democracy as popularly constructed worth struggling for, or, dying for?

Even if democracy is only a language game, should we all not be playing? The Peacemaker of the Haudenosaunee taught us that even unborn children should be playing, for democracy is about the past, present and future, about hopes, and possibilities. I believe educators must take the lead in analysing, revitalising, debating, and reclaiming a resuscitated approach to and understanding of democracy. Our classrooms and schools should be sites where the core qualities, values and possibilities of democracy are discussed, and experienced. The social, economic, and ecological injustices we face together on our shared planet can only be ameliorated through a revitalised deliberative and participative democracy struggling for a clear core set of content-based democratic ideals. As Dewey reminded us, schools are laboratories for the study of different theories of democracy, not just the popular view.

> Think not of yourselves, O Chiefs, nor of your own generation.
> Think of continuing generations of our families,
> think of our grandchildren and of those yet unborn,
> whose faces are coming from beneath the ground
>
> —THE PEACEMAKER OF THE HAUDENOSAUNEE

Notes

1. I am using critical "red" democracy in recognition of Sandy Grande's (2004) recent book *Red Pedagogy* which explores the synergies embedded in the commonalities and differences within critical democratic pedgagogy and indigineous ways of knowing, learning, living, and deciding.
2. See Mulberger & Payne(1993). Democracy's Place in World History, *Journal of World History*, Vol. 4, No. 1. pp. 23–45 and Price, J. *Reclaiming Democracy for the Longschoolhouse* (Unpublished doctoral thesis). Toronto, ON: University of Toronto, 2004.
3. See the documentary film, *The Corporation*, where Joel Bakan et al. compare the Diagnostic and Statistical Manual's definition of psychotic with the public actions and stated policies and positions of Corporations.
4. Tönnies (1957) outlined the inherent contradiction between capitalist social relations and the development of community based on a sense of belonging, custom and tradition. In his concept of *gemeinshaft*, community respect is mutual and innate in all social relations which are not based primarily upon utilitarian or economic association. In contrast *gesellschaft* communities are characterised by predatory competitive legal relations where "others" are simply a means to an economic end. Where neighbour becomes client, customer, or potential customer, employee, or investor, and all are treated mechanically, as profit-making capital units devoid of intellectual, cultural, social, spiritual and ecological value.

5. Freedom House in effect reinforces the popular view of democracy by stressing good governance and rule of law (processes) over content such as distribution of wealth, and environmental custodianship policies for example.

6. It should also be noted that for Dewey (1954) the philosophic basis of democracy was the expression of a pragmatic and productive spirit, while for the Haudenosaunee democracy is both the gift and the natural expression of the spiritual and the inherent human desire for peace and justice. In fairness, Dewey also offers an ethical argument for democracy as the most "humane condition" in *Experience and Education*.

7. Freire (1970) held the Highlander Folk School up as an example of an empowering democratic school. For Horton the purpose of education was to empower individuals to think and act for themselves and to challenge social injustice. He worked alongside black civil rights leaders including Martin Luther King, Rosa Parks, and Andrew Young, and poor white Appalachian mine workers.

8. For example: a reading of some Western writers on democracy turned up the following attempts to define or describe features of democracy: (a) it is "not majority rule: democracy [is] diffusion of power, representation of interests, recognition of minorities" (John Calhoun, as paraphrased by Roper, 1998, p. 63); (b) "government by the people; that form of government in which the sovereign power resides in the people as a whole, and is exercised either directly by them...or by officers elected by them" (Oxford English Dictionary, 1933); (c) "a form of institutionalization of continual conflicts...[and] of uncertainty, of subjecting all interests to uncertainty. . . ." (Przeworski, 1986, p. 58); (d) a regime that is "first and foremost a set of procedural rules for arriving at collective decisions in a way which accommodates and facilitates the fullest possible participation of interested parties" (Bobbio, 1987, p. 19); (e) "a system of governance in which rulers are held accountable for their actions in the public realm by citizens, acting indirectly through the competition and cooperation of their elected representatives" (Schmitter & Karl 1991, 76); (f) "a state where political decisions are taken by and with the consent, or the active participation even, of the majority of the People....[L]iberalism, though recognizing that in the last resort the 'legal majority' must prevail, tries to protect the minorities as it does the civil rights of the individual, and by much the same methods....Liberal democracy is *qualified* democracy. The ultimate right of the majority to have its way is conceded, but that way is made as rough as possible" (Finer 1997, pp. 1568–1570); (g) characterised by providing "opportunities for (1) effective participation, (2) equality in voting, (3) gaining enlightened understanding, (4) exercising final control [by the people—WR] over the agenda, and (5) inclusion of adults"; (h) political institutions that are necessary to pursue these goals are "(1) elected officials, (2) free, fair and frequent elections, (3) freedom of expression, (4) alternative sources of information, (5) associational autonomy, and (6) inclusive citizenship" (Dahl 1998, 38 & 85); (i) democracy is "governance by leaders whose authority is based on a limited mandate from a universal electorate that selects among genuine alternatives and has some rights to political participation and opposition" (Danziger, 1998, p. 159).

9. Largely unrealised goals. The exclusionary nature of Athenian "citizenship" is a sharp contrast to the equitable participation in Haudenosaunee democracy with its empowered participation of women and youth, and the absence of property or racial qualifications for full "citizenship" and suffrage.

10. Alfred, 1995; Austin, 1986; Bagley & Ruckman, 1983; Bruchac, 1995; Burton, 1983; Calloway, 1995; Cassidy, 1995; Churchill, 1993; Deloria & Lytle, 1983; Grinde & Johansen, 1995, 1996; Grinde, 1977, 1993; Hirschfelder, 1995; Howard & Rubin, 1995; Jaimes-Guerrero, 1995; Johansen, Grinde & Mann, 1996; Johansen, 1982; Joseph, 1995; Loewen, 1995; Markoff, 1996; Mihesuah, 1996; Parillo, 1996; Pommersheim, 1995; Pratt, 1996; Steinem, et al.,1998; Wagner, 1996; Zimmerman, 1996

11. See references in footnote 10.

Bibliography

Alfred, G.R. (1995). *Heeding the voices of our ancestors: Kahnawake Mohawk politics and the rise of Native nationalism.* Toronto: Oxford University Press.

Apple, M. (2002). Patriotism, pedagogy, and freedom: On the educational meanings of September 11. http://www.tcrecord.org/

Austin, A. (1986) *Ne'Ho Niyo' De: No': That's what it was like.* Lackawanna, NY: Rebco Enterprises.

Bagley, C., & Ruckman, J.A. (1983). Iroquois contributions to modern democracy and communism. *American Indian Culture & Research Journal, 7*(2), 53–72.

Bakan, J. (2004). The corporation: The pathological pursuit of profit and power. (unpublished manuscript).

Bertolo, A. (2002). Democracy and beyond. *Democracy & Nature: The International Journal of Inclusive Democracy, 8*(1). http://www.democracynature. org/dn/vol5/bertol09democracy.htm

Bobbio. N. (1987). *The future of democracy.* Minneapolis: University of Minnesota Press.

Bobiwash, R. (2001). Cultural diversity in the age of globalisation. http://www. cwis.org/260fge/rbinternet.html.

Bruchac, J. (Ed.). (1995). *New voices from the longhouse.* Greenfield, NY: Greenfield Press.

Burton, B. A.(1983). *Hail! Nene Karenna, the hymn: A novel on the founding of the Five Nations, 1550–1590.* Rochester, NY: Security Dupont Press.

Calloway, C. G.(1995). *The American Revolution in Indian country: Crisis and diversity in Native American communities.* Cambridge, UK: Cambridge University Press.

Cassidy, J.J., Jr. (1995). *Through Indian eyes: The untold story of Native American peoples.* Pleasantville, NY: Readers Digest Association.

Castoriadis, C. (1996). The democracy of procedure and of regime. *Democracy and Nature, 1* (March), 221–241.

Chase, J. S. (1983). Review of Johansen, forgotten founders (1982)]. *History: Reviews of New Books, 11*(8), 181–193.

Chomsky, N. (1987). *On power and ideology.* New York: South End Press.

Churchill, W. (1993). *From a native son.* Boston: South End Press.

Colden, C. (1902). *History of the Five Indian Nations [1765].* New York: New Amsterdam Books Company

Dahl, R. (1998). *On democracy.* New Haven, CT: Yale University Press.

de Tocqueville, A. (1835/2001). *Democracy in America.* New York: Signet Classic.

Deloria, V., Jr., & Lytle, C. (1983). *American Indians, American justice.* Austin, TX: University of Texas Press.

Dewey, J. (1938). *Experience and education.* New York: Collier Books.

Dewey, J. (1937/1958). Democracy and education in the world of today." in J. Dewey, *Philosophy of education: Problems of men,* pp. 34–45. Totawa, NJ: Littlefield, Adams.

Engles, F., & Marx, K. (1884/1942). *The origin of the family, private property and the state.* New York: International Publishers.

Erlich, P. (1986). *The machinery of nature.* New York: Simon Schuster.

Finer, S. (1997). *The history of government from the earliest times: The intermediate ages.* New York: Oxford University Press.

Fotopoulos, T. (1997). *Towards an inclusive democracy, the crisis of the growth economy and the need for a new liberatory project.* London, UK: Cassell.

Freire, P. (2004). *Pedagogy of indignation.* New York: Continuum

Goodman, J. (1992). *Elementary schooling for critical democracy.* Albany, NY: State University of New York Press.

Grande, S. (2004). *Red pedagogy: Native American social and political thought.* Lanham, MD: Rowman & Littlefield.

Graveline, F. J. (1998). *Circleworks: Transforming Eurocentric consciousness.* Nova Scotia: Fernwood Publishing

Grinde, D., & Johansen, B. E. (1995). *Ecocide of Native America: Environmental destruction of native lands and people.* Santa Fe, NM: Clear Light.

Grinde, D. (1977). *The Iroquois and the founding of the American Nation.* San Francisco: Indian Historian Press.

Grinde, D. A. Jr. (1993). The Iroquois and the development of American government. *Historical Reflections, 21*(2), 301–318.

Grinde, D. A., Jr. & Johansen, B. E. (1996). Sauce for the goose: Demand and definitions for "proof" regarding the Iroquois and democracy. *William & Mary Quarterly, 53*(3), 621–636.

Hill, P. (2001). Public education and moral monsters: A conversation with Noam Chomsky. *Our Schools/Our Selves*, January, 73–92.

Hirschfelder, A. (Ed.). (1995). *Native heritage: Personal accounts by American Indians, past and present.* New York: MacMillan.

Horton, M., & Freire, P. (Edited by B. Bell, J. Gaventa, & J. Peters). (1990). *We make the road by walking: Conversations on education and social change.* Philadelphia, PA: Temple University Press.

Johansen, B. (1982). *Forgotten founders: Benjamin Franklin, the Iroquois, and the rationale for the American revolution.* Ipswich, MA: Gambit.

Johansen, B. E., & Grinde, D. A. (1990, Summer). "The Debate Regarding Native American Precedents for Democracy: A Recent Historiography." *American Indian Culture & Research Journal 14*: 1, pp. 61-88.

Johansen, B. E., Grinde, D. A., Jr., & Mann, B. (1996). *Debating democracy: The Iroquois legacy of freedom.* Santa Fe, NM: Clear Light Publishers.

Joseph, J. A.(1995). *Remaking America: How the benevolent traditions of many cultures are transforming our national life.* San Francisco: Jossey-Bass.

Legesse, A. (2000). *Oromo democracy: An indigenous African political system.* Trenton, NJ: Red Sea Press.

Loewen, J. W. (1995). *Lies my teacher told me.* New York: The New Press.

Macedo, S. (2003). *Diversity and distrust: Civic education in a multicultural democracy.* Cambridge, MA: Harvard University Press.

Maracle, L.(1988). *I am woman: A native perspective on sociology and feminism* New York: Press Gang Publishers.

Markoff, J. (1996). *Waves of democracy: Social movements and political change.* Thousand Oaks, CA: Pine Forge Press.

McClaren, P., & Giroux, H. A. (1997). Writing from the margins: Geographies of identity, pedagogy, and power. In P. McClaren (ed.)., *Revolutionary multiculturalism: Pedagogies of dissent for the new millennium.* Boudler, CO: Westview Press.

McNeil, L. M. (2002). Private asset or public good: Education and democracy at the crossroads (Editor's introduction). *American Educational Research Journal, 39*(2), 243–248.

Mignolo, W. (2002). *The Zapatistas's theoretical revolution: Its historical, ethical, and political consequences.* Binghamton, NY: Fernand Braudel Center for the Study of Economies, Historical Systems, and Civilizations.

Mihesuah, D. A. (1996). *American Indians: Stereotypes and realities.* Atlanta, GA: Clarity Publishers.

Mohawk Nation. (1978). A basic call to consciousness: The Haudenosaunee address to the Western World. *Akwesasne Notes.* N.p.: n.d.

Montesquieu, C. (1752/1914). *The spirit of laws.* London, UK: J. Bell & Sons.

More, Thomas (1516). *Utopia.* Gutenberg Book Project, April 22, 2005 (eBook #2130) http://www.gutenberg.org/files/2130/2130-h/2130-h.htm

Mouffe, C. (2002). *Politics and passions: The stakes of democracy.* London, UK: Centre for the Study of Democracy.

Muhlberger, S. & Paine, P. (1993). Democracy's place in world history. *Journal of World History, 14*(1), 23–45.

Obder, J. & Hedrick, C. (1996). *Demokratia.* Princeton, NJ: Princeton University Press.

Pommersheim, F. (1995). *Braid of feathers: American Indian law and contemporary tribal life.* Berkeley: University of California Press.

Portelli, J., & Solomon, P. (Eds.). (2001). *The erosion of democracy in education.* Calgary, Canada: Detselig.

Pratt, S. L. (1996). The influence of the Iroquois on early American philosophy. *Transactions of the Charles S. Peirce Society, 32*(2), 275–314

Price, J. (2001). *Leading from and for the margins.* M.A. thesis. Ontario Institute for Studies in Education/University of Toronto.

Rousseau, J. J. (1762/1950). *Social contract.* G.D.H. Cole, trans.

Rousseau, J. J. (1762/1991) *Emile*, ed. Allan Bloom. London: Penguin.

Said, E. (1985). *Beginnings: Intention and method.* New York: Columbia University Press.

Simon, R. (2001) Introduction. In J. Portelli & P. Solomon (Eds.), *The erosion of democracy in education.* Calgary, Canada: Detselig.

Six Nations. (2003). *Haudenosaunee: People building a longhouse.* http://www. sixnations.org/

Spring, J. (2001). *Globalisation and educational rights: An intercivilizational analysis.* Mahwah, NJ: Lawrence Erlbaum.

Steinem, G., Mankiller, W., Navarro, M., Smith, B., & Mink, W. (1998). *Reader's guide to U.S. women's history*. Boston: Houghton Mifflin.

Tönnies, F. (1957). *Community and society: Gemeinschaft und gesellschaft*. (Trans. Charles P. Loomis). East Lansing, MI: Michigan State University Press.

Wagner, S. R. (1996). *The untold story of the Iroquois influence on early feminists: Essays by Sally Roesch Wagner*. Aberdeen, SD: Sky Carrier Press.

Watson, P., & Barber. (1988). *The struggle for democracy*. New York: Random House.

Weatherford, J. (1990). *Indian givers: How the Indians of the Americas transformed the world*. New York: Ballantine.

White, W. & Cook, P. (2001). Thunder-birds, thunder-beings, and thunder-voices: The application of traditional knowledge and children's rights in support of Aboriginal children's education. *American Review of Canadian Studies, 31*(1/2), 331–347.

Wilson, E. O. (1984). *Biophilia*. Cambridge, MA: Harvard University Press.

Zimmerman, R. (1996). *Native North America: Living wisdom*. Boston: Little-Brown.

This chapter originally appeared in *The Journal of Thought*, Vol. 42, No. 1 & 2 (Spring/Summer, 2007). Published here by permission of Caddo Gap Press.

CHAPTER TWENTY-FOUR

Delimiting the Debate

The Fordham's Attack on Democratic Values

Christopher Leahey

A new debate has emerged in educational circles on how to teach about the terrorist attacks of September 11, 2001, (9/11) and the subsequent U.S. invasions of Afghanistan and Iraq. Less than two months after 9/11, the American Council of Trustees and Alumni (ACTA), founded by Lynne Cheney, released a report titled "Defending Civilization: How Our Universities Are Failing America and What Can Be Done about It." Within this report, Anne Deal and Jerry Martin list 115 comments made at teach-ins, posted on Web sites, written on campus posters, and sung in protest songs. Administrators, professors, and students who voiced opposition to U.S. foreign policy as well as the invasion of Afghanistan were labeled radical and criticized for their moral relativism. Of particular concern to ACTA was the increase of college courses offered on Islam and terrorism. Rather than explore Islam and terrorism in a wider global context as a way to help students make sense of 9/11, ACTA called "upon colleges and universities to adopt strong core curricula that include rigorous, broad-based courses on the great works of Western civilization as well as courses on American history, America's founding documents, and America's continuing struggle to extend and defend the principles on which it was founded" (Martin and Deal 2001, 8).

If we can agree that a "democracy is more than a form of government; it is primarily a mode of associated living, of conjoint communicated experience," then it follows that our pedagogy must reflect our shared democratic values (Dewey 1944, 87). Democratic social education, broadly defined, consists of several interdependent concepts. First, democratic education recognizes teachers and students as rational people who possess the capacity to make decisions, reflect on their experiences, think critically, and act (Dewey 1944; NCSS 1994; Sorensen 1996). Second, democratic education supports young people in developing value systems and drawing on those systems in creating knowledge and presenting arguments (Matthews 1996; Newmann,

Bertocci, and Landsness 1977). Third, democratic pedagogy charges students with the responsibility to participate in our nation's political system in meaningful ways (Barber 2000; Saxe 1997). Fourth, democratic education posits that "alternative social arrangements to the status quo exist and are worthwhile" (Schor 1992; quoted in Wood 1998, 187). It is these four tenets of democratic pedagogy that I hold up as democratic ideals in the following analysis of the Thomas B. Fordham Institute's *Terrorists, Despots, and Democracy: What Our Children Need to Know* (Agresto et al. 2003).

Overview of Terrorists, Despots, and Democracy

Terrorists, Despots, and Democracy (TDD) is one of several publications produced by the Fordham Institute that are designed to influence social studies instruction. In the months after 9/11, the National Association of School Psychologists, the American Red Cross, the National Educational Association, the National Council for the Social Studies, and an online journal called *Rethinking Schools* provided a rich, yet distinctive, body of educational materials, ideas, and lessons related to terrorism and war. In the introduction to *TDD*, Chester E. Finn Jr. sharply criticizes those organizations for being "relativistic, non-judgmental (except about the United States), pacifist, and anything but patriotic" (Finn 2003, 9). A collection of twenty-eight brief essays written by historians, politicians, members of private institutes, and classroom teachers, *TDD* is prescriptive in its approach as it identifies the appropriate documents, articulates appropriate perspectives, and outlines the appropriate methods that should be drawn on when one is teaching about September 11 and the U.S. invasions of Afghanistan and Iraq. The short essays featured in *TDD* consist of four problematic themes: (1) American exceptionalism is an appropriate framework from which to study international conflict; (2) the September 11 terrorist attacks were an attack on American democratic ideals; (3) the wars in Afghanistan and Iraq are supported by just war theory; and (4) the doctrine of preemption is the only viable solution to international terrorism. Taken together, the themes serve to stifle debate about the meaning and causes of September 11, the legitimacy of the war in Iraq, and the Bush doctrine of preemption.

Theme 1: American Exceptionalism as Framework for Teaching about September 11 and the Middle East Conflict

American exceptionalism is a concept introduced in Alexis de Tocqueville's *Democracy in America*. In his five-year (1835–1840) stay in the United States, the French politician believed that the United States was unique in its representative democracy, egalitarianism, liberty, and individualism. Those who subscribe to American exceptionalism believe that the history of the United States has been exceptional in that it has largely been insulated from European conflicts stemming from feudalism, social revolutions, ethnic strife, and nationalism. Trevor McCrisken (2003) contends that American exceptionalism has two strands. The first strand represents the United States as an exemplary nation as signified by dictums such as "city on a hill," "nonentangling alliances," "anti-imperialism," "isolationism," and "fortress America." The other, often more dominant strand, is that of a missionary nation, as represented by such dictums as "manifest destiny," "imperialism," "leader of the free world," and "new world order" (McCrisken 2003, 2).

Both strands of American exceptionalism are woven throughout *TDD*. Lynne Cheney, Andrew Rotherham, Katherine Kersten, and Lucien Ellington illustrate the first strand, in which the United States is cast as an exemplary nation, contending that in educating our children about terrorism, we should center our instruction on traditional American heroes (for example, Patrick Henry, George Washington, Thomas Jefferson, Elizabeth Cady Stanton, and Martin Luther King Jr., among others) and salient historical documents (for example, the Declaration of Independence, the Constitution, the Federalist Papers, Emancipation Proclamation, Gettysburg Address, and Washington's Farewell Address). In an essay titled "How to Stop Worrying and Love American Exceptionalism," Sheldon Stern argues that we must abandon the multicultural perspective that has "[b]ecome a rationalization for the most reactionary forces in the world today" (Stern 2003, 59). In place of a multicultural perspective that explores the diversity of American experiences, Stern argues that we must teach the history and significance of American constitutionalism in an effort "provide our students with the knowledge they need to understand and preserve their freedom" (59).

The second strand of American exceptionalism, depicting the United States as not only exceptional but also as a missionary nation, is also present within *TDD*. In addition to underscoring unique history and civic ideals of the United States, the authors of *TDD* suggest that social studies educators should also recognize that the United States has a unique responsibility to "take up arms to defend our freedoms against those who have sought to take them away, to deprive others of their freedom, or to prevent others from forming a free society" (Stotsky and Schnidman 2003, 84–85). In his essay titled "Seizing This Teachable Moment," William Bennett echoes these sentiments:

> In the wake of the slaughter that took place two years ago, America was handed a unique opportunity to educate children in this country—and elsewhere—about the meanings and methods of democracy, the very meanings that inspire the wrath of our enemies who hate how we do things as much as our purposes for doing them.
>
> As I write this, children in Iraq are seeing the hand of democracy at work for the first time. We are rebuilding schools and cities, re-opening schools and restoring justice. The pinnacle of reconstruction in Iraq will be the establishment of government of, by, and for the Iraqi people. But it took our liberation with military might to actually begin this process. (Bennett 2003, 40)

Working from within the parameters of American exceptionalism, Bennett, in his discussion of September 11 and the U.S. mission to bring democracy and stability to Iraq, glosses over the intense domestic and international debates that took place before the war. Bennett's description of America's democratizing mission also fails to explain why U.S. troops have faced intense resistance throughout the occupation.

Although the authors of *TDD* direct teachers to explore those unique, positive qualities of American history, there are many negative qualities embedded within American history. Seymour Martin Lipset (1996) points out that American exceptionalism is a double-edged sword. He indicates that America's negative traits "such as income inequality, high crime rates, low levels of electoral participation, a powerful tendency to moralize which at times verges on intolerance toward political and ethnic minorities, are inherently linked to the norms and behavior of an open democratic society that seems so admirable" (Lipset 1996, 13). Tocqueville himself was cognizant of those American qualities that were antidemocratic. In commenting on how the American majority "raises formidable barriers around liberty of opinion," Tocqueville commented, "I know of no country in which there is so little independence of mind and real freedom of discussion as in America" (de Tocqueville 1988, 263). Yet, when events incompatible with the spirit of American democracy are mentioned in *TDD*, they are either dismissed as "nonsense" (as Chester Finn Jr. does of Michael Apple's suggestion to set September 11 within the context of U.S. global policies) or taken up in a way that supports American exceptionalism. For instance, Kenneth Weinstein argues that the injustices of slavery can be used as a historical example of how Americans were guilty of "looking away from tyranny" (Weinstein 2003, 26). Just as slavery "coarsened one's sensibilities…to the point that the worst injustices became tolerable," Weinstein warns us, "Americans have similarly inured themselves to the existence of tyrannies across the globe" (Weinstein 2003, 26). Thus, slavery is a useful instructional topic, not because it underscores the brutality of hundreds of years of institutionalized American slavery but because it highlights our capacity for complacency about tyranny and the need to transform "an era of relative isolation" into one "of unparalleled interventionism" (26).

The complexity of September 11 and the wars in Afghanistan and Iraq cannot be grasped from the framework of American exceptionalism because it limits the routes of exploration to those that fit neatly within the U.S. geographical borders. Ian Tyrell (1991) suggests that a global outlook for studying American history is necessary because American life has become increasingly influenced by interdependent economic relations, the development of communication systems and technology, global environmental constraints, systems of alliances, the development of international organizations, and the growth of international legal obligations (Tyrell 1991, 1044). Adopting a global outlook requires us to take a broader perspective in studying September 11 and the U.S. invasions of Afghanistan and Iraq. It requires America's exceptional qualities to be part of a larger study that includes global economics, previous U.S. interventions in the Middle East, international law, and religious doctrine.

Working from the framework of American exceptionalism also distorts history because those concepts that do not fit within the story of American progress—for example, the Alien and Sedition Acts of 1798, the internment of Japanese Americans in World War II, the McCarthyism of the cold war, or the political scandals of Watergate and the Iran-Contra Affair—are often pushed to the margins or altogether disregarded. Writing about the discord between the realities of colonial life and the historical record as it is shaped by American exceptionalism, Appleby relates the following:

> The exotic cultures of Africans and native Americans could not be incorporated into American history, for those peoples' very claims to have culture would have subverted the story of progress. The self-conscious crafters of American identity took great pride in freedom of religion, but the major religious figures of the colonial era, the Puritans of New England, openly embraced orthodoxy—banishing dissidents, whipping Baptists, even executing four Quakers. And so it went with free speech. Congress composed a Bill of Rights guaranteeing free speech, but colonial legislators had been much more likely to jail their critics than to protect their speech. And then there was the elaboration of slave codes by colonial legislators. How were those laws to be integrated into the teleology of peculiarly free people? (Appleby 1992, 425)

Just as American exceptionalism diverts attention away from the contradictions of colonial life, it also diverts our attention away from the contradictions of contemporary life. Working within the parameters of American exceptionalism, the authors of the essays found in *TDD* paper over such controversial issues as the detention and treatment of suspected terrorists at Guantanamo Bay, the no-bid military contracts awarded to the Haliburton Company, and the U.S. support of the Saudi royal family. Moreover, such controversial issues demonstrate that September 11 is much more complex than the parameters of American exceptionalism permit.

In the end, the authors of the essays found within *TDD* do not explain why American exceptionalism is an appropriate lens for studying recent events or how it promotes democratic education. Instead, the essays reflect the assumptions that students are not being taught about their democratic heritage, that the current state of instruction is a threat to our survival, and that the September 11 attacks were attacks on the U.S. commitment to freedom and democracy. Rather than limiting our study of the events of September 11 to America's exceptional qualities, Eric Foner, the prominent historian, contends that in teaching about the attacks, "[w]e need an historical framework that eschews pronouncements about our own superiority and prompts greater self-consciousness among Americans and greater knowledge of those arrayed against us" (Foner 2003, 31). Such an approach creates space for a pedagogy that widens the scope of study to include the positive and negative aspects of U.S. history and prompts us to explore U.S. history in a larger global context. Having outlined the framework of *TDD*, I now examine the other dominant themes found within the report.

Theme 2: September 11 Was an Attack on American Democratic Values

In reference to the terrorist attacks of September 11, Chester Finn Jr. writes, "In an instant we understood that the American ideals of freedom, tolerance, and individual self-determination were themselves under attack" (Finn 2003, 19). Echoing those sentiments, John Argesto contends that "Part of the reason of the worldwide attack on American ideals is so serious and so *radical* [his emphasis] is that our enemies well know that much of what we are—our libertinism, our materialism, our lack of respect for traditional values, our subordination for what they see as Divine Will—result from the very principles we hold dear, including individual liberty, equality, democracy, general prosperity, and a belief in human progress" (Agresto 2003, 76). In assuming American values to be the cause of the September 11 attacks, the authors of *TDD* limit their discussion of terrorism to specific attacks on American interests: Flight 103, the World Trade Center, the Pentagon, and the attacks on American embassies in Tanzania and Kenya. The *TDD* essayists attribute the causes of those terrorist attacks to Islam, which is rendered a religion in crisis where "powerful forces within the Islamic world community have turned the faith in an extremist, intolerant, separatist, and exclusionary direction" (Schwartz 2003, 90). Thus, Islam with its "potential for Jihad and violence—a potential that has been as significant a part of its history as tolerance and learning," is made out to be the essential cause of terrorist attacks against the United States (Klee 2003, 57). In accepting Islamic fundamentalism as the cause of recent terrorist attacks, Hanson reminds teachers that "[t]he failure to exercise moral judgment—denying that Islamic fundamentalism and fascism is a great plague on the world that would destroy the rights of women, the very notion of religious tolerance, and all the gifts of the Enlightenment is not proof of forbearance but of abject ethical aptitude" (Hanson 2003, 23).

Recent reports, however, indicate that Islamic fundamentalism may not have been the singular cause of the September 11 attacks. The most comprehensive account of the attacks is contained within *The 9/11 Commission Report*. In describing Osama bin Laden's appeal in the Islamic world, those writing *The 9/11 Commission Report* state that political instability, economic stagnation, and unpopular American foreign policies were factors in the terrorist attacks:

> His rhetoric selectively draws from multiple sources—Islam, history, and the region's political and economic malaise. He also stressed grievances against the United States widely shared in the Muslim world. He inveighed against the presence of U.S. troops in Saudi Arabia, the home of Islam's holiest sites. He spoke of the suffering as a result of the sanctions imposed after the Gulf War, and he protested U.S. support of Israel. (National Commission on Terrorist Attacks 2004, 49)

Or, let us consider Michael Scheuer's account of bin Laden's foreign policy goals:

> Bin Laden's foreign policy goals, if they are to be so termed, are six in number and easily stated. First, the end of all U.S. aid to Israel, the elimination of the Jewish state, and in its stead, the creation of an Islamic Palestinian state. Second, the withdrawal of all U.S. and Western military forces from the Arabian peninsula....Third, the end of all U.S. involvement in Afghanistan and Iraq. Fourth, the end of U.S. support for, and acquiescence in, the oppression of Muslims by the Chinese, Indian, Russian, and other governments. Fifth, restoration of full Muslim control of the Islamic world's energy resources and a return to market prices, ending the impoverishment of Muslims caused by oil prices set by Arab regimes to placate the West. Sixth, the replacement of U.S.-protected Muslim regimes that do not govern by Islam law by regimes that do. (Scheuer 2004, 210)

Although the ultimate cause of the attacks is unknown and may never be known, public opinion polls support the 9/11 Commission and Scheuer. The *Christian Century* reports "Seventy-nine percent of Muslims in this country say that U.S. foreign policy led to the September 11 terrorist attacks" (*Christian Century* 2002, 12). Similarly, a survey conducted by Zogby International found that among 2,620 Arab men and women who were interviewed, "only four percent in Saudi Arabia, six percent of Morocco and Jordan, thirteen percent in Egypt, and thirty-two percent in Lebanon had a favorable opinion of the United States. Most said, however, that they based their negative opinion on *U.S. foreign policies, not on American values*" (Younes 2003, 73; emphasis added).

Rather than engage in an open exploration of the meaning and manifestations of terrorism, the *TDD* essayists close off debate about the possible causes of the attacks by repeatedly stating that events of September 11 were an attack on American democratic values. Consequently, teachers and students are steered away from exploring the protracted U.S. role in such Middle Eastern affairs as Egypt's nationalization of the Suez Canal, the Arab-Israeli conflict, the Iran Hostage Crisis, the Iran-Iraq War, the Afghan-Soviet War, and the Persian Gulf War (Sicker 2001). Teachers and students are not allowed to explore how increasing U.S. dependence on Middle Eastern oil has shaped foreign policy or how it has led to the support of the unpopular, antidemocratic Saudi royal family (Klare 2002). Nor are teachers and students allowed to explore how global capitalism with its emphasis on consumer culture and expanding markets stands in opposition to traditional Middle Eastern tribal values (Barber 1996). Rather than explore the events of September 11 in all of their complexity, inquiry and debate are stifled as the *TDD* authors urge teachers to believe that America was attacked because of its core values of "freedom, tolerance, and individual self-determination" (Rodriguez 2003, 20).

If indeed the causes of September 11 are complex and may not be fully known for years to come, we cannot teach about such events as if we have pinpointed their cause. Rather, a democratic approach seeks to explore terrorism as a broader historical concept, with many different manifestations that vary with time and space. Walter Lacqueur explains that terrorism is the use of clandestine violence by a group for political ends that "may vary from the redress of specific 'grievances' to the overthrow of a government and taking of power, or to the liberation of a country from foreign rule" (Lacqueur 1977, 79). "Terrorists," he adds, "seek to cause political, social, and economic disruption, and for this purpose frequently engage in planned or indiscriminate murder" (79). Terrorism, of course, is a tactic that has been employed throughout history. The Jacobins used terrorism as a political tool as early as the French Revolution, and the United States itself has been victimized by domestic terror groups such as the Molly McGuires, Ku Klux Klan, Weathermen and by largely independent actors such as Timothy McVeigh and Terry Nichols. More recently, Indonesia, Israel, Kenya, Philippines, Russia, Spain, Saudi Arabia, and Turkey have been victimized by terrorist attacks. The *TDD* essayists, however, do not consider these disparate examples of terrorism relevant to understanding the events of September 11.

If students are to become knowledgeable about terrorism and capable of evaluating the current "War on Terrorism," we must not attribute simplistic causes to complex events and must offer a broader study of the various historical examples of terrorism and of how religious doctrine, economics, politics, foreign policy, and technology have made terrorism an increasingly acute threat. Students should be encouraged to explore the varied perspectives surrounding September 11. Greenhaven Press has published an accessible collection of essays representing different viewpoints titled *The Attack on America: September 11, 2001*. With that text, students explore essays and speeches from George Bush, Chalmers Johnson, William Bennett, Rudolph Giuliani, and Faisal Bodi, among others. By reviewing those essays students can freely explore the multiplicity of perspectives related to September 11, evaluate arguments and evidence, and participate in the larger debate about the future of American foreign policy and the wars in Afghanistan and Iraq.

Theme 3: The Wars in Afghanistan and Iraq Are Supported by the Just War Theory

TDD's contributors instruct teachers and students to believe that "the real core of Osama bin Laden's hatred of America is his opposition to open, secular, and democratic societies where individuals have rights that are not linked to their religion, gender, sexual orientation, or ethnicity" (Kennedy 2003, 28). Framing the terrorist attacks as attacks on American values and institutions, the essayists then justify the U.S. military response by drawing on the just war theory. In explaining the just war theory, Wilson states "its central arguments are that war cannot be used for unimportant reasons and that, in a war, it is wrong to attack innocent civilians deliberately and without being an inherent part of a campaign against military targets" (Wilson 2003, 81). In reference to critics who have raised objections to the United States bombing of civilian sections of

German and Japanese cities during World War II, Wilson contends "that argument is wrong, since the goal of these campaigns was to defeat military opponents and thus, in the long run, save lives" (Wilson 2003, 81). Likewise, Victor Davis Hanson, in comparing the civilians who were killed in the September 11 attacks to those killed in Afghanistan and Iraq, suggests that "[i]n the present conflict, we must reject the notion that the loss of innocent civilians deliberately murdered in a time of peace is somehow the same as accidental civilian deaths that occur from efforts to punish evildoers during a time of war" (Hanson 2003, 24).

For certain, just war theorists acknowledge that civilian deaths cannot always be avoided. However, by intimating that civilian deaths are justified by a military campaign or by circumstance, Wilson and Hanson fail to point out that the underlying principle of just war theory is to limit the violence of war "so that those who (regretfully) have course to lethal violence can be assured that what they are doing is not murder" (Yoder 1996, 50). James Turner Johnson, the distinguished just war theorist, explains that "[t]he principle of discrimination requires that noncombatants should not be directly, intentionally targeted, even in the course of using force that is otherwise proportionate....Means of warfare that cannot make this distinction are morally wrong, such as the use of poison gas against civilian populations to suppress dissidence or counter population bombing in an effort to undermine civilian morale" (Johnson and Weigel 1991, 31–32). In a similar fashion, Michael Walzer underscores the inviolability of civilians in the following description of "The War Convention":

> An army warring against aggression can violate the territorial integrity and political sovereignty of the aggressor state, but its soldiers cannot violate the life and liberty of enemy civilians....The war convention rests on a certain view of enemy combatants, which stipulates their battlefield equality. But it rests more deeply on a certain view of noncombatants, which holds that they are men and women with rights and that cannot be used for some military purpose, even if it is a legitimate purpose. (Walzer 1977, 136)

Thus, civilian casualties, although impossible to eliminate, are not justified by a military campaign or an effort to punish evildoers. Rather, wars must be waged to avoid civilian losses, and efforts need to be made to discriminate between combatants and noncombatants (This is spelled out in Article 3 of the Third Geneva Convention of 1949, a document noticeably absent from *TDD*).

Hanson and Wilson also fail to explain fully that the just war tradition aims to limit war by setting criteria for initiating a just war (*jus ad bellum*) as well as for waging a just war (*jus in bello*). The commonly accepted criteria for *jus ad bellum* include legitimate authority, just cause, right intent, proportionality, last resort, and using war only when there is a reasonable chance of establishing peace. The commonly accepted criteria for *jus in bello* are proportional use of force and the protection of noncombatants (Johnson 1984; Yoder 1996). In applying these two sets of criteria, Jimmy Carter, weeks before the U.S. invasion of Iraq, argued that such an invasion would not meet the criteria of a just war because all nonviolent options were not exhausted, the United States failed to connect Iraq to the September 11 terrorist attacks, and that even the most precise U.S. weapons fail to "discriminate between combatants and noncombatants" (Carter 2003, 4). Applying all just war criteria to the terrorist attacks of September 11 and the U.S. invasions of Afghanistan and Iraq forces us to explore not only the depravity of al Qaeda's terrorist attacks but also the Bush administration's justification for invading Iraq, the injustices at Abu Ghraib prison, the detention and treatment of suspected terrorists at Guantanamo Bay, and the Iraqi civilian death toll that is estimated to be in the tens of thousands (Steinfels 2004).

In the end, Wilson and Hanson slip into their own unique form of moral relativism in which the legitimacy of military intervention is not determined by standards established by international law but by the intervention's relation to the deplorable violence that provoked it. The spirit and criteria of the just war tradition, rooted in Christian doctrine, is subverted because its fundamental objective to limit war and protect civilians is used to justify violence against civilians. If we are to use just war theory as a theoretical framework in which to analyze the terrorist attacks and the wars in Afghanistan and Iraq, we must teach our students the historical development of the just war tradition, the criteria associated with initiating and waging a just war, and the international institutions—the Geneva Conventions, the Hague Peace Conferences, the Charter of the United Nations—that have supported limiting the violence of war. Once students have demonstrated an appreciation for just war tradition, a democratic pedagogy would expose them to arguments focusing on whether or not the present wars in Afghanistan and Iraq meet just war criteria.

Theme 4: The Bush Doctrine of Preemption Is the Appropriate Response to September 11

On June 1, 2002, President Bush outlined his policy of preemption to graduating cadets at the U.S. Military Academy at West Point: "If we wait for threats to fully materialize, we will have waited too long. We must take the battle to the enemy, disrupt his plans, and confront the worst threats before they emerge" (Bumiller 2002, 1.1). In discussing the doctrine of preemption, *TDD* essayist Stanley Kurtz underscores how the nature of national threats has changed from the cold war period to the present age of proliferating nuclear weapons and unexpected terrorist attacks. Kurtz rationalizes that "in a world of mass-scale terrorism and nuclear proliferation, it has become necessary to protect ourselves by displacing rogue regimes before they can develop nuclear weapons" (Kurtz 2003, 93). In constructing a historical backdrop for the doctrine of preemption, the authors of *TDD* repeatedly refer to the U.S. military campaigns of World War II as successful examples of how military intervention has brought about democracy and peace:

> In World War II, of the three Axis powers we took arms against, only Japan first struck at our homeland. But it is beyond debate that our taking up arms to defeat all three enemies of liberty made those countries better. Japan, Germany and Italy are all now thriving democracies. Their people are better off, we are better off, and the world is better off—not because of their leaders in World War II, but because of ours. (Bennett 2003, 41)

Bennett, as well as the other contributors to *TDD*, choose to build a tenuous link between Iraq and World War II while simultaneously ignoring failed American interventions in Vietnam, Haiti, and Somalia. Those historic examples, of course, reveal that there are palpable dangers associated with military intervention and that American military intervention does not always result in democratic reform.

314 | *Christopher Leahey*

More disconcerting is that Bennett and Kurtz fail to discuss how the Bush doctrine of preemption, with its emphasis on preventive war, is a departure from the cold war policies of containment and deterrence. Shortly after Bush's elaboration of the doctrine of preemption, scholars raised concerns about its legality, usefulness, and international implications. O'Hanlon, Rice, and Steinberg (2002), foreign policy experts at the Brookings Institution, explain that the Bush administration is broadening the meaning of preemption "to encompass preventive war as well, in which force may be used even without evidence of an imminent attack."

Questions have also emerged regarding the degree to which preemption "reinforces the image of the United States as too quick to use military force and to do so outside the bounds of international law and legitimacy" and whether or not the use of preventive war by the United States might increase the likelihood of other nations on the verge of war—for instance, India and Pakistan, China and Taiwan, Ethiopia and Eritrea—adopting a similar policy (O'Hanlon, Rice, and Steinberg 2002).

More recently, Arthur Schlesinger Jr., the former Kennedy adviser and prominent historian, raised questions about the legality of preventive war as he compared Bush's preventive strategy to that used by imperial Japan in rationalizing their attack on the U.S. Pacific fleet. Schlesinger argues that "the distinction between 'pre-emptive' and 'preventive' is worth preserving—it is the distinction between legality and illegality" (Schlesinger 2004, 23). Whether preemptive and preventive wars honor international law has been the center of much debate. The *American Journal of International Law* featured a forum titled "Agora: Future Implications of Iraq." Within the forum, William Howard Taft IV, Todd Buchwald, John Yoo, and Richard Gardner argue that U.N. Security Council Resolutions adopted between 1990 and 2003 authorize and justify U.S. military action in Iraq. Other scholars such as Richard Falk and Miriam Sapiro question the legality of U.S. military actions because Iraq did not pose an imminent threat and peaceful measures were not fully exhausted (see *American Journal of International Law*, vol. 97, no. 3). I suggest that teachers review those debates that reveal much about international law, U.S. policy in Iraq, and the institutions that have been created to maintain global peace and stability.

Rather than teach students to accept passively the necessity of the Bush doctrine of preemption, with its emphasis on preventive war, teachers using a democratic pedagogical approach would make such concepts the center of study. Teachers might ask students how the doctrine of preemption differs from the previous cold war policies of containment and deterrence and then investigate how the threats associated with the cold war differ from those associated with international terrorism. Students should also explore how the policy of preemption, with its emphasis on stopping a known eminent threat, differs from that of a preventive war in which force may be used without overwhelming evidence. The Six Days War fought between Israeli and Arab forces is an instructive example of preemptive war, and the 1961 U.S. invasion of Cuba's Bay of Pigs and 1983 U.S. invasion of Grenada might be useful case studies of preventive measures. Teachers and students should also explore how the doctrines of preemption and preventive war sit with the Charter of the United Nations (another body of international laws largely absent from *TDD*). The classroom debates, along with rigorous study of past policies and a full exploration of the unique threats associated with international terrorism, should be the focal point of classroom inquiry.

Conclusion

The September 11 terrorist attacks were horrific events that claimed the lives of thousands of innocent Americans. As tragic as that event was, we must not recoil from freely exploring the underlying causes of terrorism, the history of American foreign policy, or the ways in which we can create a safer, more just world. Historians (Foner 2003) and educators (Apple 2002) have suggested that a study of the events of September 11 provides a rich teaching opportunity to appraise our strengths and weaknesses and to provide educational spaces in which students are encouraged to make sense of those tragic events. In a discussion of democratic pedagogy, Paul Gagnon reminds us that in educating our children to become active citizens, "we do not ask for propaganda, for crash courses in the right attitudes, or for knee-jerk patriotic drill. We do not want to capsulize democracy's arguments in slogans, or pious texts, or bright debater's points" (Gagnon 1989, 254–55). Instead, we must "leave it to our students to apply their knowledge, values, and experiences to the world they must create" (255). These sentiments hold true today. Unfortunately, the Fordham Institute's prescriptions serve to stifle democratic inquiry because they preclude teachers and students from openly exploring debates surrounding those issues and from constructing their own understanding of the causes of the attacks, the wars in Afghanistan and Iraq, and the range of policies that might be used to thwart future attacks.

Rather than following the prescriptions offered by the Fordham Institute, teachers might turn to the National Council for the Social Studies' *Standards for Excellence and Progress* (1994) for guidance in developing appropriate instructional methods to teach about international terrorism and war. In supporting students in constructing a global perspective, NCSS suggests that teachers design curricular experiences for students that enable them "to conceptualize contexts of issues or phenomena; to consider causality; to inquire about the validity of explanations; and to create new explanations and models for grappling with persistent and/or recurring issues" (NCSS 1994, 6). In the end, it is the act of free inquiry itself that supports students in developing the knowledge, values, and experiences required for democratic citizenship.

Bibliography

Apple, M. 2002. Patriotism, pedagogy, and freedom: On the educational meanings of September 11. *Teachers College Record* 104 (8): 1760–72.

Appleby, J. 1992. Recovering America's historical diversity: Beyond exceptionalism. *Journal of American History* 79 (2): 419–31.

Agresto, J., L. Alexander, W. J. Bennett, W. Damon, L. Ellington, and C. E. Finn Jr. 2003. *Terrorists, despots, and democracy: What our children need to know.* Washington, DC: Thomas B. Fordham Institute.

Agresto, J. 2003. Passing the preamble. In Agresto, Alexander, Bennett, Damon, Ellington, and Finn 2003, 74–77.

Barber, B. 1996. *McWorld versus jihad: How globalism and tribalism are shaping the world.* New York: Ballantine Books.

———. 2000. *A passion for democracy: American essays.* Princeton, NJ: Princeton University Press.

Bennett, W. 2003. Seizing this teachable moment. In Agresto, Alexander, Bennett, Damon, Ellington, and Finn 2003, 40–42.

Bumiller, E. 2002. U.S. must act first to battle terror, Bush tells cadets. *New York Times*, June 2, Late Edition, 1.1.

Carter, J. 2003. Just war or a just war? *New York Times*, March 9, 4,13.

Cheney, L. 2003. Protecting our precious liberty. In Agresto, Alexander, Bennett, Damon, Ellington, and Finn 2003, 27–28.

The Christian century. 2002. Polled Muslims blame attack on U.S. policy. 119 (1): 12.

de Tocqueville, A. 1988. *Democracy in America*. Edited by Phillips Bradley. New York: Alfred A. Knopf.

Dewey, J. 1944. *Democracy and education*. New York: Free Press.

Dudley, W., ed. 2002. *The attack on America: September 11, 2001*. San Diego, CA: Greenhaven.

Ellington, L. 2003. Civic and historical literacy for a dangerous world. In Agresto, Alexander, Bennett, Damon, Ellington, and Finn 2003, 60–62.

Falk, R. A. 2003. What future for the U.N. charter system of war prevention? *American Journal of International Law* 97 (3): 590–99.

Finn, C. E., Jr., 2003. Introd. to Agresto, Alexander, Bennett, Damon, Ellington, and Finn 2003, 5–15.

Foner, E. 2003. Rethinking American history in a post 9/11 world. *Liberal Education* 89 (2): 30–37.

Gagnon, P. 1989. History's role in civic education: The precondition of civic intelligence. In *Educating the democratic mind*, ed. W. C. Parker, 241–62. Albany: State University of New York Press.

Gardner, R. N. 2003. Neither Bush nor the "jurisprudes." *American Journal of International Law* 97 (3): 585–90.

Hanson, V. D. 2003. Preserving America, man's greatest hope. In Agresto, Alexander, Bennett, Damon, Ellington, and Finn 2003, 23–24.

Johnson, J. T. 1984. *Can modern war be just?* New Haven, CT: Yale University Press.

Johnson, J. T., and G. Weigel. 1991. *Just war and the Gulf War*. Washington, DC: Ethics and Public Policy Center.

Kennedy, C. 2003. Defending American tolerance. In Agresto, Alexander, Bennett, Damon, Ellington, and Finn 2003, 28–29.

Kersten, K. 2003. What is "education for democracy?" In Agresto, Alexander, Bennett, Damon, Ellington, and Finn 2003, 47–49.

Klare, M. 2002. *Resource wars: The new landscape of global conflict*. New York: Owl Books.

Klee, M. B. 2003. What schools should do on September 11. In Agresto, Alexander, Bennett, Damon, Ellington, and Finn 2003, 56–57.

Kurtz, S. 2003. The doctrine of pre-emption. In Agresto, Alexander, Bennett, Damon, Ellington, and Finn 2003, 91–93.

Lacqueur, W. 1977. *Terrorism*. Boston: Little, Brown.

Lipset, S. M. 1996. *American exceptional-ism: A double-edged sword*. New York: W. W. Norton.

Martin, J. L., and A. D. Neal. 2001. *How our universities are failing America and what can be done about it*. Washington, DC: American Council of Trustees and Alumni. http://www.goacta.org/publications/Reports/ defciv.pdf (accessed February, 1, 2005).

Matthews, D. 1996. Reviewing and previewing civics. In *Educating the democratic mind*, ed. W. C. Parker, 265–86. Albany: State University of New York Press.

McCrisken, T. 2003. *American exceptionalism and the legacy of Vietnam: U.S. foreign policy since 1974*. New York: Palgrave MacMillan.

National Commission on Terrorist Attacks upon the United States. 2004. *The 9/11 commission report: Final report of the national commission on terrorist attacks upon the United States*. New York: W. W. Norton.

National Council for the Social Studies (NCSS). 1994. *Expectations for excellence: Curriculum standards for social studies*. Washington, DC: NCSS.

Newmann, F., T. Bertocci, and R. M. Landsness. 1977/1996. Skills in civic action. In *Educating the democratic mind*, ed. W. C. Parker, 223–39. Albany: State University of New York Press, 1996. Originally published in *Skills in citizen action*. Madison: Citizen Participation Curriculum Project, University of Wisconsin.

O'Hanlon, M., S. E. Rice, and J. B. Steinberg. 2002. *The new national security strategy and preemption*. Washington, DC: Brookings Institution, policy brief number 113, http://www.brookings. edu/comm/policybriefs/pb113.htm (accessed February 1, 2005).

Parker, W. C. 1996. *Educating the democratic mind*. Albany: State University of New York Press.

Rabb, T. 2003. Seeing the patterns. In Agresto, Alexander, Bennett, Damon, Ellington, and Finn 2003, 82–83.

Rodriguez, R. 2003. America: Always vulnerable, never inevitable. In Agresto, Alexander, Bennett, Damon, Ellington, and Finn 2003, 20–21.

Rotherham, A. 2003. A basic education for the post-9/11 world. In Agresto, Alexander, Bennett, Damon, Ellington, and Finn 2003, 29–31.

Sapiro, M. 2003. Iraq: The shifting sands of pre-emptive self-defense. *American Journal of International Law* 97 (3): 599–607.

Saxe, D. W. 1997. The unique mission of the social studies. In *The social studies curriculum: Purposes, problems, and possibilities*, ed. E. W. Ross. Albany: State University of New York Press.

Schlesinger, Jr., A. 2004. Seeking out monsters: By committing himself to preventive war, George Bush has overturned two centuries of U.S. thinking on global diplomacy. *Guardian*, October 19, 23.

Scheuer, M. 2004. *Imperial hubris: Why the west is losing the war on terror*. Washington, DC: Brassey's.

Schor, I. 1992. *Empowering education: Critical teaching for social change*. Chicago: University of Chicago Press.

Schwartz, S. 2003. America and the crisis of Islam. In Agresto, Alexander, Bennett, Damon, Ellington, and Finn 2003, 88–91.

Sesso, G., and J. Pyne. 2003. Five defining documents. In Agresto, Alexander, Bennett, Damon, Ellington, and Finn 2003, 77–80.

Sicker, M. 2001. *The Middle East in the twentieth century*. Westport, CT: Praeger.

Sorensen, K. 1996. Creating a democratic classroom: Empowering students within and outside school walls. In *Creating democratic classrooms: The struggle to integrate theory and practice*, ed. L. E. Beyer, 87–105. New York: Teachers College Press.

Steinfels, P. 2004. In the brutality of war, the innocents have been lost in the crossfire. *New York Times*, November 20, B6.

Stern, S. M. 2003. How to stop worrying and learn to love American exceptionalism. In Agresto, Alexander, Bennett, Damon, Ellington, and Finn 2003, 57–59.

Stotsky, S., & Schnidman, E. (2003). Democracy at home and abroad. In *Terrorists, despots, an democracy: What our children need to know* (pp. 84-86). Washington, DC: Thomas P. Fordham Institute.

Taft, W. H. IV, and T. F. Buchwald. 2003. Preemption, Iraq, and international law. *American Journal of International Law* 97 (3): 557–63.

Tyrell, I. 1991. American exceptionalism in an age of international history. *American Historical Review* 96 (4): 1031–55.

Walzer, M. 1977. *Just and unjust wars: A moral argument with historical illustrations*. New Haven, CT: Yale University Press.

Weinstein, K. 2003. The perils of complacency and limits of niceness. In Agresto, Alexander, Bennett, Damon, Ellington, and Finn 2003, 25–26.

Wilson, J. Q. 2003. What students should know about war. In Agresto, Alexander, Bennett, Damon, Ellington, and Finn 2003, 80–81.

Wood, G. H. 1998. Democracy and the curriculum. In *The curriculum: Problems, politics, and possibilities*, ed. L. E. Beyer and M. W. Apple, 177–98. Albany: State University of New York Press.

Yoder, J. H. 1996. *When war is unjust: Being honest in just-war thinking.* New York: Orbis Books.

Yoo, J. 2003. International law and the war in Iraq. *American Journal of International Law* 97 (3): 563–76.

Younes, R. 2003. Arab public opinion of U.S. takes a nosedive. *Washington Report on Middle East Affairs* 22 (4): 73.

This chapter originally appeared in *The Social Studies*, Vol. 96, No. 5 (September/October, 2005). Published here with permission of Heldref Publications.

CHAPTER TWENTY-FIVE

Civic Illiteracy and American History Textbooks

The U.S.-Veitnam War

JOHN MARCIANO

> In thirty years of "limited war"...the number of [Vietnamese] casualties perhaps totalled between 5,245,000 and 6,140,000 killed and wounded, plus 300,000 MIAs.
>
> JEFFREY KIMBALL, 1989

> At this moment of national disgrace, as American technology is running amuck in Southeast Asia, a discussion of American schools can hardly avoid noting...that these schools are the first training ground for the troops that will enforce the muted, unending terror of the status quo in the coming years of a projected American century.
>
> NOAM CHOMSKY, 1966

Introduction

A concrete illustration of civic illiteracy is the treatment of the U.S.-Vietnam War in American history textbooks, which prepare students to accept the basic purposes of that conflict. Although textbooks have improved factually since I co-authored an earlier study,[1] they still preserve one of education's essential purposes: shaping youth consciousness to foster support for U.S. aggression. The lessons of the war are important, for they have influenced subsequent U.S. actions in the Third World and public opinion. Since the end of the war, the dominant elite has tried to undermine the "Vietnam Syndrome," the term given to citizen fears of and opposition to U.S. wars abroad. To undermine this resistance, it has used the media and educational institutions to obtain support for policies in Central America and the Persian Gulf. History textbooks support the honorable intentions of U.S. policy in Vietnam as part of a larger ideological effort to

320 | *John Marciano*

ensure that aggression against weaker nations will not be disrupted by civically-literate youth.

Part I of this chapter reproduces a narrative history of the war in the language of 20 U.S. history textbooks published in the 1980s; this narrative history is then challenged in Part II."[2] Part III places the narrative within a theoretical framework that asserts that the dominant elite influences state policies through education and the mass media, and shapes the perceptions of youth and the public on vital issues of war and peace in an effort to maintain hegemonic power. While a single historical narrative cannot capture the minor differences between individual texts, it does give an accurate representation of the major assumptions and assertions presented to students. Basic beliefs about Vietnam and the U.S. role in the world are crucial here, not minor differences among authors who still agree on the ends of the nation and its foreign policy. Aside from minor editing in terms, e.g., a single spelling for Viet Cong and Viet Minh, I have tried to faithfully reproduce the history that students would have learned had they synthesized the 20 separate texts into one narrative.

Part 1: A Textbook History of the U.S.-Vietnam War

The textbook history of the war begins with French colonial rule in Vietnam, which commenced in the 1860s; it was harsh, and most peasants lost their land. The French produced and marketed opium, and fostered drug addiction among the native population. There was strong resistance from the Vietnamese, but they were brutally suppressed. During World War II, Japan invaded Vietnam and drove out the French, and many Vietnamese formed guerrilla groups to fight the Japanese. The United States aided one such group: the Viet Minh, which was led by the Soviet-trained Communist Ho Chi Minh. When the Japanese surrendered in 1945, Ho proclaimed the establishment of the Democratic Republic of Vietnam, and was recognized as head of an independent state. A strong nationalist, he used the Preamble of the U.S. Declaration of Independence in his proclamation because he wanted America's support for Vietnamese independence, but that did not happen.

France returned after World War II and regained control of Vietnam. It refused to discuss independence with the Viet Minh, but it recognized Vietnam as a Free State within the French Union. This agreement broke down, however, and fighting began in 1946. Ho appealed for U.S. support, but he received no reply. Instead, the U.S. would pay more than 70% of France's war costs because it feared Ho's Communist ties and China's expansion throughout Southeast Asia. In 1954, when the Viet Minh, supported by China, won the major battle of Dien Bien Phu, Secretary of State Dulles and Vice President Nixon urged President Eisenhower ("Ike") to support the French militarily; Dulles urged a nuclear attack. But President Eisenhower realized that he had no support from Congress and other allies, so he did not escalate U.S. involvement. The French were defeated and soon left Vietnam.

The French-Vietnamese conflict ended in 1954, when the Geneva Conference divided or temporarily divided Vietnam. The North became a Communist state led by Ho Chi Minh, supported by the Soviet Union and China; the South became a "free" government under the non-Communist Ngo Dinh Diem. The United States promised to support the 1956 elections that were to unify the nation, but Eisenhower felt they would give power to Ho and the Communists.

Therefore, he pledged military assistance to Diem, who declared himself president of South Vietnam, and the elections were canceled. The Viet Cong or Viet Communists as Diem called them then began their guerrilla campaign, supported by North Vietnam. Diem was a nationalist and Catholic who opposed both Communist domination and French colonialism; although Eisenhower had doubts about Diem, he supported the regime with CIA agents and money. In North Vietnam, Ho and the Communists took over and abolished all political opposition. Thousands of former landlords were killed or sent to forced-labor camps, and about one million people, mostly Catholics, fled to South Vietnam.

In 1960, the Viet Cong set up their own government, the National Liberation Front (NLF). In the early stages of the war, almost all of the rebels were South Vietnamese, who were encouraged and supplied in large part by North Vietnam; the North later took over much of the fighting. Not all Viet Cong were Communists—some were Buddhists who did not like Diem's support of Catholics, and nationalists who wanted a united Vietnam. Since many were Communists, however, Eisenhower sent more aid to Diem, who was not a popular ruler. With his harsh policies he brutally suppressed both Communists and non-Communists, and his lack of support among the peasantry allowed the Viet Cong to gain control of most rural areas in the South by 1960.

The administration of President John F. Kennedy (JFK) made Vietnam a major foreign policy commitment. Kennedy also had misgivings about Diem, but he expanded the number of soldiers to 15,000 or 17,000 by 1963 and also authorized combat air missions over North and South Vietnam. JFK was aware of Diem's lack of support, but escalating NLF victories increased his advisers' fear that South Vietnam would become Communist. He resisted advice to send more troops, but sent more advisers and supplies to offset North Vietnam's help to the Viet Cong, and also urged Diem to carry out reforms. Diem ruthlessly put down all political opponents, however, and Kennedy began to see that outsiders could not solve Vietnamese problems. He was reluctant to fully involve U.S. troops in combat because he feared getting bogged down in a land war as France had, but Diem's rule became increasingly harsh and the United States could no longer tolerate him. In late 1963, the South Vietnamese military received backing from the Kennedy Administration through the CIA for a coup; it seized power and murdered Diem and some of his family members. The United States had not sanctioned the murders, but it supported the coup, and had to choose either to let South Vietnam fall to the Communists, or expand American involvement. JFK chose the latter.

A rapid succession of military leaders replaced Diem, but none was interested in reform and most asked for American troops. Kennedy refused, at the risk of deepening U.S. involvement. Three weeks later, he was assassinated. At the time, however, he was considering expanding American involvement in Vietnam.

The Vietnam War escalated during President Johnson's term, especially after the Tonkin Gulf incident in August, 1964. Johnson (LBJ) told Congress that U.S. ships had been attacked without cause while on routine patrol. North Vietnam stated that the ships were inside its territorial waters, but LBJ denied this. After this attack, he ordered American planes to bomb the North, and Congress passed the Tonkin Gulf Resolution, giving him almost complete freedom of action in Vietnam. Only two Senators voted against it and few questioned LBJ's version of what happened. Attacks against North Vietnam's coastal islands had begun in February 1964, with

American support of South Vietnamese secret operations; however, Johnson did not reveal this fact to Congress or the American public. He had the Tonkin Resolution prepared by advisers three months before the attack, and it provided his legal basis for escalating the war.

When Johnson became president, South Vietnam was almost completely dependent upon U.S. aid and controlled by the military. Each new regime was corrupt and not interested in reforms. Meanwhile, Viet Cong influence continued to grow until they controlled 80 percent of the countryside. Some 30,000 North Vietnamese troops had also infiltrated the South. LBJ's advisers laid out two unpleasant choices: further military escalation, which might bring in China and the Soviet Union, or reducing the U.S. role and leaving the fighting to South Vietnam—then the Communists would take over. The U.S. was to be trapped in this dreadful predicament for seven years.

In early 1965, Johnson ordered U.S. troops into battle because South Vietnam was being defeated. The explanation for this escalation was not clear: the simplest one given was the "domino theory." Although there were few North Vietnamese troops in the South, LBJ and his advisers recalled the failure to stand up to Hitler's aggression. U.S. "credibility" was also at stake, as other free countries needed to know that we would resist aggression. North Vietnam responded to this expansion by sending more of its regular army units and supplies to assist the Viet Cong.

The United States finally got a relatively stable government in South Vietnam in General Thieu's regime, but it was also brutal and corrupt, and the Viet Cong and the North were clearly defeating his army. The Viet Cong's strength was not in weaponry but in infiltration. The United States responded with massive technological warfare, trying to defeat a "popular movement" aided by North Vietnam, the Soviet Union, and China. Equally important, however, was the Viet Cong's success with the native population, which supported them by ambush and terror. The U.S. responded by trying to "pacify" rural areas and win the "hearts and minds" of the peasantry. But it did not get the support that Vietnamese peasants gave the highly nationalistic Viet Cong. The "pacification" program was replaced by the more extreme "relocation" campaign, by which villagers were taken from their homes into refugee centers or cities. The countryside was then devastated with bombs and chemical defoliants. These toxic chemicals caused birth defects in Vietnamese children and U.S. servicemen's offspring, and led to health problems for exposed adults.

The massive U.S. bombing of North Vietnam strengthened Communist resistance, and other military efforts were also ineffective. Beginning in 1968, North Vietnam sent 100,000 troops to the South each year to replace Communist casualties. The war shattered both the North and South. In the North, air strikes were aimed at bridges and roads, but bombs are not pinpoint weapons and villagers were often the victims. But the South felt the heaviest weight, as villages were destroyed and vast areas of the country were turned into moonscapes from "carpet bombing."

By 1967 some U.S. officials began questioning the government's policy, and Secretary of Defense Robert McNamara commissioned The Pentagon Papers, a study of U.S. policy in Vietnam since World War II. It revealed that the public had been misled about Vietnam for two decades as U.S. presidents secretly waged war. McNamara resigned in 1967 and was replaced by Clark Clifford, who reviewed reports and talked with leaders who had supported the war; they now thought that the U.S. ought to get out. This caused President Johnson to reconsider his policies,

as the conflict had destroyed both Vietnam and his Great Society programs. While the war escalated, Johnson tried to negotiate a solution, and peace efforts continued into 1968. In March of
that year, with American protests against the war rising, LBJ ordered U.S. aircraft "to make no
attacks on North Vietnam." He called for peace talks, which finally began in Paris that May. This
announcement did not alter the way the war was fought, however, and bombings increased dramatically in South Vietnam.

In 1967, General Westmoreland had stated that victory was near: there was "light at the end
of the tunnel." But this hope was shattered when the Viet Cong or North Vietnamese launched
the massive Tet offensive in early 1968 throughout South Vietnam that showed astonishing
power. The offensive was very costly and they suffered terrible casualties, but it startled and
embarrassed the American military, and Westmoreland was soon relieved of his command. A
major battle took place in Hue, where Viet Cong forces murdered 3,000 South Vietnamese supporters. Although Westmoreland asserted that Tet was an American military victory, many
thought it was a psychological triumph for the Communists. The fighting included the shoot-
ing of a Viet Cong suspect on a Saigon street by a South Vietnamese officer; televised, it did more
than any single event to undermine support for the war. Tet turned American opinion against
the war, and the media raised the question of a "credibility gap." How could North Vietnam
launch such an attack if President Johnson was telling the truth? Were we backing a government
that did not have the support of its own citizens? Tet revealed that the "other war"—Saigon's effort
to win the "hearts and minds" of the Vietnamese people—was far from over.

President Nixon came to office in 1969 with a plan to bring "peace with honor" in Vietnam,
but United States involvement was to continue for four more years, becoming bloodier and
expanding geographically. An important part of the plan was training and equipping the South
Vietnamese army to take over most of the combat. This "Vietnamization" was accompanied by
increased bombing of North Vietnam and secret bombing of Cambodia and Laos. It would end
the war with honor, and South Vietnam would remain independent and non-Communist.
President Nixon and Secretary of State Kissinger thus restored the war to the situation of 1965,
with Vietnamese fighting each other. The President actually expanded the conflict in April 1970,
when he ordered a joint U.S.-South Vietnamese invasion to attack North Vietnamese "sanctu-
aries" inside Cambodia. He did not consult with Congress, and said the action was to shorten
the war. In February 1971, Nixon ordered American support of a South Vietnamese invasion
of Laos, a test of the "Vietnamization" program. It was a disaster, however: the North destroyed
the South's forces.

In early 1972, North Vietnam launched a major invasion of South Vietnam as American
troops pulled out. The U.S. did not have enough forces to win the war, but simply leaving Vietnam
would make it seem weak and untrustworthy. "Peace with honor" was not peace at any cost, as
the U.S. could not simply leave. Nixon insisted that Communist forces must leave South
Vietnam, and that it must remain independent. North Vietnam did not agree: it wanted a
united Vietnam under one government. One of the most difficult problems facing Nixon during this "Vietnamization" was the decay within the American military. Discipline among U.S.
troops was rapidly deteriorating, with desertion, drug addiction, refusal to obey orders, and the
occasional killing of unpopular officers by enlisted men.

While pursuing "Vietnamization," President Nixon tried to negotiate an end to the war.

Shortly before Nixon's re-election in November, 1972, Secretary of State Kissinger announced that "peace is at hand." It did not happen, however, because of General Thieu's strong opposition, and the peace talks were suspended. The heaviest and most destructive bombing raids of the war took place in December as docks, airfields, bus and train stations were hit. Many of the targets were in heavily populated areas, and civilian casualties were high as homes and hospitals were accidently bombed. The peace talks resumed, and on January 27, 1973, an agreement was reached. All fighting was to stop and the North was to release American POWs (Prisoners of War), and the U.S. was to withdraw completely. Nixon promised that the U.S. would respond "with full force" if the North Vietnamese broke the agreement.

The Paris Agreement called for Thieu's government to remain in power, but few thought it would last long. It was actually a death warrant for South Vietnam, which could not stand long without U.S. support. Despite U.S. assurances, it was understood that it was only a matter of time before the South. would be crushed by the North. The Paris Agreement did not produce peace or honor: it only removed the U.S. from the disastrous war. The agreement was broken by both sides, and within two years North Vietnam and the Viet Cong easily conquered South Vietnam. In March, 1975; North Vietnam began a final offensive against the powerless forces of the South, which disintegrated without the support of the U.S. Thieu appealed to President Ford for aid, and Ford appealed to Congress for funds but was refused. On April 30, 1975, Saigon fell to North Vietnam, and Vietnam was reunited under Communist rule.

The U.S. paid a terrible price for its involvement in the war, and the human and financial costs were staggering for both sides. Between 46,000 and 58,000 Americans died, and the war cost $110 to $190 billion. Between 1.2 million and 2 million Vietnamese soldiers and 2 million to 3.5 million civilians lost their lives. Millions more became refugees, and 500,000 to 1.5 million of these fled the nation. The U.S. felt a special obligation toward the Vietnamese, who had fought bravely; therefore, it took in the largest number of these "boat people." Perhaps tens of thousands lost their lives at sea. By 1979 approximately 220,000 Vietnamese refugees had come to the U.S., many of them educated and wealthy supporters of the war. The bloodbath that many feared after the Communists won did not happen, but thousands were imprisoned or resettled. The war devastated Vietnam, as millions of acres of farmland and jungle were defoliated by toxic chemicals. Today it is one of the poorest nations in the world. The U.S. tried in vain to make it a viable democratic nation, but Vietnam became a repressive regime and close ally of the Soviet Union.

Most Americans tried to forget our most unpopular war, and there was widespread cynicism toward the government and political system. Thousands of veterans were exposed to toxic chemicals, and many suffered from depression and rage. Some became addicted to alcohol and drugs and could not find or keep jobs, but most returned to normal pursuits, and the vast majority were employed. They were often met, however, with indifference or outright hostility. It took years to be accepted for what they were: patriotic soldiers who sacrificed much to support their country. After Vietnam, U.S. prestige was lower than at any time in our history, and powerful lessons can be drawn: we must find new ways to fight Communist-supported wars of "national liberation"; we should only support those who can and want to help themselves; we must never fight a conflict without a declaration of war or a ·clear-cut goal of victory; and the U.S. must confine itself to conflicts that Americans believe are vital to the nation's interest.

Part II: A Critique of the Textbook History: French Colonialism and Origins

The brutal nature of France's colonialism is freely admitted in the textbooks summarized above, but that tough language disappears when the U.S. takes over from the French. The U.S. does not engage in colonialism or imperialism; rather, it fears Ho Chi Minh's Communist ties and aids those who wish to remain "free." He is always referred to as a Communist, a Marxist, or a Soviet-trained leader. Ho was all of these, but there is no adequate explanation of why he and the Communist-led Viet Minh had such support. Students would not know that at the end of World War II, thousands of Vietnamese who gathered in Hanoi to celebrate the end of the war against Japan and the Allied victory were joined by U.S. army officers. A Vietnamese band played "The Star-Spangled Banner," and Ho Chi Minh, soon to be head of a united and independent Vietnam, linked his people's struggle against France to the American revolution. Ho believed that "the Vietnamese revolution was supported by the same spirit that had brought about American independence in 1776."[3]

The texts do not adequately explain why Ho Chi Minh and the Viet Minh had such over-whelming support in Vietnam, even though U.S. documents are available that would explain it. One of the many State Department reports concluded that Ho was regarded as "the symbol of nationalism and the struggle for freedom to the overwhelming majority of the population." This official view from the 1940s was confirmed by the 1972 congressional testimony of Abbot Low Moffat, the former chief of the Division of Southeast Asia Affairs, Department of State (1945–47):

> I have never met an American…who had met Ho Chi Minh who did not reach the same belief: that Ho Chi Minh was first and foremost a Vietnamese nationalist. He was also a Communist and believed that Communism offered the best hope for the Vietnamese people. But his loyalty was to his people.[4]

Noam Chomsky confirms Moffat's view, reviewing reports from The Pentagon Papers that discuss efforts to prove that Ho Chi Minh was a puppet of the Russians or Chinese. One 1948 State Department report found "no evidence of direct link between Ho and Moscow"[5]; another discovered a "Kremlin directed conspiracy…in virtually all countries except Vietnam."[6] Regardless of the facts, however, officials remained desperate to prove that Ho was a puppet in order to discount the indigenous nature of the Vietnamese struggle. Despite the evidence of Ho Chi Minh's leadership and respect among his people, "the internal record…reveals that United States government analysts recognized that Western intervention must destroy the most powerful nationalist movement in Indochina." A victory for Ho and the Viet Minh on behalf of the Vietnamese people "was regarded as inconsistent with American global objectives, and therefore it was necessary to define the Viet Minh as agents of foreign aggression."[7] Freedom and self-determination for the Vietnamese people were a threat to the dominant elite here; therefore, the Viet Minh–led, anti-colonial movement had to be crushed.

The texts present Chinese and Soviet support for the Viet Minh as if to imply that U.S. aid to France was needed to match Communist aid for those resisting the French. But when Pentagon figures for the period of U.S. escalation (1965–73) are used as a guide to the relative economic and military support given to each side in the war, U.S. aid to the French would have been forty times greater than Chinese-Soviet aid to the Viet Minh—which always relied on support within Vietnam against the French.[8] Students also are taught that U.S. leaders did not support French rule, which is pure fiction without a shred of evidence in the texts themselves. To the contrary, these texts reveal that the U.S. funded French colonialism.

The texts acknowledge that France agreed to recognize Vietnam as a Free State within the French Union in March, 1946. But as historian Marvin Gettleman and colleagues point out, France immediately broke the agreement when it formed a separate republic in the southern part of Vietnam—with no opposition from the U.S.[9] From that March agreement, Vietnam was a sovereign state and any aggression against it was a violation of international law. Students also learn that the U.S. considered a nuclear attack on Vietnam in 1954 to block the French defeat at Dien Bien Phu, but there is no discussion of this incredible fact. As with so many other admissions, the bare statement cannot do justice to the momentous possibility it revealed.

Geneva, Diem, and the NLF

The view created for students about the 1954 Geneva Accords is inaccurate: the Accords did not divide Vietnam and did not create the state of South Vietnam. Vietnam was recognized as one nation, with a temporary dividing line between the Viet Minh and French forces. The "Final Declaration of the Geneva Conference" is quite explicit on this point, recognizing "that the essential purpose of the agreement relating to Vietnam is to settle military questions with a view to ending hostilities and that *the military demarcation line is provisional and should not in any way be interpreted as constituting a political or territorial boundary* (emphasis added)."[10] Despite the temporary nature of this agreement, however, the *Monthly Review* points out that "the U.S. government has never hesitated to claim the Geneva Accords as the basis of the legitimacy of the South Vietnamese state whenever it has suited its purposes to do so!"[11]

In its view, this is the perspective of the former foreign policy columnist of the *New York Times*, Leslie Gelb, now an official in the Clinton Administration. Writing in the *Times* in April 1975 as the war ended, Gelb contended that "the regime of South Vietnam…was effectively created in the summer of 1954. In the spring of 1975, it is perishing." The *Monthly Review* believes that Gelb was "wrong on two counts: the Geneva Conference did *not* create 'the regime of South Vietnam,' the United States did that; and the war now ending is *not* a civil war but a war of national liberation of the Vietnamese people against the United States." [12]

The texts' claims about the oppressiveness of the regime in North Vietnam are simply mentioned, with no context or evidence provided from the documentary record for these assertions. In November 1969, President Nixon stated that the Viet Minh killed "more than 50,000 people following their takeover in the North in the 1950s.…Later, he reported that 'a half a million, by conservative estimates…were murdered or otherwise exterminated by the North Vietnamese.'"[13] Edwin E. Moise's study of land reform in North Vietnam after 1954 demolishes the prevailing view that is rehashed in the textbooks. Moise concludes that the "number of people executed during the land reform was probably in the vicinity of 5,000 [and] the slaughter of tens of thousands of innocent victims, often described in anti-Communist propaganda, never took place." These deaths were not the result of a Communist program of revenge and murder, and an "extraordinary" fact is that the errors that occurred during that period "were not covered up, or blamed on a few scapegoats, after it was over."[14] Southeast Asia scholar Gareth Porter reveals that most of the information on the land reform abuses came from a former "substantial landholder in [northern] Vietnam" who was "employed and subsidized by the Saigon Ministry of Information, CIA, and other official U.S. sources for many years."[15] None of this history is shared by our textbook authors; without it, youth cannot challenge the texts' distortions, which have become part of the standard mythology.

The texts state that hundreds of thousands of refugees fled from North Vietnam to South Vietnam after the Geneva Conference in 1954, but there is no context provided for this fact. Many were Catholics who supported the French and later Diem. These "land people" would provide the basis for early propaganda on the evils of Vietnamese Communism, creating refugees driven to seek freedom. The role of the CIA in this movement of people is not discussed, a pattern of avoidance and ignorance about that agency that continues throughout the textbooks. Journalist Robert Scheer exposed the refugee myth as "perhaps the most important one put forth by the Vietnam Lobby, a group of anti-communist intellectual, political, and religious leaders" who supported Diem and raved "about the 'miracle of democracy' flowering in South Vietnam." These refugees received millions in aid from "the United States and the Catholic Relief Agency, and they became a 'privileged minority and source of support' for Diem....They manufactured atrocity stories, aided in this endeavor by CIA agents."[16] Many of the Catholics who fled to South Vietnam after the Geneva Agreements had been "collaborators and even [had] been mobilized into 'an autonomous Vietnamese militia' that fought against the anti-French resistance led by the Viet Minh."[17] They thus fought for a French colonial regime that is considered oppressive even in the eyes of our textbook authors.

There are harsh comments on Diem's failings as leader of South Vietnam, and the texts admit that he would have lost the 1956 elections called for by the Geneva Accords, and therefore refused to hold them. But such a simple note does not do justice to this fundamental violation of the Geneva Agreements. The Pentagon Papers state that "the French urgently sought to persuade Diem to accept consultations about the elections....Britain [also]...joined France in urging Diem to talk with the Vietminh. But Diem refused," supported by the United States. He could not have blocked the elections had the U.S. upheld the Agreements. The Papers admit that before and after the Geneva Conference, the National Security Council rejected any notion of self-determination through free elections, arguing that it was "infeasible," and that "such a course of action would, in any case, lead to the loss of [Vietnam] to Communist control."[18] All of this information was known to U.S. officials; thus, they were faced with the choice of a Viet Minh victory and Vietnamese control of their own country or a policy of subversion and terrorism to impose an American-supported regime to prevent this reality.

The texts admit that Diem consolidated his power after the Geneva Conference with the aid of the CIA. From its creation in 1947, the CIA has overthrown and subverted governments perceived as threatening American (actually dominant-elite) interests in the Third World. There is nothing in these texts to help students understand why this happened in Vietnam and throughout the world. Therefore, they cannot challenge the reputed U.S. devotion to "democracy" and "freedom" with the reality of aggression and violence. Philip Agee, a former CIA agent, joins scholars like Michael Parenti in documenting this historical record, including millions in secret election funds used in Western Europe to insure that conservative forces favored by the U.S. stayed in power; and "covert actions and secret operations" to undermine internal policies, including "coups, murders [and] terrorism" in Iran, Guatemala, Cuba, Nicaragua, Angola, El Salvador and Brazil. In pursuing such policies in virtual secrecy from the public and elected officials, the CIA "violated international treaties and domestic laws." This documented history[19] of the most powerful and well-financed international terrorist organization on earth is unknown to youth because of the civic illiteracy fostered by schools, textbooks, and the mass media.

Terror and violence were the central aspects of the Diem regime, and it was this systematic terrorism that was the principal violation of the Geneva Agreements. Former Diem adviser Joseph Buttinger describes the violence used to maintain an unpopular regime in South Vietnam, including operations into regions where the NLF has great support. These resulted in the arrest of "tens of thousands of people" and the deaths of "hundreds, perhaps thousands of peasants.…Whole villages whose populations were not friendly to the government weredestroyed by artillery. These facts were kept secret from the American people."[20] U.S. officials supported this effort, and academics worked with CIA officials to train, equip, and finance Diem's forces to carry out this terror.

U.S. officials knew that Diem was running a terrorist state. Arthur Schlesinger, Jr., a Kennedy adviser during this period, admits that "Diem's authoritarianism…caused spreading discontent and then armed resistance in the countryside."[21] And The Pentagon Papers note: "Enough evidence has now been accumulated to establish that peasant resentment against Diem was extensive and well founded. Moreover, it is clear that the dislike of the Diem government was coupled with resentment toward Americans."[22] The depth of Diem's repression is thus available in the documentary record, but students would not know this from the text history. Jeffrey Race, a U.S. Army adviser in South Vietnam whose *War Comes to Long An* is a well-respected historical study of the repression of the Diem regime and the growth of the NLF revolutionary movement, shows how the regime's violence created its own demise. Despite this, it was advised and supported throughout by the U.S.[23]

Eric Bergerud's study of the Diemist terror and the indigenous resistance supports Race's conclusions. Bergerud, who Chomsky asserts believed in the "moral validity" of the war, showed that the regime "lacked legitimacy with the rural peasantry" while the "Communist-led [NLF] enjoyed widespread support." It gained such strength because the Diem regime and the U.S. would not support "fundamental change in the social or economic makeup of South Vietnam." By the end of 1965, the NLF "had won the war in Hau Nghia province [the area of his study]." Even the CIA was forced to admit that "98 percent of the insurgents in the province were local and that they neither got nor needed substantial aid from Hanoi."[24] Faced with such realities, the U.S. turned to its only option: violence. Chomsky concurs: "For Kennedy and his circle, violence raised at most tactical problems; the client regime understood that there was no other choice, despite the negative impact on villagers when Diem's agents…murdered, tortured and destroyed."[25] Both Bergerud's and Race's studies reveal that the "U.S.-imposed regime had no legitimacy in the countryside, where 80 percent of the population lived…and that only force could compensate for this lack. Both report that by 1965, when the U.S. war against South Vietnam moved to sheer devastation, the Viet Cong had won the war in the provinces they studied, with little external support." Therefore, the only logical recourse for the Diem regime and the U.S.

was "terror, then the greater incomparable violence of the invaders."[26] Diem's policies, however, are never called "murder" or "terror." The word "terror," for example, an essential part of contemporary media and political language that is always directed against nations such as Iran, Iraq, and Libya but never U.S. allies such as Guatemala and Indonesia, does not appear once in reference to U.S. or client practices in any of the total of forty-eight texts examined in my co-authored 1979 study and the present one.

Diem's support of the Vietnamese upper class is mentioned in the texts, yet this important issue is not examined even though it was a central factor in the nationalist struggle led by the NLF against foreign invaders. The war was a nationalist and class resistance of peasants against wealthy landowners and the military who sided with the invaders.

Kennedy and Vietnam

The texts repeat the Camelot rhetoric about the Kennedy administration, with comments on the President's high-minded concern for reform in both South Vietnam and Latin America. But the "reform" during his presidency included the use of CIA subversion and terror, gutting Third World nations' economic potential, siphoning billions in wealth to U.S. multinational corporations banks, and overthrowing popularly elected governments and replacing them with undemocratic regimes supported by the U.S., however devious and corrupt they may be. Chomsky, among others, has challenged the prevailing view of Kennedy that youth gain from these textbooks. U.S. support of national security states "dedicated to 'internal security' by assassination, torture, disappearance, and sometimes mass murder constituted one of the two major legacies" that Kennedy brought to Latin America; the other was the Alliance for Progress, "a statistical success and social catastrophe (apart from foreign investors and domestic elites)."[27] In Vietnam, there was a dramatic escalation of U.S. involvement under Kennedy, as he "moved on to armed attack" upon the civilian population in the south. "The assault that followed left three countries (Cambodia, Laos and Vietnam] utterly devastated with millions dead…and a record of criminal savagery that would fill many a docket, by the standards of Nuremberg."[28]

Johnson, Tonkin ,and Escalation

The "competing claims" viewpoint shapes the Tonkin Gulf incident. Johnson's assertions are simply repeated and students read that the President did not tell the "whole truth." The secret operations that began against North Vietnam in February 1964 are mentioned, but there is no suggestion that these violated international law. There is no outrage over the fact that a fabricated incident (Tonkin Gulf) fueled a war that led to the loss of millions of lives and the betrayal of democratic principles.

Edward S. Herman and Chomsky show conclusively that the dominant-elite media supported the mystification and lies that later would shape the history textbooks; they believe that the best coverage of Tonkin was found in the dissenting and leftist *National Guardian* (later the *Guardian* and no longer published) and by the late independent journalist I.F. Stone, a critic of U.S. policies in Vietnam through his *Week*.[29] Stone analyzed the testimony before the Senate

Foreign Relations Committee on August 6, 1964, of then-Secretary of Defense Robert McNamara, who claimed that "our Navy played absolutely no part in, was not associated with, was not was not aware of, any South Vietnamese actions [attacking North Vietnam] if there were any." His testimony to the same committee on February 20, 1968, however, revealed another version. "McNamara's [1968] version of the attack contradicts the melodramatic account he gave [in 1964]....It was this graphic, but (as it now appears) untrue version which helped stampede the Senate into voting the Tonkin Gulf resolution." In 1964, McNamara told the Senate that the attack "occurred at night. It appeared to be a deliberate attack in the nature of an ambush...directed against the vessels [the *Maddox* and the *Turner Joy*]. *They returned the fire.*" He spoke of "unprovoked aggression," a view that "was magnified and emotionalized" by President Johnson, who talked on national television of "this new act of aggression."[30]

The truth is not what McNamara and other officials told the country. "It is quite clear that [McNamara] and Secretary [of State] Rusk...lied...to the Senate committee [in 1964], and that McNamara [was] still trying hard to lie about it [in 1968]." On both occasions, "he withheld...many crucial facts which cast doubt on the whole story of the August [1964] attack" that was so crucial in moving the war to another level of escalation, violence, and lying.[31] The historical record to counter the official Tonkin story has been available for decades, but the textbook authors did not use it. How can youth become civically literate about this war without the facts about one of the major events that shaped it?

The texts assert that Johnson did not want to widen the war, but also that he secretly expanded the conflict to North Vietnam. Such contradictions continue in the absence of the civic and critical analysis necessary for student understanding. It is claimed that in late 1964 and early 1965 there were 30,000 North Vietnamese troops fighting in the South alongside the Viet Cong, and that beginning in 1968, the North sent in 100,000 troops per year. The first claim is false and is contradicted by information within the texts themselves as well as by The Pentagon Papers and other documents. There is no mention of mercenary troops used by the U.S. in Vietnam. Up to the time of the Tet offensive in 1968, for example, Koreans, "who were particularly brutal" toward Vietnamese civilians, outnumbered the North Vietnamese in the South.[32] The second fact is also asserted without any context or evidence that might allow students to understand why this happened: it was essentially an effort to stop the brutal repression against NLF forces and supporters in the South, many of whom were being slaughtered by South Vietnamese and U.S. troops.[33]

The use and effects of toxic chemicals on the Vietnamese and American veterans and the connection to food production and starvation are briefly mentioned, but Agent Orange is not named, and the long struggle of Vietnam veterans for some form of financial restitution and health benefits is not discussed. The chemical warfare against Vietnam is a crime worthy of a Nuremberg Tribunal, but it is not deemed worthy of examination in these texts. The authors seem undisturbed by the revelation of official lies in The Pentagon Papers, and this source is rarely mentioned. That so little attention could be given in the 1980s to the most important government document on the conflict is an incredible omission by authors with access to this material. Despite the fact that the document revealed "that the American people had been deceived about the real situation," the authors never use the word "lie" when they refer to Johnson's (or any president's) actions.

Students learn that the United States could neither win nor understand the enemy and the struggle in Vietnam. But U.S. officials had plenty of information to assess the war correctly; however, such data had to be put through the "correct" political filter, which did not allow for Vietnam pursuing its own economic and political destiny without outside domination by the U.S. These students do learn, however, that the "heart of the problem" was that the U.S. was fighting a popular movement. This fact is not investigated in order to enhance civic literacy; perhaps it might undermine the government's assumptions and practices in students' eyes. The effort to destroy a popular resistance movement against imperialism cannot be acknowledged fully for what it was, and the texts move forward, undisturbed by the weaknesses in logic and documentation of their own narrative.

The textbooks reveal that thousands of civilians were killed in bombing raids, and Vietnam "was carpeted with [bombs]…vast areas…were turned into crater-pitted moonscapes." These are horrendous admissions, but the possibility of war crimes is not even mentioned. There is not a single allusion to the Nuremberg Trials in these texts, despite the scholarship about war crimes committed during the conflict, the International War Crimes Tribunal in Stockholm, Sweden, and the Winter Soldier investigation by the Vietnam Veterans Against the War, which featured eye-witness and personal accounts by U.S. combat troops.

The advice of Clark Clifford and other members of the political and corporate elite who changed their views on the conflict is mentioned, but there is no discussion about why this shift occurred. It was totally pragmatic and cynical, rather than a response to moral concern about destroying a people and their country. Had the U.S.-Vietnam War been quick and relatively bloodless for American troops as the invasions of Grenada, Panama and Iraq, and without major protests at home, no major government official ould have opposed the war on ethical grounds. There is no discussion of the social and economic standing and influence of the leaders who advised Johnson about the war, and students are not asked whether elite self-interest and other factors were at work. The U.S. was clearly not winning and had to re-evaluate its position; thus, shifts in viewpoint had nothing to do with the war's moral premises or conduct.

Tet

The alleged murder of 3,000 South Vietnamese sympathizers by National Liberation Front (NLF) forces during the Tet Offensive in Hue in January, 1968, which was given major media attention after the My Lai massacre story broke in the U.S. in November, 1969 (nearly 21 months later), is simply passed on as the truthful version to youth. The official story is that NLF and North Vietnamese forces "deliberately…rounded up and murdered" these civilians.[34] D. Gareth Porter has also examined this alleged massacre and challenged its credibility. He argues that it is "one of the enduring myths of the Second Indochina War [that] remains essentially unchallenged." While "there is much that is not known about what happened in Hue," Porter states that there is enough information to show that what has been "conveyed to the American public by South Vietnamese and American propaganda agencies bore little resemblance to the truth, but was, on the contrary, the result of a political warfare campaign by the Saigon government, embellished by the U.S. government and accepted uncritically by the U.S. press." The original source of the data on Hue was a Political Warfare Battalion of the [Saigon] Army. "It is on the word of this body, whose specific mission is to discredit the National Liberation Front without regard to the truth, that the story of the 'massacre'…was based. Neither the number of bodies found nor the causes of death were ever confirmed by independent sources."[35]

Porter claims that American forces and not Communist executions were responsible for the greatest loss of life in Hue, concluding that the documentary evidence shows that "the official story of an indiscriminant slaughter of those unsympathetic to the NLF is a complete fabrication."[36] What happened stunned even supporters of the anti-Communist effort such as journalist Robert Shaplen, whose firsthand account supports the thesis that most of those allegedly killed by the NLF were the victims of American-Saigon assaults.

> I went to Hue and nothing I had seen during the Second World War…during the Korean War, and in Vietnam during the Indochina War or since 1965 was as terrible, in point of destruction and despair, as what I had witnessed.…Much of the city was in complete ruins.…*Nearly four thousand civilians were killed in Hue…and most of them were the victims of American air and artillery attacks.*[37]

His reports and Porter's scholarship, however, do not merit a single line in the textbook history.

The hysteria and public relations surrounding the so-called Hue massacre served a vital purpose: It obscured actual massacres that had been going on, and took people's minds off the My Lai massacre. These massacres included the CIA-sponsored "Phoenix" program, which resulted in the assassination, torture, and imprisonment of thousands of NLF guerrillas and peasants, and Operation "SPEEDY EXPRESS," a pacification program that uprooted and killed thousands of peasants in South Vietnam. Kevin P. Buckley of *Newsweek* shared his sobering conclusion on "SPEEDY": "All the evidence I gathered pointed to a clear conclusion: a staggering number of…civilians—perhaps as many as 5,000 according to one official—were killed by U.S. firepower to 'pacify' Kien Hoa [province]. The death toll there made the My Lai massacre look trifling by comparison."[38]

Nixon and "Vietnamization"

Nixon's "Vietnamization" program repeated the policies of the Diem period, with the Vietnamese fighting and dying and the U.S. aiding clients who had little popular support. Despite earlier comments admitting the possibility of an indigenous rebellion against Diem, the idea that the North was trying to conquer the South is maintained in the textbooks, as well as the concept of South Vietnam as a separate nation. Thus, the texts report on Nixon's continued effort to maintain an independent South Vietnam and to force Communist troops to leave the South.

The textbook narrative asserts that the January 1973 Paris Peace Agreement was a "death warrant" for the Thieu regime, which could not last without U.S. support. The assertion is presented without any analysis; thus, the texts ignore the annoying fact that South Vietnam was an artificial client regime like those set up by the Nazis during World War II. In the textbooks' view, the U.S. essentially abandoned South Vietnam, and it was crushed by the North. To the final moment, the fiction of two Vietnams is sustained, with one half attempting to conquer the other. The United States undermined the 1973 Paris Accords that were to end this latest war in

Vietnam, just as it had undermined the 1954 Geneva Agreements. Herman and Chomsky point out that "as the agreements were announced…the White House made an official statement, and Kissinger had a lengthy press conference in which he explained clearly that the United States was planning to reject every essential provision of the accords the administration had been compelled to sign." The media passed on this version "unquestioningly, thus guaranteeing that the Vietnamese enemy would appear to be violating the agreements if it adhered to them."[39] The U.S. thus disregarded "every essential provision of the scrap of paper it was compelled to sign in Paris." As in 1954 at Geneva, it subverted principles arrived at through negotiation in order to deny the legitimate aspirations of the Vietnamese people for independence and peace.[40]

The dissolution and drug abuse among American troops are mentioned briefly in the textbooks, a very inadequate explanation of a crucial development which had a profound impact on the course of the war. The widespread demoralization of U.S. ground troops, many of whom were African-American, Latino or working class, is not expanded into any discussion of why these troops were there in the first place, or why this decay occurred. Coupled with Vietnamese resistance and U.S. opposition at home, G.I. anti-war efforts and this demoralization helped to bring about the eventual U.S. withdrawal from Southeast Asia. Yet this development, which included widespread resistance and even mutinies among ground combat troops, is not examined to the extent it deserves.

My Lai

The major publicized U.S. atrocity of the Vietnam War elicits the briefest of comment, and the reported death toll ranges from 100 to 450 civilians. This massacre is morally equated with the NLF/NV murders in Hue during the Tet offensive. The nature and facts of these alleged crimes have been challenged; no scholar, however, has challenged the essential facts of what happened at My Lai. The pathetic coverage of the massacre and the contradictory casualty figures form another lesson in civic illiteracy for youth. How can they begin to make sense of the war if such a major incident is so poorly and erroneously reported?

The My Lai massacre was part of a much larger and systematic pattern of terrorism aimed at the rural peasantry who supported the NLF-led revolution against the Saigon regime and U.S. forces—but this organized terror elicits virtually no examination in the text history. Chomsky and Herman examine the central message of this massacre and the many larger and unpublicized massacres that were a regular part of U.S. military policy in Vietnam. Reviewing the dispatches of journalist Kevin Buckley, they contend that "on the matter of My Lai, misleadingly regarded in the West as somehow particularly evil (or perhaps a shocking exception), [it] was one of many that took place during Operation WHEELER WALLAWA. In this campaign, over 10,000 enemy were reported killed, including the victims of My Lai, who were listed in the official body count."[41] Buckley asserts that "the incident at My Lai [was] a particular gruesome application of a much wider policy which had the same effect in many places at many times."[42] The knowledge that massacres were routine policy is simply not raised with students, who leave the texts' discussion of My Lai with the impression that it was an isolated and regrettable incident and an exception to otherwise honorable policies.

Gettleman et al. point out that "the day the news broke [on My Lai]," the Army ordered an inquiry, which revealed that "war crimes" had indeed occurred there, including "individual and group acts of murder, rape, sodomy, maiming, and assault on noncombatants." The American Army had "suppressed" this information about the crimes, however, as part of "an elaborate cover-up of the massacre." The inquiry was itself suppressed and the Army still "refuses to release most of it to the public."[43] None of these facts finds its way into the textbook history.

The End and Lessons of the War

The casualty and refugee figures cited in the books vary greatly, as mentioned above. The divergent figures do not give one much confidence in these books' ability to help students form a truthful understanding of the conflict. The texts also state that there were 500,000 to more than 1.5 million refugees or "boat people"; many or perhaps tens of thousands died at sea. This death toll is widely exaggerated, another textbook claim that fosters civic-historical illiteracy among youth. The social class of the refugees coming to the U.S. is mentioned. In fact, many were wealthy, educated supporters of the war who were against legitimate Vietnamese efforts at self-determination and anti-colonialism; but this important point is never explored, another wasted opportunity for critical understanding.

In these texts, Vietnamese refugees are portrayed as helpless and worthy of U.S. assistance. By this logic, perhaps all refugees are equally deserving of sympathy and support, including slave-owners leaving the South during Reconstruction, Nazis escaping post-war Europe with help from the Catholic Church and CIA, and death-squad generals in El Salvador and Guatemala. Did these wealthy and educated Vietnamese share any responsibility for the murderous invasion of their own nation, or for aiding illegal actions that the United States held to be criminal at the Nuremberg Tribunal? There is no discussion of this question nor a deeper analysis of the "boat people" and, of course, no critical commentary about the millions of Vietnamese made refugees by the U.S.-Vietnam War. They do not deserve our concern and support, it seems, given the refusal of the U.S. to offer reparations and assistance as stipulated in the Paris Treaty.

The story of the war ends with North Vietnam "taking over" the weakened and helpless South—which had received more than $120 billion in direct economic and military aid and the support of nearly 3 million U.S. troops. The position is advanced that "Congress let them down," because our representatives did not want to appropriate more funds for our brave allies. This notion is not examined, and Congress, which did not oppose a single one of the 113 funding bills for the war from 1966 through 1973, is cast in an almost un-American role even though it supported the war to the bitter end. The "fall of Vietnam"—it is never called a "liberation"—came because the United States opposed an indigenous and democratic struggle for self-determination against foreign aggression. But students learn that a fundamental lesson was "clear to nearly everybody," namely that the U.S. could not simply withdraw from its responsibilities in the world. Only irrational critics and extremists could possibly assert that the basis of U.S. involvement in the world is domination of smaller nations to benefit the economic-political interests of the dominant elite here. Although the texts state that Vietnam's land and people had been destroyed and its agricultural economy was ravaged, students are assured that this was done in an effort to make Vietnam a viable democratic nation; sadly, it ended up as a "repressive" state allied with the Soviet Union. There is no analysis of U.S. responsibility for what eventually transpired.

Concern is voiced in the textbooks for the disaffected youth who became bitter and disillusioned about our government and political system because of the war; they and the nation would not soon recover. But, one could ask, why shouldn't they be bitter and disillusioned, and why should the nation soon recover from what it has done? As many veterans remind us, the wounds from the war cannot be healed without a truthful reckoning of our responsibility as a government and a people. The textbooks lament the distrust and cynicism directed against the government, but given the lies and contradictions admitted even in these texts, and the indisputable evidence of official lying found in The Pentagon Papers and other sources, distrust and cynicism are healthy responses to the government's cynical betrayal of democratic ideals, its citizens, and the truth.

The veterans who chose "to obey the call of their country" or, more accurately, to obey the dominant elite that claims to speak for the country, are victims of a process of civic illiteracy that begins in our schools. They did not answer the genuine call of a nation to defend freedom, but a call by an elite that defines its narrow self-interest as the nation's, and influences youth to sacrifice their lives in undemocratic and immoral causes. While the bitter legacy of the war endured by U.S. veterans is briefly mentioned in the text history as one the lessons of the conflict, it is surprising that there is no examination of the controversial POW/MIA issue. Rutgers University professor H. Bruce Franklin, an Air Force veteran and an anti-Vietnam War activist, reveals the bankruptcy of the dominant view in his book: *M.I.A. or Mythmaking in America*. At that time (1992), most people believed that "American prisoners of war [were] still being held as captives in Indochina."[44] This faith is not simply based "on political rhetoric, rumors, and the POW rescue movies," but also on material that puts forth "a coherent and superficially plausible pseudo-history compounded by self deception, amateur research, anecdotes, half truths, phony evidence, slick political and media manipulation, downright lies, and near-religious fervor." The anguish over POWs and MIAs "permeates the society, running especially strong in the working class"; it remains "the most important concern of many Vietnam veterans, displacing their own problems with unemployment, homelessness [there are thousands of homeless Vietnam vets], Agent Orange, and inadequate medical care."[45] All of these legitimate problems have been eclipsed by an unproven and blindly supported claim—testimony to the prevailing view of the conflict which serves to keep youth and citizens civically illiterate.

In spite of the national obsession with U.S. MIAs, there has been little recognition of the human cost of the war for Vietnamese families and veterans. Journalist Philip Shenon reported that the Vietnamese have some 300,000 missing from the war. They have also attempted in gentle ways to remind those here who are eager to pursue the MIA issue that "the sacrifice of Vietnamese families was greater than that of families in the U.S." If we compare the number of Vietnamese killed and wounded (1945–1975) in terms of the two countries' relative size, the equivalent toll for the U.S. would be some 31 to 37 million dead and wounded. Such an awesome human loss should cause citizens here to ponder at last the tragic legacy of this conflict. Although "the chances of finding a soldier's remains are virtually nonexistent, nearly 1,000 northern Vietnamese families apply to the Government each month for the chance to travel south to look for clues to the fate of missing relatives."[46] This reality should be kept in mind when we read about Vietnam's unwillingness to help U.S. officials find the remains of American service-men, and the Clinton administration's decision to formally recognize that nation after more than two decades of U.S. economic and political harassment.

The textbook lessons on the war do not deal adequately with the struggles faced by return-ing American veterans. Walter Capps, former director of the Center for the Study of Democratic Institutions, calls our attention to the great many suicides among Vietnam veterans—which are greater in number than the combat death toll, the hundreds of thousands who still suffer "delayed stress syndrome," the 2.5 million who were exposed to Agent Orange, the thousands who have been in jail and prison, and the 7,465 women who also served there.[47] The latter, along with Vietnamese women, receive not a line of mention in the textbooks. Carol Lynn Mithers points out that women fought and died on both sides, especially the Vietnamese: "Eight American women died in Vietnam; by 1968, according to the North Vietnamese government, 250,000 Vietnamese women fighters had been killed and 40,000 disabled."[48] Since the shoot-ing war continued for another seven years, it is evident that the casualties are much higher. The American women who served in Vietnam were "overwhelmingly white and middle class." They were all volunteers, many of whom "specifically requested assignment to Vietnam. Like the men who served, however, most knew nothing about…Vietnam [or] the politics of the war raging there."[49] Thus, civically illiterate men and women ended up fighting and dying in a conflict and country they knew little about—a tragic ending to the long indoctrination they had received.[50]

The lessons in these textbooks are many, but not one suggests that those who planned, exe-cuted, and lied about this aggression are war criminals as surely as those this nation and its allies tried at Nuremberg. The one lesson students ought to have learned is that the United States must stop invading smaller nations, but this is never presented as .a possibility for civic learning. The essential message in the texts and major media sources such as the *New York Times*, is to wage war differently and quickly next time (as the Gulf War demonstrated) and never to ask whether the U.S.-Vietnam War was unethical, unconstitutional, and undemocratic, as well as an affront to humanity and the ideals that educators share with students.

The textbook history avoids all of the dissenting lessons suggested by Chomsky. In "Visions of Righteousness," he raises issues that youth will not find in the textbooks. For example, Chomsky states that "in one of his sermons on human rights, President Carter once explained that we owe Vietnam no debt and have no responsibility to render it any assistance because 'the destruction was mutual.'" One of the "most astonishing statements in diplomatic history," it cre-ated no stir "among educated Americans" and did not diminish "Carter's standing as patron saint of human rights."[51] If youth can be made to believe that this was a "mutually destructive" war, then the ideological assault against the Vietnamese will continue in the textbooks and mass media. Chomsky contends that the "American system of indoctrination is not satisfied with 'mutual destruction' that effaces all responsibility for some of the major war crimes of the mod-ern era. Rather, the perpetrator of the crimes must be seen as the injured party." Since the essen-tial government and textbook history version of the war is that the United States was "simply defending [itself] from aggression, it makes sense to consider ourselves the victims of the Vietnamese."[52]

Final Thoughts

The history of the war in these texts reveals many terrible facts and strategic deceptions. They are similar to Robert McNamara's lament about Vietnam, in which he states that his "exceptional...vigorous, intelligent, well-meaning, patriotic" colleagues in the Kennedy and Johnson administrations—recall "the best and the brightest"—were "wrong, terribly wrong" about the war, although they acted "according to what we thought were the principles and traditions of this nation."[53] However, the textbooks essentially reproduce the dominant elite viewpoint of the conflict. The fundamental integrity of the nation and of our leaders is not subject to critical examination; it is naturally assumed that the United States was in Vietnam for honorable reasons. The possibility that the intentions of the dominant elite that led the country into war were not honorable, and were essentially played out in aggression against Chile, El Salvador, Grenada, Guatemala and Nicaragua, is simply out of bounds and not open for civic and historical examination. The doubt and uncertainty that the texts claim would "plague" the nation for years are seen as problems for educators and political leaders, not a marvelous opportunity to debate moral and political issues in a democracy, and that doubt and uncertainty are necessary for debate to occur is not considered. The struggle for such a democracy, therefore, cannot be aided by these history texts.

Part III: The History Textbook Treatment of the U.S.-Vietnam War: A Dissenting Theoretical Explanation

The textbook treatment of the U.S.-Vietnam War is an example of civic illiteracy, through which education's most important civic function has become the preparation of students to support U.S. aggression against the Third World. The textbook narrative that appears earlier in this chapter must also be placed within a theoretical context to help us understand the dominant-elite view of the war. A dissenting perspective is provided by insights on ideological hegemony that are often associated with Antonio Gramsci, who has been called "the greatest Western Marxist theorist of our century." His important theoretical and political insights have in turn been enriched by those of Paulo Freire and Chomsky.[55]

    Gramsci defines hegemony as the "'spontaneous' consent given by the great masses...to the general direction imposed on social life by the dominant [economic] group."[56] In the United States, as elsewhere, this means the dominant elite that shapes national and international policies, especially on life-and-death issues such as war. It is able to establish its views of society, war, and patriotism as the acceptable and most important ones for citizens, by influencing beliefs and ideas disseminated by schools and the media. The "national security" argument is perhaps the most powerful single example of Gramsci's theory. The needs of multinational corporations are presented as the interests of the nation, and as necessary to the defense of the country and the "free world." The underlying "truth" embedded in this ideology is that, despite resorting to questionable means, the United States acted in Vietnam, as it does everywhere in the world, from honorable moral and political motives. National leaders may stumble and err in the pursuit of noble ends, but they are always trying to do good and speak on behalf of all Americans. In Vietnam, as in the Persian Gulf, the country is committed to freedom and democracy. These are fundamental assumptions conveyed to students, but which Chomsky and others have challenged.

Chomsky's criticism of how the mass media manufacture agreement for this conception of the "national interest" should extend to our textbook authors, whose "institutional task…is to create the system of beliefs which will insure the effective engineering of consent."[57] Peter McLaren agrees with this assertion and aims his criticism directly at educational institutions: "The prevailing image of America that the schools…have promulgated is a benevolent one in which the interests of the dominant classes supposedly represent the interests of all groups.…The values and beliefs of the dominant class appear so correct that to reject them would be unnatural, a violation of common sense."[58]

Gramsci's theory of hegemony is complemented by the insights of Paulo Freire. In his major theoretical work, the *Pedagogy of the Oppressed*, Freire asserts that subordinate groups are dominated by social situations and educational institutions that make their inferior status appear legitimate. His work reminds us that education is always political, and the dominant elite always uses schools to further its own agenda. But education can also become a subversive element in the struggle over ideas, if the elite's power and influence are challenged and people begin to define the world in critically conscious terms.[59]

It can aid the process of civic literacy by helping youth to look at the world accurately, free of the nationalism and patriotism that now shape history textbooks and lessons. Freire, Gramsci, and Chomsky hold that all people have the intellectual potential for civic literacy; they can think critically about issues such as war and change the conditions that produce it—and the world. The educational system is largely a hindrance to such understanding, however, because it serves to make the interests of the dominant elite appear natural and good in the eyes of youth. This "natural" process is reflected in the textbook history on Vietnam.

An analysis of Freire and Gramsci's work reveals two basic ways in which dominant-elite views are passed on in U.S. education: an ideological form, in which the dominant elite shapes the fundamental beliefs about the social order and schools, and an ideational form, by which the content of historical issues blocks students' civic literacy. This latter process determines what is taught, and discussed. Curricular materials such as textbooks play a vital role because they can nurture or stifle critical thought. As Michael Apple argues, the actual content or ideational form reflected in textbooks is extremely powerful: "*How* is this 'legitimate' knowledge made available in schools? By and large it is made available through something to which we have paid far too little attention—the textbook.…the curriculum in most American schools is not defined by courses of study or suggested programs, but by one particular artifact, the standardized, grade-level-specific text."[60] Even though many high school students learn nothing about the U.S. Vietnam War in history classes, their textbooks remain the primary source for information on this epic tragedy. They are also training manuals for civic illiteracy on conflicts in Grenada, El Salvador, Nicaragua, Panama, and the Persian Gulf.

Gramsci's and Freire's theoretical insights are enriched by Herman and Chomsky's propaganda critique. Since history texts are an educational medium within the mass media, the Herman-Chomsky model is a powerful tool for examining textual content as a part of the larger purposes of schools. While the textbooks describe some of the problems and ruthless nature of the war, such facts are presented within the constraints of premises that maintain the integrity and honor of our country, its institutions, and leaders. Herman and Chomsky challenge this "defense-of-honor" position in their study of the media. The textbooks can be placed alongside the media because their essential task is to convince students that the Vietnam aggression was a defense of democracy and freedom that did not work; it was a mistake, a tragedy. The possibility that the war was "outright criminal aggression—a war crime—is *inexpressible*. It is not part of the spectrum of discussion [and] the idea is unthinkable."[61] Neither the media nor the texts and school lessons, however, simply "parrot" the official government line. The texts, for example, touch on many unsavory facts about U.S. aggression—though never termed as such—and criticisms are made of the means employed and the horrible results. But this treatment of the war does not confront Chomsky's conclusion: "We have no problem in perceiving the Soviet invasion of Afghanistan as brutal aggression....But the U.S. invasion of South Vietnam in the early 1960s...cannot be perceived as what it was."[62]

Notes

1. William L. Griffen and John Marciano, *Teaching the Vietnam War: A Critical Examination of School Texts and An Interpretive Comparative History Utilizing The Pentagon Papers and Other Documents* (Montclair, New Jersey: Allanheld and Osmun, 1979); reissued as *Lessons of the Vietnam War* (1984). This chapter builds upon that work.

2. The textbooks used in this chapter were obtained from the Teaching Materials Center, State University of New York at Cortland, and the Ithaca High School, Ithaca, New York: Carol Berkin and Leonard Wood, *Land of Promise* (Glenview, Illinois: Scott, Foresman, 1983); Daniel Boorstin and Brooks Mather Kelly, *A History of the United States* (Lexington, Massachusetts: Ginn, 1986); Paul Brandwein and Nancy Brauer, *The United States: Living in Our World* (San Francisco: Harcourt Brace Jovanovich, 1980); Richard C. Brown and Herbert Bass, *One Flag, One Land, Volume II* (Morristown, New Jersey: Silver Burdett Co., 1987); Joseph R. Conlin, *Our Land, Our Time* (San Diego: Coronado Publishers, 1985); Richard N. Current, T. Harry Williams, Frank Freidel, and Alan Brinkley, *American History: A Survey* (New York: McGraw-Hill, 1987); James W. Davidson and John Batchelor, *The American Nation* (Englewood Cliffs, New Jersey: Prentice Hall, 1989); Henry N. Drewry, Thomas H. O'Connor and Frank Freidel, *America Is*, 3rd Edition (Columbus, Ohio: Merrill, 1984); Henry Graff, *America: The Glorious Republic* (Boston: Houghton Mifflin, 1988); Robert P. Green, Jr., Laura L. Becker, and Robert L. Coviello, *The American Tradition: A History of the United States* (Columbus, OH: Merrill, 1984); Diane Hart and David Baker, *Spirit of Liberty: An American History* (Menlo Park, California: Addison-Wesley, 1987); Winthrop D. Jordan, Miriam Greenblatt, and John S. Bowes, *The Americans: A History of a People and a Nation* (Evanston, Illinois: McDougal, Littell & Co., 1985); Glenn M. Linden, Dean C. Brink, and Richard Huntington, *Legacy of Freedom: A History of the United States* (River Forest, Illinois: Laidlaw Brothers, 1986); Pauline Maier, *The American People: A History* (Lexington, Massachusetts: D.C. Heath, 1986); Ernest R. May, *A Proud Nation* (Evanston, Illinois: McDougal, 1985); James J. Rawls and Philip Weeks, Land of Liberty (New York: Holt; Rinehart, and Winston, 1985); Donald A. Ritchie, *Heritage of Freedom* (New York: Macmillan, 1985); Melvin Schwartz and John R. O'Connor, *The New Exploring*

American History (New York: Globe Book Company, 1981); Robert Sobel, Roger LaRaus, Linda DeLeon, and Harry P. Morris, *The Challenge of Freedom* (River Forest, Illinois: Laidlaw, 1986); Howard B. Wilder, Robert Ludlum, and Harriet McCune Brown, *This Is America's Story* (Boston: Houghton Mifflin, 1983). In this chapter, or textbook history synthesis, I have tried to reproduce the authors' view of the war as a synthesis of all the works, as if a class of American history students had woven together the twenty texts into one narrative of the conflict. Support for the text study came from the Faculty Research Program, State University of New York at Cortland.

3. Walter H. Capps, *The Unfinished War: Vietnam and the American Conscience* (Boston: Beacon Piess, 1982), 31–32.

4. Testimony of Abbot Low Moffat before the Senate Foreign Relations Committee, May 11, 1972, quoted in Griffen and Marciano, 60.

5. *The Pentagon Papers*, Senator Gravel Edition (Boston: Beacon Press, 1972) Vol. I, 243, hereafter noted as GE. Quoted in Noam Chomsky, *For Reasons of State* (New York: Vintage Press, 1973), 52.

6. GE, I, 5, 34, quoted in Ibid.

7. Chomsky, xv.

8. Congressional Record, June 3, 1974, 17391.

9. Marvin E. Gettleman, Jane Franklin, Marilyn Young, and H. Bruce Franklin, *Vietnam and America: A Documented History* (New York: Grove Press, 1985), 49.

10. "Final Declaration of the Geneva Conference" quoted in "Historic Victory in Indochina," *Monthly Review*, Vol. 27, No. 1, May 1975, 5.

11. Ibid., 6.

12. Leslie Gelb, "The U.S. and Vietnam: The Accretion of Failing Policy, *New York Times*, April 6, 1975, quoted in Ibid., 6–7.

13. Nixon quoted in Noam Chomsky and Edward S. Herman, *The Washington Connection and Third World Fascism: The Political Economy of Human Rights, Volume I* (Boston: South End Press, 1979), 341. ·

14. Edwin E. Moise, "Land Reform and Land Reform Errors in North Vietnam," *Pacific Affairs*, Spring, 1976, quoted in Ibid., 344.

15. D. Gareth Porter, "The Myth of the Bloodbath: North Vietnam's Land Reform Reconsidered," *Bulletin of Concerned Asian Scholars*, September, 1973, quoted in Ibid., 343–344.

16 Robert Scheer, *Ramparts Magazine Primer on Vietnam* (San Francisco: Ramparts Press, 1966), 21.

17. Chomsky, "The Pentagon Papers as Propaganda and History," in *The Pentagon Papers: Critical Essays*, eds. Noam Chomsky and Howard Zinn, GE, V, 188.

18. GEl, 239.

19. Philip Agee, "The CIA," Taped lecture, October 6, 1988. See William Blum, *Killing Hope: U.S. Milita, and CIA Interventions Since World War II* (Monroe, Maine: Common Courage Press, 1995).

20. Joseph Buttinger, *Vietnam: A Dragon Embattled*, 2 Vols. (New York: Praeger, 1967), 976.

21. Arthur Schlesinger, Jr., quoted in GE I, 252.

22. GE I, 252.

23 Jeffrey Race, *War Comes to Long An* (Berkeley: University of California Press, 1972), 196–197.

24. Eric Bergerud, *The Dynamics of Defeat: The Vietnam War in Hau Nghia Province* (Boulder, Colorado: Westview Press, 1991), 82.

25. Chomsky, *Rethinking Camelot: JFK, the Vietnam War, and US Political Culture* (Boston, Massachusetts:· South End Press, 1993), 59.

26. Ibid., 57.

27. Ibid., 25.

28. Ibid., 25–26.

29. Edward S. Herman and Noam Chomsky, *Manufacturing Consent: The Political Economy of the Mass Media* (New York: Pantheon, 1988), 209.

30. "All We Know Is That We Fired The First Shots," I.F. Stone's *Newsweekly*, March 4, 1968.
31. Ibid.
32. Chomsky, *Rethinking Camelot*, 43.
33. Douglas Kinnard, *War Managers* (Hanover, N.H.: University Press of New England, 1967), 37; and George McTuman Kahin, *Intervention: How America Became Involved in Vietnam* (New York: Alfred A. Knopf, 1986), 307–8, cited in Chomsky and Herman, *After the Cataclysm: Postwar Indochina & The Reconstruction of Imperial Ideology: The Political Economy of Human Rights: Volume II*, 321–2.
34. Chomsky and Herman, Ibid., 345.
35. D. Gareth Porter, "The 1968 'Hue Massacre'" Congressional Record—Senate, February 19, 1975, 3515.
36. Ibid., 3519.
37. Robert Shaplen, *Time Out of Hand* (New York: Harper and Row, 1969), 412.
38. Kevin P. Buckley, "Pacification's Deadly Price," *Newsweek*, June 19, 1972, 42–43, quoted in Griffen and Marciano, 133.
39. Herman and Chomsky, *Manufacturing Consent*, 230.
40. Ibid., 232.
41. Chomsky and Herman, *The Washington Connection and Third World Fascism*, 317.
42. Kevin Buckley, "Pacification's Deadly Price," *Newsweek*, June 19, 1972, quoted in Ibid.
43. Gettleman, et al., 404–405. See Seymour Hersh, *My Lai 4: A report on the massacre and its aftermath* (New York: Random House, 1970).
44. Bruce Franklin, *M.I.A. or Mythmaking in America* (Brooklyn, New York: Lawrence Hill Books, 1992), xii.
45. Ibid., 5–6.
46. Philip Shenon, "The Vietnamese Speak Softly of 300,000 Missing in the War," *New York Times*, November 30, 1992.
47. Walter H. Capps, *The Unfinished War: Vietnam and the American Conscience* (Boston: Beacon Press, 1982), 1.
48. Shelley Saywell, *Women in War* (Toronto: Penguin Books, 1985), 131, cited in Carol Lynn Mithers, "Missing in Action: Women Warriors in Vietnam," in Carlos Rowe and Rick Berg, eds., *Vietnam and American Culture* (New York; Columbia University Press, 1991), 81.
49. Mithers, 75.
50. A courageous minority cut through the civic illiteracy and resisted in Vietnam and military units throughout the world. See Richard Moser, *The New Winter Soldiers: GI and Veteran Dissent During the Vietnam Era* (New Brunswick, New Jersey: Rutgers University Press, 1996).
51. Chomsky, "Visions of Righteousness," in Rowe and Berg, 21.
52. Ibid.
53. Robert McNamara, *In Retrospect: The Tragedy and Lessons of Vietnam*, with Brian VanDeMark (New York: Times Books, 1995), xv–xvi. For commentary on McNamara's views, see R.W. Apple, "McNamara Recalls, and Regrets, Vietnam," *New York Times*, April 9, 1995; Max Frankel, "McNamara's Retreat," *New York Times Book Review*, April 16, 1995; and Carol Brightman and Michael Uhl, "Bombing for the Hell of it," *The Nation*, June 12, 1995.
54. Eugene Genovese, "On Antonio Gramsci," in James Weinstein and David Eakins, eds., *For a New America: Essays in History and Politics from Studies on the Left, 1959–1967* (New York: Random House, 1970), 285.
55. See Paulo Freire, *Pedagogy of the Oppressed*, Richard Schaull, ed. (New York: Herder and Herder, 1972). Freire's seminal work has moved thousands of teachers and citizens to reflect on the educational and social premises and practices in this country.
56. Antonio Gramsci, *Selections From The Prison Notebooks*, eds. Quintin Hoare and Geoffrey Nowell-Smith (New York: International Publishers, 1971), 12.

57. Noam Chomsky, in *Language and Power*, C.T. Otero, ed. (Montreal: Black Rose Books, 1988), 674.

58. Peter McLaren, *Life in Schools: An Introduction to Critical Pedagogy in the Foundations of Education*, 2nd Edition (New York: Longman, 1994), 175. See chapter 4 for more on McLaren.

59. See Richard Schaull, "Foreword" in Freire, 13–15.

60. Michael Apple, *Teachers and Texts: A Political Economy of Class and Gender Relations in Education* (New York: Routledge, 1988), 85.

61. Herman and Chomsky, *Manufacturing Consent*, 252.

62. Noam Chomsky, *Necessary Illusions: Thought Control in Democratic Societies* (Boston: South End Press, 1989), 150.

This chapter originally appeared in John Marciano, *Civic Illiteracy and Education: The Battle for the Hearts and Minds of American Youth* (New York: Peter Lang, 1997)

CHAPTER TWENTY-SIX

Critical Civic Literacy

Thinking Systemically about Peace Education

JOSEPH RAYLE

Peace Education and Critical Civic Literacy

I was asked several years ago to speak to a local peace group about peace education at my institution. To their consternation, I opened the talk with a simple question: "What do you mean
by 'peace'?" This was not an attempt at clever semantics; I wanted to draw attention to the fact
that our culture does not have a very clear conception of peace (Schell, 2003). An essential part
of a critical civic literacy that includes peace must take on the task of both defining "peace" and
bringing about the cultural changes necessary for the emergence of peace as a meaningful
value. By this, I do not intend that we arrive at some hard-and-fast definition of peace. I think
that it is essential to recognize the fact that peace, like other social processes, is dynamic and,
as such, is constantly changing and evolving; and it is highly dependent upon its context
(Hakvoort, 2010).

American education is one of the cultural vectors through which peace education can
become part of critical civic literacy. This notion of critical civic literacy is essential, as it connotes an active engagement with the ideas and processes of civic life, not just knowledge of how
these things work. Marciano (1997) pointed out that this sort of education is "political" in the
sense that it seeks to change aspects of the status quo. The stakes are high. The present lack of
civic literacy in our republic makes it shockingly easy for the power elite in this country to com-
mit our society to wars for dubious purposes. At home, it permits the growth and intrusion of
the national security apparatus into our daily lives, endangering our civil liberties. A muted citizen response to intrusions such as those permitted by the (so-called) Patriot Act only paves the
way for greater such intrusions in the future. Violence and oppression continue to be frequently
employed by various aspects of our government, and the Patriot Act is but one example. In general, our educational institutions are under attack, and intellectual freedom is at stake (Best,

Nocella, & McLaren, 2010). I shall argue here that peace education represents a very real attempt to change the status quo, from a culture that embraces violent solutions to conflicts—with the concomitant social, economic, and spiritual costs—to a culture that uses conflict as an opportunity in which new, potentially novel, non-destructive, and mutually beneficial solutions may be developed. This orientation to peace education requires a different approach to conflict that shifts from a reductionist to a relational way of thinking about peace and conflict (Rayle, 2010).

The role education plays in fostering critical civic literacy and peace education is that it is a significant social institution that influences the culture at large (Tozer, Senese, & Violas, 2007). Peace education is a rapidly developing area in academe (Harris, Shuster, et al., 2006), and peace education curriculum is emerging in school districts as well (Hakvoort, 2010). There are a number of professional associations dedicated to peace as an area of study, and many of them include subgroups that pursue the theory and practice of peace education.

This chapter has the goals of offering a working definition of peace and peace education, and providing an overview of system theory that is essential for understanding peace as a dynamic process. Part of the crisis in education is a lack of meaning or relevance for students. Students are often alienated from both the process of schooling and the ideas being taught in schools (Griffen, 2003; Gatto, 2006). This becomes particularly stark when one considers critical civic literacy. While the majority of students have a basic grasp of issues such as voting and jury service (Lutkus & Weiss, 2007), it is less clear how actively engaged with civics, peace, and the democratic process students are. Younger people tend to vote in fewer numbers, and in my experience, they tend to be thin on the ground at peace demonstrations and other political rallies. Most measures of anything that could represent critical civic literacy, particularly on the broad level, do not get at what some educators call "deep learning," which is learning that empowers students to apply ideas and information they have learned to solve meaningful problems (Bain, 2004). Indeed, in a rather disturbing study, researchers discovered that most people were unwilling to sign a petition based upon the Bill of Rights written in contemporary English on the grounds that the document was "too radical" (Loewen, 1995). Critical civic literacy must be made part of a meaningful narrative for education in order for it to be taught and accepted by students. This project, of course, runs counter to the traditional role of schooling (as opposed to education), which is to create obedient workers and good consumers (Gatto, 2008). For this reason, it must be expected that attempts to change this will be met with resistance.

Approaching these problems from a systemic framework has a number of advantages. To begin with, the framework itself represents a shift in narrative about both the purposes of education and the means through which these issues are examined (Capra, 1997). Inherent in system thinking is a new way of seeing the world. This culture's way of tackling problems is often reductionist in nature. Reductionism, while very useful in some situations, often leads us astray when we deal with complex phenomena such as education. Fixing a problem such as critical civic literacy or understanding peace requires more than simply supplying students with the right kind of information, or somehow motivating them.

There is a great deal of discussion in educational circles about the lack of student motivation. Critics such as Diane Ravitch (2010) point to a lack of student motivation as one of the problems in contemporary schools. Motivation does not somehow magically manifest itself—

it is itself an emergent property of a complex system, in this case the student-curriculum-teacher system. You can no more instill genuine motivation in students than you can cause someone to fall in love. Many factors are at work, and we must understand how these factors relate to one another if meaningful progress is going to happen. When we adopt a systems framework to examine the problem of education, it becomes necessary to understand the myriad factors involved in issues such as critical civic literacy and peace work. This involves not only identifying relevant factors, but also understanding the nature of their relationships.

System thinking opens the door to new and worthwhile ways of seeing these problems. System thinkers give us several reasons for adopting this perspective. First, it is of use in situations that require helping many actors to see the overall picture. Second, it opens new possibilities for working with problems that have been made worse by past attempts to fix them. Third, these issues interact with their surrounding natural and/or social environment. Fourth, problems whose solutions are non-obvious are amenable to system analysis (Senge, 2006). Education in general, peace education, and critical civic literacy clearly fit those criteria.

Critical civic literacy and peace education are issues that must be broadly understood by people throughout the educational system. These ideas are not simply reduced to a series of facts or skills, although facts and skills certainly do matter. To grasp their importance, policy makers, administrators, and teachers must understand the social, historical, and cultural connections involved in critical civic literacy and peace education. These things do not operate in isolation from other aspects of our socio-cultural system. Without a "big picture" perspective, these critical ideas, like so many others, get reduced to a sort of trivia test, perhaps, but not one that is particularly meaningful for either teacher or learner.

Ideas such as critical civic literacy have been a part of the educational discourse for a long time. Clearly, an important aspect of critical civic literacy is a sense of history, and schools have made strides to cover a considerable amount of history (Loewen, 2005); but these efforts frequently take the form of learning isolated facts instead of becoming familiar with processes and important arguments about history. My students, mostly teacher education candidates, complain bitterly about what sounds like a death march through un-stimulating history courses with little room for debate, interpretation, purpose, or connection with their own experiences. The issues of purpose and connection are important. Teachers should welcome the dreaded, "Why do I have to learn this?" question, because it represents an opportunity to engage with students and guide them toward connecting with whatever is being taught in order to make it personally meaningful. Many educators point out that this lack of personal meaning in education alienates students (Palmer, 2007).

By their very nature, peace education and critical civic literacy both influence, and are influenced by, other cultural forces. It is for this reason that a systemic approach in both their framing and pedagogy are worthwhile. Clearly, these problems have non-obvious solutions, or they would have been solved by now. That educators have struggled, and continue to struggle, over these questions should be evidence enough that a new way of thinking about them is called for.

In my own teaching, I have found a systemic approach useful in helping students both connect with peace education and related issues for several reasons. System theory allows the level of focus to move from level to level in the social system. It is a commonplace to say that in dealing with social problems, liberals focus on the system, and conservatives focus on the individual. I find in classroom discussions that these opposing political orientations can get in the way of developing a thorough understanding of issues. System theory allows us to bridge that gap, making it possible to consider both social forces and individual behavior, and, most importantly, how they interact. The decision to participate in the civic life of one's community, or whether or not to behave peacefully, are individual decisions, but they can only really be understood in terms of their particular milieu (Mills, 1961).

In addition to opening up conversations across lines of political difference, it is possible to bridge philosophical differences as well. Although system theory is similar in some respects to the functionalist school of sociology, it can admit and make use of ideas such as class conflict, ideology, and oppression. Further, its interdisciplinary nature allows me to draw from insights from a number of fields, even sometimes breaking down the artificial barriers that exist between disciplines, while at the same time avoiding the lack of accessibility and "real world" applicability inherent in the "rag and bone shop" (McLaren, 2007, p. 12) of postmodernism.

The concept of peace, as my experience with the peace group shows, is a bit slippery, and grappling with this is facilitated by system thinking. Writers such as Schell (2003) have explored the nature of this difficulty, but by and large, it has been under-conceptualized in our culture. Harris & Morrison (2003) set out several types of peace, both positive and negative. The characterizations of positive and negative peace refer to notions of peace that are either typified by the absence of conflict (negative peace), or the efforts to create peaceful systems and practices. These types of peace are the absence of war, a lack of structural violence, the management of interpersonal relationships without violence, holistic peace systems, intercultural peace, and inner peace. Some forms of peace are more familiar than others. For example, peace is most commonly thought of as "freedom from disturbance" (Abate & Jewel, 2001). Structural violence takes the form of the existence or organization of social institutions that prevent some members of a society from developing their potential, or even meeting their basic needs (Galtung, 1969). Common forms of structural violence are racism, sexism, and classism. There are many other examples as well.

Moving toward a positive conception of peace is facilitated by thinking of peace as a dynamic, rather than static, process. Furthermore, peace requires an ongoing effort to sustain. It is a practice, as elucidated by Mohandas Gandhi's idea of *satyagraha* (Schell, 2003). The idea of *satyagraha* moves peace and peace work from the negative connotation (i.e., absence of war) to a positive connotation, in which real activity is used to create and sustain peace. Peace becomes an action, an orientation toward the world, that necessitates both an awareness of one's myriad connections with the world (in all of its ways), and a willingness to act in a way that reflects this connection. System thinking opens the door to this way of seeing and acting.

The management of interpersonal relationships without violence is increasingly encouraged in the school environment through programs of conflict resolution (Hakvoort, 2010). This represents a shift away from the win/lose mentality that is often characteristic of conflict, and instead takes conflict as an opportunity for the affected parties to take action that helps ameliorate the conflict. It also provides students communication and interaction skills that make future violence less likely.

In order to think systemically, it is necessary to understand what systems are and how they operate. Systems thinking may be contrasted with reductionist or mechanistic thinking (Capra, 1983). Mechanistic analyses of the world involve conceptualizing things as machines. For example, it is possible to think of the human body as a machine, and analyze those parts and their functioning, largely in isolation from other parts. While this has produced some stunning breakthroughs in our understanding of human biology, in and of itself it is not sufficient for understanding human health, wellness, or disease, because of the complex biological and social nature of human beings. Similarly, schools have often been thought of as machinelike, as a sort of factory that produces students (Betts, 1992). The problem, of course, is that human learning and the educational endeavor are very complex, and these things exist in an ever-changing social and cultural environment that are constantly affecting and affected by each other.

Many of the ideas on systems were first articulated by Bertalanffy (1969). A system is a complex of interacting parts. Most systems are open in that they affect, and in turn are affected by, other systems. Systems tend to resist change, as they have feedback and control systems that maintain a system's dynamic equilibrium. Changes in systems can produce unintended consequences. Related to this, systems often have emergent properties, which are new characteristics that arise as a result of interactions within the system. Systems can be nested, which is to say that systems can be comprised of other systems. As a result of this, parts of systems, and systems themselves, can be highly interconnected.

For the educator, there are a number of practical implications of system theory. It is helpful to use these ideas not only to aid students in understanding peace education and critical civic literacy, but it is also useful in designing curriculum. A systemic approach to teaching involves helping students understand their own connection to the ideas under examination. In my own educational practice at a regional comprehensive college that serves an overwhelmingly white population, I help students understand their own connection and self-interest in understanding and dealing with racism. Most white students are uncomfortable in dealing with race, and in the case of my institution, not a few of them complain that race has somehow been "shoved down our throats" by professors unsympathetic to their own (largely imagined) plight brought about by Affirmative Action and other programs aimed at ameliorating racial inequality in our society. Taking a systemic approach, I encourage students to recognize how their daily lives are affected by a vast, interconnected web of people, both living and dead, without whose efforts their own lives would be seriously diminished. I point to the contributions made by African American inventors who, despite growing up during the era of Jim Crow, managed to develop their potential and make technological contributions that continue to benefit us today. The gamut runs from engineering to medicine, and this example leaves out much else. Then I ask them to consider first, where might we be as a society if everyone had been allowed to develop his or her potential all along? The waste of human potential, and our loss as a society, is sobering. Then I ask them to consider that there are any number of children whose needs are not met by the contemporary educational system, many of whom have the potential to make further contributions that never come to fruition. These students lose out, and often in a big way, if one considers the consequent loss of potentially life-saving or life-changing developments that are either never created or the development of which is delayed.

In addition, I help students understand that general fears arising from racist thinking often lead to the erosion of civil liberties in our society in the name of increasing our security. This can be seen in the form of the proliferation of security cameras that ostensibly protect us from crime, or the ever-intrusive nature of government agencies into citizens' lives to protect them from terrorist attacks. Finally I demonstrate how historically racism has been used to control both whites and minority groups, either by playing them off against one another in labor disputes (Zinn, 2003), or by playing on white fears about property values, resulting in "white flight" and consequent distortions in home prices (Loewen, 2005).

While I am sensitive to the fact that this particular approach does little to lessen the culture of narcissism that envelops our students, I do think that it is necessary if we are to have much hope of reaching them at all. Looking at this relationship from a systemic framework, it is likely that students will be resistant to ideas that conflict with their own worldview. Indeed, Koole, Greenberg, and Pyszcynski (2006) point out that challenges to cultural beliefs represent a serious existential threat, and as such, can provoke serious resistance. Given that students as nested systems themselves are resistant to change, it is unsurprising that they express disdain for the kind of mental leaps required of critical civic literacy because too many of their taken-for-granted assumptions are challenged. This isn't to say that students can't be reached, but one cannot expect that there will be too many "aha" moments in the classroom. As I have shared elsewhere (Patterson & Rayle, 2004), change can be a long time coming. It happens, but not in any way even remotely recognized by educational assessment.

Some Practical Implications for Peace Education

Peace education and peace building are an essential element in a globalized world. Barring some unimaginable disaster, the globalization that was set into motion in the eighties and nineties is here to stay (Friedman, 2005). There are both positive and negative implications for those we teach, but in either case, our students require the knowledge and perspective necessary to live fulfilled lives in this changing world. As Friedman points out, globalization has led to great improvements in production, access to less expensive goods and services, and an economic system integrated in such a way that there is less incentive for armed conflict between developed nation states. On the downside, globalization has resulted in the rise of corporations that possess economic resources the size of some nations, and the power and influence that comes with it. Changes in the global economy have led to serious economic dislocation in the United States. The litany of declining numbers of manufacturing jobs and the subsequent economic malaise is familiar. In this republic, one of the few checks on the runaway power of big business is a civically literate citizenry that values and works for peace.

Peace educators, by challenging structures and processes that promote inequality and oppression, prepare students to begin making their own decisions about what values they will accept and what goals they will pursue. As educators, we work in a system that militates against a sense of connection or wholeness. In fact, a great deal of effort is made toward making distinctions, cutting off individuals from each other, and even themselves (Gatto, 2008). Alienated people, as Gatto observes, are good consumers, and often good workers, in that they are unlikely to question the narrative of consumerism, or the educations they receive to prepare them for the workforce. There is no conspiracy here: There is economic rationality and the emergent results. It is unlikely that business people are out to cause chaos or harm (evidence, in fact, would suggest that they'd do well to work for peace) (Reuschlein, 2010), but as systemic effects emerge, such as selling of values, defining people, indoctrinating students with particular meanings and ideas about the good life, it would be irrational to then subvert those values. The advertising system may help perpetuate social stereotypes (guys are emotionally shallow, only interested in sex, sports, and television, for example), but then it must use these ideas in clever ways to sell products, further perpetuating the stereotypes. Peace education includes teaching students the media literacy skills required to resist and grapple with the power inherent in these messages.

The advertising system has one clear, simple message: You are not okay. Your life is somehow not good enough. This pervasive message creates a kind of discontent—almost an addiction—that cannot be easily fixed, if for no other reason than it promises what it cannot provide. Here's the scheme: You're empty: Go buy something: That something doesn't fill the void: You're empty: Repeat ad mortem (*Story of Stuff*, 2007). Nothing else in life is as important as consumption. Our major holidays revolve around consumption. Witness "Black Friday" or the ever-earlier Christmas shopping season. These things get in the way of things that are genuinely connected with human happiness. For empirical support, take a look at the World Value Survey (Gatto, 2008). There are other, more accurate, ways to measure human freedom and fulfillment than retail sales.

The problem here, from a peace perspective, is that consumerism needlessly uses resources, bringing our society into conflict with societies that possess resources needed to produce consumer goods. Consumerism not only wastes resources, the whole process detracts from things that matter: good relationships, good health, and satisfying work (Gatto, 2008).

This isn't to argue that a certain level of material comfort isn't necessary. Indeed, measures of happiness indicate that people's happiness tends to increase as their level of material comfort increases. At least this is true up to a point. There is a clear relationship early on: Where food, shelter, clothing, and other basic necessities of life are concerned, there is a clear correlation between happiness and material comfort. Beyond this level, the relationship becomes less clear. In fact, it is safe to say that more material goods wind up producing more problems than they solve.

So, how is this related to peace? Effective critical civic literacy in this regard must move from considering the civic realm such as laws and government, to understanding the connections that both sustain and contextualize them. Considering these ideas from a system theory point of view, as articulated by such thinkers as Capra (1997), can make it possible to understand peace and develop the type of critical civic literacy that makes peace possible.

Compassion arises from a sense of connection. A sense of connection comes from an awareness of the highly interconnected nature of our social worlds. The socio-cultural reality that we experience is an emergent property of the complex interplay of the dynamic processes that make up our societies, cultures, and selves. A critical civic literacy that includes peace education strengthens both.

Bibliography

Abate, F.R., & Jewell, E. (2001). *The new Oxford American dictionary*. New York: Oxford University Press.

Bain, K. (2004). *What the best college teachers do*. Cambridge, MA: Harvard University Press.

Bertalanffy, L. (1969). *General system theory: Foundations, development, applications*. New York: G. Braziller.

Best, S., Nocella, A., & McLaren, P. (2010). The rise of the academic-industrial complex and the crisis in free speech. In A., Nocella, S. Best, & P. McLaren (Eds.), *Academic repression: Reflections from the academic industrial complex*. Baltimore: A.K. Press.

Betts, F. (1992, November). How systems thinking applies to education. *Educational Leadership*, 38–41.

Capra, F. (1983). *The turning point: Science, society, and the rising culture*. New York: Bantam Books.

Capra, F. (1997). *The hidden connections: A science for sustainable living*. London: Flamingo.

Friedman, T.L. (2005). *The world is flat: A brief history of the twenty-first century*. New York: Farrar, Straus and Giroux.

Galtung, J. (1969). Violence, peace, and peace research. *Journal of Peace Research*, *6*(3), 167–191.

Gatto, J.T. (2006). *The underground history of American education: A schoolteacher's intimate investigation into the prison of modern schooling*. New York: Oxford Village Press.

Gatto, J.T. (2008). *Weapons of mass instruction: A schoolteacher's journey through the dark world of compulsory schooling*. Philadelphia: New Society Publishers.

Glassner, B. (1999). *The culture of fear: Why Americans are afraid of the wrong things*. New York: Basic Books.

Griffen, W. (2003). All the world is a stage—Time to change the plot. *Journal of Thought*, *38*(3), 87–92.

Hakvoort, I. (2010). The conflict pyramid: A holistic approach to structuring conflict resolution in schools. *Journal of Peace Education*, *7*(2), 157–169.

Harris, I., & Morrison, M. (2003). *Peace education* (2nd ed.). Jefferson, NC: McFarland & Co.

Harris, I.M., Shuster, A.L., Peace and Justice Studies Association, & International Peace Research Association. (2006). *Global directory of peace studies and conflict resolution programs*. San Francisco, CA: Peace and Justice Studies Association.

Koole, S., Greenberg, J., & Pyszcynski, T. (2006). Introducing science to the psychology of the soul: Experimental Existential psychology. *Current Directions in Psychological Science*, *15*(5), 212–216.

Loewen, J. (2005). *Sundown towns: A hidden dimension of American racism*. New York: New Press.

Loewen, J.W. (1995). *Lies my teacher told me: Everything your American history textbook got wrong*. New York: Simon & Schuster.

Lutkus, A., and Weiss, A. (2007). *The nation's report card: Civics 2006* (NCES 2007–476). U.S. Department of Education, National Center for Education Statistics. Washington, DC: U.S. Government Printing Office.

Marciano, J. (1997). *Civic illiteracy and education: The battle for the hearts and minds of American youth*. New York: Peter Lang.

McLaren, P. (2007). *Life in schools: An introduction to critical pedagogy in the foundations of education*. (5th ed.). New York: Pearson.

Mills, C.W. (1961). *The sociological imagination*. New York: Grove Press.

Palmer, P.J. (2007). *The courage to teach: Exploring the inner landscape of a teacher's life*. San Francisco, CA: Jossey-Bass.

Patterson, J.A., & Rayle, J.M. (2004). Decentering whiteness: Personal narratives of race. In G.W. Noblit, S.Y. Flores, & E.G. Murillo, Jr. (Eds.), *Postcritical ethnography: Reinscribing critique*. Cresskill, NJ: Hampton Press.

Ravitch, D. (2010). *The death and life of the great American school system: How testing and choice are undermining education*. New York: Basic Books.

Rayle, J. (2010). Peace education: A systemic framework. In A. Fitz-Gibbon (Ed.), *Positive peace: Reflections on peace education, nonviolence, and social change*. New York: Rodopi.

Reuschlein, R. (2010). Peace economics. Presentation at the annual conference of the Peace and Justice Studies Association. Winnipeg, Manitoba, Canada.

Schell, J. (2003). *The unconquerable world: Power, non-violence, and the will of the people*. New York: Metropolitan Books.

Senge, P.M. (2006). *The fifth discipline: The art and practice of the learning organization*. New York: Doubleday/Century.

The Story of stuff. Perf. Annie Leonard. Free Range Studios, 2007. Storyofstuff.com.

Tozer, S., Senese, G., & Violas, P. (2007). *School and society: Historical and contemporary perspectives*. New York: McGraw-Hill.

Zinn, H. (2003). *A people's history of the United States: 1492–present*. New York: HarperCollins.

CHAPTER TWENTY-SEVEN

The Allure of Corporate Deception and Greenwashing

Why Every Rose Has Its Thorn

CORI JAKUBIAK & MICHAEL P. MUELLER

> The process of neoliberalism has…entailed much "creative destruction," not only of prior institutional frameworks and powers…but also of divisions of labor, social relations, welfare provisions, technological mixes, ways of life and thought, reproductive activities, attachments to the land, and habits of the heart.
>
> (HARVEY, 2005, P. 3)

> The skills, aptitudes, and attitudes necessary to industrialize the earth…are not necessarily the same as those that will be needed to heal the earth or to build durable economies and good communities.
>
> (ORR, 2004, P. 27)

In the days following the tragic events of September 11, 2001, observers noted that a primary response of the U.S. government was the call for Americans to return to their "normal" practices of citizenship—that is, to return to shopping. "We've got to give people confidence to go back out and go to work, buy things, go back to the stores. Get ready for Thanksgiving, get ready for Christmas…participate in our society," announced one member of Congress (Robbins, 2005, p. 36). From the president on down to the mayor of New York City, the primary message delivered to stunned Americans in the wake of 9/11 was "to act as individuals, to spend money on themselves, to consume products and entertainment because their true mission as citizens was to bolster the economy, even if they put themselves and their savings at risk" (Sturken, 2007, p. 57). In what civic context, one might wonder, is the act of making a purchase—of a pair of jeans, a movie ticket, or a manicure—a necessary and proper form of civic engagement? Why, one might ask, would the post-9/11 American populace—a group reeling from the brutality of a surprise terrorist attack—be encouraged to "go back to the stores" as a demonstration and measure of their national solidarity, resistance, and patriotism?

In this chapter, we address how American citizenship is increasingly being defined through *consumption*. U.S. citizens are *consumer-citizens*, a people who practice their politics through the purchase of goods and services. People are constantly encouraged to engage in this practice: for example, they vote through their wallets and purses to increase healthy food options. We argue in this chapter that consumer-citizenship not only represents a broad constriction of public life, but also that it is encouraged by color-based marketing: the Madison Avenue practice of labeling goods green, pink, and so forth in order to imbue these goods with symbolic meanings. Color-based marketing implies that one can remedy resource depletion, global warming, and rising breast cancer rates—among other economic, political, social, and ecological justice issues—through the purchase of correctly hued products and services.

While educators and anthropologists have gazed critically on color-based marketing trends and the attendant consumer-citizenship it permeates (Brosius, 1999; King, 2006), little is being done in American schools to teach students how to untangle these same messages. Through their lack of curricular attention to *critical civic literacy education*, public schools inadvertently perpetuate consumer-based citizenship. National and state educational priorities and standards even pitch the primacy of the economy and developing a consumer society (e.g., National Research Council, 1996). Viewing this situation as short sighted, we organize this chapter as follows: First, we situate consumer-citizenship within *neoliberalism*, an ideological apparatus that privileges economic growth as its main priority and restructures societal relations in numerous ways. Second, we argue that corporate color-based marketing schemes such as green and pink, in their apparent benevolence, are problematic and further the aforementioned consumer-citizenship by obfuscating other, more collective, means of civic engagement. Third, we suggest that schools can and should incorporate critical civic literacy education into their regular curricula—a move that would better equip students to decipher the thorny vines of corporate messages in society. Finally, we explore some of the alternatives to consumer-based citizenship.

Neoliberalism and the Shift to Consumer Citizenship

Consumer-citizenship finds roots in the logic of *neoliberalism*, a broad, often contested, political label used to describe the pro-free market, pro-corporate, anti-big government ideology that has become hegemonic among Global North nation-states and supranational financial institutions (e.g., the World Bank and the International Monetary Fund) in the last few decades. The world order as envisioned under neoliberalism is one in which publicly funded, social service provisions are reduced or non-existent, economic growth is promoted at all costs, and the primary role of the nation-state is to regulate markets so as to promote the unfettered, global movement of capital.

Under the regime of neoliberalism, the free market is equated with freedom—indeed, with shared democracy (or "equal opportunity"). Maximizing corporate industries' chances for financial gain, through the privatization of any number of social services and through the easing of restrictive environmental and labor laws, is seen as on a par with optimizing individuals' choices and civil liberties (Harvey, 2005). Consequently, attempts to challenge neoliberalism as an ideology that puts profit before people or as a formation that harms natural systems are not only quickly discredited, but also viewed as anti-democratic. As Duggan (2003, p. 10) notes, neoliberalism is usually presented not as a particular set of interests and political interventions, but as a kind of nonpolitics—a way of being reasonable, and of promoting universally desirable forms of economic expansion and democratic government around the globe. Who could be against greater wealth and more democracy?

As a way of viewing the world, then, and as a set of conceptual priorities on which principles of governance are based, neoliberalism is stubbornly resistant to critique or amendment.

Ideas of civic engagement and what it means to be an active citizen are reframed under the auspices of neoliberalism. In the last three decades in the United States, as four successive administrations have been in thrall to neoliberal doctrines, rates of participation in community organizations and in long-standing forms of collective, public action such as political letter-writing, union membership, and protest rally attendance have declined dramatically (Putnam, 1995). Concurrently, we have witnessed a rise in a more private, individually oriented form of civic participation: consumer politics. As consumer-citizens, people exercise political expression through the purchase of goods; they fashion lifestyles for themselves based on the accumulation of particular objects or the consumption of certain experiences (Rose, 1999). Citizens are acculturated as consumers of science, technology, politics, popular culture, and media as well as consumers of particular forms of scientific recreation and ecotourism (Russell & Russon, 2007).

This self-reliant and self-shaping consumer-citizen is deemed as active within neoliberalism as s/he depends not on the state (as a passive citizen would) or on any reconfiguration of the existent social structure for happiness, security, or cultural identity. Instead, the consumer-citizen is expected—indeed, encouraged—to participate actively in the shops, places that are framed as more responsive to the collective weal than the now-outmoded, inefficient, public institutions of New Deal origin. Says Butcher (2003) on how consumer-citizenship promotes the rationalities of neoliberalism:

> traditional political channels increasingly invite cynicism, and many feel alienated from the institutions of government. Other institutions, through which individuals related to their society, have also declined—church, community and family. All this has strengthened, by default, the more individual form of politics—consumer politics. Far from the discredited institutions of government, it is as consumers that we are, apparently, free to exercise our choice in pursuit of a better world. (p. 105)

As part and parcel of consumer-citizenship, then, one is expected to shop—a lot!—and to make the right purchases as one does so. Many of these "correct" purchases are color-coded to index particular politicized or socialized meanings—a discussion to which we now turn.

Colorwashing Consumer-Citizens: Buy Green, Buy Pink

There is a trend most Americans know well: color-based marketing. In the last 30 years, we have seen a proliferation of green, pink, red, and other-hued goods, services, and experiences, all of which are designed to link commercial purchases to broader, arguably ethical, social, or political, agendas. For example, one's selection of a green, perhaps highly priced, dishwashing detergent versus a colorless, cheaper, off-brand equivalent ostensibly allows the purchaser to engage in civic action. To buy the green dishwashing detergent is to save water tables from an infusion of phosphates, while buying the non-green alternative suggests an acceptance of the status quo.

Similarly, color-based marketing offers that the purchase of something labeled pink—e.g., a bag of chips, a blender, a pair of tweezers—allows one to raise breast cancer awareness. Consumer-citizenship, aided by color-based marketing, offers the ultimate in multitasking. One can, purportedly, accomplish yesteryear's version of a sit-in while stocking up on big-box values. The color label advises one as to the cause, fostering a frenzy of hues around consumption. Some consumer-citizens even *desire* the related monikers of fashionista, shopaholic, or mall-rat, becoming specialists in the consumer-citizen appeal. These specialists then advise the public how to be successful, for example, in the rush for the stores on large-scale shopping events such as Black Friday, the day after many folks say they are *thankful* for what they already have.

Astute observers of color-based marketing point out that the origins of labeling products as colored—in particular, green—stem from the early work of modern-day public relations (PR) firms—namely, groups that work in the interest of profit rather than social or ecological justice. The underlying value of a company in relation to its investors drives the pursuits of corporate agenda. In the first decades of the 20th century, PR firms in the United States were recruited by large corporations such as Standard Oil to fend off what was then widespread anti-corporate sentiment and to fight government efforts at regulation (Karliner, 1997). As the 20th century progressed and corporations came under increasing attack for causing environmental problems, corporations directed PR firms to shift public opinion in their favor. Over time, these corporations increasingly relied on PR firms and advertising agencies for environmental whitewash or *greenwash* propaganda, which is designed to cleanse corporations of their environmentally destructive impacts and recast them as environmental advocates rather than plunderers. In the words of Karliner (1997):

> The role that the descendants of [PR firms] have played in shaping and distorting environmental issues can be traced back to the 1962 release of Rachel Carson's *Silent Spring*, the book credited with catalyzing the modern environmental movement. In response to *Silent Spring*, the Chemical Manufacturers Association (CMA, called the Association of Manufacturing Chemists at the time) recruited a young man named E. Bruce Harrison, whose job was to develop a coordinated response among the major U.S. chemical corporations to *Silent Spring*'s stinging and prophetic account of the ecological impacts of pesticides such as DDT....Harrison sowed the seeds of the corporate PR response to modern environmentalism....As the contemporary environmental movement built momentum in the mid- to late-1960s, undermining public trust in many a corporation, newly greened corporate images flooded the airwaves, newspapers, and magazines. This initial wave of greenwash was labeled ..."ecopornography." (p. 170)

As Karliner (1997) reports, late 20th-century environmental catastrophes did nothing if not further popularize and create consumer frenzy around color-based marketing. He continues:

> As the 1980s produced the Bhopal, Chernobyl, and Exxon Valdez disasters, the environmental movement gained in strength. In response, greenwash advertisements became even more numerous and more sophisticated, peaking in 1990 on the twentieth anniversary of Earth Day. It was during that year of eco-hoopla that "corporate environmentalism" came into its own in the United States. The transnationals came to recognize that increasing numbers of consumers wanted to buy green products. In fact, in the early 1990s, one poll found that 77 percent of Americans said that a corporation's environmental reputation affected what they bought....In response to this phenomenon, the corporate world went to great lengths to market itself and its products as the greenest of the green. One-fourth of all new household products that came onto the market in the United States around the time of "Earth Day 20" advertised themselves as "recyclable," "biodegradable," "ozone friendly," or "compostable." (p. 171)

In the years since Earth Day 20, green has become so commonplace that even the most outrageously polluting products are labeled as such. For example, as we write, an empty, plastic Deer Park water bottle sits on the desk nearby, hailing for selective attention with the following text: "Did you notice this bottle has an Eco-Slim cap? This is part of our ongoing effort to reduce our impact on the environment....Be Green." Given the proliferation of empty plastic water bottles currently floating in the Pacific and Atlantic Oceans (so-called trash islands), it is hard to believe that Nestlé (Deer Park is one of its subsidiaries) has not faced more public, or community, scrutiny.

The green barrage in the marketplace contains green versions of nearly everything, from green cosmetics to green supersized SUVs. But that's not all. Green advertising is also operating very covertly now. Green may take the form of ideas or things associated with being cleaner and more environmentally friendly, such as more oxygen in bottled water, nitrogen in tires (Koballa & Demir, 2010), and recycling logo forms as the bracket in DVD cases. In the case of zoos, parks, and green travel destinations, green often takes the form of protected fauna, while concomitantly what is deemphasized is the fact that, say, a zoo enclosure is too suffocating for the species it houses.

Color-based deception also goes beyond green marketing. In the last few years, we have also seen an expansion in the plethora of products labeled pink and red—motives that associate commercial items with abstract social causes such as breast cancer awareness and HIV/AIDS. While corporate greenwashing suggests that a particular product or item is green because of qualities inherent within the product, the connection between other colors and deadly disease is purely symbolic. Take Deer Park's water bottle again. With its smaller cap, it is purportedly *less* polluting than other, equivalent water bottles and is therefore a good choice purchase. In contrast, although many people think they are supporting "a cause for a cure" when they buy pink-labeled items, the pink-product market does not inherently use pink to reduce the incidence of breast cancer inasmuch as it claims to promote awareness around breast cancer as a disease (King, 2006). The strategy of marking something pink so that people think they are contributing to breast cancer research, then, is a ploy that frequently goes by the wayside not only because it obscures the transnational, corporate enclosure of an often localized public health problem (Klawiter, 2000), but also because very few people investigate how and in what ways corporations funnel money back toward breast cancer research (King, 2006). At the same time, red tee-shirts, scarves, and sweatshirts sold at The Gap do not, in themselves, reduce HIV/AIDS; rather, these red product lines entice consumer-citizens through the vague promise of promoting HIV/AIDS awareness. When one makes a red purchase, one might believe that one has actually contributed to reducing HIV/AIDS worldwide while simultaneously acquiring a new hoodie.

There has been a confluence, then, of color-based marketing with "lifestyle choice" (Rose, 1999), a phenomenon that intersects tidily with neoliberalism's prerogatives and the civic duties it mandates. If active, consumer-citizens practice their politics in the marketplace—that is, out of concern for the environment, they select disposable paper cups rather than the Styrofoam alternatives for their next tailgate—they can also agitate for broader, non-consumptive issues like better health care and disease reduction through color-coded purchases. Perhaps because statistically one out of seven American women will receive a positive breast cancer diagnosis in her lifetime

(King, 2006), the American people may feel compelled to issue civic "protests" on a daily basis: pink cleaning sponges, vacuum bags, cotton balls, potato chips, and so forth are popular purchases that many people buy and take home.

Consumer-Citizenship as Problematic

A rose by any other name, color-based marketing and the concomitant consumer-citizenship it fosters appear benign. What could be wrong with buying an apparently safer, greener alternative to standard, bleach-based bathroom cleansers? Isn't it sensitive—even morally significant—to purchase a pink-labeled kitchen mixer over an unmarked one, especially if one intends to make the purchase anyway? Who could be on the side of dirtier, more polluting cleansers, or, for that matter, against more breast cancer awareness? There are those who would argue against the medical technologies that prolong human life in the face of increasing population pressures for the Earth (Bowers, 2001) or for mandated population control because they don't argue against free choice (Wilson, 2002, 2006). Herein lies the crux. Precisely because color-based marketing and its attendant consumer-citizenship seem to epitomize liberty and free choice, these behaviors are difficult to challenge. If consumer-citizenship affords people the chance to break free from historically characteristic class, gender, or racial constraints through the purchase of self-selected, lifestyle accoutrements or the illusion that one can put pressure on corporations to make products safer or better, then why abstain from it? Should the consumer-citizenry be subject to scrutiny?

One factor to consider when looking at color-based marketing and its corollary, consumer-citizenship, is the way in which these practices redefine civic participation. If social action takes place primarily in the shops, green and pink purchase by purchase, both civic engagement and virtuosity are limited to those who can pay. Put differently, in the realm of consumer-citizenship, people with little disposable income—those who can ill afford, say, the extra $2.00 per box for green tissues made with sustainably harvested wood pulp—can neither resist indiscriminate logging nor freely express their support of the cause. Correspondingly, if breast cancer research advances through pink attentiveness and purchases, then people who lack access to pink items or the requisite funds to buy them are excluded from having a say on a significant public health problem. Activists may make matters worse by living up to the social justice agenda of inadvertently promoting consumer-citizenship by working to create "equal" opportunities for consumption. These things work together to produce a powerful underpinning for neoliberalism in the schools. Take how easy it is to stop by a McDonald's to buy a family meal rather than purchasing apparently better organic foods from Earth Fare or Trader Joe's, when the nutritional value of organics is contentious (Soltoft et al., 2010). Buying organic foods, then, is less a conversation about nutrition then it is about ascribing virtuosity and political activism to people with purchasing power.

Illuminating the ways in which the U.S. Postal Service's 1998 issue of a pink breast cancer research stamp reflects larger, neoliberal shifts in state formation and codifies consumer-citizenship and individual responsibility for breast cancer, King (2006) suggests that consumer-citizenship, in its limits, forecloses the very democracy it purports to expand. The rhetoric of consumer-based free choice as well as an ever-growing array of socially inflected consumer products obscure an examination of who, exactly, has membership in the consumer-citizenry. King writes:

The creation of the breast cancer research stamp was viewed as a way of democratizing philanthropy, of giving "all Americans" the opportunity to participate in what is popularly understood as a self-actualizing and socially productive space. Moreover, in contrast to mandatory taxes, which are widely held to quash the civic impulses of Americans and to alienate citizens both from one another and the government, voluntary leverages are seen to elicit civic participation and personalize the relationship between citizens and the state. Thus…[the] discourse of "access" and "opportunity" works to displace questions about the ability of *all* citizens to partake equally in these new forms of civic action. (p. 74)

While everyone is preoccupied with buying, King suggests, no one is looking to see who is absent from the shops. Under the guise of increasing opportunities for social and political engagement, consumer-citizenship actually restricts civic action to those with the money to spend on it.

In addition to delineating who can engage in social action, consumer-citizenship also circumscribes the ways in which people can do so. To the extent that individual civic acts of consumption are celebrated as the most appropriate, even normative, forms of civic participation, alternative, more collective—perhaps disruptive—types of social activism such as protesting, boycotting, or rallying are dismissed as childish and inappropriate (especially in the ways that Baby Boomers engaged in these practices during the Civil Rights Movement of the 1960s, for example). Observers note that media representations of people participating in non-consumptive forms of political action such as teach-ins or picket lines often portray these groups as silly, ineffectual, and even dangerous (Klein, 2002; King, 2006). Consequently, the medium obscures the message. U.S. evening news coverage of the 2000 Seattle World Trade Organization (WTO) protests, for example, focused largely on isolated, violent acts of storefront glass breakage instead of the underlying causes of protesters' ire—not limited to the WTO's consistent failure to enforce minimum labor safety standards in manufacturing sites throughout the Global South (Klein, 2002).

This "sedentarization," to use Deleuze and Guattari's (1980/1987) term, of civic engagement to the consumptive realm also has material effects. Debates over what constitutes a green product can divert attention away from the larger, structural problems that create the need for green in the first place. Brosius (1999) illustrates this point well in his ethnographic work on how a colorful, star-studded campaign to bring attention to indiscriminate logging in Sarawak, Malaysia, was effectively shut down when discussions turned from indigenous peoples' human rights to metrics of green timber certification. As Brosius reports, the nomadic Penan of Sarawak garnered worldwide media sympathy in the late 1980s—even visits from the likes of popular singer Sting and Prince Charles of Wales—through a grass-roots, activist-led campaign to halt logging on Penan ancestral lands. By erecting human blockades in front of logging trucks and succumbing to arrest, the Penan captured numerous actors' interest and exposed, to a global audience, how rainforest destruction threatens indigenous peoples' livelihoods and alters their traditional ways of life. However, once Malaysian government officials hired international PR firms to shift the contours of the debate away from concerns about Penan land tenure to technical and economic metrics of sustainable wood harvesting—i.e., what constitutes a "green dot" on a wood product—protesters' voices were silenced and logging continued unabated. Brosius writes:

At the center of the early Sarawak campaign were arresting images (in the most literal sense) of Penan…and indigenous activists.…However…as the institutional foundations of [timber] certification were established, the role that such images and individuals could play was diminished. At an [International Tropical Timber Organization] meeting in which "criteria and indicators" of sustainability are on the agenda, images of blockades and arrests are not merely irrelevant but disruptive. (p. 49)

When corporate-driven priorities dominate the focus of social events, local peoples' concerns can be muffled. In the case of the Sarawak logging campaign, corporate interest in maintaining logging practices through green timber certification supplanted Penan grass-roots activism and silenced questions about the broader relations between indigenous peoples' human rights and deforestation. A focus on the greening of products, then, can mask an interrogation of whether a given product should even be available for market-based consumption at all. This represents a form of commodity fetishism: a way of removing (and silencing) the often negative conditions and associations under which goods are produced. Many so-called green products might dissolve if educators aimed for the "cradle-to-grave" mentality of analyzing whether advertising is honest.

Consider the corporatization of breast cancer. King (2006) sees "pink" as working in a similar, attention-diverting, vein. The contemporary swell of consumer-based civic action around breast cancer issues (i.e., shelves of pink products and a focus on individually oriented, fee-requiring philanthropy such as "Race for the Cure") obscures numerous, politically charged questions about the disease as well as the collective responsibilities to it. These questions include an interrogation of the links between environmental pollutants and breast cancer, how and by whom breast cancer research is conducted in the Global North, and, as King poignantly notes, whether breast cancer awareness even matters in a context in which axes of class and race determine who lives and who dies of the disease. She states:

> The limited focus of consumer-oriented activism…shaped as it is by an ideology of individualism and an imperative for uncomplicated, snappy market slogans, has allowed for the emergence of a preoccupation with early detection to the virtual exclusion of other approaches to fighting the epidemic and a failure to address the barriers, financial and otherwise, to treatment. This has resulted in a situation in which uninsured women with breast cancer have more reliable access to screening but are frequently left with no means to receive treatment after diagnosis. (p. 118)

Constrained by the hegemony of pink, the consumer-citizen is actually *dis*engaged from breast cancer activism in several ways. Although a sparkly pink ribbon purchase might identify one as sympathetic to breast cancer awareness, it is a limited form of social action that simultaneously forecloses other, potentially more effective, modes of expressing broad-scale concerns about the origins and rise of breast cancer and dissatisfaction with the nation-states' current responses to it.

Moreover, the overall association of breast cancer with pink may very well *weaken* participatory democracy, as it affirms rather than challenges pre-existent cleavages in the civic collective. As Ehrenreich (2001) acerbically asserts, pink and its frilly accoutrements (e.g., ribbons) not only further constitute breast cancer as strictly a women's issue, but also consolidate deeply entrenched, heteronormative ideals of femininity. Observing that breast cancer patients are wont to receive items such as pink teddy bears as gifts, Ehrenreich pens: "Femininity is by its nature incompatible with full adulthood—a state of arrested development. Certainly, men diagnosed with prostate cancer do not receive gifts of Matchbox cars" (p. 46). Active civic participation is associated with full adulthood. Given the late entry of both women and African-Americans into full legal participation in U.S. society, the corporate breast cancer awareness movement's link between pink and an infantilized, pre-suffrage female is not one to be taken lightly.

Under the guises of greater freedom and wider choice, then, consumer-citizenship and its bedfellow, color-based marketing, actually narrow peoples' opportunities for participating in and actively constructing the broader social world in which they live. Because lively engagement in a consumer-citizenry is contingent upon personal, self-financed acts of consumption rather than on *esprit de corps*, consumer-citizens' foci is on their wallets, products, and people-as-products rather than on broader social questions such as why problems exist in the first place and what the role of larger, collective entities is in solving them. Although a dizzying array of color-coded goods in the marketplace might suggest infinite possibilities for self-shaping and political action, Berger (1972) explains that choices *among products* are really not choices at all:

> Every publicity image confirms and enhances every other. Publicity is not merely an assembly of competing messages: it is a language in itself which is always being used to make the same general proposal. Within publicity, choices are offered between this cream and that cream, that car and this car, but publicity as a system only makes a single proposal. It proposes to each of us that we transform ourselves, or our lives, by buying something more. This more, it proposes, will make us in some way richer—even though we will be poorer by having spent our money. (p. 131)

The panoply of consumer options, Berger suggests, actually reflects a diminishment of choice and political agency. To choose between a two-by-four bearing a green dot and an uncertified lumber piece does little to address the wider, transnational problems that rainforest destruction ultimately creates. Issues such as global climate change, increased geopolitical instability between the Global North and Global South, or rapid species extinction cannot be addressed by the marketplace alone. People who vote with their pocketbooks are, in the end, not voting on these issues at all.

Equally, if not more importantly, consumer-citizenship—indeed, neoliberalism in general—allows certain, usually privileged, individuals and groups to disavow their responsibility for and investment in the protracted vulnerability of other people and natural systems worldwide. Preoccupied with constructing their own lifestyles through color-coded purchases and primarily interpellated as shoppers, consumer-citizens need not address the more unsavory sides of the global capitalist network in which they are daily participants. So it is that exploitative labor practices, forced migration, ecological degradation, and the myth that some people are disposable (Wright, 2006)—among other consequences of what economic geographers call the globalization tendencies of late modernity (Dicken 2003)—remain perpetually outside consumer-citizens' fields of vision. In fact, as Butcher (2003) observes, the grand narrative of globalization actually encourages a sense of impotence among individual people about their personal role in the global economic grid and their ability to effect change upon it. He explains:

> Globalization is often invoked to emphasize the interconnected nature of society—we are all bound together through the market. But globalization often carries the underlying implication that the market is beyond human intervention. Hence whilst we are encouraged to see ourselves as ethical in our role as consumers, the basis on which we consume, the power relationships between nations and between social classes, appears beyond us. (p. 107)

Facing an economic globalization juggernaut that seems to possess agency and a will of its own, consumer-citizens often feel powerless. Color-coded purchases at least offer people the appearance and suggestion of taking some personal responsibility.

A final reason for looking more cautiously at consumer-citizenship and its bosom buddy, color-based marketing, is that these practices reconstitute the nation-state in a very specific way. By furthering and reinforcing neoliberal interests, consumer-based citizenship practices naturalize and reaffirm the idea that good governance is measured primarily by *market growth.* Other, arguably more social justice–oriented, metrics of institutional efficacy such as whether a nation-state's government reduces (or contributes to) social and economic inequality, furthers (or erodes) geopolitical stability, and aids (or hinders) lively community-building are swamped by the market mantra. As Hamilton (2004) observes, under contemporary conditions in which the primary role of the nation-state has shifted from providing social services to greasing economic engines at multiple scales, "[H]uman beings have become 'consumers' and human desire has been defined in terms of goods; it follows that the only way to make people happier is to provide more goods. In other words, the objective [of government] is growth" (p. 8). The logic of growth, then, fosters a climate in which a nation-state's obligations to its constituency begin and end with an expansive marketplace. In other words, if Christmas shopping is up and economic growth rates are higher than the previous year, a government is said to be doing well by society.

The limitations of the equation "economic growth equals good government" should seem fairly obvious. In the main, this perspective abdicates governments of any responsibility for preserving or supporting natural systems, building community *joie de vivre*, and taking care of its weakest members, among other utilitarian considerations of what helps to constitute the "good life" for a large number of people in any country or what promotes the prospects of the future. Despite the illusory promises of endless economic/fiscal growth, scholars have demonstrated repeatedly that increased capital accumulation does not necessarily equal more happiness, an improved quality of life, or greater security, either for people or a community (e.g., Folbre, 2001). To wit, Hamilton (2004) reports that

> the social basis of discontent in modern society is not so much lack of income; it is loneliness, boredom, depression, alienation, self-doubt and the ill-health that goes with them....Most of the problems of modern society are not the result of inadequate incomes; they are the result of social structures, ideologies, and cultural forms that prevent people from realizing their potential and leading satisfying lives in their communities. (p. 209)

In the end, the role of a representative, or delegated, government is to respond to and represent the interests of its citizens. The commonwealth may be doing itself a disservice by maintaining their enthusiasm for consumer-based citizenship. Unwittingly, consumer-citizens may be helping to develop an infrastructure in which public institutions work mainly to augment and safeguard peoples' shopping experiences rather than their present or future health and happiness.

Despite the challenges, school classrooms are places where the norms of consumer-citizenship may be challenged. Next, we discuss the possibilities of integrating critical civic literacy education into school curricula.

A Call for Critical Civic Literacy Education

According to Cook-Gumperz (2006), "Literacy is usually taken to refer not only to the ability to understand written and printed inscriptions, but also to the socio-cognitive changes that result from being literate, and from having a literate population" (p. 21). Literacy, then, operates as a social formation—one that alters people and culture, often in historically contingent, highly ideological, ways. In the 17th and 18th centuries, literacy in the United States was non-standardized. People used a plurality of oral and written literacy traditions for a variety of purposes including entertainment, education, and to challenge dominant political ideals. Consequently, apologists for the status quo often feared widespread literacy and actively prohibited its spread (think Frederick Douglass). However, once *schooled literacy*, or standardized literacy practices, became institutionalized as part of universal public schooling in the 19th century, literacy became a means of strict social control—one necessary for acculturating a compliant industrial workforce and a way of demarcating virtuous citizens from the less so (Cook-Gumperz, 2006). That is, as literacy became increasingly defined as the first two of the three R's—oral recitation and rote copying rather than a flexible, social repertoire of fluid skills one might use for self-determined purposes—it was illiteracy, not literacy, that came to be viewed as a looming social danger.

The role of literacy continues to be contested today, particularly in U.S. schools. While academics have issued calls for the recognition of a plurality of literacies including, but not limited to, multimodal literacy (Street, 1984; Gee, 1991), community-based literacy events (Heath, 1983), media literacy (Hobbs, 2007), and even hip-hop literacies (Richardson, 2006), we have also seen a federally supported rise in a "unitary account" of literacy (Collins & Blot, 2003). This is a version of literacy in which drill-based phonics are the norm, discrete skills are stressed, and reading and writing are often taught through glossy, commercial, prescriptive literacy kits (Larson, 2001). The unitary account of literacy is put forth by "pedagogical fundamentalists…who argue that in essence reading and writing are matters of decoding and encoding language in a text" (Collins & Blot, 2003, p. 173). Similar to how 19th-century schooled literacy was disproportionately the province of the poor and used to maintain social control, the contemporary unitary account of literacy (wrapped in the cloak of making schools "accountable") is disproportionately used in under-resourced classrooms. It operates as a means of teaching economically vulnerable, often minority, students lessons in rote compliance rather than critical thought (Cook-Gumperz, 2006).

Advocates of *critical literacy*, however, are engaged in an ideological struggle to take literacy back, so to speak, as a tool of social critique and personal freedom. The critical literacy perspective is primarily concerned with political empowerment, social engagement, and political agency. As Dozier, Johnston, and Rogers (2006) put it:

> Critical literacy means developing a sense that literacy is for taking social action, an awareness of how people use literacy for their own ends, and a sense of agency with respect to one's own literacy.…Critical literacy also requires…understanding the ways in which that tool [literacy] works—for example, how language is organized to reproduce race, class, and gender roles. (pp. 18–19)

Literacy from a critical perspective is about using the tools of print, text, and semiotic signs to critique and remake the world (cf. Freire, 2003). Expanding upon Dozier and colleagues' notions of critical literacy, then, we define *critical civic literacy education* as a politically engaged, socially active practice in which people use literacy skills to analyze the meanings of their own lives in relation to society and as a way to interrogate dominant notions of public life and citizenry. Critical civic literacy education prepares students to strategically attend to the social and linguistic foundations that frame them predominantly as shoppers.

Accordingly, within a critical civic literacy perspective, people can use literacy skills to interrogate apparatuses such as color-based marketing schemes that demand little more of them than that they make color-coded purchases, for example, if they are concerned about the environment. A classroom exercise in critical civic literacy education might entail examining advertisements depicting green and pink purchases and the ways in which images and print copy bespeak particular ethical commitments. Using the aforementioned Deer Park water bottle, for example, students might be asked to question whether its "smaller cap" makes it green when the bottle of the product itself is considerably wasteful. Alternately, students might be asked to read and analyze schools' mission statements and course descriptions, looking for embedded assumptions of consumer-based citizenship (e.g., foreign language courses often cite "useful for global business" as the main reason to learn Spanish or French, while school mission statements often stress the importance of creating "global entrepreneurs"). While schools certainly offer one venue for analyzing unnoticed and unchecked assumptions of consumer-citizenship, the larger educational domains of neighborhoods, grocery stores, and shopping malls may also serve as outlets of systematic influence where the unquestioned assumptions of consumerism could be examined.

In an age in which the reverberations of neoliberal policies are often felt in U.S. schools, critical civic literacy education may be more important than ever. Indeed, it is an issue of equity. Government divestments from U.S. education in the last few decades have often left certain, usually cash-strapped and urban, schools with little choice but to adopt corporate-donated books and curricula; these materials often naturalize corporate-friendly versions of the world and consumer-based citizenship. To illustrate, Karliner (1997) writes that "The American Coal Foundation provides a [free] curriculum that makes no mention of acid rain or global warming, but rather helps students 'identify the reasons coal is a good fuel choice'" (p. 187). Further, he notes that Exxon is

> rewriting the history of the Valdez oil spill for an audience of the nation's impressionable youth. While an Alaska jury was awarding 10,000 fisherfolk, 4,000 Native Alaskans and another 20,000 plaintiffs more than $5 billion in damages from Exxon, the company was distributing, free of charge, its version of the truth to 10,000 elementary school teachers, for viewing by kids who were too young to remember the devastating oil spill in Prince William Sound. While the jury determined that the spill had destroyed much of the plaintiffs' livelihood, damaging fishing and native hunting grounds, the Exxon video—which is filled with shots of stoic scientists cleaning cute, furry marine mammals—told a new generation of potential environmentalists and soon-to-be consumers that the spill did not decimate wildlife in Prince William Sound. (pp. 186–187)

Similar to the way in which neoliberal interests drive the spread of the English language worldwide—e.g., International Monetary Fund–imposed structural adjustment policies have impoverished many schools in Tanzania, leading local teachers to use donated English language books for a lack of Kiswahili ones (Vavrus, 2002)—corporations' donations of books, videos, and other curriculum materials to under-resourced U.S. schools neutralize particular social events and redirect peoples' responses to them. Given that poorer schools may have a pragmatic need to accept corporate-donated materials, the students in these schools are more inundated with corporations' versions of social events and their implicit calls to consumer-based citizenship than are the students of well-heeled institutions. In the end, then, critical civic literacy education (or lack of it) is a justice issue in the same way that literacy is. Students who come from wealthier homes and social classes in which critical civic literacy education is taught explicitly or as part of a community's norms will learn multiple ways of exercising political agency. Other students—those youth whose schools are cash-poor and more likely to rely on corporate-donated curriculum materials—may learn to be good citizens through messages marketed by the likes of Exxon.

Alternatives to Consumer-Citizenship: Life beyond the Shops

A rising call for alternatives to consumer-citizenship can be heard coming from educators and activists alike. Among them is Noddings (2005), who champions a version of civic engagement that we term here *global-environmental citizenship*. Broadly, this version of citizenship aims beyond the neoliberal agendas of nation-states, moving instead toward a global society in which all beings—people, plants, and animals—are equally connected through and similarly situated in biotic networks. As members of a global-environmental citizenry, people are just one of many living things, and their civic loyalties and obligations are to the larger, single, environmental community in which they live. Citizenry and political action in a global-environmental citizenry are enacted not through the singing of national anthems or the purchase of green products, but by protecting the environment or larger ecosystems, finding pleasure in connecting with nature, and living sustainably—and peacefully—within one's means.

Spring (2004) observes that a global-environmental citizenship is inherently radical in that it not only challenges traditional notions of the nation-state, but it also displaces "civics" with environmental education. Educating students in a global-environmental citizenship paradigm requires teaching them not about war victories or how to generate wealth on Wall Street, but rather how to derive pleasure from nature, to recognize their diminutive yet powerful roles in the biosphere, and how to be environmental stewards. He explains:

> Environmental education runs counter to the educational efforts of nation-states…and to the neoliberal policies of organizations like the World Bank.…Environmental education attempts to transform human thinking by displacing humans as the central and dominant form of life. Humans become just one species existing among other animal and plant species. In addition, environmental education teaches that the meaning and pleasure of life is dependent on the quality of human interaction with nature. (p. 162)

While the consumer-citizenship ideal measures the quality of life through material resources, cars, "bling," and one's possession of correctly colored products—even for social attractiveness—a global-environmental citizenship ethically defines the metrics of a well-lived life as the extent to which people live in harmony with their surroundings, others, and the idea that less is always more.

Another alternative to consumer-citizenship, what we call here *locally based citizenship*, draws upon the works of scholars such as Berry (1990) and Orr (2004). Locally based citizenship calls for active engagement with and intimate knowledge of one's local, immediate community: its people, its land, its animals and plant species. Advocates for locally based citizenship view "the global" as a scale beyond reach, understanding, or the purview of individual action. They call for citizenship practices that are tailored to the climate, temperament, and history of particular places. Per Berry (1990),

> The word "planetary"…refers to an abstract anxiety or an abstract passion that is desperate and useless exactly
> to the extent that it is abstract. How, after all, can anybody—any particular body—do anything to heal a
> planet? The heroes of abstraction keep galloping in on their white horses to save the planet—and they keep
> falling off in front of the grandstand. (p. 197)

Where locally based citizenship differs from global-environmental citizenship is in reminding us to attend not to the global biotic community, but to our immediate surroundings. Locally based citizenship advocates argue that problem-solving and civic action become more fully manageable from the local, community perspective. Again, Berry (1990):

> The question that must be addressed…is not how to care for the planet, but how to care for each of the
> planet's millions of human and natural neighborhoods, each of its millions of small pieces and parcels of
> land, each one of which is in some precious way different from all the others. Our understandable wish to
> preserve the planet must somehow be reduced to the scale of our competence—that is, to the wish to pre-
> serve all of its humble households and neighborhoods. (p. 200)

One benefit of locally based citizenship is that it might offer people a humane, do-able alternative in the face of a seemingly homogenizing globalization. Klein (2002) suggests that this alternative might be called "democracy":

> If centralization of power and distant decision making are emerging as the common enemies [to citizen-
> ship], there is also an emerging consensus that participatory democracy at the local level—whether through
> unions, neighborhoods, city governments, farms, villages, or aboriginal self-government—is the place to start
> building alternatives to it. The common theme is an overarching commitment to self- determination and
> diversity: cultural diversity, ecological diversity, even political diversity….What seems to be emerging
> organically is not a movement for a single global government but a vision for an increasingly connected inter-
> national network of very local initiatives, each built on reclaimed public spaces, and, through participatory
> forms of democracy, made more accountable than either corporate or state institutions. If this movement
> has an ideology it is democracy, not only at the ballot box but woven into every aspect of our lives. (p. 456)

Locally based citizenship, Klein suggests, increases overall diversity: cultural, ecological, and political. Given that consumer-citizenship thrives on the flattening of thinking—e.g., "Everybody Go Green!"—a locally based citizenship alternative means that, in the end, people may not have to sacrifice thinking for consuming.

Final Thoughts

In this chapter, we have highlighted the ways in which the rationalities of neoliberalism produce and maintain consumer-citizenship as a dominant form of civic participation in the contemporary U.S. We have argued that color-based marketing practices such as green and pink further one-track, consumer-based citizenry by conflating vigorous political action and individually oriented consumption. We have cautioned that these practices of consumer-citizenship foreclose some other, perhaps more inclusive and transformative, means of public engagement. With a nod to literacy studies, we have suggested that consumer-citizenship might be challenged by robust critical civic literacy education measures in U.S. schools. Careful to note how literacy has been historically tied to various ideologies, we have cautioned that critical civic literacy education, too, risks being inequitably distributed among attendees of inequitably resourced schools. We have connected with other educational writers to recommend alternatives to consumer-based citizenship, broadly categorized here as global-environmental and locally based citizenship.

Alternatives to consumer-citizenship offer the possibility of radically challenging the pre-eminent neoliberal paradigm. They allow more expansive visions of peoples' roles in and responsibilities to the larger (or, in some cases, smaller) communities in which they live, as well as fresh ways of understanding individual and collective freedom. Democracies have always offered people more ways to express themselves politically than merely forming a queue at a cash register. It is highly unlikely that people 100 years from now will laud us for our green shopping bags and carbon offset schemes. If the truth be told of tobacco companies, then let us critically analyze green water bottles, pink ribbons, red hoodies, and our visits to the mall. Every rose has its thorn; it is time to take the long view of history, starting now.

Bibliography

Berger, J. (1972). *Ways of seeing.* London: Penguin Books.

Berry, W. (1990). *What are people for?* New York: North Point Press.

Bowers, C.A. (2001). *Educating for eco-justice and community.* Athens: University of Georgia Press.

Brosius, J.P. (1999). Green dots, pink hearts: Displacing politics from the Malaysian Rain Forest. *American Anthropologist, 101*(1), 36–57.

Butcher, J. (2003). *The moralization of tourism: Sun, sand…and saving the world?* London: Routledge.

Collins, J., & Blot, R.K. (2003). *Literacy and literacies: Texts, power, and identity.* Cambridge: Cambridge University Press.

Cook-Gumperz, J. (2006). Literacy and schooling: An unchanging equation? In J. Cook-Gumperz (Ed.), *The social construction of literacy* (2nd ed.), (pp. 19–49). Cambridge: Cambridge University Press.

Deleuze, G., & Guattari, F. (1987). *A thousand plateaus: Capitalism and schizophrenia* (B. Massumi, Trans.). Minneapolis: University of Minnesota Press. (Original work published 1980)

Dicken, P. (2003). *Global shift: Reframing the economic map in the 21st century* (4th ed.). New York: The Guilford Press.

Dozier, C., Johnston, P., & Rogers, R. (2006). *Critical literacy/critical teaching: Tools for preparing responsive teachers.* New York: Teachers College Press.

Duggan, L. (2003). *The twilight of equality? Neoliberalism, cultural politics, and the attack on democracy.* Boston: Beacon Press.

Ehrenreich, B. (2001, November). Welcome to Cancerland: A mammogram leads to a cult of pink kitsch. *Harper's,* 43–53.

Folbre, N. (2001). *The invisible heart: Economics and family values.* New York: The New Press.

Freire, P. (2003). *Pedagogy of the oppressed* (30th anniversary ed.) (Myra Bergman Ramos, Trans.). New York: Continuum. (Original work published 1970)

Gee, J. (1991). *Social linguistics and literacies: Ideology in discourses.* Brighton: Falmer Press.

Hamilton, C. (2004). *Growth fetish.* London: Pluto Press.

Harvey, D. (2005). *A brief history of neoliberalism.* Oxford: Oxford University Press.

Heath, S.B. (1983). *Ways with words: Language, life, and work in communities and classrooms.* Cambridge: Cambridge University Press.

Hobbs, R. (2007). *Reading the media: Media literacy in high school English.* New York: Teachers College Press.

Karliner, J. (1997). *The corporate planet: Ecology and politics in the age of globalization.* San Francisco, CA: Sierra Club Books.

King, S. (2006). *Pink ribbons, inc.: Breast cancer and the politics of philanthropy.* Minneapolis: University of Minnesota Press.

Klawiter, M. (2000). From private stigma to global assembly: Transforming the terrain of breast cancer. In M. Burawoy (Ed.), *Global ethnography: Forces, connections, and imaginations in a postmodern world* (pp. 299–334). Berkeley: University of California Press.

Klein, N. (2002). *No logo*. New York: Picador.

Koballa, T.R., & Demir, A. (2010). Making high school science instruction effective. In J. DeVitis & L. DeVitis (Eds.), *Adolescent education: A reader* (pp. 343–359). New York: Peter Lang.

Larson, J. (Ed.). (2001). *Literacy as snake oil: Beyond the quick fix*. New York: Peter Lang.

National Research Council. (1996). *National science education standards*. Washington, DC: National Academies Press.

Noddings, N. (2005). Global citizenship: Promises and problems. In N. Noddings (Ed.), *Educating citizens for global awareness* (pp. 1–21). New York: Teachers College Press.

Orr, D. (2004). *Earth in mind: On education, environment, and the human prospect*. Washington, DC: Island Press.

Putnam, R.D. (1995) *Bowling alone: The collapse and revival of American community*. New York: Simon and Schuster.

Richardson, E. (2006). *Hiphop literacies*. London: Routledge.

Robbins, R.H. (2005). *Global problems and the culture of capitalism* (3rd ed.). Boston: Pearson.

Rose, N. (1999). *Powers of freedom: Reframing political thought*. Cambridge: Cambridge University Press.

Russell, C.L., & Russon, A.E. (2007). Ecotourism. In M. Bekoff (Ed.), *Encyclopedia of human-animal relationships: A global exploration of our connections with animals* (pp. 653–657). Westport, CT: Greenwood Publishing Group.

Soltoft, M., Nielsen, J., Holst Laursen, K., Husted, S., Halekoh, U., & Knuthsen, P. (2010). Effects of organic and conventional growth systems on the content of flavonoids in onions and phenolic acids in carrots and potatoes. *Journal of Agricultural and Food Chemistry, 58*(19), 10323–10329.

Spring, J. (2004). *How educational ideologies are shaping global society: Intergovernmental organizations, NGOs, and the decline of the nation-state*. Mahwah, NJ: Lawrence Erlbaum Associates.

Street, B. (1984). *Literacy in theory and practice*. Cambridge: Cambridge University Press.

Sturken, M. (2007). *Tourists of history: Memory, kitsch, and consumerism from Oklahoma City to Ground Zero*. Durham, NC: Duke University Press.

Vavrus, F. (2002). Postcoloniality and English: Exploring language policy and the politics of development in Tanzania. *TESOL Quarterly, 36*(3), 373–397.

Wilson, E.O. (2002). *The future of life*. New York: Vintage Books.

Wilson, E.O. (2006). *The Creation: An appeal to save life on earth*. New York and London: W.W. Norton & Company.

Wright, M. (2006). *Disposable women and other myths of global capitalism*. New York: Routledge.

CHAPTER TWENTY-EIGHT

Opportunities

How to More Effectivley Shape the Next
Generation of Human Beings and Citizens

KRISIT FRAGNOLI & DAVID EPSTEIN

You walk into Mrs. Jerard's fourth-grade class, and students are busy copying down notes about the three branches of New York State government from an overhead projector. The teacher is rushing to get through all four bulleted points under each branch of government. Down the hall, in Mrs. Snyder's fifth-grade class, students are rewriting the introduction of the Declaration of Independence, not changing the meaning of the document, just trying to use words that 10-year-olds might understand better.

As educators we have not yet mastered the perfect curriculum for cultivating active citizen-ship. While the above scenarios are not causing any harm to our students, they do not cre-ate active, knowledgeable, savvy citizens either. According to the International Civic Education Study (ICEA), which tested students from 24 democratic countries, our students ranked sixth in overall understanding of democratic structures. However, the report goes on to conclude that, despite the impressive ranking of students' understanding of processes and structures, students' knowledge is superficial and fact based (Ross, 2001, p. 394). The National Assessment of Educational Progress (NAEP) confirms this trend. The NAEP 2006 national assessment of civic knowledge of fourth-grade students shows higher average scores compared to the 1998 test scores; however, it provides no evidence as to the ability of students to apply the factual knowl-edge (Lutkus & Weiss, 2007).

As Americans, we have often heard the familiar, monotonous phrase by George Santayana that "those who cannot remember the past are condemned to repeat it"; yet in our education sys-tem students are continuously presented with a limited perspective of history consisting of a laun-dry list of facts, a how-to for citizenship, and a limited array of skills. Without a wide range of knowledge and skills in the classroom, children are constricted and saturated, leading them to perceive the world as narrow-minded, handicapped citizens. Facts are a part of history educa-tion; they are needed to establish historical foundations. Yet it is crucial to help students make sense out of facts and learn how to evaluate them. In exploring civic literacy in the elementary classroom, we turned to a group of diverse young adults with active civic engagement, in hopes of uncovering common threads in their educational experiences. Through a series of interviews, eight civic-minded individuals were asked to contemplate their years of schooling, especially their elementary years, reflecting back on the curriculum presented and how it affected them throughout their education and lives.

While the goal of the interviews was to better understand how civically minded and engaged citizens evolve, what developed from these rich portraits were common understandings of what it is to be civic-minded, and how life and schooling experiences enriched and promoted that civic thought and action. Among these individuals were members of various communities who had created community gardens, led student organizations, worked with autistic adults and other members of society seen as "disadvantaged," and young adults who have traveled and learned extensively around the world. These interviews included equal numbers of men and women, and consisted of four African Americans, two Jewish Americans, and two European Americans. The individuals were all within the working-class or middle-class categories, with two identifying as poor at one point in their lives and two identifying as upper middle class at one point in their lives. In interviewing these engaged citizens. many common themes emerged from their educational experiences and the ways in which these served as positive and negative influences on their development as concerned human beings and citizens.

Defining Civic Literacy

When the eight subjects were asked to define both civics and citizen there was, incredibly, a universal response and definition given. Civics was defined as that which individuals do for the common good in contributing to a society to better perfect and improve our communities. A citizen was defined as an individual within this group who is bequeathed rights by virtue of being born, or naturalized, in a nation state. It was noted that a citizen is given these rights regardless if one, in turn, gives back to the community. But it is only by virtue of other citizens who have given to the community that individual citizens are able to receive benefits from society at large, and, consequently, they should feel an obligation to a wider community and give back in some manner. Examples of giving back ranged from offering free education and tutoring to creating community gardens, teaching, working in soup kitchens, advocating for political change, etc. The only deviation in this universal response came from one subject who, when asked to define citizen, stated: "We have the choice to do good…it's an imperative that we have…beyond boundaries of country, government, and institutions. Those are all incidental" (J.W., personal communication, October 22, 2010). Similarly, another subject stressed how learning in multiple countries and interacting with people from all over the world created in her a sense of "realizing where I came from in a manner that set me apart. I was the American, but it also gave me the awareness that this [identity as an American] occurred within a larger identity as a global citizen" (J.S., personal communication, September 27, 2010).

According to the National Council of the Social Studies (NCSS):

> The aim of social studies is the promotion of civic competence—the knowledge, intellectual processes, and democratic dispositions required of students to be active and engaged participants in public life. Although

civic competence is not the only responsibility of social studies nor is it exclusive to the field, it is more central to social studies than to any other subject area in schools. By making civic competence a central aim, NCSS has long recognized the importance of educating students who are committed to the ideas and values of democracy. Civic competence rests on this commitment to democratic values, and requires the abilities to use knowledge about one's community, nation, and world; apply inquiry processes; and employ skills of data collection and analysis, collaboration, decision-making, and problem-solving. Young people who are knowledgeable, skillful, and committed to democracy are necessary to sustaining and improving our democratic way of life, and participating as members of a global community. (Executive Council, Ness, 1992, para. 2)

Elementary education is typically viewed as preparing youth for citizenship education, but we must remember that social studies education is the blending of multiple strands and disciplines: geography, political science, global studies, history, economics, and anthropology. However, we cannot neglect the fields of education, philosophy, psychology and the arts—they all play a cardinal role. Consider the rich set of skills that are required from all of these domains. The skill components of the varied disciplines are major factors that make up the eclectic definition of citizenship. Most definitions of citizenship education include a wide variety of skills. The key is to cultivate those habits of mind so that the ways of thinking that one gains through practice becomes second nature and easily tapped into when confronted with a problem, dilemma, or new information (Goldenberg, 1996).

School Experiences

Two common themes emerged from the interviews when exploring the development of civic literacy in elementary education: (1) Curriculum is driven by the white male perspective, and examples of non-whites within the social studies curriculum are viewed as add-ons to an already existing curriculum, as opposed to teaching a global perspective within a lens or framework from which the content operates; and (2) Critical and multi-perspective narratives of history result in more engaged students.

Throughout all the interviews, examples of civic curricular add-ons that lacked substance were abundant. In particular was the mention of the speed with which Civil Rights leaders and thinkers were studied, if they were studied at all, which was only in half of the interviews, and the degree to which the content lacked any historic context. One interviewee put it this way:"You read about Martin Luther King for half a page, then boom, on to the next topic. Rosa Parks gets a part of a paragraph. The historical events and stories were so superficial as to lack any meaning or power" (C.S., personal communication, September 21, 2010). When discussing Dr. Martin Luther King and other leaders, connections were not made to the national Civil Rights Movement or the existence of racism and the pursuit of equality over the preceding 100 years. In fact, the throw-in additions of minority events were done so superficially, and lacking context to such a degree, that they were perceived by many as nothing more than exoticism. A black male student who was in a suburban and largely white school stated that "There was a lot of exoticism when [minority views were examined]. I was seen as exotic in the American perspective…it [this view] was based on 'otherness'…it was very superficial…this exoticizing of people side steps their humanness" (M.A., personal communication, September 27, 2010). In nearly all examples the best scenarios in schools involved the teaching of knowledge, consisting of facts, but never of a higher understanding of how those facts connect to each elementary learner in a meaningful and contextualized manner.

In addition to curricular add-ons, students noticed the omission of positive contributions from various minorities that would contribute to civic literacy development throughout their elementary education. Musical inventions like jazz, or the Harlem Renaissance, not to mention the marginalization of female contributions in fields such as science, e.g., when Rosalind Franklin had her findings largely stolen by Crick and Watson, were passed over. Those omissions were so blatant that over 50% of those interviewed stated that they felt robbed of any voice at all. The role they often felt pressured to play was the voice of defense for "their people." This was a trying and stressful position for a young adult to be in, and in most cases resulted in them being reduced to silence, the antithesis of the goal of civic literacy (Howard, 2006) .

In contrast to this sterile presentation of minority experiences in history, many interviewees mentioned that when such positive and inspiring examples were experienced and studied, it was outside of the classroom. One example included a basket-weaving display at the Smithsonian Museum that captured the interest of a young child. It presented the complex connection between the geographic and cultural interweave of West Africa and the African American South in an artistic and content-rich global display. The number of examples similar to this one—brought out by all of the interviews—underscores just how many missed opportunities for the development of civic literacy exist in schools. Elementary classrooms could be abuzz with multiple educational experiences requiring students to explore global and cultural connections. However, many interviewees reported on the reliance of old, outdated textbooks and a plethora of bland patriotic worksheets. Every single respondent stated that such "flag-waving"[1] history was "bland and boring" (C.S., personal communication, September 21, 2010). One subject clearly captures this point:

> The way they taught American history was very biased…the way they wrote the book, it seemed as if the ideal [achievements] were very justified and the negative things that America has faced and committed, slavery [for example]…it seemed as if the tone of the textbooks were monotone [when discussing chapters in our history that may cause shame, guilt, or regret]….I always wondered how other kids in other countries are learning the same information. (C.S., personal communication, September 21, 2010)

When the subject was asked for some of his best experiences from school, he stated:

> My social studies teacher was very animated…because they were excited about it, I was too…they always tried to be impartial…someone would ask who was right and they'd say that depends on how you think of it. The "objective" reality wasn't very clear. (J.S., personal communication, September 27, 2010)

In following up on what made this social studies teacher effective at teaching content that the students were excited about, and what remained memorable into adulthood, the interviewee stated:

> It was always story telling—they were effective story tellers.…The stories always tied back [to the present]…it helped that he was familiar with the language we used. (J.S., personal communication, September 27, 2010)

In both of these narratives a dominant theme emerged: Critical and multi-perspective narratives of history resulted in more engaged students in the classroom, and more engaged citizens in the world. When asked about the potential tension between students becoming more engaged despite a historical perspective that was often self-critical (as opposed to the "flag-waving" approach), the responses were very similar. One interviewee explained the importance of understanding issues of meaning in our society:

> Why are people still poor? Unless we ask critical questions we can't explore the issues. Why haven't we fixed this? When people ask questions, and are critical, they are spurred to cause change, it's not seen as monolithic—that's the way life is, life is unfair, so why bother to try and change it? To be critical is empowering. (J.S., personal communication, September 27, 2010)

What an invaluable insight—"To be critical is empowering." In the interviews I asked if subjects thought that a critical history, in opposition to a flag-waving approach, while not being "bland and boring," might cause citizens to turn off by having very negative frames of reference for their society's history. Not only did all subjects answer that this would not be the case, they did so eloquently. One subject put it this way:

> Citizens wouldn't be turned off by a critical approach because they are still proud in the idea humans are imperfect and that we live to pursue perfection and create the perfect world. I believe that before I can succeed I have to fail. So when I'm looking at history, I'm like yes that's one more mistake we don't have to make again. (M.B., personal communication, October 9, 2010)

The concept that humans are imperfect, but continuously working toward improvement, is an interesting generalization to share with elementary children as they learn and discover about themselves and others, a developmental process that is a key component to civic literacy. However, what emerged from so many interviews were the missed opportunities in elementary classrooms to create a critical, and thus engaging, history. Yet, the impact is far-reaching; these elementary students move on to middle and high school as disengaged members of their schools and communities. As Deanna Kuhn puts it:

> Based on the time they spend in classrooms, what inferences are disadvantaged adolescents likely to make about epistemological matters of what it means to learn, to acquire knowledge, to become educated? The recent focus on standardized test preparation and performance, particularly in low-performing schools, makes one likely conception that of drilling empty facts into memory to pass a test. (Kuhn, p. 118)

Kuhn goes further than this and offers a prescription for how to attack this problem.

> If education is to be successful, adolescents must "buy in" to the enterprise, by finding some personal meaning and value in what goes on in school. At its best, education ought to go further, aiding the quest to construct meaning in life. Again, school ought to connect to life. But this ideal cannot possibly be approached unless the school experience is itself meaningful. If students cannot answer the question, "why would one want or need to know this?" they will find it difficult to direct more than superficial attention to what is being taught. (Kuhn, p. 117)

Every aspect of Kuhn's recommendation was supported in every single interview. Human beings are meaning-seeking creatures, and this is true in the context of school as well. Time and time again the feedback has been that schools are providing a content that lacks meaning, by ignoring the relevance of the vast majority of groups in the making and creation of our history, be they women, people of color, immigrants, or most any other underrepresented demographic. Indeed, the extent to which their voices are absent from the curriculum is troubling. To make matters worse, when the curriculum does include such voices it lacks any context. In one particularly poignant interview, the subject provides an explanation as to why some social studies elementary classes where unfocused and disengaged from real learning:

> When I started school I started in a classroom and we just started learning lessons and we never sat down and discussed "what we are about to do now is education and education is important for such and such reasons." No student had an idea of why being in this room all day was important. (M.B., personal communication, October 9, 2010)

The overwhelming consensus among the subjects was a feeling that elementary education should provide a foundational understanding of the purposes of schooling. Additionally it should assist in exploring the interconnectedness of the students' own biographies and histories to the content and the concept of a global community, ultimately demonstrating how they can interact with each as citizens and human beings.

Components of Practicing Citizens

Based on the subjects' reflections of their life experiences, schooling, and ideas, it becomes apparent that practicing citizens develop, convey, and apply two common domains that make up civic literacy; these are the interconnectedness of content and skills, and philosophic thought. Both components can form a dialectic relationship resulting in a civic-minded person willing to participate for the betterment of society. Elementary education can become a powerful arena in developing civic literacy by integrating these components into the curriculum.

Civic Content and Skills

Civic literacy seems to be a contentious concept in the field of education. Some believe the role of civic literacy is to develop and infuse nationalist patriotism in our youth, promoting the rights and obligations of citizens. Meanwhile, another view describes civic literacy as the need to challenge that dominant perspective in order to examine the injustice and oppression that undermine political and social equality. While both of these divergent goals of civic literacy sit at opposite ends of the spectrum when enacted as curriculum, the results are the same, i.e., non-contextualized curricular add-ons in the elementary classroom. In the first case, students may just be learning facts, a meaningless chronological display of history, sprinkled with stories and descriptions of what it looks like to be a good citizen. While on the opposite end of the spectrum, students do not have adequate historical context of past events, resulting in the inability to critically view or evaluate relevant topics. This is indeed quite a conundrum. In the first scenario, the students accumulate facts but are not drawn into active citizenship because there is no need for change or improvement. In the second instance, students might identify areas of change but are not equipped with the skills or knowledge necessary to effect change.

When considering the optimal civic literacy content for the elementary classroom, Kuhn's three stages of epistemological development shed light on this convoluted issue. In the first stage, Kuhn ascertains the understanding of knowledge as the accumulation of facts with a truth value that allows for correction of false beliefs by appeal to an external reality and source of "the truth." Therefore, "knowledge is black or white, right or wrong, highly certain, composed of discrete facts, and handed down from authorities unquestioningly" (Hofer, n.d., para. 5). All too often this is the approach that has been taken in our elementary classrooms and was an approach to curriculum often referenced with sharp criticism in our interviews. In this model, history has an "objective reality," and we can ascertain "the truth" about what occurred in any given event. Every single civically minded adult interviewed saw through this model and was extremely turned off when education was presented in this light. Kuhn refers to this epistemological model as the "absolutist" position.

In Kuhn's second stage of knowledge acquisition, "knowledge consists not of facts but of opinions, freely chosen by their holders as personal possessions, and accordingly, not open to challenge" (Kuhn, p. 121). There is an obvious equal danger in this epistemological view: If there is no sense of truth, if everything is utterly relative and a matter of opinion, then why bother learning at all? One can simply arrive at his/her own conclusions, be it via reading material or living experience. It is worth noting that not a single person interviewed who was civically engaged had adopted this viewpoint. However, it is Kuhn's third stage, the "evaluativist" stage, that matched interviewees' perceptions of epistemology, despite the common absence of this evaluativist framework being seen in the development of curriculum and thus in the classroom. This stage is one in which the students have the ability to evaluate knowledge in a recursive structure, to develop theories and understanding. Namely, "the understanding that some opinions are in fact superior to others to the extent they are better supported by argument and evidence. Rather than facts or opinions, knowledge at this level of epistemological understanding now "consists of claims which require support in a framework of alternatives, evidence, and argument" (Kuhn, p. 122). This allows students to justify various statements or arguments, while at the same time continuously reframing knowledge in light of being confronted with new perspectives. Hofer explains this recursive stage as "marked by a growing realization that there are means for justification of various positions and that this enables an individual to assert some positions with confidence even if knowledge is evolving and contingent" (2003, para. 5). Indeed, it is only at the evaluativist level that history and social sciences become a science, with hypotheses (claims) that require support, evidence, and argument with any given theory being, by nature, falsifiable (as is all good science). For this process to occur it requires an array of multiple alternatives to consider, flexibility and creativity of thought—all of which were mentioned in every interview. Only with multiple ideas to consider can we truly draw from the history of ideas. A monolithic approach, including a unicultural approach, omits the plethora of ideas and contributions of all men and women. It deprives history and humanity of its richness; it in fact reduces history to silence. Is it any wonder that such a method is perceived by students as lacking in meaning? Civic literacy education should strive to provide learning experiences that promote students' evaluativist level of epistemological knowledge: "Only at the evaluativist level are thinking and reasoning recognized as essential support for beliefs and actions. Thinking is the process that enables us to make informed choices between conflicting claims" (Kuhn, p. 122). Perhaps we should not be so surprised that critical thought was a common denominator across interviews as crucial in creating an engaged curriculum and pedagogy.

This requires us to reconsider the aims of education. According to Resnick and Nelson-LeGall (1997), properly educated citizens "believe they have the right (and the obligation) to understand things and make things work…believe that problems can be analyzed, that solutions often come from such analysis and that they are capable of that analysis…have a toolkit of problem-analysis tools and good intuitions about when to use them…know how to ask questions…seek help and get enough information to solve problems…have habits of mind that lead them to actively use the toolkit of analysis skills" (pp. 149–150). How can we expect to have civically engaged citizens, that is, citizens who have a toolkit of analytic skills and an ability to effect positive change if they have not even been taught how to think critically, to analyze problems, to consider multiple solutions? Monolithic approaches to history with all or nothing, right or wrong approaches to "the truth" will produce monolithic citizens, who see the world as it is instead of as it could be.

Philosophy

The art of philosophical thought is not typically included in the discussion of elementary education. However, according to Webster, philosophy is the "pursuit of wisdom by intellectual means and moral self-discipline." Wouldn't any parent want this type of study intertwined throughout all disciplinary studies in schools? So why isn't philosophy required in schools today? Some might say elementary students are not capable of such high-level, independent thinking and reflection. Many believe that teaching and philosophy are in conflict due to the communal nature of teaching and the "solitary act of philosophy." Rather, this is where teaching and philosophy find a beautiful confluence. Philosophy, particularly Socratic philosophy, is by nature dialogic and dialectic and fundamentally communal. Critical analysis of history that includes multiple perspectives, cultures, races, and genders is by nature Socratic in its grand conversation with different, often divergent, viewpoints. A history course that puts into conversation voices from differing times and perspectives is creating a Socratic dialogue between students and history. It brings history to life. Teaching is the active form of philosophy, not an oppositional force.

In *The Crisis in the Classroom*, Charles Silberman (1970) points to the sense of "mindlessness" that maintains the status quo throughout our educational system. He describes mindlessness as "the failure or refusal to think seriously about educational purpose, the reluctance to question established practices" (p. 11). Mindlessness exists today throughout our educational system. If a meaningless curriculum cultivating a mindless culture is the nature of our pedagogy, what should we expect of the next generation of human beings and citizens? Keep in mind Socrates's well-known maxim that "the unexamined life is not worth living." Kuhn does not identify schools as successfully assisting in exploring the good life, suggesting that education seldom provides opportunity for meaning or even an examination of beliefs. Kuhn modifies the Socrates adage by stating that "unexamined beliefs are not worth having." Civic literacy starts with the investigation of one's beliefs and values in relationship to others. Michael Oakeshott, in *The Voice of Liberal Learning*, beautifully connects these two aspects of self awareness: unexamined beliefs and the unexamined life.

> The freedom of a human being inheres in his thoughts and his emotions having had to be learned....This inseparability of learning and being human is central to our understanding of ourselves. It means that none of us is born human: each is what he learns to become....In short, this connection between learning and being human means that each man is his own self-enacted "history."...This [education] then is what we are concerned with: adventures in human self-understanding....Being human is a historic adventure which has been going on since the earth rose out of the sea, and we are concerned with this paraphernalia of learning because it is the only way we have of participating in this adventure. The ancient Greek exhortation Know Thyself meant *learn* to know thyself. It was not an exhortation to buy a book on psychology and study it; it meant, contemplate and learn from what men, from time to time, have made of this engagement of learning to be a man. (Oakeshott, 2001, p. 16).

To be a critical consumer, or a civic-minded person, is to "*learn* to know thyself." It is to work towards examined beliefs, examined history, and an examined self as they relate to wider communities and past events. Learning from history is one of the most critical ways in which we learn how we exist relationally to the self and others, be that another single individual, neighborhood, race, gender, religion, nation state, or any other category we have created to unite and divide groups of people.

Oakeshott connects the idea of knowing the self and being aware of history:

> Perhaps we may think of these components of a culture as voices, each the expression of a distinct and conditional understanding of the world and a distinct idiom of human self-understanding, and of the culture itself as these voices joined, as such voices could only be joined, in a conversation—an endless unrehearsed intellectual adventure in which, in imagination, we enter into a variety of modes of understanding the world and ourselves and are not disconcerted by the differences or dismayed by the inconclusiveness of it all (Oakeshott, 2001, p. 30).

As educators we cannot fall prey to silencing any voice within our classroom. We must be cautious and vigilant about encouraging self-awareness through expression of multiple voices. I am reminded of the introduction to *The Closing of the American Mind*, where Saul Bellow states that "when the Zulu invent a Tolstoy we will read him" (Bloom, 1987, p. 18). This statement is entirely in conflict with Socratic philosophy and evaluatist pedagogy, both of which must rely on critical analysis. Bellow sheds light on the height of an arrogant and unicultural viewpoint that is so dismissive of others that it literally leaves them uninvited to the conversation and philosophical dialogue. It reduces others to silence. It makes history dumb, mute. And even those invited to the table cannot help but be aware that their conversation is, by design, omitting and intentionally ignoring data that they may find uncomfortable. An interesting tangent was born of one interview in a seemingly innocuous question: How do you define democracy? The interviewee stated that "In order to have democracy...you have to have basic respect for the individual, each person has a voice...there must be structures/systems that are manageable...to ensure respect for the individual and so that minority voices aren't overrun" (J.S., personal communication, September 27, 2010). There is an obvious conflict between a curriculum that is so monotonous that it is described as "bland and boring" and caters largely to one group, and one with an alleged commitment to modeling and teaching democratic ideas and principles. In attempting to teach democracy and American history, we have created a curriculum whose very model undermines the principle of having basic respect for individual(s), i.e., that each person has a voice. In our curriculum, voices have been ignored or muted. How then can we expect to be nurturing the growth of future citizens engaged in a democratic society?

In contrast to this, one interviewee described her first experience on the path to finding her identity as a global citizen while participating in a Model United Nations Conference in Jerusalem, Israel. Here she was exposed to an "obvious and tangible experience of seeing the world in a more international light" by being exposed to multiple perspectives and cultures (J.S., personal communication, September 27, 2010). She was able to gain a perspective on humanity as a whole, in addition to differing communities and cultural contexts. This life-altering experience could be part of every educational experience for all students. And it is possible in all schools. This example captures the dialectical relationship of relevant curriculum infused with reflective thought and action. As educators, establishing a classroom that values knowledge and reflection of self and others is crucial. Knowledge becomes valuable unto itself in such a class, and students engage by virtue of an epistemological attitude that focuses on learning as a goal unto itself instead of a means to an end.

Dialectic Relationship

In addition to the common definition given by the eight subjects interviewed for citizen and civics, there was a common mechanism for how such conclusions were reached. All subjects spoke to the responsibility and moral obligation that citizens should have to creating a better community through critical awareness and engagement to effect change. Two subjects expanded this moral obligation to be that of a global citizen: "We have the choice to do good…it's an imperative that we have…beyond boundaries of country, government, and institutions. Those are all incidental" (J.W., personal communication, October 22, 2010). Another subject attested to that idea as well, noting that he hesitates to use the word "citizen," precisely because "the word carries ideas of exclusion and a monolithic sense of [individuals]. There is a lot of hypocrisy in the idea in how it leads to exclusion…in our own history be it women, Blacks, immigrants, etc." (M.A., personal communication, October 22, 2010).

So the obvious question is, how did all subjects arrive at an evaluativist stage of thought that prompts in them an empowerment to be critical and to attempt to effect change? A major piece of this mechanism for all subjects was the ability to see outside the self, to recognize the legitimacy of other and differing viewpoints. The evaluativist position made sense to them, based on their appreciation that there are many different kinds of people with unique stories to share. This awareness of differing viewpoints does not suffice; to recognize them as legitimate alternatives and narratives is critical (Howard, 2006). In all cases the subjects interviewed reached this level of empathy and acceptance of divergent viewpoints through a personal experience of "otherness" and being seen as "other"; for some this was as a woman or an African American. But gender and race were far from the only ways that people experienced otherness. European Americans interviewed described similar "otherness" experiences by virtue of being "brainy" and ostracized, or having a mentally ill family member, being poor, and so on. When the subjects interviewed realized in their own lives that they were often seen as "other," they evolved the ability to see the "other" narratives around them as well. We're all "others" in some way. Educating children to see critically may, in part, be making them feel uncomfortable, taking them out of their comfort zones to think and reflect on themselves as part of the whole instead of as *the* whole. This allows for a true dialectic relationship of knowledge, skills, and philosophical thought. We need to teach, model, and practice the art of thinking with our students if they are to become active, engaged, and—perhaps above all—compassionate citizens.

These components of civic knowledge exist within a dialectic relationship, interconnected and dependent on one another. Knowledge examined through a philosophical lens, while explored and analyzed with a variety of historical skills, tends not only to create new knowledge but also leads to an informed public. This requires education to redesign what is viewed as "essential" knowledge and the purpose of social studies. No longer is it important to have a common, shared history, but a view of multiple perspectives in which it is imperative to question, explore, and evaluate in a quest to develop reflective, engaged citizens. Knowing the nature of history and society, as well as the skills to critique those structures, provides the foundation and wherewithal to produce effective, caring, practicing citizens. Civic action puts civic knowledge into practice by having the practicing citizen comment or act upon her discovery. According to Osanloo (2007): "This is a bottom-up strategy that views individual duty and responsibility as the crux of maintaining and sustaining a liberal democracy. Individuals as one or in groups must voice their concerns when the system of checks and balances itself needs to be checked" (p. 191). This view of civic literacy suggests the creation of school environments that value multiple perspectives, open discussion, and critical analysis to be part of the daily curriculum. This was captured by one subject when he stated: "In order to have democracy…you have to have basic respect for the individual, each person has a voice…there must be structures/systems that are manageable…to ensure respect for the individual and so that minority voices aren't overrun (J.S., personal communication, October 1, 2010).

How would this play out in the elementary classroom? Creating interdisciplinary courses that focus on the context of ideas in depth will demonstrate how knowledge is linked and related across disciplines. In the process, we would create a higher-order thinking environment. Speaking to this critical point, nearly every interview provided the same recipe for addressing this issue, namely by establishing units of study that focus more specifically on a smaller set of ideas throughout a longer period of history, resulting in content with manifest meaning and context. Each unit of study would ask students to be savvy consumers of information in the classroom and inevitably in the real world. A savvy consumer is one who applies the skills of civic literacy, such as critical thinking, evaluation, and analysis, to make an informed decision. A decision based on various skills of analysis results in a formulation of a rational integration of interpretations of different historical developments that weighs perspectives and evidence. Critical literacy requires students to develop and utilize a variety of skills that evaluate the facts, places, people, and events that are typically considered to be school curriculum. These skills are integrated throughout the process of learning and becoming a citizen.

Ideally, elementary classrooms would be filled with individuals who are "able to evaluate expertise, reconcile theory and evidence, provide support for their claims, and re-evaluate those claims in the light of new evidence" (Hofer, 2003, para. 5). Teachers would be facilitating students in meaning making and developing participants in the shared construction of knowledge. In-depth exploration of an idea is more meaningful when that idea is also connected to our own lives in such a manner that the relationship between the individual, society, and history is manifest. When that beloved circumstance occurs, we have succeeded in creating a meaningful civic literacy curriculum and delivering that curriculum in an effective and caring manner.

Conclusion

Elementary school students come to the classroom with a natural curiosity. As educators, we need to cultivate and nurture their innate instincts, not extinguish their wondrously inquisitive characteristics. Elementary classrooms should be the arena for cultivating civic-minded members of our society. As educators, we know teachers who require rote memorization of minute facts. They often create students who are disengaged and uninformed. According to Levistik and Barton (1997), the concept of memorizing isolated facts rarely advances students' conceptual understandings. Hence, it is very difficult to separate the content that promotes civic literacy from the skills required in civic literacy. Rather, content infused with thinking skills equips students with the tools needed for informed citizenship. This requires elementary school teachers to create experiences in which children will pursue possible solutions to questions and search for clarity on issues. In short, we should encourage them to seek out information that sheds light on, or permits, a better understanding of ideas, issues, or questions that are either posed or revealed through experience (Ross, 2001). This results in thoughtful educators moving beyond the delivery of facts and dates and immerses students in civic literacy by way of authentic investigation. Perspectives of thought now become a skill set, becoming part of the larger toolkit of critical thought being fostered in our students (Foster & Padgett, 1999). Modeling and creating educational experiences that allow young people to question, explore, test, and argue their thoughts and opinions are important goals of critical pedagogy and critical civic literacy. These skills need to be taught and practiced through all disciplines and grades. Foster and Padgett (1999) capture the essence of this approach: "Genuine historical thinking demands that students learn to ask authentic questions, to select and examine historical evidence, to appreciate historical context, to evaluate divergent perspectives, and to reach, albeit tentatively, logical conclusions" (p. 2). In so doing, students begin to appreciate the interpretive and normative nature of thinking required for civic literacy.

It is our job as teachers to ensure that students think about thinking and gain an internalized realization about why knowledge is valuable and critical thinking a skill worth acquiring and perfecting. Meta-cognition is not something that students simply develop on their own as a skill, but rather is a tool that needs to be nourished by teachers and other adults.

Through civic literacy education students are offered multiple voices, multiple wisdoms, and a distinct contextual and conditional understanding of the world. What greater intellectual gift can we offer our students than the opportunity to be excited about not only their past, but that of others; to learn from all knowledge and wisdom that humans have created; and to be able to put into conversation and action different viewpoints from a diverse array of minds across the globe?

Entitlement to a voice and opinion allows students to feel comfortable expressing and exerting their voices, which will lead to feeling comfortable with the right to critique their own reality and attempt to effect social change. It was the potential for this very conversation that makes the interviewees proud participants in American society as people who, by choice, continue to live, contribute to, and partake in America. Our teaching must embrace this challenge if we are to effectively raise a new generation of citizens concerned with community and equality as a democracy is meant to be. Unfortunately, we are not there yet. As Matthew Arnold put it, "No individual life can be truly prosperous, passed…in the midst of men who suffer" (1903, page 332). Likewise, no society can be truly prosperous in the midst of communities that suffer.

Note

1. Several respondents used this term. When asked to elaborate, they talked about a presentation of U.S. history that was uncritical, largely focused on the history of America through war, and a narrative that was meant to create pride in the "superiority of American culture and modes of thinking."

Bibliography

Arnold, M. (1903). *Culture and anarchy*. Oxford. Oxford University Press.

Bloom, A. (1987). *The closing of the American mind*. New York: Simon & Schuster.

Costa, A.L., & Kallick, B. (2009). *Habits of mind across the curriculum: Practical and creative strategies for teachers*. Alexandria, VA.: Association for Supervision and Curriculum Development.

Executive Council, National Council for the Social Studies. (1992). *National curriculum standards for social studies: Executive summary*. Retrieved October 5, 2010, from http://www.socialstudies.org/standards/execsummary

Foster, S., & Padgett, C. (1999). Authentic historical inquiry in the social studies classroom. *Clearing House, 72*(6), 357–365.

Goldenberg, P. (1996). "Habits of mind" as an organizer for the curriculum. *Journal of Education, 178*(1), 13–34.

Hofer, B. (n.d.). Epistemological development. *Education.com* Retrieved December 3, 2010, from http://www.education.com/reference/article/epistemological-development/#A

Hofer, B., & Pintrich, P. (1987). The development of epistemological theories: Beliefs about knowledge and knowing and their relation to learning. *American Educational Research Association, 6*(1), 88–140. Retrieved September 11, 2010, from http://www.jstor.org/stable/1170620

Howard, G. (2006). *We can't teach what we don't know: White teachers, multiracial schools*. New York: Teachers College Press.

Kuhn, D. Educating adolescents for life. (n.d.). Unpublished draft, Teachers College, Columbia University, New York.

Levstik, L. S., & Barton, K. C. (2005). *Doing history*. Mahwah, NJ: L. Erlbaum Associates.

Lutkus, A., & Weiss, A. (2007, May 16). Publications & products. *National Center for Education Statistics (NCES) Home Page, a part of the U.S. Department of Education*. Retrieved September 11, 2010, from http://nces.ed.gov/nationsreportcard/pubs/main2006/2007476.asp

Oakeshott, M. (2001). *The voice of liberal learning*. New York: Liberty Fund.

Osanloo, A.F. (2007). Civic education post 9/11: Efficacy, cosmopolitanism, and pedagogical implications. *Social Studies Research and Practice, 2*(2), 180–195. Retrieved October 7, 2010, from www.socstrp.org/issues/getfile.cfm?volID=2&IssueID=2&ArticleID

Resnick, L., & Nelson-LeGall, S. (1997). Socializing intelligence. In L. Smith, J. Dockrell, & P. Tomlinson (Eds.), *Piaget, Vygotsky, and beyond* (pp. 145–158). Boston: Routledge & Kegan Paul.

Ross, W. (2001). Waiting for the great leap forward: From democratic principles to democratic reality. *Theory and Research in Social Education, 29*(3), 394–399.

Silberman, C.E. (1970). *Crisis in the classroom: The remaking of American education* (1st ed.). New York: Random House.

CHAPTER TWENTY-NINE

Writing to Read

Critical Civic Literacy at an Alternative High School

BETH HATT & PAUL PARKISON

In the fall of 2009, we were approached by the principal of a local alternative high school. He was passionate about improving the opportunities available to the young people at his school, especially in regard to literacy, and needed help in doing so. Could we help him? We—meaning Beth, who had previously taught in prison settings, and Paul, a previous middle school social studies and literacy teacher—decided to give it a try. Since both of us ascribe to critical pedagogical ideals, we knew we wanted to generate a project that led to more critical thinking, civic engagement, and empowerment. What we were unsure of was what notions of citizenship, critical thinking, and empowerment would mean for students who had essentially been disenfranchised and excluded from the civic space of school through their placement in an alternative setting.

We proposed beginning with an 8-week writing workshop that we would facilitate, centered upon critical civic literacy. The rest of this chapter provides an overview of the school, a brief literature review, a description of the project, and what we learned from it about critical civic literacy.

Ritz Alternative High School

The students came to the alternative school through two main channels. First, all high school age students just released from the Department of Corrections enrolled within the school district were immediately referred to the alternative high school. Second, students could be expelled from one of five local high schools and referred to the alternative high school. Based upon interviews with the teachers and social workers at the school, academic skills varied widely among students. Differentiating instruction was difficult for the teachers due to a lack of professional development. Challenges also included low attendance rates and never knowing what new students might arrive on any given day. Also, according to the social workers, drug and alcohol use were a big issue, with 60% of the population either using themselves or living in a household where drug and/or alcohol abuse occurred.

The school consisted of 101 students—58.4% boys and 41.6% girls—at the time of the Writing to Read program implementation. The school's demographic data indicate that with respect to race/ethnicity, 67% of the students were white, 32% Black or African American, and 1% Latino. Demographic data for the student population is suspect due to institutionalized biases within the school district. Mixed race and Latino populations are not recognized as readily, and self-identification has been discouraged. Sixty-eight percent of the students held IEPs. There were a total of 10 teachers with a student-teacher ratio of approximately 10.1:1 (Great Schools Inc., 2010). Demographic and socioeconomic data for the student population, as well as per-pupil expenditure data, point to part of the disenfranchisement and marginalization of this school. The school district allocates the funding provided by the state and through local property tax revenue to the students' home schools. The alternative school was allocated a fixed operating budget that was below the district per-pupil rate and did not allow for increases in student population throughout the fiscal year.

Since neither of us had previously taught in an alternative high school setting, we approached the development of the project through what we "knew" from the research literature. What follows is a brief summary of the literature that provided a foundation for the project split into three categories: citizenship, discipline, and tracking.

Citizenship

The relationship between the processes of education and the effects that these processes have upon social engagement and power of students within this system form the basis of the following discussion. De-mythologizing the school context and culture will enable students and teachers to relocate themselves within the political discussion of curriculum content and pedagogical practice. At the same time, this de-mythologizing critique draws the political neutrality of the alternative education curriculum and setting into question.

At its foundation, citizenship and participation in schooling, and any other public activity, require enduring interest in the world and the political choice of what is important and valuable to learn and understand. This is what characterizes humankind and grants meaning to life (Arendt, 1972; Benhabib, 2005; Husserl, 1962). When students and teachers become alienated (disengaged) from the educational process and the political dialogue that is brought forward within the school curriculum and setting, they cease to fully engage in the process that is meant to facilitate engagement and the development of a learning culture. Relinquishing interest and choice in what is taught and learned leads to an orientation that fits a "participatory subject" rather than a critical "democratic citizen" (Almond & Verba, 1963).

Gonzalez, Moll, and Amanti (2005) help to articulate the necessity of creating connections that facilitate engagement—bridging the everyday knowledge of the individual to the broader knowledge of the society, state, nation, and world (Banks, 2007). Crossing cultural borders helps to facilitate the type of multicultural citizenship (Kymlica, 1995) that is necessary within a pluralist, democratic culture. Gonzalez and colleagues clarify the manner in which perspectives on culture and cultural investigation have evolved:

> Increasingly, the boundedness of cultures gave way to an idea of the interculturality and hybridity of cultural practices. Often these concepts were predicated on examining borderlands, which are often riddled with emergent practices and mixed conventions that do not conform to normativity. Borderlands came to be a fertile metaphor for observing flux and fluidity, literally and metaphorically. (Gonzalez, Moll, & Amanti, 2005, p. 38)

Considerations of "Funds of Knowledge" (Gonzalez, Moll, & Amanti, 2005), "Politics of Recognition" (Benhabib, 2005; 1992; 2002; Taylor, 1998; 1994), and "Colonizing Epistemologies" (Apple, 2006; Carnoy, 1972; Fanon, 1990; Foucault, 1972; Willinsky, 1998) lead to a desire to open the public space of the Writing to Read project through a recognition of the private space perspective. In the case study being presented here, students were given the opportunity to experience educative learning (Dewey, 1916) and to make the personal connections with academic disciplines that facilitate the development of a democratic civic culture and engaged learning.

Discipline

Although there is no evidence that disciplinary removal in high school leads to improvements in the individual student's behavior or an improvement in overall school safety, it is still a commonly used practice (Skiba and Peterson, 2003). Furthermore, there is wide variation across schools and teachers regarding what behaviors result in a student actually being expelled or suspended (Wu, Pink, Crain, & Moles, 1982). Students of all backgrounds often recognize the arbitrary enforcement of suspension/expulsion and believe the practices unfairly target students based upon reputation, race/ethnicity, or income level (Brantlinger, 1991; Sheets, 1996). In fact, students of color are much more likely to be suspended and expelled even when controlling for socioeconomic status (Skiba, 2004). Additionally, when students are expelled or suspended, they are at a higher risk of dropping out (Skiba, 2004). Based upon the literature, we knew we were stepping into an environment that the literature had largely deemed ineffective and would be working with students who most likely perceived their placement at the alternative school as having occurred through an unfair process.

Furthermore, we knew we were likely to be stepping into an environment where students' schooling identities were entrenched in notions of being framed as "bad." One example of a typical misunderstanding between teachers and students is when students regularly misbehave. Often, teachers may believe students are misbehaving because they do not care about school, are disrespectful, or come from dysfunctional home environments (Banks, 2006; Honneth, 1996; Riggs & Gholar, 2009; Slater, 2002). This stereotype is frequently tied to Latino and African American youth because of their overrepresentation in office referrals, suspensions, and expulsions. Alternatively, the reality suggests many of these youth are intelligent and know the system is not fair. Consequently, they have embraced a "bad" identity as a way to save face from an often alienating and painful schooling context where they are framed as "problems" and "low achievers" (Hatt, 2007; Kohl, 1991). Ann Arnett Ferguson (2001) writes about a "punishing room" at an elementary school:

> For the children, it is a place of knowing one is not alone. The child who gets in trouble is the norm. Identities and reputations are made and remade here. It is the space in the school in which everyone is like yourself—in trouble—and you are no longer different. (p. 32)

How we think about "bad" kids needs to be shifted from an assumption that these students do not care about school to an attitude that asks why students are misbehaving and how schooling is not meeting their current needs. We began the project by attempting to avoid labeling the students at the school as "bad" and, instead, assumed traditional schooling did not meet their needs and would better meet their needs through our project.

Tracking

Tracking is the practice of placing students into groups or classes based upon *perceived* academic ability. Research has confirmed that tracking is often tied to racial, ethnic, and social class differences (Oakes, 2005). For example, Oakes and Guiton (1995) discovered that wealthy white and Asian students at three high schools were much more likely to be placed in high-status, academically rigorous courses than Latinos whose achievement was similar. Once students are placed into these courses, it can influence their own perceptions about whether or not they are "smart" and whether school is something they are good at or not (Hatt, 2007). Furthermore, the most experienced teachers are more likely to teach "gifted" classes, while the low-track classes are often taught by teachers who are new or poorly prepared in their subject area (McLaughlin & Talbert, 2001). Finally, the students in the lower-level tracks are more likely to be taught using a banking style of education that emphasizes drill, memorization, and conformity rather than creative thought, critical thinking, or individual expression (Murphy & Hallinger, 1989; Oakes, Gamoran, & Page, 1992). This style of teaching often leads to students losing motivation, rejecting the curriculum, and/or acting out in the classroom (Alschuler, 1994; MacLeod, 1987; Rubin, 2008).

In our work with the students, we wanted to avoid buying into deficit models regarding the students and to provide them with curriculum that avoided rote memorization and, instead, emphasized creative expression, critical thinking, and individuality rather than conformity. Through a funds-of-knowledge perspective, we believed the students would be bringing with them a wealth of untapped knowledge that most likely had not been valued in their previous educational settings (Costa, 2008; Gonzalez, Moll, & Amanti, 2005). We also knew students may have already developed a pattern of resisting authority, having been previously presented with curricula that emphasized control and conformity (Finn, 2009).

The Project

As a result of our consideration of the previous literature, we decided upon implementing a writing workshop format. Writing workshop is a research-based practice that allows students to become producers rather than receivers of knowledge by becoming authors themselves (Gutierrez, 2008; Riggs & Gholar, 2009; O'toole, 2008; Parkison, 2010). Furthermore, we spent the 8 weeks prior to implementing the workshop volunteering in classrooms at the high school. We wanted to get to know teachers and students and to become more familiar with the daily operations of the school. We hoped that building relationships within the school prior to beginning the project would allow for things to run more smoothly and for students to feel more comfortable with us.

Over the 8-week period, we worked with a total of 23 students, but attendance was random. Some students attended regularly, while we may have only seen others once or twice during that time period. Out of the 23, 61% (n: 14) were white and 39% (n: 9) were Black. The school district as a whole is 74% white and 14% Black, which depicts a clear over-representation of students of color at the alternative school. Males were also over-represented in our group at 78% (n: 18) versus 12% (n: 5) females. It is also important to note that out of the 5 females, 3 self-identified as lesbian. Although actual household income data was not available for each of the students, based upon the ways they described their lives beyond the classroom, the majority of the students came from low-income families.

We covered six main topics during the eight weeks:

1. What is and/or should be the purpose of public education?
2. How does your private self fit or not fit within public school?
3. What does it mean to be smart?
4. What would a declaration of student rights consist of?
5. What advice would you give to future teachers?
6. Can you identify when you started to dislike school and why?

Our ultimate goal was to encourage students to think more critically about the education they had received and were continuing to receive while also asking them to think about the purpose education served (or did not serve) in their lives. At the same time, we wanted to build their reading and writing skills, as these skills are essential for civic engagement. Admittedly, these were high expectations for an 8-week project.

We would begin each topic with a short reading, discuss the topic, and then ask the students to begin writing about their thoughts/opinions. Early on students were very resistant to writing. Some of this resistance was toward schooling altogether, while some of the resistance was also connected to insecurity about their writing skills. We then offered students a choice of writing, producing a drawing of their thoughts, or speaking their thoughts into a recorder. These options worked better with the students. We focused upon an expanded view of literacy rather than simply relying upon text production and interpretation as the only relevant mode of literacy (Gutierrez, 2008). Overwhelmingly, students chose to speak rather than write or draw what they were thinking. With student permission, we began to record our conversations regarding the topics. Toward the end of the 8 weeks, students were writing more, but we had not made it as far as we had hoped. Students were producing single paragraphs rather than full pages. However, the teachers shared with us that students were participating and more engaged during our workshops than they had witnessed previously in their own classes.

For the purposes of this chapter, we will focus upon our work with students regarding a Student Declaration of Rights. To begin the discussion, we shared with students the Universal Declaration of Human Rights (http://www.un.org/en/documents/udhr/) adopted by the General Assembly of the United Nations on December 10, 1948. Our aim was to have the students think about their own rights as human beings and also their obligation in respecting the rights of others. Additionally, as a previous middle school teacher, Paul believed in framing classroom discipline around students' rights rather than focusing upon what behaviors were not allowed. We wanted the students to consider their rights as citizens within the school community. We discovered that many of the students believed their rights had been violated at school. They especially felt they had not been listened to and that they did not have any recourse if they were mistreated by teachers. The following is an excerpt from one of our conversations on students' rights:

> *John*: They [administration] believe the teachers over everything. . . .
>
> *Dylan*: I think you should have a right, just like anyone else, you have a right to state your own opinions.
>
> *John*: When I was going to [South High School], I was in Miss, I don't remember my teacher's name, but she told the principal I slammed her into the wall. I got kicked out of school for that. And, I didn't even touch her. She snatched me by the arm and I walked out of the classroom.
>
> *Brittany*: Yeah, and to be honest…when you do get in trouble, I think there should be more than one person that should actually hear the story from different people.
>
> *John*: They don't ask the students. Everything they see, the teacher says, goes.
>
> *Dylan*: The teacher is always correct.
>
> *John*: No matter—
>
> *Dylan*: What they say, they've said to me, every time I get a referral. The teacher is always correct. The teacher never lies.
>
> *Brittany*: They're always right because—
>
> *John*: Because they're adults.
>
> *Dylan*: That's not necessarily true because just like in the world—
>
> *John*: They think that just because we're teenagers or kids, we don't know what we're talking about.

Some of the students even went on to equate teachers with cops and the mistreatment they had experienced at the hands of police officers. The following excerpt depicts these beliefs:

> *Dylan*: Just like in jail or prison, there is going to be cops in there that is not going to do what they're told. Just like whenever I got arrested, the cop, like, pretty much, just bullied me.
>
> *John*: A cop can beat you—
>
> *Dylan*: Like, they just got me out of the car, and just switched my handcuffs, and then I'd do like that, and they'd slam me down, and it was for nothing. And, stupid stuff. And, it's just, they'd think it was funny.
>
> *Beth*: So, it sounds like you feel like in a lot of ways, your rights have been violated.
>
> *Brittany*: Yeah, cuz—
>
> *Dylan*: They do.

Brittany: Yeah, sometimes, kids don't know what they're talking about, but an adult should at least take the time to listen to a child when they're talking. . . .

Dylan: You never know. The child could know what they're talking about.

In terms of developing critical civic literacy skills, the problem was not that, as marginalized students, they weren't able to critique the system, which might be true of more mainstream populations. As the previous excerpt describes, the struggle was in feeling delegitimized and silenced. By beginning with recognizing the students' lived experiences and the legitimacy of their perception of these experiences, we were able to open a critical space for the students to re-engage. The students began to assert their interests and to make and defend civic choices based upon their funds of knowledge.

Consequently, we discussed the possibility of sharing their Declaration of Student Rights with the local school board as a way to be heard. We attempted to help them think through their arguments for each of the "rights" in a way that would be well received by the school board. Students struggled with understanding how to re-structure arguments toward people in power. Speaking from the margin of civic culture presents one of the chief obstacles to re-engagement. Border pedagogy (Giroux, 1988), pedagogy of hope (Freire, 1994), and identity politics (Barber, 1992; Benhabib, 2007; Honneth, 1996; Slater, 2002) all assert the role of voice and dialogue in reclaiming the civic space necessary for engaged and critical citizenship. This was especially difficult when their rationale for the rights was grounded at times in beliefs that education was meaningless and did not serve a purpose in their lives. The following excerpt provides an example of this struggle:

Jake: Nah, we're talking about a right to rest because a lot of the classes and everything, they won't even let you have your head down.

Bryce: Or sleep, or yeah.

Paul: But you know, how would you present this argument to a group of people who are going to make a policy about school?

Jake: Policy?

Paul: You know, that we're going to say, "Okay, here are the rules for this school."

Jake: You mean, like, "This is what we've gathered up and everything?"

Paul: Because can you picture a group of adults saying, "Yeah, you could come to school and sleep?"

Jake: That would be awesome.

Paul: But I mean, can you picture a group of adults who are going to make rules and policies saying that?

Jake: I can't picture it, but like it says, you have a right to an education, and I think if you come into school, then at least, you should have a right to…if they're making you come to school, you should have a right to do that, at least sleep or something, a nap or something, because if you have a right to an education, that doesn't necessarily mean you have to have an education. It's a right.

Paul: A right is not necessarily an obligation.

Jake: Yeah.

Within this dialogue it is evident that the students, though prompted, are beginning to see the role of persuasion. Critical citizenship requires an appeal to evaluative criteria and recognition of power. It is not simply a rebellion without direction or cause (Benhabib, 2005; Kymlica, 1995).

In considering the rights the students felt they deserved but had been denied, they simply wanted to have more of a democratic educational experience. They desired a more collaborative process in determining school rules and how discipline was enforced. Rather than fitting the stereotype of "bad" students or students who "did not care" about school, they exhibited the contrary. They were students who wanted to be more involved and to have more of a voice in their education. They wanted to be respected as agents capable of participating in a more democratic community. Unfortunately, school officials largely viewed the youth as needing to be controlled and given fewer rights to encourage organizational conformity.

Regarding public schools and democracy, McCadden (1998) states:

> It [public education] is a place where democracy plays out, or in many cases does not play out: a place where voices can be heard or squelched; where power can be grabbed or shared; where people can be included or excluded, etc.…Because so much is believed to be at stake in the control and governance of public education, the tendency is, at least rhetorically and politically, toward squelching, grabbing, and excluding. (pp. 7–8)

What we observed and experienced at the alternative high school closely aligned with the research literature. We observed students being involuntarily shifted from one school to another and teachers doing the best they could with limited resources and support. The students understood the system, knew they were unfairly labeled, and were denied a voice in being able to define what a meaningful education would look like for them. The students had not experienced a democratic process in their education (Castoriadis, 1997). They felt silenced and devalued. Yet the writing workshop allowed for alternative possibilities—a chance to speak their minds, to create knowledge.

Critical Civic Literacy in the Lives of Marginalized Youth

Giroux (1988) states:

> Once the relationship between schooling and the larger society is recognized, questions about the nature and meaning of the schooling experience can be viewed from a theoretical perspective capable of illuminating the often ignored relationship between school knowledge and social control. (p. 22)

This relationship between the process of education and the effects that these processes have upon social engagement and power should not be overlooked. Schooling has become less human-centered and more focused upon competencies, standardization, and outcomes (Parkison, 2009). More than ever—and not just for the economic elite—education has become something to purchase and own. It has become less about the original purpose of public schooling with regard to the importance of an educated citizenry capable of full participation in the collective narrative of democratic governance.

Labaree (1997) discusses this shift as a move away from the goal of "democratic equality" with an emphasis on schools as *public* goods and with the aim of creating a healthy democracy. On the contrary, the politics of education have shifted to the goal of "social mobility," which frames schools as *private* goods where students become *consumers* and attempt to accrue the appropriate educational "property" to improve or maintain their own social status. Schooling becomes framed through the individual benefits it provides rather than the role it plays in supporting our democracy. These two competing paradigmatic goals for education are what allow education "to be defined as an arena that simultaneously promotes equality and adapts to inequality" (Labaree, 1997, p. 41). Under the goal of social mobility stratification, rather than equal treatment, is an acceptable outcome. Furthermore, under the goal of social mobility,

> students at all levels quickly come to the conclusion that what matters most is not the knowledge they learn in school but the credentials they acquire there....The end result is to reify the formal [external] markers of education and displace the substantive content. (Labaree, 1997, pp. 55–56)

In asserting that performance on a specified test indicates educational proficiency on the part of the student and the school, the current social mobility paradigm grounded in neo-conservatism represents a power grab within the cultural politics of education (Parkison, 2009). It expressly restricts the discussion of educational objectives and content by institutionalizing a set of standards within a non-democratic political system. The search for the validation of a particular cultural politics becomes of vital importance in identifying the potential for a shift away from the hegemonic structure of the current social mobility goal. Shifting from a search for certainty in the form of standardized test performance and the brute data that legitimate it to a search for agency within a collaborative consensus-building axiological dialogue represents the challenge of this socio-political crisis.

Many students who struggle in school, such as those at the alternative school, have struggled to acquire the more valuable credentials of schooling regarding grades, test scores, etc., and, as a result, have lost a purpose for schooling under the goal of social mobility. These students then become less likely to engage in the competition of schooling and, instead, "often look at education as a lost cause or a sucker's game" (Labaree, 1997, p. 57). In essence, the goal of social mobility "works" by effectively alienating students, especially those from low income or diverse backgrounds, from the educational process.

Finally, Labaree (1997) argues that the shift toward the goal of social mobility has resulted in watered-down citizenship training within schools. He states:

> Once seen as the overarching goal of the entire educational effort, schooling for citizenship increasingly has been confined to one part of the curriculum (social studies) or even perhaps a single course (civics)...what schools identify and reward as good citizenship in their students today is often just organizationally acceptable conduct—behaving in accordance with school rules rather than showing a predisposition toward civic virtue. (p. 67)

Critical civic literacy affords the opportunity to reassert the goal of democratic equality for public education. It is an essential step toward asking students and policy makers: education for whom and for what ends? It is a step toward realigning citizenship with notions of agency rather than organizational conformity (Banks, 2007; Castoriadis, 1997; Taylor, 1999; Thrupp, 2006).

In *Ideas: General Introduction to Pure Phenomenology*, Husserl (1962) outlines the approach that allows the philosopher (or educator) to go beyond mere appearance in the form of brute data and school report cards and to grasp essential agency in the axiological dialogue. The claim in this phenomenological analysis is that the more practitioners come to rely upon these instruments to define the effectiveness and proficiency of individual students and teachers, the more we are led to interpret students and teachers in terms of the social mobility paradigm. There is an epistemological bias built into the social mobility goal that effectively alienates a significant portion of the population that must submit to the educational system.

It is within the politics of this decision making that the lived experience of students becomes evidence of the systemic crisis that the social mobility paradigm enables. Aronowitz and Giroux offer their consideration of this epistemological stance, stating that it is "at odds with an ethical and substantive vision of what schools might be with respect to their potential for empowering both students and teachers as active and critical citizens" (Aronowitz & Giroux, 1991, p. 45). Critical civic literacy, however, is aligned with the goal of democratic equality and encourages active and critical citizens through education. It is one step toward democratic equality in our schools.

Bibliography

Almond, G.A., & Verba, S. (1963). *The civic culture: Political attitudes and democracy in five nations.* Boston: Little, Brown and Company.

Alschuler, A. (1994). *School discipline: A socially literate solution.* New York: McGraw-Hill.

Apple, M. (2006). *Educating the "right" way: Markets, standards, God, and inequality.* (2nd ed.). New York: Routledge.

Arendt, H. (1972). Crisis of the republic: Lying in politics; civil disobedience; on violence; thoughts on politics and revolution. Orlando, FL: Harcourt Brace and Company.

Aronowitz, S., & Giroux, H. (1991). Postmodern education: Politics, culture, and social criticism. Minneapolis: University of Minnesota Press.

Banks, J. (2006). *Cultural diversity and education: Foundations, curriculum, and teaching.* (5th ed.). Boston, MA: Pearson.

Banks, J.A. (2007). *Educating citizens in a multicultural society* (2nd ed.). New York: Teachers College Press.

Barber, B. (1992). *An aristocracy of everyone: The politics of education and the future of America.* New York: Ballantine Books.

Benhabib, S. (1992). *Situating the self: Gender, community, and postmodernism in contemporary ethics.* New York: Routledge.

Benhabib, S. (2002). *The claims of culture: Equality and diversity in the global era.* Princeton, NJ: Princeton University Press.

Benhabib, S. (2005). Borders, boundaries, and citizenship. *PS, Political Science & Politics, 38*(4), 673–677.

Benhabib, S. (2007). Twilight of sovereignty or the emergence of cosmopolitan norms? Rethinking citizenship in volatile times. *Citizenship Studies, 11*(1), 19–36.

Brantlinger, E. (1991). Social class distinctions in adolescents' reports of problems and punishment in school. *Behavioral Disorders, 17,* 36–46

Carnoy, M. (1972). *Education as cultural imperialism.* New York: McKay.

Castoriadis, C. (1997). Democracy as procedure and democracy as regime. *Constellations, 4.*

Costa, A.L. (2008). *The school as a home for the mind: Creating mindful curriculum, instruction, and dialogue.* (2nd ed.). Thousand Oaks, CA: Corwin Press.

Dewey, J. (1916). *Democracy and education.* New York: Macmillan.

Fanon, F. (1990). *The wretched of the Earth.* London: Penguin.

Ferguson, A.A. (2001). *Bad boys: Public schools in the making of black masculinity.* Ann Arbor: University of Michigan Press.

Finn, P. (2009). *Literacy with an attitude: Educating working-class children in their own self- interest.* Albany: State University of New York Press.

Foucault, M. (1972). *The archaeology of knowledge.* New York: Pantheon Books.

Freire, P. (1994). *Pedagogy of hope: Reviving pedagogy of the oppressed.* New York: Continuum.

Giroux, H. (1988). Border pedagogy in the age of postmodernism. *Journal of Education, 170*(3), 162–181.

Gonzalez, N., Moll, L.C., & Amanti, C. (Eds.). (2005). *Funds of knowledge: Theorizing practices in households, communities, and classrooms.* Mahwah, NJ: Lawrence Erlbaum Associates.

Great Schools Inc. (2010, May). *Great schools.* Retrieved June 25, 2010, from www.greatschools.org/cgi-bin/in/other/455#students

Gutierrez, K.D. (2008). Developing a sociocritical literacy in the third space. *Reading Research Quarterly, 43*(2), 148–164.

Hatt, B. (2007). Street smarts vs. book smarts: The figured world of smartness in the lives of marginalized, urban youth. *The Urban Review, 39*(3), 145–166.

Honneth, A. (1996). *The struggle for recognition: The moral grammar of social conflict.* Cambridge, MA: Polity Press.

Husserl, E. (1962). *Ideas: General introduction to pure phenomenology* (W.B. Gibson, Trans.). New York: Collier Books.

Kohl, H. (1991). *I won't learn from you: The role of assent in learning.* Minneapolis, MN: Milkweed Editions.

Kymlica, W. (1995). *Multicultural citizenship: A liberal theory of minority rights.* New York: Oxford University Press.

Labaree, D. (1997). Public goods, private goods: The American struggle over educational goals. *American Educational Research Journal, 34*(1), 39–81.

MacLeod, J. (1987). *Ain't no makin it.* Boulder, CO: Westview Press.

McCadden, B. (1998). *It's hard to be good: Moral complexity, construction, and connection in a kindergarten classroom.* New York: Peter Lang.

McLaughlin, M.W., & Talbert, J. (2001). *Professional communities and the work of high school teaching.* Chicago: University of Chicago Press.

Murphy, J., & Hallinger, P. (1989). Equity as access to learning: Curricular and instructional treatment differences. *Journal of Curriculum Studies, 21*(2), 129–149.

Oakes, J. (2005). *Keeping track: How schools structure inequality.* New Haven, CT: Yale University Press.

Oakes, J., Gamoran, A., & Page, R. (1992). Curriculum differentiation: Opportunities, outcomes, and meanings. In P. Jackson (Ed.), *Handbook of research on curriculum* (pp. 570–608). New York: Macmillan.

Oakes, J., & Guiton, G. (1995). Matchmaking: The dynamics of high school tracking decisions. *American Educational Research Journal, 32*(1), 3–33.

O'toole, L. (2008). Understanding individual patterns of learning: Implications for the well-being of students. *European Journal of Education, 43*(1), 71–86.

Parkison, P. (2009). Political economy of NCLB: Standards, testing and test scores. *The Educational Forum, 73*(1), 44–57.

Parkison, P. (2010). The changing role of instructors as both leaders and learners. In M.A. Fallon & S.C. Brown (Eds.), *Teaching inclusively in higher education* (pp. 77–94). Charlotte, NC: Information Age Publishing, Inc.

Riggs, E.G., & Gholar, C.R. (2009). *Strategies that promote student engagement.* (2nd ed.). Thousand Oaks, CA: Corwin Press.

Rubin, B. (2008). Detracking in context: How local constructions of ability complicate equity-geared reform. *Teachers College Record, 110*(3), 646–699.

Sheets, R.H. (1996). Urban classroom conflict: Student-teacher perception: Ethnic integrity, solidarity, and resistance. *The Urban Review, 28*, 165–183.

Skiba, R. (2004). *Zero tolerance: The assumptions and the facts.* (Education policy briefs, vol. 1, no. 2). Bloomington: Indiana University, Center for Evaluation and Education Policy.

Skiba, R., & Peterson, R. (2003). Teaching the social curriculum: School discipline as instruction. *Preventing School Failure, 47*(2), 66–73.

Slater, J. (2002). Limitations of the public space: Habitus and worldlessness. In J. Slater, S. Fain, & C. Rossatto (Eds.), *The Freirean legacy: Educating for social justice* (pp. 57–72). New York: Peter Lang.

Taylor, C. (1994). *Multiculturalism: Examining the politics of recognition.* Princeton, NJ: Princeton University Press.

Taylor, C. (1998, October). The dynamics of democratic exclusion. *Journal of Democracy*, 143–156.

Taylor, C. (1999). Democratic exclusion (and its remedies?). In R. Bhargava, A. Bagchi, & R. Sudarshan (Eds.), *Multiculturalism, liberalism and democracy* (pp. 138–163). New Delhi: Oxford University Press.

Thrupp, M. (2006). taking school context more seriously: The social justice challenge. *British Journal of Educational Studies, 54*(3), 308–328.

Willinsky, J. (1998). *Learning to divide the world: Education at empire's end.* Minneapolis and London: University of Minnesota Press.

Wu, S.C., Pink, W.T., Crain, R.L., & Moles, O. (1982). Student suspension: A critical reappraisal. *The Urban Review, 14*, 245–303.

CHAPTER THIRTY

The Civics of Language Diversity

Human Rights, Citizenship, and English-Only

JOHN E. PETROVIC

Introduction

Preparation of this chapter for the theme of this book took me back to my eighth-grade cclass. While I could visualize Mr. Kaletz in front of the class in a pink button-down shirt, tie, and gray pin-stripe slacks, I couldn't recall a single word of anything he said about civics. Trying to recall what civics was seems relevant to a chapter on critical civic literacy. Of course, I could give a generally accurate account of what I think civics is, but I wanted to recall what I was taught that it is. For that seems to be the building block on which to begin.

I went to our curriculum library and found an eighth-grade civics textbook: *Civics: Participating in Our Democracy* (Davis & Fernlund, 1993). Not my civics book but, I would have to guess, sadly, that it is probably pretty close. The subtitle of the text sums up the purpose of civics classes. In the first unit of this particular text, students are told that they "will begin to learn what it means to be an American citizen and what rights and responsibilities citizens share" (p. 1). Of course this requires, in units 2–6 respectively, an understanding of our history, the three branches of the federal government, what state and local governments do, our economic system, and our legal system. In unit 7, then, students are taught how "people make a difference."

Civics, as an area of study, provides the foundational knowledge (essentially units 2–6 from the example above) upon which students should be expected to acquire civic literacy. Civic literacy would seem to mean the habits and dispositions necessary for engaging in democratic society, a combination of the understandings of the goals of unit 1 and the habits related in unit 7. Kenneth Teitelbaum (2010) summarizes it thusly:

> Civic literacy means being well-versed in social and political knowledge, understandings, dispositions and skills. It means not only being able to essentially de-code and make meaning of the world around us but

also to employ information and abilities for active engagement with and within civic relationships and institutions. (p. 308)

Such active engagement must be guided by, as noted from the civics lesson, the rights and responsibilities we share. Here we should not have a perspective of each other merely as citizens (nameless political creatures) but also as human beings with unique backgrounds, experiences, wants, and needs. It is here that *critical* civic literacy comes into view. Critical civic literacy involves, among other things, the habit of following the emancipatory imperative of problematizing the structures that limit individual flourishing and participation as citizens and that construct our "common sense" assumptions about society and legitimate ways of being and knowing.

In this chapter, I take on the issue of language diversity as an issue of critical civic literacy. Critical civic literacy requires an understanding of the ways that the language one speaks marginalizes certain groups from civic life in and out of schools. Given the reality of linguistic diversity, the two overarching questions that I consider are: (1) what rights do/should language minority citizens enjoy, and (2) what responsibilities does the state have to its language-minority citizens?

Linguicism

One purpose of rights is to protect people from legal, political, and/or social oppression. There are many forms of oppression that might be discussed in a civics class; most typically addressed is racism. Of course, we might also talk about sexism, classism, ableism, etc. The form of oppression named in this chapter is linguicism. To begin with, I would define linguicism as a form of oppression deriving from the presumption of superiority of some languages, language varieties, or language forms over others and the assumptions made about their speakers, especially the assumptions made about speakers of non-privileged languages, language varieties, or language forms.

A simple example of linguicism is related by Rita Tenorio (1994) regarding two students in a bilingual school. Many of Tenorio's young students come to this school hearing for the first time another child speaking a language other than English. They also hear for the first time accented English. Thus, one day a student, Sean, complained to Ms. Tenorio, "I don't want to sit next to [Miguel]. He talks funny." Whether it was due to Miguel's accented English or his use of Spanish, Sean reveals the extent to which children form, uncritically, taken-for-granted assumptions about how people should be. The point here is not to blame Sean but to acknowledge that linguicism starts early, and must be addressed early at the level of the individual.

This said, we must also capture the institutionalization of linguicism and the ways that linguistic privilege is (re)produced. Tove Skutnabb-Kangas (2000) captures this in her definition of linguicism as "ideologies, structures, and practices which are used to legitimate, effectuate, regulate, and reproduce an unequal division of power and resources (both material and immaterial) between groups which are defined on the basis of language" (p. 30). In short, linguicism becomes part of the social contract.

Consider that in recent surveys two-thirds (67%) of Americans say that those who move to the United States should "adopt America's culture, language, and heritage." Seventy-nine percent (79%) say immigrants should be required to learn English before they are allowed to become citizens. Eighty-four percent (84%) of Republicans and seventy-eight percent (78%) of Democrats say that learning English should be required before citizenship is offered (Rasmussen Reports, 2005). It is unclear whether these responses reflect general agreement with current law (naturalization requirements currently include, as per section 312 of the Immigration and Naturalization Act, "An understanding of the English language, including an ability to read, write, and speak . . . simple words and phrases . . . in ordinary usage in the English language" [U.S. Citizenship and Immigration Services, 2010]) or whether they reflect a desire to make current law more restrictive, applying it not only to naturalized citizens but also to citizens by birth.

Similar ambiguity can be found in recent legislative proposals such as the "English Language Unity Act" (2009, H.R. 997), the purpose of which is "to declare English as the official language of the United States, to establish a uniform English language rule for naturalization, and to avoid misconstructions of the English language texts of the laws of the United States, pursuant to Congress's powers to provide for the general welfare of the United States and to establish a uniform rule of naturalization under article I, section 8, of the Constitution."

Attitudes such as those above reflect a general belief that English is not only the language *for* citizenship (you must learn it before becoming a citizen) but also the language *of* citizenship (you must use English in the practice of many of your rights as a citizen). Just to provide an example of viewing English as the language *of* citizenship, voters opposed to Chinese ballots in Seattle commented, "If they can't read English, they shouldn't be citizens" and "Didn't we win World War II?" (Iwasaki, 2002). (The latter comment indicates that civics should probably include more history.) In the education arena, parallel considerations occur around the issue of bilingual education versus English-only instruction. For example, in California, Arizona, and Massachusetts, ballot initiatives all but eliminated bilingual instruction.

To my mind, declaring English the official language, eliminating bilingual ballots, and doing away with bilingual education all fit the definition of linguicism provided by Skutnabb-Kangas. Furthermore, these broader issues give license to the acts and beliefs that are part of the more simple definition of linguicism I provided. Much of the motivation behind such movements is to "encourage" language minorities to learn English. There is no evidence, however, that doing any of the above would accomplish this. Indeed, there is plenty of empirical evidence to suggest that bilingual education, for example, promotes English-language learning as well or better than other educational programs (Ramirez, Yuen, & Ramey, 1991; Greene, 1997; Rolstad, Mahoney, & Glass, 2008). Nevertheless, as evidenced by the polls cited previously, linguistic assimilationism remains a dominant part of "American" ideology. Linguistic assimilationism is the idea that all language minorities should become speakers of the dominant language of their country of residence. In the United States, the assumption of linguistic assimilationists is that one nation must have one language and, thus, English-only policies must be supported politically and educationally. As former Speaker of the House Newt Gingrich once opined, "I think anybody who argues we ought to have more than one common language doesn't understand anything about how human societies operate" (Journal Graphics, Inc., 1995). In fact, however, many societies have more than one common language and the linguistically homogeneous nation that Gingrich implies simply does not exist anywhere in the world.

Drawing on the examples of voting and education, I want to address, in what I hope is a performance of critical civic literacy, the question of the permissible extent to which linguistic assim-ilationism, which, as the examples above indicate, seems to be written into the conceptualiza-tions of the social contract of the majority, can interfere with rights. On the one hand, I want to argue that there is an overemphasis (among assimilationists) on the responsibilities of citizens (or potential citizens) over their rights—the scales being balanced in most conceptualizations of citizenship. On the other hand, I want to argue that some claims of "language rights" (among language pluralists) dilute the meaning of "right" to the extent that they hold societies to polit-ical ransom. What I mean here is that providing something as a right may come at a huge price, sacrificing other more immediate societal needs. I offer a way forward by distinguishing between the necessity of both rights and goals in democratic societies.

A Note about "Inalienable" Rights

Given that rights is one of the key weights on the scales of citizenship, I think we need to recon-sider the kinds of work that "rights" can actually perform.[1] Typically, we speak of rights as being "inalienable." *Black's Law Dictionary* defines an inalienable right as one that "cannot be trans-ferred or surrendered."[2] James Nickel (2006) defines inalienable as meaning that the "holder can-not lose it temporarily or permanently by bad conduct or by voluntarily giving it up" (p. 4). Both of these definitions are practically problematic.

Randy Hewitt (2004) argues, "there is no such thing as freedom in general but rather free-dom or capacity (power) to do specific things within a given context or set of circumstances" (p. 48). Freedom is a much grander ideal in the abstract; the case is the same, I would argue, for inalienable rights. There is no such thing as an inalienable right in general. So, for example, I would note from the first definition that the need to include nontransferability in discussions of such rights is precisely because no rights are inalienable. If they were truly inalienable, the zero-sum game inherent in the concept of transfer would not obtain, since specific "rights" in the abstract do not come in finite quantities.[3] As for Nickel's definition, I think a better word for his notion of inalienable is probably inviolable. In other words, Nickel's definition suggests a moral absoluteness, immutable even by law.

The hitch here is "inalienable" (in its inviolable sense), not "right." There are many rights that we can agree on "in general." Say, the right to life. After all, "We hold these truths to be self-evident, that all men are created equal, that they are endowed by their Creator with certain unalienable [read: inviolable] rights, that among these are life, liberty and the pursuit of happi-ness." But is the right to life inviolable? By Nickel's definition, inalienability here is even less plau-sible in practice. For we (read: our duly elected representatives) take life all the time (and justify it) through capital punishment, war, and impoverishment, among myriad other ways.

But it would seem that the right to vote in a democracy should not be particularly con-tentious. Nevertheless, over the course of the experiment that is the United States, the Supreme Court "has said both that the Constitution '[u]ndeniably' protects the right to vote in state and federal elections and that the right to vote 'is not a constitutionally protected right.' According to the Court, the right to vote is the most fundamental of rights 'because [it is] preservative of all rights' and its abridgment must survive strict scrutiny'; yet the Court has also insisted that 'the Constitution . . . does not confer the right of suffrage upon any one'" (Gardner, 1997, p. 894). In short, the right to vote is utterly indeterminate.

To further make the point, a series of human rights has been identified in, for example, the Universal Declaration of Human Rights (UDHR) (General Assembly of the United Nations, 1948), that include, among other types, security rights, political rights, and social rights—none of which seems to be practically inalienable/inviolable. (From here on I use the terms "inalienable" when referring to Black's definition and inviolable when referring to Nickel's definition of inalienable.) Nevertheless, we can and must grant certain societal goods the rhetorical and often legal heft of a "right," those minimal standards by which societies should operate. Further, as James Griffin (2001) argues, rights must be understood as resistant to trade-offs. But, he goes on to point out that they shouldn't be too resistant (in other words, they shouldn't be too inalienable or too inviolable?). Given that some rights are not feasible in many countries (due primarily to lack of resources to uphold them), Nickel (2006) seemingly recognizes the point of trade-offs, arguing that "standards that outrun the abilities of many of their addressees are good candidates for normative treatment as goals" (p. 15). I think applying this distinction between rights and goals (what I will refer to as the right-goal approach) is a fruitful way to analyze two important and related issues vis-à-vis language minorities in the United States: (1) voting and bilingual ballots, and (2) education and bilingual education.

The Right to Vote

Article 21 of the UDHR states:

> Everyone has the right to take part in the government of his country, directly or through freely chosen representatives. . . . The will of the people shall be the basis of the authority of government; this will shall be expressed in periodic and genuine elections which shall be by universal and equal suffrage and shall be held by secret vote or by equivalent free voting procedures.

The indeterminacy of U.S. Supreme Court holdings notwithstanding, the vote is widely accepted as a right in general. Indeed, it is touted as a civic duty. Unlike some other aspects of citizenship, the vote is not only a privilege of citizenship but also its enactment is evidence of good citizenship ("due process," for example, is only the former). The vote is and should be a right. But note that it is inalienable (I cannot give my right to vote to someone else) but not inviolable (felons, for example, legally forfeit their right to vote).[4] But should bilingual ballots be an inviolable right? Chalsa Loo (1985) nicely sums up many of the arguments for and against bilingual ballots (see Table 1).

Notice that none of the arguments for or against bilingual ballots speaks to whether or not voting should be a right. What is subject to dispute here is when and why the right can (should) be violable. This is one of the challenges of the right-goal approach: ". . . it allows the addressee great discretion concerning when to do something about the right and how much to do" (Nickel, 2006, p. 16).

TABLE 1. Claims of Bilingual Advocates and English-only Advocates

	Bilingual Advocates	English-Only Advocates
Bilingual Ballots	encourage assimilation	discourage assimilation
	prevent discrimination	represent reverse discrimination
	assume more informed votes	erringly permit the uniformed to vote
	are cost effective	are costly
Immigrants	want to learn English	don't want to learn English
	want to integrate	don't want to integrate

The Right to Education

Arguably, education too is widely, if not universally, accepted as a right. Article 26 of the UDHR states, for example: "Everyone has the right to education. Education shall be free, at least in the elementary and fundamental stages. . . ." To the extent that one believes that the right to vote implies an informed vote, the connection to the right to education should be reasonably clear. More important to my discussion is the connection of the right to education to language rights.

One ideal of this connection is the notion of "linguistic human rights." This is a notion that has been championed by Tove Skutnabb-Kangas (among others) for more than three decades. For her, human rights "are supposed to be ONLY those rights which are so fundamental for a minimum of dignified life that no state is allowed to violate them" (Skutnabb-Kangas, 2004, p. 132, emphasis in original). For linguistic human rightists (LHR), one of these inviolable rights is bilingual education. The LHR orientation suggests that everybody has the right, among other things, to "learn the mother tongue(s) fully, orally (when physiologically possible) and in writing. This presupposes that minorities are educated mainly through the medium of their mother tongue(s), and within the state-financed educational system" (Skutnabb-Kangas, 2000, p. 502). In a previous paper (Petrovic, 2006), I argued that because of LHR views on dialects and languages (they make no distinction), the burden of their framework is overwhelming. However, even holding to lay understandings of language and dialect, the LHR still face a tremendous challenge in dealing with immense diversity within the strict "rights" framework they employ (again, such diversity is increased exponentially when one includes "dialect" among "language" rights).[5]

What Should Be a Right and What Should Be a Goal?

Voting

As regards voting, the right only has meaning if it is a right not merely to vote, but a right to vote for or against something. At first blush, this would seem to suggest that bilingual ballots, which provide explanation of what one is voting for or against, should be a right. While I am sympathetic to this argument and want to say that bilingual ballots are a right, I am reluctant to do so. I am reluctant for a variety of reasons, but mostly because of the political ransom argument.[6]

We might look at this from the analytical perspective offered in the distinction between negative and positive liberty (or freedom) provided by Isaiah Berlin (1969).[7] Briefly, Berlin posits negative freedom as the *freedom from* interference or constraints, whereas positive freedom is the *freedom to* pursue one's goals. The former refers to external constraints, in other words calling for a minimalist government. From the perspective of negative freedom it is enough for the government to protect everyone's right to vote (e.g., police might be present at voting stations to avoid voter intimidation by extremist groups). The latter refers to one's ability to pursue or act on her freedoms and might more accurately be referred to as agency or autonomy: "the capacity for critical self-reflection in the development of value systems and plans of action" (Christman, 2005, p. 87). But this conception of positive freedom does not speak to the resources or material conditions that might impact a citizen's ability to pursue her plan of action. Thus, making the concept of positive freedom more robust would suggest that it should be the responsibility of government to create the conditions for what Kai Nielsen (1985) calls "effective opportunity." This refers to freedoms, opportunities, and/or "rights" that are not just formally available but actually and meaningfully actionable.

If something is a right, it MUST be provided as an effective freedom, it seems to me. This "must" is the rub; it is the reason to appeal to a right-goal mix. For if a right must be provided (effectively), we must also consider at what cost. For example, to say that all children have the right to 12 years of free education in an impoverished country may interfere with the more basic right to life (freedom from starvation). (Here arises a problem, to my mind, with Griffin's position that rights should be resistant to trade-off but not too resistant. In this position, rights seem to collapse into goals, extra-strength goals, but goals nonetheless.)

While I am certainly sympathetic to the more robust ideal of positive freedom, consider the potential cost of the right to vote in this positive ideal. In fuller iterations, the positive ideal could come to entail government subsidies to non-English newspapers or other news sources, the dubbing or subtitling of debates in X number of languages, and the provision of bilingual ballots in X number of languages at municipal, state, and federal levels. For such provisions would certainly go a long way toward creating the material conditions necessary to promoting Berlin's more narrow notion of positive freedom as autonomy. Wealthy states should certainly consider all of these options, especially the last. But states struggling to provide even more basic rights are rightly exempt from such provisions, at least temporarily.

So where does this leave us as regards bilingual ballots? In order to avoid holding states to a political ransom (e.g., wherein the expense of providing bilingual ballots in, say, a poor country comes at the cost of other perhaps more basic rights), compromise is necessary. The vote qua right must be provided at least in the negative sense. The vote in the positive sense (one positive provision being bilingual ballots) should be a goal. At the federal level, I think the 1975 Amendment to the Voting Rights Act a good beginning compromise.[8] Among other things, the 1975 Amendment states:

> No State or political subdivision shall provide registration or voting notices, forms, instructions, assistance, or other materials or information relating to the electoral process, including ballots, only in the English language if the Director of the Census determines (i) that more than 5 percent of the citizens of voting age of such State or political subdivision are members of a single language minority. . . . (p. 19)

This five-percent rule is a good beginning compromise since it takes cost into account through the criterion of numerosity and is inherently ever-expanding in its reach. That said, it is certainly not ideal. Full, multilingual enfranchisement should be the goal as dictated by the Fourteenth Amendment to provide for the exercise of fundamental rights on an equal basis. The five-percent rule excludes great numbers of voters from the assistance pledge in the VRA. Furthermore, English-only legislation threatens the practices of jurisdictions that voluntarily go beyond the VRA's minimimal requirements. Finally, minimal as it is, the VRA is under fire from the political right (cf. Babington, 2006).

Bilingual Education

As regards bilingual education in the United States, there is no right to it *per se* (just as there is no right to education despite its general acceptance as such). In *Lau* v. *Nichols* (1974), the Supreme Court ruled simply that equal educational opportunity must be provided language-minority students. While the Court ruled that affirmative action must be taken, it suggested no specific remedy. Ironically, as the empirical support for bilingual education (over English-only methods) has grown, political support has waned.

Despite the empirical research and convincing moral claims for bilingual education, the position of LHR may not be possible in practice. As a former ESL teacher in Virginia, I recall the representation of 40 different languages in my school district. In most instances, there were very few (in some cases only one) speakers of a given language. This stretches resources quite far—even when the resources are available. However, there is understandably a lack of teachers who can teach in the necessary languages (given the number of languages) and lack of materials. Even when there are more significant numbers of students of any given language background, they are probably at different grade levels, stretching the resource problem even further. So, on the one hand, requiring the district to provide instruction to students "mainly through the medium of their mother tongue" would have been fiscally disastrous, even in this relatively wealthy district. On the other hand, there are approximately 5 million English-language learners in schools today. The United States could provide each of them with a private teacher at $53,400 each at a cost of approximately 50% of its current defense budget. The discretionary defense budget stands today at approximately $534 billion, not including the nearly $160 billion in mandatory funding (United States Department of Defense, 2009). So, providing every student a bilingual education in this way is certainly within the financial possibilities—although this strikes me as an extraordinarily high cost. However, the fact is that most language minority children are concentrated within certain states and jurisdictions. Thus, individual provision would certainly not be the norm, and the cost—in most cases—is drastically reduced to be on a par with providing English-only education.

As with bilingual ballots, bilingual education enhances and makes the basic right to education an effective opportunity. Note that it also impacts, in the longer run, the right to an informed vote. As noted, research overwhelmingly demonstrates that bilingual education is more effective (both in terms of the learning of academic content and English acquisition) than English-only education. Nevertheless, it is not clear that there is a right to the best or most effective education. Rights, again, tend toward minimal requirements. Thus, one compromise here has been to apply the numerosity criterion as well. Where there is a viable number of students who speak the same (non-majority) language at the same or similar grade levels, bilingual education should be provided. The goal should be to provide every language minority child with some instruction or instructional aid in their first language. Unlike multilingual ballots however, there is a significant financial cost to this that could result in clashes with the provision of other equally important basic rights.

Summary and Conclusion

Rights are usually (especially in wealthier countries) a matter of political will. As such, and going back to the earlier discussion of inalienability/inviolability, they will always be susceptible to political compromise. This should not necessarily be seen as a problem. Indeed, the determination of the proper mix of right-goal is properly determined through political dialogue driven by the ideal of critical civic literacy. However, the basic right that is the foundation of the right-goal mixture must be upheld. In this paper, I have argued that the right to vote and the right to education are basic rights. Both, however, can be enhanced through naming specific goals such as bilingual ballots and bilingual education. These goals are necessarily ever-shifting, and their setting must take into consideration local (read: national) conditions and the relation to the provision of other rights. They should have increasingly stringent criteria for their achievement. For example, the principle of numerosity in the provision of bilingual ballots might also be shifting. The number of different language-minority groups served expands as the numbers in the group grow. However, since the vote is an individual right, the goal should be to provide bilingual ballots (or translation service) to increasingly smaller numbers (not fewer people). Instead of requiring 100 people to speak language X before bilingual ballots are provided, the goal would be that within some time period, only 50 people would be required, then 30, and so on. This same principle of what I call "declining numerosity" would function equally well in determining the provision of bilingual education.

Within some political traditions, it is argued that "society, being composed of a plurality of persons, each with his own aims, interests, and conceptions of the good, is best arranged when it is governed by principles that do not *themselves* presuppose any particular conception of the good" (cited in Sandel, 1998, p. 1).[9] The English-only movement presupposes a conception of the good as linguistic homogeneity. It thus serves as a force behind institutionalized linguicism which, in turn, gives license to individual linguicism. Critical civic literacy requires us to consider the plurality of persons in our democracy and reconsider the institutions and policies that detract from that democracy. Blanket provisions against bilingual ballots and bilingual education detract from our democracy. While not ideal, the right-goal approach problematizes existing structures, moves us closer to a democratic ideal wherein individual flourishing and civic engagement matter, while recognizing legitimate economic constraints.

Notes

1. The broader issue here is what it is we mean by rights, especially human rights. As James Griffin (2001) notes, "it is not that the term 'human rights' has no content: it just has far too little for it to be playing the central role that it now does in our moral and political life" (p. 306).
2. *Black's* also lists "unalienable" as a synonym
3. My argument here fails when applied cross-nationally. For example, transferability makes sense in the case of, say, my transferring my right to vote in any given election to a non-citizen. This, of course, begs the question of why non-citizens should not have a right to vote, especially permanent residents but also perhaps others who, in an increasingly shrinking world in these times of globalization, have a legitimate interest and stake in the outcomes of elections in their non-home countries.
4. Note my specific use of the adverb "legally," not "rightly."
5. Note that I happen to agree with the LHR position that there is no linguistic (only political) reason to distinguish between a language and a dialect. However, this position, I believe, strengthens my subsequent argument that language in education be "demoted" from a right to a goal.
6. I should point out that this argument, when made primarily as a financial cost argument, goes against current legal precedent in the United States. As Guerra (1988) points out, "Cost efficiency . . . has not been accepted by the judiciary as a compelling governmental interest sufficient to survive even an intermediate degree of scrutiny" (p. 1434). On the one hand, I concur with the impact of the legal precedent in wealthy countries such as the United States. There is abundant evidence that the provision of multilingual ballots is not so costly as to represent a "political ransom." In the case of the United States (and many other nations), multilingual ballots certainly fall within a cost range that should be compelled. On the other hand, I think the precedent is problematic as a universal, normative position.
7. This is not to suggest that the notion of negative freedom owes completely to Berlin. John Stuart Mill's harm principle is similar. Furthermore, some notion was around well before the Christian era. In *Politics* (III, ix), for example, Aristotle argues for the virtuous state "not a mere society, having a common place, established for the prevention of mutual crime and for the sake of exchange." Here he seems to be expressing a notion, more skeletal than contemporary notions perhaps, of negative freedom.
8. Recall that the VRA of 1965 was designed to eliminate literacy tests and other tools of disenfranchisement of African Americans in the south. In effect, the VRA ensured English illiterates the right to vote; it also recognized the need for some multilingual assistance—secured with the 1975 Amendments.
9. While it is beyond the scope of this chapter, I should point out the long-standing debate in political philosophy as to whether the "right" should precede an ideal of the "good" (or vice versa) and whether such a precedence is even possible. See Gray (2000) for a discussion.

Bibliography

Babington, C. (2006, June 22). GOP rebellion stops Voting Rights Act. *Washington Post*. Available at http://www.washingtonpost.com/wpdyn/content/article/2006/06/21/AR2006062101910.html

Berlin, I. (1969). Two concepts of liberty. In I. Berlin, *Four essays on liberty*. London: Oxford University Press.

Christman, J. (2005). Saving positive freedom. *Political Theory*, *33*(1), 79–88.

Davis, J.E., & Fernlund, P.M. (1993). Civics: Participating in our democracy. New York: Addision-Wesley.

English Language Unity Act. (2009). Available at http://www.usenglish.org/view/575

Gardner, J.A. (1997). Liberty, community and the constitutional structure of political influence: A reconsideration of the right to vote. *University of Pennsylvania Law Review*, *145*(4), 893–985.

General Assembly of the United Nations. (1948). The universal declaration of human rights. Available at http://www.un.org/en/documents/udhr/

Gray, J. (2000). *Two faces of liberalism*. New York: The New Press.

Greene, J.P. (1997). A meta-analysis of the Rossell and Baker review of bilingual education research. *Bilingual Research Journal*, *21*(2,3), 103–122.

Griffin, J. (2001). First steps in an account of human rights. *European Journal of Philosophy*, *9*, 306–327.

Guerra, S. (1988). Voting rights and the Constitution: The disenfranchisement of non-English-speaking citizens. *The Yale Law Journal*, *97*(7), 1419–1437.

Hewitt, R. (2004). Priming the pump: "Educating" for market democracy. In D. Boyles (Ed.), *Schools or markets? Commercialization, privatization, and school-business partnerships* (pp. 47–58). New York: Routledge.

Iwasaki, J. (2002, October 18). Bilingual ballots draw protests. *Seattle Post Intelligencer*. Available at http://www.seattlepi.com/local/91756_language18.shtml

Journal Graphics, Inc. (Producer). (1995, September 10). *Both sides now with Jesse Jackson*. [Television broadcast]. Atlanta: Cable News Network.

Loo, C.M. (1985). The "biliterate" ballot controversy: Language acquisition and cultural shift among immigrants. *Immigration Migration Review*, *19*(3), 493–515.

Nickel, J. (2006). Human rights. *Stanford encyclopedia of philosophy*. Retrieved October 15, 2008, from http://plato.stanford.edu/entries/rights-human

Nielsen, K. (1985). *Equality and liberty: A defense of radical egalitarianism*. Totowa, NJ: Rowman and Allanheld.

Petrovic, J.E. (2006, November). Linguistic human rights and the (post)liberal conundra of dialect and language. Paper presented at the meeting of the American Educational Studies Association, Spokane, Washington.

Ramirez, J.D., Yuen, S.D., & Ramey, D.R. (1991). Final report: Longitudinal study of structured English immersion strategy, early-exit and late-exit transitional bilingual education programs for language minority children. Washington, DC: U.S. Dept. of Education and Aguirre International.

Rasmussen Reports. (2005). 79%: No English, no citizenship (2005). Available at http://legacy.rasmussenreports.com/2005/Citizenship.htm

Rolstad, K., Mahoney, K., & Glass, G. (2008). The big picture in bilingual education: A meta-analysis corrected for Gersten's coding error. *Journal of Educational Research & Policy Studies*, *8*(2), 1–15.

Skutnabb-Kangas, T. (2000). *Linguistic genocide in education or worldwide diversity and human rights?* Mahwah, NJ: Lawrence Erlbaum.

Sandel, M. (1998). *Liberalism and the limits of justice* [2nd ed.]. Cambridge: Cambridge University Press.

Skutnabb-Kangas, T. (2004). "Do not cut my tongue, let me live and die with my language." A comment on English and other languages in relation to linguistic human rights. *Journal of Language, Identity, and Education*, *3*(2), 127–134.

Teitelbaum, K. (2010). Critical civic literacy in schools: Adolescents seeking to understand and improve the(ir) world. In J. DeVitis & L. Irwin-DeVitis (Eds.), *Adolescent education: A reader* (pp. 307–322). New York: Peter Lang.

Tenorio, R. (1994). Race and respect among young children. In W. Au, B. Bigelow, & S. Karp (Eds.), *Rethinking *our classrooms* (pp. 24–28). Milwaukee, WI: Rethinking Schools, Ltd.

U.S. Citizenship and Immigration Services. (2010). Immigration and Nationality Act. Available at http://www.uscis.gov/portal/site/uscis/menuitem.eb1d4c2a3e5b9ac89243c6a7543f6d1a/?vgnextchannel=f3 829c7755cb9010VgnVCM10000045f3d6a1RCRD&vgnextoid=f3829c7755cb9010VgnVCM10000045f3 d6a1RCRD

United States Department of Defense. (2009). National defense budget estimates for FY 2010. Available at http://comptroller.defense.gov/budgetindex.html

Voting Rights Act of 1965, Public Law 89–110. Available at http://clerk.house.gov/library/reference-files/PPL_VotingRightsAct_1965.pdf

The Role of Service Learning in Critical Thinking

NANCY P. KRAFT

Imagine a school where seventh grade children are involved in an integrated project that addresses issues of homelessness and poverty and culminates in students' active involvement in organizing a food drive, working in a local soup kitchen, and making the community aware of the larger political, economic, and social issues surrounding poverty, hunger, and homelessness. This is the promise of service-learning. But in order for service-learning to raise this kind of critical consciousness in children and youth and to provide a transformative experience that spurs them to social action, it needs to be grounded in critical pedagogy processes that encourage reflection and a sense of empathy for others' situations. The key to making this happen is to create a community of learners where the students and teachers jointly investigate, through collaborative critical inquiry, issues that are of relevance to them in their lives and of broader social significance.

Critical thinking, or inquiry, is a skill that necessitates one to engage in processes of questioning beliefs, values, and assumptions that one holds about virtually everything. Yet common practice in schools, in Ira Shor's (1992) words, is to "answer questions rather than question answers." Paulo Freire (1970) has labeled this approach a "banking" education where teachers deposit information and skills in students' memory banks. Consequently the role of students is nothing more than parroting back previously deposited information. This method is especially prevalent in most compensatory education programs where the purpose is to remediate so-called disadvantaged students through drill and practice activities, rather than engaging in guided inquiry that enables them to critically question and reflect on issues that have some social meaning and significance for themselves and others in similar situations.

If our intent is to instead link learning to social action through developing students' critical thinking capacities, then what kind of practices are needed in schools to enable and encourage critical thinking? What teaching and learning practices are most likely to ensure students' abilities to engage in critical thought and discussion? What kinds of roles will teachers and other adults in schools have to assume to foster and nurture critical thinking in students? And what about the students themselves—what roles will they have to assume in order to hone these kinds of questioning skills?

This chapter seeks to answer these questions through:

1. re-conceptualizing education that is grounded in a philosophy of service-learning;
2. differentiating and critiquing alternative ways to view critical thinking;
3. illustrating how service-learning is a vehicle to encourage and enable students' critical thinking; and
4. examining what conditions are necessary in schools to foster students' critical thinking skills.

What Is Service-Learning

Educational practices that are grounded in approaches emphasizing relevance and authentic learning experiences such as service-learning have the potential to transform classrooms into centers of inquiry and students into active, rather than passive, learners. Service-learning is an approach to education that educators are using to create more authentic learning opportunities for students. According to the Alliance for Service-Learning in Education Reform (1995), service-learning is a method:

a. under which students learn and develop through active participation in thoughtfully organized service experiences that meet actual community needs and that are coordinated in collaboration with the school and community;

b. that is integrated into the students' academic curriculum or provides structured time for students to think, talk, or write about what they did and saw during the actual service activity;

c. that provides students with opportunities to use newly acquired skills and knowledge in real-life situations in their own communities; and

d. that enhances what is taught in school by extending student learning beyond the classroom into the community and helps to foster the development of a sense of caring for others.

Service-learning can take many forms depending upon community needs, student interests, and the curricular objectives of the program. All service-learning programs have certain commonalities: they integrate service with learning and feature "reflections," or student discussion and writing about their experiences. Examples of service-learning that have the potential for student involvement in social action include the following:

STUDENTS MAY WORK ON CITIZENSHIP ISSUES, SUCH AS:
*   researching voting procedures in their hometowns;
*   conducting a survey of political candidates to reflect their opinions on a variety of issues; and/or organizing a voter registration drive.

STUDENTS MAY WORK ON **ENVIRONMENTAL ISSUES,** SUCH AS:
- designing and building a nature trail;
- developing and maintaining a community garden;
- testing the water quality of a local stream or reservoir; and/or
- presenting a proposal to the state legislature for clearing up a polluted water supply.

STUDENTS MAY WORK ON **EDUCATIONAL ACTIVITIES,** SUCH AS:
- tutoring younger children;
- teaching conflict resolution skills to other students;
- researching and designing exhibits for the local natural history museum;
- preparing oral tapes of books for the blind; and/or
- producing telecasts or newspaper articles for the local media on topics of concern.

STUDENTS MAY HELP **COMMUNITY AGENCIES,** BY:
- constructing special equipment or resources like wheelchair ramps for neighborhood homes or Braille instructions for sight-impaired parents who attend school functions;
- assisting English language learners with application forms;
- cooking meals for shelters or for those who are not able to leave their homes; and/or
- installing smoke detectors for those who need them.

STUDENTS MAY WORK WITH **SENIOR CITIZENS,** BY:
- writing and producing biographies;
- collecting information to design an historic fair;
- conducting research about cultural heritage; and/or;
- creating collages that highlight significant life events in both the students' and seniors' lives.

Service-learning that is connected to the academic curriculum is integrated, coherent, and based on the belief that learning comes to life for students only when it is intimately connected to their experiences and the lives of real people. Structuring time for students to think, talk, and write about their service-learning experiences lends authenticity to the learning experience. It allows students to use their minds while encouraging them to engage in critical inquiry that requires them to reflect and process information and ideas in ways that transform their meaning. It gives schoolwork intrinsic value beyond achieving success in school, since there is a connection between the knowledge acquired and the larger social context in which the students live.

Effective service-learning programs provide structured opportunities for students to apply academic theory to real-world practice. While active or experiential learning does not necessarily guarantee that students will become critical thinkers, the potential is there. A basic tenet of service-learning requires students to reflect on their experience, discuss how the service experience ties back to their academic learning, assess how they have impacted the community through their work, and identify how their experience affects their future studies and career ambitions. Service-learning can be a vehicle through which students begin to understand concepts such as community revitalization and economic development and learn how they can use their skills and education for social action to better the community (and eventually the world) in which they live. The community values the students' contributions and students feel a sense of pride in their work.

Service-learning is not synonymous with community service. Community service, in and of itself, is beneficial to students and the community. However, service becomes far more powerful in its effects when a deliberate linkage is made with academics and learning opportunities.

Service-learning combines community needs with student interests and learning needs, and gives students opportunities to learn new roles, think more critically and analytically, and apply knowledge and skills in a systematic way.

In addition to these factors outlined by the Alliance, Billig and Kraft (1997) add that service-learning is a method that should be supported by regular assessment to provide feedback and guide improvement. To accomplish this they believe that assessment has three purposes:

1. as an indication of how well students are comprehending and applying knowledge, skills, and attitudes;
2. a means to determine how well teachers are facilitating learning and connecting content to students in meaningful, relevant and authentic ways; and
3. to provide input and establish what kind of programmatic changes are necessary to accomplish program goals.

Alternative Views about Critical Inquiry

As more and more schools are beginning to integrate service-learning into their curriculum, several key points need to be considered to make service-learning a viable approach that enables the kind of critical inquiry with the potential for social action and change. Critical thinking, however, has been viewed from various perspectives with several popular conceptions existing in schools. One is that critical thinking is an outcome of schooling. This idea of critical thinking is limiting because it negates the very nature of what it means to engage in critical thinking—it can never be finished in some final, static manner. Instead, it is a way of life that encourages one to challenge or be critical of universal truths or total certainty.

Another perspective that is popularly touted in schools has students engage in a process of logical reasoning that may or may not alter students' perceptions or beliefs about social reality. Critical thinking of this nature typically asks students to conceptualize, apply, analyze, synthesize, and/or evaluate information gathered from, or generated by observation, experience reasoning, or communication. This practice of critical thinking is nothing more than cognitive activity that asks students to engage in logical reasoning or to scrutinize arguments for assertions unsupported by empirical evidence. This mode of critical thinking does not necessarily challenge the student to analyze the information from a variety of perspectives—from the perspective of the assumptions underlying one's beliefs and behaviors—and much less from the perspective of race, class, or gender and power relationships in society.

This way of thinking about critical thinking does not alter the very basis of belief systems, as students and teachers, alike, may not even be aware that there is an alternative way of thinking about the information that is couched in a larger political, social, economic, historical, and cultural context. While thinking of this nature entails much more than the mere acquisition and retention of information alone, it is generally an uncritical reflection on the information under consideration. In this mode, schooling and the education that occurs there is more about socializing students into a way of thinking about and viewing the world.

Another perspective, that is the focus of this chapter, is a process of critical thinking that enables students to question the very basis of their own beliefs, values, and assumptions, and has the power to change the way that students' view themselves and the world. According to Brookfield "it involves calling into question the assumptions underlying our customary, habitual ways of thinking and acting and then being ready to think and act differently on the basis of this critical questioning" (1987, p. 1). It also goes beyond questioning self to questioning others, social reality, and the world, or in other words, challenging the importance of context. In Freirian terms this way of thinking has been characterized as enabling students to read the world rather than merely being able to read the word. Service-learning as a means to enable students to read the world involves teaching them how to engage in critical inquiry. Thus, critical thinking becomes a process that encourages students to pose essential critical questions such as the following, identified by Bigelow, et al. (1994) in *Rethinking Our Classrooms*:

- Who benefits and who suffers;
- Why is a given practice fair or unfair;
- What are its origins;
- What alternatives can we imagine; and
- What is required to create change?

They go on to state that through this kind of inquiry, students learn to think about the many facets of experience including advertising, cartoons, literature, legislative decisions, job structures, newspapers, movies, agricultural practices, and school life. Questioning of this nature enables students to understand how, why and who constructs knowledge and power.

In this manner, thinking critically is more than merely conceptualizing, applying, or analyzing information and making meaning of that information as it relates to one's experiences. Instead, critical thinking also involves an analysis of the surrounding people and community and an analysis of the visible and invisible messages of the world. It is a process of encoding the power structure and our role in these processes (Freire and Macedo, 1987). Critical thinking recognizes that what students learn in school does not take place in a vacuum; but rather includes the entire social, economic, cultural, political, and historical context that shapes one's position and existence in the world. In this manner, thinking critically is essential to creating and maintaining a healthy democracy. It is only through this type of inquiry that the potential for social transformation and action exists.

How Service-Learning Enables Students' Critical Thinking

One of the primary tenets of service-learning is that students engage in processes of reflection on and about their service experience. In many service-learning programs the practice of reflection means having your students think about the experience they have had, the meaning of their experiences, and how the experiences impacted their lives and the lives of other people. When service-learning programs are grounded firmly in academics, reflection serves an even broader purpose of reinforcing cognitive processes of thinking and brain functioning. Research suggests that working effectively at a challenging task requires significant amounts of reflection—a critical part of brain functioning (Diamond, 1995).

John Dewey believed that reflective thinking is the key to making experiences educational in that it links observed and experienced facts with ideas. The experiential learning cycle developed by Kolb illustrates the relationship between reflection and understanding (1984). The four parts of his cycle include:

- concrete experience where learners involve themselves fully and openly;
- reflective observation where learners are able to reflect on and observe experiences from many perspectives;
- abstract conceptualization where learners create concepts and integrate observations in logically sound theories; and
- active experimentation where learners use theories to make decisions and solve problems.

Kolb believed that learning, change, and growth occur through a process starting with experience, followed by observations and reflection on that experience, and then in-depth analysis to understand and modify behavior and/or choose new experiences. Reflections lead to change and are therefore a basic element in learning.

Reflection consists of two steps. First, it involves a process of students surfacing their tacit knowledge or beliefs and assumptions about their experiences. Second, it requires critical evaluation of the knowledge, beliefs, and assumptions to help students gain insights into their meaning systems that influence and shape their beliefs. Ultimately, the practice of reflection serves to help students either develop new knowledge, concepts, beliefs, and values, or affirm their existing beliefs. These two steps are imperative in order for students to benefit from their service-learning experience in ways that challenges them to think more critically about their involvement and how that involvement impacts themselves and others.

In this mode, service-learning has the potential to alter and change students' beliefs and value systems. But whether this occurs will be dependent on the ways in which service is structured and reflected on to compliment learning in the classroom. As illustrated in Table 1, the service component in service-learning has been conceptualized as either promoting the value of students engaged in charitable acts or helping them realize that they are capable of effecting real and meaningful change (Kahne and Westheimer 1996). Depending on the underlying goals (i.e., charity or change) of the service-learning experience, they believe that service-learning has the potential to impact students morally, politically, and intellectually. If the service-learning experience fosters charity rather than change, the emphasis in the moral domain is more likely to be about giving rather than caring. In the political domain, charitable service-learning experiences instill in students a sense of civic responsibility, i.e., experiences that demonstrate the value of altruism and the dangers of exclusive self-interest. In contrast, service experiences with an underlying focus toward change help students understand what it means to participate in a democracy and political and social activism. In addressing how service-learning can potentially impact a person's intellectual dimensions, they believe that service-learning grounded in change is more likely to foster transformational experiences for students than service-learning postured as charitable experiences.

Quality service-learning programs are those that help students engage in higher-order thinking. Transformation, however, will only occur when critical inquiry is combined with action. A process of critical inquiry that helps students surface their tacit beliefs and assumptions and evaluate these through reflection, has the potential to move students' thinking in ways that question and challenge thinking grounded in the status quo.

The simple kinds of reflections that sometimes occur in school, requiring students to engage in reflective writing and keeping journals as a means to document personal learning discoveries, often do not support academic or intellectual growth. Neither does reflection of this nature

TABLE 1. Service-Learning Goals

Charity	Moral	Political	Intellectual
	Giving	Civic duty	Additive experience
Change	Caring	Social reconstruction	Transformative experience

Source: Kahne, J. and Westheimer, J. (1996). "In the service of what? The politics of service-learning," *Phi Delta Kappan*, 77(9), 593-599.

challenge basic assumptions and alter belief systems. Standards for determining the intellectual quality of student learning and reflection are those that require students to think, to develop in-depth understanding, and to apply academic learning to important, realistic problems. Standards for promoting a sense of caring requires critical thinking that brings into question beliefs and perceptions as well as enabling a sense of critical consciousness raising.

Following are two examples that have the potential to transform students' beliefs. The first illustrates how biases and stereotypes of elderly and poor persons can be challenged and elimi-nated when students are required to engage in critical thinking and reflection as part of their ser-vice-learning experience. The second example challenges students to become political activists in questioning community attitudes toward people of color through practices concerning the bur-ial of community residents.

Example 1: Service-Learning Focused on Elderly Issues and Concerns

Middle school students from a suburban and predominantly middle-class neighborhood took on a project that involved reading stories to and interacting with elderly residents in a nearby nurs-ing home. Every other week the students visited the home and spent an hour reading to residents and listening to them share stories of their past and childhood experiences. To prepare the stu-dents for this experience and to integrate this experience into a curriculum unit that focused on the relationship between being elderly and the impact of economics on lifestyles the teacher asked his students to reflect on the questions, " What is old? How are elderly treated in this society? and What is the relationship between one's financial status and growing old?" Listing students' responses to these questions on the blackboard gave the teacher many ideas of ways he could address their responses and underlying beliefs and stereotypes they had about elderly people and the elderly poor through the science, social studies, math, and language arts curriculum using an integrated, coherent curricular approach. As the middle school science curriculum focused on nutrition, liv-ing systems and physical change, students researched caloric needs of individuals at different stages of life and how body systems change during the aging process, looking specifically at common ail-ments creating physical challenges for elderly persons. In social studies, students studied the rela-tionship between income level and access to quality medical services and nutrition programs. They also compared and contrasted perceptions of elderly persons across several cultures, both those rep-resented by the student make-up of the school and those of elderly residents living in the adja-cent inner city. In addition to these, students studied social issues such as loss of autonomy, independence, and the impact of limited incomes. They also researched how government programs and policies impacted the elderly in different social strata and the effects these policies had on elderly people who were poor. Another assignment had students critically view television programs to assess how popular culture and the media represents the elderly and the poor. Based on all their research, the students developed a survey to assess the prevalence of these issues among elderly persons in their own neighborhoods. The resulting data were tabulated and aggregated by ethnicity categories and then represented and interpreted through a variety of means such as pie charts, bar graphs, and narrative analysis. Survey results indicated differentials in access to health care and a quality of life for elderly residents dependent on a person's socio-economic status.

This unit about the effects of economics on elderly lifestyles culminated with student's writing papers that illustrated their own understandings of the impact of economic conditions on lifestyles, especially those of the elderly. Students brainstormed ways to counter negative portrayals of the elderly in this society and how to raise others' social and critical consciousness concerning the issues they had uncovered through their own investigations. Several students chose to submit these to the local paper where they were published in the editorial section. While the original intent of the project was for students to be involved in service to elderly citizens, the way the teacher structured learning and reflection resulted in a transformative experience for students. Their involvement in this project helped students come to view the elderly from a more compassionate and respectful perspective now that they realized the breadth and depth of physical and emotional challenges confronting elderly citizens. Students also took an active interest in supporting and advocating for social issues that impacted the lives of elderly people in their own community.

Example 2: Service-Learning Focused on Community Issues

The second example caused students to question and challenge community attitudes and values toward people of color through their participation in a project focusing on the restoration of a cemetery in their community. In this southern town, there were several cemeteries, one of which had been allowed to deteriorate. In visiting the cemetery and noting the names and dates of death on the headstones, students realized that people buried in this cemetery were early residents of the community who had been buried there in a fifty-year period following the Civil War. To determine who these early community residents were, the students researched local newspaper archives and conducted interviews with living relatives who were still residents of the community. To their surprise, the students came to realize that all the people in this particular cemetery were Afro-Americans and many of them had been prominent citizens in the community who had made major contributions. Their research also revealed segregation practices and early attitudes toward people of color in the community.

After engaging in lengthy research, students decided to write stories about these early residents and publish a book on local history and contributions of early residents. Since the social studies curriculum for students in the primary grades focused on an understanding of community, these middle school students wrote books that second graders could read and understand about local history. Because this school was bilingual, with French as the second language, students translated the books into French as a way to hone their own language skills and reinforce French language skills for primary children.

Their involvement in this service-learning project helped the students to understand the negative effects of segregation in the community and enabled them to better understand the issues surrounding the civil rights movement in their social studies unit and in their community. Continued discussion led the students to political action in petitioning the city council to spend resources on restoration of the Afro-American cemetery, as had been the case with the cemetery on the other side of town, where early white residents had been buried. Being successful in their campaign to restore the cemetery, students also sponsored numerous activities to raise sufficient money to replace headstones that had been destroyed or missing. This ongoing project, that continued to expand into other areas of community involvement, exemplified curriculum integration, pulling in all subject areas—math, reading, social studies, science, language arts, music, and art. The project also led to critical consciousness raising among students and community members alike, in questioning and challenging the allocation of community resources toward differentiated ethnic groups in the community. The ultimate benefit of the project was in validating people of color who had been active and productive members of the community and whose contributions would have gone unnoticed had it not been for these students who were involved in this project of giving to these former community residents " voices from the grave."

To maximize learning, as illustrated in these examples, service-learning should require students to engage in deeper, reflective analysis and processing of learning experiences. To maximize critical thinking, reflection should call into question those practices and/or policies that impact peoples' lives, often in negative ways. Reflection is a cognitive process that fosters critical thinking, problem solving, synthesis, interpretations, and evaluation—all skills considered within the realm of complex and higher-order thinking. A process of reflection will help bridge learners' past experiences and existing mental structures. As Meyers points out, this will lead learners from concrete operations to more abstract, reflective ways of thinking. He argues, " whenever teachers build bridges between concrete, everyday ideas and more abstract, academic concepts, they are fostering critical thinking" (1986, p. 77)." To nurture critical thinking and effective reflective activity, reflection should be continuous, connected, challenging, and contextualized, as shown in Table 2 on the following page (Eyler et al., 1996).

In order to foster the kind of critical thinking that reflection can bring about, teachers would have to work with students to develop their reflective thinking skills. This is generally accomplished by having students respond to open-ended questions, write in journals or learning logs, or by participating in a debriefing or sharing session about their experience. Many techniques could be used to nurture this kind of reflective thinking, among which is the use of Socratic questioning as a reflection strategy. This is an excellent process because it probes student's reasoning and thinking abilities. Eyler et al. suggest other ways that students can be encouraged to engage in reflection (1996). These include the following:

- **Reading:** case studies, books about social issues, government documents, professional journals, and classic literature;
- **Writing:** journals and logs, reflection essays, self-evaluation essays, portfolios, analysis papers, case studies, grant proposals, press releases, drafting legislation, letters to others (students, clients, self, and/or politicians), published articles (newspapers, newsletters, journals), and volunteer/agency training manuals;
- **Verbal exercise:** focus groups, informal discussion, formal class discussions, presentations, talking to

TABLE 2. Principles for Effective Student Reflection

Continuous	Must be an ongoing part of a learner's education and service involvement over the course of his/her educational career. Should include reflection before the experience, during the experience, and after the experience.
Connected	Links service to the intellectual and academic pursuits of the students. Academic pursuits add a "big picture" context to the personal encounters of each isolated service experience and help student s to search for causes and solutions to social problems.
Challenging	Requires intervention on the part of a teacher or colleagues who is prepared to pose questions and propose unfamiliar or even uncomfortable ideas for consideration by the learner.
Contextualized	The environment and method of reflection corresponds in a meaningful way to the topics and experiences that form the material for reflection.

Source: Eyler, J., Dwight, E. G. Jr., and Schmiede, A. (1996). *A Practitioner's Guide to Reflection in Service-Learning: Student Voices & Reflections*, Nashville, TN: Vanderbilt University.

other students, recruiting other volunteers, teaching a class, cooperative learning, story telling, individual conferences with faculty or project sponsors, and legislative testimony;

- **Projects and activities:** simulations, conducting interviews, art journals, role playing, collecting photos and/or creating slide presentations, watching movies and videos, presentations (involving dance, music, or theatrics), planning public relations events, analyzing or creating budgets, and program development.

Student involvement in service is a powerful experience. When service is coupled with learning and formal opportunities for reflection, students can have tremendous benefits. McPherson (1989) identifies the following outcomes of reflection:

Effective problem solving: By examining experiences, students discover ways to handle real-life problems more effectively both in their service projects and in other areas of their lives;

Lifelong learning skills: Students develop a greater ability to learn from experience by reflecting on positive and difficult experiences;

Increased sense of personal power: Through examination, students can clarify their goals and develop a variety of ways to accomplish them;

Higher-level thinking: Reflecting on service encourages students to deal with the root causes of complex issues. Students learn to look for the big picture and to analyze and synthesize what they have learned;

Academic skills: In addition to skills needed for the service project itself, reflection acts as a vehicle to link a broad range of academic skills to the students' direct experience;

Celebration: When students think about the high points and the benefits of service, they feel a sense of renewal and accomplishment;

Improved service: Students discover ways to improve the quality and quantity of their service as they examine the effects of their behavior; and

Improved program: Both teacher and students receive important feedback on strengths and weaknesses of the program.

In addition to these, reflection from a critical perspective leads to feelings of empathy and feelings of compassion toward others' reality and conditions. It is only through reflection of this nature that the potential for transformation exists.

Conditions Necessary to Foster Students' Critical Thinking Skills

The kind of critical thinking that has been discussed in this chapter is not readily practiced or easily accepted in schools. While school outcomes often refer to instilling in students a capacity to engage in critical thinking, this kind of critical thinking is one that generally does not enable students to critically reflect on their own beliefs, values, and assumptions, let alone societal norms that often perpetuate an inequitable status quo. Thinking of this nature appears to be too disruptive at all levels of the system—it often is easier to accept the status quo rather than to challenge and advocate for change. Another reason this kind of thinking does not happen so readily is because of hegemony or the dominant and "accepted" way of looking at the world. A hegemonic view of the world is informed by one's ideological perspective. If an individual's worldview has never been challenged or questioned, one may not be aware that an alternative perspective exists or one may be unwilling to question belief systems.

Yet, if one of the goals of education is to provide opportunities for children and youth to become independent and critical thinkers, then the system needs to allow teachers to be independent and critical thinkers as well. Teachers, in turn, need to model critical thinking as well as teach students how to be critical, and encourage and welcome their questioning through providing ample opportunities for them to engage in reflective analysis concerning the service and the linkages between service and learning. Conditions that are supportive of this kind of critical thinking activity include: (1) a risk-free environment that welcomes and encourages questioning and reflection; (2) giving students a sense of ownership in defining what the service-learning experience and reflective process should entail; (3) valuing reflection and allotting the necessary time to engage in continuous reflection; (4) viewing reflection as a central activity to education and what it means to be educated—moving away from the practice that there is a " right" answer; and (5) a commitment from teachers to value student judgment.

One of the first ways to start encouraging reflection and critical thinking of this magnitude is to encourage and solicit participation by students in creating a democratic classroom where students have voice in their learning experiences. Democratic classrooms are those where students are actively engaged in collaborative critical inquiry as the focus of the curriculum. In these classrooms, students take more ownership and responsibility for their own learning. Apple and Beane suggest the following conditions to help foster democracy in the classroom:

- the open flow of ideas, regardless of their popularity, that enables people to be as fully informed as possible;
- faith in the individual and collective capacity of people to create possibilities for resolving problems;
- the use of critical reflection and analysis to evaluate ideas, problems, and policies;
- concern for the welfare of others and "the common good";
- concern for the dignity and rights of individuals and minorities; and
- an understanding that democracy is not so much an "ideal" to be pursued as an " idealized" set of values that we must live by and that must guide our life as a people (1995, pp. 6–7).

Reflection and inquiry about knowledge and its relationship to the human experience assists students in making connections between what happens in school and in their own lives. Connecting the work of school with the life of communities, as exemplified through service-learning, has the potential to help students become revitalized as learners and make sense of human experience.

Democratic planning at both the school and classroom levels should be a genuine attempt to honor the rights people have to participate in making decisions that affect their lives. If one of the purposes of schooling, and programs using a service-learning approach, is to enable students to become active citizens and prepare them for participating in a democracy, then the best way to teach them to prepare for that role is to let them experience it on a daily basis in the classroom setting. Kohn (1996) believes the best way to teach decision making is to allow students to make decisions—starting in the classroom.

Other authors have recommended the kinds of conditions that are needed as part of the curriculum and learning process that will ensure reflective thinking which, in turn, is more likely to enable collaborative critical inquiry. Bigelow et al. (1994) in *Rethinking Our Classrooms* recommend situating teaching and learning practices in the following components: (1) grounded in the lives of students; (2) critical; (3) multicultural, antiracist, pro-justice; (4) participatory, experiential; (5) hopeful, joyful, kind, visionary; (6) activist; (7) academically rigorous; and (8) culturally sensitive. In a similar vein, Shor (1992) identifies a range of classroom values that should influence the process as well as the curriculum of schooling. In order to encourage the kind of critical thinking emphasized in this chapter he believes that education should be participatory, affective, focus on problem posing, situated, multicultural, dialogic, desocializing, democratic, researching, interdisciplinary, and activist.

Brookfield believes that one of the conditions necessary to foster critical thinking is to first have critical teachers (1987). Borrowing from Paulo Freire, he identifies the characteristics of competence, courage, risk taking, humility, and political clarity as necessary for teachers to be considered "critical." In defining these further Brookfield says

> Competence in communicating clearly with people and in managing group activities democratically is needed to ensure that people understand that alternative interpretations of the world are possible and that participants have a chance to explore these fully. Courage is needed to withstand the resistance to challenging assumptions that teachers who try to nudge learners away from their uncritically accepted ways of looking at the world are bound to encounter. Courage is also needed in those times when teachers face condemnation and criticism of their efforts by outsiders, and when they have to combat attempts to prevent them from engaging in this activity.
>
> Risk taking is at the heart of all creative and exciting teaching, implying as it does that teachers as well as learners are fully engaged in the education transaction. A willingness to risk experimentation in one's teaching is an important aspect of modeling change and promoting critical openness in learners. Humility is essential to teachers, lest they slip into the all-too-seductive (but appallingly arrogant) role of omniscient guru of critical thinking. Political clarity is a more controversial concept. What is politically self-evident to one person is heresy to another. To Freire, political clarity is the ability to break free from distorting perspectives imposed by oppressive groups so that we can see the inequitable and hierarchical relationships in society clearly and fully (pp. 81–82).

If educators are to engage students in critical thinking, then a different method of teaching will be required—one that moves away from the transmission or banking model that is so prevalent in schools, to a critical model of teaching and learning. Weil (1996) differentiates between these two teaching models as illustrated in Table 3. As is evident, in comparing and contrasting these two modes of education, critical teaching has the potential to transform students through connecting their individual and collective experience to broader social issues relevant to their lives. Critical teaching can create meaningful and authentic learning experiences that are powerful and energizing for students.

TABLE 3. Two Contrasting Theories of Learning: The Banking Assumption and the Critical Assumption

The Banking Assumption	The Critical Assumption
Students need to be taught what to think and this can best be done by "banking" information into the student.	Students need to be taught how to think not what to think and this is best done in an environment of inquiry where teacher is midwife as opposed to banker.
The quiet classroom, where students are bent on particular tasks is a class that resonates real learning.	The quiet classroom is generally a classroom where few learn and is too often regimented, authoritarian, and teacher based. All learning is based on communication and all communication is based on dialogue. Without collaborative dialogue there can exist few genuine opportunities to learn.
That basic skills can be taught divorced from reasoning and reduced to preformulated repetitious tasks that are orchestrated at a future time in the service of thinking.	That basic skills cannot be reduced to formula or repetition and must be taught within the context of an interdisciplinary problem posing curriculum that calls for utilization of the skills in the service of reasoning.
That learning is essentially an autodidactic activity that takes place privately as opposed to publicly.	That learning is a public, communal, dialogical, and dialectical endeavor that is done in collaboration with others and that no learning is autodidactic.
If students have no questions it is probably because we as teachers did such a good job banking that they understand what they are learning.	If students have no questions they are probably not learning. All reasoning requires dialogical reasoning, which in turn requires Socratic questioning.
An educated person in today's society is a repository of facts and details; the *Jeopardy* contestant or whiz kid of the 1950s. Essentially educated people are people who have stored a lot of information.	An educated or literate person in today's society is not a *Jeopardy* contestant or repository of content, but is a person who can reason or come to well-founded conclusions based on reasoning. This requires a new notion of what it means to be educated as we seek to help students develop insights and principles and strategies of thinking.

Conclusion

Service-learning, as a philosophy, approach and method that connects students in real and authentic ways to their families and communities, holds the promise and potential to transform schools into arenas that encourage and enable students' critical thinking skills. For this to occur, however, several things are necessary. First, teachers and students alike will have to assume new roles. It is imperative that teachers view themselves as facilitators of learning, orchestrating meaningful learning experiences for students and that they welcome and encourage students' questioning and search for truth. Students, likewise, need to be open to new experiences and willingly engage in processes of reflection that challenge and call into question the very basis of their belief systems. Second, the process of reflection that accompanies service-learning activities needs to be carefully thought out and structured so that students engage in reflective judgment (as opposed to reflective observation) and/or reflective action if they are to learn and benefit from the service-learning experience.

Bibliography

Alliance for Service-Learning in Education Reform. (1995). *Standards for School-Based and Community-Based Service-Learning Programs.* Alexandria, VA: The Close-Up Foundation.

Apple, M., and Beane, J. (Eds.). (1995). *Democratic Schools.* Washington, DC: ASCD.

Bigelow, B., Christensen, L., Karp, S., Miner, B., and Peterson, B. (1994). *Rethinking Our Classrooms: Teaching for Equity and Justice.* Milwaukee, WI: Rethinking Schools, Ltd.

Billig, S. H., and Kraft, N. P. (1997). *Linking IASA (Improving America's Schools Act Program) and Service-Learning: Planning, Implementation, and Evaluation Guide.* Denver, CO: RMC Research Corporation.

Brookfield, S. D. (1987). *Developing Critical Thinkers: Challenging Adults to Explore Alternative Ways of Thinking and Acting,* San Francisco, CA: Jossey-Bass Publishers.

Cummins, J., and Sayers, D. (1995). *Brave New Schools: Challenging Cultural Illiteracy Through Global Learning. Networks.* New York: St. Martin's Press.

Diamond, M. (1995, July/September). The significance of enrichment. *The In Report.*

Eyler, J., Dwight, E. G. Jr., and Schmiede, A. (1996). *A Practitioner's Guide to Reflection in Service-Learning: Student Voices & Reflection.* Nashville, TN: Vanderbilt University.

Freire, P., and Macedo, D. (1987). *Literacy: Reading the Word and the World,* South Hadley, MA: Bergin & Garvey.

Freire, P. (1970). *Pedagogy of the Oppressed.* New York: Seabury.

Kahne, J., and Westheimer, J. (1996). In the Service of What? The Politics of Service-Learning, *Phi Delta Kappan,* 77(9), 593–599.

Kohn, A. (1996). *Beyond Discipline: From Compliance to Community.* Alexandria, VA: ASCD.

Kolb, D. A. (1984). *Experiential Learning: Experience as the Source of Learning and Development.* Englewood Cliffs, NJ: Prentice-Hall.

McPherson, K. (1989). *Service-Learning Concept Paper.* Unpublished paper. 2034 N.E., 104th, Seattle, WA.

Meyers, C. (1986). *Teaching Students to Think Critically: A Guide for Faculty in All Disciplines.* San Francisco: Jossey-Bass, 1986.

Shor, I. (1992). *Empowering Education: Critical Teaching for Social Change,* Chicago, IL: The University of Chicago Press.

Weil, D. (1996). *Two Contrasting Theories of Learning: The Banking Assumption and the Critical Assumption.* Guadalupe, CA: The Critical Thinking Institute.

This chapter originally appeared in Danny Weil and Holly Kathleen Anderson (Eds.), *Perspectives in Critical Thinking: Essays by Teachers in Theory and Practice* (New York, Peter Lang, 2000).

CHAPTER THIRTY-TWO

Social Justice Enacted

Critical Civic Engagement in the Gay Straight Alliance

J. B. MAYO, JR.

Introduction

Students who identify as gay, lesbian, bisexual, or transgender (GLBT) face tremendous challenges and hardship in schools. According to the latest National School Climate Survey, GLBT-identified youth endure hostile environments at school where their classmates *and* teachers make homophobic comments, where the word "gay" is commonly used in a negative way, and where incidents of verbal and physical abuse directed toward them remain high as compared to students who identify as heterosexual (Kosciw, Diaz, & Greytak, 2008). Given the negative conditions they encounter, many GLBT-identified students choose to skip certain classes or full days of school, rather than endure the pain and humiliation that accompanies the abuse they experience. These students simply do not feel safe at school. Over time, this absenteeism leads to lowered educational aspirations and a lack of academic achievement (Harris Interactive, 2005; Kosciw et al., 2008). Despite growing awareness of the issues faced by GLBT-identified youth, these students report that school officials, including their teachers, often do little, if anything, to protect them from the harassment and abuse they endure.

Ironically, the very students against whom acts of discrimination and intolerance are committed are performing acts of social justice, while enacting a specialized brand of critical civic literacy. Unwilling to simply be labeled as victims of oppression, these GLBT-identified students and their allies are working toward positive social change in Gay Straight Alliance across America, which has helped mitigate some of the harmful impacts of homophobia and heterosexism. More than 3,500 GSAs exist within the United States, and their members report decreased incidence of homophobic remarks and verbal and physical harassment at school (Kosciw et al., 2008). In addition, students in schools with GSAs are less likely than students attending schools without GSAs to feel unsafe because of their sexual orientation or gender expression and are less likely to miss school because of safety concerns. GLBT-identified youth actually report a greater sense of belonging to their school community thanks to the presence of the GSA (Graybill and Morillas, 2009; Kosciw et al., 2008). These latest findings of the National School Climate Survey support the conclusions of researchers who have investigated the various roles GSAs have played since they first appeared in U.S. schools in the early 1990s. Lee (2002) finds that membership in the GSA helps improve school attendance and performance, a testament to GSAs serving as a safe space at school, and others have written about the GSA as a site of student activism, where students work to change school policies and practices in order to improve the school environment for all students (MacGillivray, 2004a; MacGillivray, 2005; McCready, 2002). GSAs do not solve all the problems faced by GLBT-identified youth and their allies, but they exemplify part of a larger solution because they positively affect the school experiences of many youth whether or not they actually attend meetings (Walls, Kane, & Wisneski, 2010). Indeed, the positive impact GSAs have had on students' lives is based, in part, on the GSA becoming a site where club members engage in critical civic literacy in the hopes of promoting social justice at school and in the larger community.

For the purposes of this chapter, I will focus on the activities of two distinct GSAs located in two different parts of the country and whose members engaged in meaningful, transformative work eight years apart, which indicates consistency of purpose and action over time. One of the highlighted groups performed its critical civic literacy activities in Charlottesville, Virginia, in 2001; the other GSA enacted its form of critical civic literacy in 2009 in Minneapolis, Minnesota. In both cases, students' engagement pushed their schools and their communities forward along the path toward social justice.

The GSA at Monticello High School

Monticello High School is a public school within the Albemarle County (Virginia) school district but placed geographically within the city of Charlottesville. Like other public high schools in Virginia, it houses grades 9 through 12 and offers a variety of academic programs, including Standard, Academic/Advanced, Honors, Dual Enrollment, and Advanced Placement programs. Monticello High School also offers cooperative education programs with Piedmont Virginia Community College, and it boasts a wide array of extracurricular activities, including an Air Force Junior ROTC Program, the only student-run Shakespeare Company in Albemarle County, and a host of honor societies and student-run clubs (Monticello High School website, 2010). Included on the current listing of student clubs is the GSA, which now stands for Gay Student Alliance. During the time of my involvement with the group, it was known as the Gay Straight Alliance.

Similar to today, students who attended Monticello High School in 2001–2002 represented several social and economic classes, but the majority came from families that were working class or lower middle class. And though the city of Charlottesville was a politically liberal pocket surrounded by a large area of conservative-thinking citizens, Monticello High School students' families represented a mixed bag of fiscal conservatism and progressivism on many social issues. At the time of my observations of and involvement with the GSA at Monticello High School (2001–2002), it was led by two co-sponsors, an English teacher who identified as a straight ally and her student teacher who identified as an out lesbian. The regular membership during the spring 2002 school term included a small number of students who identified as white, mostly female, and either lesbian, gay, or bisexual. The one male student, Colin, identified as gay, and there were no transgender students in the group. All of the GSA students were in grades 10–12, but one recent graduate who attended a local postsecondary school came to meetings on occasion as well.

At the time, the GSA at Monticello High School was one of only three such groups in the region, including city and county school districts. The other GSA was located at a private school called Tandem Friends School, and another local high school had an Amnesty International group that sometimes discussed issues similar to those discussed at Monticello's GSA. The alliance at Monticello started in 1999, one year after Monticello High school opened, at the request of a student who had been denied permission to do a National History Day Project on the history of gay activists and Harvey Milk, in particular. Soon after, this student sought out open-minded faculty members to sponsor the group and found that one young English teacher, Maria, was willing to take on the responsibility of sponsorship. During the 2001–2002 school term, GSA membership included several straight-identified allies who attended meetings during the fall semester, but could not attend meetings during the spring 2002 term. The sponsor surmised that the spring sports practice schedule kept many of those students from attending, but other factors may have kept them from attending as well.

The GSA at the Blake School

Like Monticello High School, the Blake School houses grades 9–12, but unlike Monticello, it stands as an Independent School known for its advanced Arts Program, as a site of privilege, and where the majority of its graduated seniors attend top-ranked colleges and universities across the United States. Members of the class of 2009 now attend Harvard, Tufts, Oberlin, Duke, and the University of Virginia, among other highly rated institutions. The Blake School professes a strong commitment to diversity. On its website one finds the following statements:

> The Blake School defines diversity as the human facets of race, ethnicity, national origin, geography, religion, gender, affectional or sexual orientation, age, physical ability, and marital, parental or economic status. We celebrate diversity in its many forms because it is our steadfast belief that multiple perspectives and experiences are core to educational excellence and strengthen a school community (The Blake School, 2010).

Though "celebrated," diversity is not the norm among the adults who work there and the students who attend Blake. The vast majority of its students, staff, and administration are white, able-bodied, Christian, and identify as heterosexual. In addition, students' parents have the means to pay an annual tuition at Blake that rivals the amount of money paid for tuition at the local, public university. Yet, an ethos of social justice and critical examination of race, gender, privilege, and sexual orientation exists among a significant core group of its faculty and administration. The Gay Straight Alliance at Blake is one site where much of the critical examination takes place.

The GSA at the Blake School School officially started in 2000, but its origins began a year earlier when a small group of faculty members and students attended the National March for Lesbian and Gay Rights on October 14, 1999. According to one of the faculty members who attended this historic event, "We were sufficiently inspired [by what we saw at the march] that we started a GSA" upon our return (Interview, J.J., May 28, 2009). This faculty member, and soon-to-be advisor of the GSA, indicated that the policies at Blake "were always ahead" of other similar schools, recalling that "Blake had a non-discrimination clause when [she] came here [in 1999] that included sexual orientation and gender identity" (Interview, J.J., May 28, 2009). She also shared that the school guaranteed benefits to domestic partners long before other educational institutions in the area. For these reasons, queer faculty enjoyed a level of job protection and feelings of safety unknown to their colleagues in nearby educational settings. Consequently, queer and questioning students also felt safe to engage in conversations about their sexual orientations with trusted teachers *before* the GSA officially started.

Little controversy surrounded the founding of Blake's GSA, but its early years did not run smoothly. Membership consisted of only four or five students, who were not interested in having conversations focused on GLBT issues. According to the advisor, "They simply wanted a comfortable place to have lunch together and gossip. We struggled to have discussions, and it was hard to keep them on track" (Interview, J.J., May 28, 2009). More challenging, however, were the actions of unknown assailants who sabotaged the advisor's repeated attempts to advertise meetings. According to the advisor, "I would put up posters advertising the GSA and by the time I would get around the school, half of them would be torn down. I don't know if this was done by students or colleagues or by other staff members" (Interview, J.J., May 28, 2009). Eventually, the advisor enlisted the support of faculty members to keep the posters from being torn down, convincing a few people to post signs on the inside of glass doors so that they would be better protected. Over time, support grew for the GSA as students began to come out and/or show support for queer issues. Then in 2004, an unexpected watershed moment occurred in the history of Blake's GSA, the re-election of George W. Bush as President of the United States. The advisor stated it this way:

> It was the whole marriage agenda! I put these signs up that read, "Do you want to talk about gay marriage? Come to GSA!" And it was like all of a sudden, I had people who I had never seen before. I think they [the students] just needed an agenda. Meetings have been huge ever since with standing-room-only kinds of crowds. (Interview, J.J., May 28, 2009)

Attendance at GSA meetings certainly fluctuated during my year of observations at Blake, but the average weekly attendance over two lunch periods typically ranged from 30–40, numbers that included both students and teachers. Attendees definitely enjoy eating lunch together, but the gossip of times past has been replaced with discussions of meaningful issues, analysis of various print and television ads, conversation centered on current events related to GLBT issues, and reflections on personal triumphs and disappointments.

Methodology

Though I embarked upon these two GSAs at different points in time, I faced two similar challenges, namely, gaining access to students and earning their trust. As a former middle school teacher at one of the feeder schools for Monticello High School, mine was a familiar face to many students and teachers there. At the time of the project, I served as a University Supervisor for preservice teachers, which offered me a legitimate reason for being at school: I was there to observe student teachers. While true that one of the co-sponsors of the GSA was a student teacher, nobody seemed to notice that she was placed in an English classroom, while I was a teacher of the social studies. This bit of deception was also aided by the fact that GSA meetings took place after school on Monday afternoons and most students only knew about the meetings by word of mouth. Besides, attending GSA meetings was certainly not the hot ticket in 2001–2002, and the group managed to fly under nonparticipating students' radar for the most part. Therefore, my presence was never questioned. Once I began attending meetings, the participating students quickly gave me their trust once I shared personal stories with them about my experiences as a closeted middle school teacher and when it became obvious that I was a friend to both of their co-sponsors.

The scenario at the Blake School was completely different. I was now a university professor with no personal ties to the students or the school community: I was a stranger to all, with the exception of a few teachers. During the spring semester of 2008, a colleague of mine and I worked with several teachers in the social studies department, helping them create authentic assessments for their students. Over that 4-month period, I noticed that several of the teachers' classroom doors were adorned with multicolored rainbow stickers, the sign of a safe space for students of all sexual orientations and gender expressions. Upon further inquiry, I learned that the school had an active GSA and that the stickers represented part of the advocacy work performed by GSA members and their longtime advisor, J.J., an out lesbian Spanish instructor and veteran teacher of 25 years. After some lengthy conversation with her toward the end of that semester, she invited me to attend a GSA meeting the following week. I eagerly accepted the invitation and discovered a group of students and teachers that met weekly to discuss various topics and plan a host of activities that took place throughout the year. I was excited to discover this group, but saddened that the school year was wrapping up. Sensing both my excitement and disappointment, J.J. invited me to return on a regular, weekly basis to GSA meetings the following year.

For the first several weeks, I simply attended the meetings without saying much, while listening to students' stories and observing their interactions. Identified simply as "J.J.'s friend from the university," I attained a level of trust from the participating members who clearly respected J.J.'s judgment. My presence, in fact, was not unusual because several teachers and staff members from Blake also attended meetings. In time, I began to share my story as a former middle school teacher, openly gay professor, and one with a keen interest in the inner workings of various gay-straight alliances.

Having gained the trust of the advisors and the GSA participants in both locations, I began collecting field notes and observations without fear that my presence was drastically changing the normal flow of their meetings and conversations. I attended GSA meetings at Monticello High School from February to June of 2002 and at the Blake School for the entire school year (September 2008–May 2009), collecting my last field notes in May 2009. In both cases, I conducted semi-structured interviews with GSA members and the advisors. All of the interviews took place on campus either during or after school when students were free from academic responsibilities, lasted from 60–90 minutes, and were audiotaped. I transcribed all interviews verbatim and sent copies to participants via electronic mail for member checking purposes (Lincoln & Guba, 1985).

Critical Civic Literacy

Teitelbaum (2010) offers a clear definition of critical civic literacy, making use of analogy. Literacy is commonly understood as the ability to read, write, speak, and listen in meaningful ways. Therefore, *civic* literacy, he says, "means being well-versed in social and political knowledge, understandings, dispositions, and skills" (Teitelbaum, 2010). Civic literacy goes beyond simple meaning making of the world around us; instead it includes making use of information to actively engage civic relationships and institutions. In other words, civic literacy means that one has become actively engaged as a democratic citizen. And *critical* civic literacy goes a step further in that it entails students actively questioning assumptions about what it means to be a democratic citizen and even who counts as a citizen in our society. A critical civic literacy perspective allows students to closely interrogate historical and current events, allowing them to focus on ways that they can participate in the process of creating positive changes toward the ultimate goal of promoting social justice. Critical civic literacy allows students to move beyond what Westheimer & Kahne (2004) call the participatory citizen to becoming a justice-oriented citizen, one who is particularly concerned with exposing and undoing systems of privilege and oppression in the hopes of attaining equity for all. In both the GSA at Monticello High School and at the Blake School, students displayed dispositions and engaged in activities that exemplified critical civic literacy.

Critical Civic Literacy at Monticello High School

During the fall semester of 2001, a controversy was brewing within the Albemarle County School District that would eventually impact the GSA at Monticello High School. Sexual orientation was not part of the non-discrimination policy for the Albemarle County School District, and several community organizations, including the Virginia Organizing Project (VOP), aimed to change this policy. Opponents claimed that language prohibiting sexual harassment was sufficient to protect all county employees, regardless of their sexual identity, but closeted GLBT teachers and their allies knew differently. In school districts across the nation where specific language to protect gay teachers did not exist, GLBT-identified faculty and staff members faced on-the-job discrimination and harassment from colleagues, administrators, and parents who claimed moral opposition to their "lifestyle." This scenario played out prominently in rural school districts across the South like Albemarle County.

As the evening approached for the Albemarle County School Board's discussion and vote on whether or not to add sexual orientation to the district's non-discrimination policy, students at Monticello High School's GSA kept a watchful eye on the local news. In the weeks leading up to the vote, several students who identified as straight allies attended GSA meetings, revealing a level of interest that had not been seen before. When asked about this campaign and the GSAs role in it, Jenny, the GSA co-sponsor, responded:

> In the fall, the mission was more kind of political, it was to gain official status as a group. And so we worked hard to get sexual orientation added to the non-discrimination policy. I was talking to all the students in my classes and trying to get them to come to meetings. We ended up getting a really large group, but they were all allies, which was fantastic. (Interview, Jenny, April 3, 2002)

Maria, the other co-sponsor of the GSA, added, "We did this more political action in the fall when it was more of a direct issue. We did this to actively educate and inform [the students] and raise awareness about gay issues in school" (Interview, Maria, April 10, 2002). GSA members engaged in conversations about the meaning behind having a non-discrimination policy that contained specific language. In their discussions, students examined what it would mean for closeted GLBT teachers to feel more protected, and they decided to take action. Students created posters showing their support and many prepared short statements in preparation for the upcoming school board meeting. Thanks, in part, to the efforts of the more politicized GSA in the fall, the Albemarle County School Board passed the measure to add sexual orientation to the county's non-discrimination policy.[1] Many students from Monticello High School spoke in favor of passing this measure: every student who spoke was an active member of the GSA.

Later in the year, the co-sponsors reflected on the meaning they and the students made about their participation in the non-discrimination policy vote, revealing an unexpected consequence of their political activism. Jenny commented, "I think on the one hand, it was more exciting in the fall because we were doing stuff. I felt like we were making big strides" (Interview, Jenny, April 3, 2002). But during the course of the fall semester, some of the gay and lesbian members of the group felt as if their safe space had been violated. They were very supportive of having a rush of new people join the GSA in support of changing the district policy, but at the same time, they suddenly felt less safe, as new students had access to their previously semiprivate meeting space and could potentially figure out (or make assumptions about) their sexual identities. Because most of the gay and lesbian students were not officially "out" at school, this became a huge issue for them.

With this revelation, Jenny hoped to bring the two groups together more in the spring semester. Following the School Board's decision and the celebration held at Maria's house one evening soon thereafter, Jenny showed the movie *After Stonewall* to give the students some perspective on what being a part of the GSA was really about. She hoped to maintain the interest of the straight allies by making them feel like a part of a modern civil rights movement. At the same time, this allowed the gay and lesbian members of the group to discuss and interrogate issues pertinent to them. It was Jenny's hope that the allies would take a more personal interest in the issues faced by their gay and lesbian peers, and that more trust would be built between them. Unfortunately, Jenny's goal never fully materialized because many of the students who had been invigorated by the events leading up to the School Board vote during the fall term could no longer attend meetings in the spring.

The two co-sponsors of Monticello High School's Gay Straight Alliance both cared very deeply for the students involved, and they each played a major role in developing the critical civic literacy displayed by the students. Maria, in particular, demonstrated her individual motivation for her passionate leadership, which became apparent during my observations of and discussions with her. As a young, self-proclaimed liberal-thinking person, Maria enjoyed having a cause for which to fight. She was absolutely ecstatic about the School Board's decision to add sexual orientation to Albemarle County's non-discrimination policy and described that event as "really rewarding." Maria did not diminish the importance of maintaining a safe space for gay and lesbian students, but her focus remained the larger cause. When asked what had been the most rewarding aspect of her involvement with the GSA, she did not hesitate to say:

> Well, honestly being involved with this group of kids has been one of the most rewarding things I've done in schools…because the kids who are in the group are so passionate about it. It's just been *great* to be working with kids who are there and willing to do what it takes, to take a stand and be political—so that has been incredible! (Interview, April 10, 2002)

It became apparent to me that a majority of the students Maria described as "willing to do what it takes" and "take a stand and be political" were mostly those students who identified as straight allies, an identity she shared with them.

After the more "activist" mission in the fall became less important to the GSA members who desired a re-focus on the safe-space mission, Maria continued to advocate for action. As a member of Monticello High School's Equity and Diversity Committee, she strongly endorsed and promoted the Sexuality Awareness Day that was held on May 24, 2002, and she made this clear in the meetings by giving it a prominent place on the agenda. What fueled this activism was the need to continually justify her position as sponsor of a group that was deemed controversial at the time. If the "school board stuff" was a highlight for the year, the biggest challenge Maria faced was "getting up enough of my own courage to say 'Alright, I am the sponsor of this group, and I'm going to help promote its cause without being afraid of the consequences of doing that.' I mean in a sense, I've had to come out as the sponsor of this group…and out as an active supporter of gay rights" (Interview, Maria, April 10, 2002). Sponsoring the GSA caused Maria to face a variety of judgments from her colleagues and other students. Therefore, it became extremely important to wear the activist banner with pride as a means of justification for her involvement. Just as it was scary for straight allies to participate in the GSA for fear of being perceived as gay, it was also challenging for Maria as a single female working with a lesbian co-sponsor and with students who were all perceived to be gay by outsiders. Maria once commented about being the sponsor, "It has made me stand up for things that I really believe in. You know, it's made me feel safe." Maria felt "safe" to support a cause and a group that is controversial as long as activism was central to the group's mission. Maria's observations and my interpretation of her commentary do not imply that GLBT-identified students did not engage in critical civic literacy along with their straight allies during the fall semester. It does indicate, however, a preference felt by gay students to have a safe space at school, especially at a time and place where being openly gay was not a viable option for most of them.

Critical Civic Literacy at Blake: Community Activism

The call to student activism rests at the foundation for the GSA at the Blake School. It cultivates students' identity as community activist, a role performed by students regardless of their sexual orientation or designation as ally. Each school term, GSA members at Blake participate in a wide range of school and community events. Some of these events include: the school-wide Club Fair, the "Find Another Word" Campaign, The National Day of Silence, Coming OUT Day, and panel discussions at both an affiliated middle school and a local university. According to the GSA advisor, participation in these events allows students to "take action for social change, trying to achieve some kind of social justice" at school and in the surrounding community (Interview, J.J., May 28, 2009). Six members of the GSA participated in a panel discussion at a local university, fielding questions from graduate-level education students. The panel enlightened these future classroom teachers about the importance of supporting or starting a gay-straight alliance at their future schools. They also stressed the importance of realizing that not all of their future students will identify as heterosexual and that many will have GLBT family members and friends. In addition, nearly one-third of the student body at Blake participated in the National Day of Silence in recognition of the "silence faced by lesbian, gay, bisexual, and transgender people and their allies in schools caused by name-calling, bullying, and harassment" (Day of Silence, http://www.dayofsilence.org/index.cfm), and a small busload of GSA students attended Lobby Day at the State Capitol in support of gay rights. There, students spoke with local government officials about extending the right to marry for *all* people.

In all these examples of activism, students engaged in activities closely connected to current events in their local and school communities that were of keen interest to them. The participating GSA members examined and challenged the behaviors and attitudes of area adults and their schoolmates, noting that ignorance rather than malice informed many of their homophobic views. These activities also afforded students time to reflect on their own beliefs and offered them opportunities to transform beliefs into action. Staying silent for a day may be viewed by some as passive inaction, but certainly educating future teachers about GSAs, attending Lobby Day—where they carried pro-GLBT banners and participated in a public rally covered by the local media—and speaking to public officials about GLBT rights constitutes direct, intentional movement toward an activist identity, one that flourished in the space created at GSA meetings back at Blake. Casual supporters were transformed into "gung-ho allies," students willing to speak loudly and clearly about their beliefs (Interview, Karen, May 28, 2009). Quoting one male ally, "It has equipped me with confidence to convey my message about sexual orientation and gender issues. I can now converse openly, with intelligence. Before [coming to GSA], I got sucked into society's homophobia, but I will no longer be a bystander" (Fieldnotes, May 14, 2009). This student and his peers experienced personal growth and transformation while enacting critical civic literacy.

Concluding Thoughts

Clearly, students' engagement in critical civic literacy happens inside and outside of the classroom and school settings. Though academic core and elective courses, most notably social studies or service learning classes, offer students many opportunities to participate in said activities, the actions taken by students in both the GSA at Monticello High School and at the Blake School indicate that extracurricular clubs and organizations offer students opportunities as well. Of great significance, the GSA students, those who identified as heterosexual allies and members of the GLBT community, all came together around issues that mattered to them. The issues were not necessarily steeped in controversy, but were, instead, issues of fairness and indicated what students believed was the right thing to do. Too often, issues centered on sexuality and gender expression are clumped together as "controversial" issues in schools, scaring away teachers who may be weary of conservative-minded colleagues, administrators, and parents. The GSA members at Blake and Monticello High School demonstrated that a critical civic literacy approach to issues of importance allowed them to skirt any would-be controversy in the name of furthering the cause of social justice. With the appropriate guidance and modeling from their GSA advisers, these students understood at a very young age a basic principle of fairness that has taken our national leaders far too long to understand. Though Don't Ask Don't Tell as an official policy in the United States Armed Forces has finally come to an end, the GLBT community still faces injustice on many fronts, not the least of which are marriage rights, hospital visitation rights, and adoption rights, among many others. Perhaps our nation's leaders should take time to visit schools where GSAs are doing similar work that is akin to the work performed at Blake and at Monticello High School. Perhaps a lesson in critical civic literacy will encourage them to act more boldly to live out the promise made so long ago by this nation's founders: with liberty and justice for all.

Note

1. On February 5, 2010, Governor Robert F. McDonnell signed an executive order bagring discrimination in the state workforce, but his order did not include sexual orientation. The Republican Governor does not believe state entities should include language not officially adopted by the General Assembly of Virginia. This executive order essentially removed sexual orientation from the Albemarle County School District's nondiscrimination policy.

Bibliography

The Blake School (2010). Official school website: http://www.blakeschool.org/

Constas, M.A. (1992). Qualitative analysis as a public event: The documentation of category development procedures. *American Educational Research Journal, 29*(2), 253–266.

Cosier, K. (2009). Creating safe schools for queer youth. In W. Ayers, T. Quinn, & D. Stovall (Eds.), *Handbook of social justice in education* (pp. 285–303). New York: Routledge.

Crocco, M.S. (2001). The missing discourse about gender and sexuality in the social studies. *Theory into Practice, 40*(1), 65–71.

Crocco, M.S. (2002). Homophobic hallways: Is anyone listening? *Theory and Research in Social Education, 30*(2), 217–232.

Gamson, J. (2000). Sexualities, queer theory, and qualitative research. In N.K. Denzin & Y.S. Lincoln (Eds.), *Handbook of qualitative research* (pp. 347–365). Thousand Oaks, CA: Sage Publications.

Grace, A.P., & Wells, K. (2007, May). *Victims no more: Trends enabling resilience in sexual minority students.* Invited paper included in the background papers for the Canadian Teachers' Federations' "Education for Social Justice: From the Margin to the Margin Conference" (pp. 79–88). Ottawa, Ontario.

Graybill, E., & Morillas, C. (2009). *School climate for lesbian, gay, bisexual, and transgender youth: An overview of the literature* [white paper, electronic version]. Retrieved from Georgia State University Center for School Safety, School Climate, and Classroom Management website: http://education.gsu.edu/schoolsafety/

Halverson, E.R. (2005). InsideOut: Facilitating gay youth identity development through a performance-based youth organization. *Identity, 5*(1), 67–90.

Harris Interactive and GLSEN. (2005). *From teasing to torment: School climate in America, a survey of students and teachers.* New York: Gay, Lesbian, and Straight Education Network.

Helderman, R.S. (2010, February 10). Virginia governor's anti-bias order removes language regarding sexual orientation. *The Washington Post,* B04.

Khayatt, D. (1997). Sex and the teacher: Should we come out in class? *Harvard Educational Review, 67*(1), 126–143.

Kosciw, J.G., Diaz, E.M., & Greytak, E.A. (2008). *2007 National School Climate Survey: The experiences of lesbian, gay, bisexual and transgender youth in our nation's schools.* New York: Gay, Lesbian, and Straight Education Network.

Lahelma, E. (2004). Tolerance and understanding? Students and teachers reflect on differences at school. *Educational Research and Evaluation, 10*(1), 3–19.

Lee, C. (2002, February/March). The impact of belonging to a gay/straight alliance. *The High School Journal, 85*(3), 13–27.

Lincoln, Y.S., & Guba, E.G. (1985). *Naturalistic inquiry.* Beverly Hills, CA: Sage.

Linville, D. (2009). Queer theory and teen sexuality: Unclear lines. In Jean Anyon, *Theory and educational research: Toward critical social explanation* (pp. 153–177). New York: Routledge.

Macgillivray, I.K. (2004a). Gay rights and school policy: A case study in community factors that facilitate or impede educational change. *International Journal of Qualitative Studies in Education, 17,* 348–370.

MacGillivray, I.K. (2004b). *Sexual orientation & school policy: A practical guide for teachers, administrators, and community activists.* Lanham, MD: Rowman & Littlefield Publishers, Inc.

MacGillivray, I.K. (2005). Shaping democratic identities and building citizenship skills through student activism: Mexico's first gay-straight alliance. *Equity & Excellence in Education, 38*(4), 320–330.

MacGillivray, I.K. (2007). *Gay straight alliances: A handbook for students, educators, and parents.* New York: Harrington Park Press.

Martino, W. (2005). I could not speak my heart: Education and social justice for gay and lesbian youth. *Canadian Journal of Education, 28*(3), 549–555.

Mayo, C. (2009). Access and obstacles: Gay straight alliances attempt to alter school communities. In W. Ayers, T. Quinn, & D. Stovall (Eds.), *Handbook of social justice in education* (pp. 319–331). New York: Routledge.

McCready, L. (2002). Making space for diverse adolescent male identities in schools. *Knowledge Quest, 30*(5), 37–39.

McCreary, J.B. (2001). Getting clubbed over a club. *Journal of Cases in Educational Leadership, 4*(1), 37–56.

Miles, M.B., & Huberman, a.m. (1994). *Qualitative data analysis.* Thousand Oaks, CA: Sage.

Monticello High School. Official school website: http://schoolcenter.k12albemarle.org/education/school/school.php?sectionid=19

Morris, M. (2005). Queer life and school culture: Troubling genders. *Multicultural Education, 12*(3), 8–13.

The National Day of Silence (n.d.) http://www.dayofsilence.org/index.cfm

Owens, R.E. (1998). *Queer kids: The challenges and promise for gay, lesbian, and bisexual youth.* Binghamton, NY: Harrington Park Press.

Payne, E.C. (2009). Stand up, keep quiet, talk back: Agency, resistance, and possibility in the school stories of lesbian youth. In W. Ayers, T. Quinn, & D. Stovall (Eds.), *Handbook of social justice in education* (pp. 304–318). New York: Routledge.

Peters, A.J. (2003). Isolation or inclusion: Creating safe spaces for lesbian and gay youth. *Families in Society, 84*(3), 331–337.

Talburt, S., & Steinburg, S. (2000). *Thinking queer: Sexuality, culture, and education.* New York: Peter Lang.

Teitelbaum, K. (2010). Critical civic literacy in schools: Adolescents seeking to understand and improve the(ir) world. In J. Devitis & L. Irwin-DeVitis (Eds.), *Adolescent education: A reader* (pp. 307–322). New York: Peter Lang.

The Trevor Project: http://www.thetrevorproject.org/home2.aspx

Walls, N.E., Kane, S.B., & Wisneski, H. (2010). Gay-straight alliances and school experiences of sexual minority youth. *Youth & Society, 41*(3), 307–332.

Westheimer, J., & Kahne, J. (2004). What kind of citizen? The politics of educating for democracy. *American Educational Research Journal, 41*(2), 237–269.

CHAPTER THIRTY-THREE

Framing Adolescents, Their Schools and Culture

Contested Worldviews

LINDA IRWIN-DEVITIS

How you think about adolescents is shaped by deeply held, largely subconscious worldviews about family. Worldviews about family inform our beliefs about adolescents and influence the ways we relate to adolescents in the family, school, agency, or any other setting. The argument I am making in this chapter—and the challenge for us all—is to examine our beliefs and predispositions and their foundations. I will build upon Lakoff's work on family-based worldviews and how the values privileged by a worldview inform current policies toward adolescents, their schools and their cultures. How do our views impact our professional roles and relationships with adolescents (as well as our parenting)?

The chapter begins with an overview of historical and current lamentations on adolescents. Then the discussion focuses on the changing goals of adolescent education in America—contrasting the views shared when our nation was founded to the current stated educational purposes. With that background established, the chapter explores our understanding of adolescence and adolescent policies within the context of the theories of family worldviews, and overarching frames that shape thinking across a wide variety of issues including adolescence and education. Finally, the chapter explores what might happen if we bring deeply held worldviews to the surface, consciously deconstructing those frames, worldviews and values, and begins a conversation on a progressive "reframing" of adolescence and adolescent policies. Such a reframing has the potential to bring the changes many progressive educators and other professionals believe are needed. Progressive policies whose purpose is to increase the well-being, aspirations and outcomes of all adolescents, their families and communities are possible within the American value system. These progressive policies encourage the development of students and citizens who are engaged and well-prepared for creating fulfilled, productive lives in caring communities.

Young People Are Out of Control (and so were you!)

"What is happening to our young people? They disrespect their elders; they disobey their parents. They ignore the law. They riot in the streets inflamed with wild notions. Their morals are decaying. What is to become of them?" Plato's words are not much different from editorials, conversations in teachers' break rooms, and portrayals of teens in movies, television, print, and popular culture. With the advent of social networking, these despairing conclusions are amply illustrated with disturbing self-portraits on social networks such as Facebook and MySpace. Teen problems and pathologies are often a major portion of nonfiction bestsellers, texts, and parenting guides on adolescence: Pipher's (1995) *Reviving Ophelia: Saving the Selves of Adolescent Girls;* Simmons' (2001) *Odd Girl Out: The Hidden Culture of Aggression in Girls;* Straus' (2007) *Adolescent Girls in Crisis: Intervention and Hope;* Miller's (2008) *Getting Played: African American Girls, Urban Inequality and Gendered Violence;* Tyre's (2009) *The Trouble with Boys: A Surprising Report Card on our Sons, Their Problems at School, and What Parents and Educator's Must Do;* and Saval's and Sax's (2009) *The Secret Lives of Boys: Inside the Raw Emotional World of Male Teens Boys Adrift: The Five Factors Driving the Epidemic of Unmotivated Boys and Underachieving Young Men.* While there are certainly books on healthy, happy, successful adolescents, the bestsellers tend to focus on adolescent angst, surging hormones and the dangerous transition from childhood to adulthood that has the status of "common wisdom."

Adolescence was defined as a time of *sturm und drang* by G. Stanley Hall (Hall, G. S., 1931/2008) the first modern psychologist to study the period between childhood and adulthood, and the impacts of wayward adolescents on the future of society. Philosophers, psychologists, parents, professionals, economists, and business elites often think of adolescence as a time of risk—and so do many adolescents and anxious parents:

> Across America today, adolescents are confronting pressures to use alcohol, cigarettes, or other drugs and to have sex at earlier ages. Many are depressed: about a third of adolescents report they have contemplated suicide. Others are growing up lacking the competence to handle interpersonal conflict without resorting to violence. By age seventeen, about a quarter of all adolescents have engaged in behaviors that are harmful or dangerous to themselves and others: getting pregnant, using drugs, taking part in antisocial activity, and failing in school. Altogether, nearly half of American adolescents are at high or moderate risk of seriously damaging their life chances. The damage may be near term and vivid, or it may be delayed, like a time bomb set in youth. The Carnegie Commission on Adolescence (1995)

It is true that adolescence is a time of transition; increasing responsibility; enormous physical, social and emotional changes; brain developmen;, and searching for identity; however, these changes are normal, developmental, and not dissimilar from childhood transitional periods and adult transitional periods. Males (1996), Rothstein (1998) and Bracey (2009) are some of the scholars who argue against the popular hysteria of lost youth and schools in crisis. Many professionals and parents, however, are prepared to see a perilous and rocky road threatening to wreck adolescents' lives; and such views have an impact on our beliefs, behaviors and policies.

Education as the Key to American Economic Dominance

In addition to beliefs about adolescent development, there are other, more recent, additions to Americans' "common wisdom" about the purposes of adolescent education. Like the historical beliefs informing our ideas of adolescent development discussed above, current beliefs about the purposes of education are pervasive, and have recently assumed a dominance overshadowing or completely expunging historical beliefs about the purpose of American education.

Jefferson spoke often about the purposes of American education:

> No other sure foundation can be devised for the preservation of freedom and happiness....Preach a crusade against ignorance; establish and improve the law for educating the common people. Let our countrymen know that the people alone can protect us against the evils [of misgovernment]. Thomas Jefferson to George Wythe, 1786.

In a similar vein, James Madison stated: "Learned institutions ought to be favorite objects with every free people. They throw that light over the public mind which is the best security against crafty and dangerous encroachments on the public liberty." George Washington Carver was also clear in his view of the purpose and power of education, "Education is the key to unlock the golden door of freedom." G. K. Chesterton added, "Education is simply the soul of a society as it passes from one generation to another." Horace Mann believed that "A human being is not attaining his full heights until he is educated." John Dewey often affirmed his firm beliefs about the purpose of education, "Education, therefore, is a process of living and not a preparation for future living." Franklin D. Roosevelt also spoke of the worth of education, "Knowledge—that is, education in its true sense—is our best protection against unreasoning prejudice and panic-making fear, whether engendered by special interest, illiberal minorities, or panic-stricken leaders." His wife Eleanor (1930) was even more specific:

> What is the purpose of education? This question agitates scholars, teachers, statesmen, every group, in fact, of thoughtful men and women. The conventional answer is the acquisition of knowledge, the reading of books, and the learning of facts. Perhaps because there are so many books and the branches of knowledge in which we can learn facts are so multitudinous today, we begin to hear more frequently that the function of education is to give children a desire to learn and to teach them how to use their minds and where to go to acquire facts when their curiosity is aroused. Even more all-embracing than this is the statement made not long ago, before a group of English headmasters, by the Archbishop of York, that "the true purpose of education is to produce citizens."

In these various quotes from some of our most influential leaders and thinkers, the overriding themes connected to public education are citizenship, freedom, and a path toward happiness. Then came Sputnik, a time of great fear, and a renewed focus on American education.

Adolescents: A Threat to Our National Security

Since *A Nation at Risk* (1983), there has been an increasing focus on economic rationales for education: work-force development has become the mantra from not only business interests, but also educators and education policymakers, and it has had the greatest impact upon the shape of adolescent education. Historically, the American notion of "common schools" was to prepare a citizenry (although largely restricted to white males) who were prepared to assume their rightful roles in a democratic republic.

Linking outcomes of adolescent education to economic dominance of the nation is again in vogue. *Tough Choices or Tough Times (New Commission on the Skills of the American Workforce,* 2007) states:

> "We have failed to motivate most of our students to take tough courses and work hard, thus missing one of the most important drivers of success in the best-performing nations."

Our morality, our national security and everything in between seem to rest on the shoulders of adolescents in our society. Scholars challenge the conclusions of these recurrent exhortations with their scapegoating and overwrought language of crisis, but their work is largely unknown to the public and ignored by the media. Therefore, progressive rebuttal has had little impact on policy or perception. There are strong rebuttals about the ability of our society to produce high-paying positions for all students even if they achieve a postsecondary education (Aronowitz & DeFazio, 1994; Gee, Hall & Lankshear, 1996). Our census data (2009) tell us that the greatest job growth (in real numbers) in 2008–09 was in the fields of personal and home health and care aides (773,000), that require only short-term training. In fact, of the new jobs created, 52% require short to moderate on-the-job training, another 6% require an associate's or specialized post–high school training, 35% require a bachelor's degree and 7% require an advanced degree.

Perhaps adolescents are more perceptive than many pundits: they look around and see where there are jobs in their neighborhoods. Yet, we continue to hear that unless America's high school completion and college going rates improve, we will be risking our national future. As adolescents' education has taken on an increasingly vocational purpose, the notions of education as preparation for citizenship, freedom, democratic participation, fulfillment and happiness have increasingly disappeared in educational policy and planning. The "road," or "race," to economic security through higher educational attainment has been defined by standards, high-stakes tests, fewer curricular options, tighter regulation of teaching and learning, fewer opportunities to explore beyond the basic curriculum, zero tolerance for disruptions, and teachers and principals who are increasingly focused on test scores. Educational goals of increasing adolescents' independence, democratic participation, individual exploration, and freedom of choice are few and far between in low-performing schools.

Drop-out rates escalate even as restrictions tighten. Those students who do navigate the system are prepared to follow instructions, prepare for tests, acquire facts—and in these "sanctioned" schools, it is rare to find a teacher or leader who remembers Bronowski's admonition: "It is important that students bring a certain ragamuffin, barefoot, irreverence to their studies; they are not here to worship what is known, but to question it."

As for the "declining morality" among America's adolescents, multiple sources report declining drug use, more than a decade of declining teen pregnancy rates, and little evidence of a marked increase in teen sexual activity. Urban and rural schools, where rates of violence, drug use and early sexual activity are increasing, are the often the least democratic, offering little opportunity for individual exploration and the practice of freedom. These are typically schools where citizenship is defined as simply obeying the rules. They are often places where training trumps teaching. They are largely the antithesis of what one wise (anonymous) person shared, "An educational system isn't worth a great deal if it teaches young people how to make a living but doesn't teach them how to make a life."

In spite of the hysteria of national reports and the continuing critique of public education and the next generation, most 'tweens and teens survive and thrive; and the majority emulate the values and aspirations of their families and communities. There are teens, especially those who are poor or in abusive situations, who are in serious trouble, teens whose lives, health and future are at serious risk. Is such dysfunction endemic to adolescence or attributable to the context and climate in which adolescents live, work and go to school? Is our overarching devotion to education as primarily a vehicle for economic survival helping or interfering with educational attainment? Is our impoverished and limited view of education partly responsible for the problems it claims to address? In some (mostly poor, often minority) communities, adolescence is pathologized; public education is vilified; and educators are denigrated. As we move further into No Child Left Behind, "Race to the Top" (the new competition among states for federal dollars to improve teaching and teacher evaluation, experiment with alternative systems for teacher salaries, implement better student data-tracking systems, and encourage charter school formation), a national curriculum, and the directions set by the Gates Foundation, the Business Roundtable and an activist U.S. Education Department, we hear less and less about the historical aims and purposes of education in our society. Indeed, the reigning "crisis" and the emphasis on public education is a major agenda item of those conservatives whose ideas are being implemented into policies from NCLB to choice issues, including charters and vouchers to accountability of schools, without any attention to societal factors that influence the students who attend. There are many and varied explanations for this conservative emphasis on education policy—and for good reason. As Kumashiro (2008) asserts: "public education has the potential to change the very conditions that have benefited certain groups. It is not surprising then, that in recent years, the Right has launched a series of policy initiatives that aim to undermine public education." He goes on to conclude, "The right is successfully reframing common sense in education" (pp. 6–7).

Some influential federal and corporate leaders and their followers attribute individual and societal problems primarily to adolescent development: lack of personal responsibility on the part of teens, their families and failing schools; the education bureaucracy; teacher incompetence; and inadequate accountability. Those ideas are "common wisdom," they shape institutional responses, and lead to divergent actions or inaction in schools, courtrooms, legislatures and think tanks. Progressive parents, educators, and citizens respond with research, statistics, issue papers, and monographs. Rarely are they influential in the debates at local, state and federal levels.

More often, progressive educators subvert the systems to provide schools that honor democratic participation, minimize the impact of federal and state mandates, and focus on the historical values and goals of education for full, active, respectful, questioning citizenship. The opportunities for this joyful subversion are fewer as the federal and state accountability apparatus expands—and disproportionately impacts low-performing schools and districts. Progressive teachers, scholars, parents and adolescents themselves are silenced: their voices, research and values have so little impact in shaping institutional policies toward adolescents. Why?

The shifting purpose for public education from citizenship to economic survival (or hege-mony) is certainly one reason that progressive ideas are marginalized, but I suggest there is another deeper reason that is identified in George Lakoff's work on family metaphors and worldviews.

Worldviews, Adolescents, and Social Policy

How we think of adolescents, individually and collectively, is influenced by the historical and pop-ular contexts mentioned above; but our views of teens and 'tweens are also shaped by deeper frames that shape our worldview. There are distinctive worldviews (meta-frames) that shape and divide our individual opinions, beliefs and actions. These worldviews predispose our willingness to see young people as basically worthy of adult mentoring and second chances or to punish them as adults deserving retribution for disobedience. The tensions among worldviews and our con-ceptions of adolescence are reflected in dysfunctional and contradictory impulses, not only in Hall's description of adolescent psyches, but also in our policies, and too often in unyielding dis-agreements about, what is in the best interests of young people. These are the arguments that I will be making in this chapter using Lakoff's definitions of framing and metaphor from a cog-nitive science perspective.

When we think of an adolescent, what images and words come to mind? Those thoughts and words are evidence of the frame(s) we use to think about adolescents. The collective frames regarding adolescents are very powerful in shaping the actions of parents, teachers, and policy-makers whose decisions influence the lives and futures of young people who are within their sphere of influence. The frames defining adolescents are influenced by larger frames or world-views, largely unconscious to the individual, held by adolescents themselves, as well as their par-ents, their teachers, and policymakers. These worldviews influence and define most, if not all, aspects of a person's values, beliefs and understandings.

Linguistic framing activates the generally unconscious mental structures that shape our understandings of a topic, a concept, a role, and a worldview. The skillful, sometimes invisible, use of frames is a key aspect of work in marketing, politics, and any type of persuasion. In order to create social change, George Lakoff (and other scientists who investigate the linguistic aspects of cognition and belief systems) indicates that social activists must "reframe" arguments. The next section of this chapter explores Lakoff's notion of family worldviews more fully, applies it to understandings of adolescence, and concludes with some suggestions for reframing our understandings of adolescence, and our social policies and practices that shape American ado-lescent education.

Frames, Family Metaphors ,and World Views

In his most popular book exploring the ubiquity of frames, *Don't Think of an Elephant* (2004), Lakoff asks his readers to try not to think about an elephant after reading the book title. He reit-erates, "Whatever you do, do **not** think of an elephant." (p. 3) As he notes, and as you are expe-riencing currently, once a "frame" such as "elephant" is activated, you cannot force yourself not to see the big, heavy animal with its ivory tusks, huge eyes, and long trunk. We each have our own set of frames about elephants and once those are activated, our minds fall into those frames without any conscious effort—and getting out of the frame is extremely difficult once it is activated.

Lakoff's earlier work focused on metaphors (1980) as central to our ability to make meaning. Drawing upon that work, Lakoff attempted to find the metaphors (organizing ideas, meta-narratives) that would explain the seemingly unrelated positions of American conservatives (and liberals) on key issues. Lakoff (2002) eventually began to see divergent family metaphors that could explain the seemingly incoherent pastiche of political views that unite people as conservatives (or progressives) and sometimes divide them from each other. Lakoff's primary interest in these metaphors was understanding seemingly contradictory and inconsistent political stances on issues that unite conservatives (and liberals.) "I remembered a paper that one of my students had written some years back that showed that we all have a metaphor for the nation as a family. We have Founding Fathers. The Daughters of the American Revolution. We "send our sons" to war…Given the existence of the metaphor linking the nation to the family, I asked the next question: If there are two different understandings of the nation do they come from two different understandings of family." (2004, p. 5.)

Lakoff found that divergent moral and political views could originate in the potent metaphor of nation/government as family.[1] These divergent metaphors of family (and nation/government) embody certain values and beliefs and form the basis for moral reasoning. The first of the family metaphors that provides the foundation of conservative thought is the *strict-father family*. The other metaphor, the *nurturing-parent family*, explains and unifies most progressive positions and understandings.[2]

The *strict-father family model* is built upon the notion of a traditional family with an authoritative father supporting and protecting the family, i.e., setting and enforcing rules. The mother is responsible for the care of children and house and upholding the father's rules. Children must respect and obey their parents. Such obedience will enable children to be accountable and self-reliant. Parental love is part of the strict-father model, but it never outweighs parental authority. Successful children become self-reliant and independent. Thus adolescents/young adults are to be independent and make their own way, and parents no longer to meddle in their lives since parental work is done (Lakoff, 2002, p. 33). Moral strength and authority are primary in the patriarchal family. Nurturance and empathy are also important, but they are never allowed to interfere with the strict father's moral strength and authority. In this family metaphor, the pursuit of self-interest coming from self-discipline allows one to achieve self-reliance. Meritocracy is a central pillar of "strict-father" views—one earns and gets what one deserves on the basis of individual talent and work.

In the *nurturing-parent family model*, empathy, nurturance and love are dominant and parenting is shared, not hierarchical. It is expected that being cared for, nurtured, and demonstrating and expecting empathy and respect will enable children to become responsible and self-disciplined. Nurturing families teach and model respect for those within and beyond the family. Nurturance also implies protection, support, and strength from both parents, who share responsibilities for all aspects of family life and child-rearing. Dialogue and explanations between parents and children are crucial since children need to understand parental decisions. Nurturing parenting requires understanding children as individuals, including their interests, values, and right to individuality. In this model, the moral pursuit of self-interest and fulfillment can only be realized by the practice of empathy and nurturance of others. In fact, empathy and nurturance are the basis of self-fulfillment and moral authority (Lakoff, 2002, p. 34)

Lakoff, while clearly identifying himself as a progressive, does not discuss these different family models as right or wrong, better or worse. Rather, he explores their explanatory power to make sense of a variety of outwardly contradictory positions and stances. Using Lakoff's competing views of family, one can examine the competing frames of adolescence and the resulting policies and practices regarding adolescence. These divergent family metaphors provide a theoretical base to explore the boundaries and contradictions that competing frames impose on parents, teachers and policymakers.

A recent example of the "strict-father model" is making the news. Congress and the media are engaged in debating the abortion provisions in the health care reform bill. The "strict-father model" may be seen in the statement from the Catholic Diocese of Washington, D.C., about the health care reform bill. The bishop of the Washington diocese said if the bill pays for abortion services as part of the public option,[3] the social services work of the D.C. Catholic Charities will be suspended. This is a clear example of a "strict-father model," valuing obedience to church doctrine on abortion more than empathy for those in need. This position puzzles or outrages those, both Catholic and not, who value empathy in the "nurturing-family model" over the obedience demanded by "the strict father."

In addition, the model of obedience to the "father" elucidates the reluctance to provide sex education or contraception. The strict father's authority also explains policies requiring parental notification for adolescents seeking abortions. Drug, alcohol, and tobacco addictions are seen as "disobedience" and a "failure of self discipline;" and the key intervention is punishment in a "strict-father" worldview. The adolescent's opinion is not sought and often ignored or cut off when offered. The failure is within the adolescent, the punishment is the father's duty, and the future is solely up to the adolescent to work out herself. While the "nurturing-family" view strongly supports protecting adolescents from these destructive forces, the responses are more likely to include counseling, support, rehabilitation, and nurturance in addition to or in place of punishment. When punishment is involved, the "nurturing" model involves the adolescent in discussion and strategizing how to change behavior and collaboratively explores the kinds of support the adolescent herself identifies as important in her future success.

In education policy, we encounter some interesting examples of this conflict between worldviews. "Stric- father" approaches are seen in Arne Duncan's and President Obama's words and policies, which are generally consistent with those of President George W. Bush, albeit better funded. A "strict-father" worldview promotes the top-down setting of policy we are seeing in the criteria for "Race to the Top (RTTT)." RTTT affirms high-stakes testing, although with more realistic and psychometrically valid ways of measuring individual students, schools, districts and states. There are still "report cards" which demonstrate obedience, or lack thereof, to the top-down mandates and competition in which not only schools, but also states, are winners and losers. In President Obama's controversial television speech to the nation's school children, the themes of "individual responsibility" and "personal accountability" far outweighed a more nuanced discussion of a social contract with America's young people. A social contract is based upon mutual responsibility (student, family, school, and society) and goes far beyond tests, report cards, and increasingly empty promises of "the American Dream."

Similarly, in Secretary Duncan's relentless attacks on teacher education, he plays the role of the "strict father" who is reprimanding the "mother" who is charged with carrying out his dictates obediently and without any expectation of input. There is no doubt that ardent supporters of education from both "strict-father" and "nurturing-family" perspectives expect high achievement and rigorous standards. The differences most often lie in choosing a set of strategies to achieve the goals and sometimes in the motives underlying the goals.

These policies are distressing at face value; more importantly, they are incompatible with what we know about successful schools. Schools that are able to educate all children, close the achievement gap, and attract and keep great teachers and leaders are nurturing schools, like those that live the values in the National Middle School Association's *This We Believe* (2003), a wonderfully written example of the nurturing family model for educating adolescents in middle schools. The vision of middle schools as nurturing places for adolescents was, at best, incompletely enacted in our nation's schools over the last several decades. That nurturing vision met vigorous opposition from the Education Department under President George W. Bush. *This We Believe* violated the "strict-father" views of NCLB. NCLB emphasized teacher-centered classrooms, implementing a curriculum and standards set by the "father" (state departments and district offices) and enforced through standardization, regulation, and sanctions. NCLB mandates left little time for student-centered, democratic classrooms and schools. NCLB contains no provisions for students' exploration of their talents, roles and place in society. *This We Believe*, rather than prescribing the outcomes, promoted team-centered schools with democratic structures that honored teachers' professionalism, collaboration, and input in school-wide policies and procedures. Schools based upon *This We Believe* and a nurturing family worldview work to ensure student success in a climate that values relationship and, models responsibility and empathy while protecting students with an orderly environment. Such schools facilitate students' increasing self-governance and place less emphasis on inflexible, "zero tolerance rules." The research on effective high schools highlighted the importance of commitments to strong relationships among all stakeholders (leaders, teachers, students, parents, and community), mutual respect, individualized curriculum, participatory decision making, and high expectations. These school characteristics were associated with the highest levels of achievement and satisfaction among students, teachers, and leaders. However, these nurturing family values collide with NCLB's test-driven accountability, school report cards, and sanctions. RTTT, Obama's major initiative, only affirms the top-down, "strict=father" model of educational reform with its emphasis on competition among the states for better tests, stricter accountability, and repetition of the perennial call for better teachers and better teacher preparation.

Family Metaphors as They Shape Views of Adolescents in Popular Culture, Education, and Social Policy

The implications of these disparate views of family are reflected in the debates that frame the views of adolescence in our culture and in policy debates:

	Strict Father Model	Nurturing Family Model
Popular culture	Supporting strict limits on alcohol and tobacco sales to minors; protecting minors from certain movies and books, including censoring print and web access; restricting access to contraception, including parental notification in abortion; banning exposure to ideas and options inconsistent with the strict father family's values.	Negotiating rules and responsibilities; modeling and expecting democratic and respectful discussion of issues in family relations with empathy, flexibility, and active listening; emphasizing adolescent apprenticeship in decision-making and recognition of adolescent voice in decision-making.
Adolescent development	Advocating firm guidance and boundaries with strict consequences to protect adolescents from mistakes and from straying beyond their appropriate role in the strict father family—obedient and unquestioning adherence; designating LBGT as deviant behavior, as something to be corrected, a personal failing, and a practice for which an adolescent can be forced to leave the family.	Suggesting adolescents need to experiment within safe contexts, make mistakes without adult consequences, negotiate boundaries with parents and adults, and explore and challenge as they practice independent thought; honoring difference in a variety of ways, including LBGT youth.
Textbooks on adolescence and parenting guides	Discussing adolescent pathologies, the stress and turmoil of identity formation and physical change; suggesting "tough love" approaches.	Emphasizing identity development, experimentation, freedom to explore roles and new responsibilities.
Education policy	Setting standards; implementing high-stakes assessments; using graduation tests; tracking; making early decisions on vocational versus college-bound tracks; establishing a clear hierarchy with rules and enforcement in the hands of adults; enforcing zero tolerance; emphasizing top-down decision-making and curriculum mandates; emphasizing teacher-dominated classroom management with rule-dominated adult supervision rather than promoting student self-management, democratic approaches to discipline.	Practicing genuine "middle school philosophy" which values relationships and individualism; creating small schools movement; using a student-centered curriculum; practicing democratic decision-making with significant student voice in classroom management and curriculum.
Criminal justice	Trying adolescents as adults; reluctance to remove adolescents from family, even in cases of parental abuse and neglect	Emphasizing rehabilitation; welfare of the adolescent and adolescent voice as well as parental rights.

Implications for Teachers of Adolescents

The vast majority of adolescents, in families and schools that are nurturing, navigate their 'tween and teen years without major trauma. The voices of adolescents who do not "fit the model" of expectations fare very differently, depending upon the schools and classrooms where they are expected to learn and grow. Those voices, and other research, strongly suggest that teachers of adolescents who work with their students, respect them as individuals, and provide nurturance are able to motivate students to far greater achievement, self-confidence and increased aspirations. These voices come from school professionals (individually and, more importantly, collectively) who understand that certain students have or lack privileges that make meritocracy a dubious model and indeed a potentially dangerous one when students come from vastly different backgrounds, cultures, languages, discourses (Gee, 2008) homes and neighborhoods. These educators are able to create "nurturing" instructional climates and educative communities that are conducive to greater learning and better social and psychological outcomes for all adolescents.

Implications for Adolescent Advocates

In many ways, this chapter reflects the assumption that you, the reader, will evaluate the research, claims, and logical consistency of the arguments I have presented, judge their merits, and, if found worthy, they may have some impact on your thinking and practice. That assumption, applied to you, may be accurate; but, increasingly, educational progressives who hold the "nurturing family" value system are finding their arguments having little impact in policy or practice.

If you responded to the ideas presented with an "ah-ha" reaction and a feeling of reaffirmation, it is likely you share many of the values of the "nurturing family." If you found yourself questioning the article, disagreeing with its assumptions, doubting the research presented and the conclusions drawn, it is likely that you do not share the "nurturing family" worldview and my argument that "nurturance" is key to good adolescent education and policy. This leads back to George Lakoff's seminal work on how we make decisions—largely on our basic worldview and the hierarchy of values that we hold as individuals and only secondarily on evidence as viewed through our worldview frames and their associated values.

In many ways, Lakoff's work on the power of values over logic, worldviews over specific issues, and the failure of progressive educators to respond effectively to the conservative educational policies of the last decade complements current work in cognitive psychology and behavioral economics (Ariely, 2009; Levitt and Dubner, 2005; Thaler, 2009: Brafman, 2009); Lehrer, 2009) challenging the Enlightenment view of the rational individual operating to maximize self-interest. In this new realm of cognitive science Willingham (2009), we are far from rational, i.e., not designed to think, but rather to operate on a series of scripts, frames and memories that shape our responses and behavior in ways that are largely unconscious. "Discourses" (Gee, 2008)—ways of believing, thinking, talking and being—are similar to the scripts and memory sequences cited by Willingham. Both Discourses and memory scripts are largely unconscious and do not require or invite "thinking." The scripts that Willingham (2009) describes are being researched though *f*MRI work; however, Discourses lend themselves to linguistic analysis both by researchers and, though less sophisticated, by teachers, other professionals, parents and adolescents themselves. I suggest that a person's "Discourses" can be examined, reflected upon, embraced or discarded to some degree. However, these Discourses operate within the family worldview that is dominant (and largely operating below consciousness) for the individual, i.e., the dominant family metaphor is lived in specific sets of beliefs and behaviors. The power of these dominant worldviews, strict father or nurturing parent, are so strongly and deeply held that they override "rational" analysis and logical argument. Research and theories that contradict these deeply held views rarely have the impact needed to make or accept the changes advocated.

Well-written, cogent issue analysis (the forte of many progressives and academics) will not be sufficient. Critiques of conservative adolescent policies, no matter how well-argued, will only reinforce the conservative frames that dominate current policies and discussions. By arguing for a different, or more effective, type of accountability, we are using the conservative frame and reinforcing the argument that the major flaw of adolescent education is the lack of accountability. By citing the research that graduation tests disproportionately have a negative impact on high school graduation by low- income, minority students with statistics and graphs, we are not challenging the "personal responsibility," "meritocracy" and "accountability" motifs of the "strict-father" family. In reality, I am just pointing to results that are acceptable and deserved within that worldview. By citing recidivism rates for "boot camps" and early incarceration, we argue for more empathy, which works with other progressives, but is trumped by perceived lack of "obedience" and "personal responsibility" in the "strict-father" model. By arguing for protection of LBGT adolescents and acceptance of families that are not "traditional," we are assaulting the very foundation of the "strict-father family" worldview.

When these worldviews (deeply held and largely below the level of conscious and rational thought) are challenged it is clear that the Enlightenment view of human beings as rational actors is inaccurate. The research-based argument has had modest impact upon federal education policy. When qualitative, historical, and ethnographic research contradicted the "strict-father" view, it was officially ousted from recognition as valid research for guiding educational policy. The textbook example is the "scientifically based reading instruction" (SBRI) push in Reading First National Institute of Child Health and Human Development, 2000). Purportedly based upon the National Reading Panel Report, a close reading of the report itself and an examination of implementation of federal and state regulations put forth in the name of the report bear little consistency and many contradictions. Adolescent literacy programs were expected to adapt to SBRI findings that were never intended for use with students who were not beginning readers, and in many cases were inconsistent with the findings of the NRP report itself. The appeal of SBRI, the avowed authority prescribing interventions for an admittedly serious problem of inadequate literacy performance, was the "answer" coming from above which merely needed consistent implementation by classroom teachers. The reality is that even many original SBRI supporters, including Grover Norquist, admitted that, though the model had robust implementation, sufficient time to demonstrate impact, and a rigorous longitudinal evaluation, Reading First failed to improve reading skills of beginning readers. The multibillion-dollar Reading First Initiative certainly made no impact on older students who lacked the literacy skills needed for success.

Current research from Harvard (Hill & Chao, 2009) on parent involvement also indicates that the NCLB requirement for parental involvement, modeled on meta-analysis largely comprised of elementary school research, has not been successful in improving adolescents' success. Hill's findings on secondary parent involvement suggest that adolescents benefit most through parental communication of high expectations for achievement and fostering career aspirations and through linking school learning to real life. This research also indicates that the transition from middle to high school is a key time and that communication between schools, parents, and adolescents is an important factor. Again, we have a "strict-father," top-down policy overgeneralizing the research available from elementary school studies and tying school accountability to parent involvement without a carefully researched, nuanced understanding of what kind of involvement is most appropriate for parents, teachers, 'tweens, and teens.

Reframing Adolescent Education and Policy

Given current top-down accountability, high-stakes assessment and the move toward federal curriculum mandates, which are all based upon a "strict-father" model, how can progressive educators be heard? If George Lakoff's (2004, 2008) work has any salience, perhaps the most important message for adolescent advocates is that we must make "nurturing-family" arguments based upon American values present since the earliest days of our country. Only through consistent and ubiquitous narratives emphasizing these values will advocates find the arguments and language frames that will be persuasive, unify progressive issues in a larger vision and, at the same time, be influential in policymaking and in reshaping "common wisdom."

By connecting individual issues, arguments, and policy positions to a common set of values, we can be more effective advocates. These values are not strictly "contested" values and are shared to some degree by almost every American. Some examples of these shared progressive values are: the American commitment to public education as necessary for an engaged and informed citizenry; protection of our children and adolescents; adolescents' ability to practice engaged citizenship by participating in democratic decision making, collaborative goal setting, teamwork, and reflection upon their own behaviors and understandings, needs, and wants; the understanding of our founding fathers that we find success in shared efforts and common commitments; unity and a sense of common purpose as Franklin D. Roosevelt eloquently inspired in his fireside chats; and, perhaps most importantly, the nurturance, caring and empathy that are pre-eminent in all major religious, spiritual and moral traditions.

These values, while often contested, prevailed in the Civil Rights Movement of the '50's and '60's, the New Deal, and Lyndon Johnson's Great Society. While all of these movements had flaws, both in conception and implementation, they were endorsed by the majority of Americans because they invoked the basic values associated with the nurturing-family worldview: empathy, community, caring, an equal playing field, the right to be different (Kumashiro, 2008), safety and security through common purpose, creating engaged and active citizenry through public education, and measuring success through the growth of individuals and communities in health, happiness, and security as well as economic strength. This list is doubtless incomplete and in need to word-smithing. It is meant as a first step, wading into the moral issues inherent in adolescent policy in education, criminal justice, and other social issues and anchoring our arguments in values that are clear and powerful. Adolescent advocates must set a progressive agenda, a unifying narrative in which powerful research and analysis, including the variety of issues raised in this book and others, can penetrate the "strict-father" worldview. This agenda includes head-on challenges to the pre-eminence of economic goals as the overriding purpose of education, educational policy and educational practice.

The "strict-father" worldview has led to policies that are detrimental for many adolescents, families, communities and the professionals who work with them. The "strict-father" worldview contradicts the deeply held moral convictions of many Americans who continue to fight or subvert the system. As policies become more entrenched and representative of the "strict-father" worldview and more instantiated in poor and minority institutions deemed "failing," the "strict-father" policies will lead many students to resist and drop out. (That dire consequence has already happened and continues to happen.) Others will learn obedience in a top-down hierarchy with little opportunity for democratic participation, little modeling of empathy and compassion, and a restricted sense of who they are and what they might become.

If this is to change, progressives must reach out to the vast majority of Americans who value both empathy and obedience. Progressives must create a narrative elevating the long tradition of progressive values in American thought and policy—empathy and compassion, freedom and engaged citizenship.

Notes

This chapter is partially revised from a chapter with the same title which appeared in Joseph L. DeVitis and Linda Irwin-DeVitis, eds., *Adolescent Education: A Reader* (New York: Peter Lang, 2010).

1. Lakoff does not equate *parenting* and *political views.* He also warns that individuals may vary between the views depending upon issues and may also vary over time. Even with these important caveats, Lakoff still makes a persuasive case that these guiding views of *family,* and by extension *nation,* have important explanatory power to elucidate political beliefs and values.
2. For a fascinating popular exploration of these family metaphors in American politics, read Lakoff's (2004) *Don't Think of an Elephant: Know Your Values and Frame the Debate.* For a more scholarly examination, *Moral Politics* (2002) provides a more thorough, research-based examination.
3. The Hyde Amendment already bars the use of government money for abortions.

Bibliography

Ariely, Dan. (2009). *Predictably irrational: The hidden forces that shape our decisions.* New York: Harper.
Aronowitz, S., & DeFazio, W. (1994). *Jobless future: Sci-tech and the dogma of work.* Minneapolis: University of Minnesota Press.
Bracey, Gerald W. (2009) *Education hell: Rhetoric versus reality.* Alexandria, VA: Educational Research Service.
Brafman, Ori & Rom Brafman. (2009). *Sway: The irresistible pull of Irrational behavior.* New York: Broadway Business.
Bronowski, J. (1976). *The ascent of man.* Boston: Little, Brown.
Carnegie Council on Adolescent Development (1995). *Great transitions: Preparing adolescents for a new century.* New York: Carnegie Corporation of New York.
Carver, G. W. (1991). In Kremer, G. R. (Ed.). *George Washington Carver: In his own words.* Columbia, MO: University of Missouri Press.
Chesterton, G. K. (1987). In Marlin, G. J., Rabatin, R. P., & Swan, J. L. (Eds.). *The quotable Chesterton: A topical compilation of the wit, wisdom and satire of G. K. Chesterton.* Garden City, NY: Image Books.
DeNavas, W., Carmen, B., Proctor, D., & Smith, J. C. (2009). *Income, poverty, and health insurance coverage in the United States: 2009.* Washington, DC: U. S. Census Bureau.
Dewey, J. (1897). My pedagogic creed. *School Journal, 54* (January): 77-80.
Gee, James P. (2008). *Social linguistics and literacies: Ideology in discourses, 3rd. Ed.* New York: Routledge.
Gee, J., Hall, G., & Lankshear, C. (1996). *The new work order.* Boulder, CO: Westview.
Hall, G. S. (1931/2008). *Adolescence—Its psychology and its relations to physiology, anthropology, sociology, sex, crime, and religion.* Bel Air, CA: Hesperides Press.
Hill, N. E. & Chao, R. K. (Eds.) (2009). *Families, schools, and the adolescent: Connecting research, Policy, and practice.* New York: Teachers College Press.
Jefferson, T. (1786). In B. B. Oberg (Ed.) *The papers of Thomas Jefferson*, 10:244. Princeton, NJ: Princeton University Library.

Kumashiro, Kevin K. (2008). *The seduction of common sense: How the right has framed the debate on America's schools.* New York: Teachers College Press.

Lakoff, George & Mark Johnson. (1980). *Metaphors we live by.* Chicago: University of Chicago Press.

Lakoff, George. (2002). *Moral politics: How liberals and conservatives think,* 2nd ed. Chicago: University of Chicago Press.

Lakoff, George. (2004). *Don't think of an elephant! Know your values and Frame the debate.* White River Junction, VT: Chelsea Green Publishing.

Lakoff, George and The Rockridge Institute. (2006). *Thinking points: Communicating our American values and vision.* New York: Farrar, Straus & Giroux.

Lakoff, George. (2008). *The political mind: A cognitive scientist's guide to Your brain and its politics.* New York: Penguin Books.

Lehrer, Jonah. (2009). *How we decide.* New York: Houghton Mifflin.

Levitt, Steven D. & Stephen J. Dubner. (2005). *Freakonomics: A rogue economist explores the hidden side of everything.* New York: Morrow.

Madison, J. (author) & Meyers, M. (Ed.) *The mind of the founder: Sources of the political thought of James Madison.* Waltham, MA: Brandeis University Press.

Males, Mark A. (1996). *Scapegoat generation: America's war on adolescents.* Monroe, ME: Common Courage Press.

Mann, H. (2002). In M. Engelbreit (Ed.). *Words for teachers to live by.* Kansas City, MO: Andrews McMeel.

National Commission on Excellence in Education. (1983). *A nation at risk: The imperative for educational reform.* Washington, DC: National Institute for Education.

National Institute of Child Health and Human Development. (2000). *Report of the National Reading Panel. Teaching children to read: An evidence-based assessment of the scientific research literature on reading and its implications for reading instruction* (NIH Publication No. 00–4769). Washington, DC: U.S. Government Printing Office.

National Middle School Association (2003). *This we believe: Keys to educating young adolescents.* Westerville, OH: National Middle School Association.

New Commission on the Skills of the American Workforce. (2007) *Tough choices or tough times.* Washington, DC: National Center on Education and the Economy.

Pipher, N. (1995). Reviving Ophelia: *Saving the selves of adolescent girls.* New York Riverhead Books.

Roosevelt, E. (2003). In Wigal, D. (Ed.). *The Wisdom of Eleanor Roosevelt.* New York: Citadel Press.

Roosevelt, F. D. (1965). In Taylor, E., & Parks, L. F. (Eds.). *Memorable quotations of Franklin D. Roosevelt.* New York: Crowell.

Rothstein, Richard. (1998). *The way we were: The myths and realities of America's student achievement.* New York: Century Foundation Press.

Rothstein, Richard. (2004). *Class and schools: Using social, economic and educational reform to close the Black-white achievement gap.* New York: Teachers College Press.

Savil, M. (2009). *The secret lives of boys: Inside the raw emotional world of male teen boys adrift: The five factors driving the epidemic of unmotivated boys and underachieving young men.* New York: Basic Books.

Simmons, R. (2001). *Odd girl out: The hidden culture of aggression in girls.* Boston: Mariner Books.

Straus, M. B. (2007). *Adolescent girls in crisis: Intervention and hope.* New York: W. W. Norton.

Thaler, Richard H. & Cass Sunstein. (2009). *Nudge: Improving our decisions about health, wealth and happiness.* New York: Penguin.

Tyre, P. (2009). *The trouble with boys: A surprising report card on our sons, their problems at school, and what parents and educators must do.* New York: Three Rivers Press

Willingham, Daniel T. (2009). *Why students don't like school: A cognitive scientist answers questions about how the mind works and what it means for the classroom.* New York: Jossey-Bass.

This chapter originally appeared in Joseph L. DeVitis & Linda Irwin-DeVitis (Eds.), *Adolescent Education: A Reader* (New York: Peter Lang, 2010).

CHAPTER THIRTY-FOUR

The Futility of Ideological Conflict in Teacher Education

DANIEL P. LISTON

Introduction

When faced with the question: Should we prepare teachers to engage in critical civic literacy? I encounter two clear, opposing, and resolute replies. One answer is affirmative, the other negative. The skeletal responses follow.

For many teacher educators who embrace a "critical" identity, the answer is a resounding, heartfelt, committed, and enthusiastic, "Yes!" Their argument goes something like this: We live in a democratic nation, committed to the ideals of equality, justice, and freedom for all. Democracy entails particular principles and practices, institutional arrangements, kinds of political engagement, and identifiable individual dispositions. In the United States we honor the principle of individual inalienable rights, and embrace justice and equality. Certain practices follow. We are prohibited from restricting citizens' rights to due process or limiting citizens' access to schooling based on race, creed, or class. We maintain the rights of citizens to participate in their local, regional and national public institutions. Given the complex terrain of our democratic society, it takes a civic education to prepare future citizens to understand our democratic institutions and processes as well as to practice their future roles. And it requires a *critical* civic education to transform the harms created when justice and equality are not attained: when an individual, or group's, class, race, gender, or sexual identity restricts its political or educational franchise. In short, critical civic literacy promises to empower and transform when structural obstacles impede. Critical civic literacy enables students to see the power structures clearly and learn how to battle them effectively. Given the need for, and promise of, critical civic literacy, we must prepare our teachers so as to properly engage and educate their students. Those appear to be some of the main features of the positive response.

The negative reply goes something like this: We should prepare future teachers to engage their students in civic education but not a critical one. We need to educate all students, our future citizens, in the history and current features of this, our democratic experiment. Civic education relates the structure and processes of our democratic institutions and way of life, and students— as members of this society—need to understand these aspects. This includes the promise and perils of our democratic institutions. But there really isn't a place in our public schools for what some have called "critical" civic education. The term "critical" needs to be recognized for what it is: it connotes a politically liberal, generally leftist, point of view. It presumes a social and political landscape determined by the structural forces of class domination, racial discrimination, and gender inequality. Critical civic literacy inserts our public school students into this ideologically constrained terrain and asks them to transform the world and themselves. Public schools should not function as the staging grounds for particular political ideologies, and the "critical" in critical civic education all too often operates in this stealth manner. It is not an education—it is an imposition, an inculcation, and could easily turn into an indoctrination.

These two responses capture some of the messiness of public education and, by extension, the teacher education terrain. And while these (admittedly) pointed caricatures don't quite illustrate the nuances, vagaries, and complexities of the professional educational landscape, together they depict a central underlying challenge of teacher education: How should we prepare future teachers for problematic schools while acknowledging distinct and sometimes competing educational goals? The two elaborated arguments underscore distinct interpretations of the societal and educational obstacles, and the remedies proposed to address those obstacles. The first argument maintains that we should prepare teachers to transform the ills and inequities of a racist, capitalist, and undemocratic school system. In contrast, one could ask: Is that a defensible delineation of teachers' educational tasks? Are these ills structural features of our current social context, unfortunate outcomes, or the result of complex cultural dimensions? Should teachers be construed as transformative political agents? And the second argument posits that we should enable teachers to provide their students with the intellectual and cultural capital, skills, and understandings necessary to navigate the current problematic but not irredeemably flawed system. In contrast, one could ask: If skills and understandings are to be distributed, are we reproducing the inequities of our social system? Are some skills appropriate for some students and other skills for other students? Who or what decides the distributive rationale and mechanisms? Is there a middle ground between these two positions? Reasonable and well-intentioned individuals have and will differ on these contentious matters.

Much depends on how we define education, teaching, and learning, and consequently how we construe teacher preparation. Here I will argue that it is time to move on from the interminable ideological battles over the ends and means of education and teacher education. It is time to recognize that many of the key concepts and corresponding practices associated with education are "essentially contested." Reasonable individuals have embraced and argued for very distinct conceptions of education appropriate within a democracy. It seems a single "right" or "defensible" educational approach does not exist. Instead, a plurality of divergent approaches can be compared, contrasted, and evaluated for their suitability to particular democratic social and political settings and local contexts. In today's public school setting (with charter schools and voucher programs included) we have a variety of educational approaches, including core knowledge schools; Montessori-based K–12 approaches; "Knowledge Is Power Program" efforts (KIPP); International Baccalaureate offerings; and school-without-walls expeditionary learning programs.[1] Although much of public schooling can be aptly described as conservative and traditional, various programs exist. Conceptually and programmatically, we can identify substantial and reasonable progressive (e.g., Dewey and Sizer[2]), conservative (e.g., Fish and Hirsch[3]), radical (e.g., Moses and Freire[4]), and spiritual (e.g., Lantieri and Palmer[5]) understandings of what it means to educate and teach (as well as various hybrids and combinations of these four traditions). Neither teacher educators nor other concerned critics and citizens can justifiably dictate a single and universally preferred pathway for any particular context in our democratic educational, political, and moral landscape. We need to be more circumspect in our determination of how we educate (and train) our future and present teachers, and we should offer more varied conceptual and practical professional development pathways from which teachers can choose.

This proposed approach will not satisfy all. Most education faculty believe they should and can determine the direction for prospective teachers. Most maintain that teachers should become "progressive" curricular, instructional, and political reform agents.[6] Their more conservative (and traditional) critics assert otherwise: Teachers should know their subject matter and be able to impart that content. This debate occurs within and around a university teacher education context that is increasingly viewed as ineffective and broken. Given those practical and conceptual obstacles, I will argue that we need to: (1) recognize the essentially contested nature of teaching and learning, highlight the central features of the dominant and competing educational conceptions (e.g., progressive and traditional), and underscore the predominantly narrow and progressive stance of the teacher education profession; (2) come to terms with the present ineffectiveness of university-based teacher education; and (3) embrace and develop a professional preparation sequence grounded in a humanist, liberal arts orientation that would enable students (prospective teachers) to examine their core values. Here is my skeletal professional sequence proposal: an initial preparatory (training) phase, emphasizing basic instructional and curricular approaches that would come after the liberal arts component and that would be followed (after substantial work in the field) by the opportunity for teachers to choose from among distinct professional development paths (i.e., professional communities of practice representing the varied conceptions of education and teaching—including critical civic literacy).

Essentially Contested Traditions of Education and the Progressive Ideology of Teacher Education

Fifty years ago W.B. Gallie[7] claimed that the content of particular normative and philosophical concepts was "essentially contested." In brief, Gallie maintained that certain concepts (e.g., art, God, beauty, justice, and democracy) entail widespread disagreement about their particular content, and this disagreement cannot be resolved by appeal to common usage, empirical evidence, or logic. Education, it seems, is one of those concepts. Traditions of education tend to embody distinct and at times competing notions of "the good life" or valued educational ends; they construe teaching, learning, and the curriculum differentially as well as present varied views about what it means to be both teacher and student. We have, in effect, a variety of educational traditions (and corresponding notions of teaching, learning, and the curriculum) that contrast, conflict, and compete with one another. At least four distinct educational traditions can be highlighted: the conservative, progressive, radical, and spiritual approaches.

Conservatives (e.g., E.D. Hirsch, Paul Hirst, Stanley Fish, and Michael Oakeshott[8]) maintain that a proper education needs to convey to students accumulated knowledge and cognitive frameworks that have guided and engaged others. Knowledge, as either information or discipline-based frameworks, provides maps to various understandings of our world. Students are changed when they engage these understandings and become more fully human when they reflectively participate in the human conversation. Progressives (e.g., John Dewey, Eleanor Duckworth, Deborah Meier, and Theodore Sizer[9]) fear that such a conservative education is an undue imposition—it molds students in ways that don't fit and may be unbecoming. Progressives believe that we need to create educational contexts for students so that their search for meaning can be bridged with past searches for meaning (the disciplines or habits of mind) and so that the student can find his or her way in this world. As a result, the student develops more fully as a human being. Radicals (e.g., Paulo Freire, Bob Moses, George Counts, and bell hooks[10]) argue that existing traditional forms of education reproduce an unjust social order and that both schools and the larger society must be transformed. A qualitatively different social and political order, one structured to serve all people equally, is needed; and it is the goal of students and teachers alike to achieve that political and educational order. Empowerment is key, and critical exploration of extant power structures necessary. More recently others (e.g., Dwayne Huebner, Linda Lantiere, and Parker Palmer[11]) have offered a view of education as a spiritual journey through which we come to know our true selves and our place in this temporal, utterly immanent, perhaps more transcendent realm. In this spiritual tradition, human growth is achieved when we come to embrace both a faith in ourselves and a greater good. While all of these traditions maintain that student growth is central to the concept of education, each tradition defines that growth in significantly different ways.

It would take us too far afield to delve into the intricacies of how education represents an example of an essentially contested concept. In Gallie's original text, he identified seven criteria that delineated the features of essentially contested concepts.[12] These features include reference to appraisiveness (the concept conveys a valued achievement); internal complexity; diverse describability; openness of meaning; reciprocal recognition (of various contending interpretations); existence of exemplars; and progressive competition. Without delving into Gallie's framework, I will simply claim that the concept of education, as delineated within these four traditions, entails widespread disagreement about its content and that this disagreement cannot be resolved by appeal to common usage, empirical evidence, or logic. Others have argued for and examined education as an essentially contested concept and, for the time being, I'll assume it is an apt characterization.[13] For my purposes these arguments underscore the existence of reasonable and quite varied definitions of what constitutes "education." They also point to the futility of unabated rhetorical clashes asserting the moral, political, or educational primacy of one position over another.[14]

While this variety of educational definitions exists, schools of education and the teacher education profession promote a single, if somewhat ill-defined, educational orientation.[15] It is a variation of the progressive approach with a strong concern for social justice. It construes education as a form of student meaning making, in which the students' interests are wedded to the subject matter to create meaningful adventures in learning. Whether the inspiration is drawn from Dewey's iconic *The Child and the Curriculum*, the 1960's "open classroom" movement, the 1990's elementary and high school reform efforts of Theodore Sizer or Deborah Meier,[16] or the discipline-based curriculum reform efforts of our more recent past, the ed school notion of progressivism emphasizes communities of "student-centered learning." A proper education should invite students to make sense of their world. Accompanying the emphasis on student meaning is a view of the teacher as a professional—a skilled individual with key instructional and curricular decision-making capacities. Even for its proponents, this conception of education is seen as a somewhat romantic, not institutionally steeped, vision that emphasizes the joys and engagements of learning and teaching. Incorporated within this progressive stance is a focus on "social justice"—an examination of the ways in which schooling contributes to the vast array of injustices in democratic societies.

This progressive view of teaching and learning collides with the more traditional view of teaching and learning that prevails in the public schools and with the larger public. It is a view that focuses on students' and teachers' mastery of subject matter and disciplinary learning, the achievement of classroom and school order, as well as the command of cultural and intellectual capital. The central idea is that students learn so as to master important material and to develop their ability to navigate capably the worlds beyond schools. It is a view that has been articulated by more politically conservative individuals, who view the mastery of knowledge and disciplinary understanding as more important than student meaning making and individual student effort as central to educational achievement. E.D. Hirsch, Chester Finn, and Diane Ravitch have articulated these views and criticized ed schools' reliance on the progressive stance.[17]

One upshot of this progressive-traditional rift is that the university-based teacher education enterprise is construed as ineffectual, out of touch, and ideologically driven. It is not a grossly inaccurate depiction. More and more politicians, journalists, and philanthropists[18] construe schools of education as contributing to, rather than solving, our nation's educational woes. Even prominent teacher educators recognize the need for substantial ed school change.[19] When Arne Duncan, U.S. Secretary of Education, spoke at Teachers College, Columbia University, on October 22, 2009, he focused on the failures of our teacher preparation efforts. Duncan admitted that a few of the nation's teacher education programs are engaged in remarkable efforts, but he went on to say that

> by almost any standard, many if not most of the nation's 1,450 schools, colleges, and departments of education are doing a mediocre job of preparing teachers for the realities of the 21st-century classroom. America's university-based teacher preparation programs need revolutionary change—not evolutionary tinkering.[20]

And part of the problem, according to Duncan, is the ideological blinders worn by school of education faculty. Duncan maintains that U.S. teacher education is, for the most part, "subjective, obscure, faddish . . . out-of-touch, politically correct" and fails to address our nation's schools' most pressing problems. Duncan went on to argue that ed school professional efforts are ideologically constrained. While his depiction may be a bit harsh and extreme, he provided a telling and emblematic anecdote. He relayed that:

> English professor E.D. Hirsch, the father of the acclaimed, content-rich Core Knowledge Program, got his own taste of the ideological blinders at colleges of education when he chose to teach an ed school course on the causes and cure of the achievement gap. Having authored the 1987 bestseller, *Cultural Literacy*, Hirsch anticipated that his course would be oversubscribed. But three years in a row, only 10 or so students enrolled. Finally, one of Hirsch's students informed him that other professors in the ed school were encouraging students to shun the course because it ran counter to their pedagogical beliefs.[21]

Unfortunately, the attitudes that kept Hirsch's enrollment numbers low are not unique to that particular university. It seems to be a problem endemic within schools, colleges, and departments of education. When university-sponsored teacher preparation programs preclude and exclude a significant representation of the diversity of educational ideas and practices, their legitimacy is seriously undermined. It may be time for ed schools to reconsider "business as usual," especially when the most politically liberal and progressive federal administration in years joins and contributes to the ed school critiques.

The Problems with Teacher Education

University-sponsored teacher education has been in existence for some 100 years. Given this history and legacy, one would think that we would have a substantial response to the central questions: How do we prepare prospective teachers for teaching? Should we encourage, educate, and train them to engage in critical civic literacy? One would think that, after more than a century of teacher preparation, we would have secured an answer to the first question; and, with that answer in hand, we could progress toward responding to the second one. But that's not the case. Teacher education has proved, for the most part, to be ideologically narrow and rigid, and pragmatically ineffectual.[22] In spite of the ideological adherence to progressive educational tenets, the reality is that teacher education never has been quite sure of its scope, methods, or institutional location. This historical fact has resurfaced recently in the controversy surrounding the degree to which our departments, schools, and colleges of education are (in)adequately preparing future teachers. During the past few years the teacher education industry has come under renewed critical scrutiny from prominent members within its ranks as well as those outside. Arthur Levine (formerly Teachers College, Columbia University, president) recently published the findings from his study "Educating School Teachers. The Education Schools Project."[23] Any call for teacher education to embrace "critical civic literacy" must first address these sorts of criticism before heading down the path to critical engagement.

Levine, in the second of four reports dealing with the state of our country's schools of education, recounts the results of an ambitious study. He examines the state of teacher preparation, utilizing a number of distinct data sources, including surveys of school principals as well as school of education deans, faculty, and alumni; a Northwest Evaluation Association Study examining the linkages among teacher preparation, teachers and public school student growth; and a series of site visits at 28 different teacher preparation programs. While the research basis for his report is not flaw-free (and I will look at some of the issues below), my central focus is on Levine's critique.

Teacher education in the United States has been, and continues to be, characterized by a series of conflicts and conundrums. These conflicts can be posed as questions: Are we preparing candidates for a craft or a profession? Should they be prepared on the job in schools or beforehand in institutions of higher education? What is the proper preparatory blend, i.e., between a practice-based orientation and a theoretical framing of teaching, learning, and schooling? Should such preparation occur in the public schools, a university setting, or something more akin to a normal school context? Will state regulation or deregulation encourage the profession to become clearer about its professional vision? Levine maintains that the teacher education profession has been and continues to be caught in the middle of these conflicting purposes and understandings. Despite the progressive framing, we are a profession without a clear programmatic plan for teacher preparation.

Levine and others before him have argued that teacher education seems confused about its purposes and means.[24] Levine writes:

> There is a schism over the how's and when's of teacher education between those who believe teaching is a profession like law or medicine, requiring a substantial amount of education before an individual can become a practitioner, and those who think teaching is a craft like journalism, which is learned principally on the job.[25]

Whether candidates travel the professional or craft path, they confront a dizzying variety of options. Unfortunately, Levine maintains, the profession has offered neither central conceptual threads nor a practical, programmatic, professional backbone.[26] Levine argues that we are a profession confused about what to profess. This confusion results in basic inadequacy.

The teacher education curriculum is in disarray. "Overall, the result is a curriculum incapable of achieving desired outcomes because of the ambiguity of its goals and unable to educate teachers effectively because of the split between academic and clinical instruction, with an overemphasis on the academic."[27] We lack coherence and direction in our teacher preparation curriculum. And our teacher education faculty are disconnected within their university setting. The faculty

> hold a place between the arts and sciences and the schools, but they are not a part of either. They are natural allies of policy makers, practitioners, and scholars, but are embraced by none and their research is ignored or criticized by each. The lack of rigorous self-assessment of the nation's teacher education programs exacerbates those conditions.[28]

In addition to programmatic confusion, Levine observes that there are great disparities in institutional quality. The weakest group of universities, Masters level I institutions, produce 54% of the teachers. Levine maintains that they are "weaker academically than the other two major producers of teachers. As a group, they have lower admission standards, professors with lesser credentials, and produce less effective graduates in the classroom."[29] Levine summarizes his survey findings:

> The inescapable conclusion is that the nation's teacher education programs are not adequately preparing their students in competencies that principals say they need and that schools of education regard as their responsibility to teach.[30]

Principals, those who oversee the teacher education graduates, are not generally satisfied with ed school graduates.

Certainly one could quibble over the basis for some of Levine's claims and the manner in which he casts them. The NWEA study is not well delineated, and the manner in which Levine analyzes his data and draws his inferences appears, at times, quite shaky. The data collection process utilized for the 28 site studies and the basis for the selection of the 4 exemplary programs could be more helpfully specified. But Levine's main point, the gist of his research effort, is a charge that has not changed in the last 50 to 60 years. Levine's assessment of university-based teacher education as an enterprise that is confused, and conflicted, and one characterized (by others) as ideologically misdirected is also a view that is shared by many outside of the profession and must be taken more seriously by those of us within the enterprise.

The Liberal Arts as a Basis for Teacher Education

Given the deeply contested nature of our educational proposals, the growing ideological divide between ed schools and the larger public, and the disarray of our current university-based teacher education practices, a proposal to prepare all teachers for critical cultural literacy would be ill advised and ineffective. Something much more basic, more structurally differentiated, and better attuned to the noted issues and obstacles is needed. In what remains, I offer a rudimentary outline for teacher education reform. It is one that: integrates different elements of varied educational traditions; asserts and recognizes the importance of the *teacher* in teacher education; appreciates the need for basic instructional and curricular training; and incorporates distinct professional pathways for subsequent professional development. In short, I propose that our preparation for teachers include a strong liberal arts component, followed by basic training in the skills and arts of teaching, to be further developed by teachers choosing and pursuing distinct professional pathways (modeled after diverse educational conceptions and existing professional development efforts, e.g., Core Knowledge; Algebra Project; Courage to Teach; and others). Here I focus on the rationale for the liberal arts component as a foundational element in teacher education and speak very briefly about the subsequent training and professional development features. Since the liberal arts component provides the backbone for this professional preparation and addresses squarely the essentially contested nature of education, it seems the most appropriate place to start.

What is the value of a liberal arts education? Most justifications underscore the need for students to examine varied disciplinary frameworks and to gain sufficient knowledge of the world.[31] A liberal arts education enables its graduates to think cogently and clearly, understand the power and illumination of distinct disciplinary lenses, and to master basic understandings of our natural, social, and cultural worlds. For prospective teachers, a sound liberal arts education should ensure content and skill acquisition as well as disciplinary mastery: teachers need to know well the content and disciplines they teach. With some tweaking, those traditional justifications might work here. But recent work by Mark Edmundson underscores the role of the liberal arts, specifically the humanities, in enabling students to examine their core values.[32] And it is this core value component that seems particularly critical in the preparation of teachers. As a humanist, Edmundson asks: Why read? We read, he writes, so as to discover ourselves and others, and to come to know previously unrecognized aspects of our selves and the world. Each one of us is unique and yet, at the same time, we experience common human refrains and themes. We learn these individual and shared themes so that we might get a glimpse of who we are and what we might become. In *Why Read?* Edmundson outlines the central educational elements that encourage this discovery. The basic element is an education that challenges students to consider their central or ultimate values by posing critical questions about what they value and how they ought to live. Given the contentious nature of our essentially contested educational concepts, this seems a promising path. In so many ways "we teach who we are." This approach to liberal arts education should enable prospective teachers to understand who they are and enable them to choose their educational path.

Challenging Beliefs and Values:

Edmundson relates that a valuable liberal arts education is one that guides us along our central life questions: How should I live my life? What are my purposes? What is work that matters? How do I picture God? Why should I go to school? Should I marry? Whom should I marry? Should I have a family? What sort of parent do I want to be? It is risky and at times difficult and messy stuff. But these questions begin to get at students' core values, or what Edmundson (following Richard Rorty) calls individuals' "Final Narratives." Final narratives are the stories we tell ourselves when things that really matter are questioned. For prospective teachers, such final narratives arise in response to such questions as: Why do schools produce such unequal results and what is my role in it—as student, teacher, or parent? Students' responses to these questions begin to unveil their values, as well as their view of themselves, the larger social world, and their possible role in it. When students respond that parents and schools pass along culturally variable skills to children and students, or indicate that our society's schools reproduce existing inequalities, or that such inequalities belie a natural order—these sorts of answers begin to unveil students' understandings. This liberal arts education offers alternative narratives that challenge students' received views and enlarges or redirects their circle of meaning. It does so in a manner that engages feeling and intellect, does not presuppose a particular answer, and relies—in some way—on an inner eye, an inner self.

Mind and Heart:

Edmundson relates that a humanistic approach to education invites students to empathize with a reading, a character, a point of view. Students are asked to imagine what it looks and feels like to be a character or hold a particular perspective. In doing so, the classroom can become disordered and complicated—neither pristine nor analytically precise. By posing significant questions about students' final narratives, and offering substantial works that shed light on alternatives to those narratives, thus enlarging students' circles of understanding, this liberal arts education walks into promising but messy territory. He writes:

> The process of human growth—when it entails growth of the heart as well as of the mind—is never particularly clean or abstract. To grow it is necessary that all of our human qualities come into play, and if some of those qualities are not pretty, then so be it. But to keep them to the side so as to preserve our professional

dignity—that is too much of a sacrifice. (Men and women die every day, perish in the inner life . . . for lack of what we have to offer.)[33]

Developing the inner life and facilitating human growth require that we fuse mind and heart, and Edmundson's humanist education recognizes this.

No sSngle, Right Direction:

Many teachers believe they know where students ought to head—the values they should hold, the kinds of people they should become. Most of us want our students to be decent human beings. But we frequently want something more, something much more specific. In teacher education, many faculty want to help prospective teachers become reform-oriented teachers, committed to an ideal of social justice and deep content understanding. As teacher educators, we "know" what they should fight for and we put them on that path. Edmundson disagrees. A humanist education does not stipulate the particular valued ends students should develop. Edmundson once asked another humanities professor what he tried to achieve in the classroom, and this professor indicated that he had particular dispositions in mind. He encouraged greater skepticism and cultural enlargement so that students could become more "humane . . . more sensitive, more community minded, less materialistic, more civilized." As appealing as these dispositions might seem, Edmundson thought this route wasn't such a good idea. He writes:

> It strikes me as a very bad idea for us teachers to have a preexisting image of how we want our students to turn out, even as potentially attractive an idea as this teacher was offering. No I think what we need is for people to understand who and what they are now, then to be open to changing into their own highest mode of being. And that highest mode is something that they must identify by themselves, through encounters with the best that has been known and thought. We all have promise in us; it is up to education to reveal that promise, and to help it unfold. The power that is in you, says Emerson, is new in nature. And the best way to release that power is to let students confront viable versions of experience and take their choices.[34]

Too many of us, it seems, are unwilling to let the students view viable versions and choose. We want to construe which versions are commendable and worth pursuing. We have little faith in students' inner selves. Edmundson embraces that faith and asks us to do the same, if, that is, we are to pursue a truly humanist and liberal arts orientation.

The Inner Self and Truth:

Talk about an inner self stretches the content of many academics' somewhat brittle metaphysical catalogue. Add to this talk of an inner self a search for "truth" and it seems we begin to herald an outmoded epistemological quest and certainly a misguided educational journey. But Edmundson's conception of educational transformation will have it no other way. A proper education is geared toward human transformation and offers literary, historical, and philosophical works that matter. "Works that matter work differently. Such works . . . can do many things, but preeminent among them is their capacity to offer truth."[35] And what are these truths? How do we find them and what do we do with them? Edmundson explains:

What I am asking when I ask of a major work (for only major works will sustain this question) whether it is true is quite simply this: Can you live it? Can you put it into action? Can you speak—or adapt—the language of this work, use it to talk to both yourself and others so as to live better? Is this work desirable as a source of belief? Or at the very least, can it influence your existing beliefs in consequential ways?[36]

In this liberal arts, prospective teachers should be asked what kind of teachers they want to become. We should offer them major works that pose the following questions: What view of education and teaching allows me to live and teach better—to serve students best? Can I live this version of a teacher, and how might I put it into action? Students' responses to these consequential questions lie in the interplay, in a significant sense, between these works that offer truths and the source that lies within each of them.

For many academics the proposal that great works offer some version of truth is ludicrous and outmoded. We have discarded conceptions of truth in scholarship and education. Why try to bring truth back in? Edmundson suggests:

For the simple reason that for many people, the truths—the circle, the vision of experience—that they've encountered through socialization is inadequate. It doesn't put them into a satisfying relation to experience. That truth does not give them what they want. It does not help them make a contribution to their society. It does not, to advance another step, even allow for a clear sense of the tensions between themselves and the existing social norms, the prevailing doxa . . . most people who go to literature and the liberal arts . . . demand other, better ways to apprehend the world—that is, ways that are better for them.[37]

There is throughout Edmundson's text an abiding faith that most students have within them the power for discernment—for taking major works, examining their truths, and asking of themselves and others important life questions.

Concluding Futility

I've asserted that a preferred sequence in teacher education is one that begins with a liberal arts basis, followed by basic instructional and curricular training, and further developed by the pursuit of distinct educational professional development pathways. I developed this sequence in response to the question: Should we prepare future teachers to engage in critical civic literacy? I've only begun the response here. Further work is required; multiple questions remain. In a world of essentially contested educational plans, how can one approach trump all others? Should this preparation occur within universities, public schools, both, or neither? What would this "basic training" look like, and how would it relate to current school practices? What do we do with ed schools? These questions await further exploration. But one question seems to be resolved: Should we prepare future teachers to engage in critical civic literacy? Yes—but only after those individuals have been prepared to make that choice for themselves and have other options available.

Notes

1. See, for example, http://www.coreknowledge.org/ and http://www.mrsh.org/index.php; http://clark.cps-k12.0rg/ and http://ncme-ne.org/; http://www.kipp.org/; http://www.ibo.org/; and http://www.kurthahnschool.org/

2. John Dewey, *The Child and the Curriculum* (Chicago: University of Chicago Press, [1902] 1956), and Theodore Sizer, *Horace's School* (New York: Houghton Mifflin, 1992).

3. Stanley Fish, *Save the World on Your Own Time* (New York: Oxford, 2008), and E.D. Hirsch, *The Schools We Need and Why We Don't Have Them* (New York: Doubleday, 1996).

4. Robert Moses, *Radical Equations* (Boston: Beacon Press, 2001), and Paulo Freire, *Pedagogy of the Oppressed* (New York: Continuum, [1970] 2006).

5. Linda Lantieri (ed.), *Schools with Spirit* (Boston: Beacon Press, 2001), and Parker Palmer, *The Courage to Teach* (San Francisco, CA: Jossey-Bass, 2007).

6. See, for example, David Labaree, *The Trouble with Ed Schools* (New Haven, CT: Yale University Press, 2004).

7. W.B. Gallie, "Essentially Contested Concepts," *Proceedings of the Aristotelian Society*, Vol. 56 (1956), pp. 167–198. See also D. Collier, F. Hidalgo, & A. Maciuceanu, "Essentially Contested Concepts: Debates and Applications," *Journal of Political Ideologies*, Vol. 11, No. 3 (October 2006), pp. 211–246.

8. See, for examples: E.D. Hirsch, *The Schools We Need* (New York: Random House, 1999); Paul Hirst, "Liberal Education and the Nature of Knowledge." In *Philosophical Analysis and Education*, ed. R.D. Archambault (New York: Humanities Press, 1965); Stanley Fish, *Save the World on Your Own Time* (New York: Oxford, 2008); and Michael Oakeshott, *The Voice of Liberal Learning*, ed. Timothy Fuller (New Haven, CT: Yale University Press, 1989).

9. See for examples: John Dewey, *The Child and the Curriculum* (Chicago, University of Chicago Press, [1902] 1956); Eleanor Duckworth, *"The having of wonderful ideas" & other essays on teaching & learning* (New York: Teachers College Press, 1996); Deborah Meir, *The Power of Their Ideas* (Boston: Beacon Press, 1996); and Theodore Sizer, *Horace's School* (New York: Houghton Mifflin, 1996).

10. See, for examples: George Counts, *Dare the Schools Build a New Social Order?* (New York: John Day, 1932); Paulo Freire, *Pedagogy of the Oppressed* (New York: Seabury Press, 1974); Robert Moses, *Radical Equations* (Boston: Beacon Press, 2001); and bell hooks, *Teaching to Transgress* (New York: Routledge, 1994).

11. See, for examples: Dwayne Huebner, *The Lure of the Transcendent: Collected Essays by Dwayne E. Huebner*, ed. Vikki Hillis (Mahwah, NJ: Lawrence Erlbaum, 1999); Linda Lantieri (ed.), *Schools with Spirit* (Boston: Beacon Press, 2001), and Parker Palmer, *The Courage to Teach* (San Francisco, CA: Jossey-Bass, 1998).

12. Collier et al., "Essentially Contested Concepts," is helpful here.

13. See, for example, R.S. Peters, "Democratic Values and Educational Aims," *Teachers College Record*, Vol. 80, No. 3 (1979), pp. 463–482; and A. Hartnell and M. Naish, *Theory and Practice of Education*, vol. 1 (London: Heinemann, 1976), pp. 79–94.

14. By viewing education as an essentially contested concept I do not mean to imply that reasonable and defensible claims cannot be put forward. We need not accept a simple conceptual relativism. By acknowledging the contested nature of any educational project, my hope is that a greater tolerance for the variety of distinct educational options will develop. This may be naïve. But having observed the incessant ed-school posturing, self-congratulation (individual and organizational), and demonizing of others (conservatives as "evil")—it would seem helpful to change games.

15. Labaree, *The Trouble with Ed Schools*.

16. Sizer, *Horace's School*; and Meier, *The Power of Their Ideas*.

17. A rich source of this material can be found at: http://www.edexcellence.net/, the website for the Thomas B. Fordham Institute, a conservative think tank.

18. For examples see Arne Duncan, http://www.ed.gov/news/speeches/2009/10/10222009.html; Jay Matthews, *Work Hard, Be Nice* (Chapel Hill, NC: Algonquin Books, 2009), p. 267; and A. Hartocolis, "Who Needs Education Schools?" *New York Times Education Life* (July 31, 2005), pp. 24–28.

19. See: Deborah Ball, "The Case for Ed Schools and the Challenge," The Dewitt Wallace Readers' Digest distinguished lecture presented at the annual meeting of the American Educational Research Association, Chicago, April 2007; and D. Ball and F. Forzani, "The Work of Teaching and the Challenge for Teacher Education," *Journal of Teacher Education*, Vol. 60, No. 5 (2009), pp. 497–511. See also Kenneth Zeichner, "Rethinking College and University-Based Teacher Education" Draft, December 2010.

20. http://www.ed.gov/news/speeches/2009/10/10222009.html

21. http://www.ed.gov/news/speeches/2009/10/10222009.html

22. In what follows I focus on Levine's criticisms. There certainly are features of university-based teacher educa-tion that produce positive results. For example, see: S. Wilson and E. Tamir, "The Evolving Field of Teacher Education," in M. Cochran-Smith, S. Feiman-Nemser, and J. McIntyre (eds.), *Handbook of Research on Teacher Education* (New York: Routledge, 2008), pp. 908–935; and G. Sykes, T. Bird, M. Kennedy, "Teacher Education Its Problems and Some Prospects," *Journal of Teacher Education*, Vol. 61, No. 5 (2010), pp. 464–476.

23. Arthur Levine, *Educating School Teachers. The Education Schools Project*, 2006. http://www.edschools.org/teacher_report.htm

24. See Geraldine Clifford and James Guthrie, *Ed School* (Chicago: University of Chicago Press, 1988), and The Holmes Group, *Tomorrow's Teachers: A Report of the Holmes Group* (East Lansing, MI: The Holmes Group, 1986).

25. Levine, *Educating School Teachers*, p. 13.

26. Labaree, *The Trouble with Ed Schools*, observes that strong ideological framings do not ensure coherent program-matic offerings.

27. Levine, *Educating School Teachers*, pp. 43–44.

28. Ibid, p. 53.

29. Ibid, p. 71.

30. Ibid, p. 33.

31. Hirst, "Liberal Education," is a powerful example here.

32. Mark Edmundson, *Why Read?* (New York: Bloomsbury, 2004).

33. Ibid, p. 67.

34. Ibid, p. 86.

35. Ibid, p. 51.

36. Ibid, p. 56.

37. Ibid, p. 52.

CHAPTER THIRTY-FIVE

The "Theology of Neutrality" and the "Middle-Class" Curriculum of Teacher Education

Threats to Critical Civic Literacy

JOSEPH C. WEGWERT

A Parable of Practice

I teach in a teacher education program at a public university that graduates 3 out of 4 teacher candidates in the state. At some point near the beginning of the semester in my teacher education course—often in the first or second meeting—I ask my students if they wish to influence the lives of the young people they will teach. Although a few students seem initially cautious by what they probably perceive as a "trick" question, the overwhelming proportion of students unhesitatingly raise their hands high in the air. They **do** wish to influence the children they will teach. In the ensuing discussion, many students elaborate on the ways in which they want to influence children—how they behave and interact with one another; how they encounter knowledge; how they resolve conflicts; how they seek to persevere; what they value. My preservice teacher candidates hope, in other words, to powerfully impact their students' lives.

"Well, then, that's that," I say, "Clearly, you understand that, as a teacher, you are not neutral." The question of teacher neutrality: raised and dispatched. Yes? No. Not so fast. Almost immediately my students begin to try to find some ways out of the proverbial corner they have found themselves painted into. They point out that they wish to influence children's behaviors and choices but do not wish to impose their own values; they wish to help students understand the complexities of the world around them but do not wish to share their own political or social perspectives; they wish to connect current issues to the lives of their students but wish to avoid controversial topics that might violate or challenge students' cultural or family norms and, thereby, create student "discomfort."

Introduction

It is here, then, at the nexus of neutrality and purpose, that my students most display their middle-class identities—their dispositions towards maintaining the status quo while invoking a distorted, 21st-century social gospel. Of course, this is and always has been rhetorical code for, at the least, normalizing middle-class aspirations and, at the most, passive acceptance of the regulating role of middle-class values. In the current cultural context, a critical teacher education program, essential for the development of critical civic literacy for teachers and students, requires surfacing and de-constructing the anti-democratic and anti-intellectual tendencies of a pervasive neo-liberal rationality rooted in middle-class values that, in the name of civility, eschew not just controversy but complexity itself.

This chapter examines the question of critical civic literacy by theorizing a circular—reproductive—effect as middle-class high school students encounter a citizenship curriculum that aligns with and supports the imperatives of neo-liberal capitalism and the essential roles of middle-class professionals, including public school teachers, within corporatist institutions. Middle-class students often encounter socialization into dominant ideological frameworks that privilege individualism, meritocracy, and neutrality (Agostinone-Wilson, 2006), offering affirmations of their own cultural system of common sense (Geertz, 1975). I argue that since teacher education disproportionately draws candidates from the middle class, these attachments often manifest for students as certainties of "common sense." These middle-class certainties, without disruption, serve to reify dominant values and contexts and marginalize the lives and experiences of those who fall outside, especially below, middle-class status (Schutz, 2008).

The basis of this theorizing draws on analysis generated from a study that examined the curriculum and performance of citizenship in a suburban, middle-class school.[1] Using ethnographic methods and critical theoretical frameworks the study focused on social studies classrooms and the larger context of the culture of a suburban Midwestern high school, Covington Woods High School (a pseudonym). The central research question asked how the formal and informal curricula of school and social studies classrooms served to frame, communicate, socialize and perform the discursive, symbolic, ritualized, and conceptual constructs of citizenship. The data sets used in this study came from observations in social studies classrooms and common areas (cafeteria, hallways, and library), building and district meetings, and interviews with the social studies teachers and school administrators at Covington Woods High School (CWHS). These data pointed to an overarching formal and informal curriculum of the *middle-class promise*, lessons that modeled for these middle-class students how middle-class professionals (teachers) operate in the context of a corporatized institution. Many students in teacher education programs come from this middle-class context and, I argue, carry with them these lessons of the *middle-class promise*.

This chapter begins by locating my own long-standing involvement and investment with the issues of citizenship and civic literacy and then, briefly examines the American civic landscape. Next, it moves into the realm of schools and civic education and examines the citizenship curriculum of a suburban, middle-class high school attending especially to the civic lessons of identity and performance. Finally, I explore the education/socialization of preservice teacher candidates, returning to the opening narrative, and how the teacher education curriculum of "professionalism" taps into cultural beliefs and discursive practices around the nature of knowledge, the cult of individualism, the centrality of instrumental rationality, and the tendencies toward an ontological pessimism. These elements all contribute toward a professional identity that produces an impoverished civic literacy and ubiquitous civic passivity.

Although this chapter connects to the long-standing and continuing conversation of teacher neutrality in the context of citizenship education (Agostinone-Wilson, 2005; Applebaum, 2009; Bartolome, 1994, 2008; Giroux, 1981; Hess, 2009; Kelly, 1986; Kelly & Brandes, 2001), its central point explores why the myth of teacher neutrality has such ideological staying power and how this ideological intransigence reinforces curricular and pedagogical conditions that produce/reproduce impoverished, thin conceptions of democratic citizenship. At the center of this inquiry, then, is an assertion that the current state of civic education fails to produce critical civic literacy and civic performance throughout the United States reflects this fact.

A Personal Journey: Beginning Lessons

In some manner or another I have been thinking about and working on questions of citizenship and critical civic literacy since I was a student in high school. Interestingly, those beginnings had nothing whatsoever to do with what I was learning about government and politics in my high school classrooms, a standard curriculum of structure/function marinated in an unreflective patriotism. Rather, during those years I cut my political teeth, outside the classroom, on the presidential campaign of 1972 and the subsequent civic tremors that accompanied the combined effects of the debacle of Vietnam, the tainted Nixon presidency, and Watergate. Political events during that time produced what was called a "credibility gap" between the government and the American people. For me, however, the "credibility gap" was most powerfully manifested in the gulf between the civic curriculum of my school and the lessons I learned participating in the political context of the times.

By the mid-1970s, in contrast to the political activism of the 1960s, the whole nation seemed frozen in a civic stupor. Apathy served as a favorite topic of many pundits, columnists, and other purveyors of cultural and national decline and doom. Commentators warned how the late "baby-boomers," those of the television generation, too young for anti-war marches and civil rights demonstrations, might well be civically stunted by the seemingly unrelenting waves of political corruption and the concomitant emotional and literal resignations.

My youthful involvement with political activism led, not surprisingly, to an undergraduate degree in political science with an emphasis on American government and politics and, some years later, a graduate degree in American history. I began my career of teaching citizenship in the fall of 1977. In preparing for that career and as I moved through it, I thought a good deal about the intersection between the civic apathy pervading American culture and my chosen profession. My first teaching experience involved teaching American government to high school seniors only three years younger than their novice instructor. For many of these young people, American government and physical education were their only classes at school that first semester I taught. Many lived in the reality of work, 40 hours per week for some, in an increasingly sluggish economy.

Assigned to teach the Constitution and functions of government, I struggled to make those structures and workings of the national government come alive to my classes of largely working-class students in a sprawling urban high school. The Constitutional "miracle in Philadelphia" so uncritically celebrated by the students' textbooks provided little connection either to their work life or to the post-Watergate political convulsions playing out in the news. More out of desperation than creativity I veered off the prescribed curricular path and offered up a more critical discussion of governmental privilege, in general, and Congressional privileges and perquisites, in particular. At that point, I saw a spark of student interest flicker and then erupt into a blaze of passionate but thoughtful and righteous anger. Student responses varied depending on the issue but the general theme of elite privilege and perks drew significant interest and critique.

In short, the information and context we explored rang more truthfully—matched students' sensibilities more accurately—about the world around them than did the textbook narrative. Although I didn't entirely or clearly recognize it at the time, the "credibility gap" my students experienced paralleled my own high school experience. In retrospect, these were early lessons that pointed to the only way I have ever found—in over 30 years of teaching—to draw students toward critical civic literacy: Young people live in the real world. To the extent that the adults in schools offer a false or a heavily distorted narrative of reality, young people regard "school knowledge" as something unworthy of their serious engagement. Students must be invited into—not "protected" from—the real world of power. "Letting students in on" the complexities and contradictions of the world around them serves as a prerequisite for critical civic literacy.

Civic Performance: A Cultural Analysis

The immediate post-Watergate context in which I began my teaching career saw an upsurge in concern for disaffection from political life, especially among the nation's youth. Very quickly, however, this concern for America's civic malaise became enveloped within a broader cultural critique of civic education and questions of civic competence. Indeed, cultural anxiety over civic apathy and competence has served to define much of the discourse around citizenship education for the last several decades and continues as one of the few constants of contemporary American political life (Giroux, 2003; Marciano, 1997; Ravitch & Finn, 1987; Schlesinger, 1992). Although surface agreement might exist on this point across the political spectrum, it is clear that what cultural conservatives consider civic competence differs significantly from that envisioned by progressives. Nonetheless, American culture has trained its quick-fix, self-improvement fetish on notions of civic crisis, spawning innumerable civic "makeover" strategies. A Google search of "citizenship initiatives" garners 4.7 million hits. "Fixing" the broken condition of American civic performance is more than a cottage industry; it involves corporations, foundations, legislatures, the publishing industry, and, of course, volunteer organizations.

Aside from this cultural fascination, it is from the evidence and effects of civic performance that questions about civic socialization draw their potency and, increasingly, their urgency. In this regard, there is much evidence to suggest that the United States is in a state of civic crisis: a crisis of democracy (performance) as well as a crisis of civic education in our schools (socialization). These dual crises represent not parallels but linkages, manifestations of an increasingly permeable boundary between the mediated and corporatized culture of American society and the life of schools—between impoverished civic performance and anemic civic curriculum.

Contemporary performances of citizenship demonstrate an ongoing and intensifying pattern of civic passivity in which not even a majority of the citizens of the world's self-proclaimed "premiere" democracy participate as voters and far fewer embrace a more activist—that is, a more authentically democratic—civic identity. In this civic environment, words such as "freedom," "change," "leadership," "democracy," and "progress" serve as floating signifiers that mutate to meet the hegemonic imperatives of the immediate context. This dynamic produces an ironic context for political dialogue characterized by a potent anti-intellectualism—a dialogue in which complexity becomes suspect doubletalk while over-simplification and sloganeering performs as welcomed evidence of determined commitment (Jensen, 2004; Kaminer, 1999; Popen, 2002).

In a society increasingly characterized by a culture of fear, a containment of discourse, an encroaching privatization of the public sphere, and a hyper-individualism, American citizens appear not only disinclined but incapable of responding to the very real threats posed to the health of American democracy. This disquieting acquiescence and civic passivity describe a public sphere increasingly characterized by unabashed government propaganda, outright lies, and manipulation of news. Indeed, Americans are immersed in an increasingly technological and ideological hyper-reality where misinformation, misdirection, and denial manifest in political disequilibrium and where the deliberate fragmentation of knowledge, meaning, and purpose promotes a "social vertigo—[a] depoliticization of perception" (Kincheloe, 2001, p. 62). The cultural and ideological phenomenon of re-framing what is—re-casting experiences, history, and knowledge—is a defining characteristic of an emergent neo-liberal corporate hegemony. At its core, this agenda produces a domestication of citizenship—a domestication of ideas, of participation, and, ultimately, of our collective humanity (Rodriguez, 2006).

So, if there is a real crisis of civic competence—and I think there is—then it is crucial that we not be confused about the source of the problem or misled by false solutions. The current political and ideological milieu suggests a sustained and systemic crisis of democratic citizenship and calls for thoughtful and creative analysis about how civic socialization takes place and what roles school culture, schools curriculum, and classroom pedagogies, in particular, play in this process.

Civic Education: The Context of Schools

As cultural workers, public school teachers are also storytellers, communicators, and interpreters to their students of American culture and of the world beyond. Yet, teachers and the schools they inhabit operate within the boundaries of a cultural script that serves to reproduce dominant social and economic relations (Giroux, 1981; Loewen, 1995; Quantz, 2003). Teachers play a significant role in communicating cultural narratives complicit in the hegemonic project of corporate power. Indeed, one of the most potent narratives perpetuated by schools is one about schools themselves: a cultural narrative of opportunity and equality and one of meritocracy that locates schools as a level playing field for individual achievement and as the single most important social institution for the health and success of America's historic experiment in democracy. The place of public schools in the dominant story of America's unfolding democracy continues to provide much of the foundational layer of the hegemonic work that schools perform.

In many ways, the cultural jeremiad of American public schooling serves as a template for the stories—the component parts of an overarching, dominant narrative—one that character-izes much of the civic curriculum enacted in schools. Social studies teachers, perhaps more than any of their colleagues, operate as professional storytellers. The "storying" of citizenship in social studies classes, in particular, involves narratives woven into the very fabric of nationhood and civic membership, the very raison d'être (at least rhetorically) for public schools (Kincheloe, 2001).

The civic curriculum demanded by the imperatives of an increasingly virulent form of neo-liberalism moves from the broader cultural sphere into the schoolhouse door. The stories that dominate American society—stories told largely through a mediated culture—intersect, filter, and translate in powerful ways the civic and historical narratives offered in schools. Here we see a potent layering of story—one that informs, shapes, and limits the discursive and imaginary pos-sibilities students encounter. Here we see a curriculum that distances students from their largely undemocratic experiences both within and beyond the boundaries of school. The ideological and discursive cross-pollination between schooling's curriculum of "democratic citizenship" and the wider civic curriculum in a mediated culture socializes students into passive consumption of that very contradiction—normalizing relations of domination and authority situated within domi-nant cultural narratives of democracy and individual agency.

The standard of civic education, then, serves to normalize the distorted narratives of equal-ity and agency that students and citizens frequently encounter. The suppression and marginal-ization of students' own reflexivity about their lives in school and beyond reflect an increasingly seamless connection to the narratives produced and disseminated by corporate media through a variety of hegemonic outlets—including public schools, one of the most pervasive and acces-sible distributors of dominant ideology. Consequently, the social studies curriculum and teach-ers of social studies play a central and restricting role in students' civic socialization.

A Study of Civic Socialization[2]

This section of the chapter draws on data that surfaced in a study about the civic curriculum of a suburban Midwest, middle-class high school (enrollment of 2,100 students). These data from discussions, interviews, and observations regarding both the Pledge of Allegiance ritual and the larger civic lessons found in the social studies classrooms and common areas of Covington Woods High School point to a broad civic curriculum I call the *middle-class promise*.[3] The cen-tral lesson this curriculum offered to students was the lesson of *compliance*—a distinctly middle-class notion of *compliance* that acknowledges choice and self-interest, reifies privilege and common sense (Lukacs, 1971), and offers *success*. In these ways, the varying ecologies of school-ing contribute toward different educational experiences for students from working, middle, and affluent-professional social classes (Anyon, 1980, 1981). According to Anyon, these schooling experiences reflect the work lives of a given social class: students in working-class communities often come face to face and go toe-to-toe with a curriculum of obedience that marginalizes and threatens; students in middle-class schools, on the other hand, often encounter a curriculum of compliance that validates family and cultural patterns, practices, and beliefs (Anyon, 1980, 1981; Brantlinger, 2003).

Within the context of CWHS, the curriculum of compliance was embedded in a *middle-class promise* that offered *success* through an ideologically proscribed pedagogy. Social studies teachers taught and modeled the importance of *navigating the middle* in a corporatized institution where *rituals and discourses of distance* shaped students' encounters with the meanings and implications of citizenship in the American polity. Students encountered pedagogical practices that contained powerful curricular messages. They experienced a *curriculum of pedagogy* that actualized the lessons embedded in the *middle-class promise*.

The Middle-Class Promise: Navigating the Middle

Navigating the middle emerged as a theme in teacher discourse as well as in the classroom interactions revealed in this study. In a broad sense, navigating the middle refers to ways in which the social studies teachers at CWHS articulated their own decision-making processes, the ways in which they performed or modeled in the classroom as middle-class professionals, and the ways in which they interacted with students in the classroom context. Within the corporatized institution that is CWHS, teachers performed and modeled two categories of behavior and decision-making that suggest strategies for navigating the middle, and in so doing, protecting and securing the "self" in the corporatized culture of a middle-class school.

The first of these categories for *navigating the middle* might be described as *staying between the lines*. That is, social studies teachers participated in discursive and performative frameworks that avoided the ideological margins delineated by the culture and community of CWHS. Most of the social studies teachers recognized, articulated, and aligned their teaching to the restrictive parameters that bounded their curricular and pedagogical choices. This dynamic was most dramatically illustrated by the pervasive tendency toward technical curriculum. In classroom after classroom, social studies teachers engaged in curriculum without controversy, curriculum largely devoid of both context and complexity. In government classes, especially, students encountered a civic education grounded in structures and functions, where the core of civic identity is rooted in the individual and the quintessential civic act is voting.

The data generated from interviews with social studies staff illustrated different categories or levels of responses concerning the teachers' beliefs about the core elements of citizenship education. The vast proportion of the social studies teachers at CWHS located the essential elements of civic education within the realm of technical information or background knowledge necessary to understand the workings of government and the fundamentals of contemporary political issues. With only a few exceptions, the social studies staff viewed voting as the core of responsible civic behavior. Indeed, several teachers emphasized low voter turnout as evidence of the need for the kind of civic education their courses offered. Their perspectives about what was needed in civic education were often grounded in their articulated frustration with the passivity that characterizes civic culture in the United States.

At CWHS, the centrality of voting in understanding civic performance steered the curricular and pedagogical practices in technical and procedural directions. These practices operated to narrow students' political field of vision, thereby serving to individualize civic responsibility, isolate civic behavior, eschew complexity, and virtually ignore the public element of civic life. In this framework, competing political perspectives were classified as distasteful but unavoidable dysfunctions to be resolved through procedures devoid of interest. Left behind were understandings of democratic life in which competing political visions meet in the public square and are submitted to the reasoned scrutiny of public debate and discourse (Calhoun, 1992). Foundational to the dominating curricular and pedagogical dynamics at CWHS was the belief embraced by many of the social studies teachers that students' lack of background knowledge stunts their analytical capacities. For students, this results in repeated messages of limited and deferred political agency.

The second category of *navigating the middle* in the corporatized institution of CWHS might be described as *self-regulation*. Social studies teachers exhibited careful and strategic attention to their own displays of attitude and disposition as they engaged in and modeled a management of self called for by the demands, both real and perceived, of the CWHS administration and the wider community. This curriculum manifested in efforts to manage controversy when it occurred or, more commonly, to carefully script lesson content and choreograph student interactions so as to practice a carefully managed civility. The resultant classroom interactions were framed as—but looked nothing like—democratic discourse.

For a number of social studies teachers, the idea of minimizing, or managing, controversy in the classroom shaped their own behaviors toward focusing students on the content at hand, attempting a non-political stance themselves, and recognizing and accommodating the institutional and community parameters that framed the context of their practice. Central to this process was the element of compliance. Compliance within the corporatized context of CWHS extended beyond mere obedience; indeed, compliance was tied to elements of self and notions of identity as performed in the institutional context and culture. Social studies teachers at CWHS exhibited some differences in perspective and pedagogies, but permeating all their conversation and classroom interactions was a palpable attachment to, and discourse toward, student success. That is not to say that social studies teachers inflated grades or made the curricular path easy for students. Quite the contrary: students were constantly involved in producing study guides, worksheets, review questions, reading summaries, vocabulary lists; they regularly faced ongoing surveillance and accountability with quizzes or tests in each class. In all this, including their apparent willingness to fail students who consistently neglected to fulfill these requirements, the social studies teachers at CWHS conveyed, in a variety of ways, the importance of compliance and its absolute viability as a powerful avenue toward success.

The context of this broader pedagogical framework in the social studies classrooms at CWHS, one that emphasizes technical knowledge, defines democracy as a government of procedures (Sandel, 1984), and is grounded in an impoverished estimation of student capabilities, also suggests undercurrents of concern and fear about the powerful influences of community sensibilities, real or imagined, as well as a professional ethic steeped in the ideological value of neutrality. These concerns led many of the social studies teachers at CWHS to carefully regulate the behavior of their students and themselves. Teachers engaged in strategies of self-management as they worked to submerge their own beliefs and attend to the dominant ideological proclivities of the community. They sought to avoid conflict with the administration by closely adhering to curricular guidelines and attending to test scores. Social studies teachers at CWHS articulated a concern for compliance that included but extended beyond their own well-being. They clearly felt a commitment to help their students access success; compliance was perceived as a gate-keeping mechanism that provided entrée to student success.

The Middle-Class Promise: Rituals and Discourses of Distance

Rituals and discourses of distance describe a second major theme in teacher discourses and classroom interactions that surfaced in this study. Rituals and discourses of distance refer to the ways in which social studies teachers at CWHS talked about and narrated the dynamics of historical and social change, ways in which teachers performed and modeled for students the deployment of skills and knowledge on behalf of their corporatized employers and the habits of compliance and the ideological subordination embedded in the curricular and procedural patterns that define classroom interactions and teacher behaviors.

The social studies teachers at CWHS engaged in selling ideological labor power (Reid, 2003; Schmidt, 2000). That is, they made decisions, applied knowledge, and sought to steer student learning in directions consistent with the imperatives of neoliberal capitalism (Apple, 2001a, 2001b). As middle-class professionals, the social studies teachers in this study acted not merely to convey information and support the maintenance of the institution of which they were a part but also acted to shape their pedagogical encounters and their curricular offerings in ways that drew students into practice as middle-class professionals—practice in the procedures, attitudes, and discourses that define and empower specialized knowledge workers of the corporation (Schmidt, 2000; Quantz, 2003).

Grounded in a discourse of individualism and a ubiquitous de-contextualization, the middle-class curriculum in the social studies classrooms at CWHS invited students into an analytical frame that eschewed complexity and connections, marginalizing students' own understandings and offering them instead a dominant rationality designed to alienate students from issues of power, structures of inequity, and the efficacy of their own experiences. This dominant rationality calls forth an ideological subordination (Schmidt, 2000) that denies materiality and dismisses, as merely contentious, competing visions of society. Students are lulled into a false sense of historical change in which the lesson of America-as-accomplished narrows not only the range of ideas and values that characterized the historical past (Loewen, 1995) but also limits the varied discursive and imaginary possibilities that might lie ahead (Zinn, 1993, 1997). The recurrent theme of limited possibilities has as its discursive counterpart a powerful, hegemonic embrace of the status quo, treating alternative thinking as irrationality (Marcuse & Kellner, 2001).

An instrumental culture serves to narrow possibility (Marcuse and Kellner, 2001), promoting in its stead an ontological inevitability: a powerful and pervasive artifact of the market logic embedded in neo-liberal rationality (Apple, 2001a, 2001b). The discourse of inevitability is one that often emerges in teachers' explanations about the limits and obstacles that shape their practice. Social studies teachers at CWHS could readily name and thoughtfully frame the obstacles to a more critical civic literacy—ideologically based community pressures, institutional culture of compliance, and regulatory surveillance from the state. Yet just as quickly they reified those very conditions, distancing their own understandings from the possibilities of action. At CWHS, such ideological subordination of the first order was modeled by social studies teachers and instantiated for students. It was couched in narrowed narratives of possibility in which possibilities were rooted in choices without power and where the only dissent permitted was ineffectual dissent.

For those positioned to benefit from the dominant rationality, notions of critical public agency are of less individual significance. More important is the significance of status and success in the dominant rationality. For many teachers, then, a curriculum of the middle-class professional requires enculturation into practices and procedures that privilege a kind of compliance that both regulates and rewards. Essential to this curriculum are lessons about the centrality of surrender—acceptance of a narrowed and instrumental agency that eschews engagement with the discourse of change and the logic of possibility.

The choices made by the social studies teachers in the CWHS study reveal the significant role of middle-class professionals in reinforcing the efficacy of ideological boundaries within the corporatized institution. To frame teaching as the delivery of technical knowledge, largely devoid of contextual complexity, permits teachers to distance themselves and those they serve from any factors or conditions that rest outside the instrumental parameters of the organization. To deny the value-laden and power-directed nature of curriculum gives teachers permission to perform as technicians (Kincheloe, 1999). The social field of the technical privileges the context of the individual. The day-to-day curriculum of the technical allows teachers to rely on discourse and rituals that distance them from students, that distance students from one another, and that distance students from the very experiences and meanings they bring to or encounter in school.

A Note on Interaction Patterns

In my efforts to understand the dialectical relationship between school and society, between the school curriculum of citizenship and the realities of an increasingly anti-intellectual and anti-democratic society, this study inquired into teachers' views about democratic civic education, about what was required for education for democracy. Teachers consistently reported their views that good, democratic citizens must have grounding in a knowledge base about government and history AND they must practice the skills of debate and analysis around current events and issues of controversy.

Drawing on the notion of "interaction patterns" as harbingers of ritual (Quantz, 2003), this study attended to both the spoken and unspoken classroom dynamics between students and teachers. In one respect, I was looking for patterns that could be found in *all* of the social studies classes visited. Indeed, one of the most striking commonalities across classrooms had to do with the role of current events. What emerged was a ubiquitous pattern of absolute *avoidance* of current events discussion. In not one of the classroom visits in this study did I hear a teacher initiate discussion, invite discussion, or refer to previous discussion of current political or cultural events. Of course, this is not to say that such discussions did not or do not take place in the social studies classrooms at CWHS. It is simply, but not unimportantly, to say that such discussions were not observed, nor did they appear to have a place of significance in the social studies curriculum. Interview data with the social studies staff suggest this avoidance was not circumstantial but purposeful—that it revealed a commonplace artifact of *navigating the middle* in this middle-class school. Discussions of current events offer and require opportunities for the kind of pedagogical practices that allow spontaneity, that anticipate and tolerate unpredictability, and that require flexibility. These pedagogical skills were neither demonstrated, nor acknowledged, by a preponderance of the social studies staff at CWHS.

A second pattern noted in *all* the observed classrooms, on every occasion, was the *presence* of the discourse of surveillance and accountability. That is, in every one of the classroom visits in this study, I heard teachers call students' attention to the topic of assessment and accountability. Teachers' comments ranged from quick references to rather extended explanations—and, occasionally, a substantial lecture—regarding upcoming quizzes, tests, or homework assignments. Although these are not unusual or unexpected interactions to find in high school social studies classrooms, the ways in which these interactions communicated expectations about *surveillance* and *accountability* in the corporate context revealed a significant element in the curriculum of middle-class professionals. That is, for the most part, these references to impending mechanisms of assessment and accountability were accompanied by statements overtly connecting those very mechanisms to strategies of individual *success*. Social studies teachers at CWHS found occasion, in every classroom encounter observed, to locate the lesson or activity within the broader framework of accountability *and* to link that framework to a system of advantages and privileges reserved for those who comply with established expectations.

Summary

At every turn this study revealed patterns of explicit and implicit curriculum that offered to these largely privileged students the middle-class promise. The ever-present message was that this system of schooling (the cultural and historical narratives embedded in the curriculum, the grades, the weights of those grades, the class ranks, the extra-curriculars, the extra credit, the National Honor Society, the walk-in-the-park community service requirements, and even the quizzes, tests, progress reports, and state proficiency tests) was all about positioning for advantage; and that this was a system designed to advantage them and, by extension, disadvantage others. The "promise" had an implicit, sometimes explicit, quid pro quo: Follow the rules, meet the expectations, jump through the seemingly meaningless hoops—in short, *be compliant*—and you will reap the benefits of this system, a system designed for your advantage. What an incredibly important message for the future professional managerial class of neo-liberal transnational capitalism to learn!

A civic corollary to the middle-class promise made to these privileged students is that citizenship in the context of the neo-liberal corporation and society requires neither an attachment to, nor a deep understanding of, democratic life (Boggs, 2000; Brown, 2003). The civic curriculum at CWHS was less a curriculum of democratic citizenship than a curriculum of *middle-class membership*: a curriculum offering lessons in the sensibilities of entitlement and moderation that define middle-class identity in American culture.

The Bridge to (Critical) Nowhere: The Middle-Class Promise and Teacher Education

The discussion that follows is rooted in a critical framework that calls for re-constituted teacher education programs designed to fulfill the promise of education for democracy. Drawing on experiences and insights from over two decades in the secondary classroom and a third decade in the teacher education classroom at the university level—and in the context of the lessons of *the middle-class promise*—I want to connect the foregoing discussion to the current role of teacher education programs in perpetuating a version of professional identity that poorly serves the goal of critical civic literacy. Specifically, I suggest there are core elements of the dominant teacher education curriculum that serve to inhibit critical civic literacy and that these elements resonate powerfully with the predominantly middle-class students drawn to teacher education. Teaching for democracy means teaching for agency and critique; teaching for agency and critique means teaching against a dominant culture that eschews the intellectual and social activism embedded in complexity and context and instead embraces the intellectual and social passivity embedded in a culture of consumption, spectacle, and voyeurism. In short, before we can construct a powerful teacher education curriculum—what to *teach*—we must carefully consider those civically debilitating cultural "truths" that require *un-teaching*.

Reflecting dominant cultural constructions, the standard university teacher education program is steeped in neutrality, individualism, proceduralism, and passivity. These elements inhibit a more critical teacher education curriculum and more critical public school classrooms. Specifically, the core construct of *professionalism* in teacher identity rests on a larger, culturally grounded epistemological objectivism that separates knowledge from power (neutrality), that de-contextualizes social relations from material conditions (individualism), that privileges instrumental rationality over questions of purpose and value (proceduralism), and that, thereby, inhibits the inclinations and skills required for imagined possibilities (passivity).

Neutrality in teacher education—in the curricula of curriculum, assessment, and instruction—is the proverbial elephant in the living room. It is not that the term neutrality is never used in teacher education; quite the contrary, it is widely used but seldom curricularized. It is an unquestioned, accepted truth at the core of professional identity, and to challenge its truth is to disparage professionalism; yet it is, in itself, evidence of unprofessionalism. However, challenges to the hegemony of teacher neutrality, though muted, have long existed. Over 70 years ago Stanford University professor Harold Hand offered one of the rare critiques of the ideology of teacher neutrality. In the fifth lecture of the William Henry Snyder Lectureship of Los Angeles City College, Hand critically but grudgingly acknowledged to his audience the central role of the "theology of neutrality" in teacher identity:

> Both from without and from within the profession, teachers engaged in the work of social education have time without number been told that their task is "impartially" to serve "the American public"…[and that] documenting this article in our received educational faith is about as unnecessary as documenting the fact that the sun rises and sets, so prevalent is the belief that educators should be "neutral." Impartiality has in fact become one of the most firmly entrenched stereotypes in our folklore of education. Proof of this contention is to be found in the fact that at least 9 out of every 10 educators would feel that his integrity as a teacher had been impugned were it charged that he had introduced bias into his instruction, so completely immersed are we in the theology of neutrality. (Hand, 1940, pp. 15–16)

In this way, the ideology of professionalism has long served to regulate behavior, to distance critical analysis, and to enforce compliance. In new ways, however, this identity of domestication is critically important for middle-class professionals in the context of neo-liberal corporate institutions. Neoliberal assumptions increasingly give shape to the culture and curriculum of schools. This dynamic is even more central in middle-class schools in which the enculturation of the new class of managers into the logic of neo-liberalism defines nearly all aspects of the school experience. This "new managerialism" is reflected in a corporatized curriculum in middle-class schools. As the new managerialism operates in schools to implement the neo-liberal agenda of improved economic efficiency, accountability and, hence, competitiveness in the global market, it shapes the curricular, pedagogical, and discursive experiences of teachers and students (Beckmann and Cooper, 2004; Agostinone-Wilson, 2006; Apple, 2001a). As members of the cadre of middle-class professionals, teachers instruct as well as perform the role of expert knowledge worker in the neo-liberal economy and curriculum:

> As Roger Dale reminds us, "the market" acts as a metaphor rather than an explicit guide for action. It is not denotative, but connotative. Thus, it must itself be "marketed" to those who will exist in it and live with its effects [quoted in Menter *et al.* (1997, p. 27)]. Markets are marketed, are made legitimate, by a depoliticising strategy. They are said to be natural and neutral, and governed by effort and merit. And those opposed to them are by definition, hence, also opposed to effort and merit. (Apple, 2001b, p. 413)

The discursive power of neutrality has the politically potent effect of de-contextualization: distancing knowledge, individuals, and events from historical, cultural and material conditions and contexts. Yet, even as a civic curriculum of instrumental knowledge and distorted cultural narratives conflicts with students' real-world experiences, the ideological power embedded in the discursive constructs of individualism and meritocracy provide an ontological safety net for middle-class students that anesthetizes critical analysis and domesticates civic agency. In the teacher education classroom, this dynamic produces students who are ideologically entrenched in an autonomous individualism, viewing schools, students, and pedagogical practices through the lens of their own experience. This privileging of individual experience over context serves to normalize middle-class values, reinforcing powerful but problematic assumptions about competition, equity, and meritocracy. Middle-class teacher candidates are quick to attribute students' poor academic performance to individualistic issues of motivation and family life. This often manifests in claims that low-performing students come from "bad families" where "parents don't value education." Conversely, they see their own successes as a function of individual talents and the benefit of "supportive parents" who, themselves, have worked hard and been successful. This individualistic analytical frame serves to normalize middle-class experiences and values, to effectively naturalize or submerge structures and practices of privilege, and to mask the marginalization of those below the middle class.

An ideological corollary to autonomous individualism is a commitment to a culturally pervasive instrumental rationality. The educational testing, ranking, and sorting that are artifacts of the cultural accountability fetish serve to "evidence" the meritocratic assumptions and beliefs that naturalize an individualistic lens. Bartolome (1994) points to the technical thinking about student learning that results in marginalization:

> The solution to the problem of academic underachievement tends to be constructed in primarily methodological and mechanistic terms dislodged from the sociocultural reality that shapes it....[It] is erroneous to assume that blind replication of instructional programs or teacher mastery of particular teaching methods, in and of themselves, will guarantee successful student learning, especially when we are discussing populations that have historically been mistreated and miseducated by the schools. (pp. 173–174)

Giroux (1981) suggests that the instrumentalism embedded in school life reflects a deeper cultural embrace of objectivism. It is this objectivism that "elevates methodology to the status of a truth and sets aside questions about moral purposes as matters of individual opinion" (p. 51). Submerging questions of purpose, meaning, and value threatens to cultivate a civic field that "so restricts the realm of ideas as to subjugate intellect to the service of particular ends; much is lost, including reflectiveness, critique, judgment, and ethical action" (Howley et al., 1995, p. 30). In short, one of the effects of the *middle-class promise* is to suggest an "'end of ideology' thesis…that tacitly supports deeply conservative views about human nature, society, knowledge, and social action" (Giroux, 1981, p. 51).

Conclusion

The middle-class civic curriculum of compliance is saturated in the black and white logic of a de-contextualized, individualistic instrumental rationality; it is manufactured further by the deployment of neo-liberal mechanisms of self-regulation attached to professional identity; finally, cultural narratives tightly weave the ideological fabric into a blanket of naturalized middle-class assumptions that promise comfort and security but instead smother intellect under the weight of a tyranny of inevitability and limited possibilities. As civic education, a curriculum of compliance is a recipe for passivity. As middle-class students find their way into teacher education programs, these identifiers and parameters of professionalism are further entrained, producing docile employees of the "corporation." The curriculum of corporate citizenship directs students away from epistemological contingency, away from the combative arena of political struggle and questions of social justice, away from, in short, a contested and dynamic conception of the public sphere. Until and unless teacher education programs help students critically interrogate the undemocratic and anti-intellectual elements of the curriculum of the middle-class promise that teacher candidates bring with them, the opportunities to build strong capacities for critical civic literacy will remain distant and impoverished.

Notes

1. See Joseph C. Wegwert, Democracy without Dialogue: A Civic Curriculum of "The Middle Class Promise" for Citizens of the Corporation, *Unpublished Ph.D. Dissertation*, Miami University, Oxford, Ohio, 2008.
2. Portions of this section also appear in J. Wegwert, "GLBTQ Youth and the Hidden Curriculum of Citizenship Education: A 'Day of Silence' in a Suburban High School" in D. Carlson & D. Roseboro, (Eds.), *The sexuality curriculum and youth culture*, Peter Lang, 2011.
3. The central participants in this study included the eleven social studies staff at CWHS and the students in the observed social studies classes. More peripheral to these central participants were the two administrators interviewed—the principal and an assistant principal. Two other groups, again, less central, but important nonetheless in providing context and in surfacing broader themes, were the students and staff observed in non-classroom settings. These settings included the common areas of CWHS. In addition, at the very beginning of this study I observed three meetings—a district-wide staff meeting, a CWHS faculty meeting, and a CWHS Social Studies Department meeting. Participants in these meetings included members of central administration and building administrators, teachers, and employees from across the district as well as staff members from all departments at CWHS. For a more complete discussion of the data and research themes, see Wegwert, Democracy without Dialogue.

Bibliography

Agostinone-Wilson, F. (2005). Fair and balanced to death: Confronting the cult of neutrality in the teacher education classroom. *Journal for Critical Education Policy Studies*, 3(1), Available online at http://www.jceps.com/?pageID=article&articleID=37

Agostinone-Wilson, F. (2006). Downsized discourse: Classroom management, neoliberalism, and the shaping of correct workplace attitude. *Journal for Critical Education Policy Studies*, 4(2), Available online at http://www.jceps.com/?pageID=article&articleID=69

Applebaum, B. (2009). Is teaching for social justice a "liberal bias"? *Teachers College Record*, 111(2), 376–408.

Anyon, J. (1980). Social class and the hidden curriculum of work. *Journal of Education*, 162(1), 67–92.

Anyon, J. (1981). Social class and school knowledge. *Curriculum Inquiry*, 11, 3–42.

Apple, M. (2001a). *Educating the "right" way: Markets, standards, God, and inequality.* New York: RoutledgeFalmer.

Apple, M. (2001b). Comparing neo-liberal projects and inequality in education. *Comparative Education*, 37(4), 409–423.

Bartolome, L. (1994, Summer). Beyond the methods fetish: Toward a humanizing pedagogy. *Harvard Educational Review*, 64(2), 173–194.

Bartolome, L. (2008). Introduction: Beyond the fog of ideology. In Bartolome, L. (Ed.) *Ideologies in education: Unmasking the trap of teacher neutrality.* New York: Peter Lang.

Beckmann, A., & Cooper, C. (2004, September). "Globalization," the new managerialism and education: Rethinkng the purpose of education in Britain. *Journal for Critical Education Policy Studies*, 2(2), Available online at http://www.jceps.com/?pageID=article&articleID=31

Boggs, C. (2000). *The end of politics: Corporate politics and the decline of the public sphere.* New York: Guilford.

Brantlinger, E. (2003). *Dividing classes: How the middle class negotiates and rationalizes school advantage.* New York: RoutledgeFalmer.

Brown, W. (2003). Neo-liberalism and the end of liberal democracy. *Theory and Event*, 7(1). Available at: http://muse.jhu.edu/journals/theory_and_event/v007/7.1brown.html

Calhoun, C. (1992). Introduction: Habermas and the public square. In C. Calhoun (Ed.), *Habermas and the public square* (pp. 1–48). Cambridge, MA: The MIT Press.

Geertz, C. (1975). Common sense as a cultural system. *Antioch Review*, 33, 5–26.

Giroux, H. (1981). *Ideology, culture, and the process of schooling.* Philadelphia, PA: Temple University Press.

Giroux, H. (2003). *The abandoned generation: Democracy beyond the culture of fear.* New York: Palgrave Macmillan.

Hand, H. (1940). *Neutrality in social education: An aspect of the educator's world of make believe.* Los Angeles, CA: The College Press.

Hess, D. (2009). *Controversy in the classroom: The democratic power of discussion.* New York: Routledge.

Howley, C., Howley, A., & Pendarvis E. (1995). *Out of our minds: Anti-intellectualism* and talent development in American schooling. New York: Teachers College Press.

Jensen, R. (2004). *Citizens of the empire: The struggle to claim our humanity.* San Francisco, CA: City Lights.

Kaminer, W. (1999). *Sleeping with extra-terrestrials: The rise of irrationalism and perils of piety.* New York: Vintage Books.

Kelly, D., & Brandes, G. (2001). Shifting out of "neutral": Beginning teachers' struggles with teaching for social justice. *Canadian Journal of Education*, 26(4), 437–454.

Kelly, T. (1986). Discussing controversial issues: Four perspectives on the teacher's role. *Theory and Research in Social Education*, 14(2), 113–138.

Kincheloe, J. (1999). The foundations of a democratic educational psychology. In Kincheloe, J., Steinberg, S. & Villaverde, L. (Eds.) *Rethinking Intelligence.* New York: Routledge.

Kincheloe, J. (2001). *Getting beyond the facts: Teaching social studies/social sciences in the twenty-first century.* New York: Peter Lang.

Loewen, J. (1995). *Lies my teacher told me: Everything your American history textbook got wrong.* New York: New Press.

Lukacs, G. (1971). *History and class consciousness.* London: Merlin.

Marciano, J. (1997). *Civic illiteracy and education.* New York: Peter Lang.

Marcuse, H., & Kellner, D. (2001). *Towards a critical theory of society*. London; New York: Routledge.

Popen, S. (2002). Democratic pedagogy and the discourse of containment. *Anthropology & Education Quarterly*, 33(3), 383–394.

Quantz, R. A. (2003). The Puzzlemasters: Performing the mundane, searching for intellect, and living in the belly of the corporation. *The Review of Education, Pedagogy, and Cultural Studies*, 25, 95–137.

Ravitch, D. and Finn, C. (1987). *What do our 17-year-olds know?* A report on the first national assessment of history and literature. New York: Harper & Row.

Reid, A. (2003). Understanding teachers' work: Is there still a place for labour process theory? *British Journal of Sociology of Education*. 24(5), 559–573.

Rodriguez, A. (2006). Rejecting mediocrity and the politics of domestication. *Journal of Curriculum Theorizing*, 21(3), 47–59.

Sandel, M. (1984). The procedural republic and the unencumbered self. *Political Theory* 12(1), pp. 81–96.

Schlesinger, Jr., A. (1992). *The disuniting of America.* New York: W. W. Norton.

Schmidt, J. (2000). *Disciplined minds.* Lanham, MD: Rowman & Littlefield.

Schutz, A. (2008). Social class and social action: The middle-class bias of democratic theory in education. *Teachers College Record*, 110(2), 405–442.

Zinn, H. (1993). *Failure to quit: Reflections of an optimistic historian.* Monroe, ME: Common Courage.

Zinn, H. (1997). *A people's history of the United States* (Teaching ed.). New York: New Press.

CHAPTER THIRTY-SIX

(Re)imaging Activism

Educating Teachers for Change

JESSICA A. HEYBACH & ERIC C. SHEFFIELD

> The educational problem is not wholly intellectual in nature. Our Progressive schools therefore cannot rest content with giving children an opportunity to study contemporary society in all of its aspects. This of course must be done, but I am convinced that they should go much farther. If the schools are to be really effective, they must become centers for the building, and not merely for the contemplation, of our civilization. This does not mean that we should endeavor to promote particular reforms through the educational system. We should, however, give to our children a vision of the possibilities which lie ahead and endeavor to enlist their loyalties and enthusiasms in the realization of the vision. Also our social institutions and practices, all of them, should be critically examined in the light of such a vision.[1]
>
> —GEORGE COUNTS, 1932

Introduction

George Counts' familiar fiery invocation to teachers and schools contains an equally strong corollary for teacher educators and programs: educate teachers such that they see themselves as essential agents of critical social examination, and as activists for social change. This sense of teacher identity as change agent is particularly important within the American democratic framework—a framework that calls on schools to develop in young people a deep sense of democratic "citizenship."[2] Thus, the perennial question arises in teacher education: can teachers foster in others dispositions they themselves do not possess?

Though the U.S. Constitution provides no clear definition of citizenship, it does include specific citizen protections—protections that point to a more robust understanding beyond that of blind allegiance and uncritical governmental support. Of particular importance on this count are the rights of free speech and free assembly, both of which have been successfully utilized in important social change movements throughout our history, and are reflective of Henry David Thoreau's notions of civil disobedience.[3] However, we believe the activism-for-change portion of American democratic citizenship, most clearly encouraged by our constitutionally protected rights of free speech and free assembly (as well as the more mundane right to vote), have eroded of late. In its place has developed a rather uncritical "America-right-or-wrong," nationalistic sentiment that is antithetical to democratic citizenship and to Counts' suggestion that contemporary social institutions be continually and critically examined via formal schooling.

In this chapter we posit that the disposition of activism in teacher education, and by extension in P-12 schooling, has atrophied, in part, because of the climate created by contemporary educational policies. No Child Left Behind (NCLB) and Race to the Top (RTT), in particular, have seeped into teacher education programs and been the driving forces behind the P-12 experiences of most current teacher education students. We believe that NCLB and, now, RTT, are reflective of what Paulo Freire called "banking"[4] education. Both policies emphasize rote memorization and transmission of information rather than the authentic emotional engagement that is necessary for a critical/cognitive analysis of contemporary social institutions and practices (or what Freire called "conscientization").[5] In avoiding emotionally difficult content that prompts deep reflection, the individual transformation necessary to promote a robust social transformation is repressed. The results of such banking forms of teaching and learning are anaesthetized educational experiences, sanitized public discourse, and paralyzed social action. We also suggest that teacher educators are in a unique position to encourage thoughtful emotional engagement and criticality in our schools, and in so doing, to reinvigorate in America's polity the disposition toward activism-for-change.

As the means to encourage the (re)imagining of activist citizenship, we argue that teachers and students take up Counts' invitation to critically examine existing social institutions and practices via what Deborah Britzman has called "difficult knowledge."[6] The engagement with difficult knowledge, an extension of John Dewey's conception of powerful learning experiences sourced in "felt difficulties," can, we believe, transform individuals such that they are disposed to act in the world to change it. Finally, we suggest that the self-transformation which can lead to broad social-transformation is best accomplished within a "classroom" structure based on the notion that the self and the social, or the "psyche" and the "city," are intimately connected and interdependent.[7]

The Impact of Difficult Knowledge: A Vignette

> Reflecting back on this class, hearing what my fellow cohort members said, I almost wanted to walk out and quit the program. I was irate. I really was. I was irate…I was upset…it was very discouraging…but now that I've had like 5 months to reflect…it was an experience that I learned through . . .
>
> —SHELBY, (RESEARCH PARTICIPANT)

We present the following vignette excerpted from a qualitative study conducted with preservice Master of Arts in Teaching (MAT) graduate students. These students engaged the images and words of Chicano artist Malaquias Montoya regarding war and globalization. One of the inter-viewees was educated in the NCLB era of American education, and the other in Canada. Montoya's exhibition, entitled *Globalization & War—The Aftermath*, employs a deeply tragic aes-thetic to provoke the engagement of spectators around issues of war, poverty, globalization, and torture at the Abu Ghraib prison in Iraq. He provides these words to clarify the intent of his work:

> With this exhibition I hope to convey the consequences of power and war, a universal story that involves peoples of all cultures and nationalities. This work presents a mirror for viewers to see themselves in portraits that focus on the human spirit at its most vulnerable, in the shadows between obliteration, devastation, and survival. My hope is that the viewer is unable to observe it without feeling some *cul-pability* in these continued acts of violence that have been carried out in our name by our elected lead-ers (our emphasis).[8]

Montoya's images clearly affected the psyche of the students involved in the study, and what tran-spired was uncomfortable and heated, political and aesthetic—it was difficult knowledge.

Two of the participants from the larger group study volunteered to participate in a paired interview to draw out and highlight their experience with Montoya's images and the resulting classroom conversations. They were asked to discuss an image from Montoya's exhibition that had the most affect on them, and the image above emerged as the contested object at the center of the following interview transcript:[9]

Shelby:	I find it very agitating and disrespectful. And how I view that is I see a box that says the USA on it where somebody who may not…I assume that looking at the face that they might not be American and they are migrating. They might be migrating because they are fleeing, or they are migrating because they might be coming to a different country for other opportunities. I just think that it is absolutely disgusting. It is very degrading to the American flag. To me…it's a symbol more of what America represents which is a whole other issue I don't want to go into. This just makes me sick. I've said this throughout the whole thing. I've said this artist should be thankful that he's not…ya know…that this is accepted…the point of what it is…[pause]. But the great value is in having these conversations…and bringing up these different viewpoints that is what he is getting at. Personally, with my experience and my family, as a military family…we went through a lot to uphold…ya know…to serve and protect…to coin the term [laughter]…I just hate it (the image).
Researcher:	Is your whole family military?
Shelby:	My grandparents, but not my dad. He was drafted, but he had three kidneys and received a medical discharge.…my husband's family is all military too.
Researcher:	So a long tradition?
Shelby:	Yes…but I'm a sheep, not a sheep dog. I could never be in the military.
Researcher:	What do you think about the image [to Emma]?
Emma:	[to Shelby] I'm shocked by the reaction to the flag on the feet. Your reaction…and it's not…[pause]. It's just different…I see him as a displaced person, a refugee, needing assistance, needing help, getting help by the American…um…needing shoes. And just seeing the flag as useful…I can understand the image, but I never really associated it with…ya know.…I never associated the flag on the feet as patriotic…or anything that was against patriotic…but that's me…it just comes from a different viewpoint. I don't really hold the same attachment to the U.S. flag or to the two flag Canadians, we are not patriotic…we tried to incorporate a flag day…the government tried to give anyone flags to fly them, it just didn't fly…[laughter]…Really they were giving them away…it just didn't go over…we don't have…we just don't have the same culture.
Shelby:	The American flag is never supposed to touch the ground.
Emma:	I know.
Shelby:	And now someone is walking on it. I mean . . .
Emma:	Well, *all* flags are not to touch the ground…but I mean, this is someone who is possibly in need of something. A displaced person because of war, and this could be a box of supplies. That is what we sent to "Convoy of Hope" for Haiti…they are just making use of what they got. But that's me. I think your views are interesting. It makes me question everything. . . .

Shelby:	interesting, I never noticed it looks like rope (pointing to the man's feet in the image)
Emma:	yeah, he has to tie them on. He might have miles to walk and this might protect him from sores or something…I don't know. I've never been homeless…I had to stay the night in an airport on Sunday, it was awful and I was so distraught by that, and I was totally like…I had my little airport voucher, had everything. But…[pause] I've never been displaced. I get upset from not making my flight home but imagine having children and dogs [laughter] and not having a place to go because of war or natural occurrence…I mean…I just think you use what you have, to do what you have to do. [Inaudible] [Laughter]

This brief excerpt offers a portal into the complicated connection between psyche and city—self and other—that surrounds dialogues of difficult knowledge. This interview followed a whole class discussion of the artist's work and the implications such images have for the development of citizenship, in and out of the classroom. Yet, the whole group discussion led to a very distraught Shelby who chose not to speak up for her beliefs. Other students, far more familiar with Shelby than the researcher, looked to her to participate and speak her mind. As the researcher asked for counter opinions, scanning the room for raised hands, none were found—silence prevailed. In the follow-up interview Shelby noted the following fall-out as a result of the heated political debate that took place months prior:

Shelby:	For me…the summer class redirected my thought process. It was kind of like having cold water thrown on my face…I thought I knew my own thoughts, and now I'm starting from scratch…[Laughter]
Emma:	Shelby that's what every experience is. I learn things everyday from just being down here, from living here, that I didn't know…Even my own biases are changed. I've talked to you about the confederate flag. It's flown just south of here…as you know. I hold it as a symbol of fear and hatred. Hatred from the people who fly it, which they think of it as a historical deal…I'm gonna have to work my whole life to not see kids' heritage as…um…racist, and living a life of hate. So, I think ya know…these questions…I *really* wanted you to talk that day [directed to Shelby] [laughter].
Shelby:	I would have been very impolite . . .
Emma:	That's what we need sometimes to have that brought out. Take a breath, everyone think, and then discuss further. I don't think we have to attack each other. The discussion. The dialogue. We need more.
Shelby:	It is. The people I was agitated with were coming up to me consoling me…I had my core group, but people…[Laughter]
Emma:	I wish you would have said something.
Shelby:	I let other people suppress my thoughts.

This exchange points to the educative potential that we believe difficult knowledge holds for self- and social transformation—for a reinvigorated notion of democratic citizenship. It also provides some insight into how patterns of sanitized discourse and emotionally barren curriculum in classrooms can restrict the self- and social transformation required of a robust activist citizenship. We find Emma's commentary on the confederate flag telling in this regard; as she suggests, she will have to "work" her "whole life not to see kids' heritage as racist"—certainly an instance of ongoing and future "activism." Furthermore, we believe that Shelby's habitual discomfort with discussing difficult knowledge was learned and not an inherent state of being. As a learned disposition, Shelby's reticence might be reconstructed and become a vigorous disposition of engagement, rather than one of disengagement, denial, and silence.

Dewey on Emotion, Belief, Critical Reflection and Experience

The above discussion, particularly in light of Counts' suggestion that teachers and students should critically analyze contemporary social institutions, directs us to the work of John Dewey; more specifically, to his notions of critical reflection and his understanding of experience as continual and transformative. Dewey's work is also the basis for an extended and somewhat more radicalized aesthetic pedagogy suggested in Britzman's notion of "difficult knowledge."

Dewey explains his understanding of critical reflection or analysis in the following:

> So much for the general features of a reflective experience. They are (i) perplexity, confusion, doubt, due to the fact that one is implicated in an incomplete situation whose full character is not yet determined; (ii) a conjectural anticipation—a tentative interpretation of the given elements, attributing to them a tendency to effect certain consequences; (iii) a careful survey (examination, inspection, exploration, analysis) of all attainable consideration which will define and clarify the problem in hand; (iv) a consequent elaboration of the tentative hypothesis to make it more precise and more consistent, because squaring with a wider range of facts; (v) taking one stand upon the projected hypothesis as a plan of action which is applied to the existing state of affairs: doing something overtly to bring about the anticipated result, and thereby testing the hypothesis.[10]

Importantly for our later argument, Dewey elsewhere describes this "perplexity," "confusion," and "doubt" as "an undefined uneasiness and shock" that leads "later to a definite attempt to find out what is the matter."[11] Robert R. Sherman describes this initial emotional interest as intrigue, revolt, or elation, noting that "our guts are tense, our heads ache, we pace the floor and our voices rise."[12] As to our core concern, that of reinvigorating American citizenship as activist-oriented, there are important psyche and city implications in Dewey's understanding of reflection sourced in emotionally charged interests.

First, with regard to self-transformation—the psyche—Dewey makes clear that sans an emotionally charged, even shocking, interest, there is no source for critically reflective self-transformation. Sheffield, Medina, and Cornelius-White suggest an even darker result when banking models supplant emotionally-sourced pedagogies such as those implied in Dewey's understanding above:

> This disembodied [banking] type of education creates in teachers and students what Stanley Milgram calls an "agentic state," one "in which he [or she] defines himself [or herself] in a manner that renders him [her] open to regulations by a person of higher status."[13]

This "agentic" state described by Milgram is manifested in Shelby's self-understanding that "I let other people suppress my thoughts." The danger of repressing, or as Shelby calls it, suppressing, the emotionally laden discourse that difficult knowledge entails lends itself to a loss of agency—a loss that can prevent the self-transformation that we suggest is essential to robust citizen activism.

Dewey himself seemed well aware of the dangers to self when emotionally sourced critical reflection is not the core catalyst in educational practice and when the city becomes oppressive of the psyche. He distinguished "belief" from critical thought in noting that beliefs

> grow up unconsciously and without reference to the attainment of correct belief. They are picked up—we know not how. From obscure sources and by unnoticed channels they insinuate themselves into acceptance and become unconsciously a part of our mental furniture. Tradition, instruction, imitation or appeal to our own advantage, or fall in with a strong passion—are responsible for them. Such thoughts are prejudices, that is, prejudgments, not judgments proper that rest upon a survey of evidence….The agent does not see or foresee the end for which he is acting, nor the results produced by his behaving in one way rather than in another. *He does not "know what he is about"*[14] (our emphasis).

Certainly the "America-right-or-wrong" nationalistic sentiment is one such unquestioned belief—built up from we know not where—and is sourced, in part, in ignoring Counts' invitation to criticality and by avoiding difficult knowledge in both teacher education and P-12 school settings. Critical reflection as the source for self-transformation suggests that, rather than leaving beliefs unquestioned, "we must be willing to sustain and protract that state of doubt which is the stimulus to thorough inquiry, so as not to accept an idea or make positive assertion of a belief until justifying reasons have been found."[15]

As to our second concern—that of acting to transform the city—Dewey's description of critical reflection has a much more straightforward implication: critical action aims at reconstructing the deconstructed self, to retrieve our lost emotional comfort. When there is no discomfort, there is no reason to act self-reconstructively and, therefore, no activism that challenges the status quo and transforms the city. This point explains our contention that banking methods of teaching and learning serve less-than-active forms of citizenship as teachers avoid emotionally difficult knowledge—the kind of knowledge that leads to the critical/cognitive analysis of contemporary (and historic) institutional practices of the city. In sanitizing educational discourse, emotionally challenging knowledge is repressed and selves are left relatively unchanged as beliefs are further entrenched rather than reflectively challenged. The reluctance to act-for-change takes root and grows into a weakened conception of democratic citizenship—one that tends to support the status quo.

Equally important to an activist-oriented education, as well as to Britzman's conception of difficult knowledge, is Dewey's contention that experience, as the source of any educational endeavor, is both continual and transformative. As to the continual nature of experience, Dewey writes, "the principle of continuity of experience means that every experience both takes up something from those which have gone before and modifies in some way the quality of those which come after;"[16] additionally, not taking into account the continually connected nature of experience can lead to "miseducative" endeavors:

> How many students, for example, were rendered callous to ideas, and how many lost the impetus to learn because of the way in which learning was experienced by them? How many acquired special skills by means of automatic drill so that their power of judgment and capacity to act intelligently in new situations was

limited? How many found what they did learn so foreign to the situations of life outside the school as to give them *no power of control over the latter* [our emphasis].[17]

The continual nature of experience is deeply neglected in banking pedagogies and clearly produces students comfortable with passive forms of citizenship. The creation of students who are "callous" and "scatterbrained;" who are unable to reflect and then act for change results from beliefs unexamined, rather than from psyche- and city-critical thought and action.

As to the transformative nature of experience understood as continual, educational and otherwise, Dewey writes:

> The basic characteristic of habit is that every experience enacted and undergone modifies the one who acts and undergoes, while this modification affects, whether we wish it or not, the quality of subsequent experiences. For it is a somewhat different person who enters into them. It [habit] covers the formation of attitudes, basic sensitivities and ways of meeting and responding to all the conditions which we meet in living.[18]

We suppose it is really no surprise that the activist portion of citizenship has been unfortunately reduced and repressed given educational policy realities. Instead of the critical self- and institutional reflection required for the development of a habitually transformative psyche and city polity, schooling experiences, both P-12 and teacher education, have become dull endeavors of routine and regurgitation of facts. These experiences *continue* into life generally as beliefs are further entrenched in the refusal to consider difficult knowledge. We believe Shelby's initial habitual reticence toward engagement of such difficult knowledge is clearly a manifestation of the routinization found in contemporary school policy and practice; Emma's reaction to the confederate flag, on the other hand, indicates how truly "educative" experiences continue on into life generally as an orientation toward acting.

Against Comfort: Difficult Knowledge in the Classroom

In light of what appears to be a deep commitment to the status quo through sanitized discourse and the feeling of simply "getting through" an experience, Deborah Britzman suggests that what is most important in Dewey's construction of experience as continual and transformative is his concern with

> the work of shaping and interpreting experience, and whether such interpretations lead to transformative knowledge about the self and the social world. Continuity, as a criterion for experience, refers to the connectedness we feel toward our social practice and activities, and whether we see ourselves as authors of, rather than as authored by, our experience. Dewey distinguishes this form of *continuity* from *routinization*, when the repetition of activity desensitizes us and undermines our critical capacity to transform it into something more than going through the motions [emphasis hers].[19]

As we suggest below, we believe by utilizing what Britzman elsewhere describes as difficult knowledge that teacher candidates can develop the habit of self-transformation essential to the civic engagement required for active citizenship.

Britzman puts forth a theory of knowledge that must find a more prominent place in teacher education given the contradictory (often tragic) realities of contemporary lived experiences. Her theory illuminates the powerful internal struggles that resist learning to teach for change, as difficult knowledge demands a shattering of self to make way for the construction of something not yet defined. Britzman reminds educators to consider what is not learned, what is lost, and how individuals must learn to make meaning through resistance and fractures between the psyche and the city. Learning to teach for change requires the abandonment of certain long-held beliefs that occur at both the conscious and unconscious levels. Nothing about this endeavor is comfortable. As Shelby poignantly stated, "It was kind of like having cold water thrown on my face."

When faced with difficult knowledge, many respond with anxieties, defensiveness, or a silent "putting up with" only to quickly discard all disequilibrium when the experience has ceased. In the case of teacher education, in particular, how often do authentic spaces exist to sort out these myriad emotions that occur both in the content and the process of learning to teach? Britzman argues that teacher education has yet to "grapple with a theory of knowledge that can analyze fractures, profound social violence, decisions of disregard, and how from such devastations, psychological significance can be made."[20] What happens to the teacher candidate who learns to see the world more clearly? The students in the qualitative study viewed images of war, torture, and social agony—they witnessed an alternative, critical, and difficult set of visuals. Not only did they witness the pain of the other, but also the trauma of being witness to a history that is not their own (at least on a conscious level).

Difficult knowledge may not only pull one away from emotional comfort, but it pulls one away from the known and definable. Britzman places difficult knowledge in the affective realm—a "borderline" between thought and emotion:

> Something in between the fault lines that suture thought, and yet something that also threatens thought from within. The threat has something to do with the speculation that while affect is a statement of need, its force is prior to its representation. We feel before we know, and this uncertainty allows affect its strange movement: Affect must wander aimlessly; it arrives too soon; it is too encrypted with other scenes to count upon understanding. The affect that may propel identifications is subject to this flaw in that, without knowledge, identification can only depend upon the urge to make familiar what is, after all, outside the range of understanding.[21]

As any teacher knows, curriculum of this kind is often met with profound silence, guilt, and defensiveness rather than understanding. Easily these educational encounters become ones of missed opportunity and futility, a sort of curricular trauma. Britzman agrees, arguing "what makes trauma traumatic is the incapacity to respond adequately, accompanied by the feelings of profound hopelessness and loss, and a sense that no other person or group will intervene."[22] Again, the individual potentially *feels* the difficult knowledge, but does not dare *act* in the community to change such social reality.

Britzman's analysis builds upon Adorno's seminal piece, *Education after Auschwitz.*[23] Adorno sets education against barbarism, a state of being, and speaks to the inadequate responses exhibited by both the individual and society to such atrocities as the Holocaust. In many ways, the Holocaust, as curricular content, is already known and neatly compartmentalized in the psyche of many students. Our inquiry suggests that as difficult knowledge approaches the current lived experiences of the students, the degree of felt trauma and inadequacy increases. For example, whereas students might exhibit disgust at the actions taken during the Holocaust due to repetition of exposure, are students willing to engage the Abu Ghraib prison scandal with the same criticality? In utilizing Britzman's "difficult knowledge," we argue that education must embrace aesthetic, rather than anesthetic, educational experiences to address such knowledge, and fight against passive forms of citizenship. Unfortunately, current educational practice at all levels is more reflective of an anesthetic, or banking, epistemology—one that numbs our students into conformity and obedience—an agentic state.

"Classroom" Community

None of what we suggest above, as a pedagogical *theory* of emotional engagement—an engagement that can transform individuals and thereby inform an activist conception of citizenship—explains the practicalities of classroom context within which a pedagogy of difficult knowledge can flourish. Certainly Shelby and Emma's conversation points to the essential need for establishing a classroom context that is built on the understanding that selves are constructed, and experientially reconstructed, in the dialogical relationship of psyche with city. Just as curricular decisions relative to difficult knowledge fall (or should fall) to the teacher, constructing the broad classroom context does as well. The teacher must remain ever mindful that experiential context is vital to individual transformation, and as we have suggested throughout, individual transformation is vital to a reinvigorated activist notion of citizenship.

In considering the outward and the inward interaction of psyche and city, Dewey reminds educators that

> assured and integrated individuality is the product of definite social relationships and publicly acknowledged functions.…If his ideas and beliefs are not the spontaneous function of a communal life in which he shares, a seeming consensus will be secured as a substitute by artificial and mechanical means.[24]

With this in mind, Dewey suggests that teachers

> be on the alert to see what attitudes and habitual tendencies are being created…be able to judge what attitudes are actually conducive to continual growth…that sympathetic understanding of individuals as individual which gives him an idea of what is actually going on in the minds of those who are learning.…be aware of the general principle of the shaping of actual experience by environing conditions.[25]

Early in his career Dewey called such an event "interaction," and later on "transaction," between psyche and city. A space where selves can be (re)imagined and (re)constructed and where educational growth is fomented. With particular regard to difficult knowledge, a non-repressive classroom community environment, one that encourages such a psyche-city transaction, is essential.

To successfully construct such a classroom environment, we suggest teachers do so from an evolved conception of democratic liberalism—one grounded in a "freedom-to" conception of human liberty, reminiscent of Dewey's renascent liberalism, similar to Barbara Thayer-Bacon's "relational pluralistic democracy always-in-the-making" and mindful of Amy Gutmann's "restriction" against repressing discourse about conceptions of the good life. At heart, what each of the above reminds us of is that selves are created and recreated in the milieu of what George

Herbert Mead called the "generalized other."[26] That is, it is in the transaction between psyche and city that both are transformed and it is in that transaction that the disposition toward an activist citizenship might be encouraged in our students via the engagement of difficult knowledge.

Briefly, the classroom community context that we suggest here is essentially grounded in an understanding of human liberty as "positive" (freedom to) rather than "negative" (freedom from). This distinction is most notably explained by political philosopher Isaiah Berlin. About negative liberty Berlin writes: "I am normally said to be free to the degree to which no human being interferes with my activity. Political liberty in this sense is simply the area within which a man can do what he wants."[27] Positive liberty, on the other hand, is derived from our "wish to be a subject, not an object; to be moved by reasons, by conscious purposes"—a very human "wish to be somebody, not nobody; a doer—deciding, not being decided for" rather than as "a thing, or an animal, or a slave incapable of playing a human role, that is, of conceiving goals and policies of my own and realizing them."[28]

At first blush such a distinction seems minor at best; however, on closer analysis, positive liberty is reflective of the interactive process between self and other, psyche and city that we have discussed throughout. Positive liberty essentializes the process within which psyches and cities are constructed and reconstructed via the transaction between self and other. Positive liberty implies a development of self that is communal; an accomplishing of individual human aspirations that can only be achieved *through* community rather than *exclusion from* it. Negative liberty, on the other hand, suggests that freedom is entailed in the very exclusion that positive liberty entails; and, as Paul Theobald convincingly argues, negative liberty leads away from intradependence in its support of a rather radical form of selfish individualism.[29] Again, Emma and Shelby's commentary is telling: Emma wanted discourse; Shelby, at least in the initial experience, simply opted out. With Emma and Shelby in mind, we make the following practical classroom suggestions implied by a freedom to conception of community with regard to difficult knowledge.

First and foremost, such a classroom environment can only be developed when teachers move increasingly away from banking forms of education. As Freire correctly argues, "Implicit in the banking concept is the assumption of a dichotomy between human beings and the world: a person is merely in the world, not with the world or with others; the individual is spectator, not re-creator." Practically speaking, the engagement of difficult knowledge greatly limits the appropriateness of such traditional practices as lecture, worksheets, memorization, "skills" training and other forms of knowledge transmission. Difficult knowledge also entails teachers abdicating much, or all, of their traditional "power" manifested in such traditional practices and in its place allowing community and individual interest to drive classroom "doings."

Secondly, teachers must encourage, rather than repress, all reasonable discussions of the good life. As Amy Gutmann points out, democracy has as its core goal "conscious social reproduction" and, as such, democracy holds that disagreement is a virtue, rather than something to be avoided.[30] Non-repressive forms of teaching also ensure that the emotional engagement implicated in the use of difficult knowledge will, in fact, be a core driving force for classroom practice steeped in a pedagogy of difficult knowledge.

Non-repressive forms of teaching and learning require a degree of civility and, at the same time, must not be such that the civility limits emotionally charged discourse. Each extreme holds the danger of closing down, rather than encouraging, valuable conversation. As Shelby suggests above, her fear of being "impolite," or of offending her classmates, leads her to retreat in silence; and, as Emma suggests, "That's what we need sometimes to have that brought out. Take a breath, everyone think, and then discuss further. I don't think we have to attack each other. The discussion. The dialogue. We need more." This kind of open discourse suggests more nontraditional approaches, including whole class discussions, small group interactions, individual journaling, one-on-one interactions, and so forth—all of which are antithetical to NCLB and RTT modes of memorizing facts and regurgitating them—and all of which, we believe, can be an essential part of re-encouraging a vibrant civic activism.

Finally, we suggest that the above challenges to psyche and the ensuing attempts at self-reconstruction that will result from the engagement with difficult knowledge will be manifested in broader city actions only with encouragement; and such encouragement must include examination of how such action might be carried out and, then, the opportunities to do so. In practice, it means encouraging teachers to see their classroom and students as part of, rather than apart from, the broader community; and it means providing opportunities to engage in civic activism in the broader community. In this way the engagement of difficult knowledge can in fact reinvigorate citizenship as activist oriented and aide in the creation of a vibrant democracy.

Concluding Remarks

We have suggested that contemporary educational policy and practice, as most clearly manifested in NCLB and RTT, have anaesthetized schooling in the United States. We further believe that the resulting banking forms of teaching and learning have led to a retreat from an activist understanding of democratic citizenship. To remedy the erosion of such activism, we have suggested that an emotionally powerful pedagogy of engagement—one that can reinvigorate our conception and practice of citizenship toward more activism—can be found in incorporating what Deborah Britzman calls difficult knowledge into our classrooms at every level. This engagement with difficult knowledge, we believe, can only succeed if we first engage future educators in such difficult knowledge experiences such that they both see its value and are then encouraged to utilize it in their future classrooms. Finally, we believe that such a pedagogy speaks to the possibility of a reformulated understanding of teaching and learning for democratic citizenship as an aesthetic itself…but that is a conversation for another time . . .

Notes

1. George S. Counts, *Dare the School Build a New Social Order?* Carbondale: Southern Illinois University Press, (1978/1932), 25.
2. We want to be clear here in our agreement with Counts: no particular reform should be promoted but a general disposition toward social critique and action should.
3. Henry David Thoreau, *On the Duty of Civil Disobedience*. Radford, VA: Wilder Publications (2008/1849).
4. Paulo Freire, *Pedagogy of the Oppressed*. New York: Continuum (2000/1970), 71.
5. Freire defines conscientization as "learning to perceive social, political, and economic contradictions, and to take action against the oppressive elements of reality." Freire, *Pedagogy of the Oppressed.*

6. Britzman has defined difficult knowledge as "a concept meant to signify both representations of social trau-mas in curriculum and the individual's encounters with them in pedagogy." Deborah Britzman, *Lost Subjects, Contested Objects: Toward a Psychoanalytic Inquiry of Learning*. Albany, NY: SUNY Press. Alice Pitt & Deborah Britzman, "Speculations on Qualities of Difficult Knowledge in Teaching and Learning: An Experiment in Psychoanalytic Research." *Qualitative Studies in Education* 16.6 (2003): 755–76.

7. Jonathan Lear, "Inside and Outside the Republic." *Plato's Republic: Critical Essays.* ed. Richard Kraut (Lanham, MD: Rowman and Littlefield Publishers, 1997): 64.

8. Malaquias Montoya, *War and Globalization—The Aftermath*. (2008). Accessed at: http://www.malaquiasmon-toya.com/Catalogue_Montoya_G&W.pdf, p. 8.

9. To view the image in color and the entire collection of images that students viewed in the study, access the fol-lowing site: http://www.malaquiasmontoya.com/Catalogue_Montoya_G&W.pdf.

10. John Dewey, *Democracy and Education*. New York: MacMillan Co. (1944/1916), 153.

11. John Dewey. *How We Think*. Mineola, NY: Dover Publications, Inc., 1997/1910), 72.

12. Robert R. Sherman. "Philosophy with Guts." *Journal of Thought* vol. 20 no. 2 summer (1985): 3.

13. Stanley Milgram. *Obedience to Authority: An Experimental View*. New York, NY: Harper and Row (1974), 54. As cited in Eric C. Sheffield, Yolanda Medina & Jeffrey Cornelius-White, "Emotion, Reflection, and Activism: Educating for Peace in and for Democracy." *Infactis Pax*, forthcoming special issue.

14. Dewey. *How We Think*, 4 & 14.

15. John Dewey. *How We Think: A Restatement of the Relation of Reflective Thinking to the Educative Process*. Boston: D. C. Heath and Company (1933). 16.

16. John Dewey, *Experience and Education*. New York: Touchstone (1997/1938), 35

17. Ibid., 27.

18. *Experience and Education,* 35.

19. Deborah P. Britzman, *Practice Makes Practice: A Critical Study of Learning to Teach*. New York: State University of New York Press (2003), 50.

20. Deborah Britzman, (2000). "Teacher Education in the Confusion of our Times." *Journal of Teacher Education* 51(3), 200.

21. Deborah Britzman, "If the Story Cannot End: Deferred Action, Ambivalence, and Difficult Knowledge," In *Between Hope & Despair: Pedagogy and the Remembrance of Historical Trauma.* Eds., Roger I. Simon, Sharon Rosenberg, Cludia Eppert (Lanham, MD: Rowman & Littlefield, 2000), 43.

22. Ibid., 202.

23. Theodore Adorno, "Education after Auschwitz." in *Critical Models: Interventions and Catchwords* (191–204). (H. W. Pickford, Trans.). New York: Columbia University Press. (1998).

24. John Dewey, *Individualism Old and New* (Amherst, NY: Prometheus, 1999 [1930]), 26.

25. *Experience and Education*, 39–40.

26. *John Dewey: The Later Works* by Jo Ann Boydston, edit. Carbondale, IL: Southern Illinois University Press (1935), 5–65; Barbara Thayer-Bacon, "Beyond Liberal Democracy: Dewey's Renascent Liberalism," *Education and Culture* 22 (2) (2006), 19–30; Amy Gutmann, *Democratic Education*. Princeton: Princeton University Press (1987); George Herbert Mead, *Mind, Self and Society from the Standpoint of a Social Behaviorist*. Chicago: University of Chicago Press (1934).

27. Isaiah Berlin. *Four Essays on Liberty* (Oxford: Oxford University Press, 1969), 121.

28. Ibid., 123.

29. Paul Theobald. *Teaching the Commons* (Boulder, CO: Westview Press, 1997), 61.

30. Gutman. *Democratic Education*,7.

CHAPTER THIRTY-SEVEN

Renewing Democracy in Schools

NEL NODDINGS

Today's school reform efforts aim almost exclusively at increasing the academic achievement of students. Despite their narrow focus, reform efforts are usually "systemic" in that they address the whole complex—uniform and precise standards, governance, and mechanisms of accountability. But they often fall short in promoting the discourse that lies at the heart of education in a liberal democracy: What experience do students need in order to become engaged participants in democratic life? How can education develop the capacity for making well-informed choices? If liberal public discussion is a foundation for democracy, how can schools promote such discussion?[1] What pedagogical methods are compatible with the aims of democratic education?

In contrast to systemic reform efforts, programs aimed at renewal identify the central purposes and processes of democratic education, attempt to interpret them in contemporary terms, and seek to strengthen them.[2] I do not mean to contrast programs of reform and renewal too sharply. Many in both camps are fine programs. But the idea of renewal is different. It attends to the underlying ideals and purposes of democratic education. It takes seriously the judgment of John Dewey that a democratic society "must have a type of education which gives individuals a personal interest in social relationships and control, and the habits of mind which secure social changes without introducing disorder."[3]

In this article, I will address just two problems that we face in trying to renew democratic education. I will argue that the movement for uniform standards may actually handicap efforts to renew democracy in the schools 1) by eliminating many of the legitimate choices that students should be guided in making and 2) by failing to encourage the sort of rational political discussion that provides the very foundation of liberal democracy.

Making Choices

Choice figures prominently in liberal/democratic theories. Some political theorists make it absolutely central to liberalism.[4] Others name a different theme (e.g., preserving diversity) as primary, but no liberal theorist can deny the importance of choice in liberal democracies. "Liberal," as I am using it here, is not to be understood as, in common parlance, the opposite of "conservative" but rather as reference to a philosophical/political heritage shared by both present-day liberals and conservatives. In liberal/democratic societies, the rights and privileges of individuals are taken seriously; freedom and equality are the watchwords.

It is not simply that citizens of such democracies are expected to make intelligent choices in voting; more important, they are left to their own guidance on a wide range of life choices. Educational theories that put great emphasis on preparation for voting miss the very point of that ritual.[5] Most of us do not care terribly whether those who represent us in government are (temporarily) Republicans or Democrats, although we may work toward the election of one party or the other. What rightly concerns us is the maintenance of a form of government under which our right to make choices is held sacred. The choice of where to live, with whom to associate, what sort of work to do, which professionals to consult, which merchants to patronize, how to spend our leisure time, how to worship, what to read...these are choices we cherish. Voting is often little more than a powerful sign that we do cherish these choices.

Because we live in a liberal/democratic society (albeit an imperfect one), political education is a necessity. Amy Gutmann puts it this way: "We can conclude that 'political education'—the cultivation of the virtues, knowledge, and skills necessary for political participation—has moral primacy over other purposes of public education in a democratic society."[6]

Most of us can give assent to this statement even though we might disagree on exactly what is meant by "political" or "democratic." Without attempting a precise definition of either term (a task far too large for this space), I want to make it clear that I am using "political education" in a very broad sense. I do not mean by it simply participation in public life, however important such activity may be. Rather, I mean an education that enhances the likelihood that students will have both richly satisfying personal lives and the willingness to promote such lives for others. It is precisely because we live in a democratic society that such a description of political education is essential. We need to have not only the knowledge and skills for public participation but also those for how to "get about" in an environment of political freedom.

Oddly, liberal theorists often have less to say about education than theorists from other perspectives. Totalitarian thinkers, for example, have usually put great and consistent emphasis on education. One reason for this neglect by liberal theorists may be that systematic education seems to require coercion, and coercion is incompatible with the liberal/democratic spirit. John Stuart Mill, for example, excluded children, dependent young, and "barbarians" from the basic liberal principle of noninterference.[7] He seemed to believe that all those people who had not yet reached a mature rationality might reasonably be coerced for their own good.

In contrast with Mill, Dewey wrote extensively on liberalism and the need for an education consistent with liberalism—one that would provide students with the kinds of experience that would contribute to the personal interests and habits of mind needed for democratic life. A main point of contention between Dewey and traditional educators, such as Robert Maynard Hutchins, centered on exactly this issue: Are students best prepared for democratic life by absorbing a rigorous body of carefully prescribed material, or must they have actual experience with democratic processes? The issue generates a whole set of problems ranging over cognitive, affective, and social domains.

Arguments of this sort have raged in the U.S. for more than 100 years.[8] The faculty psychology (or mental discipline) school that was so popular in the 19th century held that the mind had to be exercised vigorously and that the best materials to provide this exercise were the standard disciplines. An interesting variation on mental discipline was suggested by Charles William Eliot, the Harvard president who presided over the Committee of Ten. Eliot defended electives for students on the ground that sustained study—not prolonged study of particular subjects—is what produces the appropriate mental exercise. This theme is echoed in much of Dewey's work. He, too, believed that engaged, sustained study of almost any topic would produce the growth and discipline we seek in education. Further, Dewey held that students' involvement in the choice of topics, projects, and objectives for their own learning was an essential part of what I am calling political education.

The difference of opinion persists today, but the establishment of national standards threatens to suppress discussion. No responsible educator advocates a hodgepodge of unconnected topics as a curriculum, but many of us agree with Dewey that there should be a way to avoid coercion and still provide a rich curriculum that can be varied according to the needs and interests of individual students. Continuity is clearly important, but it can be secured by guidance and discussion; it need not be a product of coercion.[9]

If Eliot was right in his early defense of electives (he seems to have changed his mind later), there is no sensible reason for eliminating them and moving to a "one size fits all" curriculum. However, it has been argued that allowing students to choose their own courses will encourage some to downgrade their own education. The answer to this objection is not to resort to coercion "for their own good" but to ensure that every course offered is worthwhile. An open and rigorous discussion of national standards could be very useful here. Such discussion could encourage educators to think along the following lines: What goals should all courses further? Which of many desirable goals does this particular course promote? If its content is highly constrained (e.g., jewelry making, introductory algebra), is there a way that it can be expanded to include some history, aesthetics, reading, writing, or other material deemed important? How will the methods of teaching and learning contribute to the growth of democratic character?

If every course the high school offers were to be worthwhile in the sense just described, we would not have to worry about students' making choices that would downgrade their education. We would still face the problem of continuity, however, and we would be required to supply much more information about our courses than we usually do at the high school level. An adequate political education should help students to make well-informed choices. I am not suggesting that students be allowed to exercise blind desire. Indeed, it is because a free society makes it possible for people to follow their blind desires (within their means) that education in a democracy must prepare students to make sound choices. To choose wisely among even fine possibilities requires information. In addition, it requires a relationship between teachers and students that will make it possible for teachers to guide each student responsibly. The flow of information is bi-directional. The student needs information about what the school offers; the teacher needs information about the student in order to guide him or her effectively.

Another argument against a curriculum rich in electives is that students may change their minds by the end of high school and regret that they are not better prepared for college. This worry cannot be brushed aside, but it can be answered thoughtfully. Because we live in a credentialed society, students who have chosen nontraditional courses may find themselves "unprepared" for immediate entry into college, but the power they have acquired in controlling their own studies should make it relatively easy for them to gain the further preparation required. Many such students are better prepared for the actual work of college than the sizable number of youngsters who graduate now with "approved" courses that have, in fact, left them totally unprepared for the rigors of college. If we are looking for a national disgrace, it is not to be found in the fact that too few students take "rigorous" courses but rather in the fact that so many take them and learn so little from them. Responsible educators cannot simply declare credentials unimportant, and we have to be sure that students understand the likely consequences of their choices. But we can also launch a campaign to get colleges to experiment a bit by admitting students with nontraditional preparation. Democratic societies have long professed faith in sound scientific practices, and yet our educational efforts are obstinately conservative. Changing one's mind, one's occupation, one's way of life is enormously attractive in a liberal democracy. Schooling should reflect this cherished privilege.

High school students should be encouraged to make well-informed choices not only of the courses they will take but also of the standards they will attempt to meet within each course. Again, teachers should not turn over the entire matter of standards to students, but it is entirely reasonable to establish several sets of standards for a given course, each carefully constructed to match the purposes of the students who choose to take the course. The provision of variable standards does not necessitate tracking; it can be done within heterogeneous classes. The important point, from the perspective of political education, is that students understand how the standards they are working toward fit their own purposes. To urge all students to do equally well in all subjects is foolish. In addition to being impractical, it is an invitation to mediocrity.

A program of the sort I am suggesting here—one in which students get equal credit for well-done work in art, photography, or algebra—is sometimes criticized as anti-intellectual. This criticism, too, has to be taken seriously. Too often the accusation serves as a conversation stopper. Anti-intellectual? Horrors! But what do we mean by "intellectual"? If we mean that creditable school work should invite critical thought, proficient use of language, and an increase in cultural literacy, then, as I argued above, every course should be "intellectual." But if we mean that an accredited course of study must comprise a specified body of content in order to be intellectual, then what I am advocating is clearly anti-intellectual. This too is an old debate—one that may also be foreclosed by the standards movement. Instead of closing down debate with prescribed objectives for all students, a democratic society would do better to make responsible choice available within its public school system.[10]

Liberal Political Discussion

Several writers have recently noted that democracies seem to maintain themselves and thrive in societies marked by a tradition of liberal public discourse.[11] If this is true, democratic education should give students appropriate practice in such discourse. There is a language to be learned, a form, a whole practice. It could be argued—and has been, at least implicitly—that with sufficient knowledge, the only practice needed is that involved in debating academic questions. Examples of such questions might be: Was Jefferson a liberal? To what extent were the Framers of the U.S. Constitution influenced by economic factors? These questions are interesting to some students, and they certainly can be engaged in a way that introduces students to the forms of public discourse. But they may not matter to many students, and a mark of public discourse is that it arises around issues, things that matter to those speaking.

It would seem, then, that the best practice would invite students to discuss issues of current importance—importance to them, if possible. No one can guarantee that any particular issue will be important to every student in a given class, but educators can make an effort to share questions that are relevant both to the general public and to students.

Consider, for example, what might be done with the question of whether both evolution and creationism should be taught in public schools.[12] This is a question that is debated by some school boards, but only the decision, in the form of a specified curriculum, is conveyed to students. Why not encourage students to investigate all sides of the question? Are there scientifically defensible objections to evolution? Is there more than one version of evolution theory? What are the issues that separate versions?

Students should also have an opportunity to learn something about the history of evolutionary theory, about the great debates—including the fiery exchange between Bishop Wilberforce and Thomas Henry Huxley, in which Huxley suggested strongly that he would rather share ancestry with apes than with Wilberforce. If students are then convinced that Wilberforce was a dimwitted reactionary, they should be encouraged to learn something about his enlightened social views and his father's fight against slavery. Similarly, when students study the Scopes trial, they should be invited to find out more about both William Jennings Bryan and Clarence Darrow. The biographies of both men are fascinating. Reading about Darrow, for example, students may become interested in the question of determinism versus free will.

The subtopics that arise in a free and full discussion of evolution are almost endless. For example, does human language represent a limitation on the continuity hypothesis? That is, can human language be shown to be continuous with animal communication, or is it what some scholars have called a "true emergent"? Students who are interested in animal behavior might choose to study this topic in considerable depth.

When creationism is discussed, students should be encouraged to examine the two creation stories that appear in Genesis. In one (1:27), God creates "man in his own image…male and female created he them." In the second (2:7–23), God first creates Adam and then makes Eve from Adam's rib. Why has this second version been so popular among preachers and storytellers? Why have feminists objected so strongly to it? Does the first version suggest, as Elizabeth Cady Stanton insisted, that God is both female and male? Does the second lead ineluctably to a Judeo-Christian endorsement of the ancient myths that equated the creation of woman with the advent of evil in the world? High school girls often need a special intellectual interest, and this set of topics may thrill many of them. It provides a stimulating introduction to feminist thought.

In addition to the Judeo-Christian creation stories, other such stories should be told. There are wonderful African, Chinese, and Native American creation stories, and these too would provide excellent centers for further study.

Many students will also be attracted to the study of social Darwinism and its pernicious effects on women and non-Europeans. The doctrines of Herbert Spencer, Carl Vogt, Paul Mobius, Edward Clarke, and Darwin himself perpetuated the notions that females are inferior to males, that non-Europeans are inferior to Europeans (northern Europeans), and that most of the poor deserve their misery because of deficient character or constitution. The damage done by these doctrines is incalculable. Again, the number of subtopics that arise from the stem of social Darwinism is impressive.

Instead of battling behind closed doors over whether to teach evolution or creationism, we should bring the debate into the classroom. In doing so, we might begin to see the foolishness of separating school subjects as sharply as we do. Why fight over whether creationism should be mentioned in science class? The topics mentioned above are of great human interest. They create an opportunity for interdisciplinary study and team-teaching. But they can and should be discussed in science classes as well. Willingness to do so signals to students that science is a significant part of liberal studies—studies that initiate students into the practices of a democratic society.

Imagine how much "cultural literacy" students might gain in a unit of study such as this. Working on their own projects, listening to others, trying to fit whatever direct instruction they receive with the material they are learning on their own, they will come across names, events, and concepts that will add immeasurably to their store of knowledge. I am not suggesting that we depend on "incidental learning" for the entire curriculum, but I do think we underestimate the power and scope of such learning. Material that we "pick up" while fully engaged in inquiry is likely to remain with us longer than that which we learn for the purpose of passing a test.

The main point to be made from this example is that the practice in liberal public discourse needed for the maintenance of a successful democracy can be provided in such a way that the questions to be debated are relevant, exciting, intellectually challenging, and culturally rich. Judiciously selected topics also offer the kind of choice that students need to become self-reliant learners.

In addition to a host of questions that are current on the public agenda, students should discuss those that are directly relevant to their own condition.[13] Why, for example, are they required to study algebra and geometry? What arguments are offered and how valid are they? Is it true that most occupations today require the use of algebra? Is it true that people who are competent in algebra and geometry make higher salaries than those who are not? If this is true, is it because mathematical skills are actually in demand or is it largely a result of a credentialing system? On a question such as this last, students should be encouraged to recognize and talk about partial truths.

If it is argued that academic mathematics should be studied because it is a great cultural achievement and might even be regarded as one of the foundations on which great modern civilizations have been built, then what about other institutions and practices that have made significant contributions? What role has been played by the development of the home as a private place? By the modern family? By changing conceptions of child rearing? Why are these topics not part of the standard curriculum? And if mathematics is so vital to cultural development, why do we not study its history, its uses in warfare and politics, its aesthetics, its appearances in literature, the biographies of mathematicians, the historical exclusion of women from its study, and a host of other topics usually identified with culturally rich material?

We have to be careful when we engage in this kind of political education. We want to encourage free and honest discussion, but we should avoid messages that destroy hope and induce cynicism. Some forms of radical pedagogy are too one-sided and leave students with the notion that everything good about their nation and their schooling is but a myth. Further, radical pedagogies sometimes assume that it is legitimate to enlist students in particular campaigns for social transformation, and some teachers become angry and resentful when students resist their revolutionary messages. In political education for democratic living, students should have the right to resist such pressure. We should want them to know that there are groups working hard for (and against) various changes in our society, and we should share with them the strongest arguments on all sides. Such pedagogical generosity should be characteristic of democratic education. It does not require us to be completely neutral. Sometimes, teachers should state frankly where they stand and why, but they should not silence voices that disagree.

Another word of caution is well taken here. Often students who have not yet mastered the standard forms of language and whose cultural practices differ from the rational discussions described here are silenced automatically. Their participation should be strongly encouraged, and classroom conversation should be extended to include this set of problems too. When students use emotional forms of rhetoric, their contributions should be accepted, but further inquiry should be prompted. Who else takes this point of view? What is the logic of the argument? What conditions induce it? What can be said in opposition? If we traded cultural positions, might you react as emotionally as I do? To accept the contributions of marginalized students does not require teachers to abdicate their responsibility for helping these students to learn standard forms. To reject some arguments as unfounded does not require us to reject the students who make them. Political education in a free society must be designed to help students achieve freedom in both their public and private lives.

When liberal discussion is used to promote inquiry, critical thinking, reflective commitment, and personal autonomy, students are likely to feel more in control of their own schooling. It won't hurt them to hear that much of what they are taught in schools will be useless in everyday life. They need to know that they are living in a highly credentialed society and that the tie between credential and competence is thought by many to be weak. In an adequately politicized classroom, students may begin to experience school as a place to which they can bring some meaning. School will no longer be experienced as a compulsory act in a theater of the absurd.

Notes

1. See Fareed Zakaria, "The Rise of Illiberal Democracy," *Foreign Affairs*, November/December 1997, pp. 22–43; see also Robert D. Kaplan, "Was Democracy Just a Moment?," *Atlantic Monthly*, December 1997, pp. 55–80.
2. See Roger Soder, ed., *Democracy, Education, and the Schools* (San Francisco: Jossey-Bass, 1996).
3. John Dewey, Democracy and Education (1916; New York: Macmillan, 1944), p. 99.
4. The best-known example is John Rawls, *A Theory of Justice* (Cambridge, MA: Harvard University Press, 1971); see also idem, *Political Liberalism* (New York: Columbia University Press, 1993).
5. For one who puts too much emphasis on voting, see Mortimer J. Adler, *The Paideia Proposal* (New York: Macmillan, 1982).
6. Amy Gutmann, *Democratic Education* (Princeton, NJ: Princeton University Press, 1987), p. 287.

7. See John Stuart Mill, *On Liberty and Utilitarianism* (1859; New York: Bantam Books, 1993).

8. See Herbert Kliebard, *The Struggle for the American Curriculum* (New York: Routledge, 1995).

9. For some ideas on how to accomplish this, see Nel Noddings, *The Challenge to Care in Schools* (New York: Teachers College Press, 1992).

10. Howard Gardner seems to be suggesting something along these lines in his letter to the editor, *Education Week,* 5 August 1998, pp. 45, 53.

11. See Zakaria, op. cit.; and Kaplan, op. cit.

12. See Nel Noddings, *Educating for Intelligent Belief or Unbelief* (New York: Teachers College Press, 1993).

13. See Nel Noddings, "Politicizing the Mathematics Classroom," in Sal Restivo, Jean Paul Van Bendegem, and Roland Fischer, eds., *Math Worlds: Philosophical and Social Studies of Mathematics and Mathematics Education* (Albany: State University of New York Press, 1993), pp. 150–61.

This chapter originally appeared in *Phi Delta Kappan*, Vol. 80, No. 8 (April, 1999). Published here by permission of Phi Delta Kappa International.

Contributors

Bull, Barry L.   Barry L. Bull is a professor of philosophy of education and education policy studies at Indiana University, Bloomington. His research focuses on the moral and political justification of public policies in education. He has published on such subjects as standards-based school reform, government control of schools, school finance, civic education, teacher professional development, the professionalization of teaching, and education for the gifted and talented. His most recent book is *Social Justice in Education: An Introduction* (Palgrave Macmillan, 2008).

Camicia, Steven P.   Steven P. Camicia is an assistant professor of social studies education in the School of Teacher Education and Leadership, College of Education and Human Services, Utah State University. His research focuses on curriculum and instruction in the areas of perspective consciousness, social justice, global education, queer theory, postcolonial theory, and democratic decision-making processes.

Cooley, Aaron.   Aaron Cooley teaches in the Master of Arts in Public Policy program at New England College in Henniker, New Hampshire. He has worked at the North Carolina General Assembly and in the North Carolina Governor's Office of Education Policy. His doctorate in education is from the University of North Carolina at Chapel Hill. His research interests focus on democracy, education, and public policy. His articles have appeared in *Educational Research Quarterly, Educational Studies, Southern California Interdisciplinary Law Journal, Journal of Educational Policy, International Journal of Philosophical Studies, Journal of Popular Culture,* and *Political Studies Review.*

DeVitis, Joseph L.   Joseph L. DeVitis is a visiting professor of educational foundations at Old Dominion University in Norfolk, Virginia. Recipient of the Distinguished Alumni Award from the College of Education, University of Illinois at Urbana-Champaign, he is a past president of the American Educational Studies Association, the Council of Learned Societies in Education, and the Society of Professors of Education. A wide-ranging scholar and public intellectual, his major focus is on educational policy and the social foundations of education. His most recent books are *Character and Moral Education: A Reader* (Peter Lang, 2011), edited with Tianlong Yu, and *Adolescent Education: A Reader* (Peter Lang, 2010), edited with Linda Irwin-DeVitis.

Epstein, David.   David Epstein has been a teacher for ten years, working with students of all ages from kindergarten to higher education. He has taught students from all over the world, including a vibrant mix of Israelis and Palestinians, as well as at a charter school in Chicago's South Side, operated by The University of Chicago. A fellow at Northwestern University's School of Education and Social Policy in Evanston, Illinois, he is currently completing a master's degree at The College of Saint Rose in Albany, New York.

Fragnoli, Kristi.   Kristi Fragnoli is an associate professor in the School of Education at The College of Saint Rose in Albany, New York. She has been involved in multiple forms of research and educational community dialogue. She has co-authored, with Sandra Mathison, the chapter, "Social Studies Assessment," in *Social Studies Curriculum: Purposes, Problems, and Possibilities*, edited by E. Wayne Ross (SUNY Press, 2006). She was also the lead educator for the development of the New York State Archives' web-based teacher resource, *Throughout the Ages*, which received the American Association for State and Local Leadership in History Award for Merit.

Franklin, Barry M.   Barry M. Franklin is a professor of education and assistant dean for Global Teacher Education in the School of Teacher Education and Leadership. College of Education and Human Services, Utah State University. He is also an adjunct professor of history at Utah State. His research is in the areas of curriculum reform, policy, and history, with a focus on urban schools. His most recent books are *Curriculum, Community, and Urban School Reform* (Palgrave Macmillan, 2010) and *The Death of the Comprehensive High School? Historical, Contemporary, and Comparative Perspectives* (Palgrave Macmillan, 2007), co-authored with Gary McCulloch.

Giroux, Henry A.   Henry A. Giroux is the Global TV Network Chair Professor at McMaster University, Ontario, Canada, in the English and Cultural Studies Department. His primary academic areas are cultural studies, youth studies, critical pedagogy, popular culture, media studies, social theory, and the politics of higher education. He is a prolific author of books and articles. His most recent books are *Politics After Hope: Obama and the Crisis of Youth, Race and Democracy* (Paradigm, 2010); *Youth in a Suspect Society: Democracy or Disposability?* (Palgrave Macmillan, 2010); *Against the Terror of Neoliberalism: Politics Beyond the Age of Greed* (Paradigm, 2008); and *The University in Chains: Confronting the Military-Industrial-Academic Complex* (Paradigm, 2007).

Hatt, Beth.   Beth Hatt is an associate professor of multicultural education at the University of Southern Indiana in Evansville. Her scholarship is grounded in understanding issues of equity and diversity in education. Her primary interests include examining youths' lives caught between the institutions of schools and prisons.

Heilman, Elizabeth E. Elizabeth E. Heilman is an associate professor of teacher education at Michigan State University. Her work explores how social and political imaginations are shaped and how various philosophies, research traditions, and educational policies influence democracy, social justice, and critical democratic and global education. Her recent books include *Reclaiming Education for Democracy: Thinking Beyond No Child Left Behind* (Routledge, 2009) and *Social Studies and Diversity Education: What We Do and Why We Do It* (Routledge, 2010), with Paul Shaker.

Heybach, Jessica A. Jessica Heybach is an assistant professor of education at Aurora University, Aurora, Illinois and a doctoral candidate in curriculum and instruction at Northern Illinois University in DeKalb. She holds master's degrees in elementary education and foundations of education from Northern Illinois and a B.A. in art from DePaul University. Her research interests include critical theory, aesthetics, and philosophy of education.

Houser, Neil. Neil Houser is a professor of social studies and integrated arts education in the Department of Instructional Leadership and Academic Curriculum at the University of Oklahoma. His research and teaching focus on critical civic education, integrated arts education, environmental education, and issues of teacher empowerment. He taught fifth grade in Fairfield, California, and worked for several years in Fresno County Juvenile Hall before moving into teacher education. He has been nominated for a number of teaching awards and, in 1997 and 2007, was named University of Oklahoma College of Education Teacher of the Year.

Hursh, David. David Hursh is an associate professor in the Warner Graduate School of Education at the University of Rochester. His research focuses on educational reform within the context of wider social policies, particularly the rise of neoliberalism, and teaching about energy, climate change, and environmental health. He has taught on the latter topics in schools in upstate New York and Kimpala, Uganda. He has published in the *American Educational Research Journal*, the *British Educational Research Journal, Educational Studies*, and *Educational Researcher*. His most recent book is *High-Stakes Testing and the Decline of Teaching and Learning: The Real Crisis in Education* (Rowman & Littlefield, 2008). His co-edited book on environmental and human health will be published in 2011.

Irwin-DeVitis, Linda. Linda Irwin-DeVitis is dean and professor of teaching and learning at the Darden College of Education, Old Dominion University in Norfolk, Virginia. She specializes in reading, language arts, adolescent literacy, teacher education, and critique of political constructions of literacy. She has written for such journals as *ALAN Review, Educational Studies*, and *Educational Theory*. Her most recent book, edited with Joseph L. DeVitis, is *Adolescent Education: A Reader* (Peter Lang, 2010).

Jakubiak, Cori. Cori Jakubiak is an ESOL teacher in the Morgan County Schools in Madison, Georgia, and a doctoral candidate in the Department of Language and Literacy at the University of Georgia. Her dissertation research focuses on the social phenomenon of *English language voluntourism*, a form of short-term, international voluntary service in which people from the Global North provide English language lessons in the Global South as a form of international development.

Kahne, Joseph. Joseph Kahne is John and Martha Davidson Chair, Director of the Civic Engagement Research Group, and professor of education at Mills College in Oakland, California. His professional interests include democracy and education, digital media and public participation, urban education change and school policy, service learning, and youth development.

Kincheloe, Joe L. Joe L. Kincheloe was the Canada Research Chair at the McGill University Faculty of Education. He was the author of numerous books and articles about pedagogy, education and social justice, racism, class bias and sexism, issues of cognition and cultural context, and educational reform. His most recent books include *Teaching Against Islamophobia*, edited with Shirley S. Steinberg and Christopher D. Stonebanks (Peter Lang, 2010); *Knowledge and Critical Pedagogy: An Introduction* (Springer, 2008); *Critical Pedagogy: Where Are We Now?* authored with Peter McLaren (Peter Lang, 2007); *Teaching City Kids*, edited with Kecia Hayes (Peter Lang, 2006); and *Critical Constructivism Primer* (Peter Lang, 2005).

Kraft, Nancy P. Nancy P. Kraft is a senior research associate with RMC Research Corporation in Denver, Colorado. Her research includes how to enable students, teachers, and parents to possess voice and ownership in the educational process. She has written on authentic instruction, philosophies of service-learning, Indian education, and programs for diverse youth communities. She received her doctorate in educational policy studies from the University of Wisconsin, Madison.

Kuntz, Aaron M. Aaron M. Kuntz is an assistant professor of qualitative research methods in the College of Education, University of Alabama, Tuscaloosa. His research interests include critical geography, academic citizenship and activism, and critical inquiry. He received his doctorate in education at the University of Massachusetts, Amherst.

Kunzman, Robert. Robert Kunzman is a professor of education at Indiana University, Bloomington. He studies the intersection of religion, citizenship, and education. His most recent books are *Write These Laws on Your Children: Inside the World of Conservative Christian Homeschooling* (Beacon Press, 2009) and *Grappling with the Good: Talking About Religion and Morality in Public Schools* (SUNY Press, 2006).

Lazere, Donald. Donald Lazere is a professor emeritus of English at California Polytechnic State University in San Luis Obispo and has most recently taught at the University of Tennessee, Knoxville. His textbook *Reading and Writing for Civic Literacy: The Critical Citizen's Guide to Argumentative Writing* was published by Paradigm in 2005, and in a condensed edition in 2009. His articles in the politics of literacy and education have appeared in many scholarly and journalistic periodicals. The article published in this volume was developed from a column in *The Chronicle of Higher Education.*

Leahey, Christopher. Christopher Leahey presently teaches world history and geography in upstate New York, where he is also a co-advisor to a community service organization of 90 students who work to support underprivileged/invisible members of the community. His research interests focus on democratic education, critical theory, and civic literacy. His articles have appeared in *Social Education* and *The Social Studies*. He is the author of *Whitewashing War:*

Historical Myth, Corporate Textbooks, and Possibilities for Democratic Education (Teachers College Press, 2010).

Liston, Daniel P. Daniel P. Liston is a professor of education at the University of Colorado at Boulder. His scholarly work has examined the social and political context of schooling, teacher education, and curriculum theory. He employs analytic philosophy, social theory, and literary texts and commentaries to explore educational terrains. His current scholarship focuses on the role of reason and emotion in teaching as well as features of contemplative teaching. Recently he served as editor (with Hilda Borko and Jennie Whitcomb) of the *Journal of Teacher Education* and is now the co-director (with Paul Michalec) of Colorado Courage to Teach and Lead, a program of professional renewal for teachers, clergy, and school and community leaders. His most recent book, edited with James W. Garrison, is *Teaching, Learning, and Loving: Reclaiming Passion in Educational Practice* (Routledge, 2003).

Marciano, John. John Marciano is an associate professor emeritus of education at the State University of New York at Cortland. His teaching and scholarly interests are in the social and historical foundations of education. An activist, teacher, and scholar, he is co-author, with William L. Griffen, of *Teaching the Vietnam War: A Critical Examination of School Texts and An Interpretive Comparative History Utilizing* The Pentagon Papers *and Other Documents* (Montclair, NJ: Allanheld and Osmun, 1979), reissued as *Lessons of the Vietnam War* (1984).

Mayo, J. B., Jr. J. B. Mayo, Jr., is an assistant professor of social studies education at the University of Minnesota. His research interests center on the inclusion of gender and GLBTQ topics and issues within the social studies and their intersections with multiculultural education. He coordinates the M.Ed. program in social studies at Minnesota and teaches an advanced methods course, a civic discourse class, and a course on multicultural and global issues, all within the context of secondary social studies. A former middle school teacher for six years, he serves on the executive board of the College and University Faculty Assembly (CUFA) of the National Council for the Social Studies (NCSS).

McKnight, Andrew Nunn. Andrew Nunn McKnight is an associate professor of educational foundations at the University of Alabama at Birmingham. His research interests involve the application of philosophical and qualitative research methods to contemporary educational and cultural issues, specifically with regard to equity for urban students, ethics, and the emotional context of schooling.

Middaugh, Ellen. Ellen Middaugh is a research associate in education at Mills College in Oakland, California. She has written on civic engagement in youth, civic and democratic education, service-learning, and moral development. She received a doctorate in human development from the University of California, Berkeley.

Mueller, Michael P. Michael P. Mueller is an assistant professor of science education at the University of Georgia. His environmental philosophy questions and analyzes how privileged cultural thinking patterns form one's relations with others, including nonhuman species and physical environments. He encourages teachers to think about their responsibility for cultural diversity, biodiversity, natural habitats, and nature's harmony. His most recent book is *Cultural Studies and Environmentalism: The Confluence of EcoJustice, Place-based (Science) Education and Indigenous Knowledge Systems* (Springer, 2010).

Mulcahy, Cara M. Cara M. Mulcahy is an associate professor in the Department of Reading and Language Arts at Central Connecticut State University in New Britain. She teaches courses on content area reading and literacy in the elementary and secondary grades. Formerly a middle school language arts and social studies teacher, she writes on adolescent literature and literacy, critical literacy and pedagogy, social justice, and diversity.

Noddings, Nel. Nel Noddings is Lee L. Jacks Professor of Education, Emerita, at Stanford University. She is a past president of the National Academy of Education, the Philosophy of Education Society, and the John Dewey Society. A wide-ranging scholar, she has written on the concept of caring, ethics and education, feminist issues, spirituality, constructivism, and the concepts of evil and happiness. Her most recent books include *When School Reform Goes Wrong* (Teachers College Press, 2007); *Critical Lessons: What Our Schools Should Teach* (Cambridge University Press, 2007); *Philosophy of Education,* 2nd ed. (Westview Press, 2006); *Educating Citizens for Global Awareness* (Teachers College Press, 2005); and *Happiness and Education* (Cambridge University Press, 2004).

Parkison, Paul. Paul Parkison is an associate professor and chair of the Department of Teacher Education and director of Core Curriculum Assessment at the University of Southern Indiana in Evansville. He was a social studies teacher at the middle and secondary school levels for eleven years before entering academe.

Petrovic, John E. John E. Petrovic is an associate professor in the Department of Educational Leadership, Policy, and Technology Studies at The University of Alabama, Tuscaloosa. He teachers and writes in the areas of philosophy of education, policy studies, and multiculturalism, specializing in language policy in education. He has published in a variety of journals in those areas and is the editor of *International Perspectives on Bilingual Education: Policy, Practice, and Controversy* (Information Age Press, 2010). He is also editor for the Philosophy of Education book series with Information Age Press.

Price, Jason M. C. Jason M. C. Price is an assistant professor in the Faculty of Education at the University of Victoria, Vancouver Island, British Columbia, in Canada. His academic interests include community and culture, new media and education, democracy and pedagogy, social and economic justice, indigenous education, students' rights and freedoms, anti-racist education, and secondary social studies. He is a former K-12 teacher, administrator and alternative school founder and a member of the Distinguished Alumni of Trent University, Peterborough, Ontario.

Rayle, Joseph. Joseph Rayle is an associate professor in the Department of Foundations and Social Advocacy in the School of Education at the State University of New York at Cortland. He is a member of the advisory board for SUNY-Cortland's Center for Ethics, Peace, and Social Justice, where he is currently involved in efforts to develop a Peace Studies major. He received his doctorate in education from the University of North Carolina at Chapel Hill.

Ross, E. Wayne. E. Wayne Ross is a professor in the Department of Curriculum and Pedagogy at the University of British Columbia, Vancouver, Canada. His recent books include *Critical Theories, Radical Pedagogies, and Social Education* (Sense Publishers, 2010), with Abraham DeLeon; *Battleground Schools,* with Sandra Mathison (Greenwood, 2007); *Neoliberalism and Education Reform,* with Rich Gibson (Hampton Press, 2007); and *Image and Education: Teaching in the Face of the New Disciplinarity* (Peter Lang, 2003), with Kevin D. Vinson. He also co-edits the online journals *Critical Education, Workplace: A Journal for Academic Labor,* and *Cultural Logic.*

Sheffield, Eric C. Eric C. Sheffield is an associate professor of foundations of education in the Department of Reading, Foundations, and Technology at Missouri State University in Springfield. He is also assistant director of the Academy for Educational Studies and serves as the editor of its online journal, *Critical Questions in Education.* He is co-editor of three recent books: *The Role of Religion in 21st Century Public Schools* (Peter Lang, 2009), with Steven Jones; *Challenges to Academic Freedom Past and Present (Anu Books, 2008);* and *Why Kids Hate School* (Kendall Hunt, 2007), with Steven Jones and Cathy Pearman. His newest book is *"Strong" Community Service Learning: Philosophical Perspectives* (Peter Lang, 2011).

Smith, Dianne. Dianne Smith is chair and professor in the Division of Urban Leadership and Policy Studies at the University of Missouri—Kansas City. Her research interests focus on urban education, social foundations of education, feminist theory, and curriculum theory and development. She is the author of *Womanlish Black Girls: Dancing Contradictions of Resistance* (Peter Lang, 2003).

Smith, Pamela K. Pamela K. Smith is an associate professor of education at Eastern Michigan University in Ypsilanti, where she teaches in the Departments of Teacher Education and Women's and Gender Studies. Her principal fields of study are curriculum theory and the social foundations of education. She is co-editor of *Educational Studies* and *PowerPlay: A Journal of Educational Justice.*

Smyth, John. John Smyth is a research professor of education at the University of Ballarat in Australia. His scholarly interests include social justice and policy, sociology of students' lives and teachers' work, socially critical policy ethnographies of communities and schools, and school and community activism. He has received the Palmer O. Johnston Award from the American Educational Research Association. His most recent books are *"Hanging in with the Kids" in Tough Times: Engagement in Contexts of Educational Disadvantage in the Relational School* (Peter Lang, 2010), with Barry Down and Peter McInerney; *Activist and Socially Critical School and Community Renewal: Social Justice in Exploitative Times* (Sense, 2009); *Critically Engaged Learning: Connecting to Young Lives* (Peter Lang, 2008), with Lawrence Angus, Barry Down, and Peter McInerney; *Teachers in the Middle: Reclaiming the Wasteland of the Adolescent Years of Schooling* (Peter Lang, 2007); and *"Dropping Out," Drifting Off, and Being Excluded: Becoming Somebody Without School* (Peter Lang, 2004), with Robert Hattam.

Stedman, Lawrence C. Lawrence C. Stedman is an associate professor in the School of Education at the State University of New York at Binghamton. He has worked as a district policy analyst, secondary school teacher, VISTA volunteer.and program evaluator. His research involves the national and international assessments of education; federal policy and contemporary school reform; historical trends in literacy, achievement, and general knowledge; and the transformation of the high school in the 20th century. His work has appeared in the *Brookings Papers on Education Policy, Critical Education, Educational Researcher, Educational Theory, Reading Research Quarterly,* and *Urban Education.*

Teitelbaum, Kenneth. Kenneth Teitelbaum is Dean of the Watson School of Education and a professor of educational foundations and secondary education at the University of North Carolina at Wilmington. He is a former high school social studies teacher and has taught courses in curriculum studies, social studies education, foundations of education, and multicultural education. His research interests center on critical reflection on teacher education and the work of teachers, school knowledge in current and historical contexts, and school reform as it relates to democracy, social justice, and diversity. He has recently published in the *Journal of Curriculum Studies, Journal of Curriculum and Pedagogy, Teacher Education and Practice, History of Education Quarterly,* and *Planning and Changing.*

Vinson, Kevin D. Kevin D. Vinson is a senior lecturer in the Faculty of Humanities and Education at the University of the West Indies at Cave Hill, Barbados. He is the co-author of *Image and Education: Teaching in the Face of the New Disciplinarity* and the co-editor of *Defending Public Schools: Curriculum* (Praeger, 2008), both with E. Wayne Ross. His scholarship has also appeared in *Theory and Research in Social Education* and *The Journal of Critical Education Policy Studies,* among others.

Washington, Elizabeth Yeager. Elizabeth Yeager Washington is a professor of social studies education at the University of Florida in Gainesville, where she teaches secondary social studies, civics, and global studies methods courses. Her research involves issues in civic education/civic engagement, professional development for civic educators, and the teaching and learning of history. She is a Senior Fellow of the Florida Joint Center for Citizenship, where her work focuses on professional development for new middle school civics teachers. Also, she is a past editor of *Theory and Research in Social Education* (2001–2007).

Washington, Ray W. Ray W. Washington is a former journalist for the New York Times Company in Florida, including many years as a roving columnist for the *Times* and later as a reporter for *The Gainesville Sun,* covering politics and higher education for the paper. He now practices law in Gainesville and the surrounding communities, primarily in the areas of criminal defense and civil due process indigent representation.

Wegwert, Joseph C. Joseph C. Wegwert is an assistant professor in the Department of Teaching and Learning at Northern Arizona University. He taught secondary school level social studies for 22 years. His research interests and publications include works on constructions of civic identity in school contexts, queer issues in education, and social justice in teacher education curricula. He is a founding member of the Arizona LGBTQA Higher Education Network. His Ph.D. in curriculum is from Miami University of Ohio.

Westheimer, Joel. Joel Westheimer is University Research Chair in Sociology of Education and a professor of education at the University of Ottawa in Canada. He is co-founder and executive director of *Democratic Dialogue*. He has written widely on democratic engagement, activism, social justice, service learning, and community in education. He has also received numerous honors for his writing and research, including the Canadian Education Association's Whitworth Award, the Daniel E. Griffiths Award for Excellence in Education Research, and the Jason Millman Award. He is the author of *Pledging Allegiance: The Politics of Patriotism in America's Schools* (Teachers College Press, 2007).